Theory and Applications of Natural Language Processing

Aims and Scope

The field of Natural Language Processing (NLP) has expanded explosively over the past decade: growing bodies of available data, novel fields of applications, emerging areas and new connections to neighboring fields have all led to increasing output and to diversification of research.

"Theory and Applications of Natural Language Processing" is a series of volumes dedicated to selected topics in NLP and Language Technology. It focuses on the most recent advances in all areas of the computational modeling and processing of speech and text across languages and domains. Due to the rapid pace of development, the diversity of approaches and application scenarios are scattered in an ever-growing mass of conference proceedings, making entry into the field difficult for both students and potential users. Volumes in the series facilitate this first step and can be used as a teaching aid, advanced-level information resource or a point of reference.

The series encourages the submission of research monographs, contributed volumes and surveys, lecture notes and textbooks covering research frontiers on all relevant topics, offering a platform for the rapid publication of cutting-edge research as well as for comprehensive monographs that cover the full range of research on specific problem areas.

The topics include applications of NLP techniques to gain insights into the use and functioning of language, as well as the use of language technology in applications that enable communication, knowledge management and discovery such as natural language generation, information retrieval, question-answering, machine translation, localization and related fields.

The books are available in printed and electronic (e-book) form:

* Downloadable on your PC, e-reader or iPad
* Enhanced by Electronic Supplementary Material, such as algorithms, demonstrations, software, images and videos
* Available online within an extensive network of academic and corporate R&D libraries worldwide
* Never out of print thanks to innovative print-on-demand services
* Competitively priced print editions for eBook customers thanks to MyCopy service http://www.springer.com/librarians/e-content/mycopy

More information about this series at http://www.springer.com/series/8899

Massimo Poesio • Roland Stuckardt •
Yannick Versley
Editors

Anaphora Resolution

Algorithms, Resources, and Applications

Editors
Massimo Poesio
Trento, Italy

Roland Stuckardt
Frankfurt am Main, Germany

Yannick Versley
Heidelberg, Germany

ISSN 2192-032X ISSN 2192-0338 (electronic)
Theory and Applications of Natural Language Processing
ISBN 978-3-662-56907-8 ISBN 978-3-662-47909-4 (eBook)
DOI 10.1007/978-3-662-47909-4

Printed on acid-free paper

This Springer imprint is published by Springer Nature
The registered company is Springer-Verlag GmbH Berlin Heidelberg

Preface

More than 10 years have passed since Mitkov's book on anaphora resolution in 2002, and the area of computational anaphora resolution has since made substantial progress through effective use of machine learning, lexical and encyclopedic knowledge, constraint solving techniques and more, and a much improved understanding of evaluation issues that has made it possible to compare systems and approaches from different people in a meaningful way.

The goal of this volume is to provide the reader with an accessible yet thorough path through these late developments, providing comprehensive background where needed but also giving the detail and perspective that only people who have been at the forefront of these developments can deliver. We as editors, along with the numerous chapter authors who have contributed their knowledge and perspective, have given our best to provide future readers with what they need as practitioners to make sense of the possibilities of coreference and anaphora resolution or as researchers to get up to speed with this substantial and interesting field in a minimum of time.

We would like to thank Olga Chiarcos and Federica Corradi Dell'Acqua, our editors at Springer Nature, who demonstrated a really admirable patience and faith in the book project, thus contributing greatly to the eventually successful completion of this long-running endeavor. Credit goes as well to Professor Eduard Hovy for his constructive comments on the original book proposal, which proved to be very helpful for the further enhancement and fine adjustment of this monograph's structure and contents. Last not least, we are particularly indebted to our authors for providing contributions of such high quality, and we are especially grateful to Marta Recasens and Sameer Pradhan, who spontaneously took over responsibility for several chapters more than originally envisaged.

Essex, UK
Frankfurt, Germany
Heidelberg, Germany
Summer 2015

Massimo Poesio
Roland Stuckardt
Yannick Versley

Contents

List of Contributors

Shane Bergsma Department of Computer Science, University of Saskatchewan, JHU Center of Excellence, Saskatoon, Baltimore, Canada

Anders Björkelund IMS Universität Stuttgart, Stuttgart, Germany

Veronique Hoste University College Ghent, Ghent, Belgium

Mijail Kabadjov School of Computer Science and Electronic Engineering, University of Essex, Colchester, UK

Xiaoqiang Luo LinkedIn Inc., New York, NY, USA

Vincent Ng University of Texas at Dallas, Richardson, TX, USA

Massimo Poesio School of Computer Science and Electronic Engineering, University of Essex, Colchester, UK

Simone Ponzetto University of Mannheim, Mannheim, Germany

Sameer Pradhan Boulder Learning, Inc., Boulder, CO, USA

Marta Recasens Google Inc., Mountain View, CA, USA

Nick Rizzolo Google Inc., San Francisco, CA, USA

Kepa Rodriguez Yad Vashem Archives, Jerusalem, Israel

Dan Roth University of Illinois at Urbana/Champaign, Champaign, IL, USA

Josef Steinberger Faculty of Applied Sciences, Department of Computer Science and Engineering, NTIS Centre, University of West Bohemia, Pilsen, Czech Republic

Roland Stuckardt IT-Beratung, Sprachtechnologie, Medienanalyse, Frankfurt am Main, Germany

Olga Uryupina DISI University of Trento, Trento, Italy

Yannick Versley ICL University of Heidelberg, Heidelberg, Germany

Renata Vieira Universidade Católica do Rio Grande do Sul, Porto Alegre, Brazil

Roberto Zanoli Fondazione Bruno Kessler, Trento, Italy

Introduction

Roland Stuckardt

Abstract In this introductory chapter, a synopsis of the book content will be given, the intended audience will be delineated, and an introduction into the historical development of the research field of anaphora resolution will be featured. Moreover, informative summaries of all book chapters will be provided.

Keywords Anaphora resolution • Coreference resolution • Discourse processing • History of anaphora processing research

1 Synopsis

This book documents the recent advances in a key research area of computational linguistics that has received wide attention in the past 12 years: anaphora resolution. Recent research has led to a rapid progress that by now is documented by a plethora of individual research papers that appeared in diverse conference proceedings and journals. Time has come to consolidate the recently gained insights by editing a monograph that provides a unified and independent view of the respective algorithms, resources, and applications, thus capturing the state-of-the-art of computational anaphora processing.

While the first work on computational anaphora resolution dates back to the 1960s and 1970s, the scope of these early approaches was generally limited to particular application scenarios of limited complexity. It took until the mid of the 1990s for truly robust, operational approaches working on unrestricted input to become available. Development and implementation of these algorithms was largely related to research on information extraction, text summarization, question answering, and machine translation, as approaches to these generic application cases commonly resort to coreference information. Robust software for automatic anaphora processing thus embodies an enabling technology for a large number of particular applications in diverse economically relevant domains and is hence regarded to be of high commercial value.

R. Stuckardt (✉)
IT-Beratung, Sprachtechnologie, Medienanalyse, D-60433, Frankfurt am Main, Germany
e-mail: roland@stuckardt.de

M. Poesio et al. (eds.), *Anaphora Resolution*, Theory and Applications of Natural Language Processing, DOI 10.1007/978-3-662-47909-4_1

The theoretical research on local coherence, focusing, salience, centering, and discourse structure that was predominant in the 1980s and early 1990s played a central role for establishing an in-depth understanding of the phenomenon of anaphora, and, thus, of the subtleties to be taken into account by adequate algorithms. Regarding, however, operational approaches to anaphora resolution, the appearance of shared resources—in particular: corpora annotated with coreference information, evaluation criteria, evaluation tools, and evaluation campaigns—can be regarded the critical factor for success. Noticeably, it is these resources that today constitute the proper base for enhanced, empirically grounded studies on discourse theory.

The book surveys the recent advances in research, focusing on practical, operational approaches and their applications. In **Part I (Background)**, it provides a general introduction, which succinctly summarizes the linguistic, cognitive, and computational foundations of anaphora processing and the key classical rule- and machine-learning-based anaphora resolution algorithms. Acknowledging the central importance of shared resources, **Part II (Resources)** covers annotated corpora, formal evaluation, preprocessing technology, and off-the-shelf anaphora resolution systems. **Part III (Algorithms)** provides a thorough description of state-of-the-art anaphora resolution algorithms, covering enhanced machine learning methods as well as techniques for accomplishing important subtasks such as mention detection and acquisition of relevant knowledge. **Part IV (Applications)** deals with a selection of important anaphora and coreference resolution applications, discussing particular scenarios in diverse domains and distilling a best-practice model for systematically approaching new application cases. In the concluding **Part V (Outlook)**, based on a survey conducted among the contributing authors, the prospects of the research field of anaphora processing will be discussed, identifying promising new areas of interdisciplinary cooperation and emerging application scenarios.

In the remaining part of this introductory chapter, the history of anaphora processing research shall be briefly reviewed. Five phases, which are characterized by particular research paradigms, will be identified, and initial references to landmark work will be given. This book surveys the current phase 5, for which the name **post-modern phase** will be coined. As an introduction to the book, the most important developments in this phase will be outlined, and a synopsis of the different book chapters will be given.

An initial note on terminology: the term **anaphora resolution**, which is used in the book title, is to be understood in a broad sense, i.e., as to comprise all varieties of anaphora processing, including determination of individual antecedents, coreference resolution (= determination of mention sets referring to the same entity), and auxiliary tasks such as discourse-new detection, expletive *it* identification, etc. Moreover, strictly speaking, it would be adequate to speak of *anaphor* instead of anaphora resolution, as a linguistic phenomenon—such as anaphora—cannot be "resolved" itself; rather, it is the particular instance of anaphora, viz., the anaphor (ic expression), that is the subject of our resolution efforts. As, however, the term *anaphora resolution* is now widely accepted, it shall as well be employed in this book.

2 Intended Audience

This monograph is laid out to be useful both as an accompanying text for advanced lectures in computational linguistics, natural language engineering, and computer science, and as a reference book for research and self-study. It addresses an audience that includes academic researchers, university lecturers, postgraduate students, advanced undergraduate students, industrial researchers, and software engineers. While the book is aimed at documenting the recent advances in anaphora resolution, it is laid out to be self-contained, as it includes a brief, yet comprehensive introduction to the research field, providing definitions of all relevant theoretical notions and bibliographic references to key previous work. The material should be accessible to readers with moderate previous knowledge in computational linguistics and natural language processing, but without expertise in anaphora resolution.

3 Previous Research

A closer look at the history of the research field of anaphora resolution reveals that the previous work can be coarsely divided into the following five phases, each of which being characterized by a particular focal point of research, or a prevailing *research paradigm*.[1] Inevitably, the selection of references to typical work given in this brief introduction is non-exhaustive and, to a certain extent, subjective; it can be said, however, that the referenced papers and monographs are among the most frequently cited work about anaphora resolution and insofar recognized as key by the research community. A comprehensive survey of previous work will be given below in the Background part.

3.1 Very Early Work (1964–1981): The Phase of Knowledge-Rich, Domain-Specific Processing

Considerations focus on nominal and pronominal (i.e. object) anaphora. Anaphora resolution is considered as a particular subtask of natural language processing in the

[1] It goes without saying that this division into phases is, to a certain extent, fuzzy, as there are commonly cases of "vanguard" or "traditional" research that are not representative for a particular phase.

application context of machine translation or expert systems. Well known examples are Bobrow's STUDENT system [4], Winograd's SHRDLU/Blocksworld [38], and Woods's LUNAR system [39]; the anaphora resolution approaches are rule-based, typically employing basic pattern-matching techniques tailored to resolve instances of anaphora that are specific to the application domain under consideration.

At conceptual level, there is the early influential work [37] of Wilks on preference semantics in the context of a project on English-French machine translation. Instances of pronominal anaphora are classified into four categories of increasing difficulty.

The end of this research phase is marked by the seminal publication of the **"Naive" Algorithm** for pronoun resolution by **Hobbs** [12], which, in fact, can be considered as an indicator of a shift of paradigm, as it discards the domain-specific, typically knowledge-intensive techniques in favor of a knowledge-poor approach that is based on linguistic, i.e., syntactic, information.

This very early work has been thoroughly documented in Graeme Hirst's survey [11]. Moreover, Chap. 4 of the monograph [19] by Ruslan Mitkov summarizes this research phase.

3.2 Early Work (1982–1987): The Shallow Processing Phase

Recognizing that the typical approaches developed in the 1970s are based on deep domain-specific knowledge and thus lack the degree of scalability and robustness required by real-world applications, there have been efforts to overcome these limitations by resorting to more shallow (essentially linguistic) knowledge. Among the most influential work in this regard is the **Shallow Processing Anaphor Resolver (SPAR)** approach of **Carter** [7]. While this approach chiefly resorts to more shallow knowledge indeed, it yet exhibits some of the major limitations of its ancestors: considerations are confined to interpreting documents of a comparatively simple *Story* domain; moreover, the approach recurs to a model of discourse focus by Sidner that has merely been partially formalized.

On the theoretical side, there has been extensive research on issues of focusing and discourse structure, among which is the influential work by Sidner [29–31] and Grosz and Sidner [9]. Moreover, the foundations of centering theory were laid (Grosz, Joshi and Weinstein [10]). Still, however, the great majority of these theoretical models lacked the degree of formalization necessary for exploiting them algorithmically as successful strategies in operational approaches to anaphora resolution. For instance, the respective early work [5] by Brennan, Friedman and Pollard, who investigated how to implement the rules of centering theory, yet left open diverse questions.

Besides the above-cited primary literature on focusing and discourse structure, the PhD work of Carter [7] embodies an excellent introduction to the research carried out in these years.

3.3 *The Consolidation Phase (1988–1994)*

During this period, there have been further advances towards a robust, operational account of anaphora processing. At architectural level, there has been the influential contribution [6] by Carbonell and Brown, who described a multi-strategy approach to anaphora resolution, according to which a set of strong criteria (restrictions) followed by a set of weak criteria (preferences) should be applied to eventually select the antecedent candidate considered most plausible. However, while a number of particular restrictions and preferences are suggested, the approach yet lacks the necessary degree of scalability, as the type of knowledge required by some of the criteria (e.g., thematic roles) cannot be assumed to be generally available if unrestricted text is to be processed.

Nonetheless, due to its compelling modularity, the multi-strategy approach has been very influential; in fact, it can be considered the architectural ancestor of many of the subsequently published approaches. In particular, this holds for the landmark work [15] of **Lappin and Leass**, who describe the **pronoun resolution algorithm RAP** (Resolution of Anaphora Procedure), which is built according to the multi-strategy paradigm. By considering strategies that are essentially based on syntactic knowledge, they go one further step ahead towards a truly operational solution. As, however, their approach requires complete syntactic parses, it still isn't readily applicable for processing arbitrary text. Nevertheless, this work can be regarded a milestone, as it consolidates the knowledge gathered so-far about (more or less) operational, robust anaphora resolution and formally describes an algorithm at a level of detail that enables reimplementation.

Correspondingly, the Lappin and Leass publication [15] is among the most cited papers on anaphora resolution; it is highly recommended as a reading for anyone who wants to enter into this research field. Chapter 5 of Mitkov's monograph [19] is another good source regarding the research during the consolidation phase.

3.4 *The Resources-Driven, or Robustification Phase (1995–2001)*

In this period, the final major measures towards truly robust, operational anaphora resolution were taken. **Kennedy and Boguraev** [14] described an approach that is an immediate descendant of Lappin and Leass's RAP algorithm. In recognizing the limitations of state-of-the-art parsing technology, they reformulated RAP's syntax-based strategies—in particular, the syntactic disjoint reference filter—as regular-expression-based rules in order to make them applicable to the output of a robust part-of-speech tagger. The result was a truly shallow approach to pronominal anaphora resolution that doesn't require a parser.

Another bunch of important work has been solicited by including the **coreference (= CO) task** in the information extraction evaluation contests **MUC-6** [24] and **MUC-7** [27] held by DARPA. As coreference resolution is an immediate spin-off product of, and is commonly conducted by anaphora resolution, these contests decisively fostered the development of robust algorithms for resolving third-person pronouns, names, and common nouns/definite descriptions. Among the most important achievements of the CO task contest are coreference-annotated corpora and the operationalization of a corpus-based evaluation scenario [36], which, at the first time, allowed a completely formal and repeatable comparison of fully implemented coreference resolution systems. It is thus the resources—annotation standards, annotation tools, evaluation criteria beyond simple accuracy, evaluation tools—which are now held available by institutions such as the Linguistic Data Consortium, that constitute the key contribution of the CO contests.

Beyond enabling evaluation of coreference resolution systems according to the MUC CO task definition, these annotated corpora turned out to be the mainspring for a paradigmatic turn towards **corpus-based approaches** to anaphora resolution. Since then, a great variety of machine learning and statistical methods have been investigated as devices for automatically determining respective strategies. Among the most influential work is the comprehensive research by Soon et al. [32], who employ supervised decision tree learning over the MUC-6 and MUC-7 corpora.[2] The availability of annotated corpora even fostered the further refinement of the classical Lappin and Leass style rule-based approaches, resulting in robust descendants of the RAP algorithm: Mitkov [17] developed the fundamentals of his MARS system, and Stuckardt [34] described the ROSANA system, which employs an algorithm for robustly verifying syntactic disjoint reference conditions on partial parses. Evaluation as well has been an issue of further research. Various authors emphasized the shortcomings of MUC's model-theoretic coreference scoring scheme [36], particularly its limited degree of expressiveness with respect to the task of anaphora resolution, and suggested respective refinements (e.g., Bagga and Baldwin [3], Mitkov [18], and Stuckardt [34]).

Besides the abundant research on robust, operational approaches dealing, in particular, with pronouns, there has been further important practical and conceptual work. Extensive empirical studies on particular types of non-pronominal anaphora have been carried out, e.g., work on definite descriptions (Poesio and Vieira [22] and Vieira and Poesio [35]) and on bridging anaphora (Poesio, Vieira and Teufel [23]). Research on centering theory continued as well; e.g., there have been the well-recognized publications by Strube and Hahn [33] on functional centering and by Kameyama [13] on intrasentential centering.

[2]In fact, there is as well some pre-MUC research, in which other, typically smaller corpora are used (dating back to 1994 and 1995, e.g. Connolly et al. [8], Aone and Bennett [1, 2], and McCarthy and Lehnert [16]). Moreover, there are a few approaches that explore techniques of unsupervised learning.

The key achievement of this research phase is the final step towards truly robust, operational approaches. It thus seems adequate to speak of the **"robustification" phase**, or, in emphasizing the central role of annotated corpora and formal evaluation, the **resources-driven phase**. Covering theory and empirical investigations as well as algorithms and resources, the monograph [19] by Mitkov documents this period. Further influential publications are provided by the special issue of the Computational Linguistics journal on computational anaphora resolution [21] and by the proceedings of various dedicated conferences (e.g., the *Discourse Anaphora and Anaphor Resolution Colloquia DAARC* [25, 26, 28] and the *ACL Workshop on Operational Factors in Practical, Robust Anaphora Resolution for Unrestricted Texts* [20]).

4 Recent Developments: The Post-modern Phase (2002–)

This is the phase of recent developments, which is to be documented by this book. It shall thus be discussed in a dedicated section.

As a survey of recent work on anaphor and coreference resolution shows, corpora annotated with referential information continue to play a key role. While there is ongoing theoretical research that employs constructed sample sentences and relies on acceptability judgments of informants, the corpus-based, empirical research that employs shared resources definitely prevails. This holds with respect to both practical/application-oriented and conceptual work, since annotated corpora are not only of central importance to developing algorithms and applications, but as well to the evaluation and further refinement of theoretical models.

There is a continuing predominance of empirical, corpus-based and machine learning (ML) work. However, it turns out to be difficult to single out a particular attribute that brings to the point the current trend in anaphora processing research. Taking the achievements of the robustification phase as the point of departure, present work deals with diverse issues:

- off-the-shelf anaphora resolution systems—that is, readily available software solutions (as components of NLP toolkits etc.) providing an appropriately designed API so that they can be immediately employed as components of application systems;
- off-the shelf technology for preprocessing text to be subjected to anaphora resolution—this includes enhanced ML- and rule-based approaches to perform important subtasks specific to the anaphora resolution task such as entity mention detection;
- further annotated corpora in diverse domains and languages;
- enhanced multi-layered corpus annotation schemes and the respective state-of-the-art software tools for annotating corpora;
- further enhancement of evaluation methodology and environments—in particular, to foster comparability of evaluation results by providing standardized

preprocessing tools and evaluation criteria (as part of a suitable evaluation test bed);

- refined metrics such as B-cubed, CEAF and BLANC that overcome some limitations of the classical MUC coreference resolution scoring scheme;
- important post-MUC evaluation campaigns (ACE, SemEval, i2b2, CoNLL) featuring anaphora-processing-related competitions;
- refined generic ML-based anaphora resolution methods such as the entity-mention, mention-ranking, and cluster-ranking models that resolve particular limitations (e.g., the coreference clustering/transitivity problem) of the basic mention-pair model;
- enhanced mathematical frameworks such as Integer Linear Programming for dealing with the coreference clustering/transitivity issue in an even more general sense;
- dedicated algorithms that deal with important subproblems of anaphora processing—for instance, detecting non-referential (expletive) expressions and discourse-new entity mentions based on enhanced corpus-based methods such as Support Vector Machines and Maximum Entropy classifiers;
- enhanced sources of evidence for both ML- and rule-based approaches—in particular, lexical and encyclopedic knowledge to be exploited as additional preferential factors or to resolve instances of bridging anaphora etc.; furthermore, refined supervised as well as unsupervised techniques for extracting this knowledge from state-of-the-art resources such as Wikipedia, WordNet, and OntoNotes;
- large-scale knowledge acquisition methods for particular sources of evidence—for instance, the gender and number features as referred to in the classical agreement constraint;
- refined general techniques for applying anaphora processing to accomplish diverse generic tasks; for instance, important recent advances in coreference-based single- and multi-document summarization have been obtained by augmenting a mathematical summarization framework based on Latent Semantic Analysis (LSA) with referential information provided by a state-of-the-art off-the-shelf anaphora resolver;
- particular application scenarios in diverse domains, among which are biomedicine, medicine, legal domain, and the news/media sector—substantiating that anaphora processing technology combined with domain-specific resources (such as domain-annotated corpora and custom-made preprocessing technology) can be put to good use in economically highly relevant application scenarios;
- emerging best-practice language engineering knowledge on how to systematically approach new application scenarios.

The list illustrates the high bandwidth of current research. While ML-based approaches are predominant in general research, hybrid and rule-based approaches continue to play a role—at the very least for tackling application-scenario-related particular problems. There is thus an apparent plurality of algorithms, methods, and models. Since much depends upon the application case—e.g., the anaphora processing required, the text sorts to be processed, the distribution and relative importance of particular types of anaphoric expressions, whether appropriate domain knowledge is available—there is no unique best approach.

The situation thus calls for a second consolidation phase, which should decisively benefit from a systematic appraisal of the recent advances in algorithms, resources, and—last not least—applications. Emphasizing the apparent eclecticism in present-day work, it is suggested to speak of the current research period as the **post-modern phase**.

The above-listed subject matters of recent research can be logically divided into three topics, which constitute the framework of the subsequent survey:

- **resources**—covering annotated corpora, evaluation criteria, evaluation tools, preprocessing technology, and readily available off-the-shelf systems;
- **algorithms**—discussing the state-of-the-art anaphora processing methods and related key techniques;
- **applications**—looking at particular anaphora processing applications in a broad range of domains, eventually distilling a procedure model for systematically approaching novel application scenarios.

Completed with a succinct introduction to the linguistic, cognitive, and computational foundations of anaphora processing, which includes a description of the key classical rule- and ML-based algorithms, this book thus comprises four parts.

5 Overview of the Chapters

The introduction shall be complemented with brief summaries of all following chapters. The exposition aims at providing an integrated overview of the book, that is, making visible how each individual contribution fits into the global content structure by adding cross-references to related chapters wherever appropriate.

Part I: Background features two chapters:

With his chapter—"**Linguistic and Cognitive Evidence about Anaphora**"—**Massimo Poesio** features an introduction to the conceptual backgrounds of the research field by looking at the linguistics of anaphora and the evidence to be employed to interpreting anaphora. Anaphors are characterized as expressions the interpretation of which depends upon the linguistic context; the focus is on the type of anaphora most commonly considered in research: referring noun phrases. The key concepts are defined, including the main types of relations between anaphor and antecedent and the formal notion of discourse model. The exposition is complemented with a statistics about types of anaphoric expressions and relations in diverse corpora. In the second part of the chapter, Poesio identifies the most important factors (constraints and preferences) deemed relevant for interpreting anaphoric expressions, and looks at evidence from corpora and psycholinguistics in favor of these factors. This includes a description of the main models of local focus, distinguishing between discrete and activation-based approaches and discussing important recent empirical findings about particular theories.

Moving on, with their chapter—"**Early Approaches to Anaphora Resolution: Theoretically Inspired and Heuristic-Based**"—towards the operational treatment of anaphora, **Massimo Poesio, Roland Stuckardt, Yannick Versley and Renata Vieira** provide a comprehensive introduction into some very influential early anaphora resolution algorithms, ranging from the seminal syntax-based algorithm by Hobbs, which marked the start of the shallow processing research phase, to the first robust rule-based or data-driven approaches, which were developed during the resources-driven, or robustification phase. This includes the concise description of a cornucopia of prominent algorithms and systems for pronoun as well as definite description resolution, among which are Sidner's approach, the centering algorithm by Brennan, Friedman, and Pollard, the very influential graded salience approach RAP by Lappin and Leass, the enhanced approaches to centering by Strube and Tetreault, the definite description resolution approach by Vieira and Poesio, as well as some robust descendants that work on imperfect information such as Kennedy and Boguraev's shallow implementation of RAP, Baldwin's high-precision resolver CogNIAC, Mitkov's MARS approach, Stuckardt's pronoun resolution system ROSANA implementing robust syntactic disjoint reference, and the MUC systems FASTUS by Kameyama et al. and LaSIE by Gaizauskas et al. The exposition is complemented with a brief description of one important recent approach: the Stanford Sieve by Raghunathan et al.

Part II: Resources comprises five chapters:

The huge advances in the development of operational anaphora and coreference resolution systems since the mid of the 1990s would not have been possible without appropriate resources having become available, one key component of which are corpora annotated with anaphoric relations. These corpora as well as the associated methodology and technology are of central relevance because they constitute enablers for the comparative and reproducible evaluation of competing systems as well as for the development of corpus-based approaches that employ supervised learning. The comprehensive survey given in chapter—"**Annotated Corpora and Annotation Tools**"—by **Massimo Poesio, Sameer Pradhan, Marta Recasens, Kepa Rodriguez and Yannick Versley** ranges from the corpora and guidelines developed for the Message Understanding Conferences MUC-6 (1996) and MUC-7 (1998), which have been seminal to the field, to the resources that have been recently made available as part of the 2010 SemEval evaluation campaign. All fundamental design decisions regarding annotation formats and standards are described. The relevant properties of the corpora are presented in a uniform and well-structured way, thus enabling the reader to quickly identify, and eventually access, the resources best-suited to be employed for her particular research and development purposes. Another key contribution of this chapter consists of a description of three useful, widely used and freely available annotation tools (CALLISTO, MMAX2, and Palinka), which can be employed if own annotation work turns out to be indispensable, that is, in case that none of the readily available corpora can be reused, which might be due to diverging text genres and/or application domains, or because another language or a new type of anaphoric relation shall be investigated.

The development of the model-theoretic coreference resolution scoring scheme [36] for the MUC competitions decisively fostered the advances in robust anaphora resolution. There are, however, various shortcomings of the MUC metric, which led to the proposal of diverse refinements, among which are suggestions to distinguish between subtasks (that is, to separately evaluate preprocessing/entity mention extraction and coreference resolution proper), or to appropriately enhance the coreference scoring scheme. In their chapter—"**Evaluation Metrics**"—**Xiaoqiang Luo** and **Sameer Pradhan** take a detailed look at the MUC metric and three of its most widely recognized successors, namely: B-cubed, CEAF, and BLANC. Based on an instructive introduction to the intricacies of coreference and anaphora resolution evaluation (e.g., the evaluation-technical treatment of spurious and "forgotten" markables), they identify and thoroughly compare the pros and cons of the different metrics. This chapter gives the reader the indispensable methodological background to decide which metric to choose as the diagnostic instrument of choice for a given evaluation goal.

Providing an environment for assessing implemented systems, evaluation campaigns have played—and continue to play—a decisive role for the development of natural language processing technology. Their purposes are multifaceted: (1) initiating and furthering the implementation of robust, truly operational systems; (2) providing standardized definitions of diverse tasks; (3) defining respective language data annotation standards and evaluation measures, thus enabling the construction of shared resources (annotated corpora and evaluation tools), performance assessment of individual systems and, in particular, a valid comparison of competing systems; (4) directing the development into particular directions of interest (tasks to be performed, languages to be covered, domains and genres to be considered); (5) bringing together the research community, bundling national and international research efforts through standardization and synchronization. With their chapter—"**Evaluation Campaigns**"—**Marta Recasens and Sameer Pradhan** provide an in-depth description of evaluation campaigns featuring anaphora and coreference processing tasks, looking, in particular, at the seminal evaluation efforts at the DARPA Message Understanding Conferences (MUC-6, MUC-7) and at follow-up events such as the Automatic Content Extraction (ACE) program, SemEval-2010, i2b2-2011, and CoNLL-2011/2012, which have brought about a stepwise refinement and diversification of task definitions, evaluation scenarios, and evaluation measures. The facets of these contests are summarized and compared, covering languages and corpora to be processed, type of reference processing to be conducted, evaluation measures applied, and results obtained. Some issues that are critical from an evaluation-technical point of view are looked at in detail: (a) mention detection—in particular, whether automatic mention detection forms part of the task, or whether reference processing should be performed based on pre-annotated mentions; (b) definition of mention boundaries; (c) preprocessing information—again, to what extent external resources and/or pre-annotations are employed. These issues are critical as they have strong implications regarding level of performance to be expected and comparability of results reported at different evaluation campaigns. Thus, a more global view of the evaluation topic is provided that transcends the above discussion of the formal properties of individual metrics and annotation schemes.

Corpus-based as well as rule-based approaches to anaphora resolution resort to a wide range of evidence, spanning from surface-based via linguistic/syntactic to semantic/encyclopedic knowledge. This evidence is to be employed for accomplishing the diverse subtasks of anaphora resolution, among which are entity mention extraction, anaphoricity detection, and antecedent assignment. Constructing entity mention descriptions that encapsulate the necessary knowledge thus requires the availability of respective robust preprocessing components. In their chapter—"**Preprocessing Technology**"—**Olga Uryupina and Roberto Zanoli** take a detailed look at the preprocessing pipeline that is typically employed in coreference resolution systems, comprising the whole gamut of subtasks: raw text extraction, tokenization, part-of-speech tagging, parsing, entity mention detection, and encyclopedic knowledge extraction. They discuss each subtask in detail, that is, they delineate the problem, and they give references to readily available software modules. They then focus on the key task of entity mention construction, taking a detailed look at respective recent rule- and ML-based research, eventually arriving at a practical solution that accomplishes entity mention construction based on corpus-based methods by employing a publicly available SVM software package. Useful cross-references are included that elucidate the role that entity mention detection plays in diverse coreference evaluation contests.

From the perspective of typical applications in the fields of information extraction, text summarization, machine translation etc., anaphora resolution systems can themselves be considered as yet more complex preprocessing components at the semantic analysis layer. With their chapter—"**Off-the-Shelf Tools**"—**Yannick Versley and Anders Björkelund** provide an appraisal of respective leading edge multilingual off-the-shelf solutions, discussing in detail the systems BART, dCoref (which comes as part of the Stanford CoreNLP Suite), as well as the purely machine-learning-based systems IMSCoref and HOTCoref. Among the key regards in which these solutions differ are employed input and output formats, encapsulated language-specific preprocessing components, implemented anaphora resolution algorithms, and interfaces to machine learning packages. Björkelund and Versley give a detailed account of pros and cons of the different formats for annotating linguistic data supported by the considered systems; moreover, they discuss how to employ internal or external preprocessing components, and how to train one's own language and domain-specific anaphora resolution classifiers by interfacing to external machine learning toolkits. The chapter concludes with the outline of a checklist-based approach to choosing, adapting, and integrating an off-the-shelf coreference processing technology that is most suitable for a new application scenario.

Part III: Algorithms consists of six chapters:

As recent research focuses on machine-learning-based anaphora resolution, the first chapter of Part III is devoted to discussing the architectural base of a substantial class of supervised approaches: in her chapter—"**The Mention-Pair Model**"—**Veronique Hoste** investigates the mention-pair model, which recasts noun phrase coreference resolution as a two-step procedure consisting of an initial ML-based coreference classification step over (anaphor, antecedent candidate) mention pairs followed by a coreference class clustering step. Looking at the preprocessing required, comparing strategies for selecting properly balanced sets of positive and negative training instances, discussing how to select informative features that prove useful for the classification task, and elaborating upon how to choose a suitable off-the-shelf machine learner and a clustering mechanism, all key issues are considered. Details about the most influential incarnations of the mention-pair model are given, looking, in particular, at the Soon et al. algorithm [32]. As the Soon et al. approach now serves as the standard baseline for ML-based coreference resolution, many researchers regard it as the "Hobbs's algorithm of the early 21st century". However, the mention-pair model is identified to exhibit some weaknesses as well. This leads to the definition of respectively refined alternative models, which will be discussed in the subsequent chapters.

In the last decade, a number of further advanced ML approaches to coreference resolution have been developed that aim at overcoming the weaknesses of the mention-pair model. In his chapter—"**Advanced Machine Learning Models for Coreference Resolution**"—**Vincent Ng** starts with observing two major issues to be dealt with: (1) limitations in expressiveness—as the mention-pair model merely looks at particular coreference class instances (viz., mentions), it does not take into account non-local properties pertaining to the coreference classes, that is, it does not pay sufficient attention to clustering; (2) no ranking of candidate antecedents—while, in general, the model predicts whether a particular antecedent candidate should or should not be interpreted as coreferential with the anaphor under consideration, it does not say which particular candidate is most plausible. Ng then gives a comprehensive survey of enhanced approaches to resolving these two major issues. Cluster sensitivity is obtained by employing the entity-mention model, that is, by learning ML models over pairs (m,C) of mentions and coreference clusters represented by feature sets that include cluster-level attributes; diverse particular approaches and further enhancements employing different learning and clustering algorithms are specified and discussed in detail. Determining the relative probability of antecedent candidates can be accomplished by resorting to the mention-ranking model—a different line of refinement of the mention-pair model, according to which coreference resolution is interpreted as a ranking rather than classification task. Eventually, Ng describes important recent developments in ML-based coreference resolution, including some hybrid (cluster-ranking-model) approaches that combine the entity-mention and the mention-ranking model, thus exhibiting desirable cluster-sensitivity as well as candidate ranking capabilities. The discussion covers as well some recent advanced approaches that combine ML-based coreference classification and ranking with related tasks such as mention recognition, anaphoricity and discourse-new detection—tasks that might well be performed together and thus dealt with by a joint ML model.

At present, common corpus-based approaches consider the task of anaphora and coreference resolution chiefly at mention-pair level, not paying sufficient attention to coreference class clustering. As possible interdependency between individual interpretation decisions is not adequately accounted for, these approaches fall short of deriving a globally optimal solution, or they might even generate an overall inconsistent interpretation. Restricting considerations to particular types of evidence (such as syntactic disjoint reference conditions), this issue was already recognized and successfully resolved by some early rule-based algorithms. However, today's prevalence and success of statistical approaches to natural language processing that integrate diverse potentially interdependent types of evidence hints at investigating a more general account of how to search for a consistent and globally optimal interpretation. In their chapter—"**Integer Linear Programming for Coreference Resolution**"—**Nick Rizzolo and Dan Roth** consider this challenge as a constraint-optimization problem. Specifically, they investigate how the problem can be rendered in terms of Integer Linear Programming (ILP), a mathematical framework enabling an efficient solution of linear optimization problems requiring whole-number solutions, given that some formal conditions are satisfied. In the approach they develop, the statistical mention-pair coreference model that has been learned beforehand is mapped to an ILP model's linear objective function; interdependency is then encoded as a set of linear constraints and objective function add-ons that model the transitivity conditions. Going into the mathematical details of ILP, discussing the computational implications, and identifying possible tractability issues, several explicit and implicit solutions to enforcing these conditions are specified. The chapter concludes with an account of how the techniques developed can be employed even more generally to integrating and enforcing transitivity conditions over the predictions of various statistical models that address closely related and interdependent NLP problems (coreference, anaphoricity, named entity classification). As this approach enhances the system components' interpretation quality as well as overall robustness, some well-known disadvantages of sequential NLP architectures are avoided.

As the agreement constraint is known to be among the most useful criteria for interpreting anaphoric nominal expressions, it is directly or indirectly employed by the large majority of practical approaches. Seemingly an easy-to-implement strategy, empirical evaluations of operational approaches on large-scale corpora proved that general availability of the evidence referred to—number and gender features of nouns including names—cannot be taken granted, as the employed standard resources, among which are WordNet, named entity recognition technology, and list data, are generally insufficient. In his chapter—"**Extracting Anaphoric Agreement Properties from Corpora**"—**Shane Bergsma** investigates the thus important challenge of how to automatically extract nominal agreement properties from annotated or raw text. Diverse algorithms are considered, ranging from simple heuristics to large-scale supervised, semi-supervised, and unsupervised machine-learning approaches. References to publicly available number/gender databases, which have been computed according to these approaches, are included; anaphora resolution systems can thus employ these resources as off-the-shelf components. This illustrates that the described enhanced knowledge acquisition strategies eventually contribute to the repository of reusable resources that are discussed in Part II of the book.

Recognizing which linguistic expressions are referring, and which referring expressions are anaphoric, are important subproblems of anaphora resolution. They are to be solved in order to decide which expressions constitute mentions and to further distinguish between two classes of mentions (discourse-new vs. anaphoric), since only mentions of the latter class require an antecedent and are hence to be subjected to anaphora resolution proper. Regarding object anaphora, the most important instances of non-referring expressions are expletive occurrences of the pronoun *it*; referring, but non-anaphoric mentions are contributed by discourse-new definite descriptions, through which new referents (constituting antecedent candidates) are introduced into the discourse. In their chapter—**"Detecting Non-Reference and Non-Anaphoricity"—Olga Uryupina, Mijail Kabadjov and Massimo Poesio** describe a methodological framework for the corpus-based detection of expletive pronouns and discourse-new mentions and investigate several particular approaches that are based on this framework. In a first case study, they thoroughly discuss recent work on discourse-new detection, comparing the employment of Support Vector Machine vs. Maximum Entropy classifiers. In a second case study, they take an in-depth look at various state-of-the-art approaches to expletive detection. Methodological and technical issues are covered in full detail, e.g., how to cross-validate the results, how to test for statistical significance, and which resources (SVM and MaxEnt software packages, preprocessing tools for feature extraction) to employ for implementation and evaluation.

Semantic evidence is generally recognized to play a key role for enhancing anaphora and coreference resolution performance beyond baseline level. Semantic compatibility conditions between anaphor and antecedent apply to both pronoun and definite description resolution. With their chapter—**"Using Lexical and Encyclopedic Knowledge"—Yannick Versley, Massimo Poesio and Simone Ponzetto** give a survey of state-of-the-art approaches to exploit lexical and encyclopedic knowledge, ranging from basic gender and animacy compatibility checks for pronouns via context-sensitive selectional preference patterns to enhanced criteria for definite description interpretation that make use of lexical relations such as synonymy, hypernymy, and instance-class. The techniques and strategies that they describe employ a broad range of resources, among which are gender tables, semi-annotated dictionaries (Wikipedia, DBpedia), enhanced hand-crafted resources (WordNet, OntoNotes), more specific lexical resources (FrameNet, VerbNet) and referentially annotated corpora; both supervised and unsupervised techniques for mining semantic relations from corpora are applied. According to their survey of recent research, and contrary to some earlier findings, resorting to a larger and richer semantic knowledge might well yield moderate performance gains, the measurement of which, however, requires the application of realistic evaluation settings; this recent success seems as well to be fostered by the application of some recent enhanced machine-learning models for anaphora processing, which can make better use of the semantically enriched feature sets, and by the quality and quantity of the semantic resources (corpora, dictionaries) themselves. Once again, this illustrates the central importance of statistical methods and shared resources such as evaluation standards, corpora, taxonomies, semantic preprocessing modules, and lexical/encyclopedic knowledge.

Part IV: Applications provides the following two chapters:

Automatic text summarization is among the most important applications of anaphora and coreference resolution. Since automatic summarization itself constitutes a target task of diverse evaluation contests, it has received wide attention by recent research. In their chapter—"**Coreference Applications to Summarization**"—**Josef Steinberger, Mijail Kabadjov, and Massimo Poesio** consider strategies and techniques to employing coreference and anaphora resolution information for both single-document and multi-document summarization, looking at two particular use cases of referential evidence: improving the selection of informative content, and establishing or enhancing coherence of the extract through coreference-based post-processing (substitution) techniques which ensure that anaphoric expressions occurring in the summary remain comprehensible. They focus on recent research, looking, in particular, at a summarization framework based on Latent Semantic Analysis (LSA), investigating how this framework can be successfully enhanced by supplementing lexical evidence with coreference information as made available by state-of-the-art off-the-shelf anaphora and coreference resolution systems, and giving full technical details of the approaches followed. Steinberger and Kabadjov describe diverse methods for evaluating the contribution of referential evidence, referring to appropriate summarization evaluation metrics. Eventually, they identify some particularly promising ways to employing referential evidence for automatic summarization, confirming that both single-document and multi-document summarization can benefit from properly applied referential evidence; moreover, according to their results, a high-precision resolver should be employed for coherence-enhancing post-processing.

Finally, with his chapter—"**Towards a Procedure Model for Developing Anaphora Processing Applications**"—**Roland Stuckardt** moves one step further towards real-world applications, providing a survey of particular cases in diverse highly relevant domains, among which are biomedicine, medicine, and legal domain. He suggests that the design of an appropriate anaphora processing technology should be based on a detailed understanding of the particular application scenario that goes well beyond the mere recognition of the generic application type (information extraction, text summarization, etc.). As elucidated by the survey, supplementary resources such as corpora annotated with domain information and domain entity databases play an important role for case-specific anaphora processing. Summing up these insights, Stuckardt eventually distils a procedure model that is designed to assist the natural language engineer in systematically approaching novel application scenarios. He concludes by proposing that the procedure model should as well be employed as a framework for publicly documenting application-related anaphora processing work, fostering progress of the discipline by enhancing visibility and comparability of approaches, eventually enabling reuse of previous work related to similar scenarios.

The final Part V: Outlook features one concluding chapter:

The book shall be concluded with a brief discussion of the prospects of the research field of anaphora processing, identifying promising directions of further research, new application scenarios, and interdisciplinary cooperation. In order to obtain the broadest-possible view of the discipline's future, an inspiring survey with respective pertinent questions has been conducted among all contributors to this book in order to poll their individual opinions. In this final chapter—"**Challenges and Directions of Further Research**"—which thus gathers contributions by **multiple authors**, the received answers will be summarized and evaluated.

References

1. Aone, C., Bennett, S.W.: Evaluating automated and manual acquisition of anaphora resolution strategies. In: Proceedings of the 33rd Annual Meeting of the ACL, Santa Cruz, pp. 122–129 (1995)
2. Aone, C., Bennett, S.W.: Applying machine learning to anaphora resolution. In: Wermter, S., Riloff, E., Scheler, G. (eds.) Connectionist, Statistical and Symbolic Approaches to Learning for Natural Language Processing, pp. 302–314. Springer, Berlin (1996)
3. Bagga, A., Baldwin, B.: Algorithms for scoring coreference chains. In: Proceedings of the Workshop on Linguistic Coreference at the First International Conference on Language Resources and Evaluation (LREC'98), Granada (1998)
4. Bobrow, D.G.: A question-answering system for high school algebra word problems. In: AFIPS Conference Proceedings, vol. 26, pp. 591–614. Spartan, Baltimore (1964)
5. Brennan, S.E., Friedman, M.W., Pollard, C.J.: A centering approach to pronouns. In: Proceedings of the 25th Annual Meeting on Association for Computational Linguistics, pp. 155–162. Association for Computational Linguistics, Morristown (1987). doi:http://dx.doi.org/10.3115/981175.981197
6. Carbonell, J.G., Brown, R.D.: Anaphora resolution: a multi-strategy approach. In: Proceedings of the 12th International Conference on Computational Linguistics (COLING), Budapest, pp. 96–101 (1988)
7. Carter, D.: Interpreting Anaphora in Natural Language Texts. Ellis Horwood, Chichester (1987)
8. Connolly, D., Burger, J.D., Day, D.S.: A machine-learning approach to anaphoric reference. In: Proceedings of the International Conference on New Methods in Language Processing (NEMLAP), Manchester (1994)
9. Grosz, B.J., Sidner, C.L.: Attention, intentions, and the structure of discourse. Comput. Linguist. **12**(3), 175–204 (1986)
10. Grosz, B.J., Joshi, A.K., Weinstein, S.: Providing a unified account of definite noun phrases in discourse. In: Proceedings of the 21st Annual Meeting on Association for Computational Linguistics, pp. 44–50. Association for Computational Linguistics, Morristown (1983). doi:http://dx.doi.org/10.3115/981311.981320
11. Hirst, G.: Anaphora in Natural Language Understanding. A Survey. LNCS, vol. 119. Springer, Berlin/Heidelberg (1982)
12. Hobbs, J.R.: Resolving pronoun references. Lingua **44**, 311–338 (1978)

13. Kameyama, M.: Intrasentential centering: a case study. In: Walker, M.A., Joshi, A.K., Prince, E.F. (eds.) Centering Theory in Discourse, pp. 89–112. Clarendon Press, Oxford (1998)
14. Kennedy, C., Boguraev, B.: Anaphora for everyone: pronominal anaphora resolution without a parser. In: Proceedings of the 16th International Conference on Computational Linguistics (COLING), Copenhagen, pp. 113–118 (1996)
15. Lappin, S., Leass, H.J.: An algorithm for pronominal anaphora resolution. Comput. Linguist. **20**(4), 535–561 (1994)
16. McCarthy, J.F., Lehnert, W.G.: Using decision trees for coreference resolution. In: Proceedings of the 14th International Joint Conference on Artificial Intelligence (IJCAI'95), Montreal (1995)
17. Mitkov, R.: Robust pronoun resolution with limited knowledge. In: Proceedings of the 17th International Conference on Computational Linguistics (COLING'98/ACL'98), Montreal, pp. 869–875 (1998)
18. Mitkov, R.: Towards a more consistent and comprehensive evaluation of anaphora resolution algorithms and systems. Appl. Artif. Intell. **15**(3), 253–276 (2001)
19. Mitkov, R.: Anaphora Resolution. Longman, London/New York (2002)
20. Mitkov, R., Boguraev, B. (eds.): Proceedings of the ACL'97/EACL'97 Workshop on Operational Factors in Practical, Robust Anaphor Resolution for Unrestricted Texts, Madrid (1997). ACLWS1997
21. Mitkov, R., Boguraev, B., Lappin, S. (eds.): Computational Linguistics: Special Issue on Computational Anaphora Resolution, vol. 27. MIT press, Cambridge (2001)
22. Poesio, M., Vieira, R.: A corpus-based investigation of definite description use. Comput. Linguist. **24**(2), 183–216 (1998)
23. Poesio, M., Vieira, R., Teufel, S.: Resolving bridging references in unrestricted text. In: Proceedings of the ACL'97/EACL'97 Workshop on Operational Factors in Practical, Robust Anaphora Resolution for Unrestricted Texts, Madrid, July 1997, pp. 1–6 (1997)
24. Proceedings of the 6th Message Understanding Conference (MUC-6). Morgan Kaufmann, San Francisco (1996)
25. Proceedings of the Discourse Anaphora and Anaphor Resolution Colloquium (DAARC 1996), Lancaster (1996)
26. Proceedings of the 2nd Discourse Anaphora and Anaphor Resolution Colloquium (DAARC 1998), Lancaster (1998)
27. Proceedings of the 7th Message Understanding Conference (MUC-7) (1998)
28. Proceedings of the 3rd Discourse Anaphora and Anaphor Resolution Colloquium (DAARC 2000), Lancaster (2000)
29. Sidner, C.L.: Towards a computational theory of definite anaphora comprehension in english discourse. Technical report, Massachusetts Institute of Technology, Cambridge (1979)
30. Sidner, C.L.: Focusing for interpretation of pronouns. Am. J. Comput. Linguist. **7**(4), 217–231 (1981)
31. Sidner, C.L.: Focusing in the comprehension of definite anaphora. In: Brady, M., Berwick, R.C. (eds.) Computational Models of Discourse. MIT, Cambridge (1983)
32. Soon, W.M., Ng, H.T., Lim, D.C.Y.: A machine learning approach to coreference resolution of noun phrases. Comput. Linguist. **27**(4), 521–544 (2001)
33. Strube, M., Hahn, U.: Functional centering. In: Proceedings of the 34th Annual Meeting of the Association for Computational Linguistics, pp. 270–277. Association for Computational Linguistics, Morristown (1996). doi:http://dx.doi.org/10.3115/981863.981899
34. Stuckardt, R.: Design and enhanced evaluation of a robust anaphor resolution algorithm. Comput. Linguist. **27**(4), 479–506 (2001)
35. Vieira, R., Poesio, M.: Corpus-based development and evaluation of a system for processing definite descriptions. In: Proceedings of the 18th Conference on Computational Linguistics, pp. 899–903. Association for Computational Linguistics, Morristown (2000). doi:http://dx.doi.org/10.3115/992730.992776

36. Vilain, M., Burger, J., Aberdeen, J., Connolly, D., Hirschman, L.: A model-theoretic coreference scoring scheme. In: Proceedings of the 6th Message Understanding Conference (MUC-6), pp. 45–52. Morgan Kaufmann, San Francisco (1996). doi:http://dx.doi.org/10.3115/1072399.1072405
37. Wilks, Y.: Preference semantics. Stanford AI Laboratory Memo AIM-206, Stanford University (1973)
38. Winograd, T.: Understanding Natural Language. Academic, New York/Edinburgh University Press, Edinburgh (1972)
39. Woods, W.A., Kaplan, R.M., Nash-Webber., B.L.: The lunar sciences natural language information system: final report. Bolt Beranek and Newman, Cambridge (1972)

Part I
Background

Linguistic and Cognitive Evidence About Anaphora

Massimo Poesio

Abstract Linguistics and psychology provide us with a theoretical analysis of what anaphoric expressions mean, and evidence about how their interpretation is recovered in context—in particular, which information is used. In this chapter we discuss this evidence. Respective key concepts will be defined, including the main types of relations between anaphor and antecedent and the formal notion of discourse model. Moreover, the most important factors (constraints and preferences) will be identified that are deemed relevant for interpreting anaphoric expressions, and it will be looked at evidence from corpora and psycholinguistics in favor of these factors. This includes a description of the main models of local focus, distinguishing between discrete and activation-based approaches.

Keywords Linguistic and cognitive evidence about anaphora cognitive linguistics • Psycholinguistics • Anaphora resolution

1 Introduction

Linguistics and psychology provide us with theoretical analyses of what anaphoric expressions mean, and evidence about how their interpretation is recovered in context—in particular, which information is used. In this chapter we review this work, as a background to the following chapters.

In the second section of the chapter we review the linguistic theories of anaphora. First of all, we introduce the notion of **anaphora** in terms of the notion of **context dependence**. Next, we discuss the differences between different **types of anaphoric expressions**, and the different types of **anaphoric relations**. We then present the most widely accepted view of the semantics of anaphoric expressions, according to which they are interpreted with respect to a **discourse model** dynamically constructed as the discourse progresses. Finally, we review some of the most debated terminological issues concerning anaphora—above all, the difference between anaphora and **coreference**.

M. Poesio (✉)
University of Essex, Colchester, UK

M. Poesio et al. (eds.), *Anaphora Resolution*, Theory and Applications of Natural Language Processing, DOI 10.1007/978-3-662-47909-4_2

In the third section, we review psychological work on the interpretation of anaphoric expressions. We first discuss so-called **constraints** on anaphoric interpretation: morphological (e.g., gender), syntactic (e.g., the binding constraints) and semantic. Next, we discuss three types of **preferences** that have been found to play a role: semantic, syntactic (e.g., **parallelism**), and **salience**. In particular, we discuss salience at length, has it has been the focus of much study in computational linguistics.

2 The Linguistics of Anaphora

2.1 Context Dependence

The interpretation of many natural language expressions depends on the context of interpretation; in particular, the interpretation of many noun phrases depends on the entities mentioned in the **linguistic context**—the previous utterances and their content. Such dependency on the entities in the linguistic context is particularly obvious in the case of pronouns, whose interpretation entirely depends on them, as illustrated by the following dialogue fragment from the TRAINS dialogues [61]. In this example, the very same expression, personal pronoun *it*, is interpreted in totally different ways in utterances 3.1 (where it refers to engine E2) and 5.4 (where it refers to engine E1). Demonstrative pronouns as well may depend on entities introduced in the linguistic context, as illustrated by demonstrative *that* in 4.3. We will use the term **anaphoric** to indicate expressions that depend on the linguistic context, i.e., on objects explicitly mentioned or objects whose existence can be inferred from what has been said.

	1.1	M	:	all right system
	1.2		:	we've got a more complicated problem
	1.4		:	first thing _I'd_ like you to do
	1.5		:	is send engine E2 off with a boxcar to Corning to pick up oranges
	1.6		:	uh as soon as possible
	2.1	S	:	okay
	3.1	M	:	and while it's there it should pick up the tanker
(1)	4.1	S	:	okay
	4.2		:	and that can get
	4.3		:	we can get that done by three
	5.1	M	:	good
	5.3		:	can we please send engine E1 over to Dansville to pick up a boxcar
	5.4		:	and then send it right back to Avon
	6.1	S	:	okay
	6.2		:	it'll get back to Avon at 6

But pronouns are not the only noun phrases whose interpretation depends on the entities in the context (1) also contains the definite NP *the tanker* in 3.1, whose interpretation depends on the **visual context**, which in the TRAINS dialogues is a map of the 'TRAINS world' shared between the participants. *The tanker* has not been mentioned before, but it's on this map, and therefore it is shared and has high salience and can be referred to [22]; this type of context dependence is usually called **(visual) deixis.**[1] Such examples illustrate the fact that the noun phrases in these examples are better viewed as depending on what is usually called the **discourse situation** or **utterance situation** [7], that includes both the linguistic context and the surroundings in which the participants operate.[2] Following the terminology of Discourse Representation Theory (DRT) [76], we will call the set of entities introduced in the discourse situation U, for 'Universe of Discourse'. There is plenty of work in CL on interpreting references to the visual context [9, 81, 85, 99, 100], but this work falls outside the scope of this book, in which we will focus on anaphora.

More in general, the interpretation of noun phrases depends on the **domain of interpretation**: the particular set of objects under discussion. Indeed, under the most widely accepted theory about their meaning [84], the interpretation of proper names only depends on the domain of interpretation, because proper names are **directly referring**: they are the natural language encoding of logical constants, and therefore the object they are referring to is directly encoded in their semantics (as opposed to being recovered from the discourse situation). Under this view, the process of interpreting proper names would be completely different from that of interpreting pronouns and nominals. The interpretation of the second mention of *Avon* in (1), for instance, would not be obtained by finding an antecedent in the discourse situation, but it would come straight from the lexical semantics of proper name *Avon*—or, more plausibly, through a pragmatic process of identifying the appropriate domain of interpretation, and the object referred to within that domain. (For instance, the proper name *David Mitchell* in (2a) refers to a different object than the proper name *David Mitchell* in (2b).)

(2) a. David Mitchell (born 12 January 1969) is an English novelist. He has written four novels, two of which were shortlisted for the Booker Prize.
b. David Mitchell (born 14 July 1974) is a British actor, comedian and writer. He is one half of the comedy duo Mitchell and Webb, alongside Robert Webb, whom he met at Cambridge University.

The conclusion that the two instances of proper name *Avon* are mentions of the same object would be obtained indirectly, through the fact that they both refer to the same object: it would be a genuine 'coreference' task.

There is plenty of work in CL on disambiguating direct references to the domain of interpretation, particularly now that Wikipedia provides unique identifiers for many objects—e.g., the two interpretations of *David Mitchell* above correspond to

[1] Visual deixis is a type of **exophora**, but this term is not much used in CL.

[2] There are some constraints on what can be referred to in this way [120]; see below for a discussion of visual focus.

different Wikipedia pages [13, 27]—but this work, as well, falls outside the scope of this book, and even CL systems concentrating on identifying links between named entities do not identify coreference indirectly through the reference of proper names, whereas systems that attempt to interpret all noun phrases still need to model the context-modifying effect of proper names as they make antecedents available for pronouns and nominals.[3]

The choice of the domain of interpretation also affects the interpretation of nominals by fixing their **domain of quantification**—the set of objects of the type specified by the nominal complex which are included in the domain of interpretation [24, 97]. For instance, what makes the use of definite NP *the tanker* in (1) felicitous is the fact that the domain of quantification of nominal **tanker** consists of a single object (in the TRAINS dialogues the domain of interpretation coincides with the visual context).[4] The domain of quantification can also be specified by the linguistic context. In the following example, the expression *most employees* is evaluated with respect to the firm mentioned in the first sentence, whereas *the management* is interpreted as the management of the firm.

(3) Kim worked for 3 years in a large firm. Most employees were friendly, but the management was very distant.

However, we are not aware of much work on identifying the domain of quantification of a nominal apart from [99, 100].

2.2 Types of Context-Dependent Expressions

Nominals are not the only expressions whose interpretation is dependent on the linguistic or visual context in the sense above. Other examples include expressions that could be viewed as the analogous for the verbal interpretation domain of pronouns, such as **pro-verbs** like *did* in (4a) and **ellipsis** such as **gapping** in (4b). But just as pronouns are only the most extreme example of context-dependence among nominals, full verbal expressions have a context-dependent component as well. In (4c), for instance, the time of listening to the messages is pragmatically determined by the discourse [30, 76, 96].

(4) a. Kim is making the same mistakes that I did.
  b. Kim brought the wine, and Robin _ the cheese.
  c. Kim arrived home. She listened to the messages on her answering machine.

[3] We will also note that the direct reference theory of proper names is being challenged again [43].

[4] Readers may have noticed that the interpretation of expressions like *tanker* is 'context dependent' also in the sense that it depends on the sense of the word *tanker* intended in the circumstances of utterance. We will not be concerned here with this sense of context dependence, but only with expressions that are context dependent in that their interpretation depends on the entities contained in universe of discourse U.

A great deal of interest was paid to ellipsis in the early years of computational linguistics [28, 135, 137] but modern corpus-based work on the interpretation of anaphoric expressions in computational linguistics (and psycholinguistics) tends to focus on the identification of the antecedents of nominal expressions, primarily because of the lack of annotated resources for studying other types of anaphora.[5] For this reason, we will concentrate on nominal anaphoric expressions in this chapter.

Noun phrases can play four main types of **semantic function**:

Referring — Following the terminology used in functional linguistics and natural language generation, we will use the term **referring noun phrases** to indicate noun phrases that introduce new entities in a discourse, or require a link to previously introduced entities. Examples include sentences like *A train arrived soon after*, where *A train* introduces a new discourse entity; or *It left immediately*, where *it* refers to a previously introduced entity. We discuss referring noun phrases and their semantics in greater detail below.[6]

Quantificational — Quantificational noun phrases denote relations between the set of objects denoted by the nominal complex and the set of objects denoted by the verbal phrase: e.g., in *Few trains arrived in time*, the quantificational noun phrase *few trains* expresses a relation between the set of trains and the set of objects arriving late—namely, that few of the members of the first set are members of the second set as well:

$$\mathbf{few}(\lambda x.\mathbf{train}(x), \lambda\, x.\mathbf{arrive\text{-}late}(x))$$

Predicative — Predicative noun phrases express properties of objects. For instance, in *Kim is a preacher*, the noun phrase *a preacher* expresses a property of Kim (as opposed to referring to a second object).

Expletive — In languages like English, where verbal arguments always have be filled on syntactic grounds, forms like *it* and *there* can also be used to express semantically vacuous **expletives** as well as pronouns, as in example (5).

(5) It is half past two.

One should keep in mind that these distinctions are not always easy to make, even for humans [104, 109]. For instance, pronoun *it* in utterance 37.7 in fragment (6),

[5] A notable exception is the work by Hardt, e.g., [60]. Also, the presence of a VP ellipsis detection and resolution task at SEMEVAL-2010 indicates a renewed interest.

[6] This sense of 'referring noun phrase' is clearly distinct from the sense in which the term 'referring' is used in the philosophical and semantics literature.

also from the TRAINS dialogues, could be interpreted either as an expletive or as a reference to the proposed action of 'going through Dansville'.

	37.1	M	:	um
				[5sec]
	37.2		:	oh kay
	37.3		:	um
(6)	37.4		:	...then I guess we might as well go through Dansville
	37.5		:	so
	37.6		:	th / dz / cn / dyou /
	37.7		:	does it seem like a reasonable alternative to
	37.8		:	dealing with the engine that's hanging out in Elmira

An example of difficulty in classifying a noun phrase as predicative or referring is the underlined NP in (7), which would seem to be coreferring with Mr. Hoffman, yet appears to be playing more of a predicative role.

(7) Mr. Lieber, the actor who plays Mr. Hoffman, says he was concerned at first that the script would "misrepresent an astute political mind, one that I admired," but that his concerns were allayed.
The producers, he says, did a good job of depicting someone "who had done so much, but who was also a manic-depressive."

Finally, whether a noun phrase is considered referring or quantificational is often a matter of the particular theory chosen: for instance, in some theories all nominals are considered quantifiers, whereas in DRT and other theories, definites and indefinites are considered of a different type from other nominals.

Predicative noun phrases usually depend less on the universe of discourse U than other types of nominals (although they can depend on context in other respects of course). Thus, our interest in predicative NPs in this book will be limited to the fact that as many types of noun phrases can be used referentially in some contexts and predicatively in others, an anaphora resolution system must distinguish between the two types of NPs, hence the distinction must be reflected in anaphoric annotation schemes [102, 111]. Quantificational NPs are often context dependent, but in the sense that their domain of quantification is contextually specified, as discussed above. We will therefore concentrate here on referring expressions, and on the problem of selecting the discourse entity they are associated with, that is generally called **anchor** in the most general case, and **antecedent** in the case the relation between the referring expression and the anchor is one of identity (see below).

There are many varieties of referring noun phrases, which differ primarily according to the rules that govern their anaphoric behavior [19, 37, 39, 57, 113]. Such varieties include:

Reflexives, as in *John bought himself a parrot*[7];
Pronouns, which in turn can be divided into

[7]Reflexives are also known as 'anaphors' in Binding theory (see below).

- **Definite pronouns** such as *he* or *she*, as in *Ross bought {a radiometer/three kilograms of after-dinner mints} and gave {it / them} to Nadia for her birthday.* [65]
- **Indefinite pronouns** such as *one* in *Kim bought a t-shirt so Robin decided to buy one as well* [135].
- **Demonstrative pronouns** such as *that* in example (1), utterance 4.3.

Nominals, i.e., noun phrases that have a noun as head, such as *a man*, *a woman*, and *the man* in (8).

(8) A man and a woman came into my shop yesterday. The man wore a baseball hat.

Proper names, such as *Kim* and *Robin* in *Kim and Robin are good friends even though Kim likes sports whereas Robin prefers reading.*

There is a certain degree of cross-lingual variety in the forms that can be used to realize these types of anaphoric expressions. Reflexives and personal pronouns can be realized as **incorporated anaphors** in several Romance languages (e.g., Catalan, Italian, Portuguese, Spanish) and as **zero anaphors** in these languages as well as Japanese. Incorporated anaphors are cases of anaphoric reference in which the anaphoric expression is expressed by an affix of another expression, e.g., a verb, as in the following example from Italian, where clitic suffix *lo* refers back to Giovanni.

(9) a. [IT] Giovanni$_i$ e' in ritardo così mi ha chiesto se posso incontrar[lo]$_i$ al cinema.
b. [EN] John$_i$ is late so he$_i$ asked me if I can meet him$_i$ at the movies.

Zero anaphors are cases of anaphoric reference in which one argument is unrealized, as in the following examples from Italian and Japanese.

(10) a. [EN] [John]$_i$ went to visit some friends. On the way, [he]$_i$ bought some wine.
b. [IT] [Giovanni]$_i$ andò a far visita a degli amici. Per via, ϕ_i comprò del vino.
c. [JA] [John]$_i$-wa yujin-o houmon-sita. Tochu-de ϕ_i wain-o ka-tta.

As said above, proper names differ from other referring noun phrases from a semantic point of view, in that they are directly referring rather than referring to an entity introduced in the linguistic context; demonstratives, as well, can be directly referring (both pronouns and nominals) [77]. In this book however we will concentrate on methods for establishing coreference rather than identifying the referent of noun phrases, thus these claims about proper names and demonstratives will be primarily of interest in that they suggest that such nominals will often used to introduce new entities in the linguistic context. But this is true for nominals as well, as shown by (11) (from the 1993 TRAINS corpus; reported by J. Gundel) where *the maximum number of boxcars of oranges that I can get to Bath by 7 a.m. tomorrow morning* is not anaphoric—indeed, most studies find that a majority of definite NPs serve this purpose [35, 109]. (We discuss some statistics about the distribution of referring NPs in corpora below.)

(11)

S	hello can I help you
U	yeah I want t- I want to determine the maximum number of boxcars of oranges that I can get to Bath by 7 a.m. tomorrow morning so hm so I guess all the boxcars will have to go through oran- through Corning because that's where the orange juice factory is

Another difference between types of referring expressions intensively discussed in Linguistics is that between reflexives and (personal) pronouns, illustrated by (12), in which *herself* must corefer with *Susan*, but *her* cannot, has been investigated in depth in generative syntax, even leading to the development of a whole new Chomskyan paradigm in the 1980s (Government and Binding) [19, 113].

(12) Susan considered herself fortunate to meet her.

Several researchers have concerned themselves with the factors influencing the choice among multiple admissible linguistic forms [1, 4, 39, 57, 98, 101].

Gundel et al. [57] investigated in depth the difference between personal and demonstrative pronouns (i.e., the difference between *it* and *that*) using corpus data (see also [89, 98]), whereas several papers by Garrod and colleagues (e.g., [39]) discuss behavioral evidence concerning the difference between definites and pronouns and between definites and proper names. We will discuss these differences in the following section.

It is important for the purposes of the following discussion to point out that no form of referring expression is invariably referring or invariably context dependent. Even pronouns can sometimes be non-referring, as shown by the example of expletives.

2.3 Relation Between Anchor and Antecedent

The relation between a context-dependent referring expression and its anchor need not be one of identity of reference, as seen so far. Indefinite pronouns *one* and *another* generally stand in an **identity of sense** relation with their anchor: they refer to a different object of the same type, as in (13). Definite pronouns may also be used in the same way, as in so-called **paycheck pronouns** from famous example (14).

When the anchor is a quantified expression, as in (15), a pronoun with that anchor behaves like a variable in a procedure that gets repeatedly called over the elements specified by the restriction of the quantifier; that the relation between the pronoun and its anchor is not of identity in these cases is seen most clearly when the quantifier is downward entailing, like *no* in this case. We talk in these cases of **bound anaphora**.

Finally, in **associative anaphora**, the context-dependent nominal is related to its anchor by a relation such as part-of, as in (16). In these cases, to identify the antecedent a **bridging inference** is generally required [21, 123, 131].

(13) Sally admired Sue's jacket, so she got one for Christmas [37].
(14) The man who gave his paycheck to his wife is wiser than the man who gave it to his mistress [79].
(15) No Italian ever believes that the referee treated his team fairly.
(16) We saw a flat yesterday. The kitchen is very spacious but the garden is very small.

Identifying the exact relation between an anaphor and its anchor is not always easy [104, 109, 130]. This difficulty is illustrated by examples like the following, from the WSJ portion of the ARRAU corpus, where the possessive description *its machines* in sentence (17e) could refer either to the 'three small personal computers' introduced in sentence 1, or to the entire range of computers sold by Texas Instruments (thus paralleling the reference to the machines sold by Compaq in the previous clause), but it's not clear which. We refer to these cases as cases of **underspecified identity**.[8]

(17) a. Texas Instruments Inc., once a pioneer in portable computer technology, today will make a bid to reassert itself in that business by unveiling three small personal computers.
b. The announcements are scheduled to be made in Temple, Texas, and include a so-called "notebook" PC that weighs less than seven pounds, has a built-in hard disk drive and is powered by Intel Corp.'s 286 microprocessor.
c. That introduction comes only 2 weeks after Compaq Computer Corp., believing it had a lead of 3–6 months on competitors, introduced the first U.S. notebook computer with such features.
d. Despite the inevitable comparison with Compaq, however, Texas Instruments' new notebook won't be a direct competitor.
e. While Compaq sells its machines to businesses through computer retailers, Texas Instruments will be selling most of its machines to the industrial market and to value-added resellers and original-equipment manufacturers.

A range of types of anaphoric references in which the exact semantic relation between anaphor and antecedent is particularly complex to identify, and would require a more sophisticated theory of entities, was discussed by Versley [130] and by Recasens et al. [112]. The examples listed by Recasens and colleagues range from cases such as (18a), in which different stages of an individual are mentioned [15], to cases such as (18b), in which different facets of an individual are considered.

(18) a. On homecoming night [Postville] feels like Hometown, USA ... For those who prefer [the old Postville], Mayor John Hyman has a simple answer.
b. "[Your father]$_i$ was the greatest, but [he]$_i$ was also one of us," commented an anonymous old lady while she was shaking Alessandro's hand—[Gassman]'s$_i$ best-known son.
"I will miss [the actor]$_{i_1}$, but I will be lacking [my father]$_{i_2}$ especially," he said.

[8]Recasens [112] used the term **quasi-identity** for these cases.

2.4 Discourse Models

One point that the examples so far should have already made clear is that the universe of discourse U used to identify the anchor Z of a context-dependent referring expression only includes a subset of the objects of a certain type, among which the entities explicitly mentioned in the previous discourse seem especially prominent: for instance, when interpreting *the man* in (8), the only man considered seem to be the one mentioned earlier. (This perception is backed up by psychological research [37]). Such considerations are one of the main arguments for the so-called **discourse model** hypothesis [36, 37, 62, 74, 75, 79, 121, 135] and for **dynamic** models of discourse interpretation. The discourse model hypothesis states that context dependent expressions are interpreted with respect to a discourse model which is built up dynamically while processing a discourse, and which includes the objects that have been mentioned (the universe of discourse U introduced above). This hypothesis may at first sight seem to be vacuous or even circular, stating that context dependent expressions are interpreted with respect to the context in which they are encountered. But in fact three important claims were made in this literature. First, that the context used to interpret utterances is itself continuously updated, and that this **update potential** needs to be modelled as well. Second, that the objects included in the universe of discourse/discourse model are not limited to those explicitly mentioned. The following examples illustrate the fact that a number of objects that can be 'constructed' or 'inferred' out of the explicitly mentioned objects can also serve as antecedents for context dependent nominals, including sets of objects like the set of John and Mary in (19), or propositions and other abstract objects like the fact that the court does not believe a certain female individual in (20). In fact, the implicitly mentioned object may have been introduced in a very indirect way only, as in the case of (21), where *the government* clearly refers to the government of Korea, but the country itself has not yet been mentioned either in the text or the title. These implicitly mentioned objects constitute what Grosz [51] called the '**implicit focus**' of a discourse.

(19) John and Mary came to dinner last night. They are a nice couple.

(20) We believe her, the court does not, and that resolves the matter. (NY Times, 5/24/00, reported by J. Gundel)

(21) For the Parks and millions of other young Koreans, the long-cherished dream of home ownership has become a cruel illusion. For the government, it has become a highly volatile political issue. [109]

The idea of discourse model, originally formulated by Karttunen [79], was then developed by Sanford and Garrod [121] and Garnham [37] in psycholinguistics, and made more formal, by, among others, Heim [62] and Kamp [75] in theoretical linguistics, and by Webber [135] in computational linguistics.

The theories developed by Heim and Kamp collectively took the name of Discourse Representation Theory (DRT); DRT has become the best known linguistic theory of the semantics of anaphora, and has served as the basis for the most extensive treatment of anaphora proposed in linguistics, [76], as well as many computational models. In DRT, a discourse model is a pair of a set of discourse referents and a set of conditions (statements) about these discourse referents:

$$\langle x_1 \ldots x_n, c_1 \ldots c_n \rangle$$

represented in the linear notation of Muskens [93] as

$$[x_1 \ldots x_n | c_1 \ldots c_n].$$

For instance, suppose A addresses utterance (22a) to B in an empty discourse model.[9] Then according to DRT update algorithms such as those proposed in [76, 93], when we process this utterance, we update the existing discourse model with information contributed by this utterance: that an entity, engine e3, has been mentioned (hence a discourse referent x_1 'representing' that entity gets introduced in the discourse model); and that 'we' (speaker A and addressee B) are supposed to take x_1. This fact, as well as the fact that x_1 is an engine, are new conditions added to the discourse model. The resulting discourse model is as in (22b). Note in particular that interpreting nominal expression *engine E3* has resulted in a new discourse referent being added to the universe of discourse U. (Here and elsewhere we will ignore illocutionary force and simply treat all utterances as statements.)

(22) a. We're gonna take engine E3
b. $[x_1 | x_1 = e_3, \mathbf{engine}(x_1), \mathbf{take}(A + B, x_1)]$

This discourse model is the context in which the interpretation of the following utterance takes place. Say that (22a) is followed by (23a), which contains a pronoun. This pronoun has only one interpretation in the discourse model in (22b)—as having discourse entity x_1 as antecedent. Interpreting utterance (23a)—i.e., establishing that an instruction to send engine E3 to Corning—leads to a second update of the discourse model; the resulting model is as in (23b) and contains, in addition to the discourse entities and the conditions already present in (22b), new discourse entities and new conditions on these entities.

(23) a. and shove it to Corning
b. $[x_1, x_2, x_3 | x_1 = e_3, x_2 = x_1, x_3 = \mathit{corning}, \mathbf{engine}(x_1), \mathbf{take}(A + B, x_1), \mathbf{send}(A + B, x_2, x_3)]$

Two key contributions of dynamic theories of anaphora developed in formal linguistics have been to show that the construction of such discourse models can be characterized in a formal way, and that the resulting interpretations can be assigned a semantics just as in the case of interpretations proposed for other semantic phenomena. The original approach to discourse model construction proposed by Heim [62] and Kamp [75]—and later spelled out in painstaking detail by Kamp and Reyle [76]—was highly idiosyncratic, but later work demonstrated that the methods

[9] An extreme abstraction!

of syntax-driven meaning composition used in mainstream formal semantics can be used to develop a theory of discourse model construction as well [50, 63, 93, 118].

These formal approaches to discourse model construction center around the idea of **file card**. According to Heim [63], a discourse model can be seen as a collection of file cards, each representing the information about a single discourse entity introduced in the discourse. More precisely, in most recent versions of DRT, mentions of referring expressions are interpreted as follows:

indefinite (a P, some P):	a new file card x_i is added to the discourse model and asserted to be of type **p**. This update is formally written $[x_i, |\mathbf{p}(x_i)]$.
proper names:	as a result of a reference to object b via a proper name, a new file card x_i is added to the discourse model and asserted to be identical with b. This update is formally written $[x_i, |x_i = b]$. (See for instance proper name *Corning* in (23).)
pronouns:	a new file card x_i is added to the discourse model and noted as needing resolution via the condition $x_i =?$. This update is formally written $[x_i, |x_i =?]$. Resolution leads to this condition being replaced with an equality with the file card of the anchor. (See for instance pronoun *it* in (23).)
definite nominals (the P, that P):	this is the type of referring expression on which there is the least agreement. Most researchers believe that definite descriptions have a **uniqueness presupposition**: the existence of an object of type P is presupposed instead of asserted, and furthermore this object is meant to be unique [6, 117]. This semantics can be translated as follows: a new file card x_i is added to the discourse model and asserted to be identical with the unique object of type **p** (in the context). This update is formally written $[x_i, |x_i = \iota y.\mathbf{p}(y)]$.

Crucially for what follows, the file card for discourse entity x contains all information that is known in the context about x. Thus for instance after reading the first sentence of example (24) our Universe of Discourse will contain an entity x_i whose file card will contain the information that her name is Miss Watson, that she is the sister of the widow, that she is an old maid, etc.

(24) The widow's sister, Miss Watson, a tolerable slim old maid, with goggles on, had just come to live with her, and took a set at me now with a spelling-book.
She worked me middling hard for about an hour, ...(from M. Twain, *Huckleberry Finn*).

The notion of file cards, or discourse entities, played a crucial role in work on anaphora resolution of the 1980s and early 1990s [90, 105, 132, 135] but then took a back seat to more primitive notions such as single anaphor-antecedent links, although it is now being revived, as we will see in chapter "Advanced Machine Learning Models for Coreference Resolution".

A crucial feature of these theories is that DRSs are logic representations with their own truth conditions, different although equivalent to traditional first-order logic, and from which inferences can be made. For instance, (22b) is equivalent to the pseudo-existential statement that there is an object, this object is identical to e_3, and that A+B take this object. The existence of a deductive system over these representations is essential because many cases of anaphora resolution require complex inference, as we will see in a moment.

DRT has been used to develop accounts of a range of anaphoric phenomena beyond the simple case of nominal reference to antecedents introduced by nominals, covering reference to events as in (25a), to plurals as in (25b), or to more abstract objects such as propositions as in (25c).

(25) a. John met Mary. <u>That</u> happened at 3 o'clock.
b. John saw Mary. <u>They</u> had gone to school together.
c. John met Mary. <u>This fact</u> stroke him as strange ....

Kamp and Reyle [76] and others provide detailed treatments of anaphora to events and plurals. Their treatment of reference to events is based on the assumption that events are individuals that introduce discourse referents in the common ground, as in (26).

(26) a. John met Mary. <u>That</u> happened at 3 o'clock.
b. $[x_1, x_2, e_1, x_3 | x_1 = john, x_2 = mary, e_1 : \textbf{meet}(x_1, x_2),$
$x_3 @ 3pm, x_3 = e_1]$

By contrast, Kamp and Reyle's analysis of plurals, like that of most researchers in the area, is based on the assumption that resolving such references (i.e., finding an anchor for discourse entity x_3 in (27b)) requires bridging inferences on the discourse model as a result of which the model is augmented with new objects. In the case of plurals, these new objects are sets or groups, such as new object x_4, defined as $x_1 + x_2$ in (27c). In the case of propositional references, these new objects are propositions. Resolving the discourse referent x_3 in (27e) requires introducing a new propositional variable K_1, as in (27f). As already discussed, one of the key claims of the discourse model hypothesis is that resolving anaphoric references in general requires inferences on the discourse model.

(27) a. John met Mary. They had gone to school together.

b. $[x_1, x_2, e_1, e_2, x_3 | x_1 = john, x_2 = mary, e_1 : \mathbf{meet}(x_1, x_2),$
$e_2 : \mathbf{gone\text{-}to\text{-}school\text{-}together}(x_3)]$

c. $[x_1, x_2, e_1, e_2, x_3, x_4 | x_1 = john, x_2 = mary, e_1 : \mathbf{meet}(x_1, x_2),$
$e_2 : \mathbf{gone\text{-}to\text{-}school\text{-}together}(x_3), x_4 = x_1 + x_2, x_3 = x_4]$

d. We believe her, the court does not, and that resolves the matter.

e. $[x_1, s_1, x_2, s_2 | s_1 : \mathbf{believe}(we, x_1),$
$\mathbf{court}(x_2), \neg s_2 : \mathbf{believe}(x_2, x_1)]$

f. $[x_1, s_1, x_2, s_2, x_3, e_1, K_1 | s_1 : \mathbf{believe}(we, x_1),$
$\mathbf{court}(x_2), K_1 : [\neg s_2 : \mathbf{believe}(x_2, x_1)], \mathbf{matter}(x_4),$
$e_1 : \mathbf{resolves}(x_3, x_4), x_3 = K_1]$

Little or no work has been done within statistical approaches to anaphora resolution on creating plural objects out of singular mentions as antecedents of plural anaphors. Some research on reference to events has been carried out after the creation of the OntoNotes corpus.

Even richer, if less formalized, models (usually called **mental models** instead) of **discourse models** were proposed in psycholinguistics on the basis of work by Bransford et al., Garnham, and Sanford and Garrod, among others [11, 37, 121]. Such models are assumed to encode the results of rich inference and to be more distant from language than the models usually assumed in computational and theoretical linguistics.

2.5 *Statistics About Anaphora from Corpora*

Statistics from anaphorically annotated corpora can give a rough quantitative indication of the relative importance of different types of nominal anaphoric phenomena.

Kabadjov [72] reports several statistics about the relative frequency of different types of nominals in the GNOME corpus and the Vieira-Poesio corpus. The GNOME corpus ([103]; see also chapter "Annotated Corpora and Annotation Tools") was designed to study local and global salience [107, 108] and in particular, their effect on generation, including text structuring [78], aggregation [18] and determining the form of referring expressions [101]. It consists of texts from three different genres widely studied in NLG: museum labels, pharmaceutical leaflets, and tutorial dialogues.

The subset of the GNOME corpus analyzed by Kabadjov includes 3354 NPs, classified into 28 mutually exclusive types. The five most frequent types are bare-np, the-np and the-pn, pers-pro, pn and a-np, representing 22 %, 18 %, 10 %, 10 %, and 8 % of the total, respectively.

Concerning the types of relations, the part of the GNOME corpus studied by Kabadjov includes 2075 anaphoric relations; of these, 1161 (56 %) are identity relations, whereas the rest are bridging. Among the anaphors, 44 % of all anaphors related to their antecedent by an identity relation are pronouns (of which 27 % personal pronouns and 17 % possessive pronouns), 16 % are definite descriptions, and 10 % are proper names. Conversely, 97 % of possessive pronouns are anaphoric, as are 95 % of pers-pro, 38 % of proper names, and 30 % of definite descriptions.

The anaphoricity (or lack thereof) of pronouns has been studied in a number of papers concerned with detecting expletives. Evans [34] collected statistics from 77 texts from the SUSANNE and BNC corpus chosen to sample a variety of genres, and which contained 3171 examples of *it*. Of these, he classified 67.9 % as being nominal anaphoric, 26.8 % expletives, 2.2 % used in idiomatic/stereotypical constructions, 2 % discourse topic mentions, 0.8 % clause anaphoric, 0.1 % cataphoric. Very similar figures are reported by Boyd et al. [10], who studied expletives in text as well (the BNC sampler corpus). Of the 2337 instances of *it* in their corpus, 646 (28 %) are expletives. Arguably the most careful analysis of the distribution of pronouns has been carried out by Müller [92], who studied the distribution of third-person pronouns *it*, *this* and *that* in multi-party dialogue. Müller asked his coders to classify these pronouns as either 'normal' (i.e. referring to either a nominal or clausal antecedent), 'extrapos-it' and 'prop-it' (two types of expletives), 'vague' (i.e., referring but without a clearly identifiable antecedent), 'discarded' (i.e., included in utterances that were not continued) and 'other'. For *it*, he found that of the around 1,000 cases in his corpus, about 62.5 % were classified as referential (of which 57.8 % were 'normal' and 4.7 % 'vague') and 37.5 % as either expletive or discarded (22 % as 'discarded', 15.5 % as expletive). He also observed however significant disagreements on the classification ($\kappa = 0.61$ see Table 1 for overall percentages).

The distribution of the antecedents of pronouns—whether they are introduced by NPs or more indirectly—was studied by [14, 32, 58, 98]. Eckert and Strube found that around 22 % of the pronouns in their corpus (Switchboard) had a non-NP antecedent, whereas 33 % had no antecedent at all. Byron reported that 16 % of pronouns in her corpus had non-NP antecedents. Gundel et al. analyzed 2000 personal pronouns in the Santa Barbara Corpus of Spoken American English and

Table 1 Anaphors and degree of anaphoricity in written text: summary

Type of anaphoric expression	Percentage of total (of anaphors) (%)	Percentage anaphoric	Source
Pronouns	44		Kabadjov [72]
Personal pronouns	27	95 %	Kabadjov [72]
it		68–72 %	Evans, Boyd et al.
Possessive pronouns	17	95 %	Kabadjov [72]
Definites	16	30 %[Gnome]	Kabadjov
		–40 %[WSJ]	Poesio and Vieira
(First mention)		50 %[WSJ]	Poesio and Vieira
(Bridging)		10 %[WSJ]	Poesio and Vieira
Proper names	10	38 %	Kabadjov [72]

found that 16 % lacked an NP antecedent: around 5 % had a non-NP antecedent, 4.5 % were expletives, and 4.2 % had what Gundel et al. call 'inferrable' antecedent, like *she* in the following example, that refers to the mother of the kids just mentioned.

(28) [Talking about how the kids across the street threw paint in their yard.] Those kids are just—And she's pregnant with another one. (2.294)

An extensive study of the uses of definite descriptions was carried out by Poesio and Vieira [109], who were particularly concerned with the percentage of definite descriptions that were first mention, as opposed to anaphoric. Poesio and Vieira carried out two experiments in which definite descriptions were classified according to two slightly different schemes. In both cases, they found that around 50 % of definite descriptions were first mention, around 40 % were anaphoric, and 10 % bridging. However, Poesio and Vieira also raised the issue of agreement on classification, only finding reasonable agreement among their coders on the distinction between first mention and anaphoric ($\kappa = 0.76$) with finer distinctions leading to more disagreements, and the distinction between bridging and first mention in particular being difficult.

2.6 Anaphora vs. Coreference and Other Terminological Issues

We conclude this section on the linguistics of anaphora with some additional discussion of terminological issues, and in particular of the use of the terms 'anaphora' and 'coreference'. As we said above, we use the term **anaphoric** to indicate expressions whose interpretation depends on objects introduced in universe of discourse *U* either by virtue of being explicitly mentioned (like *engine E3* in (22)) or by being inferred (as in the cases of plurals and propositional anaphora). As we said, in this book we will primarily be concerned with these expressions and this characterization of the interpretation problem. However, quite a lot of other terms are used in the literature and there is a great degree of confusion about their use, so a few remarks on these issues are in order.

First of all, note that this use of the term 'anaphoric'—although, we would argue, the most common in linguistics—is not the only use of the term. Many researchers use the term to indicate links at the *textual* level of representation (i.e., between expressions rather than with respect to discourse entities)—indeed, this seems to be the use of the term in the well-known [29]. Other researchers use the term anaphora to indicate the study of pronominal interpretation, reserving the term coreference for the study of anaphoric reference via proper names.

Second, with the first MUC initiative the term **coreference** was introduced for a task which is closely related (although not identical with) the task of anaphoric resolution. As a result, the term 'coreference' has become in CL virtually synonymous with anaphora. Unfortunately, the term coreference has a technical meaning in formal semantics, which has caused all sorts of discussions [29]. To add to the confusion, the term coreference is used in different ways in formal linguistics and in functional linguistics.

As we saw earlier in this section, in formal semantics the term 'reference' is used to indicate the relation between an expression of the language and an object in the world, if any: proper names are the typical example of expression which is referring in this sense. Two expressions are thus **co-referring** if they refer to the same object. However, not all expressions in the language, and not even all the nominal expressions that we called 'referring' earlier on, are referring in this sense, yet this does not prevent them serving as antecedents of anaphoric expressions. A typical example are expressions occurring in hypothetical or negated contexts, as shown in the examples in (29) [95]: neither the hammer mentioned in (29a) nor the car mentioned in (29a) exist, yet they can happily serve as antecedents of anaphoric expressions.

(29) a. If I had a hammer I would use it to break your head.
b. I can't buy a car—I wouldn't know where to put it.

Viceversa, there are expressions which are coreferent but are not anaphoric in the sense discussed above—e.g., references to *Barack Obama* in distinct conversations, or in distinct documents, are co-referring (the term used in the case of documents is **cross-document coreference**) but not anaphoric (because distinct universes of discourse are built during each conversation).

This distinction between coreference and anaphora is the reason why computational linguists have generally preferred to avoid the term coreference and introduce other ones [29, 123]. We should however note that in other types of linguistics—particularly in systemic functional grammar and related functional frameworks—the term coreference is used in an entirely different manner [57, 59]. In these frameworks, there is no notion of 'reference to the world': all we can do is to refer to objects in our cognitive state—i.e., discourse referents—and therefore the term 'coreferring' is synonymous with 'anaphoric' in the sense here. And indeed, the use of the term 'referring expression' as in this section comes from this tradition, via NLG. (For further discussion of the notion of 'reference in the world,' see [112].)

As the CL use of the term coreference is here to stay, we will note here that the 'coreference task' as defined by the MUC guidelines [64] is not the same as coreference either in the sense of formal semantics or in the sense of functional linguistics. Given the focus on applications, most instantiations of the 'coreference task' concentrate on entities of a restricted number of semantic classes frequently occurring in newspaper text (persons, organisations, locations, events, vehicles, weapons and facilities in the case of the Automatic Content Extraction (ACE) effort, or include the marking of textual relations that would not necessarily be viewed as 'coreference' in linguistics. The most discussed example [29] is that of the relation between *John* and *a fool* in (30).

(30) John is a fool.

In linguistics, the relation is typically seen as one of predication—being a fool is viewed as a property of John, as discussed earlier in this section. In the MUC/ACE guidelines, the relation is marked as coreference. The problem is that coreference is generally taken to be transitive so these guidelines result in John, 'Mayor of Buffalo', and 'Senator for New York' being coreferent in (31).

(31) John was mayor of Buffalo last year and is now Senator for New York.

3 The Interpretation of Anaphoric Expressions: Evidence from Corpora and Psycholinguistics

As illustrated by example (32), anaphoric expressions can and often are ambiguous in context, and the 'one sense per context' assumption does not apply to this case of ambiguity. Starting with the second sentence, there are two potential antecedents masculine in gender, that become three the next sentence if the system does not recognize that *the skipper of a minesweeper* is an apposition on *his father*). After the fifth sentence, a third potential antecedent appears, the sailor.

(32) Maupin recalls his mother trying to shield him from his father's excesses.
"Your father doesn't mean it,", she would console him.
When Maupin was born, his father was in the thick of battle, the skipper of a minesweeper.
He didn't see his son for 2 years.
He learned of his birth from a sailor on another ship, by semaphore.
"I got very sentimental about 6 months ago, and asked him to tell me exactly where he was when he found out." (From *The Guardian Weekend*, August 15th, 1998, p. 22.)

Interpreting anaphoric expressions—i.e., resolving this ambiguity—requires a combination of many different types of information, as illustrated by the example above. One of the strongest factors is gender: for instance, *she* in the second sentence is totally unambiguous. Commonsense knowledge can be an equally strong factor: clearly *Maupin* and *his father* cannot corefer if *his* is taken to have *Maupin* as its antecedent. Syntactic constraints also play a role: even if *his son* was replaced with *him* in sentence four (obtaining *he didn't see him*), coreference between subject and object would still be ruled out. Other types of disambiguation depend on factors that appear to behave more like preferences than hard constraints. For instance, the preferred interpretation for pronoun *He* at the beginning of the fourth sentence would seem to be Maupin's father rather than Maupin himself, but that preference appears to be more the result of the preference for pronouns in subject position to refer to antecedents in subject position than a hard constraint or complex reasoning. The same motivation seems to justify the preference for pronoun *He* in the subject position of the following sentence. This difference between **constraints** and **preferences** plays an important role in many computational models of anaphora resolution and is also followed in standard expositions such as [91] so we'll follow it here even though there is not conclusive evidence about the existence of two distinct mechanisms. In this section we will discuss these constraints and preferences and the psychological evidence in their favor; in the following sections we will discuss evidence coming from computational work.

3.1 Constraints

Much of the early linguistic work on anaphora focused on the identification of morphological and syntactic **constraints** on the interpretation of anaphoric expressions. Among these constrains the better known are **agreement constraints** (syntactic and semantic) and **binding constraints**. We will now discuss in turn each of these constraints and the evidence from psycholinguistics of their importance in anaphora resolution.

Morphological constraints Agreement constraints include gender, number and person constraints. We have an example of **gender constraint** in (32): *him* in the second sentence can only refer to Maupin or his father, not to his mother. The role of gender matching has been intensively studied in psychology [5, 33, 38]. Such studies demonstrated that gender affects disambiguation very early, and considered also the differences in gender use between languages with semantic gender such as English and languages with syntactic gender such as Italian or Spanish. As we will see in the other chapters, most modern anaphora resolution systems do incorporate agreement constraints. The problems such systems encounter are that gender is not always used consistently: witness cases like (33), an error reported in [128] but due to erroneous use of pronoun *its* to refer to *a customer*:

(33) to get a customer's 1100 parcel-a-week load to its doorstep

Even when gender is not used erroneously, systems run into difficulties when pronouns are used to refer to entities referred to using uncommon proper names, as in the examples in (34).

(34) a. Maja arrived to the airport. [Maja a man] He ...
b. John brought Maja to the airport. [Maja a small dog] It ...

This second problem can be in part addressed by attempting to infer the gender of unknown names [8, 41] but more in general it is clear that people can often infer gender from context (see [25] and other references mentioned by [37], p. 67).

There has been much less psycholinguistic work on the role of number constraints, but several studies have compared the relative difficulty of interpreting plural and singular anaphoric references (e.g., [48]), and Clifton and Ferreira [23] showed that plural pronoun *they* was equally easy to read following a conjoined noun phrase (*Bill and Sue met*) than when the antecedents were syntactically divided (*Bill met Sue*) suggesting that the antecedent for the plural pronoun was found in the discourse model instead of in the syntactic representation. In Computational Linguistics, the main problem with number are nouns which are syntactically singular but semantically plural such as *the Union* in (35).

(35) The Union said that they would withdraw from negotations until further notice.

Syntactic constraints The study of constraints on anaphoric reference played an important role in the development of modern generative linguistics, to the point of giving the name to one of its best-known paradigms, Government and Binding theory [19]. The aim of this work was understanding why pronoun *him* cannot corefer with *John* in (36a) (the asterisk indicates that the sentence is ungrammatical under the interpretation specified by the indexing) whereas reflexive *himself* must obligatorily be interpreted as referring to *John* in (36b).

(36) a. *John$_i$ likes him$_i$.
b. John$_i$ likes himself$_i$

Langacker [86] proposed an account based on a relation that he called **command** holding between nodes in a syntactic tree. The definition of the relation was subsequently refined by Lasnik [88] and then by Reinhart [113], who introduced the **c-command** relation, defined as follows:

Definition 1 Node A c-commands node B iff

1. A $\neq$ B
2. A does not dominate B and B does not dominate A, and
3. every X that dominates A also dominates B.

For instance, in the following tree, A does not c-command anything, B c-commands C, C c-commands B, D c-commands E, and E c-commands D.

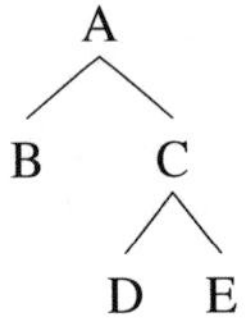

The c-command relation is at the heart of the classic definition of what is now called the **binding theory** due to [19], which is articulated around three Principles. Principle A specifies constraints on reflexives and reciprocals (rather misleadingly called 'anaphors'), and says that they must have a c-commanding antecedent in their **governing category** (the smallest clause or noun phrase in which they are included). Principle B states that pronouns cannot have an antecedent in this governing category. Together, Principles A and B claim that reflexives and pronouns are in complementary distribution. Finally, Principle C states that R-expressions—proper names and nominals—cannot have c-commanding antecedents.

Binding theory subsequently underwent numerous revisions to address empirical limitations of the 1981 version. In [20] the alternative notion of **m-command** was introduced. In HPSG, an alternative definition of **o-command** was introduced based on argument structure instead of phrase structure [110], to account for exceptions to binding theory in so-called picture NPs, as in (37).

(37) John was going to get even with Mary. That picture of himself in the paper would really annoy her, as would the other stunts he had planned.

But perhaps the main development after [19] was the proposal by Reinhart and Reuland [115] that some reflexives are **logophors**, i.e., have discourse antecedents—examples being cases like *himself* in (38a), which is grammatical, in contrast with the ungrammaticality in (38b).

(38) a. Bill_i told us that Elisabeth had invited Charles and himself_i
b. * Bill_i told us that Elisabeth had invited himself_i

Substantial experimental testing of binding constraints has been carried out over the years. Nicol and Swinney [94] using a priming technique found that only associates of *the doctor* would be primed by *himself* in (39a), whereas only associates of *the skier* would be primed by *him* in (39b).

(39) a. The boxer told the skier that the doctor for the team would blame himself for the recent injury.
b. The boxer told the skier that the doctor for the team would blame him for the recent injury.

Gordon and Hendrick [47] found broad support for Principles A and B of binding theory but poor support for Principle C. Runner et al. [119] found confirmation that many reflexives in picture NPs behave like logophors.

Semantic constraints The main semantic constraint on anaphoric reference is the so-called **scope constraint**, that prevents anaphoric reference to antecedents introduced in the scope of downward-entailing operators [79]. Thus, in (40a), the reference in the second sentence to the car introduced in the scope of a negation is claimed to be infelicitous. In (40b), the car can be referred to within the conditional, but now outside it. (40c), illustrates that anaphoric reference to indefinites in the scope of models is problematic [79, 116].

(40) a. John doesn't have a car. * It is in the garage.
b. If John has a car, he doesn't use it much. * Let's drive it around the park.
c. A wolf might have come in. *It ate John first. [116]

Semantic constraints have recently become the object of interest among psycholinguists because ERP experiments[10] is showing that examples of anaphoric reference like those in (40) result in so-called 'semantic' violation effects (i.e., N400 effects)—see, e.g., [31] for such effects in cases like (40c).

3.2 *Preferences*

By themselves, linguistic constraints do not eliminate anaphoric ambiguity. None of the constraints discussed above would prevent interpreting *him* in the second

[10]The experimental paradigm of *event-related potentials* look for correlations between text that subjects read and brain activity as measured by EEG.

sentence of (32) as referring to Maupin's father. Neither do these constraints rule out interpreting *He* in the fourth sentence as referring to Maupin instead of his father. Yet these interpretations are clearly **dispreferred**. Much research has been carried out on the factors determining such preferences.

Commonsense knowledge One such factor is plausibility based on commonsense knowledge. One of the best known illustrations of the effect of plausibility is the minimal pair in (41), due to Winograd and also reported in [123]. The only difference between (41a) and (41b) is the verb in the second clause, but that change is sufficient to change the preference from the council (in (41a)) to the women (in (41b)).

(41) a. The city council refused the women a permit because they feared violence.
b. The city council refused the women a permit because they advocated violence.

One type of plausibility effect intensively studied in the literature is the so-called **implicit causality** effect [40, 125]. Garvey and Caramazza [40] observed that subjects, when asked to write a continuation to a sentence like (42), would tend to continue in a way consistent with *he* being Bill (i.e., by assuming the *because* clause explains why Bill is to blame).

(42) John blamed Bill because he ...

Stevenson et al. [125] found that these preferences are affected by the thematic structure of the verb (so that agent-patient verbs behave differently from experience-stimulus ones) and by the connective.

In a forced choice experiment, Kehler et al. [80] presented subjects with a short discourse and a question uncovering the subjects' interpretation of a pronoun in the second sentence, as in (43).

(43) Samuel threatened Justin with a knife, and he blindfolded Erin with a scarf.
Who blindfolded Erin?

Kehler et al. found that in discourses with one semantically coherent interpretation, this interpretation was chosen regardless of other salience factors, whereas in sentences where both interpretations were equally plausible, subjects' choice of interpretation more or less reflected general salience.

Another simple form of preference carried by verbs are so-called **selectional restrictions**: restrictions on the type of argument a verb may have. Their effect is shown by minimal pair (44), from Mitkov [91]. In (44a), the preferred antecedent for *it* is the computer, presumably because *disconnect* prefers an electric appliance. In (44b), however, the preferred antecedent for *it* is the disk, because *copied* prefers an information-carrying device.

(44) a. George removed the disk from the computer and then disconnected it.
b. George removed the disk from the computer and then copied it.

Because of evidence such as that above the early models of anaphora resolution in CL concentrated on developing theories of commonsense reasoning [17, 70, 136] (this work is surveyed in chapter "Early Approaches to Anaphora Resolution: Theoretically Inspired and Heuristic-Based"), but there is clear evidence that other factors are at play as well. In (45a), one could argue that it's more plausible for Bill to know the combination of his own safe—yet the interpretation that has John as antecedent of *he* is clearly preferred. And if commonsense reasoning was the only factor determining anaphoric resolution, then (45b) should not be funny—the reason it is that the preferred interpretation for *it* is as referring to the head rather than the bomb.

(45) a. John can open Bill's safe—he knows the combination [68]
b. If an incendiary bomb drops near you, don't lose your head. Put it in a bucket and cover it with sand [65]

Syntactic Preferences The next factor obviously playing a role in anaphora resolution is syntactic structure and syntactic preferences. Corpus statistics suggest that in most English corpora, about 60–70 % of pronouns occur in subject position, and of these, around 70 % have an antecedent also realized in subject position. This preference for pronouns in subject position to refer to antecedents in subject position has been called **subject assignment** and has been extensively studied in psycholinguistics [12, 26].

Researchers also observed a preference for object pronouns to refer to antecedents in object position, suggesting a preference for **parallel** interpretations [73, 122]. Parallelism effects were studied, among others, by Smyth et al. [124], who showed that the closer the syntactic function, the stronger the effect; and by Stevenson et al. [126], who observed a similar phenomenon, but a much stronger preference for subject pronouns than for object pronouns (80–60 %).

Researchers including Smyth and Stevenson and colleagues also hypothesized that parallelism might be semantic rather than syntactic in nature; this approach was developed by Hobbs and Kehler [69], among others.

Salience Another factor that clearly plays a role in anaphora resolution is **salience**, at least in its simplest form of **recency**: generally speaking, more recently introduced entities are more likely antecedents. Hobbs [67] reported that in his corpus, 90 % of all pronoun antecedents were in the current sentence, and 98 % in the current or the previous sentence, although there was no fixed distance beyond which no antecedent could be found (one pronominal antecedent was found 9 sentences back). This importance of the antecedents in the current and previous sentence for pronouns has been confirmed by every study of referential distance , if with slightly different figures: e.g., Hitzeman and Poesio [66] found that around 8 % of pronoun antecedents in their corpora were not in the current or previous sentence. Distance is less important for other types of anaphoric expressions: e.g., Givon [45] found that 25 % of definite antecedents were in the current clause, 60 % in the current or previous 20 clauses, but 40 % were further apart. Vieira [131] found that a window of 5 was optimal for definites. This is true cross-linguistically [44]

This is not to say, however, that choosing the most recently mentioned antecedent is an effective strategy, as several studies suggest that this strategy would have mediocre results: e.g., Tetreault [128] reports that choosing the most recent antecedent for pronouns that satisfies gender number and binding constraints would result in a 60 % accuracy. On the contrary, there is a lot of evidence for a **first**

Fig. 1 The materials from [3]

AT THE CINEMA

Jenny found the film rather boring.
The projectionist had to keep changing reels.
It was supposed to be a silent classic.
a. Ten minutes later the film was forgotten
Ten hours later the film was forgotten
b. She was fast asleep
c. He was fast asleep

mention advantage—a preference to refer to first mentioned entities in a sentence [42, 46]. Combined, these results provide support for a search strategy like that proposed by Hobbs [67]: going back one sentence at a time, then left-to-right. (See chapter "Early Approaches to Anaphora Resolution: Theoretically Inspired and Heuristic-Based" for discussion.)

A stronger version of the claim that there are differences of salience between entities is the hypothesis that attentional mechanisms of the type found in visual interpretation also affect the interpretation of anaphoric expressions. Authors such as Grosz [51], Linde [89], Sanford and Garrod [121], and others have claimed that linguistic **focusing** mechanisms exist and play an important role in the choice of an antecedent for anaphoric expressions. Gundel et al. [57] and others suggested that such mechanisms also affect production, and in particular, the choice of form of referring expression.

The best-known theory of this type is the framework proposed by Grosz and Sidner [54] and articulated in two levels: the **global focus** specifying the articulation of a discourse into segments, and the **local focus** of salience specifying how utterance by utterance the relative salience of entities changes. That discourses are segmented according to 'topics' or the episodic organization of the story is widely accepted and backed up by evidence such as that presented by Anderson et al. [3]. Anderson and colleagues presented their subjects with a passage like in Fig. 1, introducing a main character (in this case, female) and a secondary character (in this case, male) tied to the scenario. This first passage was followed either by a sentence expressing immediate continuation of the episode (*Ten minutes later ...*) or by one indicating that the story had moved on (*Ten hours later ...*). Finally, the subjects were presented with either a sentence referring to the main entity, or to one referring to the scenario entity. Anderson et al. found an entity x delay effect: after the sentence expressing immediate continuation there was no difference in processing a pronoun referring to the main entity or a pronoun referring to the scenario entity, but when the text indicated a longer delay (and hence, a closure of the previous episode) the pronominal reference to the scenario entity was harder to process.

Grosz and Sidner [54] add the further hypothesis that this segmentation is hierarchical and that it is parasitical upon the intentional structure of the discourse—the intentions that the participants are trying to achieve. Grosz and Sidner proposed that the global focus is like a stack; by contrast, Walker [133] proposes a cache model. The two models were evaluated by Poesio et al. [107] in terms of the way they limit accessibility. Knott et al. [83] argued that the intentional structure proposed by Grosz and Sidner, while perhaps appropriate for task-oriented dialogue, is not appropriate for many types of text.

The second level of attention is the so-called **local focus**. According to Grosz and Sidner and other researchers including Linde, Garrod and Sanford, and others, at every moment during a conversation or while reading text some entities are more salient than the others and are preferred antecedents for pronominalization and other types of anaphoric reference. Sidner [123] proposed the first detailed theory of the local focus, articulated around two distinct foci: the **discourse focus**, meant to account for the phenomena normally explained in terms of the notion of 'discourse topic' [55, 114, 129] is usually introduced. In (46), the meeting with Ira is the discourse focus and serves as privileged antecedent for certain types of anaphoric reference.

(46) a. I want to schedule a meeting with Ira.
  b. It should be at 3p.m.
  c. We can get together in his office

Sidner also introduced an **actor focus**, supposed to capture some of the effects accounted in previous theories through subject assignment, such (47).

(47) John gave a lot of work to Bill. He often helps friends this way.

According to Sidner, the local focus changes after every sentence as a result of mention and coreference. Extremely complex algorithms are provided for both foci and for their use for anaphoric reference.

Centering theory [53] was originally proposed as just a simplified version of Sidner's theory of the local focus [52] but eventually it evolved in a theory of its own—in fact, the dominant paradigm for theorizing about salience in computational linguistics and, to some extent, in psycholinguistics and corpus linguistics as well (see, e.g., the papers in Walker et al. [134]). According to Centering, every **utterance** updates the local focus by introducing new **forward looking centers** (mentions of discourse entities) and updating the focal structure. Forward looking centers are **ranked**: this means that each utterance has a most highly ranked entity, called **Preferred Center** (CP), which corresponds broadly to Sidner's actor focus. In addition, Centering hypothesizes the existence of an object playing the role of the discourse topic or discourse focus: the **backward looking center**, defined as follows:

Constraint 3 CB(U_i), the **Backward-Looking Center** of utterance U_i, is the highest ranked element of CF(U_{i-1}) that is realized in U_i.

Several psychological experiments have been dedicated to testing the claims of Centering, and in particular those concerning pronominalization, known as Rule 1:

Rule 1 If any CF in an utterance is pronominalized, the CB is.

Hudson and Tanenhaus [71] found a clear preference for subjects, which could however also be accounted for in terms of subject assignment. Gordon and colleagues carried out a series of experiments that, they argued, demonstrated certain features of the theory. Gordon et al. [46], for instance, revealed a **repeated name penalty**—a preference for avoiding repeating full names when an entity is mentioned in subject or first mention position, and using pronouns instead. Thus for instance Gordon et al. found an increase in reading time when processing sentences b–c of (48), with respect to reading sentences b–c of ex:RNP:2 in which the proper name in subject position *Bruno* has been replaced by pronoun *He*.

(48) a. Bruno was the bully of the neighborhood.
b. Bruno chased Tommy all the way home from school one day.
c. Bruno watched Tommy hide behind a big tree and start to cy.
d. Bruno yelled at Tommy so loudly that the neighbors came outside.

(49) a. Bruno was the bully of the neighborhood.
b. He chased Tommy all the way home from school one day.
c. He watched Tommy hide behind a big tree and start to cy.
d. He yelled at Tommy so loudly that the neighbors came outside.

Poesio et al. [108] carried out a systematic corpus-based investigation of the claims of Centering, that revealed among other things that entity coherence between utterances is much less strong than expected, so that the majority of utterances do not have a CB. Gundel et al. [57] proposed an account of the factors affecting the choice of NP based on a theory of salience with some similarities to Centering but also some important differences. Gundel et al. argued that the choice of NP form is the result of a process that, among other factors, takes into account the **cognitive status** of the entities being referred. Gundel et al.'s theory distinguishes several levels of 'givenness', including **in focus**, **activated**, **familiar** and several levels of lexical acquaintance. 'Activation' corresponds to Grosz and Sidner's implicit focus, and 'in focus' is related to the notion of CB and CP, except that more than one entity may be in focus and there may also be no entity in focus (for the relation between Gundel et al.'s theory and Centering see [56, 106]).

In addition to these **discrete** models of salience, **activation-based** models have also been proposed in which there is no fixed number of foci, but in which all entities have a level of activation [2, 82, 87, 127, 128].

Models that integrate salience and commonsense knowledge have also been proposed, such as Carter's [16]. Carter combined Sidner's theory of focus with Wilks' causal reasoning. Among psychologists, the interaction of Centering with commonsense preferences has been studied by Gordon and Scearce [49], who found evidence that pronouns are interpreted according to Centering first and only later is commonsense knowledge used.

4 Conclusion

In this chapter we introduced, first of all, some terminology and linguistic facts about anaphora that will play a key role throughout the book, providing in particular definitions of linguistic context, anaphora and coreference, and antecedent. We saw that even though virtually all methods discussed in this book will be concerned with identifying the nominal-introduced antecedents of nominal anaphoric expressions, not all anaphoric expressions are nominals, and not all of their antecedents are introduced by nominals. We also saw that not all nominals are anaphoric, or even referring—NPs can be used with a referring, quantificational, predicative, and expletive function. Finally, we introduced the notion of discourse model—the space in which antecedents of anaphoric expressions are searched—and of file card—the properties attributed to a discourse entity in a discourse model.

We next discussed some of the factors affecting the interpretation of anaphoric expressions, distinguishing between constraints—hard factors ruling our certain interpretations—and preferences that simply rank interpretations. Among the constraints we mentioned agreement constraints, syntactic constraints including those from binding theory, and semantic constraints. Among the preferences we discussed lexical and commonsense knowledge, syntactic preferences such as parallelism, and salience preferences, such as recency, first mention advantage, and focusing, distinguishing between local and global focusing effects, and introducing the Grosz/Sidner framework that is among the best known formulations of focusing effects.

Acknowledgements This work was supported in part by the SENSEI project (FP7-ICT 610916).

References

1. Almor, A.: Noun-phrase anaphora and focus: the informational load hypothesis. Psychol. Rev. **106**, 748–765 (1999)
2. Alshawi, H.: Memory and Context for Language Interpretation. Cambridge University Press, Cambridge (1987)
3. Anderson, A., Garrod, S., Sanford, A.: The accessibility of pronominal antecedents as a function of episode shifts in narrative text. Q. J. Exp. Psychol. **35**, 427–440 (1983)
4. Ariel, M.: Accessing Noun-Phrase Antecedents. Croom Helm Linguistics Series. Routledge, London/New York (1990)
5. Arnold, J.E., Eisenband, J.G., Brown-Schmidt, S., Trueswell, J.C.: The immediate use of gender information: eyetracking evidence of the time-course of pronoun resolution. Cognition **76**, B13–B26 (2000)
6. Barker, C.: Possessive descriptions. Ph.D. thesis, University of California at Santa Cruz, Santa Cruz (1991)
7. Barwise, J., Perry, J.: Situations and Attitudes. MIT, Cambridge (1983)
8. Bergsma, S.: Automatic acquisition of gender information for anaphora resolution. In: Proceedings of 18th Conference of the Canadian Society for Computational Studies of Intelligence, Victoria, pp. 342–353 (2005)
9. Beun, R., Cremers, A.: Object reference in a shared domain of conversation. Pragmat. Cognit. **6**(1/2), 121–152 (1998)
10. Boyd, A., Gegg-Harrison, W., Byron, D.: Identifying non-referential it: a machine learning approach incorporating linguistically motivated patterns. In: Proceedings of the ACL Workshop on Feature Selection for Machine Learning in NLP, Ann Arbor, pp. 40–47 (2005)
11. Bransford, J., Barclay, J.R., Franks, J.J.: Sentence memory: a constructive vs. interpretive approach. Cogn. Psychol. **3**, 193–209 (1972)

12. Broadbent, D.E.: In Defence of Empirical Psychology. Methuen, London (1973)
13. Bunescu, R., Pasca, M.: Using encyclopedic knowledge for named entity disambiguation. In: Proceedings of the EACL, Trento (2006)
14. Byron, D.: Resolving pronominal references to abstract entities. In: Proceedings of the ACL, Philadelphia, pp. 80–87 (2002)
15. Carlson, G.N.: An unified analysis of the English bare plural. Linguist. Philos. **1**, 413–457 (1977)
16. Carter, D.M.: Interpreting Anaphors in Natural Language Texts. Ellis Horwood, Chichester (1987)
17. Charniak, E.: Towards a model of children's story comprehension. Ph.D. thesis, MIT (1972). Available as MIT AI Lab TR-266
18. Cheng, H.: Modelling aggregation motivated interactions in descriptive text generation. Ph.D. thesis, Division of Informatics, the University of Edinburgh, Edinburgh (2001)
19. Chomsky, N.: Lectures on Government and Binding. Foris, Dordrecht (1981)
20. Chomsky, N.: Barriers. MIT, Cambridge (1986)
21. Clark, H.H.: Bridging. In: Johnson-Laird, P.N., Wason, P. (eds.) Thinking: Readings in Cognitive Science, pp. 411–420. Cambridge University Press, London/New York (1977)
22. Clark, H.H., Marshall, C.R.: Definite reference and mutual knowledge. In: Joshi, A., Webber, B., Sag, I. (eds.) Elements of Discourse Understanding. Cambridge University Press, New York (1981)
23. Clifton, C.J., Ferreira, F.: Discourse structure and anaphora: some experimental results. In: Coltheart, M. (ed.) Attention and Performance XII: The Psychology of Reading, pp. 635–654. Lawrence Erlbaum, Hove (1987)
24. Cooper, R.: The role of situations in generalized quantifiers. In: Lappin, S. (ed.) Handbook of Contemporary Semantic Theory, chap. 3, pp. 65–86. Blackwell, Oxford (1996)
25. Cornish, F.: Anaphoric pronouns: under linguistic control or signalling particular discourse representations? J. Semant. **5**(3), 233–260 (1986)
26. Crawley, R.J., Stevenson, R.A., Kleinman, D.: The use of heuristic strategies in the comprehension of pronouns. J. Psycholinguist. Res. **19**, 245–264 (1990)
27. Csomai, A., Mihalcea, R.: Linking documents to encyclopedic knowledge. IEEE Intell. Syst. **23**, 34 (2008). Special issue on Natural Language Processing for the Web
28. Dalrymple, M., Shieber, S.M., Pereira, F.C.N.: Ellipsis and higher-order unification. Linguist. Philos. **14**(4), 399–452 (1991)
29. van Deemter, K., Kibble, R.: On coreferring: coreference in MUC and related annotation schemes. Comput. Linguist. **26**(4), 629–637 (2000). Squib
30. Dowty, D.R.: The effects of aspectual class on the temporal structure of discourse: semantics or pragmatics? Linguist. Philos. **9**(1), 37–61 (1986)
31. Dwivedi, V.D., Phillips, N.A., Laguë-Beauvais, M., Baum, S.R.: An electrophysiological study of mood, modal context, and anaphora. Brain Res. **1117**, 135–153 (2006)
32. Eckert, M., Strube, M.: Dialogue acts, synchronising units and anaphora resolution. J. Semant. **17**(1), 51–89 (2001)
33. Ehrlich, K., Rayner, K.: Pronoun assignment and semantic integration during reading: eye movements and immediacy of processing. J. Verbal Learn. Verbal Behav. **22**, 75–87 (1983)
34. Evans, R.: Applying machine learning toward an automatic classification of it. Lit. Linguist. Comput. **16**(1), 45–57 (2001)
35. Fraurud, K.: Definiteness and the processing of NPs in natural discourse. J. Semant. **7**, 395–433 (1990)
36. Garnham, A.: On-Line Construction of Representations of the Content of Texts. Reproduced by Indiana University Linguistics Club, Bloomington (1982)
37. Garnham, A.: Mental Models and the Interpretation of Anaphora. Psychology Press, Hove (2001)
38. Garnham, A., Oakhill, J.V., Ehrlich, M.F., Carreiras, M.: Representation and process in the interpretation of pronouns. J. Mem. Lang. **34**, 41–62 (1995)

39. Garrod, S.C.: Resolving pronouns and other anaphoric devices: the case for diversity in discourse processing. In: Clifton, C., Frazier, L., Rayner, K. (eds.) Perspectives in Sentence Processing. Lawrence Erlbaum, Hillsdale (1994)
40. Garvey, C., Caramazza, A.: Implicit causality in verbs. Linguist. Inq. **5**, 459–464 (1974)
41. Ge, N., Hale, J., Charniak, E.: A statistical approach to anaphora resolution. In: Proceedings of the WVLC/EMNLP, Granada (1998)
42. Gernsbacher, M.A., Hargreaves, D.: Accessing sentence participants: the advantage of first mention. J. Mem. Lang. **27**, 699–717 (1988)
43. Geurts, B.: Good news about the description theory of names. J. Semant. **14**(4), 319–348 (1997)
44. Givon, T. (ed.): Topic Continuity in Discourse: A Quantitative Cross-Language Study. John Benjamins, Amsterdam/Philadelphia (1983)
45. Givon, T.: The grammar of referential coherence as mental processing instructions. Linguistics **30**, 5–56 (1992)
46. Gordon, P.C., Grosz, B.J., Gillion, L.A.: Pronouns, names, and the centering of attention in discourse. Cogn. Sci. **17**, 311–348 (1993)
47. Gordon, P.C., Hendrick, R.: Intuitive knowledge of linguistic coreference. Cognition **62**, 325–370 (1997)
48. Gordon, P.C., Hendrick, R., Ledoux, K., Yang, C.L.: Processing of reference and the structure of language: an analysis of complex noun phrases. Lang. Cogn. Process. **14**(4), 353–379 (1999)
49. Gordon, P.C., Scearce, K.A.: Pronominalization and discourse coherence, discourse structure and pronoun interpretation. Mem. Cogn. **23**, 313–323 (1995)
50. Groenendijk, J., Stokhof, M.: Dynamic predicate logic. Linguist. Philos. **14**, 39–100 (1991)
51. Grosz, B.J.: The representation and use of focus in dialogue understanding. Ph.D. thesis, Stanford University (1977)
52. Grosz, B., Joshi, A., Weinstein, S.: Providing a unified account of definite noun phrases in discourse. In: Proceedings of the ACL-83, Cambridge, pp. 44–50 (1983)
53. Grosz, B.J., Joshi, A.K., Weinstein, S.: Centering: a framework for modeling the local coherence of discourse. Comput. Linguist. **21**(2), 202–225 (1995). The paper originally appeared as an unpublished manuscript in 1986
54. Grosz, B.J., Sidner, C.L.: Attention, intention, and the structure of discourse. Comput. Linguist. **12**(3), 175–204 (1986)
55. Gundel, J.K.: The role of topic and comment in linguistic theory. Ph.D. thesis, University of Texas at Austin (1974). Reprinted by Garland Publishing, New York/London (1988)
56. Gundel, J.K.: Centering theory and the givenness hierarchy: towards a synthesis. In: Walker, M.A., Joshi, A.K., Prince, E.F. (eds.) Centering Theory in Discourse, chap. 10, pp. 183–198. Oxford University Press, New York (1998)
57. Gundel, J.K., Hedberg, N., Zacharski, R.: Cognitive status and the form of referring expressions in discourse. Language **69**(2), 274–307 (1993)
58. Gundel, J.K., Hedberg, N., Zacharski, R.: Pronouns without explicit antecedents: how do we know when a pronoun is referential? In: Proceedings of DAARC, Lisbon (2002)
59. Halliday, M.A.K., Hasan, R.: Cohesion in English. Longman, London (1976)
60. Hardt, D.: An empirical approach to VP ellipsis. Comput. Linguist. **23**(4), 525–541 (1997)
61. Heeman, P.A., Allen, J.F.: The TRAINS-93 dialogues. TRAINS technical note TN 94-2, Department of Computer Science, University of Rochester, Rochester (1995)
62. Heim, I.: The semantics of definite and indefinite noun phrases. Ph.D. thesis, University of Massachusetts at Amherst (1982)
63. Heim, I.: File change semantics and the familiarity theory of definiteness. In: Bauerle, R., Schwarze, C., von Stechow, A. (eds.) Meaning, Use and Interpretation of Language. de Gruyter, Berlin (1983)
64. Hirschman, L.: MUC-7 coreference task definition, version 3.0. In: Chinchor, N. (ed.) Proceedings of the 7th Message Understanding Conference (1998). Available at http://www.muc.saic.com/proceedings/muc_7_toc.html

65. Hirst, G.: Anaphora in Natural Language Understanding: A Survey. Lecture Notes in Computer Science, vol. 119. Springer, Berlin (1981)
66. Hitzeman, J., Poesio, M.: Long-distance pronominalisation and global focus. In: Proceedings of ACL/COLING, Montreal, vol. 1, pp. 550–556 (1998)
67. Hobbs, J.R.: Resolving pronoun references. Lingua **44**, 311–338 (1978)
68. Hobbs, J.R.: Coherence and coreference. Cogn. Sci. **3**, 67–90 (1979)
69. Hobbs, J.R., Kehler, A.: A theory of parallelism and the case of VP ellipsis. In: Proceedings of 8th EACL, Madrid, pp. 394–401 (1997)
70. Hobbs, J.R., Stickel, M., Appelt, D., Martin, P.: Interpretation as abduction. Artif. Intell. J. **63**, 69–142 (1993)
71. Hudson-D'Zmura, S., Tanenhaus, M.K.: Assigning antecedents to ambiguous pronouns: the role of the center of attention as the default assignment. In: Walker, M.A., Joshi, A.K., Prince, E.F. (eds.) Centering in Discourse, pp. 199–226. Oxford University Press, New York (1998)
72. Kabadjov, M.A.: Task-oriented evaluation of anaphora resolution. Ph.D. thesis, Department of Computing and Electronic Systems, University of Essex, Colchester (2007)
73. Kameyama, M.: Zero anaphora: the case of Japanese. Ph.D. thesis, Stanford University, Stanford (1985)
74. Kamp, H.: Events, instant and temporal reference. In: Bauerle, R., Egli, U., von Stechow, A. (eds.) Semantics from Different Points of View, pp. 376–417. Springer, Berlin/New York (1979)
75. Kamp, H.: A theory of truth and semantic representation. In: Groenendijk, J., Janssen, T., Stokhof, M. (eds.) Formal Methods in the Study of Language. Mathematical Centre, Amsterdam (1981)
76. Kamp, H., Reyle, U.: From Discourse to Logic. D. Reidel, Dordrecht (1993)
77. Kaplan, D.: Demonstratives. an essay on the semantics, logic, metaphysics and epistemology of demonstratives and other indexicals (1977). Unpublished manuscript, University of California, Los Angeles
78. Karamanis, N.: Entity coherence for descriptive text structuring. Ph.D. thesis, University of Edinburgh, Informatics (2003)
79. Karttunen, L.: Discourse referents. In: McCawley, J. (ed.) Syntax and Semantics 7 – Notes from the Linguistic Underground, pp. 363–385. Academic, New York (1976)
80. Kehler, A., Kertz, L., Rohde, H., Elman, J.: Coherence and coreference revisited. J. Semant. **25**(1), 1–44 (2008)
81. Kelleher, J., Costello, F., van Genabith, J.: Dynamically updating and interrelating representations of visual and linguistic discourse. Artif. Intell. **167**, 62–102 (2005)
82. Klapholz, D., Lockman, A.: Contextual reference resolution. Am. J. Comput. Linguist. microfiche 36 (1975)
83. Knott, A., Oberlander, J., O'Donnell, M., Mellish, C.: Beyond elaboration: the interaction of relations and focus in coherent text. In: Sanders, T., Schilperoord, J., Spooren, W. (eds.) Text Representation: Linguistic and Psycholinguistic Aspects, pp. 181–196. John Benjamins, Amsterdam/Philadelphia (2001)
84. Kripke, S.A.: Naming and necessity. In: Davidson, D., Harman, G. (eds.) Semantics of Natural Language, pp. 253–355. Reidel, Dordrecht (1972)
85. Landragin, F., De Angeli, A., Wolff, F., Lopez, P., Romary, L.: Relevance and perceptual constraints in multimodal referring actions. In: van Deemter, K., Kibble, R. (eds.) Information Sharing: Reference and Presupposition in Language Generation and Interpretation, pp. 395–413. CSLI, Stanford (2002)
86. Langacker, R.: Pronominalization and the chain of command. In: Reibel, D., Schane, S. (eds.) Modern Studies in English. Prentice-Hall, Englewood Cliffs (1969)
87. Lappin, S., Leass, H.J.: An algorithm for pronominal anaphora resolution. Comput. Linguist. **20**(4), 535–562 (1994)
88. Lasnik, H.: Remarks on coreference. Linguist. Inq. **2**(1), 1–22 (1976)
89. Linde, C.: Focus of attention and the choice of pronouns in discourse. In: Givon, T. (ed.) Syntax and Semantics, vol. 12. Academic, New York/London (1979)

90. Luperfoy, S.: The representation of multimodal user interface dialogues using discourse pegs. In: ACL-92, pp. 22–31. University of Delaware, Newark (1992)
91. Mitkov, R.: Anaphora Resolution. Longman, London/New York (2002)
92. Müller, M.C.: Fully automatic resolution of it, this and that in unrestricted multy-party dialog. Ph.D. thesis, Universität Tübingen (2008)
93. Muskens, R.A.: Combining Montague semantics and discourse representation. Linguist. Philos. **19**, 143–186 (1996)
94. Nicol, J., Swinney, D.A.: The role of structure in coreference assignment during sentence comprehension. J. Psycholinguist. Res. **18**, 5–19 (1989). Special Issue on Sentence Processing
95. Partee, B.H.: Opacity, coreference, and pronouns. In: Davidson, D., Harman, G. (eds.) Semantics for Natural Language, pp. 415–441. D. Reidel, Dordrecht/Holland (1972)
96. Partee, B.H.: Some structural analogies between tenses and pronouns in English. J. Philos. **70**, 601–609 (1973)
97. Partee, B.H.: Quantificational structures and compositionality. In: Bach, E., Jelinek, E., Kratzer, A., Partee, B.H. (eds.) Quantification in Natural Languages. Kluwer Academic, Dordrecht/Boston (1995)
98. Passonneau, R.J.: Getting and keeping the center of attention. In: Bates, M., Weischedel, R.M. (eds.) Challenges in Natural Language Processing, chap. 7, pp. 179–227. Cambridge University Press, Cambridge/New York (1993)
99. Poesio, M.: A situation-theoretic formalization of definite description interpretation in plan elaboration dialogues. In: Aczel, P., Israel, D., Katagiri, Y., Peters, S. (eds.) Situation Theory and Its Applications, vol. 3, chap. 12, pp. 339–374. CSLI, Stanford (1993)
100. Poesio, M.: Discourse interpretation and the scope of operators. Ph.D. thesis, Department of Computer Science, University of Rochester, Rochester (1994)
101. Poesio, M.: Annotating a corpus to develop and evaluate discourse entity realization algorithms: issues and preliminary results. In: Proceedings of the 2nd LREC, Athens, pp. 211–218 (2000)
102. Poesio, M.: Discourse annotation and semantic annotation in the GNOME corpus. In: Proceedings of the ACL Workshop on Discourse Annotation, Barcelona, pp. 72–79 (2004)
103. Poesio, M.: The MATE/GNOME scheme for anaphoric annotation, revisited. In: Proceedings of SIGDIAL, Boston (2004)
104. Poesio, M., Artstein, R.: The reliability of anaphoric annotation, reconsidered: taking ambiguity into account. In: Meyers, A. (ed.) Proceedings of ACL Workshop on Frontiers in Corpus Annotation, Ann Arbor, pp. 76–83 (2005)
105. Poesio, M., Kabadjov, M.A.: A general-purpose, off the shelf anaphoric resolver. In: Proceedings of LREC, Lisbon, pp. 653–656 (2004)
106. Poesio, M., Modjeska, N.N.: Focus, activation, and this-noun phrases: an empirical study. In: Branco, A., McEnery, R., Mitkov, R. (eds.) Anaphora Processing, pp. 429–442. John Benjamins, Amsterdam/Philadelphia (2005)
107. Poesio, M., Patel, A., Di Eugenio, B.: Discourse structure and anaphora in tutorial dialogues: an empirical analysis of two theories of the global focus. Res. Lang. Comput. **4**, 229–257 (2006). Special Issue on Generation and Dialogue
108. Poesio, M., Stevenson, R., Di Eugenio, B., Hitzeman, J.M.: Centering: a parametric theory and its instantiations. Comput. Linguist. **30**(3), 309–363 (2004)
109. Poesio, M., Vieira, R.: A corpus-based investigation of definite description use. Comput. Linguist. **24**(2), 183–216 (1998). Also available as Research Paper CCS-RP-71, Centre for Cognitive Science, University of Edinburgh
110. Pollard, C., Sag, I.A.: Head-Driven Phrase Structure Grammar. University of Chicago Press, Chicago (1994)
111. Pradhan, S.S., Ramshaw, L., Weischedel, R., MacBride, J., Micciulla, L.: Unrestricted coreference: identifying entities and events in ontonotes. In: Proceedings of IEEE International Conference on Semantic Computing (ICSC), Irvine (2007)
112. Recasens, M., Hovy, E., Antònia Martí, M.: Identity, non-identity, and near-identity: addressing the complexity of coreference. Lingua **121**(6), 1138–1152 (2011)

113. Reinhart, T.: The syntactic domain of anaphora. Ph.D. thesis, MIT, Cambridge (1976)
114. Reinhart, T.: Pragmatics and linguistics: an analysis of sentence topics. Philosophica **27**(1), 53–94 (1981). Also distributed by Indiana University Linguistics Club
115. Reinhart, T., Reuland, E.: Reflexivity. Linguist. Inq. **24**, 657–720 (1993)
116. Roberts, C.: Modal subordination and pronominal anaphora in discourse. Linguist. Philos. **12**, 683–721 (1989)
117. Roberts, C.: Uniqueness presuppositions in english definite noun phrases. Linguist. Philos. **26**(3), 287–350 (2003)
118. Rooth, M.: Noun phrase interpretation in Montague grammar, file change semantics, and situation semantics. In: Gärdenfors, P. (ed.) Generalized Quantifiers, pp. 237–268. D. Reidel, Dordrecht (1987)
119. Runner, J.T., Sussman, R.S., Tanenhaus, M.K.: Assignment of reference to reflexives and pronouns in picture noun phrases: evidence from eye movements. Cognition **81**, 1–13 (2003)
120. Sag, I.A., Hankamer, J.: Toward a theory of anaphoric processing. Linguist. Philos. **7**, 325–345 (1984)
121. Sanford, A.J., Garrod, S.C.: Understanding Written Language. Wiley, Chichester (1981)
122. Sheldon, A.: The role of parallel function in the acquisition of relative clauses in English. J. Verbal Learn. Verbal Behav. **13**, 272–281 (1974)
123. Sidner, C.L.: Towards a computational theory of definite anaphora comprehension in English discourse. Ph.D. thesis, MIT (1979)
124. Smyth, R.: Grammatical determinants of ambiguous pronoun resolution. J. Psycholinguist. Res. **23**, 197–229 (1994)
125. Stevenson, R.J., Crawley, R.A., Kleinman, D.: Thematic roles, focus, and the representation of events. Lang. Cogn. Process. **9**, 519–548 (1994)
126. Stevenson, R.J., Nelson, A.W.R., Stenning, K.: The role of parallelism in strategies of pronoun comprehension. Lang. Cogn. Process. **38**, 393–418 (1995)
127. Strube, M.: Never look back: an alternative to centering. In: Proceedings of COLING-ACL, Montreal, pp. 1251–1257 (1998)
128. Tetreault, J.R.: A corpus-based evaluation of centering and pronoun resolution. Comput. Linguist. **27**(4), 507–520 (2001)
129. Vallduvi, E.: Information packaging: a survey. Research paper RP-44, HCRC, University of Edinburgh (1993)
130. Versley, Y.: Vagueness and referential ambiguity in a large-scale annotated corpus. Res. Lang. Comput. **6**(3–4), 333–353 (2008)
131. Vieira, R.: Definite description resolution in unrestricted texts. Ph.D. thesis, Centre for Cognitive Science, University of Edinburgh (1998)
132. Vieira, R., Poesio, M.: An empirically-based system for processing definite descriptions. Comput. Linguist. **26**(4), 539–593 (2000)
133. Walker, M.A.: Centering, anaphora resolution, and discourse structure. In: Walker, M.A., Joshi, A.K., Prince, E.F. (eds.) Centering Theory in Discourse, chap. 19, pp. 401–435. Oxford University Press, New York (1998)
134. Walker, M.A., Joshi, A.K., Prince, E.F. (eds.): Centering Theory in Discourse. Clarendon Press, Oxford (1998)
135. Webber, B.L.: A Formal Approach to Discourse Anaphora. Garland, New York (1979)
136. Wilks, Y.A.: An intelligent analyzer and understander of English. Commun. ACM **18**(5), 264–274 (1975). Reprinted in Readings in Natural Language Processing. Morgan Kaufmann
137. Woods, W.A., Kaplan, R., Nash-Webber, B.: The lunar sciences natural language information system: final report. Report 2378, BBN, Cambridge (1972)

Early Approaches to Anaphora Resolution: Theoretically Inspired and Heuristic-Based

Massimo Poesio, Roland Stuckardt, Yannick Versley, and Renata Vieira

Abstract This chapter summarizes the most influential non-statistical approaches to anaphora resolution. Much of the very early work focused on *personal pronouns* and was based on theoretical proposals concerning anaphora and its interpretation developed in linguistics (e.g., the effect of syntax or semantics on anaphora) and/or psychology (e.g., on the effect of salience or commonsense knowledge). Such systems assumed the resolver would have *perfect information* available – e.g., on the syntactic structure of the sentence, or the properties of concepts and instances – and as a result, tended to be very brittle (a notable exception being Hobbs' 'naive' algorithm for pronoun resolution). In the first part of this chapter we cover in detail some of these theoretically-motivated algorithms, such as Hobbs' and Sidner's, and briefly survey a number of other ones. The availability of the first corpora in the mid-1990s (see chapter "Annotated Corpora and Annotation Tools") led to the development of the first systems able to operate on a larger scale, and to a widening of the range of anaphoric expressions handled. The fundamental property of these systems was the ability to carry out resolution on the basis of imperfect information only, using a variety of *heuristics*. In the second part of this chapter, we cover a number of these heuristic-based algorithms. Some of the ideas developed in these heuristic-based systems have come back and are the basis for systems developed in the last few years; of these, we will discuss in some detail the Stanford Deterministic Coreference System.

M. Poesio (✉)
University of Essex, Colchester, UK
e-mail: poesio@essex.ac.uk

R. Stuckardt
IT-Beratung, Sprachtechnologie, Medienanalyse, D-60433, Frankfurt am Main, Germany
e-mail: roland@stuckardt.de

Y. Versley
Ruprecht-Karls-Universität Heidelberg, Heidelberg, Germany
e-mail: versley@cl.uni-heidelberg.de

R. Vieira
Universidade Católica do Rio Grande do Sul, Porto Alegre, Brazil
e-mail: renata.vieira@pucrs.br

M. Poesio et al. (eds.), *Anaphora Resolution*, Theory and Applications of Natural Language Processing, DOI 10.1007/978-3-662-47909-4_3

Keywords Early approaches data-driven approaches • Rule-based approaches • Anaphora resolution

1 Introduction

Between the 1960s and the mid 1990s a great number of computational models of anaphora resolution were developed, implementing the theories of the effect on anaphora of syntactic, commonsense, and discourse knowledge discussed in the chapter "Linguistic and Cognitive Evidence About Anaphora". There are substantial differences between these models in terms of their theoretical assumptions (some models assume that anaphora resolution is entirely a matter of commonsense knowledge, others that it is almost entirely a matter of syntactic information) and their level of formality (some models are very linguistically and formally oriented, others are very much pragmatically oriented); but they covered quite a lot of ground, so that it is fair to say that most of what we know today about anaphora resolution was introduced as part of the development of these models. For this reason it makes sense to briefly cover these approaches before moving on more recent work. Of these proposals, this chapter covers in some detail Hobbs' and Sidner's algorithms; and, more briefly, the commonsense-based algorithms of Charniak and Wilks, Lappin and Leass' algorithm, and other Centering-based algorithms. Our discussion will be short and focusing on the main ideas introduced in this work, many of which still valuable (and not yet incorporated in recent work). More in-depth discussion can be found in earlier surveys, such as [27, 54].

However, these models all have two aspects in common that set them apart from later work: (i) no large scale evaluation was attempted: the models were either purely theoretical, or the implementation was a proof of concept (the larger evaluation attempts, such as Hobbs', consider a few hundred cases); (ii) development was guided near-exclusively by the researcher's own intuitions, rather than by annotated texts from the targeted domain. The Message Understanding Conferences (MUC), and the development of the first medium-scale annotated resources, allowed researchers in the field to overcome these early limitations. Other key research, which marked as well the beginning of the resources-driven, or robustification phase, dealt with the issue of how to arrive at truly operational implementations of important anaphora resolution strategies – here, we will take an in-depth look at Stuckardt's ROSANA system that accomplishes robust syntactic disjoint reference. In the remaining part of this chapter, we will then cover in some detail the two most influential heuristic pronoun resolution systems – Baldwin's CoGNIAC and Mitkov's MARS – and the Vieira and Poesio algorithm, one of the first to resolve *definite descriptions* on a large scale. We also review briefly the two best-performing systems that participated in the first 'coreference' resolution evaluation campaigns, FASTUS and LaSIE. Heuristic-based systems are still competitive; of the modern systems, we will discuss in some detail the Stanford Deterministic Coreference System.

Thus, we will survey the key approaches, algorithms, and systems of all past research stages as identified in chapter "Introduction", covering the knowledge-rich, domain-specific phase, the shallow processing phase, the consolidation phase, the resources-driven, or robustification phase, and the post-modern phase.

2 Hobbs' 'Naive' Syntax-Based Algorithm

We saw in chapter "Linguistic and Cognitive Evidence About Anaphora" that (morpho) syntactic information plays an important role both in filtering certain types of interpretation (gender, binding constraints) and in determining preferred interpretations (subject assignment, parallelism). Several algorithms have been developed that incorporate these types of syntactic knowledge for anaphora resolution, in particular for the resolution of pronouns.

The earliest and best-known of these syntax-based algorithms is the pronoun resolution algorithm proposed by [28]. This algorithm, still often used as a baseline, traverses the **surface parse tree** breadth-first, left-to-right, and then going backwards one sentence at a time, looking for an antecedent matching the pronoun in gender and number. (See Algorithm 1.)

The algorithm incorporates both syntactic constraints, in particular from binding theory, and preferences, in particular subject and preference for first mentioned entities. Steps 2 and 3 ensure that no NP within the same binding domain as a pronoun will be chosen as antecedent for that pronoun, in that step 3 requires another NP or S node to occur in between the top node (node X) and any candidate: thus for example [NP John] will not be chosen as a candidate antecedent of pronoun *him* in example (1).

(1)

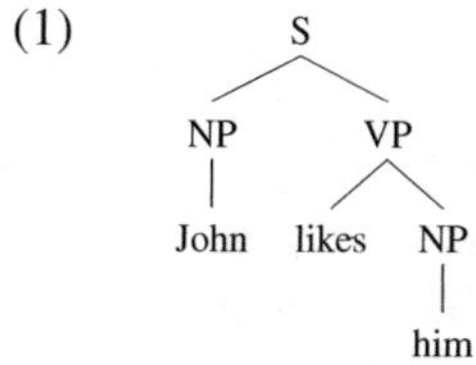

Because the search is breadth-first, left-to-right, NPs to the left and higher in the node will be preferred over NPs to the right and more deeply embedded, which is consistent both with the results of [19] concerning the effects of first mention and with the proposals and results of, e.g., [74] and [51] concerning the preference for antecedents in matrix clauses.

Hobbs was possibly the first anaphora resolution researcher to attempt a formal evaluation of his algorithm. He tested it (by hand, apparently) with 100 pronoun examples from three different genres (a historical text, a novel, and a news article) achieving 88.3 % accuracy, on the assumption of perfect parsing. Hobbs also claimed that with the addition of selection restrictions, his algorithm could achieve 91.7 % accuracy. Several subsequent larger-scale evaluations showed that when perfect syntactic knowledge is available (i.e., using syntactically hand-annotated

Algorithm 1 Hobbs' algorithm

```
1: Begin at the NP node immediately dominating the pronoun.
2: Go up the tree to the first NP or S node encountered. Call this node X, and call the path used
   to reach it p.
3: Traverse all branches below node X to the left of path p in a left-to-right breadth-first fashion.
   Propose as the antecedent any NP node that is encountered which has an NP or S node between
   it and X.
4: if node X is the highest node in the sentence then
5:     traverse the surface parse trees of previous sentences in the text in order of recency, the
       most recent first; each tree is traversed in a left-to-right, breadth-first manner, and when an
       NP is encountered, it is proposed as antecedent
6: else
7:     (X is not the highest node in the sentence) continue to step 9.
8: end if
9: From node X, go up the tree to the first NP or S node encountered. Call this new node X, and
   call the path traversed to reach it p.
10: if X is an NP node and if the path p to X did not pass through the N node that X immediately
    dominates then
11:     propose X as the antecedent
12: end if
13: Traverse all branches below node X to the left of path p in a left-to-right, breadth-first manner.
    Propose any NP node encountered as the antecedent.
14: if X is an S node then
15:     traverse all branches of node X to the right of path p in a left-to-right, breadth-first manner,
        but do not go below any NP or S node encountered.
16:     Propose any NP node encountered as the antecedent.
17: end if
18: Go to step 4
```

corpora) the algorithm is very competitive, if not quite as accurate as these initial figures would suggest. Lappin and Leass [45] observed an accuracy of 82 % over 360 pronouns from their corpus of computer manuals for their reimplementation of the algorithm. Tetrault [75] found an accuracy of 76.8 % over the 1694 pronouns in the Ge et al. corpus of news text from the Penn Treebank, and of 80.1 % over 511 pronouns from fictional texts. Hobbs' algorithm was also tested in a study by [50], who found reading time evidence for a left-to-right top-down breadth-first search for antecedents.

3 Approaches Based on Commonsense Knowledge

Although Hobbs developed his algorithm already in the 1970s, it can in fact be seen as a very early indicator of a research paradigm shift, moving towards shallow processing strategies that are chiefly based on less knowledge-rich sources of evidence. But before moving further towards considering other increasingly knowledge-poor approaches, let's briefly look at some very early work, which accomplishes anaphora processing based on knowledge-rich strategies.

Much of the initial work on anaphora resolution both in computational linguistics and in psychology was devoted to providing an account of the effects of **common-sense knowledge** on anaphoric interpretation discussed in chapter "Linguistic and Cognitive Evidence About Anaphora" and exemplified, e.g., by (2) (from [88]).

(2) a. The city council denied the women a permit because they feared violence.
b. The city council denied the women a permit because they advocated violence.

In this section, we briefly discuss the most influential among these early models; for more recent work, see chapter "Using Lexical and Encyclopedic Knowledge".

3.1 Charniak

In his dissertation [9], Charniak proposed a model of the use of inference in language comprehension largely motivated by problems in the interpretation of anaphora. For instance, the model aimed at explaining why in (3b) pronoun *it* is interpreted as referring to the piggy bank, whereas pronoun it in (3e) is interpreted as referring to the nickel.

(3) a. Janet wanted a nickel.
b. She went to her room to get her piggy bank, and found it.
c. At first, she couldn't get the nickel out.
d. So she shook the piggy bank again.
e. Finally, it came out.

Charniak developed a system called DSP (Deep Semantic Processing) taking as input the hand-coded assertions that a hypothetical semantic interpreter would produce for the sentences in an example like (3) and would carry out a number of deductive inferences that would resolve the anaphoric references as a byproduct. The deductive inferences were formulated in terms of PLANNER, one of the first languages for theorem proving developed in AI [25]. Charniak's account of the interpretation of (3e) involved a 'demon' (inference rule in PLANNER) that allowed to conclude that a possible binding for an object X that comes out is a coin Y contained in a piggy bank Z that gets shaken. An integral part of Charniak's proposal is an extensive theory of 'piggy banks' accounting for a number of other examples depending for their resolution on our knowledge about piggy banks.

Charniak's proposal was only partially implemented, not systematically evaluated, and has a number of known problems – e.g., the mechanism he proposed to choose among alternative inference paths in case more than one interpretation is possible is not very convincing – is possibly the first systematic attempt at providing a computational account of inference in anaphora resolution. In subsequent work (e.g., [10]) Charniak developed systems using frames in the sense of [52] to account for 'situational' bridging references such as *the aisles* and *the checkout counter* in (4).

(4) a. Jack went to the supermarket.
b. He got a cart and started going up and down the aisles.
c. He took the goods to the checkout counter and left.

3.2 Wilks

In [86, 87] and a number of other publications, Wilks presented an 'intelligent analyzer and understander of English' able to interpret English paragraphs and translate them into French via conversion into an interlingua based on Wilks' **Preference Semantics**. The system included an interesting treatment of anaphora resolution, and in particular of the role of semantics and commonsense knowledge.

Wilks's system did not use syntactic information. Instead, interpretation was carried out by slotting the **lexical templates** encoding the lexical semantics of the words in the sentence into **basic templates** – generic semantic templates for sentences (e.g., `[MAN FORCE MAN]`).[1] Selectional restrictions played an important role at this stage, e.g., in identifying the correct lexical template among those of an ambiguous word like *crook* to slot in the basic template for a sentence like *The policeman interrogated the crook*. At the next stage, **paraplates** expressing the interpretation of prepositions, other functional words, and connectives were used to combine together the basic templates thus enriched.

Wilks classified pronouns depending on the stage at which they are interpreted within this architecture. **Type A** pronouns are those that can resolved using 'shallow' semantic knowledge at the stage in which selectional restrictions are applied, as in (5), where the selectional restrictions specified by the lexical template for *hungry* are sufficient to choose *the monkeys* as the antecedent for *they*.

(5) Give the bananas to the monkeys, they must be very hungry.

Other cases, called **Type B** pronouns by Wilks, require deeper inference. For instance, in (6), both whisky and glasses can 'feel warm'; in order to choose among antecedents it is necessary to carry out the inference that if object X gets drank by person Y, X ends in Y's stomach. According to Wilks, such inference can be carried out using lexical semantics only. To resolve such cases, Wilks' system entered a so-called **extended mode** in which such inferences were carried out by enriching the initial template through a process called **extraction**.

(6) John drank whisky from a glass. It felt warm in his stomach.

Finally, Wilks proposed that proper inference rules, that he called **Common Sense Inference Rules**, were needed to interpret pronouns like *it* in (7). The CSIR used in this case would conclude that when animal X ingests liquid Y it may be led to evaluate Y.

[1] In Preference Semantics, semantics is expressed in terms of a small number of **semantic primitives** like `FORCE`.

(7) John drank whisky from a glass. It was good.

Wilks' system was not properly evaluated, but the implementation of his approach to use semantics and commonsense knowledge for pronoun resolution was re-implemented and integrated with Sidner's account of salience [66] by Carter [8]; we will discuss this system below.

3.3 Hobbs, Hobbs and Kehler

The most systematic account of the use of inference in anaphora resolution can be found in Hobbs' work starting from the 'second algorithm' proposed in his dissertation [29][2] and expanded in a series of papers eventually leading to the theory of 'local pragmatics' (Hobbs, J.R.: Discourse and inference, unpublished draft, 1986) [31] incorporated in the 'interpretation as abduction' framework in which the whole of natural language interpretation was formulated as abductive inference process [33].

To illustrate this proposal, let us consider the theory of the mutual effect of discourse connectives and coreference started with [30], and its treatment of example (2). We will follow the discussion in [41], a recent investigation of the predictions of Hobbs' theory using the methods of cognitive psychology. Let S1 be the sentence *The city council denied the demonstrators a permit*, and let this sentence have the semantic interpretation

(8) $deny(city\_council, demonstrators, permit)$

Let S2 be the continuation sentence (different in the two cases). According to Kehler et al. (and to Hobbs), connective *because* signals an **Explanation** relation between S1 and S2 in both versions of (2). Hobbs' formalization of **Explanation** is as follows:

> **Explanation**: Infer P from the assertion of S1 and Q from the assertion of S2, where normally $Q \rightarrow P$.

In order for the explanation of S1 in terms of S2 to be justified, some underlying axioms must exist that, simplifying a lot, could be expressed as the single following axiom:

(9) $fear(X, V) \wedge advocate(Y, V) \wedge enable\_to\_cause(Z, Y, V) \rightarrow deny(X, Y, Z)$

Axiom (9) says that if X (the city council) fears V (the violence), Y (the demonstrators) advocate V, and Z (the permit) enables Y to cause V, then we can 'plausiby infer' that X may deny Y to Z. According to Hobbs, in a situation in which axiom (8) has been asserted, and (9) is part of commonsense knowledge about

[2] In which the algorithm discussed in Sect. 2 and since known as "Hobbs' algorithm" was in fact presented as a baseline against which to evaluate the more sophisticated algorithm using commonsense knowledge.

the possible reasons for denial, abductive inference simultaneously establishes the existence of an **Explanation** while binding the council to X, the violence to V, the demonstrators to Y and therefore resolving pronoun *they* to the appropriate entity in both versions of S2. Clearly, such a theory does provide a convincing account for examples like (2), but a system based on such theory must be provided with axioms like (9).[3]

4 Salience: Sidner's Algorithm

The effect of recency on anaphoric interpretation is easy to notice; as a result, some mechanism to incorporate such preferences in anaphora resolution systems was present from the very early days and at least since the **history lists** of Winograd's SHRDLU [88] – data structures that store the potential antecedents most recently introduced first so that candidates are tested in the reverse order of introduction. As discussed in chapter "Linguistic and Cognitive Evidence About Anaphora", however, simply choosing the most recently mentioned matching antecedent is not a particularly effective strategy, and already Hobbs' algorithm incorporates a more sophisticated notion of recency, sentence based and taking the first mention effect into account. The evidence about the effects on anaphoric interpretation of salience (as opposed to simple recency) discussed in chapter "Linguistic and Cognitive Evidence About Anaphora", and in particular the work by [21, 48] and [65], motivated a great deal of research in computational linguistics producing models of anaphora resolution incorporating theories of salience [1, 6, 36, 45, 64, 66, 70, 71, 74, 75, 83–85]. Of these, the algorithms proposed in [66] and further developed by [8] and [74] arguably remain to this day the most detailed model of the effects of salience on anaphora resolution although their performance is unclear given that only a small-scale evaluation was attempted. We discuss these algorithms, which are representatives of the phase of (comparatively) shallow processing, in the present section and more recent salience-based algorithms in the next.

4.1 Sidner's Computational Model of Focus

The central component of Sidner's theory is a discourse model with two key structural aspects:

---

[3]For an alternative account of the inference process leading to the establishment of coherence relations (although, to our knowledge, not of example (2)) see [4]. Systems making heavy use of such inferences for natural language interpretation were actually implemented by SRI, some of which also participated at the early MUC competitions, see e.g., [2, 32].

- the organization of the entities in a semantic network inspired by the work of Charniak, although very few details about its organization are given in the original dissertation (see discussion of Carter's work in which this aspect of the theory was fleshed out below);
- data structures keeping track of which entities are currently most in focus. This aspect of the theory is the one which has had the greatest influence on subsequent research, in particular on the development of Centering (see next paragraph).

Sidner's theory of local focus is articulated around three main data structures: the **discourse focus**, her implementation of the notion of 'discourse topic' (see discussion in chapter "Linguistic and Cognitive Evidence About Anaphora"); the **actor focus**, accounting for the effects of thematic role preferences or subject assignment; and a ranked list of the entities mentioned in the last sentence. In addition, stacks of previous discourse foci, actor foci, and sentence foci lists are maintained. The first substantial part of Sidner's model are detailed algorithms that specify how each of these structures is updated as a discourse progresses. Unfortunately there is no space here to discuss those algorithms (the algorithm for discourse focus update alone runs for two pages).

The second part of the model are algorithms that specify how the several focus structures she proposes are used in anaphoric interpretation. Sidner subscribed to an extreme version of the 'bottom up' view of anaphora interpretation favored by psycholinguist: her model not only includes separate algorithms for each type of anaphoric expression, but also different algorithms for the same anaphoric expression depending on its (semantic) position. I.e., she doesn't simply provide different algorithms for demonstrative and personal pronouns, but three different algorithms for personal pronouns in agent position, non-agent position, and possessive position. These algorithms differ regarding which local focus structures are accessed, and in which order. Again we do not have sufficient space for presenting all of these algorithms, but for illustration, the version of her algorithm for resolving third person pronouns in non-agent position from [67] is shown in Algorithm 2.

No evaluation of the theory was provided in Sidner's thesis apart from discussing how it would work with several examples, but an evaluation was carried out by Carter.

4.2 Carter's SPAR System

Sidner's algorithms were partially implemented as part of the PAL system ('Personal Assistant Language Understanding Program') at MIT, and in the TDUS system at SRI (see [27] for an extensive discussion of PAL), but the most complete implementation of the theory was Carter's SPAR system [8].

SPAR is based on what Carter calls the **shallow processing hypothesis**, which limits calls to commonsense inference as much as possible since they are expensive and not very reliable. The system works by first producing all initial semantic

Algorithm 2 Sidner's algorithm for third person pronouns in non-agent position

If the pronoun under interpretation appears in a thematic position other than AGENT, then

if there is no Discourse Focus (DF) **then**
    check if there are focus sets; if so, then hypothesize that the focus set serves as cospecification.
end if
if (Recency rule) the pronoun occurs first in the sentence and the last element of the Discourse Focus List (DFL) is an NP **then**
    hypothesize a co specification between the pronoun and that DFL.
end if
if (Discourse Focus) the pronoun is plural and the DF is singular **then**
    hypothesize that the pronoun co specifies with the DF and an element of the DFL or the focus stack.
end if
Hypothesize that the pronoun co specifies with the DF.
if several objects associated with the DF are acceptable as co specification, and the pronoun is plural **then**
    hypothesize a plural co specification; otherwise, predict that the pronoun was used ambiguously.
end if
if only one element associated with the DF is acceptable as co specification **then**
    hypothesize the co specification.
end if
Hypothesize DFL as co specification.
(Actor Focus) Hypothesize AF or PAF as co specification.

interpretations of a sentence, expressed as formulas in Wilks' Preference Semantics formalism [86, 87] in which anaphors are left unresolved; and then attempting to resolve all the anaphors in each reading using Sidner's methods, and assigning to each reading a score which depends in part on how many anaphors have been successfully resolved and how many initial suggestions have been rejected. (It is at this point that Sidner's 'normal' inference is invoked, rejecting interpretations for anaphors that do not satisfy some pretty basic commonsense knowledge – see below.) The readings are then filtered, eliminating all those that do not satisfy configurational constraints (i.e., Reinhart's binding conditions); of those that remain, only the highest-scoring are accepted. If there is more than one such reading, then 'special' inference mode is entered, in the form of Wilks' causal inference rules [87]. These rules are used to modify the previous scores. If still more than one reading has the same score, tie-breaking 'weak' heuristics are used. In what follows, we will briefly discuss Carter's modifications to Sidner's theory, how SPAR integrates salience and commonsense knowledge, and the results of his evaluation.

Carter's modifications to Sidner's theory The first modification to Sidner's theory proposed by Carter is to eliminate the Recency Rule (see Algorithm 2) which, according to him, systematically led to worse results. The second modification concerns the treatment of intrasentential anaphors, for which Sidner made no provision. Other researchers who tackled this problem – in particular Suri and

McCoy (discussed next) and Kameyama – proposed to deal with intra-sentential anaphora by updating the focus registers at additional points inside the sentence, instead of just at the end of each sentence. By contrast, in SPAR intrasentential anaphors are handled by making some intrasentential antecedents temporarily available by adding them to the DFL and AFL, and by modifying the rules for resolving third-person pronouns so that they also consider these antecedents, in addition to those stored in the other focus registers proposed by Sidner. One advantage of this approach is that it can also be used for intraclausal anaphora.

Interaction with Commonsense Reasoning Carter's approach to using reasoning to resolve pronouns follows from Wilks', who proposed that the following steps are followed:

1. collect the candidates that match the pronoun syntactically;
2. apply selectional restrictions;
3. use analytic inference rules to derive equivalent propositions and then try to derive an interpretation for pronouns by matching these propositions with the original ones;
4. use commonsense inference rules again to infer new propositions and try to find matching antecedents.

These steps are in a progression from strong syntactic constraints to weak commonsense inferences. Also, the first two steps can be performed separately on the candidates for each pronoun, whereas the last two can only be performed starting from a complete interpretation for the sentence (i.e., one in which an hypothesis about each anaphor has been made). As a consequence, Carter proposes to identify what Sidner calls 'normal' inference mode with the first two steps, which are then performed for every pronoun; and what she calls 'special' inference mode with the second two steps, which are only performed after a set of candidates for all anaphoric expressions has been constructed, and if more than one interpretation is still possible.

Evaluation SPAR was tested with two types of texts. The first set includes 40 short texts (one to three sentences), written by Carter himself to test SPAR's capabilities; all anaphors in these texts are resolved correctly. The second set consists of 23 texts written by others, of average length nine sentences, and containing 242 pronouns in total; of these, 226 (= 93 %) are resolved correctly.

4.3 Suri and McCoy

Suri and McCoy [74] proposed a revision of Sidner's theory called RAFT/RAPR. Just as in Sidner's theory, two foci are maintained for each sentence in RAFT/RAPR: the Subject Focus (SF) (corresponding to Sidner's Actor Focus) and the Current Focus (CF) (corresponding to Sidner's Discourse Focus). The two foci often refer to distinct objects, although that need not be the case.

Another characteristic that RAFT/RAPR inherits from Sidner's theory is that in addition to a Current Focus, a Subject Focus, and two lists of Potential Foci, the data structures assumed by the pronoun resolution and focus tracking algorithms also include stacks of all the information computed in previous sentences, i.e., a CF stack, a SF stack, a PFL stack, and a PSFL stack. Finally, the pronoun resolution algorithm proposed by Suri and McCoy, like Sidner's, is based on the assumption that hypotheses are generated one at a time, and accepted or rejected by commonsense reasoning.

The first change to Sidner's theory introduced by Suri and McCoy is the replacement of thematic relations with grammatical functions both in the Focusing Algorithm and in the Pronoun Interpretation Algorithm. Thus, the SF is defined as the subject of the sentence; the FA for computing the CF relies on syntactic notions rather than thematic roles. And in Suri and McCoy's version of the PIA, unlike in Sidner's, a distinction is made between subject and non-subject pronouns, rather than between AGENT and non-AGENT ones. A second important modification is that Suri and McCoy, like Carter, extend Sidner's algorithms to include complex sentences.

5 Other Salience-Based Algorithms: Centering Based and Activation-Based Models

Two main families of computational models of salience alternative to Sidner's have been developed in Computational Linguistics. Most of the best known work has been developed within the framework of Centering theory [22], which has also been the theoretical foundation for a great deal of work in natural language generation [12, 40, 44]. As discussed in chapter "Linguistic and Cognitive Evidence About Anaphora", Centering was originally intended as a simplification of Sidner's model in which only one focus was present, although in practice a 'second focus' is still present in most algorithms based on Centering. In anaphora resolution, the two best known algorithms based on Centering theory were developed by Brennan et al. [6] and by Strube and Hahn [71].

The second family includes models which view salience as a graded notion: instead of as discrete set of 'foci', such models assign a degree of salience to all discourse entities. The earliest such model known to us is from Kantor [27] but the best-known algorithm of this type is RAP by Lappin and Leass [45], which we will discuss in some detail in this section, whereas in Sect. 6 we will discuss in detail the ROSANA algorithm that aims to make Lappin and Leass' approach work in knowledge-poor settings. Referring to the terminology introduced in chapter "Introduction", we are now considering representatives of the consolidation phase and the resources-driven, or robustification phase.

5.1 The Centering Algorithm by Brennan, Friedman, and Pollard

The algorithm proposed by Brennan et al. (henceforth: BFP) takes as input utterance u_n and updates the local focus by choosing the pair

$$\langle CB_n, [CF_n^1, \ldots, CF_n^m] \rangle$$

which is most consistent with the claims of Centering. This is done in a generate-filter-rank fashion:

1. Produce all possible $\langle CB_n, [CF_n^1, \ldots, CF_n^m] \rangle$ pairs. This is done by computing the CFs – which in turn involves generating all interpretations for the anaphoric expressions in utterance u_n – and ranking them.
2. Filter all pairs which are ruled out either by hard constraints (e.g., of the binding theory) or by the constraints of Centering (see chapter "Linguistic and Cognitive Evidence About Anaphora"): that if any CF is pronominalized, the CB is; and that the CB should be the most highly ranked element of the CF list of u_{n-1} that is realized in u_n. The CFs are ranked according to grammatical function, with subjects ranking more highly than objects, and these than adjuncts.
3. Finally, the remaining pairs are ranked according to the preferences among transitions: namely, that maintaining the same CB as the most highly ranked (**continuing**) is preferred over maintaining the CB, but in less prominent position (**retaining**) which in turn is preferred over changing the CB (**shifting**).

The BFP algorithm has been extremely influential. Some of its features are grounded in solid empirical evidence – e.g., [59] found very few exceptions for the preference for pronominalizing the CB if any other entity is pronominalized – but other characteristics found less empirical verification: e.g., there is little behavioral evidence for the preferences among transitions [19] and real texts do not appear to be consistent with such preference either [59]. BFP did not themselves provide an evaluation of the algorithm, but [83] evaluated it by hand comparing its performance for pronouns with that of Hobbs' algorithm, over the same texts used by Hobbs. The BFP algorithm performed slightly better than Hobbs' on the narrative texts (90 % accuracy vs. 88 %), whereas Hobbs' algorithm performed slightly better over the task-oriented dialogues (51 % vs. 49 %) and clearly better with the news data (89 % vs. 79 %), the difference coming from Hobbs' algorithm preference for intrasentential antecedents, whereas the BFP algorithm tended to prefer intersentential ones. However, Tetreault's more extensive (and automatic) evaluation in [75] suggests that the performance of Hobbs' algorithm is actually rather better than that of the BFP algorithm: Hobbs achieved 80.1 % accuracy with fictional texts vs. 46.4 % for BFP, whereas with news articles, Hobbs achieved 76.8% accuracy vs. 59.4 % for BFP.

In the algorithm proposed by [71], ranking by grammatical function is replaced by 'functional' ranking, i.e., ranking according to the taxonomy of given-new information proposed by [60]: (hearer) old entities (i.e., anaphoric entities and entities referred to using proper names) are ranked more highly than 'mediated' (i.e., bridging) references, and these more highly than hearer-new entities. Strube and Hahn evaluated the performance of their algorithm by hand for both English and German, using both narrative and newspaper texts for a total of around 600 pronouns for each language, and comparing the accuracy with that of the BFP algorithm. The performance using functional ranking was higher than using grammatical function ranking for both languages. For English, they obtained 80.9 % accuracy as opposed to 76 % for BFP, whereas for German, they achieved 83.7 % with functional ranking vs. 74.8 % with grammatical function ranking. The good performance of functional ranking was confirmed by the corpus study of [59], which found that the parameter configuration with functional ranking was the one for which most of Centering's hypotheses were supported by the evidence.

5.2 The Graded Salience Approach of Lappin and Leass

An alternative account of salience effects is centered around the notion of **activation**. Whereas Sidner's focusing theory and Centering account for salience effects by stipulating a discrete number of items in focus (the discourse focus, the CB, etc.), activation-based models assume that every discourse entity has a certain level of activation on a graded scale (often values in the range 0…1), updated after every utterance, and that it is this level of activation that determines the likelihood of that entity being referred to. Activation-based models are less discussed, but in fact most commonly used in anaphora resolution systems than discrete models of salience.

The first known system of this type was proposed by [39] (see also [27] for discussion), but the best known models are the MEMORY system proposed by [1] (which also includes a detailed theory of semantic network use in anaphora resolution), and the RAP pronoun resolution algorithm proposed by [45], that builds on Alshawi's work but includes several innovations, above all the first extensive treatment of expletives, and has become one of the best known pronoun resolution algorithms in CL. RAP also incorporates a sophisticated treatment of binding constraints.

Lappin and Leass's algorithm is another good example of the *generate-filter-rank* model of anaphora resolution. RAP takes as input the output of a full parser, and uses the syntactic information to filter antecedents according to binding constraints, specifically (i) antecedents of non-reflexives when the pronoun occurs in the argument, adjunct or NP domain of the potential antecedent (e.g. *John*$_i$ *wants to see him*$_{*i}$, *She*$_i$ *sat near her*$_{*i}$, *John*$_i$*'s portrait of him*$_{*i}$), and (ii) non-pronominal antecedents that are contained in the governing phrase of the pronoun (*He*$_i$ *believes that the man*$_{*i}$ *is amusing*, *His*$_i$ *portrait of John*$_{*i}$). Reflexive pronouns are instead resolved to an antecedent that fulfills the binding criteria.

Of all the candidates that pass the syntactic filter and are number and gender compatible with the pronoun, the one with the highest *salience weight* is selected, breaking ties by selecting the closest antecedent.

Each mention receives an initial salience weight, consisting of:

- A *sentence recency* weight, which is always 100.
- Additional weights for mentions not occurring in dispreferred position such as embedded in a PP (*head noun emphasis*, 80), or in a topicalized adverbial PP (*Non-adverbial emphasis*, 50).
- A weight depending on the grammatical function (80 for subjects, 50 for direct objects, 40 for indirect objects or oblique complements). Predicates in existential constructions also receive a weight (70).

The weight for each antecedent mention is halved for each sentence boundary that is between anaphor and then summed across all the members of the coreference chain of a candidate. To this salience value for the discourse entity, two local factors are added: one for parallelism of grammatical roles (35) and a penalty for cataphora (−175), which is applied to antecedent candidates that appear *after* the anaphoric pronoun.

Lappin and Leass evaluated RAP using 360 previously unseen examples from computer manuals. RAP finds the correct antecedent for 310 pronouns, 86 % of the total (74 % of intersentential cases and 89 % of intrasentential cases). Without the combination of salience degradation and grammatical function/parallelism preferences, the performance gets significantly worse (59 % and 64 %, respectively), whereas other factors seem to have a much smaller impact (4 % loss in accuracy for a deactivation of the coreference chains features, 2 % loss for a deactivation of the cataphora penalty). By contrast, their reimplementation of Hobbs's algorithm achieves 82 % accuracy on the same data.

5.3 The Shallow Implementation of RAP by Kennedy and Boguraev

Lappin and Leass use deep linguistic information in three places: firstly, to determine binding-based incompatibility and restrictions on the resolution of reflexives; secondly, to assign salience weights based on grammatical functions; thirdly, they use the parser's lexicon to assign the gender of full noun phrases. An approach based on shallow processing would have to approximate the syntax-based constraints based on the information in partial parses, and use a heuristic approach to reach full coverage for gender determination. Kennedy and Boguraev [42] use a Constraint Grammar parser that determines morphological tags and grammatical functions and allows the identification of NP chunks, but does not yield enough information for constructing a complete tree, and report 75 % resolution accuracy for news text, citing incomplete gender information and quoted passages as the most important source of errors.

Kennedy and Boguraev don't provide formal descriptions of the rules they employ for robustly emulating the syntactic disjoint reference conditions on the Constraint Grammar parses. However, as this is definitely a key issue for robust, truly operational anaphora resolution, we will take a look on another thorough solution below in Sect. 6, providing an in-depth description of the ROSANA algorithm by Stuckardt, which works on potentially fragmentary *full* parses.

5.4 Centering ff.: The Algorithms by Strube and Tetreault

The algorithms proposed by [70] and [75] were inspired by Centering, but are in fact a version of the activation models in which activation scores (a partial order) are replaced by a list (a total order).

Tetreault's algorithm, Left-to-Right Centering (LRC), shown in Algorithm 3, is the simplest and yet arguably the most effective algorithm inspired by Centering. It combines the idea of ranking of CFs from Centering with several ideas from Hobbs' algorithm.

Tetreault evaluated his algorithm using a corpus of texts from two genres: news articles (a subset of the Penn Treebank containing 1694 pronouns annotated by [18]), and fictional texts (also from the Penn Treebank, for a total of 511 pronouns). Tetreault also compared his algorithm with a variety of baselines, and with reimplementations of the BFP and Hobbs algorithms. On news articles, LRC achieved an accuracy of 80.4 %, as opposed to 59.4 % for BFP and 76.8 % for

Algorithm 3 Tetreault's LRC algorithm

```
for all U_n do
    parse U_n
    for all CF_i in the parse tree of U_n traversed breadth-first, left-to-right do
        if CF_i is a pronoun then
            search intrasententially in CF-partial(U_n), the list of CFs found so far in U_n, an
            antecedent that meets feature and binding constraints.
            if found matching antecedent then
                move to the next pronoun in U_n
            else
                search intersententially in CF(U_{n-1}) an antecedent that meets feature and binding
                constraints.
            end if
        else
            add CF_i to CF-partial(U_n)
        end if
    end for
end for
```

Hobbs. On fiction, LRC achieved 81.1 % accuracy, compared with 80.1 % of Hobbs and 46.4 % of BFP.

6 Robust Syntactic Disjoint Reference: Stuckardt's ROSANA System

In recognizing that the Lappin and Leass algorithm [45] is not applicable in knowledge-poor scenarios as it requires full and unambiguous parses, the ROSANA[4] algorithm by Stuckardt aims at generalizing the *generate-filter-rank* approach in order to make it work on partial (in the sense of fragmentary) parses. The focus is on respectively restating the syntactic disjoint reference conditions (derived from principles A, B, C and the i-within-i constraint of Binding Theory (BT)) so that as much configurational evidence as possible is exploited. Compared to the above-mentioned approach of Kennedy and Boguraev [43], which employs heuristic rules to partially reconstruct constituent structure from the results of a shallower preprocessing, it is thus aimed at exploiting syntactic evidence in the best possible way. ROSANA resorts to the potentially fragmentary parses derived by the robust FDG parser for English of Järvinen and Tapanainen (1997: [35]).[5]

In Fig. 1, the *filtering* and *ranking/selection* phases of the ROSANA algorithm are specified. There are three main steps: *(1) candidate filtering*, *(2) candidate scoring and sorting*, and *(3) antecedent selection*. In the filtering step, standard restrictions such as number-gender agreement and syntactic disjoint reference criteria are applied. In the scoring and sorting (= ranking) step, a numerical plausibility score comprising various factors is computed for each remaining candidate; in particular, this includes a graded salience weight similar to that employed by Lappin and Leass. Finally, in the selection step, for each anaphor, the highest scoring candidate that has survived filtering is chosen; as there might be interdependencies between the individual antecedent decisions, special care is taken to avoid conflicting antecedent assignments.

It would be beyond the scope of this exposition to describe these steps in full detail; the reader is referred to Stuckardt (2001: [72]) for further information on, e.g., how ROSANA implements graded salience, and how it identifies anaphors to be resolved and antecedent candidates in the preceding *generate* phase. However, some more space shall be allocated to discussing the key issue of robust syntactic disjoint reference implementation. In the respective filtering step 1b, which, by definition, considers intrasentential candidates only, two cases are distinguished: anaphor and candidate occur in the same subtree of the (possibly fragmentary) parse, vs. anaphor and candidate occur in different subtrees. It is the latter condition that signifies

---

[4] ROSANA = **Ro**bust **S**yntax-Based Interpretation of **Ana**phoric Expressions.

[5] The FDG parser is the predecessor of the commercially available Connexor Machinese Syntax parser (www.connexor.com).

1. *Candidate Filtering*: for each anaphoric NP α, determine the set of admissible antecedents γ:
   a. verify morphosyntactic or lexical agreement with γ;
   b. if the antecedent candidate γ is intrasentential:
      - if α and γ belong to the same syntactic fragment, then verify that
         i. the binding restriction of α is constructively satisfied,
         ii. the binding restriction of γ is not violated,
         iii. no i-within-i configuration results;
      - else (α and γ belong to different syntactic fragments) *try the rule patterns*:
         iv. if one of the patterns [E2], [E3a], [E3b], [E4], or [F2] is matched, then some binding restrictions are violated,
         v. else if one of the two i-within-i rule patterns applies, then some binding restrictions are violated,
         vi. else if pattern [E1a], [E1b], or [F1] applies, then the binding restrictions of α and γ are satisfied,
         vii. else (*no rule pattern applies*) assume heuristically that the binding restrictions of α and γ are satisfied;
   c. if α is a type B pronoun, antecedent candidate γ is intrasentential, and, with respect to surface order, γ *follows* α, verify that γ is *definite*.

2. *Candidate scoring and sorting*:
   a. for each remaining anaphor-candidate pair (α_i, γ_j): based on a set of preference heuristics, determine the numerical plausibility score $v(\alpha_i, \gamma_j)$.
   If the binding-theoretic admissibility was approved *heuristically* in step 1(b)vii, then reduce the plausibility score $v(\alpha_i, \gamma_j)$ by a constant value;
   b. for each anaphor α: sort candidates γ_j according to decreasing plausibility $v(\alpha, \gamma_j)$;
   c. Sort the anaphors α according to decreasing plausibility of their respective best antecedent candidates.

3. *Antecedent Selection*: consider anaphors α in the order determined in step 2c. Suggest antecedent candidates $\gamma_j(\alpha)$ in the order determined in step 2b.
Select $\gamma_j(\alpha)$ as candidate if there is no interdependency, i.e. if
   a. the morphosyntactic features of α and $\gamma_j(\alpha)$ are still compatible,
   b. for all occurrences $\delta_{\gamma_j(\alpha)}$ and δ_α the coindexing of which with $\gamma_j(\alpha)$ and (respectively) α has been determined in the *current* invocation of the algorithm: the coindexing of $\delta_{\gamma_j(\alpha)}$ and δ_α, which results transitively when choosing $\gamma_j(\alpha)$ as antecedent for α, does neither violate the binding principles nor the i-within-i condition, i.e.
      - if $\delta_{\gamma_j(\alpha)}$ and δ_α belong to the same syntactic fragment, then, for both occurrences, verify the respective binding conditions and the i-within-i condition according to steps 1(b)ii and 1(b)iii,
      - else if $\delta_{\gamma_j(\alpha)}$ and δ_α belong to different syntactic fragments, then proceed according to steps 1(b)iv, 1(b)v, 1(b)vi, and 1(b)vii (with the exception of the rule patterns [F2], [E2], and [E4], by means of which binding principle A is *constructively* verified).

   (The case $\delta_{\gamma_j(\alpha)} = \gamma_j(\alpha) \wedge \delta_\alpha = \alpha$ does not need to be reconsidered.)

Fig. 1 Stuckardt's ROSANA algorithm – candidate filtering and ranking/selection phases

$$
\begin{array}{lll}
\text{[F1]} & \surd & \{\ldots F_i = [\ldots bc(\gamma)(\ldots \gamma_{typeB} \ldots) \ldots],..,F_j = [\ldots bc(\alpha)(\ldots \alpha_{typeB} \ldots) \ldots]\ldots\} \\
\text{[F2]} & * & \{\ldots F_i = [\ldots bn(\gamma)(\ldots \gamma_{typeA/B/C} \ldots)..],..,F_j = [\ldots bc(\alpha)(\ldots \alpha_{typeA} \ldots)..]\ldots\} \\
\text{[E1a]} & \surd & \{\ldots F_d = [\ldots \gamma_{typeA/B/C} \ldots],\ldots,F_e = [\ldots bc(\alpha)(\ldots \alpha_{typeB} \ldots) \ldots]\ldots\} \\
\text{[E1b]} & \surd & \{\ldots F_d = [\ldots \alpha_{typeB/C} \ldots],\ldots,F_e = [\ldots bc(\gamma)(\ldots \gamma_{typeB} \ldots) \ldots]\ldots\} \\
\text{[E2]} & * & \{\ldots F_d = [\ldots \gamma_{typeA/B/C} \ldots],\ldots,F_e = [\ldots bc(\alpha)(\ldots \alpha_{typeA} \ldots) \ldots]\ldots\} \\
\text{[E3a]} & * & \{\ldots F_d = [\ldots \gamma_{typeA/B/C} \ldots],\ldots,F_e = [\ldots \alpha_{typeC} \ldots]\ldots\}, \\
 & & \text{if } \gamma \text{ c-commands } \alpha \text{ regardless of the attachment choice} \\
\text{[E3b]} & * & \{\ldots F_d = [\ldots \alpha_{typeA/B/C} \ldots],\ldots,F_e = [\ldots \gamma_{typeC} \ldots]\ldots\}, \\
 & & \text{if } \alpha \text{ c-commands } \gamma \text{ regardless of the attachment choice} \\
\text{[E4]} & * & \{\ldots F_d = [\ldots \alpha_{typeA} \ldots],\ldots,F_e = [\ldots bn(\gamma)(\ldots \gamma_{typeA/B/C} \ldots) \ldots]
\end{array}
$$

Fig. 2 Rule patterns employed by ROSANA for robust binding constraint verification

the application case of a set of **rule patterns** specifically designed to emulate the syntactic disjoint reference conditions on incomplete parses, i.e., parse fragments as typically occurring due to structural (PP, adverbial clause, etc.) ambiguities. To look at one particular case, *rule pattern [F2]*[6]

$$* \quad \{\ldots F_i = [\ldots bn(\gamma)(\ldots \gamma_{typeA/B/C} \ldots) \ldots],\ldots, F_j = [\ldots bc(\alpha)(\ldots \alpha_{typeA} \ldots) \ldots]\ldots\}$$

applies for reflexive (= BT type A) pronouns α that occur in syntactic fragments F_j which contain their binding categories $bc(\alpha)$. Any candidate γ of arbitrary BT type (A, B, or C) that occurs in a different fragment F_i containing its branching node $bn(\gamma)$ can be discarded (pattern prediction: $*$) since it is impossible to structurally conjoin the two fragments in a way that γ, as required by BP A of α, locally binds α: in case the anaphor's fragment is subordinated under the candidate's fragment, the presence of $bc(\alpha)$ ensures that no relation of *local* binding holds; in the opposite case, the presence of $bn(\gamma)$ rules out that a relation of c-command may be established.

The complete set of patterns employed by ROSANA to robustly implement the syntactic disjoint reference conditions is displayed in Fig. 2[7]; their binding-theoretic background is explicated in Fig. 3.[8]

In the antecedent selection step, individual antecedents are iteratively chosen in the order of decreasing plausibility, employing a greedy strategy. Two additional tests check for compatibility with the decisions made so far. In particular, step 3b accounts for the proper verification of the syntactic disjoint reference conditions,

[6]Notational conventions: round brackets delimit constituents; square brackets emphasize fragment (= parse subtree) boundaries.

[7]Between fragments named F_d and F_e, an embedding relation is assumed, requiring that the parser provides the additional information that the latter fragment is subordinated to the former.

[8]The two additional basic patterns that are employed in step 1(b)v for verifying the i-within-i condition of BT are specified in Stuckardt (2001: [72])

[F1] BP B of α / γ is satisfied	γ does not *locally* bind α $\wedge$ α does not *locally* bind γ
[F2] BP A of α is violated	γ does not *locally* bind α $\vee$ γ does not c-command α
[E1a] BP B of α is satisfied	γ does not *locally* bind α
[E1b] BP B of γ is satisfied	α does not *locally* bind γ
[E2] BP A of α is violated	γ does not *locally* bind α
[E3a] BP C of α is violated	γ c-commands α
[E3b] BP C of γ is violated	α c-commands γ
[E4] BP A of α is violated	γ does not c-command α

Fig. 3 Binding-theoretic background of the ROSANA rule patterns

which characterize valid index *distributions* rather than valid individual relations of anaphoric resumption. To give an example, in the case

John informs Jerome that he will call him tomorrow.

the antecedent decisions *John* ← *he* and *John* ← *him* are both individually admissible, as the binding conditions of anaphor (BP B) and antecedent (BP C) are satisfied; however, combining these decisions would lead to the unacceptable index assignment

* John$_i$ informs Jerome$_j$ that he$_i$ will call him$_i$ tomorrow.

as the binding condition of the type B pronoun *him* gets *transitively* violated. Again, the test distinguishes between whether anaphor and antecedent candidate occur in the same or in different parse fragments, applying the above patterns where appropriate. Regarding the binding condition of type A pronouns (reflexives, reciprocals), care has to be taken not to be overly restrictive, taking into account that further non-local coindexings are admissible as long as there is one local antecedent as constructively demanded by BP A:

John$_i$ says that he$_i$ shaves himself$_i$.

ROSANA has been fully implemented[9] and automatically evaluated on a mid-sized corpus of referentially annotated news agency press releases. Evaluation has been carried out employing diverse measures, including model-theoretic coreference scoring ([82], $(P, R) = (0.81, 0.68)$), immediate antecedents (accuracy of 0.71 for third-person non-possessives, and 0.76 for third-person possessives), and nonpronominal antecedents (accuracy of 0.68 and 0.66, respectively). According to an error case breakdown by Stuckardt, none of the seven incorrect antecedent choices that are due to failures of the syntactic disjoint reference strategy (out of a

[9]See www.stuckardt.de/index.php/anaphernresolution.html for details about the distribution; there is as well an implementation available for the German language, which works on the output of the Connexor Machinese Syntax parser.

total of 246 wrong antecedent choices) are caused by wrong predictions of its robust operationalization, which is still partly heuristic; rather, these failures are identified to be caused by wrong (in contrast to partial) parsing results, among which cases of wrongly interpreted ambiguous relative clauses are prevailing. Stuckardt thus concludes that the robust implementation of syntactic disjoint reference is nearly optimal, identifying the possibility of a further slight improvement based on an employment of a more defensive parsing strategy.

7 Heuristic Approaches: Pronoun Resolution

Both ROSANA and Boguraev and Kennedy's reimplementation of RAP are early representatives of the resources-driven, or robustification phase, which began around 1995. In those years, the focus of Computational Linguistics started to shift towards algorithms and systems whose performance could be evaluated over larger datasets. In anaphora resolution, as well, the ability to carry out larger-scale evaluation started to be considered essential. This led to the development of a new generation of algorithms and systems that could be evaluated in this way. Such algorithms typically did not assume that perfect syntactic knowledge or commonsense knowledge were available, as neither large-scale full parsing, nor large-scale lexical resources, were possible at the time. Instead, **heuristic** methods were employed to get around these limitations.

In this section we discuss two other well known heuristic algorithms for pronoun resolution, which are typical examples for the resources-driven, or robustification phase: CogNIAC, due to Breck Baldwin [5] and MARS, due to Mitkov [53]. In the next, we will discuss the Vieira/Poesio algorithm for definite description resolution, which is also one of the first examples of an approach based on machine learning.

7.1 CogNIAC

CogNIAC was designed around the assumption that Hobbs' conclusion in [29] that anaphora resolution necessarily requires commonsense knowledge was incorrect or, at least, overly pessimistic, and that there is a sub-class of pronominal anaphora that does not require general purpose reasoning. Like most other **knowledge poor** systems discussed above and in this section, CogNIAC only requires part-of- speech tagging, recognition of noun phrases, and agreement information; it can use full parse trees if available.

What makes CogNIAC historically important is that it pioneered the 'precision first' approach to anaphora resolution that still underlies the best performing anaphora resolution systems, and, in particular, the Stanford Sieve approach discussed later in this section [47, 63]. CogNIAC resolves pronouns by applying a series of rules ordered so that the most reliable (over a set of 200 'training' pronouns) apply first. Another sense in which CogNIAC is precision oriented is that its basic version does not attempt to resolve all pronouns, but only those to which rules of sufficient precision apply. The six rules, with their performance on the 'training' pronouns, are as follows:

1. **UNIQUE IN DISCOURSE**: if there is a single matching antecedent i in the read-in portion of the entire discourse, then pick i as the antecedent.
   Accuracy: 8 correct, 0 incorrect
2. **REFLEXIVE** Pick nearest possible antecedent in read-in portion of current sentence if the anaphor is a reflexive pronoun.
   Example of application: Mariana motioned for Sarah to seat herself on a two-seater lounge.
   Accuracy: 16 correct, 1 incorrect
3. **UNIQUE IN CURRENT + PRIOR** If there is a single possible antecedent i in the prior sentence and the read-in portion of the current sentence, then pick i as the antecedent.
   Example of application: Rupert Murdoch's News Corp. confirmed his interest in buying back the ailing New York Post. But analysts said that if he winds up bidding for the paper,....
   Accuracy: 114 correct, and 2 incorrect
4. **POSSESSIVE PRO** If the anaphor is a possessive pronoun and there is a single exact string match i of the possessive in the prior sentence, then pick i as the antecedent.
   Accuracy: 114 correct, and 2 incorrect
5. **UNIQUE CURRENT SENTENCE** If there is a single possible antecedent in the read-in portion of the current sentence, then pick i as the antecedent.
   Accuracy: 21 correct, and 1 incorrect
6. **UNIQUE SUBJECT/SUBJECT PRONOUN** If the subject of the prior sentence contains a single possible antecedent i, and the anaphor is the subject of its sentence, then pick i as the antecedent.
   Example of application: Besides, if he provoked Malek, uncertainties were introduced, of which there were already far too many. He noticed the supervisor enter the lounge ...
   Accuracy: 11 correct, and 0 incorrect

In [5], CogNIAC was systematically evaluated on narrative texts (where its performance was compared with that of Hobbs' naive algorithm, finding similar performance), on WSJ texts (achieving a recall of 78 % and precision of 89 %), and over the 30 articles in the MUC-6 test data (CogNIAC was the pronoun resolution component of the University of Pennsylvania's MUC-6 submission) achieving a recall of 75 % and a precision of 73 %.

7.2 MARS

Mitkov's MARS, like CogNIAC, is based on the assumption that a great number of pronouns can be resolved using what Mitkov calls **knowledge-poor** methods ([53]; see also Chapter 7 of [55]). Specifically, MARS relies only on the output of a Part-of-Speech tagger and of a parser–Conexor's FDG dependency parser [35],also used by ROSANA.

And indeed, MARS can be viewed as a stripped-down version of ROSANA: choose as actual antecedent the one among the potential antecedents that matches the pronoun in gender and number and has the higher 'score'. More specifically, MARS consists of five steps:

1. Parse the text using the FDG parser, that extracts parts-of-speech, lemmas, syntactic function, number, and dependency relations between the NPs.
2. Identify the pronouns to be processed. MARS only attempts to resolve third person personal and possessive pronouns; non-anaphoric instances of *it* are identified using Evans' algorithm [13].
3. The **competing candidates** of every pronoun identified in phase 2 are extracted. These are the NPs in the current and preceding two sentences that match the pronoun in gender and number and pass three **syntax filters** derived from [43].
4. The **antecedent indicators** (14 in total) are applied to each potential candidate to compute its score.
5. The candidate with the highest score is chosen. If two candidates have an equal score, the most recent candidate is chosen.

The heart of MARS are the rules for calculating the antecedent indicators. These rules are heuristics expressing preferences deriving from syntax, lexical/commonsense knowledge, and salience, and can either increase ('boost') the score of a candidate antecedent or decrease ('impede') it. Examples of boosting indicators include:

- *First noun phrase*: this indicator increments the score of the first NP in a sentence by +1 – i.e., it aims to capture the first mention advantage (as discussed in chapter "Linguistic and Cognitive Evidence About Anaphora").
- *Indicating verbs*: this indicator increases by +1 the score of NPs that immediately follow certain verbs – on the basis of evidence about the so-called **implicit causality** effect [17, 69].

Examples of impeding indicators are

- *Indefiniteness*: The score of indefinite NPs is decreased by 1 by this indicator, in keeping with evidence that definite NPs are more salient.

Referential distance is an example of an indicator that can either increase or decrease the score of a potential antecedent: antecedents preceding the pronoun but occurring in the same sentence have their score increased by +2, antecedents in the previous sentence by +1, antecedents in the sentence before that by 0, and all other antecedents have their score decreased by 1.

Different versions of MARS incorporating slightly different syntax filters and indicators were developed and evaluated for English, Arabic, Polish and Bulgarian. The English version was evaluated on a corpus of eight computer hardware/software technical manuals, containing a total of 247,401 tokens and 2263 anaphoric pronouns. The best success rate was 61.55 %. The Bulgarian version was evaluated on texts from two different domains containing a total of 221 pronouns, achieving a success rate of 75.7 %.

MARS has been very influential, and versions of the algorithm have also been incorporated in platforms such as GUITAR [56].

8 Definite Descriptions: The Vieira and Poesio Algorithm

Most of the approaches and algorithms described in the chapter so far, whether theoretically inspired or heuristic-based, deal mainly or exclusively with pronominal anaphora; insofar as they cover noun phrases and proper nouns (e.g., in terms of Binding Theory: type C occurrences), the resolution heuristics employed (e.g., string matching) are quite simple and surface-oriented. (The two exceptions are Sidner's algorithm, which covers all definite noun phrases, and Hobbs' commonsense-knowledge based approach, which covers all noun phrases.) There are two reasons for this focus on pronouns: a theoretical one – pronominal anaphora is much more governed by grammatical competence that full nominal anaphora – and a practical one – interpreting pronouns depends less on lexical, commonsense and encyclopedic knowledge than other types of anaphoric interpretation; hence, shallow approaches are more likely to achieve good results for this type of anaphora. By contrast, Vieira and Poesio [57, 58, 76–81] deliberately focused on definite descriptions in their research, as the type of nominal anaphora most likely to lead to interesting findings about the effect of lexical and commonsense knowledge on anaphoric interpretation. In contrast to pronouns, which only encode grammatical information and degree of salience, definite descriptions such as *the man*, or *the city* encode much more information. As such, they are often used to realize subsequent mentions for expressions that are less salient because they are farer away and/or because they are non-animate, and the choice of potential antecedents is far greater. In addition, definite noun phrases that are sufficiently informative (*the president of Peru, the man I met yesterday*) can be non-anaphoric/discourse-new (i.e., correspond to a newly introduced entity). In this section, we discuss their system(s).

8.1 Corpus Analysis

The system developed by Vieira and Poesio was the first anaphora resolution system based on a systematic corpus annotation (of around 1,400 definite descriptions in the WSJ portion of the Penn Treebank) [57, 76] employing a reliability analysis in the sense of [7]. The annotation was designed to identify the major classes of definite descriptions so as to plan the effort. Familiarity-based theories (e.g., [24]) would predict that the majority of definite descriptions would be anaphoric; this would suggest putting most of the time on improving the resolution of anaphoric definites, as indeed done by most systems previously. By contrast, uniqueness-based theories (e.g., [49, 61]) would view anaphoric definites as only one type of definite description, and not necessarily the main one.

Vieira and Poesio's corpus annotation provided support for a uniqueness-based analysis. Only between 30 % and 40 % of definite descriptions in the corpus could be considered discourse-old in the sense of Prince; between 60 % and 70 % were discourse-new, including larger-situation definites (*the Iran-Iraq war*), unfamiliar cases (*the result of the analysis is* ...) and associative descriptions (also known as bridging, see below). The analysis of bridging references carried out by Vieira, Teufel and Poesio [58, 81] also identified those cases of associative description that could be reliably identified and resolved using lexical resources such as WordNet [14].

As a result, the system(s) developed by Vieira and Poesio [76, 78–80] include three types of methods: a set of heuristics to determine whether a definite description is likely to be discourse-new; a second set of heuristics to determine if a noun phrase in the preceding text is likely to be the antecedent to the (suspected) anaphoric definite noun phrase; and finally, heuristics relying on WordNet to identify the possible **anchors** of bridging references. We discuss each type of method in turn.

8.2 Heuristics for Recognizing Discourse-New Definite Descriptions

Discourse-new descriptions include, first of all, those definites that [23] called **larger situation uses** – terms whose uniqueness can be established on the basis of encyclopedic knowledge, such as *the pope*, *the moon*, *the sky*, or terms that have only one, or only one salient, referent for their class, such as time references (*hour*, *time*, *month*). In general, recognizing such cases requires encyclopedic knowledge; Vieira and Poesio's system used instead a series of heuristics. First of all, the system used a small list of such terms. Second, the system included a heuristic to classify as larger situation definites whose modifiers included a named entity (*the Iran-Iraq war*) or a numerical modifier (*the 1987 stock-market crash*).

Both [49] and [23] also discussed however a number of additional categories of discourse-new definites that could be recognized without recourse to encyclopedic knowledge. A first example are superlatives such as *the richest* and other definites modified by ordinals such as *first* or by modifiers such as *only* or *best*. The use of such definites presupposes a unique first (only, or best) element of a given universe, as in

(10) Mr. Ramirez just got *the first raise he can remember in 8 years*, to $8.50 an hour from $8.

Hawkins [23] grouped such definites into a class of definites relying on **special predicate** premodifiers, and Vieira and Poesio's system included a heuristic that suggested that definites with one of those modifiers are discourse-new.

Another category of non-large situation discourse-new definites are those whose head is a **functional predicate with complement**. This includes predicates such as *result*, *fact*, or *idea*, which are interpreted as nonanaphoric when they have a complement (typically a clause):

(11) Mr. Dinkins also has failed to allay Jewish voters' fears about his association with the Rev. Jesse Jackson, despite *the fact that few local non-Jewish politicians have been as vocal for Jewish causes in the past 20 years as Mr. Dinkins has.*

Vieira and Poesio's system included a list of such functional predicates.

Finally, Vieira and Poesio's system include syntax-based methods to recognize postmodifiers typical of discourse-new noun phrases, particularly **restrictive postmodifiers** and **appositions**. As pointed out by Hawkins, definites modified by relative clauses which are introduced by relative pronouns (such as *who, whom, which, where, when, why*, or *that*) are typically discourse new. Other indicators of discourse novelty are non-finite clauses or prepositional phrases when they occur as postmodifiers.

Much subsequent research has been carried out exploring discourse new detection; this research is discussed in a separate chapter "Detecting Non-reference and Non-anaphoricity".

8.3 Anaphoric Definites, Same-Head Antecedent

The simplest heuristic in the resolution of definite description is to look for a potential antecedent which has the same head as the head of the definite description (e.g., *a mushroom – the mushroom*). Vieira and Poesio's system includes additional heuristics to improve the precision of the resolution.

Firstly, **segmentation heuristics** filter out potential antecedents that are not salient enough or too far away – corresponding to the intuition that a referent introduced in the second sentence of an article may have been forgotten when the reader is at the 50th sentence of the article. In its simplest form, such a heuristic may filter out any potential antecedents that are more than n sentences away. However, such a hard constraint filters out a considerable number of correct antecedents. Vieira and Poesio therefore use additional criteria in their **loose segmentation** heuristic. This heuristic admits potential antecedents from outside the given window (typically four sentences) if the antecedent is either (i) a subsequent mention (corresponding to the intuition that subsequent mentions are somehow entrenched and do not fade out of memory as quickly) or (ii) string-identical (including the article) to the previous mention.

Secondly, **compatibility heuristics** attempt to deal with the fact that noun phrases with the same noun head are sometimes not valid antecedents when they have incompatible modifiers: For example, *a blue car* is not a valid antecedent for *the red car*, or that *software from the US* and *the software from India* cannot co-refer.

Vieira and Poesio's heuristics consider both premodifiers and postmodifiers, and generally treat modifiers as incompatible when they have different surface strings. Their heuristic admits certain kinds of subset/superset relations for the modifiers of an antecedent:

- When the premodifiers of the antecedent are a superset of the premodifiers of the definite description (e.g. *the colored car* to *a blue car*)
- When a possible antecedent has no premodifiers at all (in which case the additional premodifiers of the definite description are assumed to include new information about an old referent, as in resolving *the lost check* to *a check*).

If there are multiple potential same-head antecedents, the closest one is chosen (**recency heuristic**).

8.4 Bridging Descriptions

The antecedent of many anaphoric definite descriptions has a nominal head that differs from that of the definite description. This is one example of bridging reference [11]. Vieira and Poesio's system includes methods for dealing with this class of bridging references (for which Vieira and Poesio use the term **coreferent bridging**) as well as for some types of **associative bridging**. In their corpus, about 15 % of definite descriptions belong to their "bridging" category, against about 30 % of all definite descriptions that have a same-head antecedent.

Some cases of coreferent bridging depend on lexical knowledge about lexical or conceptual relations that is available from WordNet. This includes the case in which the two head nouns are synonyms of each other (*suit* vs. *lawsuit*), or when the head noun of the antecedent is a hyponym of the head noun of the anaphor (as in *dollar* vs. *currency*). In the case of near-synonymy, the synsets may also be coordinate sisters, i.e., direct hyponyms of a common hyperonym (e.g., *home* and *house*).

Another heuristic for coreferent bridging proposed by Vieira and Poesio concerns references to **named entities**, as in *Pinkerton Inc.* subsequently mentioned as *the company*. To recognize such links, Vieira and Poesio use a combination of a named entity recognizer (which detects named entities and categorizes them as either person, location, or organization) and the conceptual knowledge in WordNet. Coreference is assumed when the definite description is a hyponym of a synset that is indicative for one of the named entity categories (in particular, *country*, *city*, *state*, *continent*, *language* or *person*), and the postulated antecedent has this particular named entity type. To aid this process, the output of the named entity recognizer is refined by using full name mentions such as *Mr. Morishita* to assign a named entity type to ambiguous shortened mentions such as *Morishita*.

In cases of associative bridging, one heuristic relies on **meronymy** relations in WordNet, such as *the living room* being a part of *the flat*.

In several cases, a bridging description that is not introduced by a noun phrase can be recovered from syntactic material, such as cases in which a bridging antecedent is a **prenominal modifier** of the antecedent (*the discount packages* as antecedent to *the discounts*), but also cases in which the antecedent to a definite description is a **verb phrase** such as the clause *Kadane oil is currently drilling two oil wells* licensing a subsequent definite noun phrase *the activity*.

Yet other cases, such as definite descriptions that are licensed through discourse topic or other means (as in *the industry* in a text referring to oil companies) or more general world knowledge, are completely out of the reach of heuristics such as those proposed by Vieira and Poesio both because they present challenges for the annotation [57] and because the necessary lexical/commonsense knowledge was not available.

8.5 Putting It All Together

The overall architecture of the Poesio/Vieira system is very simple. The system goes through the text sentence by sentence. Whenever a new sentence is encountered, the segmentation window is updated, and all mentions extracted.[10] The system then heuristically identifies all definite descriptions; all the other NPs, except for pronouns, are taken to be discourse-new, and to introduce a new **file card** (the internal representation of discourse entities). The system then uses a decision-tree (hand-coded or learned, see below) to classify each definite description as discourse-new or discourse-old using the heuristics; a new file card is created for every definite description classified as discourse-new, whereas the information for discourse-old entities is added to the file card of their antecedent.

Both the selection of the specific heuristics to be included in the decision tree, and the overall order of the heuristics, were carried out empirically, using a corpus of about 1,000 annotated definite descriptions for development, and a test set consisting of about 400 definite descriptions for testing. We summarize some of results here; see [76] for details.

Choosing among different variants of a heuristics Vieira and Poesio found that their loose segmentation with recency heuristic (81.44 % F for a loose 4-sentence

[10]Sentences and mentions are gold, extracted from the Penn Treebank annotation. The mentions and heuristically aligned with the output of a NE recognizer.

window) works considerably better than only using recency (79.62 % F), which in turn works better than just using a hard distance cutoff (69.76 % F for a strict window).

In the realm of compatibility heuristics, they show that the system using the two heuristics (requiring that the antecedent either contains a superset of the definite description's modifiers, or has none at all) works better (with, again, 81.44 % F) than a version that does not check modifier compatibility (80.19 % F) or that only allows antecedents with a superset of the definite description's modifiers (79.12 % F).

The heuristics for first-mention uses of definite descriptions show varying precision ranging from 75 % to 93 % for most heuristics (postmodification, apposition, names, time references, unexplanatory modifiers) on the training data. Vieira and Poesio identify problem sources in copula construction (where the distinction between subject and predicate in sentences such as 12 is not always clear), and in restrictive premodification, which can also carry new information about an old antecedent:

(12) a. *The key man* seems to be the campaign manager, Mr. Lynch.
 b. in the fear that an aftershock will jolt *the house* again.
 ...
 As Ms. Johnson stands outside *the Hammock house* after winding up her chorse there, the house begins to creak and sway.

In the realm of bridging descriptions, WordNet relations generally have a precision ranging from 36 % (synonymy) to 20 % (coordinate sisters). Vieira and Poesio conclude that the knowledge encoded in WordNet is not sufficient to interpret all semantic relations that are involved in bridging resolution.

Optimal configuration of the heuristics Vieira and Poesio ended up with seven heuristics for identifying discourse-new definites and resolving same-head anaphoric definites, as well as additional heuristics for resolving bridging descriptions. These heuristics were employed to develop three variants of their system, all of which based on decision trees:

1. A version ignoring bridging references and only attempting to identify discourse-new and discourse-old descriptions and to resolve the latter, in which the decision tree specifying the order of the heuristics was determined by their precision, as in CoGNIAC (see Fig. 4). (This version is called 'Version 1' in [80].)
2. A second version including the methods for resolving bridging references, called Version 2 in the paper;
3. A third version also ignoring bridging references, but in which the decision tree specifying the order of the heuristics was determined using the ID3 decision tree learning algorithm [62], using the development corpus as training data.

The performance of the three versions is compared in Table 1. As shown in the Table, Version 1 of the algorithm with the hand-coded decision tree achieves an overall F of 0.62. Version 2 achieves the same overall F, but with a higher precision and a lower recall. Version 1 with an automatically learned decision tree achieves a much higher F (0.75) as it assigns a DN classification to all NPs for which no other

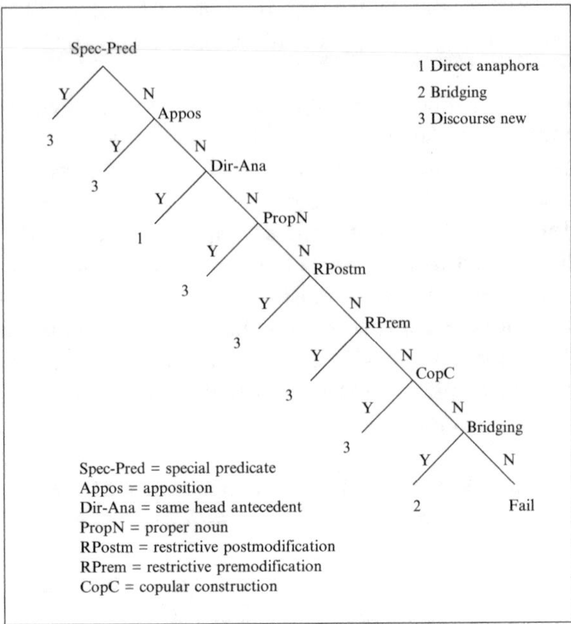

Fig. 4 Hand-coded decision tree of version 1

Table 1 Comparison between the three versions of the Vieira and Poesio system

Version	P	R	F
Version 1 (hand-coded)	73	56	62
Version 2	70	57	62
Version 1 (ID3)	75	75	75
Version 1 (hand-coded + DN default)	**77**	**77**	**77**

rule applies. The best overall results (F = 0.77) are obtained by a variant of the hand-coded form of Version 1 that also automatically classifies as DN all definites that haven't been given any other classification.

Examining the differences between the hand-coded and automatically learned decision tree, Vieira and Poesio found that the only difference was in the very first test: whereas the hand-coded version starts by checking whether the NP contains special premodifiers, the automatically learned version starts by checking if a same-head antecedent exists. This is especially interesting at the light of the subsequent work on non-anaphoricity detection discussed in chapters "The Mention-Pair Model", "Advanced Machine Learning Models for Coreference Resolution" and "Detecting Non-reference and Non-anaphoricity".

9 Rule-Based and Heuristic Systems in the MUC 6 and MUC 7 Coreference Task

The approaches and systems presented in the earlier sections of this chapter are for the most part focused on a specific type of anaphoric reference – pronouns for the historical proposals by Hobbs, Charniak, the algorithms based on centering, and more recent algorithms such as Lappin and Leass' RAP, MARS, and CoGNIAC; and definite descriptions in the case of Vieira and Poesio's resolution approach. This narrow focus was motivated by evidence highlighting how differently each type of anaphoric expression behaves both from a linguistic and from a processing perspective; but the result were systems unable to handle the complexity of full anaphoric reference. This all changed with the sixth and seventh edition of the Message Understanding Conferences, where a **Coreference (CO) Task** was introduced [20, 26]. In order to achieve a high performance in those evaluation campaigns, an *integrated account* of pronominal and definite description resolution, discourse-new detection, proper name recognition/classification/matching, and a differential treatment of text regions turns out to be required, thus making this problem considerably harder than the mere implementation of a high-accuracy pronoun resolver.

In this section, we will discuss first the coreference component of the FASTUS system [3], developed by Kameyama [37]. Kameyama's system was the best performing system in the MUC-6 evaluation, with a MUC F-measure of 0.65.[11] Next, we will discuss the coreference component of the LaSIE II system. The LaSIE systems [15, 34] participated at both MUC-6 and MUC-7. LaSIE-II was the best-performing system in the MUC-7 coreference task, with an F-measure of 0.618.[12]

In having triggered the development of these important full-fledged coreference resolvers, the MUC CO Task Evaluations can be regarded as *the* decisive momentum towards resources-driven, robust anaphora processing.

9.1 The FASTUS System by Kameyama et al.

The key characteristic of the rule-based system developed by [37] for MUC-6 is that it builds on the finite-state grammar developed for the FASTUS system, versions of which participated in several editions of MUC [3]. FASTUS yields a chunking analysis of the text which is highly accurate in the presence of complex noun chunks, but does not produce the type of hierarchical structure that, e.g. Hobbs' or Lappin

[11]Soon et al.'s system [68], the first successful machine learning approach, discussed in chapter "The Mention-Pair Model", obtained an F score of 0.63 for this dataset. As we will see in the rest of this chapter and in the following chapters of the book, it is still the case for coreference that a rule-based system can achieve state-of-the-art performance.

[12]Soon et al.'s system obtained an F of 0.605.

and Leass' approaches for pronoun resolution or the approach of Vieira and Poesio for definite descriptions, presuppose. The anaphora resolution system described in [37], therefore, approximates appositional/copular constructions and (originally syntactic) salience within the pattern-based approach in FASTUS. Kameyama points out that these approximations lead to a loss of precision with respect to perfect or good parses used in other systems; however, the loss due to this approximation approach is not as large as one could imagine, and the most obvious cases where a syntactic analysis would help (reflexives and disjoint reference filtering) are relatively infrequent.

Mention detection Kameyama's system takes mentions (**template entities**) as input which, besides their span, already have some linguistic features that are useful for subsequent processing:

- the determiner or pronoun type (definite, indefinite, or pronominal);
- grammatical number (singular or plural, or a modifying cardinal expression);
- head string and modifiers of the mention's noun chunk;
- a semantic class that is assigned based on the head, and comes from a shallow hierarchy;
- sentence and paragraph positions;
- information about the enclosing text region (headline or main text);

Information about the enclosing **text region** is used to model the assumptions for text-region accessibility that were employed in the MUC-6 annotation, namely that a mention in the *headline* region can be coreferring with a mention from the text, whereas mentions in the *text* region can be resolved to any preceding mention within the *text* region.

Resolution strategy The system has different resolution strategies based on the type of the mention, using different heuristic constraints for pronouns, definite descriptions, and names.

For **pronouns**, a narrow three-sentence window is enforced (respectively, only the current sentence is used for reflexives), together with consistency constraints for *number* and *semantic sort*, and subsequently ranked based on a left-right ranking order (see below).

Plural pronouns (*they*, *we*) are considered consistent with singular organization antecedents. First person pronouns (*I*, *we*) are allowed to be resolved as intrasentential cataphora (i.e., to a later mention in the same sentence), unlike non-pronouns or other types of pronouns.

The resolution of **definite noun phrases** relies on a window size of ten sentences, together with a *sort consistency* constraint that requires the sort of the anaporic definite noun phrase to be equal or more general than the sort of the antecedent candidate. This would allow *the company* as a subsequent mention of *the automaker* but not vice versa. Similar in spirit to Vieira and Poesio's approach, anaphor-antecedent pairs with known-inconsistent modifiers (for example *French* and *British*) are filtered out.

For **proper names**, the entire previous text is considered. The semantic class of names is provided by FASTUS' heuristics for recognizing specific-type names (persons, locations or organizations), as well as unknown names.

The system considers both *shortened names* (alias) which have a selective substring of the full name (e.g. *Colonial* for *Colonial Beef*), but also *acronyms* which have a subsequence of the initial characters of a name (e.g., *GM* for *General Motors*). For names with an unknown semantic class, the *merging of entities* in the resolution process makes sure that previously unknown aliases of entities for which the semantic class is known also get the semantic class information from their previous mention.

The **salience ordering** used by Kameyama's system is similar to the Left-Right Centering approach for pronouns as proposed by [75] in that it uses sentence information and surface order, but not the kind of hierarchical syntactic structure that earlier approaches would require.

Here, the *preceding part of the same sentence* is ordered left to right (i.e., topicalized phrases and subjects first), followed by the *immediately preceding* sentence, also in left-to-right order. Other preceding sentences (up to the resolution window, which depends on the expression type of the mention).

Evaluation Overall, Kameyama's system scored 59 % recall and 72 % precision (F = 0.65) in the official MUC-6 evaluation, which was the best overall performance [73]. In the 1997 article Kameyama also includes a more detailed breakdown of the performance by the type of mention. Intra-sentential third person pronouns (27 mentions) are resolved with 78 % precision, whereas inter-sentential third person pronouns (33 % precision, 6 mentions) and first/second person pronouns (20 % precision, 5 mentions) are more difficult. The system achieves a precision of 69 % in the resolution of proper names (32 resolved mentions), and a considerably lower figure of 46 % for definite descriptions (61 occurrences).[13]

9.2 *Coreference in the LaSIE Systems*

The LaSIE [15] and LaSIE-II [34] systems, developed at the University of Sheffield, participated in MUC-6 and MUC-7, respectively.

The systems share the same broad approach. They are both implemented using a very modular and very general pipeline architecture not focused solely on the MUC tasks but including all the traditional components of an NLP system, from tokenizer to POS tagger to (statistical) parser to NE tagger to semantic interpreter including wordsense disambiguation to a coreference component. One of the main

[13]This figure cannot be compared to the figures obtained by Vieira and Poesio, because the latter evaluate the *resolution accuracy* for definite descriptions, whereas Kameyama's evaluation requires both correct identification of a discourse-old noun phrase and the identification of the correct antecedent to be counted.

differences between LaSIE and LaSIE-II is that the pipeline used for LaSIE became the basis for the GATE NLP platform, which in turn became the basis for LaSIE-II. The systems also share the basis philosophy, aptly described by Humphreys et al. [34] as threading "a pragmatic middle way between shallow vs deep analysis" resulting in the employment of "an eclectic mixture of techniques".

From an anaphora resolution perspective, the most significant aspect of the LaSIE systems is that they attempt to build a full **discourse model** in the sense advocated by linguists and psychologists [16, 38]: i.e., these systems not only (i) attempt to link every mention to an existing discourse entity, or to create a new one otherwise, as done as well by the Vieira/Poesio system; but they also (ii) attempt to expand the bare-bones model consisting of these discourse entities into a proper domain model using an ontology.

The coreference component of LaSIE II is for the most part is a incremental development of the system incorporated in LaSIE-I, but it extends the earlier system to include

- look for antecedents not just in the current and previous paragraph but also further away–according to Humphreys et al. this resulted in a 2 % increase in recall with no significant effect on precision;
- methods for 'resolving' mentions occurring in copula constructions such as *the Navy's first-line fighter* in *The F-14 "Tomcat" is the Navy's first-line fighter* which, as discussed in chapters "Linguistic and Cognitive Evidence About Anaphora" and "Annotated Corpora and Annotation Tools", are treated as cases of 'coreference' in MUC;
- methods for resolving some cases of cataphora, and 'bare noun' coreference;
- methods for resolving som cases of NPs occurring in coordination (e.g., *John* and *his boys* in *John and his boys*) introduce new discourse entities.

Both systems performed very well at the coreference task. LaSIE-I achieved a R = 0.51, P = 0.71, F = 0.59 at MUC-6 (third highest) whereas LaSIE-II was the best system at the coreference task in MUC-7, obtaining R = 0.56, P = 0.69, F = 0.62.

10 Modern Heuristic-Based Approaches: The Stanford Deterministic Coreference Resolution System

The heuristic approach to the development of coreference systems is thriving. Many such systems are still being developed; indeed, the Stanford Deterministic Coreference Resolution System,[14] based on the so-called 'Stanford Sieve' approach [46, 47, 63] – a version of the 'precision-first' approach pioneered by CogNIAC and also adopted by MARS and the Vieira-Poesio system, was the best performing

[14]http://nlp.stanford.edu/software/dcoref.shtml

system at the CoNLL 2011 coreference shared task [46]; at CoNLL 2012, two of the three best-performing systems (namely, Fernandes et al. **[REF FIXME]** as well as Chen and Ng **[REF FIXME]**) were hybrid models that used machine learning on top of the resolutions of the Sieve model.[15]

In fact, these modern, hybrid approaches perfectly illustrate the eclecticism that is prevailing in current research, thus evidencing that it is justified to speak of the current research period, as suggested in chapter "Introduction", as the post-modern phase.

The architecture of the Stanford DCR is articulated around two main stages: a high recall (and highly precise) mention detection component based on Stanford CoreNLP, a high quality NLP pipeline[16]; and a coreference resolution stage consisting of 10 components called (**sieves**) analogous to CoGNIAC's rules and also ordered from the highest precision to lowest precision. The operation of the coreference resolution stage is based on the following principles:

- The system keeps track of **entities** (i.e., the discourse entities of systems such LaSIE: sets of mentions that have already been determined to belong together), while keeping track of properties such as number, gender, animacy, and named entity type.
- Each sieve operates on entities rather than mentions, and on the whole discourse, rather than on a sentence or a paragraph at a time.
- The system also keeps track of **cannot-link** constraints that have been added at various steps – i.e., for two entities, components can both add **must-link** constraints (merge the entities) or **cannot-link** constraints (such that the entities cannot be merged by any downstream component).
- For sieves that compare two mentions, the system keeps track of a "representative" mention in each cluster (typically the first one, as it is usually the longest, whereas subsequent mentions are shortened or only expressed as pronouns).

The ten sieves are:

1. *Speaker Identification*: This sieve first identifies **speakers**, then matches first and second pronouns to these speakers.
2. *Exact Match*: This sieve links together two mentions only if they contain exactly the same text, including both determiners and modifiers.
3. *Relaxed String Match*: This sieve links together two mentions only if they contain exactly the same text after dropping the postmodifiers.
4. *Precise Constructs*: This sieve links together two mentions if they occur in one of a series of high precision constructs: e.g., if they are in an appositive construction (*[the speaker of the House], [Mr. Smith]* ...), or if both mentions are tagged as NNP and one of them is an acronym of the other.

[15]The CoNLL coreference shared tasks are discussed in detail in chapter "Evaluation Campaigns".

[16]http://nlp.stanford.edu/software/corenlp.shtml

5. *Strict Head Match*: This sieve links together a mention with a candidate antecedent entity if *all* of a number of constraints are satisfied: (a) the head of the mention matches any of the heads of the candidate antecedent; (b) all non-stop words of the mention are included in the non-stop words of the candidate antecedent; (c) all mention modifiers are included among the modifiers of the candidate antecedent; and (d) the two mentions are not in an i-within-i situation, i.e., one is not a child in the other.
6. *Variants of Strict Head Match*: Sieve 6 relaxes the 'compatible modifiers only' constraint in the previous sieve, whereas Sieve 7 relaxes the 'word inclusion' constraint.
7. *Proper Head Match*: This sieve links two proper noun mentions if their head words match and a few other constraints apply.
8. *Relaxed Head Match*: This sieve relaxes the requirement that the head word of the mention must match a head word of the candidate antecedent entity.
9. *Pronoun resolution*: Finally, pronouns are resolved, by finding candidates matching the pronoun in number, gender, person, animacy, and NER label, and at most three sentences distant.

The Stanford Deterministic Coreference System achieved the highest MELA score (59.5) at the CONLL 2011 coreference shared task; and has been extensively evaluated on a variety of other datasets, always achieving state-of-the-art results.

11 Conclusions

In this chapter we have covered in some detail most of the best-known non-statistical approaches to anaphora resolution. As seen discussing the Stanford Deterministic Coreference System, such approaches still achieve state-of-the-art performance, and very few new ideas about the linguistic features playing a role in anaphora resolution have been introduced in more recent systems; but the thrust of the research in the field has moved towards statistical methods. The remaining chapters will focus on these approaches.

References

1. Alshawi, H.: Memory and Context for Language Interpretation. Cambridge University Press, Cambridge (1987)
2. Alshawi, H. (ed.): The Core Language Engine. MIT, Cambridge (1992)
3. Appelt, D.E., Hobbs, J.R., Bear, J., Israel, D., Kameyama, M., Tyson, M.: Fastus: a finite-state processor for information extraction from real-world text. In: Proceedings of IJCAI, Chambery (1993)
4. Asher, N., Lascarides, A.: The Logic of Conversation. Cambridge University Press, Cambridge (2003)

5. Baldwin, B.: Cogniac: a high precision pronoun resolution engine. In: Proceedings of the ACL'97/EACL'97 Workshop on Operational Factors in Practical, Robust Anaphora Resolution, Madrid, pp. 38–45 (1997)
6. Brennan, S., Friedman, M., Pollard, C.: A centering approach to pronouns. In: Proceedings of the 25th ACL, Stanford, pp. 155–162 (1987)
7. Carletta, J.: Assessing agreement on classification tasks: the kappa statistic. Comput. Linguist. **22**(2), 249–254 (1996)
8. Carter, D.M.: Interpreting Anaphors in Natural Language Texts. Ellis Horwood, Chichester (1987)
9. Charniak, E.: Towards a model of children's story comprehension. Ph.D. thesis, MIT (1972). Available as MIT AI Lab TR-266
10. Charniak, E.: Organization and inference in a frame-like system of commonsense knowledge. In: Proceedings of TINLAP, Cambridge, pp. 42–51 (1975)
11. Clark, H.H.: Bridging. In: Schank, R.C., Nash-Webber, B.L. (eds.) Proceedings of the 1975 Workshop on Theoretical Issues in Natural Language Processing, pp. 169–174. Association for Computing Machinery, Cambridge (1975)
12. Dale, R.: Generating Referring Expressions. MIT, Cambridge (1992)
13. Evans, R.: Applying machine learning toward an automatic classification of it. Lit. Linguist. Comput. **16**(1), 45–57 (2001)
14. Fellbaum, C. (ed.): WordNet: An Electronic Lexical Database. MIT, Cambridge (1998)
15. Gaizauskas, R., Wakao, T., Humphreys, K., Cunningham, H., Wilks, Y.: University of Sheffield: description of the LaSIE System as used for MUC-6. In: Proceedings of the Sixth Message Understanding Conference (MUC-6), pp. 207–220. Morgan Kauffmann, San Francisco (1995)
16. Garnham, A.: Mental Models and the Interpretation of Anaphora. Psychology Press, Hove (2001)
17. Garvey, C., Caramazza, A.: Implicit causality in verbs. Linguist. Inq. **5**, 459–464 (1974)
18. Ge, N., Hale, J., Charniak, E.: A statistical approach to anaphora resolution. In: Proceedings of WVLC/EMNLP (1998)
19. Gordon, P.C., Grosz, B.J., Gillion, L.A.: Pronouns, names, and the centering of attention in discourse. Cogn. Sci. **17**, 311–348 (1993)
20. Grishman, R., Sundheim, B.: Design of the MUC-6 evaluation. In: Proceedings of the Sixth Message Understanding Conference (MUC-6), Columbia (1995)
21. Grosz, B.J.: The representation and use of focus in dialogue understanding. Ph.D. thesis, Stanford University (1977)
22. Grosz, B.J., Joshi, A.K., Weinstein, S.: Centering: a framework for modeling the local coherence of discourse. Comput. Linguist. **21**(2), 202–225 (1995). The paper originally appeared as an unpublished manuscript in 1986
23. Hawkins, J.: Definiteness and Indefiniteness. Croom Helm, London (1978)
24. Heim, I.: The semantics of definite and indefinite noun phrases. Ph.D. thesis, University of Massachusetts at Amherst (1982)
25. Hewitt, C.: Planner: a language for proving theorems in robots. In: Proceedings of IJCAI, Washington DC, pp. 295–302 (1969)
26. Hirschman, L., Chinchor, N.: MUC-7 coreference task definition (version 3.0). In: Proceedings of the 7th Message Understanding Conference. http://www-nlpir.nist.gov/related_projects/muc/proceedings/co_task.html (1997)
27. Hirst, G.: Discourse-oriented anaphora resolution: a review. Comput. Linguist. **7**, 85–98 (1981)
28. Hobbs, J.: Resolving pronoun references. Lingua **44**, 311–338 (1978)
29. Hobbs, J.R.: Pronoun resolution. Research Note 76-1, City College, City University of New York (1976)
30. Hobbs, J.R.: Coherence and coreference. Cogn. Sci. **3**, 67–90 (1979)
31. Hobbs, J.R., Martin, P.: Local pragmatics. In: Proceedings of IJCAI-87, Milano, pp. 520–523 (1987)

32. Hobbs, J.R., Appelt, D.E., Bear, J., Tyson, M., Magerman, D.: The TACITUS system: the muc-3 experience. SRI Technical Note 511, SRI International, Menlo Park (1991)
33. Hobbs, J.R., Stickel, M., Appelt, D., Martin, P.: Interpretation as abduction. Artif. Intell. **63**, 69–142 (1993)
34. Humphreys, K., Gaizauskas, R., Azzam, S., Huyck, C., Mitchell, B., Cunningham, H., Wilks, Y.: University of Sheffield: description of the LaSIE-II system as used for muc-7. In: Proceedings of MUC-7, Fairfax (1998)
35. Järvinen, T., Tapanainen, P.: A dependency parser for English. Technical report TR-1, Department of General Linguistics, University of Helsinki (1997)
36. Kameyama, M.: Zero anaphora: the case of Japanese. Ph.D. thesis, Stanford University, Stanford (1985)
37. Kameyama, M.: Recognizing referential links: an information extraction perspective. In: ACL Workshop on Operational Factors in Practical, Robust Anaphora Resolution for Unrestricted Texts (1997)
38. Kamp, H., Reyle, U.: From Discourse to Logic. Kluwer Academic, Dordrecht (1993)
39. Kantor, R.N.: The management and comprehension of discourse connection by pronouns in English. Ph.D. thesis, Department of Linguistics, Ohio State University (1977)
40. Karamanis, N., Poesio, M., Oberlander, J., Mellish, C.: Evaluating centering for information ordering using corpora. Comput. Linguist. **35**(1), 29–46 (2009)
41. Kehler, A., Kertz, L., Rohde, H., Elman, J.: Coherence and coreference revisited. J. Semant. **25**(1), 1–44 (2008)
42. Kennedy, C., Boguraev, B.: Anaphora for everyone: pronominal anaphora resolution without a parser. In: COLING 1996, Copenhagen (1996)
43. Kennedy, C., Boguraev, B.: Anaphora for everyone: pronominal anaphora resolution without a parser. In: Proceedings of the 16th International Conference on Computational Linguistics (COLING), Copenhagen, pp 113–118 (1996)
44. Kibble, R., Power, R.: An integrated framework for text planning and pronominalization. In: Proceedings of the International Conference on Natural Language Generation (INLG), Mitzpe Ramon (2000)
45. Lappin, S., Leass, H.: An algorithm for pronominal anaphora resolution. Comput. Linguist. **20**(4), 535–561 (1994)
46. Lee, H., Peirsman, Y., Chang, A., Chambers, N., Surdeanu, M., Jurafsky, D.: Stanford's multi-pass sieve coreference resolution system at the CoNLL-2011 shared task. In: Proceedings of the CoNLL 2011 Shared Task, Portland (2011)
47. Lee, H., Chang, A., Peirsman, Y., Chambers, N., Surdeanu, M., Jurafsky, D.: Deterministic coreference resolution based on entity-centric, precision-ranked rules. Comput. Linguist. **39**(4), 885–916 (2013)
48. Linde, C.: Focus of attention and the choice of pronouns in discourse. In: Givon, T. (ed.) Syntax and Semantics, vol. 12. Academic, New York/London (1979)
49. Löbner, S.: Definites. J. Semant. **4**, 279–326 (1985)
50. Matthews, A., Chodorow, M.S.: Pronoun resolution in two-clause sentences: effects of ambiguity, antecedent location, and depth of embedding. J. Mem. Lang. **27**, 245–260 (1988)
51. Miltsakaki, E.: Towards an aposynthesis of topic continuity and intrasentential anaphora. Comput. Linguist. **28**(3), 319–355 (2002)
52. Minsky, M.: A framework for representing knowledge. In: Winston, P.H. (ed.) The Psychology of Computer Vision. McGraw-Hill, New York, pp. 211–277 (1975)
53. Mitkov, R.: Robust pronoun resolution with limited knowledge. In: Proceedings of the 18th COLING, Montreal, pp. 869–875 (1998)
54. Mitkov, R.: Anaphora Resolution. Longman, London/New York (2002)
55. Mitkov, R.: Anaphora resolution. In: Mitkov, R. (ed.) Oxford Handbook of Computational Linguistics. Oxford University Press, Oxford (2005)
56. Poesio, M., Kabadjov, M.A.: A general-purpose, off-the-shelf anaphora resolution module: implementation and preliminary evaluation. In: LREC 2004. http://privatewww.essex.ac.uk/~malexa/html_files/files/LREC2004.pdf (2004)

57. Poesio, M., Vieira, R.: A corpus-based investigation of definite description use. Comput. Linguist. **24**(2), 183–216 (1998)
58. Poesio, M., Vieira, R., Teufel, S.: Resolving bridging descriptions in unrestricted text. In: ACL-97 Workshop on Operational Factors in Practical, Robust, Anaphora Resolution For Unrestricted Texts (1997)
59. Poesio, M., Stevenson, R., Di Eugenio, B., Hitzeman, J.M.: Centering: a parametric theory and its instantiations. Comput. Linguist. **30**(3), 309–363 (2004)
60. Prince, E.F.: Toward a taxonomy of given-new information. In: Cole, P. (ed.) Radical Pragmatics, pp. 223–256. Academic, New York (1981)
61. Prince, E.F.: The ZPG letter: subjects, definiteness and information-status. In: Thompson, S., Mann, W. (eds.) Discourse Description: Diverse Analyses of a Fund Raising Text. John Benjamins, Amsterdam (1992)
62. Quinlan, J.R.: Induction of decision trees. Mach. Learn. **1**(1), 81–106 (1986)
63. Raghunathan, K., Lee, H., Rangarajan, S., Chambers, N., Surdeanu, M., Jurafsky, D., Manning, C.: A multi-pass sieve for coreference resolution. In: Proceedings of EMNLP, pp. 492–501. MIT, Boston (2010)
64. Reichman, R.: Getting Computers to Talk Like You and Me. MIT, Cambridge (1985)
65. Sanford, A.J., Garrod, S.C.: Understanding Written Language. Wiley, Chichester (1981)
66. Sidner, C.L.: Towards a computational theory of definite anaphora comprehension in English discourse. Ph.D. thesis, MIT (1979)
67. Sidner, C.L.: Focusing in the comprehension of definite anaphora. In: Brady, M., Berwick, R. (eds.) Computational Models of Discourse. MIT, Cambridge (1983)
68. Soon, W.M., Ng, H.T., Lim, D.C.Y.: A machine learning approach to coreference resolution of noun phrases. Comput. Linguist. **27**(4), 521–544 (2001). http://acl.eldoc.ub.rug.nl/mirror/J/J01/J01-4004.pdf
69. Stevenson, R.J., Crawley, R.A., Kleinman, D.: Thematic roles, focus, and the representation of events. Lang. Cogn. Process. **9**, 519–548 (1994)
70. Strube, M.: Never look back: an alternative to centering. In: Proceedings of COLING-ACL, Montreal, pp. 1251–1257 (1998)
71. Strube, M., Hahn, U.: Functional centering–grounding referential coherence in information structure. Comput. Linguist. **25**(3), 309–344 (1999)
72. Stuckardt, R.: Design and enhanced evaluation of a robust anaphor resolution algorithm. Comput. Linguist. **27**(4), 479–506 (2001)
73. Sundheim, B.M.: Overview of the results of the MUC-6 evaluation. In: Proceedings of the Sixth Message Understanding Conference (MUC-6), Columbia, pp. 13–31 (1995)
74. Suri, L.Z., McCoy, K.F.: RAFT/RAPR and centering: a comparison and discussion of problems related to processing complex sentences. Comput. Linguist. **20**(2), 301–317 (1994)
75. Tetrault, J.: A corpus-based evaluation of centering and pronoun resolution. Comput. Linguist. **27**(4), 507–520 (2001)
76. Vieira, R.: Definite description resolution in unrestricted texts. Ph.D. thesis, Centre for Cognitive Science, University of Edinburgh (1998)
77. Vieira, R., Poesio, M.: Corpus-based approaches to NLP: a practical prototype. In: Anais do XVI Congresso da Sociedade Brasileira de Computa cão (1996)
78. Vieira, R., Poesio, M.: Processing definite descriptions in corpora. In: Botley, S., McEnery, M. (eds.) Corpus-Based and Computational Approaches to Discourse Anaphora. UCL Press, London (1997)
79. Vieira, R., Poesio, M.: Corpus-based development and evaluation of a system for processing definite descriptions. In: Proceedings of 18th COLING, Saarbruecken (2000)
80. Vieira, R., Poesio, M.: An empirically based system for processing definite descriptions. Comput. Linguist. **26**(4), 539–593 (2000)
81. Vieira, R., Teufel, S.: Towards resolution of bridging descriptions. In: ACL-EACL, Madrid (1997)

82. Vilain, M., Burger, J., Aberdeen, J., Connolly, D., Hirschman, L.: A model-theoretic coreference scoring scheme. In: Proceedings of the 6th Message Understanding Conference (MUC-6), pp. 45–52. Morgan Kaufmann, San Francisco (1996). doi:http://dx.doi.org/10.3115/1072399.1072405
83. Walker, M.A.: Evaluating discourse processing algorithms. In: Proceedings of ACL, Manchester, pp. 251–261 (1989)
84. Walker, M.A., Iida, M., Cote, S.: Japanese discourse and the process of centering. Comput. Linguist. **20**(2), 193–232 (1994)
85. Walker, M.A., Joshi, A.K., Prince, E.F. (eds.): Centering Theory in Discourse. Clarendon Press, Oxford (1998)
86. Wilks, Y.A.: An intelligent analyzer and understander of English. Commun. ACM **18**(5), 264–274 (1975). Reprinted in Readings in Natural Language Processing, Morgan Kaufmann
87. Wilks, Y.A.: A preferential pattern-matching semantics for natural language. Artif. Intell. J. **6**, 53–74 (1975)
88. Winograd, T.: Understanding Natural Language. Academic, New York (1972)

Part II
Resources

Annotated Corpora and Annotation Tools

Massimo Poesio, Sameer Pradhan, Marta Recasens, Kepa Rodriguez, and Yannick Versley

Abstract In this chapter we review the currently available corpora to study anaphoric interpretation, and the tools that can be used to create new ones. A comprehensive survey of annotated corpora will be given, which ranges from the corpora and guidelines developed for the Message Understanding Conferences MUC-6 (1996) and MUC-7 (1998), which have been seminal to the field, to the resources that have been recently made available as part of the 2010 SemEval evaluation campaign. All fundamental design decisions regarding annotation formats and standards are described, and the relevant properties of the corpora are presented in a uniform and well-structured way. Moreover, three useful, widely used and freely available annotation tools (CALLISTO, MMAX2, and Palinka) will be described. They can be employed if own annotation work turns out to be indispensable.

Keywords Annotated corpora and annotation tools annotated corpora • Annotation tools • Linguistic resources

---

M. Poesio (✉)
University of Essex, Wivenhoe Park, Colchester, UK
e-mail: poesio@essex.ac.uk

S. Pradhan
Boulder Learning, Inc., Boulder, CO, USA
e-mail: pradhan@boulderlearning.com; pradhan@cemantix.org

M. Recasens
Google Inc., Stanford, CA, USA
e-mail: recasens@google.com

K.-J. Rodriguez
Yad Vashem Archives, Jerusalem, Israel

Y. Versley
University of Heidelberg, Heidelberg, Germany
e-mail: versley@cl.uni-heidelberg.de

M. Poesio et al. (eds.), *Anaphora Resolution*, Theory and Applications of Natural Language Processing, DOI 10.1007/978-3-662-47909-4_4

1 Introduction

In the 1990s, the desire to use anaphora resolution in practical applications, especially in the then-nascent field of information extraction, led to a shift in focus in anaphora resolution research towards a more empirical approach to the problem. This more empirical focus also led to the creation of the first medium-size annotated corpora, which allowed for data-driven development of resolution procedures and machine learning approaches.

These changes were primarily brought about by the Message Understanding Conferences (MUC), a DARPA-funded initiative where researchers would compare the quality of their information extraction systems on an annotated corpus provided by funding agencies. MUC introduced the **coreference resolution task** already discussed in chapters "Linguistic and Cognitive Evidence About Anaphora" and "Early Approaches to Anaphora Resolution: Theoretically Inspired and Heuristic-Based", and hosted two evaluations of coreference resolution systems, MUC-6 [23] and MUC-7 [14], where annotated corpora were provided to the participants. In parallel with the development of the corpora, guidelines for the annotation of coreference were created and a common evaluation procedure for the comparative evaluation was developed. The availability of these corpora, and of common evaluation metrics, made it possible to train and test coreference resolution systems on the same datasets, and therefore to compare their results. These efforts had a tremendous influence on the field and their influence can be seen in subsequent evaluation campaigns such as the Automatic Content Extraction (ACE) initiative.[1] As a result, it is not an exaggeration to talk of a pre-MUC and post-MUC period in research on coreference and more in general on anaphora resolution.

In this chapter we present a detailed survey of some of the proposals concerning the annotation of corpora with anaphoric and coreference information and their use for evaluation of data-driven approaches to anaphora resolution.

2 Annotating Anaphora: An Overview of the Options

In a data-driven perspective, the design of the annotation scheme acquires a crucial importance. This is because linguistic data annotated with anaphoric information are used both to evaluate the performance of data-driven anaphoric resolvers (cf. chapter "Evaluation Metrics"), and to train supervised systems, the most popular machine-learning approach to this problem (cf. chapters "The Mention-Pair Model", "Advanced Machine Learning Models for Coreference Resolution, and" "Integer Linear Programming for Coreference Resolution"). So the annotation scheme defines what the problem of anaphora resolution is, and what is the linguistic

[1] http://www.nist.gov/speech/tests/ace/index.html

phenomenon to be learned from the data. We begin the chapter by briefly discussing some of the decisions to be made while designing an annotation scheme, the choices made in some of the best known schemes including both initiative-oriented schemes for English such as MUC and ACE, and more general-purpose schemes. We also mention the most controversial issues.

2.1 *Markables*

One of the controversial issues in defining a coding scheme for anaphora is the definition of **markable** or **mention**—the unit of text to be chosen as mention of an entity. This definition depends on both syntactic and semantic factors.

Syntactic characterization of markables As discussed in chapter "Linguistic and Cognitive Evidence About Anaphora", most current work on anaphora focuses on NP anaphora, i.e., anaphoric relations expressed with noun phrases. As a result, most coding schemes for anaphoric and coreference corpora ask coders to only consider noun phrases as markables, with a few exceptions discussed below. In fact, some of the early coding schemes focused on a subset of all NPs: e.g., only pronouns (as in the corpora created by [9, 20, 26] or in the early versions of the Prague Dependendency Treebank [41]) or only definite descriptions (as in the Vieira-Poesio corpus, [62]). Most modern schemes, however, require coders to mark all anaphoric expressions realized with noun phrases, the main restrictions being semantic (see below).

A second type of syntactic restriction concerns the boundaries of markables. Most coding schemes, including those for MUC, ACE, MATE, GNOME, ARRAU, LIVEMEMORIES and ONTONOTES, require coders to mark the entire noun phrase[2] with all postmodifiers (1a). The alternative is to mark noun phrases just up to the head and leave postmodifiers out of the markable, as in (1b).

(1) a. It is more important to preserve high inter-annotator agreement than to capture [every possible phenomenon that could fall under the heading of "coreference"].

b. It is more important to preserve high inter-annotator agreement than to capture [every possible phenomenon] that could fall under the heading of "coreference".

However, this tendency to mark the noun phrase in its entirety raises markable identification problems for systems: because of pre-processing errors such as parsing inaccuracies, the phrases annotated in the gold standard and those automatically identified by a system can be partially misaligned, e.g., they may

[2]As discussed in chapter "Linguistic and Cognitive Evidence About Anaphora", many types of expressions in language are anaphoric to a degree, but the type of anaphoric reference most studied in computational linguistics, by far, is anaphoric reference via noun phrases, so in this chapter, as in the rest of the book, we will focus on coding schemes and corpora for NP anaphoric reference.

differ on which postmodifiers of a noun are included in the markable. In order not to penalize anaphora resolution systems on the incorrect identification of the markable boundaries, the decision was taken in MUC to instruct coders to mark the maximal span of a noun phrase, and, in addition, to identify its head in a separate attribute called MIN. In this way, systems in MUC could also be evaluated in a relaxed evaluation setting where they received credit for markable identification based only on the matching of heads and minimal spans—the rationale being that the full set of modifiers can be optionally recovered later with the help of separate syntactic information. In ACE, the head and the minimal extent required to guarantee correct identification were marked separately, in the HEAD and EXTENT attributes, respectively. In subsequent proposals, annotators have also been generally required to annotate the NP with all its modifiers [54, 56, 67], but heads/minimal spans are not always annotated (e.g., ONTONOTES), and in some annotation projects only parts of the NP are annotated.

Most schemes include some exceptions to the rule of annotating only NPs. One type of constituent treated as markable in many schemes are noun premodifiers. In linguistics, it is generally thought that such modifiers do not add discourse referents to the discourse model, i.e., are **anaphoric islands** [63], on the grounds of contrasts such as that between (2a), which is generally considered acceptable, and (2b), which is generally considered ungrammatical.

(2) a. Hunters of [animals]$_i$ tend to like [them]$_i$.
b. *[Animal]$_i$ hunters tend to like [them]$_i$.

However, [81] proposed a rather different account of these data, pointing out first of all that such positions not only do not block anaphoric reference in general—see (3a)—but that also nominal modification is possible at least in certain cases, as shown in (3b). They proposed that whereas in a subset of these examples anaphoric reference is indeed blocked, in general the possibility to refer depends on pragmatic factors.

(3) a. Millions of [Oprah Winfrey]$_i$ fans were thoroughly confused last week when, during [her]$_i$ show, [she]$_i$ emotionally denied and denounced a vile rumour about [herself]$_i$.
b. I had a [paper]$_j$ route once but my boss told me I took too long to deliver [them]$_j$.

Many, if not most, coding schemes for anaphoric reference require coders to annotate at least some cases of reference to antecedents introduced by prenominal modifiers. For instance, the MUC guidelines state that prenominal modifiers are markables only if the coreference chain contains one element that is not a modifier. Thus, *drug* is a markable in (4a), but *contract drilling* is not in (4b).

(4) a. He was accused of money laundering and [drug]$_i$ trafficking. However, the trade in [drugs]$_i$...
b. Ocean Drilling & Exploration Co. will sell its [contract drilling] business. ... Ocean Drilling said it will offer 15–20% of the [contract drilling] business through an initial public offering in the near future.

Similar instructions are found in the ARRAU and GNOME guidelines, where coders are also required to annotate *drug* and *drugs* in (4a) as generic. It should be noted, however, that this 'on-demand' annotation makes mention detection difficult for systems as they cannot simply rely on syntactic structure, and not many systems are good at identifying generic cases.

Another class of markables not associated with (realized) NPs are **incorporated anaphors** in Romance languages (see chapter "Linguistic and Cognitive Evidence About Anaphora"). As a reminder, incorporated anaphors are cases of anaphoric reference in which the anaphoric expression is expressed by an affix to another expression, e.g., a verb, as in the following example from Italian, where clitic suffix *lo* refers back to Giovanni.

(5) a. [IT] Giovanni$_i$ e' in ritardo così mi ha chiesto se posso incontrar[lo]$_i$ al cinema.
b. [EN] John$_i$ is late so he$_i$ asked me if I can meet him$_i$ at the movies.

A second class of anaphors that may cause problems from the point of view of markable identification are **zero anaphors**—cases of anaphoric reference in which one argument is unrealized, as in the following examples from Italian and Japanese.

(6) a. [IT] [Giovanni]$_i$ andò a far visita a degli amici. Per via, ϕ_i comprò del vino.
b. [JA] [John]$_i$-wa yujin-o houmon-sita. Tochu-de ϕ_i wain-o ka-tta.
c. [EN] [John]$_i$ went to visit some friends. On the way, [he]$_i$ bought some wine.

Such markables can be a problem for markup-based annotation (i.e., annotation in which markables are chunks of text), depending on the limitations of the annotation tool (see Sect. 4.1). They are not a problem when anaphoric annotation piggybacks on a syntactically and morphologically annotated layer which serves as a base layer, as in the case of ANCORA [69], the Prague Dependency Treebank [25], or ONTONOTES [67, 82]. This ideal situation is however rather uncommon among existing annotated corpora. Even when the base layer is text, as it is often the case, these expressions are not particularly problematic when standoff is based on character offset, as done in the NAIST corpus of anaphora in Japanese [34], annotated using Tagrin,[3] or in annotations using CALLISTO.[4] This is because with standoff, markables can point to a subset of the verbal expression (i.e., *-lo* in (5a)) or to a zero-length string before the markable (5b). However, with token standoff, some convention has to be introduced to associate those anaphors with other markables. A common approach is to mark the nearest verbal constituent, as proposed in the MATE guidelines and done in the Italian LIVEMEMORIES corpus [70]. In (7), the verbal form *dargli*, which includes the incorporated clitic *-gli* referring to Giovanni, would be treated as a markable of type `verbal`, and it would be annotated as anaphoric to Giovanni.

---

[3]http://kagonma.org/tagrin/

[4]http://mitre.github.io/callisto/index.html

(7) [Giovanni]$_i$ è un seccatore. Non [dargli]$_i$ retta.
[John]$_i$ is a nuisance. Do not pay any attention to [him]$_i$.

The last syntactic (but also semantic) restriction on markables that we will discuss are cases of anaphoric reference in which the antecedent is not introduced by an NP, as in cases of so-called **event reference** and **discourse deixis**, discussed in chapter "Linguistic and Cognitive Evidence About Anaphora". In the example of event anaphora in (8), the pronoun *it* refers to the event of John breaking his leg, not introduced by a nominal; in the example of discourse deixis in (9), the demonstrative pronoun *that* in B's statement refers to the proposition asserted by A in her previous utterance. These types of anaphora were not annotated in the MUC or ACE corpora (see, e.g., [29]), or in most existing corpora, but event anaphora is annotated in ONTONOTES, and discourse deixis in the ARRAU corpus.

(8) John broke his leg yesterday.
It happened while he was skiing.

(9) A: John broke his leg yesterday.
B: That's not true – I saw him this morning and he seemed fine to me.

A particularly intricate issue with defining markables is what to do with coordination, which we discuss in Sect. 2.3.

Semantic restrictions on markables From a semantic perspective, a coding scheme may either require coders to annotate mentions of all types of entities, or of a subset of them only. In the context of information extraction applications, coreference resolution is most important for members of a small number of **semantic classes** that are relevant for the domain at hand. Many early machine-learning approaches such as [44] and [2], only concerned themselves with organizations and persons. As a result, the guidelines for the ACE coreference annotation, for instance, identified seven types of entities as most relevant (PERSON, ORGANIZATION, GEO/SOCIAL/POLITICAL ENTITY, LOCATION, FACILITY, VEHICLE, WEAPON) and only asked annotators to annotate mentions of those types [42].

One benefit of narrowly focusing on a small number of (presumably) well-behaved semantic classes is that identity or non-identity is usually straightforward to determine, whereas it may be very difficult to decide for abstract or vague objects. The disadvantage is that anaphoric resolvers trained on these data will not be very useful in different domains. For instance, artifacts other than vehicles and weapons are not annotated in the ACE corpora, but these turn out to be a key entity type in one of the GNOME [54] domains, namely museum objects.

Coding schemes may also choose to only mark NPs fulfilling certain semantic functions. As discussed in chapter "Linguistic and Cognitive Evidence About Anaphora", nominal expressions can play at least four types of semantic function: **referring**, **quantificational**, **predicative**, or **expletive**. In many coding schemes, coders are instructed not to mark expletives (e.g., MUC [29]). In such schemes, predicative NPs are generally markables, but they are marked as coreferent with the referring NPs they are predicated about—i.e., referring and predicative mentions are treated as having the same function. More recent schemes generally make the distinction between coreference and predication. In some schemes (e.g., ANCORA,

ONTONOTES), a different relation is used for marking attributive cases (e.g., appositive NPs are annotated as ATTRIBUTE of the encompassing NP). In other schemes (e.g., ARRAU), no relation is marked between the predicative NP and the referring NP of which it specifies a property. In some of these schemes (including ACE, GNOME, and ARRAU), special attributes are used to mark the semantic function of the markable. In ACE, the CLASS attribute was used to specify whether a markable is referential or attributive, and in the case of referential markables, whether it is generic or not [1]. In GNOME, the LF_TYPE attribute was used to mark the logical form interpretation of the markable: term, predicate, quantifier, or coordination, whereas the reference attribute specified terms as being directly referring, bound, or non-referring [54]. In ARRAU, these two attributes are merged in a single reference attribute.

2.2 *Anaphoric Relations*

In the MUC coding scheme, annotators were asked to mark only the anaphoric relations involving entities introduced by NPs and mentioned using NPs or nominal modifiers, but none of the other anaphoric relations discussed in chapter "Linguistic and Cognitive Evidence About Anaphora": associative relations, cases of identity of sense, and relations where the anaphor or the antecedent are not both explicitly introduced as part of a noun phrase. The reason was the difficulty in annotating such relations already discussed in chapter "Linguistic and Cognitive Evidence About Anaphora". Annotation efforts that include associative anaphora are DRAMA (Passonneau, R.J.: Instructions for applying discourse reference annotation for multiple applications (DRAMA). Unpublished manuscript, 1997), the UCREL scheme developed at the University of Lancaster [6], and a number of schemes implementing the MATE guidelines, in particular the GNOME annotation [54]. Discourse deixis was annotated in ARRAU [56].

As discussed in chapter "Linguistic and Cognitive Evidence About Anaphora" and again in Sect. 2.1, NPs can perform different semantic functions but not all coding schemes distinguish between such functions. A famously controversial aspect of the definition of the coreference task in MUC was the proposal to annotate as coreferent appositive and copula constructions, which would normally be considered cases of predication. This drew criticism from researchers such as van Deemter and Kibble [16], since the inclusion of intensional descriptions leads to counter-intuitive effects in cases such as the following one:

(10) [Henry Higgins], who was formerly [sales director of Sudsy Soaps], became [president of Dreamy Detergents].

In this example, following the guidelines would lead to "*sales director of Sudsy Soaps*" and "*president of Dreamy Detergents*" being annotated as coreferent. This conflation of anaphoricity and predication has been abandoned in more recent coding schemes, following the guidelines proposed by the Discourse Resource Initiative (Passonneau, R.J.: Instructions for applying discourse reference annotation for multiple applications (DRAMA). Unpublished manuscript, 1997) and the MATE project [54]. The coding schemes developed for the GNOME and ARRAU corpora [56] and for the corpora used in the 2010 SEMEVAL competition (ANCORA [69], COREA [27], TüBa-D/Z [28], LiveMemories [70], ONTONOTES [67, 82]), and for the CONLL-2011 and CONLL-2012 shared tasks (ONTONOTES), all distinguish between (transitive) coreference and (directed, non-transitive) predication. In some of these corpora (e.g., ARRAU), predication is simply not marked, whereas in other corpora (e.g., GNOME and ONTONOTES) it is marked as a different type of link.

A particularly difficult issue is **metonymy**, as in the following example.

(11) *Paris* rejected the "logic of ultimatums".

In this example, the NP *Paris* is not used to refer to a geographical entity (the city of Paris) but to a (political) entity linked to Paris by a systematic relation. This example could be interpreted roughly as meaning:

> A French government official made a statement to the effect that the official French position regarding the "logic of ultimatums" is of disapproval.

Such examples raise two types of issues. Semantically, the coder must decide what type of entity should be assigned to the markable. From the point of view of anaphoric annotation, the guidelines should specify whether the markable *Paris* in (11) has to be annotated as coreferent to other mentions of any of the following entities:

1. the city of Paris;
2. the country of France (as a geographic entity);
3. the French government ;
4. the government official uttering the sentence

Different (partial) solutions have been adopted for this problem. The ACE guidelines resolve the ambiguity between 2 and 3 by assuming a semantic class of so-called **geopolitical entities** (GPEs), i.e., a conflation of a country, its government, and its inhabitants. In ONTONOTES, the diametrically opposite solution was chosen: metonymies are distinguished from other uses of an NP, e.g., coreferential ones. Thus, in a document that contains the sentences:

(12) [$_1$ South Korea] is a country in southeastern Asia. ... [$_2$ South Korea] has signed the agreement.

the annotation guidelines require to distinguish between "South Korea" mentioned as a country (1) and its metonymous use referring to the South Korean government (2).

2.3 Coordination and Plurals

The semantics of **coordination** and **plurals** is reasonably well understood, but it is not straightforward to annotate anaphoric relations involving coordinated or plural

NPs, especially in a way that current anaphora resolution models could be trained to resolve them.

Coordinations like *John and Mary* in (13a) are generally considered NPs, and therefore treated in most coding schemes as markables. It is therefore possible in such cases to mark plural *they* as having the conjunction as antecedent. However, plurals can also have **split antecedents**–they can refer to a plural entity consisting of two entities introduced separately, but not previously mentioned (13b).

(13) a. [[John]$_i$ and [Mary]$_j$]$_k$ went to the movies. [They]$_k$ saw *Turtle Diary*.
b. [John]$_i$ went to the movies with [Mary]$_j$. [They]$_k$ saw *Turtle Diary*.

Clearly, there are many different ways in which to annotate anaphoricity information in these cases, and therefore different solutions have been adopted in the existing coding schemes. In MUC, ACE, and ONTONOTES, the coordinated NP is marked as the antecedent of *they* in (13a), but no antecedent is marked for *they* in (13b).

GNOME and ARRAU tried to treat the two cases of plural reference in a uniform way, but different solutions were adopted. In GNOME, the antecedents of plural pronouns are always marked using the associative relation **has-element**: both in (13a) and (13b), no identity relation is marked for *they*, but both *John* and *Mary* are marked as elements of the set denoted by the plural. In ANCORA and ARRAU, the possibility offered by the ANCORAPIPE and MMAX2 annotation tools (see Sect. 4.1) to annotate split antecedents was used: in both examples, plural *they* is marked as having John and Mary as antecedents.

3 Corpora Annotated with Anaphoric Information

3.1 The MUC *Corpora*

The sixth and seventh editions of the Message Understanding Conference (MUC-6 and MUC-7) introduced two 'Semantic Evaluation' (SEMEVAL) tasks in addition to the template-filling tasks evaluated at previous editions of the MUC competition: coreference and named entity disambiguation [24]. To this end, new datasets were created which, in the case of coreference, were the first corpora of any size available for training and evaluating coreference resolution systems. The dataset created for MUC-6 consists of 25 articles from the Wall Street Journal on negotiations of labor disputes and corporate management succession, for a total of around 30,000 words. The MUC-7 dataset consists of a similar amount of data on airplane crashes and rocket/missile launches. Now that larger resources exist, these two corpora are not widely used anymore except for comparison with older systems, but the task definition developed for their creation is still very influential.

Markup Scheme The MUC corpora are annotated using inline SGML. Every markable that belongs to a coreference chain is identified with a `<COREF>` tag; `<COREF>` elements have three attributes: `ID` number, `TYPE` (always filled with

IDENT) and REF. The first mention of a coref chain uses the attribute id to assign an ID to the coreference chain, and every subsequent mention uses the attribute REF to specify the coreference chain to which it belongs. There is an optional attribute, STATUS, that always takes the value OPT and marks optional links, like predications.

(14)
```
<COREF ID="100">Lawson Mardon Group Ltd.</COREF>
said <COREF ID="101" TYPE="IDENT"
REF="100">it</COREF> ...
```

Guidelines The annotation scheme developed for MUC [29] virtually defined the focus for research on anaphora resolution and coreference for the 15 years after. The scheme is focused on coreference between NPs. Only cases of nominal mention of discourse entities are considered; no other type of relation (no identity of sense or bridging relation, for instance). No relations where the anaphor or the antecedent are not both explicitly introduced as part of a NP are considered either (i.e., no ellipsis, and no reference to implicitly mentioned objects as in discourse deixis).

Markable Definition Syntactically, annotators were asked to consider as markables NPs and nouns occurring in certain positions. Pronouns include both personal pronouns (including possessive pronouns) and demonstrative pronouns. Dates, percentages and currency expressions are considered nominal phrases.

Markables are defined as the maximal projections of the noun phrase, i.e., they include all pre-and post modifiers like non-restrictive relative clauses, prepositional phrases, etc. This definition of markable, while linguistically justified, could make system evaluation overly strict given that most mention extraction systems encounter difficulty at identifying all modifiers. Thus, in order to facilitate aligning the markables in the gold standard and the markables produced by a system, the MUC coding scheme introduced the solution discussed in Sect. 2.1—each markable is annotated with a MIN attribute containing the head of the NP (15).

(15)
```
But <COREF ID="42" MIN="planes">military training
planes</COREF> make up to ...
```

If the head of the markable is a multi-word named entity, like *Julius Cesar* in (16), the entire named entity is specified as the value of MIN.

(16)
```
<COREF ID="1" MIN="Julius Caesar">Julius Caesar,
<COREF ID="2" REF="1" MIN="emperor" TYPE="IDENT">
the/a well-known emperor, </COREF></COREF>
```

All and only mentions of entities which are introduced by an NP and are mentioned more than once are considered as markables: i.e., singletons are not annotated, and more entity types are considered than those specified in the guidelines for named entity annotation.[5] However, embedded named entities are not considered as markables: for example, the two occurrences of *Iowa* in (17) are not marked as coreferent, since the first one is a substring of a named entity.

[5]These are persons, organizations, locations, temporal expressions, and numerical expressions—see, e.g., [22].

(17) [Equitable of Iowa Cos.]. . . . located in [Iowa]

In the case of conjoined NPs, both the individual NPs and the coordinated NP are potential markables, as shown in (18).

(18) [[the two Croatians] and [Brown]]

However, in the case of coordinated NPs, there isn't an obvious notion of 'head' other than perhaps the coordination itself (*and*). This is not a noun however, making the annotation of the MIN attribute problematic. Different solutions to this problem were adopted in MUC6 and MUC7. The MUC6 guidelines [21] prescribe not to treat as markables coordinated NPs that can have more than one head. The MUC7 guidelines [29], by contrast, propose to assign a coordinated head to such NPs: e.g., in example (18), the MIN should be the span "Croatians and Brown" as in (19).

(19)
```
<COREF ID="59" MIN="Croatians and Brown">
<COREF ID="56" TYPE="IDENT" REF="14"
MIN="Croatians"> The two Croatians</COREF>
and
<COREF ID="57" TYPE="IDENT" REF="39">Brown</COREF>
```

Notice that the span of MIN in this example does not correspond to any linguistic category.

Range of relations Apart from the simple examples mentioned above, the coders were also asked to consider the following as cases of coreference:

- Bound anaphora, as in
  [Most computational linguists] prefer [their] own parsers
  or
  [Every TV network] reported [its] profits yesterday. [They] plan to release full quarterly statements tomorrow.
- More controversially (see above and chapter "Linguistic and Cognitive Evidence About Anaphora"), the coders were asked to consider many cases of predication as cases of coreference. This includes most cases of appositions, as in
  [Julius Cesar], [the well known emperor]
  This identity of reference is to be represented by a coreference link between the appositional phrase, "the well-known emperor", and the ENTIRE NP, "Julius Caesar, the/a well-known emperor" (20):

  (20)
  ```
  <COREF ID="1" MIN="Julius Caesar">Julius Caesar,
  <COREF ID="2" REF="1" MIN="emperor" TYPE="IDENT">
  the/a well-known emperor,</COREF>
  </COREF>
  ```

  Other predicative nominals, such as copular constructions, are also annotated as coreferent.
  [Bill Clinton] is [the President of the United States].
- Functions and values. Coders were required to link the most recent value to the function. In (21), coders were required to link [$3.85] and [The stock price]. (Again, see above why this is bound to cause problems in general.)

(21) [The stock price] fell from [$4.02] to [$3.85];

Availability Both MUC corpora are available from the Linguistic Data Consortium (LDC).

3.2 The ACE Corpora

The Automatic Content Extraction program (ACE),[6] was, like MUC (of which it forms the natural continuation), an initiative of the US government to promote content extraction technology, and in particular the identification of entities, relations, and events in text [17]. The program was articulated around evaluations of systems performing these tasks; many such evaluations took place from 2000 to 2008, supporting the annotation of data in three different languages—Arabic, Chinese and English. The ACE-2 and ACE-2005 Entity Detection and Tracking (EDT) English corpora, in particular, replaced the MUC corpora as the de facto standards for 'coreference.'

Markup Scheme The corpora are marked up using the **ACE Pilot Format** (APF), a standoff XML markup format in which a base file contains the text with some inline SGML annotation; information about entities and their mentions is stored in a separate file with indices which refer to character positions in the base file. Anaphoric information in APF is organized around entities: all entities annotated in the document are identified with `<ENTITY>` elements, and each mention of entity *e* is then recorded as a child `<ENTITY_MENTION>` element of the `<ENTITY>` element for *e*.

Each mention is annotated with the attribute `TYPE`, with three possible values: `NAM` for named entities, `NOM` for NPs with a common noun as head, and `PRO` for pronouns. Each `<ENTITY_MENTION>` element has two children: the `<EXTENT>`, which specifies the character span in the base file realizing that mention, and also contains the string of characters; and the `<HEAD>` element, which specifies the span of characters and contains the string of the syntactic head of the NP. The markup for mentions is shown in (22).

(22)
```
<entity_mention ID="2-5" TYPE="NOM">
<extent>
<charseq START="1621" END="1671">an assistant
director at the Oregon Zoo in Portland</charseq>
</extent>
<head>
<charseq START="1634" END="1641">director</charseq>
</head>
</entity_mention>
```

[6] http://www.itl.nist.gov/iad/mig//tests/ace/

If the head is a named entity realized by more than one word, the full named entity is the head of the markable (23).

(23)
```
<entity_mention ID="1-2" TYPE="NAM">
<extent>
<charseq START="1573" END="1609">American Zoo and
Aquarium Association</charseq>
</extent>
<head>
<charseq START="1573" END="1609">American Zoo and
Aquarium Association</charseq>
</head>
</entity_mention>
```

Guidelines In contrast to the MUC annotation scheme, the ACE annotation scheme for entity detection and tracking focuses on a small number of semantic classes considered particularly relevant for information extraction: persons, organizations, locations, geopolitical entities, weapons, and vehicles [42]. (See discussion of semantic restrictions in Sect. 2.1.) These classes have changed over the years: the first editions focused on five classes (facilities, geopolitical entities, locations, organizations, and persons), and the later editions on seven (facilities, geopolitical entities, locations, organizations, persons, vehicles, and weapons).

The ACE guidelines follow fairly closely the MUC guidelines, but include additional specifications as they were used for Arabic and Chinese as well as English data.

Markable Definition One of the issues addressed in the ACE annotation guidelines is the problem of metonymy (see above). In (24), the mention *Iraq* refers to the country as a geographical entity, whereas in a further sentence of the same text (25), the mention *Iraq* refers to the political and economical institutions of the country.

(24) Russia's opposition to the use of force in **Iraq** is the latest in a series of foreign policy disputes with the United States.

(25) Russia, its economy in chaos, desperately needs the cash and also hopes for big new contracts with **Iraq** when sanctions end.

The solution proposed in the ACE guidelines to ensure consistency in the annotation is the creation of a **Geopolitical Entity** (GPE) category, which merges the meaning of the country as a physical place, the institution that governs the country, and the inhabitants.

Range of relations Like the MUC guidelines, the ACE guidelines require annotating cases of nominal predication via apposition and copular clauses as cases of coreference. For instance, in (26), the mention *"an Asian power"* is marked as coreferent with *"China"*.

(26) Today , *China* is **an Asian power** and rightfully so.

Similarly, in the ACE annotation appositions are marked as coreferent with the main NP. For instance, in (27) the markable *deputy prosecutor of the war crimes tribunal* corefers with the full NP.

(27) Graham Blewitt , deputy prosecutor of the war crimes tribunal[a]

[a]npaper 9801.139

Availability All ACE corpora are distributed through LDC. A useful summary of the available resources is at https://www.ldc.upenn.edu/collaborations/past-projects/ace/annotation-tasks-and-specifications.

3.3 The DRI *and* MATE *Guidelines*

The **Discourse Resource Initiative** (Passonneau, R.J.: Instructions for applying discourse reference annotation for multiple applications (DRAMA). Unpublished manuscript, 1997) and the MATE project [54] started a re-examination of coding schemes for anaphora, leading to the schemes adopted in most of the more recent anaphoric annotation efforts, including GNOME [54], ARRAU [56], and ONTONOTES [64, 67, 82] for English, COREA [27] for Dutch, the Potsdam Commentary Corpus [40] and TüBa-D/Z corpus [28] for German, ANCORA for Catalan and Spanish [69], and LIVEMEMORIES [70] for Italian.

These schemes tend to be more linguistically inspired and less domain-oriented than the MUC and ACE schemes. All NPs are annotated, instead of only the mentions of a selected number of entity types, and markable boundaries tend to follow NP boundaries. From a semantic perspective, all of these annotation schemes distinguish between identity and predication, and some of these schemes attempt to mark a richer range of anaphoric relations, including associative relations (e.g., GNOME, ARRAU, COREA) or some types of discourse deixis—e.g., reference to events in ONTONOTES, or reference to abstract objects in ARRAU. Many such corpora also include annotations of other properties of mentions, such as agreement features. Also, agreement studies are generally carried out. The most recent evaluation campaigns for anaphora have used corpora of this type.

In this Section we discuss the MATE guidelines and the GNOME corpus; we will then discuss ARRAU and LIVEMEMORIES, the Prague Dependency Treebank, ANCORA, and ONTONOTES in separate sections.

The MATE Markup Scheme The objective of the *Multilevel Annotation Tools Engineering* (MATE) project was to develop an annotation workbench supporting multilevel annotation in dialogue [45]. The project built on XML standoff technology developed in the MULTEXT project [32], and in particular on its application in the MapTask corpus [36]. The levels to be supported by the workbench included morphosyntax, prosody, dialogue acts, coreference, and disfluencies; for each of these levels a document was produced analyzing the needs of that type of annotation, and proposing a markup scheme that could support those needs.

The MATE proposals for coreference [39, 57] were based on an analysis of the best known coding schemes of the time, including MUC-style coreference, the more general notion of anaphoric reference and associative anaphora, supported by

DRAMA (the scheme developed by Passonneau for the Discourse Resource Initiative) (Passonneau, R.J.: Instructions for applying discourse reference annotation for multiple applications (DRAMA). Unpublished manuscript, 1997), and the MapTask reference scheme [4] supporting reference proper, i.e., mention of objects in the visual situation which may or may not have been linguistically introduced. The analysis also took into account the problems with the MUC scheme identified in work such as [16].

The markup scheme derived from this analysis incorporated not only devices to support MUC-style annotation, but also the annotation of an arbitrary number of anaphoric relations between a mention and previous entities through the use of linking elements derived from the `LINK` elements from the Text Encoding Initiative (TEI) [73], as well as the `UNIVERSE` device developed in the area of multimodal reference annotation to associate `IDs` to non-linguistic entities [8]. The markup also aimed at covering zero anaphora in languages other than English, and discourse deixis through the use of the `SEG` element, also developed by TEI.

The `coref` level for anaphora and coreference has two main elements: a `<coref:de>` tag for mentions, and a separate `<coref:link>` element to mark anaphoric relations. The use of these elements is illustrated in Fig. 1. The MATE markup relied on so-called **token** standoff as in the MapTask, where the elements of the level file (`coref.xml` in Fig. 1) point to tokens in the base file using hyperlinks (`words.xml` in Fig. 1).

The form of `coref:link` proposed in MATE differed from that used in TEI by being structured–the `coref:link` only specifies the anaphor and the relation between anaphor and antecedent, the selected mention of the antecedent is marked using a separate `coref:anchor` element so as to allow coders to mark antecedent ambiguity (see discussion of the ARRAU coding scheme below).

The coreference markup scheme proposed in [39] was not implemented in the MATE toolkit, but using standoff for anaphoric annotation has become fairly standard. Aspects of the MATE markup scheme directly influenced the design of the markup scheme supported by the MMAX2 annotation tool discussed below [48]. Other types of standoff are supported by CALLISTO and other annotation tools based on the ATLAS architecture [5].

The GNOME Corpus The MATE proposals only identified a range of options without deciding among the alternatives. The GNOME corpus[7] [52, 54] was the first corpus annotated according to a coding scheme chosen among those options and using (a variant of) the markup scheme proposed in MATE. It was annotated to support research on the effect of local and global salience on the generation of referring expressions [59, 60].[8] The corpus consists of documents from three domains: the Museum Domain, including museum labels and material from museum catalogues; the Pharma Domain, consisting of several medicine leaflets; and the Sherlock

[7]http://cswww.essex.ac.uk/Research/nle/corpora/GNOME/

[8]The corpus was also subsequently used to study text structuring [38] and aggregation [13] as well as anaphora resolution [37].

Fig. 1 Mentions and links in the MATE markup scheme

```
words.xml
...
<word  ID="w1">we</word>
<word  ID="w2">'re</word>
<word  ID="w3">gonna</word>
<word  ID="w4">take</word>
<word  ID="w5">the</word>
<word  ID="w6">engine</word>
<word  ID="w7">E3</word>
<word  ID="w8">and</word>
<word  ID="w9">shove</word>
<word  ID="w10">it/word>
<word  ID="w11">over/word>
<word  ID="w12">to/word>
<word  ID="w13">Corning/word>
...

coref.xml:
...

<coref:de  ID="de00"  href="words.xml#id(w1)"/>
<coref:de  ID="de01"  href="words.xml#id(w5)..id(w7)"/>
<coref:de  ID="de02"  href="words.xml#id(w10)"/>
<coref:de  ID="de03"  href="words.xml#id(w13)"/>

<coref:link  href="coref.xml#id(de02)"   type="ident">
        <coref:anchor  href="coref.xml#id(de01)"/>
</coref:link>
```

domain, consisting of tutorial dialogues collected as part of the Sherlock project at the University of Pittsburgh and whose discourse structure was annotated according to Relational Discourse Analysis, or RDA [46]. The aim was to have around 5,000 markables for each domain; the total size of the corpus is around 40,000 tokens.

Markup Scheme Due to the lack of availability of annotation tools supporting standoff (the MATE toolkit was only completed after the end of the GNOME annotation), an inline version of the MATE markup scheme was used. Attributes were marked for the elements `s` (sentences), `unit` (local update candidates), `ne` (the equivalent of the `coref:de` element of the MATE markup scheme), and `mod` (NP modifiers).

Anaphoric information was annotated through separate `ANTE` elements implementing the `COREF:LINK` elements of the MATE scheme. The `ANTE` elements had two attributes: `CURRENT` (the ID of the anaphor) and `REL` (the relation holding between the entity referred to by the anaphor and the antecedent entity in the discourse model). The embedded `ANCHOR` element coded the last mention of the antecedent. (See Fig. 2.) Multiple `ANCHOR` elements indicated ambiguity.

Guidelines As the corpus was annotated to study salience, a lot of information was annotated besides information about anaphoric relations, including information

```
<NE ID="ne07">Scottish-born, Canadian based jeweller, Alison
Bailey-Smith</NE>
....
<NE ID="ne08"> <NE ID="ne09">Her</NE> materials</NE>
...
<ANTE   CURRENT="ne09"  REL="ident">
        <ANCHOR  ANTECEDENT="ne07"  />
</ANTE>
```

Fig. 2 Markup of anaphoric information in the GNOME corpus using separate and structured links

```
<ne id="ne109"
    cat="this-np" per="per3" num="sing" gen="neut" gf="np-mod"
    lftype="term" reference="direct"
    onto="concrete" ani="inanimate" structure="atom"
    count="count-yes" generic="generic-no"
    deix="deix-yes" loeb="disc-function">
    this  monumental  cabinet </ne>
```

Fig. 3 Morphosyntactic, semantic and discourse information about mentions in the GNOME corpus.

about document structure, potential local update units (the 'utterances' of Centering), and a variety of information about mentions. This includes morphosyntactic information (gender, number and person, grammatical function), semantic information (semantic function, semantic type—abstract or concrete, animate or inanimate, etc.—whether the object referred to is singular, mass or plural, functionality, genericity, etc.) and discourse information (e.g., whether the markable performed a deictic reference) [53, 54]. The information annotated for the `ne` element is shown in Fig. 3.

One of the key contributions of the work on GNOME was the decision to only annotate information that could be coded reliably [3, 10]. In particular, a systematic investigation was carried out of the types of associative ('bridging') relations that could be reliably annotated, building on the earlier work by Poesio and Vieira [62]. Separate reliability studies were carried out for all the attributes.

Availability At present the GNOME corpus is available from the authors (see website at previous page); a MMAX2 version will soon become available through the Anaphoric Bank.

3.4 *The* ARRAU *and* LIVEMEMORIES *Corpora*

The objectives of the ARRAU project[9] were to further investigate 'difficult' cases of anaphoric reference, and in particular, ambiguous anaphoric expressions and cases of discourse deixis [61]. This required looking in greater detail than earlier work at agreement on anaphoric reference as κ was not appropriate [3]. These investigations led to the development of a coding scheme that was then employed for annotating the ARRAU corpus [56]. This corpus was also intended to include texts from genres not traditionally covered by anaphoric corpora, in particular dialogue and narrative, and therefore includes a full annotation of the task-oriented dialogues in the TRAINS-93 corpus,[10] and the complete collection of spoken narratives in the Pear Stories [12], often used to study salience. The corpus also includes news articles (the entire subset of the Penn Treebank that was annotated in the RST treebank [11]) and additional documents from the GNOME genres. The ARRAU guidelines were then adapted to annotate anaphora in Italian, and the LIVEMEMORIES corpus was created [70].

Markup Scheme ARRAU and LIVEMEMORIES were annotated using the MMAX2 annotation tool discussed in Sect. 1. MMAX2 is based on token standoff technology: the annotated anaphoric information is stored in a `phrase` level whose markables point to a base layer in which each token is represented by a separate XML element. Because of the need to encode ambiguity and bridging references, anaphoric information is encoded using MMAX2 **pointers** instead of set-based attributes. The phrase layer also contains a number of attributes encoding semantic information.

Guidelines The coding scheme inherits several aspects of the GNOME coding scheme, although with fewer attributes, but adding the ability to annotate discourse deixis, and more extensive provision for annotating ambiguity—for instance, the possibility of marking an ambiguity between a discourse-new and discourse-old reading, which was not possible with the GNOME scheme. The reliability of the coding scheme for ambiguity was also tested, with inconclusive results however [55].

Markable Definition In ARRAU, all NPs are coded as markables at the `phrase` level. In addition, possessive pronouns are marked as well, and all premodifiers are marked when the entity referred to is mentioned again, e.g., in the case of the proper name *US* in (28a), and when the premodifier refers to a kind, like *exchange-rate* in (28b). Singletons are also marked as markables that are part of coreference chains.

[9]http://cswww.essex.ac.uk/Research/nle/arrau/

[10]http://www.ldc.upenn.edu/Catalog/catalogEntry.jsp?catalogId=LDC95S25

(28) a. ... The Treasury Department said that the [US]$_i$ trade deficit may worsen next year after 2 years of significant improvement.... The statement was the [US]$_i$'s government first acknowledgment of what other groups, such as the International Monetary Fund, have been predicting for months.

b. The Treasury report, which is required annually by a provision of the 1988 trade act, again took South Korea to task for its [exchange-rate]$_i$ policies. "We believe there have continued to be indications of [exchange-rate]$_i$ manipulation ... ...

The full NP is marked with all its modifiers; in addition, a `min` attribute is marked, as in the MUC corpora.

All markables at this level are annotated for morphosyntactic agreement (gender, number and person), grammatical function (following the GNOME scheme), and `reference` (the values being non-referring, discourse-new, and discourse-old). Non-referring markables include expletives and predicative NPs (as standard), but also, more controversially, quantifiers and coordination. Referring mentions (mentions of discourse-new and discourse-old entities) also have a `category` attribute specifying the semantic type of the entity: `person`, `animate`, `concrete`, `organization`, `space`, `time`, `numerical`, `plan` (for actions), or `abstract`. Referring mentions also have a genericity attribute, also annotated following the GNOME guidelines.

Range of relations All referring NPs are marked as either `new` or `old`. If marked as `old`, an antecedent can be identified, either of type `phrase` (already mentioned using an NP) or `segment` (not mentioned using an NP, in cases of discourse deixis). Referring NPs can be marked as ambiguous between a discourse-new and a discourse-old interpretation; discourse-old NPs can be marked as ambiguous between a discourse-deictic and a `phrase` reading; and both `phrase` and `segment` markables can be marked as ambiguous between two distinct interpretations. In addition, referring NPs can be marked as **related** to a previously mentioned discourse entity (associative or bridging anaphors). Associative descriptions were identified following the GNOME guidelines, but the type of relation was not explicitly marked.

Availability The ARRAU corpus is available from LDC; it will also be made available through the Anaphoric Bank.[11]

The LIVEMEMORIES Corpus The ARRAU guidelines were adapted to create the LIVEMEMORIES corpus of anaphora in Italian, containing texts from Wikipedia and blogs released through a Creative Commons license.

The main distinguishing feature of the LIVEMEMORIES coding scheme with respect to that of ARRAU is the incorporation of the MATE/VENEX proposals concerning incorporated clitics and zeros in standoff schemes whose base layer is words (instead of an annotation of morphologically decomposed argument

[11]The anaphorically annotated versions of LDC corpora such as the RST Discourse Treebank and the TRAINS-93 corpus require previous purchase of the original corpora.

structure, as in the Prague Dependency Treebank, discussed below). In the LIVEMEMORIES corpus there are two types of markables: **nominal** markables, for nominal expressions and clitic particles, and **verbal** markables for zeros and incorporated clitics. The type of markable is specified by the `markable_type` attribute. In the case of a zero, the first element of the verbal complex following the position of the zero is identified as a verbal markable; in the case of an incorporated clitic, the verbal element is that to which the clitic is incorporated. Example (29) shows examples of nominal markables (with index $_n$) and verbal markables (with index $_v$).

(29) …[Il giudice]$_n$ [gli]$_{n_i}$ nego' [questa richiesta]$_n$ e procedette invece ad acquistare [alcuni indumenti da [fargli]$_{v_i}$ indossare]$_n$
The judge [to-him] rejected this request and proceeded instead to buy some clothes to make-[to-him] wear.

The attribute `verbal_type` specifies the type of verbal markable: either `clitic` or `empty_subject`. In case multiple clitics are incorporated in the same verbal element (as in *darglielo*), multiple verbal markables are created. The annotation was used as the basis for the proposals concerning zero resolution in Italian and Japanese by [35].

An early annotation of about half of the Wikipedia subset of the LIVEMEMORIES corpus was used for the SEMEVAL-2010 coreference evaluation and is available in CONLL-style tabular format as part of that dataset. The entire corpus was used for the EVALITA-2011 evaluation of Italian resources. The entire corpus is available through the Anaphoric Bank.

3.5 The Prague Dependency Treebank

The Prague Dependency Treebank 2.0[12] (PDT 2.0) [25] is a corpus of samples from the Czech National Corpus (news and scientific articles) annotated according to the specifications of **Functional Generative Description**, a linguistic formalism developed by the Prague School since the 1960s [71]. The annotation involves three levels:

m-layer The morphological layer contains POS and morphological information–Czech being a highly inflected language. This is available for over two million words.

a-layer The analytic layer specifies the surface syntactic structure of the sentence in the form of a dependency tree. This is available for around 1.5 million words.

t-layer The tectogrammatical layer specifies predicate-argument structure, topic-focus articulation, and coreference (pronouns only).

Until the recent release of ONTONOTES version 5.0, the PDT 2.0 was the largest anaphorically annotated corpus (although only anaphoric relations involving

[12] http://ufal.mff.cuni.cz/pdt2.0/

pronouns were annotated), and is still arguably the most advanced corpus from a linguistic and technologic perspective. We limit our discussion here to the anaphoric annotation as discussed in [41].

Markup Scheme Each annotation layer builds on (and is linked to) the previous layer as shown in Fig. 4, the PDT representation of the Czech sentence *Byl by šel dolesa*, *He-was would went to forest.*

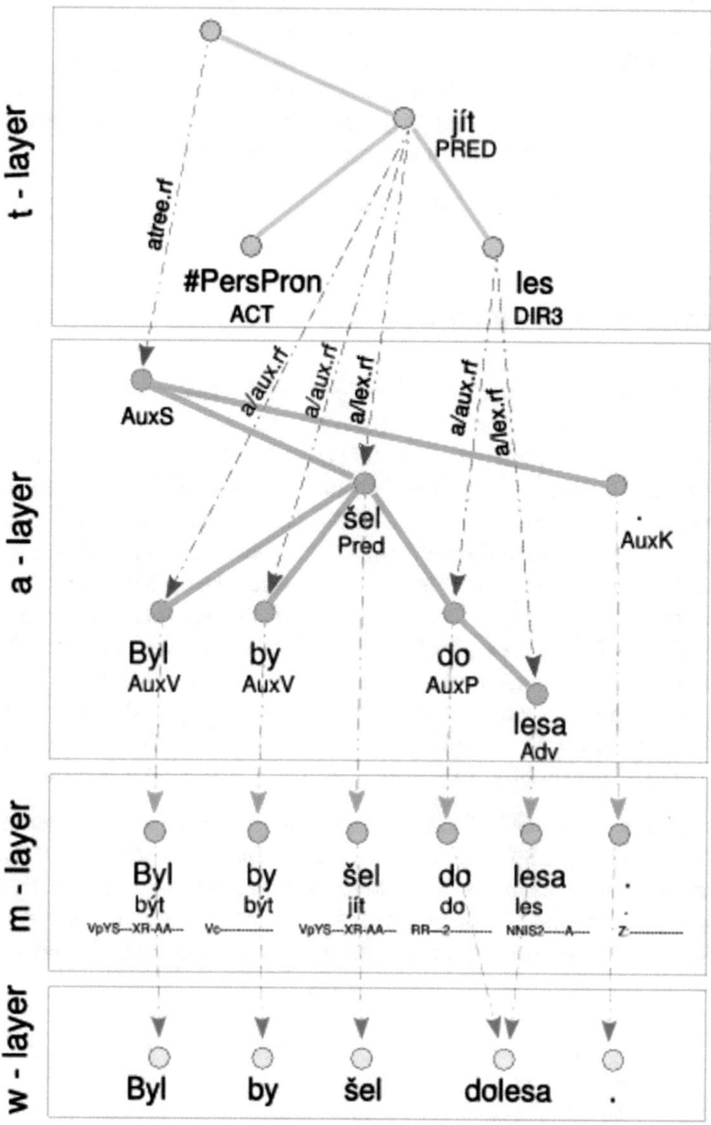

Fig. 4 The three annotation layers in the Prague Dependency Treebank

A variety of markup formats were used in the past for the layers, but the PDT 2.0 was standardized on PML, an XML format designed for linguistic annotation. The m-layer is annotated completely automatically; the a-layer and t-layer are annotated semi-automatically, by first running an automatic annotator and then having the coders correct mistakes and add information. The markup is however completely transparent to the coders, who annotate using a dedicated annotation tool called TRED.

Guidelines Two types of anaphoric information is annotated: **grammatical** coreference (control verbs, reflexives, relative pronouns) and **textual** coreference. Only personal and demonstrative pronouns are annotated, but a very wide variety of types of (identity) anaphoric reference are annotated, including not just reference to antecedents introduced by nominals, but also discourse deixis and **exophoric** reference to entities that are part of common knowledge [41].

Availability The PDT is available through LDC.

3.6 The ANCORA *Corpora*

The Annotated Corpora (ANCORA)[13] of Spanish and Catalan are the result of years of annotation at different linguistic levels [76]. The corpora began as an initiative by the University of Barcelona, the Technical University of Catalonia, and the University of Alicante to create two half-million-word treebanks for Spanish and Catalan that could be used as training and test data for supervised machine learning, and as input for corpus-based linguistic studies. The initiative was continued by the University of Barcelona in an effort to further enrich the corpora with grammatical relations, argument structures, thematic roles, semantic verb classes, named entities, WordNet nominal senses, and, more recently, coreference relations [69].[14] ANCORA are the first and largest corpora of Spanish and Catalan with coreference information including not only pronouns but all NPs. The two datasets, ANCORA-CO-Es and ANCORA-CO-Ca, consist of newspaper and newswire articles from *El Periódico* newspaper, the Spanish EFE news agency, and the Catalan ACN news agency.

Markup Scheme The different layers of annotation, including coreference, are all marked up with inline XML tags. Unlike other corpora like MUC and ACE that began from scratch, markables in ANCORA were identified based on the already existing syntactic annotations (see below for the list of syntactic nodes that were considered as markables). All referring mentions, including singletons, are annotated with an

[13]http://clic.ub.edu/corpus/en

[14]The portion of ANCORA annotated with coreference information (ANCORA-CO) amounts to a total of 400,000 words for each language.

`entityref` attribute. If two or more mentions refer to the same entity, they all receive an `entity` attribute with the same ID value. The second and subsequent mentions in a coreference chain include a `coreftype` attribute that specifies the type of relation with the previous mention. The morphosyntactic and semantic markup of mentions is illustrated in (30) for the NP *el Consejo_de_Seguridad* 'the Security_Council'. The markup of coreference information is shown in (31).

(30)
```
<sn arg="arg0" entityref="ne" func="suj"
ne="organization" tem="agt"> <spec gen="m"
num="s">
<d gen="m" lem="el" num="s" postype="article"
wd="el"/> </spec> <grup.nom gen="m" num="s">
<n lem="Consejo_de_Seguridad" ne="organization"
postype="proper" wd="Consejo_de_Seguridad"/>
</grup.nom> </sn>
```

(31)
```
<sn entity="entity5" entityref="ne"> el
Consejo_de_
Seguridad </sn> no recogió en <d coreftype="ident"
entity="entity5" entityref="spec" wd="su"/>
declaración ...
```
[The Security_Council]$_i$ did-not include in [[their]$_i$ declaration]$_j$ ...

Alternatively, ANCORA is also available in the CONLL-style tabular format that was used for the SEMEVAL-2010 task on coreference resolution [68]. See Sect. 3.8 below for further details.

Guidelines The annotation scheme that was used for ANCORA is inspired by the MATE guidelines (Sect. 3.3), as the resulting corpus was meant to be a comprehensive language resource rather than to serve the purpose of a specific evaluation campaign. Thus, the definition of both markables and coreference relations was linguistically motivated.

Markable Definition As already mentioned, the coreference annotation in ANCORA benefits from the existing syntactic annotation and asks annotators to consider as markables the following five syntactic nodes: (i) NPs (including elliptical subjects[15]), (ii) nominal groups in a conjoined NP, (iii) relative pronouns, (iv) possessive determiners, and (v) possessive pronouns. Additionally, non-nominal nodes (i.e., verbs, clauses, and sentences) are annotated if they are the antecedents in a discourse-deixis relation. A verb can also be annotated if it contains an incorporated clitic. Relying on the (manual) syntactic level ensures that markables include all premodifiers and postmodifiers; no `MIN` attribute is annotated.

---

[15]Elliptical subjects were manually inserted as part of the treebank.

To filter out the NP nodes that are not referential, the attribute `entityref` takes the values `ne`, `spec` or `nne` for referential mentions. The first value identifies named entities (e.g., *Barcelona*) belonging to six semantic types: person, organization, location, date, number, and others (publications, prizes, etc.). The second value identifies mentions that are not a named entity in form (e.g., pronouns, NP headed by a common noun), but that corefer with an NE. The third value indicates mentions that neither are a named entity in form nor refer to a named entity. The `entityref` attribute is included for both singletons and coreferent mentions, thus making it possible to extract singletons. Non-referential mentions (e.g., predicates) either lack this attribute or receive the value `lex` if they are (within) a lexicalized expression, like *cats* and *dogs* in *to rain cats and dogs*.

Range of Relations Of the range of relations proposed in MATE, ANCORA focused on three, which correspond to the three values that the attribute `coreftype` can take: `ident` (referential identity), `pred` (predication), and `dx` (discourse deixis). Following the MATE proposal, predication is separated from referential identity, and discourse deixis is also annotated, but bridging relations are not.

All the mentions with an `entityref` value of `ne`, `spec` or `nne` can participate in a relation of identity (32) or discourse deixis (33), whereas predicative relations (34) involve a non-referential mention, namely one lacking `entityref`. Identity relations that have a split antecedent (see (13b) above) are annotated by creating an entity that is the sum of two or more entities. In discourse deixis, the extent of the discourse segment is identified according to the syntactic annotation, thus it must correspond to one of the available phrasal nodes at the verbal, clausal or sentential level.

(32) a. [ES] Sobre la ausencia de [Argentina]$_i$ en la reunión, sólo se informó de que hubo una comunicación de los servicios sanitarios de [ese país]$_i$.
b. [EN] On the absence of [Argentina]$_i$ in the meeting, it was only reported that there was a communication from the health services of [that country]$_i$.

(33) a. [ES] …algunos expertos calculan [que el precio del crudo … llegará a 40 dólares a_finales_de este año]$_i$, pero que la OPEP hará “todo lo posible para que [eso]$_i$ no ocurra”.
b. [EN] Some experts estimate [that oil prices will reach $40 by the end of this year]$_i$, but that OPEC will do “everything to ensure that [this]$_i$ does not happen”.

(34) a. [ES] …una posible fusión de la operadora española con [British_Telecom [(BT)]$_i$]$_i$
b. [EN] A possible merger of the Spanish operator with [British_Telecom [(BT)]$_i$]$_i$

Additionally, predicative relations and discourse deixis take the attribute `corefsubtype` that specifies further semantic information. Predicates are either `definite` (i.e., identifying) or `indefinite` (i.e., non-identifying). Discourse-deictic mentions can refer to the same `token` as the antecedent, the same event `type` as the antecedent, or the `proposition` (the actual words) of the antecedent, which is often the case with speech verbs (e.g., *He didn't say **this***).

Availability The ANCORA corpora are freely available from http://clic.ub.edu/corpus/en. The column-based version that was used in SEMEVAL-2010 can be downloaded at http://stel.ub.edu/semeval2010-coref/download.

3.7 ONTONOTES

The ONTONOTES project [64, 82] created a multilingual corpus of large-scale, accurate, and integrated annotation of multiple levels of the shallow semantic structure in text. It spans multiple genres across three languages—English, Chinese and Arabic. The English and Chinese portions contain 1.6M words and 1M words, respectively, from newswire, broadcast news, broadcast conversation, web text, and telephone conversation. An English translation of the New Testament was also annotated as a pivot corpus to facilitate machine-translation research. The Arabic portion is relatively small, comprising 300k of newswire text. It is the largest corpus of English, Chinese and Arabic annotated with coreference. Such multi-layer annotations, with complex, cross-layer dependencies, demand a robust, efficient, scalable mechanism for storing them while providing efficient, convenient, integrated access to the underlying structure. To this effect, it uses a relational database representation that captures both the inter- and intra-layer dependencies and also provides an object-oriented API[16] for efficient, multi-tiered access to the data [64].

The coreference portion of ONTONOTES captures general anaphoric coreference that covers entities and events not limited to noun phrases, or a limited set of entity types [65–67]. The aim of the project was to annotate linguistic coreference using the most literal interpretation of the text at a very high degree of consistency, even if it meant departing from a particular linguistic theory. Two different types of coreference are distinguished: Identical (`IDENT`), and Appositive (`APPOS`). Appositives are treated separately because they function as attributions; the `IDENT` type is used for anaphoric coreference, meaning links between pronominal, nominal,

[16]http://cemantix.org/software/ontonotes-db-tool.html

and named mentions of specific referents. It does not include mentions of generic, underspecified, or abstract entities. All the data was double blind annotated and adjudicated.

Markup Scheme The corpus is annotated using inline SGML, similar to the MUC corpus except that the MIN mention span is not identified as there is gold treebank infomation from which one can derive the syntactic head. Every markable that belongs to a coreference chain is identified with a <COREF> tag; <COREF> elements have three attributes: (i) ID, the identifier for a mention; (ii) TYPE, which can be IDENT or APPOS; and (iii) SUBTYPE, which is only for the APPOS types, and can be either HEAD or ATTRIB. The first mention of a coreference chain uses the attribute ID to assign an ID to the coreference chain, and every subsequent mention uses the same ID to specify the coreference chain to which it belongs. In case of conversational data and web data, where speaker or writer could be identified, it was captured in the SPEAKER attribute.

The majority of the ONTONOTES annotation is based on the tokens in the treebank. However, a solution was needed for identifying partial-token mentions, such as *Walmart* in tokens such as *Pro-Walmart*; or *India* and *Japan* in a token such as *India/Japan*, which are not separated into distinct tokens during treebanking. This was not a problem for CALLISTO, the annotation tool, but reconciling sub-token spans with the SGML markup needed to be addressed. This was done by using two optional attributes, S_OFF and E_OFF, that identified the start and end offset of the string. Many a times, the partial token is either a prefix or a suffix, and so usually only one of these two attributes need to be specified, and the other attribute defaults to either zero (for S_OFF) or the length of the mention in characters (for E_OFF). For example, in the case of *Pro-Walmart*, the mention *Walmart* is identified with a S_OFF of 4, and the E_OFF is absent. And, for *India* in *India/Japan*, the S_OFF is absent, and the E_OFF is 5, whereas for *Japan*, the S_OFF is 6, and E_OFF is absent.

Some of the broadcast and telephone conversation documents were very long as they typically include transcriptions of recordings of entire shows that cover various topics. Full-document coreference annotation was not an option. Therefore, the documents were manually segmented into multiple parts, breaking along story boundaries as much as possible, and these were annotated independently of each other, and therefore the coreference chains do not carry information across parts. Each part is encoded in a separate TEXT segment with a PARTNO attribute.

Example (35) shows a sample markup of an ONTONOTES document.

(35)

```
<DOC DOCNO="bc/cnn/00/cnn_0003@0003@cnn@bc@en@on">
<TEXT PARTNO="000">
...
<COREF ID="26" TYPE="IDENT" E_OFF="1"
SPEAKER="Linda_Hamilton">
I-</COREF> <COREF ID="26" TYPE="IDENT"
SPEAKER="Linda_Hamilton">I
</COREF> ’m sure 0 there is *?* .
```

I- I ’m sure 0 there is *?* .

```
Um if <COREF ID="26" TYPE="IDENT"
SPEAKER="Linda_Hamilton">I
</COREF> were <COREF ID="14" TYPE="IDENT" SPEAKER=
"caller_7">you </COREF> , because <COREF ID="26"
TYPE="IDENT"
SPEAKER="Linda_Hamilton">I</COREF> do n’t know
<COREF ID="43"
TYPE="IDENT">that number</COREF> off hand um
<COREF ID="14"
TYPE="IDENT" SPEAKER="caller_7">you</COREF> can
call
<COREF ID="70" TYPE="IDENT">the University of
Medicine
and Dentistry in <COREF ID="50" TYPE="IDENT">New
Jersey</COREF>
</COREF> .
```

Um if I were you , because , I do n’t know that number off hand um you can call the University of Medicine and Dentistry in New Jersey .

```
Um oh <COREF ID="74" TYPE="IDENT">they</COREF>
would have *-1
to know where in <COREF ID="50" TYPE="IDENT">New
Jersey</COREF>
then .
```

Um oh they would have *-1 to know where in New Jersey then .

```
...
</TEXT>
</DOC>
```

Guidelines The ONTONOTES coreference guidelines are mostly inspired by the MUC and ACE tasks, and are consistent with the DRAMA/MATE ideas. As in MUC, all NPs—irrespective of their semantic type—are linked with coreferent NPs, and *singleton* entities are left out. We look now at some salient aspects of the guidelines.

Generics are not considered as markables unless they are referred to by neighboring pronouns. Generic nominal mentions can be linked with referring pronouns and other definite mentions, but are not linked to other generic nominal mentions. This allows coreference between the bolded mentions in (36) and (37), but not in (38).

(36) **Officials** said **they** are tired of making the same statements.

(37) **Meetings** are most productive when **they** are held in the morning. **Those meetings**, however, generally have the worst attendance.

(38) Allergan Inc. said it received approval to sell the PhacoFlex intraocular lens, the first foldable silicone lens available for ***cataract surgery**. The lens foldability enables it to be inserted in smaller incisions than are now possible for ***cataract surgery**.

Pronouns Pleonastic pronouns and generic *you* are not treated as markables.

Premodifiers Only non-adjectival premodifiers can be markables. Proper nouns that are morphologically adjectival are treated as adjectives. For example, adjectival forms of GPEs such as *Chinese* in *the Chinese leader*, are not linked. Thus, *United States* in *the United States policy* can be linked with another mention of the same entity, but not *American* in *the American policy.* GPEs and nationality acronyms (e.g., *U.S.S.R.* or *U.S.*) are also considered as adjectival. Premodifier acronyms are marbles unless they refer to a nationality. Thus, *FBI* is a markable in (39), but not *U.S.* in (40). cannot.

(39) **FBI** spokesman

(40) ***U.S.** spokesman

Events In addition to NP entities, events described by NPs and verbs are annotated as well. Only events that are (usually) introduced by a verb and then coreferred using an NP were annotated in order to keep the task manageable. This includes morphologically related nominalizations, *grew* and *the strong growth* in (41), and NPs that refer to the same event, even if they are lexically distinct from the verb (42).

(41) Sales of passenger cars **grew** 22 %. **The strong growth** followed year-to-year increases.

(42) Japan's domestic sales of cars, trucks and buses in October **rose** 18 % from a year earlier to 500,004 units. **The strong growth** followed year-to-year increases of 21 % in August and 12 % in September.

Copular and Predicative Copular and predicative constructions as well as small clause constructions are not markables: a separate attributive link is used for them.

Like copulas, small clause constructions are not marked. Example (43) is treated as if the copula were present (*John considers Fred to be an idiot.*)

(43) John considers ***Fred** ***an idiot**.

Appositives are not marbles, but marked with special labels. For example, in (44), an `APPOS`(itive) link is annotated between *Washington* (marked as `HEAD`) and *the capital city* (marked as `ATTRIB` (ute)). The intended semantic connection is then filled by supplying the implicit copula. An `APPOS` chain contains at least one `HEAD` mention and one or more `ATTRIB` mentions.

(44) **Washington** $_{\mathtt{HEAD}}$, **the capital city**$_{\mathtt{ATTRIB}}$, is on the East coast.

When the entity to which an appositive refers is also mentioned elsewhere, only the single span containing the entire appositive construction is included in the larger `IDENT` chain. None of the nested NP spans are linked. In example (45), the entire span can be linked to later mentions of Richard Godown.

(45) Richard Godown, president of the Industrial Biotechnology Association

Metonymy As mentioned in Sect. 2.2, metonymic referents were treated as separate entities to meet the required level of annotation consistency.
Part/Whole and other associative relations were not annotated.
Zero Anaphora For the most part the guidelines are language independent. However, unlike English, Chinese and Arabic are pro-drop languages, in which pronouns may be omitted and filled from the context. The treebank introduces and tags all these constituents. All these (i.e., `*` and `*pro*`) were considered as markables.

Markable Definition Since all the text in ONTONOTES had been treebanked prior to coreference annotation, hand-tagged NPs were available. From the point of view of consistency and completeness, the starting set of markables was based on the hand-tagged NPs. In addition, all relative pronouns (`PRP$`), which do not usually constitute an NP by themselves, were considered as markables. There were two type of markables that were later added by the annotators: verbs triggering an eventive chain (the head verb was annotated as a markable), and portions of flat non-NP constituents (usually names) in an NP: these were marked and tagged, but constitute a very small portion (˜2 %) of the total markables.

Since there was a hand-tagged treebank underlying the annotations, the syntactic heads of the markables could be determined with high enough accuracy, and so the `MIN` attribute from MUC was not added. Similarly to MUC, it was difficult to identify the head in case of conjunctive constructions. In the spoken genre, there are often pronominal references to the speaker(s) and, given that the speaker metadata was available, this was tagged alongside the sentence during annotation, which made it easier for the annotators to disambiguate the pronouns. One of the pronouns is connected to the speaker metadata markable, thus speaker information is propagated throughout the coreference chain.

Agreement Table 1 shows the inter-annotator and annotator-adjudicator agreement on all the genres in ONTONOTES.

Table 1 Inter annotator (A1 and A2) and adjudicator (ADJ) agreement for the coreference layer in ONTONOTES, measured in terms of the MUC score

Language	Genre	A1 − A2	A1 − ADJ	A2 − ADJ
English	Newswire [NW]	80.9	85.2	88.3
	Broadcast news [BN]	78.6	83.5	89.4
	Broadcast conversation [BC]	86.7	91.6	93.7
	Magazine [MZ]	78.4	83.2	88.8
	Weblogs and newsgroups [WB]	85.9	92.2	91.2
	Telephone conversation [TC]	81.3	94.1	84.7
	Pivot text [PT] (New testament)	89.4	96.0	92.0
Chinese	Newswire [NW]	73.6	84.8	75.1
	Broadcast news [BN]	80.5	86.4	91.6
	Broadcast conversation [BC]	84.1	90.7	91.2
	Magazine [MZ]	74.9	81.2	80.0
	Weblogs and newsgroups [WB]	87.6	92.3	93.5
	Telephone conversation [TC]	65.6	86.6	77.1
Arabic	Newswire	73.8	88.1	75.6

Type	Description
Annotator Error	An annotator error. This is a catch-all category for cases of errors that do not fit in the other categories.
Genuine Ambiguity	This is just genuinely ambiguous. Often the case with pronouns that have no clear antecedent (especially this & that)
Generics	One person thought this was a generic mention, and the other person didn't
Guidelines	The guidelines need to be clear about this example
Callisto Layout	Something to do with the usage/design of CALLISTO
Referents	Each annotator thought this was referring to two completely different things
Possessives	One person did not mark this possessive
Verb	One person did not mark this verb
Pre Modifiers	One person did not mark this Pre Modifier
Appositive	One person did not mark this appositive
Extent	Both people marked the same entity, but one person's mention was longer
Copula	Disagreement arose because this mention is part of a copular structure a) Either each annotator marked a different half of the copula b) Or one annotator unnecessarily marked both

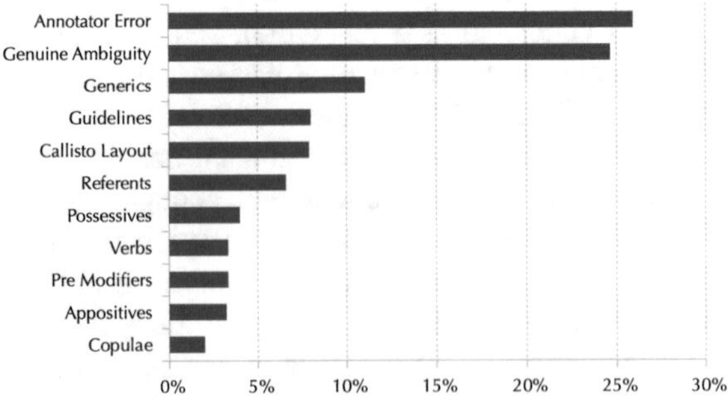

Fig. 5 Frequency of each type of disagreement

A set of 15k disagreements in various parts of the data were classified into one of the categories shown in Fig. 5. Genuine ambiguity and annotator error were the biggest contributors—the latter of which is usually captured during adjudication, thus showing the increased agreement between the adjudicated version and the individual version.

Availability ONTONOTES is available free of charge for research purposes from LDC.

3.8 *The* SEMEVAL-*2010 Task 1 Corpus*

The 2010 edition of the SEMEVAL evaluation campaign included a multilingual coreference resolution task[17] [68]. The datasets used for the task included subsets of the COREA corpus for Dutch (104,000 words), the ANCORA corpora for Spanish (380,000 words) and Catalan (345,000 words), the LIVEMEMORIES corpus for Italian (140,000 words), the Tüba/DZ corpus for German (455,000 words), and the ONTONOTES corpus for English (120,000 words).

The most valuable contribution of the task was to convert all the datasets to a common format and annotate them in the most similar and consistent manner,[18] thus providing a multilingual corpus of coreference that can be easily used to train and test coreference resolution systems for different languages, and to compare their results. Unlike the corpora used in MUC and ACE, all NPs are considered, singletons[19] are included, and predicative relations are not annotated. A further asset of the corpus is that it contains both gold-standard and automatically predicted morphosyntactic and semantic information.

Markup Scheme The SEMEVAL-2010 Task 1 datasets are formatted following the CONLL-style tabular format based on dependency relations. There is one line per token, and the different layers of annotation for each token are displayed across multiple tabular-separated columns. Although not all the datasets include every layer of linguistic annotation, they usually contain the token ID in the sentence, the actual token, lemma, part of speech, morphological features (e.g., number, gender, tense), head, dependency relation, named entity type, predicate semantic class, semantic dependency, and coreference information. Apart from the first two columns and the last column (containing coreference relations), columns are repeated for each level of linguistic information to provide the gold-standard and automatically predicted information.

Coreference relations are represented in open-close notation with the entity number in parentheses. Every entity has an ID, and every mention is marked with the ID of the entity it refers to: an opening parenthesis indicates the first token of the mention, whereas a closing parenthesis indicates the last token of the mention. If a

[17] http://stel.ub.edu/semeval2010-coref

[18] The morphosyntactic and semantic tag sets differ between languages.

[19] In the case of ONTONOTES, the singletons were heuristically added.

```
1  Inherent  _ _ JJ  _ JJ  _ 5  _ PRD      _ _ _ _          _ arg2 _   _ _ _
2  in        _ _ IN  _ IN  _ 1  _ LOC      _ _ _ _          _ _   _    _ _ _
3  the       _ _ DT  _ DT  _ 4  _ NMOD     _ _ _ _          _ _   _    _ _ (18
4  law       _ _ NN  _ NN  _ 2  _ PMOD     _ _ _ _          _ _   _    _ _ 18)
5  is        _ _ VBZ _ VBZ _ 0  _ sentence _ _ _ be.01      _ _   _    _ _ _
6  the       _ _ DT  _ DT  _ 7  _ NMOD     _ _ _ _          _ _   _    _ _ (423|(380
7  vision    _ _ NN  _ NN  _ 5  _ SBJ      _ _ _ _          _ arg1 _   _ _ _
8  of        _ _ IN  _ IN  _ 7  _ NMOD     _ _ _ _          _ _   _    _ _ _
9  high      _ _ JJ  _ JJ  _ 10 _ NMOD     _ _ _ _          _ _   _    _ _ (38
10 standards _ _ NNS _ NNS _ 8  _ PMOD     _ _ _ _          _ _   _    _ _ 38)
11 ,         _ _ ,   _ ,   _ 7  _ P        _ _ _ _          _ _   _    _ _ 380)
12 and       _ _ CC  _ CC  _ 7  _ COORD    _ _ _ _          _ _   _    _ _ _
13 money     _ _ NN  _ NN  _ 12 _ CONJ     _ _ _ _          _ _   _    _ _ (421
14 to        _ _ TO  _ TO  _ 13 _ NMOD     _ _ _ _          _ _   _    _ _ _
15 meet      _ _ VB  _ VB  _ 14 _ IM       _ _ _ meet.01    _ _   _    _ _ _
16 the       _ _ DT  _ DT  _ 17 _ NMOD     _ _ _ _          _ _   _    _ _ (38
17 standards _ _ NNS _ NNS _ 15 _ OBJ      _ _ _ _          _ _   arg1 _ _ 38)|421)|423)
18 .         _ _ .   _ .   _ 5  _ P        _ _ _ _          _ _   _    _ _ _
```

Fig. 6 Markup of morphosyntactic, semantic and coreferential information in the SemEval-2010 Task 1 corpus

mention consists of one single token, the opening and closing parentheses appear in the same line separated by the entity ID. If a token belongs to more than one mention, a pipe symbol separates the multiple entity IDs. Figure 6 illustrates the markup. Note the coreference relation between *high standards* and *the standards* with entity ID: 38.

Guidelines None of the datasets was developed explicitly for the SemEval task, thus the guidelines largely correspond to those of the respective source corpora. However, to make the evaluation as fair as possible between the different languages, the task organizers laid down a few principles that are summarized in this section. In some cases, the annotation of the source corpora had to be partially adapted or modified.

Markable Definition Markables include all NPs and possessive determiners. Singletons also receive an entity ID. Non-referential NPs (e.g., predicates, appositions, expletive pronouns, etc.) are not annotated. Although an effort was made to ensure consistency between the different annotation schemes, datasets differ slightly. For instance, the Dutch dataset only contains singletons for named entities, and expletive pronouns are annotated as singletons in the English dataset.

Range of Relations The goal of the task was the development of systems that would solve the relations of referential identity between NPs. As a result, the only relation annotated in the datasets is referential identity, excluding predicates, discourse deixis, event anaphora, and bridging relations.

Availability After the evaluation campaign, the organizers made freely available the development, training and test datasets of Catalan, Dutch, Italian, and Spanish at http://stel.ub.edu/semeval2010-coref/download. To acquire the German dataset, an Archiv-DVD from the tageszeitung must be purchased; detailed instructions are provided in the package with the rest of datasets. The English dataset is distributed by LDC.

3.9 Other Genres and Domain-Specific Corpora

Like most areas of Computational Linguistics, anaphora resolution is mainly focused on the genre of written news. All the corpora discussed or mentioned so far are collections of either news or broadcast data, and tend to focus on written language, with a few exceptions. Among the English corpora mentioned, GNOME is the one not focused on news: its three subcollections consist of pharmaceutical leaflets, museum catalogues and tutorial dialogues. ARRAU includes, in addition to a portion of the Wall Street Journal section of the Penn Treebank, the GNOME corpus as a subset, and also contains the TRAINS corpus and other dialogue material; and ONTONOTES also includes material from telephone conversations. Some substantial resources have however been created for other genres. They are briefly reviewed In this Section.

Spoken dialogue and online conversations There are few corpora of anaphora in dialogue apart from those just mentioned, and they have generally been created for comparative studies of *it* vs. demonstratives *this* and LINGEXthat. Müller annotated the ICSI meeting corpus for a study of this type [47]. Navarretta [49] created the DAD corpora of abstract anaphora in Danish and Italian[20] that also focus on the study of demonstratives and pronouns.

More recently, more and more attention has been paid to online forums and other types of social media that can be seen as forming a type of 'textual conversation'. The LIVEMEMORIES ANAPHORA corpus discussed above [70] includes annotations of blogs in Italian as well as of Wikipedia pages. The SENSEI corpus, under construction, consists of annotations of online forums in English (from *The Guardian* newspaper) and Italian (from *La Repubblica* newspaper).

Technical and Scientifical Domains Finally, there are anaphorically annotated corpora of technical and scientifical text. The NLP4EVENTS) corpus from the University of Wolverhampton is a collection of computer manuals. The domain with the most substantially anaphorically annotated corpora is Bio NLP. The best-known resource in this area is the GENIA corpus,[21] that was also annotated for coreference in the GENIA-MEDCO project[22] [75]. This annotation was used for the 2011 BioNLP

[20]http://www.cst.dk/dad/

[21]http://www.nactem.ac.uk/genia/

[22]http://nlp.i2r.a-star.edu.sg/medco.html

Shared Task on Coreference. Other anaphoric annotations of biomedical corpora have been carried out by Gasperin et al. [19] and as part of the creation of the Colorado Richly Annotated Full Text (CRAFT) corpus [7].

3.10 A Summary of Available Resources

Table 2 summarizes the corpora annotated with anaphora coreference we are aware of, with references to the main publications and sites with information. Ongoing

Table 2 Anaphorically annotated corpora in different languages

Language	Name	Reference	Size (words)
Arabic	ACE-2005[a]	[80]	100k
	ONTONOTES 5.0[b]	[83]	300k
Bengali	ICON	[72]	
Catalan	ANCORA-CO-Ca[c]	[69]	400k
Chinese	ACE-2005	[80]	≈200k
	ONTONOTES 5.0	[83]	1200k
Czech	Prague dependency Treebank 2.0[d]	[25]	≈800k
Dutch	COREA[e]	[27]	325k
English	MUC-6[f]	[23]	30k
	MUC-7[g]	[14]	30k
	GNOME[h]	[54]	40k
	ACE-2[i]		180K
	ACE-2005[j]	[80]	400k
	NP4Events[k]	[26]	50k
	ARRAU 2.0[l]	[56]	300k
	ICSI meeting corpus (dialogue)	[47]	
	GENIA-MEDCO (pronouns)[m]	[50]	800 documents
	ONTONOTES 5.0	[83]	1450k
	Phrase detectives	[31]	320k
French	CRISTAL-GRESEC/XRCE corpus (pronouns)[n]	[77]	1000k
	DEDE (definite descriptions)[o]	[18]	50k
German	Potsdam commentary corpus[p]	[74]	33k
	TüBa-D/Z[q]	[28]	600k
Hindi	ICON	[72]	
Italian	VENEX	[58]	40k
	i-Cab[r]	[43]	250k
	LIVEMEMORIES 1.0[s]	[70]	250k

(continued)

Table 2 (continued)

Language	Name	Reference	Size (words)
Japanese	NAIST text corpus[t]	[34]	38k sentences
Portuguese	Summ-It[u]	[15]	50 documents
Russian	RU-EVAL		
Spanish	ANCORA-CO-ES	[69]	400k
Tamil	ICON	[72]	
Tibetan	Tusnelda (B11)	[79]	<15k

[a]https://www.ldc.upenn.edu/collaborations/past-projects/ace/annotation-tasks-and-specifications
[b]https://catalog.ldc.upenn.edu/LDC2013T19
[c]http://clic.ub.edu/ancora/
[d]http://ufal.mff.cuni.cz/pdt2.0/
[e]http://www.clips.ua.ac.be/~iris/corea.html
[f]http://www.ldc.upenn.edu/Catalog/CatalogEntry.jsp?catalogId=LDC2003T13
[g]http://ldc.upenn.edu/Catalog/CatalogEntry.jsp?catalogId=LDC2001T02
[h]http://cswww.essex.ac.uk/Research/nle/corpora/GNOME/
[i]https://www.ldc.upenn.edu/collaborations/past-projects/ace/annotation-tasks-and-specifications
[j]https://www.ldc.upenn.edu/collaborations/past-projects/ace/annotation-tasks-and-specifications
[k]http://clg.wlv.ac.uk/projects/NP4E/#corpus
[l]https://catalog.ldc.upenn.edu/LDC2013T22
[m]http://www-tsujii.is.s.u-tokyo.ac.jp/GENIA/home/wiki.cgi?page=Coreference+Annotation
[n]http://catalog.elra.info/product_info.php?products_id=634&language=en
[o]http://www.cnrtl.fr/corpus/dede/
[p]http://www-old.ling.uni-potsdam.de/cl/cl/res/forsch_pcc.en.html
[q]http://www.sfs.uni-tuebingen.de/tuebadz.shtml
[r]http://www.celct.it/projects/icab.php
[s]http://www.anaphoricbank.org
[t]http://cl.naist.jp/nldata/corpus/
[u]http://www.inf.pucrs.br/~linatural/procacosa.html

efforts as part of the Anaphoric Bank initiative[23] aim at making some of these anaphorically annotated corpora available in compatible markup formats. Some data are also available from the SEMEVAL-2010 site.[24]

4 Annotating Anaphora

As shown in Table 2, there are today quite a few corpora annotated with anaphoric information, and for many different languages, so researchers whose only interest is to develop and test domain-independent anaphoric resolvers, especially for English but also for many other languages including Arabic, Bengali, Catalan, Chinese, Czech, Danish, Dutch, German, Hindi, Italian and Spanish, have the

[23]http://www.anaphoricbank.org

[24]http://stel.ub.edu/semeval2010-coref/

resources to do so. However, there are many languages, genres, and domains for which resources are still lacking. Those interested in non-NP anaphora (e.g., ellipsis) and/or in these other languages, genres and domains, will therefore need to annotate their own data. This Section briefly discusses what this involves, beginning with a discussion of what tools are available, then discussing coding schemes for anaphora and agreement, and markable identification; for a more extensive discussion of annotation practice in general and anaphoric annotation in general, we recommend [33].

4.1 Annotation Tools

The annotation of anaphora is a complex task. Related spans in the text need to be marked and set in relation to each other. Since a whole span of text has to be considered at once when looking for an antecedent, and visualization of (all) coreference chains is not always possible or desirable, care has to be taken to ensure the consistency of the annotated data and to support the annotation with adequate tools, which can help to ease common tasks (e.g., going back in the text to look for a same-head antecedent), lighten the cognitive load necessary for the annotation, and also help maintain consistency with formal specifications. The choice of tools also crucially affects the type of markup that can be used.

The organization of our discussion of the available corpora in Sect. 3 reflects the fact that anaphoric annotation can be divided into two more or less distinct phases: (i) the identification of markables in the text, and (ii) the identification of anaphoric relations between the entities realized by these mentions. For the latter task, two models can be used. One is *link-based*, the annotator marks the antecedent of a given NP by linking the anaphor and antecedent; the other model is *set-based*, where the annotator puts the elements of a coreference chain together into one group of markables. Both link-based and set-based annotation models have their quirks: in link-based annotation models, it is necessary to specify which antecedent the annotators should mark (either the closest, or the first one in the coreference chain, or—for definite NPs—the closest non-pronominal antecedent). Set-based annotation, on the other hand, does not easily allow marking uncertainty on the links.

Many anaphora annotation projects have been carried out using purpose-developed tools, such as TRED for the Prague Dependency Treebank.[25] In addition, there are a number of tools for 'generic' anaphoric annotation. Given this abundance of freely downloadable tools, which support the most typical coding schemes and UNICODE, developing one's own tool should only be considered as a last option. (There is always the risk of spending most of the time in the project creating the annotation tool.)

[25]http://ufal.mff.cuni.cz/~pajas/tred/

In the following, we present some of the best known freely downloadable annotation tools. (See also the annotation wiki at http://annotation.exmaralda.org/index.php/Linguistic_Annotation for links to additional information.)

CALLISTO CALLISTO[26] was the tool used for all ACE annotation tasks and for the ONTONOTES annotation project. It uses a form of character standoff based on the ATLAS architecture, jointly developed by LDC, MITRE and NIST [5], which in turn is based on the idea of **annotation graphs**. The basic annotation procedure involves selecting ('swiping') two markables in the main pane, and then specifying the relation between the two markables. CALLISTO is highly customizable, allowing for instance to specify whether coders can select words or characters, and a variety of export formats, such as APF used in ACE (see Sect. 3.2).

MMAX2 MMAX2[27] [48] uses token standoff, i.e., a standoff file format where one file (the *words* file) contains a list of the tokens, while other files (the *markable* files) contain one or multiple annotation layers, where an annotation layer contains exactly one type of markable—for example, it is possible to use one annotation layer for coreference annotation while using another annotation layer for annotation of discourse connectives. MMAX2 allows the user to specify the attributes of markables in a schema file where the kind of attribute (nominal, freetext) and the possible attribute values (for nominal attributes) can be described.

PALINKA PALINKA [51] is specifically geared towards coreference annotation. It uses an inline XML format that does not allow overlapping markables, and at the same time offers an interaction mode that is challenging for novices, but that offers significant efficiency gains for expert annotators through avoidance of drag gestures (it is possible to mark a markable span through multiple clicks, which is significantly faster, but less intuitive, than marking the span by a click-and-drag gesture), and efficient keyboard shortcuts. PALINKA also allows the user to specify attributes for markables and markable relations.

ANCORAPIPE ANCORAPIPE[28] is the tool used for annotating ANCORA with different layers of annotation, including coreference information. It is a Java-based plug-in for Eclipse. It can be combined with Eclipse's version-control plug-in to make it possible for several annotators to work simultaneously and easily synchronize their work. ANCORAPIPE takes XML documents as input. For coreference, it follows the set-based annotation model, showing a list of all the entities in a document and the (coreferent) mentions in each of them. Annotations can be added by inserting mentions into entities, or merging, splitting and deleting entities. ANCORAPIPE also includes a generic search tool that uses XPath expressions, and supports exporting the data into different formats for analysis such as Excel and CSV.

---

[26]http://callisto.mitre.org/

[27]http://mmax2.sourceforge.net/

[28]http://clic.ub.edu/ancorapipe/

Summary All the annotation tools discussed here (and others) offer the flexibility for adapting to specific annotation goals, as well as the required interaction for making annotation efficient, including visual display of markable chains (all tools offer a list view for markable chains that allows grasping quickly all the markables from a set) and a search function for text (which is especially helpful for name coreference where mention strings are similar or identical, but the mentions in a chain are far apart). Since they are available as freeware or open source and run on all major platforms, they should definitely be taken into consideration before taking on the risk of developing another annotation tool or using a simple XML or plaintext editor.

4.2 Markup and Coding Scheme

Markup Most corpora with anaphoric information are stored in XML format.[29] The corpora in XML format are generally stored using a standoff representation—either character-based, as in the corpora created using ATLAS-based tools like CALLISTO, or token standoff, as in the corpora created using MMAX2.

As discussed above, for languages with phonetically unrealized anaphoric expressions (**zeros**) like Italian and Japanese, if argument structure is being annotated at the same time and appropriate annotation tools are available, the corpus creators should consider using the argument structure annotation as the base level, as done, e.g., in the Prague Dependency Treebank or ANCORA.

Coding scheme The most common options for anaphoric annotation have been discussed in Sect. 2. There are two basic options in terms of mention selection: either annotating only the entities that are most relevant for a given domain, ACE style, or annotating all NPs, as done in most other corpora. The MUC7 guidelines [29] still provide a very useful analysis of potential difficulties in mention identification. Most corpora require coders to mark the entire NP boundary.

In terms of anaphoric relations, most corpora focus only on NP anaphora with antecedents introduced by NPs; most coding guidelines provide detailed examples for this type of annotation. Guidelines for bridging were produced by, e.g., DRAMA, GNOME,[30] ARRAU, and DEDE [18].

Markable attributes useful for anaphora include grammatical function, agreement features, and semantic features, ontological category first of all. Most modern anaphoric annotations, and most notably, ANCORA, ONTONOTES and the Prague Dependency Treebank, are carried out in combination with the annotation of other levels, which provide some of this additional information about markables. Virtually all annotation efforts rely at least on (semi-)automatic constituency or dependency

[29] A notable exception is the ONTONOTES corpus, where all semantic levels are stored in a unified format in a database [64].

[30] http://cswww.essex.ac.uk/Research/nle/corpora/GNOME/anno_manual_4.htm

annotation. Including named entity type information is also a very good idea, especially if automatic tools to do so are available for the particular language and domain. Anaphora annotation projects that have to create all information by hand could look at the GNOME guidelines for suggestions.

Agreement The design of the coding scheme should be informed by awareness of what can be reliably annotated. While some of the initial efforts, such as MUC, reported agreement scores,[31] many of the more recent ones–most notably, the ACE campaign—do not [3]. In-depth studies of agreement on anaphoric annotations have been carried out by [62] and as part of the development of the GNOME and ARRAU [56] corpora. The results suggest that reasonable agreement can be obtained on the distinction between discourse-old and discourse-new, but that annotating bridging reference requires identifying very clearly the subset of bridging relations of interest. Any attempt at marking more complex types of anaphoric information should be accompanied by a study of the agreement between annotators.

The GNOME annotation effort also involved an extensive evaluation of the reliability of other types of information (grammatical function, agreement, semantic features, etc.) [54].

4.3 Annotation Procedure

(Semi-)Automatic Steps Carrying out as much of the work automatically is essential to create a resource of adequate size given the constraints most efforts work under. The aspect of the process that can be automated to a greater extent is the identification of markables,[32] but the accuracy of parsers still typically requires that coders be able to correct markable boundaries by hand.

Named entity taggers of reasonable quality also exist for many languages, at least for unrestricted domains. Last but not least, the accuracy of dependency parsing is now such that grammatical function identification can also be by and large carried out automatically.

Guidelines Not all annotation projects produce written guidelines, but experience suggests it is very useful to do so both to carry out agreement studies and to help coders. Most large scale annotation efforts have provided useful examples that could be adapted.

[31]In MUC and other projects, the MUC scoring metric was used (see chapter "Evaluation Campaigns"). The MUC-6 annotators reached an agreement level of $F_1 = 0.83$ [30], comparable with later efforts such as the German TüBa-D/Z corpus ($F_1 = 0.83$, [78]), or the Dutch COREA corpus ($F_1 = 0.76$, [27]), which relied on more refined annotation guidelines.

[32]Researchers working on languages for which not even chunkers exist need to be aware that the corpora they create will probably only be usable for linguistic studies.

Multiple Coding and Checking Checking the output from coders is essential for quality checking. In projects with substantial financial support like ONTONOTES, all documents are coded twice and the annotations reconciled. This is unlikely to be possible for most projects, but we would recommend that the researchers leading the effort check at least 10 % of the annotation produced by their coders, and have at least 10 % of the documents doubly coded.

5 Conclusions

The availability of resources for studying anaphora resolution has greatly improved in recent years, to the extent that researchers interested in the development of computational models of anaphora resolution have now resources comparable to those available to the developers of parsers and predicate argument structure analyzers, and not just for English but also for a variety of other languages including at least Arabic, Bengali, Chinese, Catalan, Czech, Danish, Dutch, French, German, Hindi, Italian, Japanese, Spanish, and Tamil. This effort, however, has also revealed that many aspects of anaphora are still poorly understood from a theoretical perspective, and that the situation is not so good for genres other than news.

Acknowledgements This work was supported in part by a PhD studentship offered by Cogito/Expert Systems (Kepa Rodriguez), in part by the LIVEMEMORIES project (Poesio), and in part by the SENSEI project (Poesio).

References

1. ACE: Annotation guidelines for entity detection and tracking (EDT) (2004). Version 4.2.6
2. Aone, C., Bennett, S.: Evaluating automated and manual acquisition of anaphora resolution strategies. In: Proceedings of ACL, Cambridge (1995)
3. Artstein, R., Poesio, M.: Inter-coder agreement for computational linguistics. Comput. Linguist. **34**(4), 555–596 (2008). An early version of this paper has been circulating since 2005 as "Kappa^3 = Alpha (or Beta)". This version is still available from the ARRAU website
4. Bard, E.G., Anderson, A.H., Sotillo, C., Aylett, M., Doherty-Sneddon, G., Newlands, A.: Controlling the intelligibility of referring expressions. J. Mem. Lang. **42**, 1–22 (2000)
5. Bird, S., Day, D., Garofolo, J., Henderson, J., Laprun, C., Liberman, M.: Atlas: a flexible and extensible architecture for linguistic annotation. http://arxiv.org/abs/cs/0007022 (2000)
6. Botley, S.P.: Indirect anaphora: testing the limits of corpus-based linguistics. Int. J. Corpus Linguist. **11**(1), 73–112 (2006)
7. Bretonnel Cohen, K., Verspoor, K., Bada, M., Funk, C., Hunter, L.: The Colorado richly annotated full text (CRAFT) corpus: multi-model annotation in the biomedical domain. In: Ide, N., Pustejovsky, J. (eds.) Handbook of Linguistic Annotation. Springer, Berlin (forthcoming)
8. Bruneseaux, F., Romary, L.: Codage des références et coréférences dans le dialogues homme-machine. In: Proceedings of ACH-ALLC, Kingston (1997)
9. Byron, D.: Resolving pronominal references to abstract entities. In: Proceedings of the ACL, Philadelphia, pp. 80–87 (2002)

10. Carletta, J.: Assessing agreement on classification tasks: the kappa statistic. Comput. Linguist. **22**(2), 249–254 (1996)
11. Carlson, L., Marcu, D., Okurowski, M.E.: Building a discourse-tagged corpus in the framework of rhetorical structure theory. In: van Kuppevelt, J., Smith, R. (eds.) Current Directions in Discourse and Dialogue, pp. 85–112. Kluwer Academic, Dordrecht/Boston (2003)
12. Chafe, W.L.: The Pear Stories: Cognitive, Cultural and Linguistic Aspects of Narrative Production. Ablex, Norwood (1980)
13. Cheng, H.: Modelling aggregation motivated interactions in descriptive text generation. Ph.D. thesis, Division of Informatics, the University of Edinburgh, Edinburgh (2001)
14. Chinchor, N.A.: Overview of MUC-7/MET-2. In: Proceedings of the Seventh Message Understanding Conference (MUC-7), Fairfax (1998)
15. Collovini, S., Carbonel, T., Thielsen Fuchs, J., Coelho, J.C., Rino, L., Vieira, R.: Summit: um corpus anotado com informa cões discursivas visando à sumariza cão automática. In: 52nd Workshop em Tecnologia da Informa cão e da Linguagem Humana (TIL'2007), Rio de Janeiro (2007)
16. van Deemter, K., Kibble, R.: On coreferring: coreference in MUC and related annotation schemes. Comput. Linguist. **26**(4), 629–637 (2000). Squib
17. Doddington, G., Mitchell, A., Przybocki, M., Ramshaw, L., Strassell, S., Weischedel, R.: The automatic content extraction (ACE) program–tasks, data, and evaluation. In: Proceedings of LREC, Athens (2000)
18. Gardent, C., Manuélian, H.: Création d'un corpus annoté pour le traitement des déscriptions d éfinies. Traitement Automatique des Langues **46**(1), 115–140 (2005). http://www.loria.fr/~gardent/publis/tal2005.pdf
19. Gasperin, C., Karamanis, N., Seal, R.: Annotation of anaphoric relations in biomedical full-text articles using a domain-relevant scheme. In: Proceedings of DAARC 2007, Lagos, pp. 19–24 (2007)
20. Ge, N., Hale, J., Charniak, E.: A statistical approach to anaphora resolution. In: Proceedings of Sixth Workshop on Very Large Corpora (WVLC/EMNLP) (1998)
21. Grishman, R.: Coreference task definition. Technical report, NYU (1995). http://www.cs.nyu.edu/cs/faculty/grishman/COtask21.book_1.html
22. Grishman, R.: Named entity task definition. Technical report, NYU (1995). http://www.cs.nyu.edu/cs/faculty/grishman/NEtask20.book_1.html
23. Grishman, R., Sundheim, B.: Design of the MUC-6 evalutation. In: Proceedings of the Sixth Message Understanding Conference (MUC-6), Columbia (1995)
24. Grishman, R., Sundheim, B.: Message understanding conference-6: a brief history. In: Proceedings of the 16th COLING, COLING '96, pp. 466–471. Association for Computational Linguistics, Stroudsburg (1996). doi:http://dx.doi.org/10.3115/992628.992709
25. Hajič, J., Böhmová, A., Hajičová, E., Vidová-Hladká, B.: The Prague dependency treebank: a three-level annotation scenario. In: Abeillé, A. (ed.) Treebanks: Building and Using Parsed Corpora, pp. 103–127. Kluwer Academic, Amsterdam (2000)
26. Hasler, L., Orasan, C., Naumann, K.: NPs for events: experiments in coreference annotation. In: Proceedings of LREC, Genoa (2006)
27. Hendrickx, I., Bouma, G., Coppens, F., Daelemans, W., Hoste, V., Kloosterman, G., Mineur, A.M., Van Der Vloet, J., Verschelde, J.L.: A coreference corpus and resolution system for Dutch. In: Proceedings of LREC, Marrakech (2008)
28. Hinrichs, E., Kübler, S., Naumann, K.: A unified representation for morphological, syntactic, semantic and referential annotations. In: ACL Workshop on Frontiers in Corpus Annotation II: Pie in the Sky, Ann Arbor (2005)
29. Hirschman, L.: MUC-7 coreference task definition, version 3.0. In: Chinchor, N. (ed.) Proceedings of the 7th Message Understanding Conference (1998). Available at http://www.muc.saic.com/proceedings/muc_7_toc.html
30. Hirschman, L., Robinson, P., Burger, J., Vilain, M.: Automating coreference: the role of automated training data. In: Proceedings of AAAI Spring Symposium on Applying Machine Learning to Discourse Processing (1997). http://arxiv.org/pdf/cmp-lg/9803001

31. http://dl.acm.org/citation.cfm?id=2448119
32. Ide, N.: Corpus encoding standard: SGML guidelines for encoding linguistic corpora. In: Proceedings of LREC, Granada (1998)
33. Ide, N., Pustejovsky, J. (eds.): Handbook of Linguistic Annotation. Springer, Berlin (forthcoming)
34. Iida, R., Komachi, M., Inui, K., Matsumoto, Y.: Annotating a Japanese text corpus with predicate-argument and coreference relations. In: Proceeding of the ACL Linguistic Annotation Workshop (LAW), Prague, pp. 132–139 (2007)
35. Iida, R., Poesio, M.: A cross-lingual ILP solution to zero anaphora resolution. In: Proceedings of ACL. ACL, Boulder (2011)
36. Isard, A.: An XML architecture for the HCRC map task corpus. In: Kühnlein, P., Rieser, H., Zeevat, H. (eds.) Proceedings of BI-DIALOG (2001)
37. Kabadjov, M.A.: Task-oriented evaluation of anaphora resolution. Ph.D. thesis, Department of Computing and Electronic Systems, University of Essex, Colchester (2007)
38. Karamanis, N.: Entity coherence for descriptive text structuring. Ph.D. thesis, University of Edinburgh, Informatics (2003)
39. Klein, M., Bernsen, N.O., Davies, S., Dybkjaer, L., Garrido, J., Kasch, H., Mengel, A., Pirelli, V., Poesio, M., Quazza, S., Soria, C.: Supported coding schemes. Deliverable 1.1, The MATE Consortium. mate.nis.sdu.dk/about/deliverables.html (1998)
40. Krasavina, O., Chiarcos, C.: The potsdam coreference scheme. In: Proceedings of the 1st Linguistic Annotation Workshop, pp. 156–163 (2007)
41. Kučová, L., Hajičová, E.: Coreferential relations in the prague dependency treebank. In: Proceedings of DAARC, pp. 94–102 (2004)
42. LDC: ACE (Automatic Content Extraction) English annotation guidelines for entities, version 5.6.1 (2004)
43. Magnini, B., Pianta, E., Girardi, C., Negri, M., Romano, L., Speranza, M., Lenzi, V.B., Sprugnoli, R.: I-cab: the italian content annotation bank. In: Proceedings of LREC, Genoa (2006)
44. McCarthy, J.F., Lehnert, W.G.: Using decision trees for coreference resolution. In: Proceedings of IJCAI, Monréal (1995)
45. McKelvie, D., Isard, A., Mengel, A., Moeller, M.B., Grosse, M., Klein, M.: The MATE workbench – an annotation tool for XML corpora. Speech Commun. **33**(1–2), 97–112 (2001)
46. Moser, M., Moore, J.D.: Toward a synthesis of two accounts of discourse structure. Comput. Linguist. **22**(3), 409–419 (1996)
47. Müller, M.C.: Fully automatic resolution of it, this and that in unrestricted multy-party dialog. Ph.D. thesis, Universität Tübingen (2008)
48. Müller, C., Strube, M.: Multi-level annotation of linguistic data with mmax2. In: Braun, S., Kohn, K., Mukherjee, J. (eds.) Corpus Technology and Language Pedagogy. New Resources, New Tools, New Methods. English Corpus Linguistics, vol. 3, pp. 197–214. Peter Lang, New York (2006)
49. Navaretta, C.: Pronominal types and abstract reference in the Danish and Italian DAD Corpora. In: Proceedings of the Second Workshop on Anaphora Resolution (WAR II), Bergen. NEALT Proceedings Series, vol. 2, pp. 63–71 (2008)
50. Nguyen, N.L.T., Kim, J.D., Tsujii, J.: Challenges in pronoun resolution system for biomedical text. In: Proceedings of LREC, Marrakech (2008)
51. Orasan, C.: Palinka: a highly customizable tool for discourse annotation. In: Proceedings of the 4th SIGdial Workshop on Discourse and Dialogue, Sapporo (2003)
52. Poesio, M.: Annotating a corpus to develop and evaluate discourse entity realization algorithms: issues and preliminary results. In: Proceedings of the 2nd LREC, Athens, pp. 211–218 (2000)
53. Poesio, M.: The GNOME Annotation Scheme Manual. University of Edinburgh, HCRC and Informatics, Scotland, fourth version edn. (2000). Available from http://cswww.essex.ac.uk/Research/nle/corpora/GNOME/anno_manual_4.htm

54. Poesio, M.: The MATE/GNOME scheme for anaphoric annotation, revisited. In: Proceedings of SIGDIAL, Boston (2004)
55. Poesio, M., Artstein, R.: The reliability of anaphoric annotation, reconsidered: taking ambiguity into account. In: Meyers, A. (ed.) Proceedings of ACL Workshop on Frontiers in Corpus Annotation, Ann Arbor, pp. 76–83 (2005)
56. Poesio, M., Artstein, R.: Anaphoric annotation in the arrau corpus. In: Proceedings of LREC, Marrakesh (2008)
57. Poesio, M., Bruneseaux, F., Romary, L.: The MATE meta-scheme for coreference in dialogues in multiple languages. In: Walker, M. (ed.) Proceedings of the ACL Workshop on Standards and Tools for Discourse Tagging, College Park, pp. 65–74 (1999)
58. Poesio, M., Delmonte, R., Bristot, A., Chiran, L., Tonelli, S.: The VENEX corpus of anaphoric information in spoken and written Italian (2004, in preparation). Available online at http://cswww.essex.ac.uk/staff/poesio/publications/VENEX04.pdf
59. Poesio, M., Patel, A., Di Eugenio, B.: Discourse structure and anaphora in tutorial dialogues: an empirical analysis of two theories of the global focus. Res. Lang. Comput. **4**, 229–257 (2006). Special Issue on Generation and Dialogue
60. Poesio, M., Stevenson, R., Di Eugenio, B., Hitzeman, J.M.: Centering: a parametric theory and its instantiations. Comput. Linguist. **30**(3), 309–363 (2004)
61. Poesio, M., Sturt, P., Arstein, R., Filik, R.: Underspecification and anaphora: theoretical issues and preliminary evidence. Discourse Process. **42**(2), 157–175 (2006)
62. Poesio, M., Vieira, R.: A corpus-based investigation of definite description use. Comput. Linguist. **24**(2), 183–216 (1998). Also available as Research Paper CCS-RP-71, Centre for Cognitive Science, University of Edinburgh
63. Postal, P.M.: Anaphoric islands. In: Binnick, R.I., et al. (ed.) Papers from the Fifth Regional Meeting of the Chicago Linguistic Society, pp. 205–235. University of Chicago, Chicago (1969)
64. Pradhan, S.S., Hovy, E., Marcus, M., Palmer, M., Ramshaw, L., Weischedel, R.: Ontonotes: a unified relational semantic representation. Int. J. Semant. Comput. **1**(4), 405–419 (2007)
65. Pradhan, S., Marcus, M., Palmer, M., Ramshaw, L., Weischedel, R., Xue, N.: CoNLL-2011 shared task: modeling unrestricted coreference in ontonotes. In: Proceedings of the Fifteenth Conference on Computational Natural Language Learning (CoNLL 2011), Portland (2011)
66. Pradhan, S., Moschitti, A., Xue, N., Uryupina, O., Zhang, Y.: Conll-2012 shared task: modeling multilingual unrestricted coreference in ontonotes. In: Joint Conference on EMNLP and CoNLL – Shared Task, pp. 1–40. Association for Computational Linguistics, Jeju Island (2012). http://www.aclweb.org/anthology/W12-4501
67. Pradhan, S., Ramshaw, L., Weischedel, R., MacBride, J., Micciulla, L.: Unrestricted coreference: indentifying entities and events in OntoNotes. In: Proceedings of the IEEE International Conference on Semantic Computing (ICSC), Irvine (2007)
68. Recasens, M., Màrquez, L., Sapena, E., Martí, M.A., Taulé, M., Hoste, V., Poesio, M., Versley, Y.: Semeval-2010 task 1: coreference resolution in multiple languages. In: Proceedings of SEMEVAL, Uppsala (2010)
69. Recasens, M., Martí, M.A.: Ancora-co: coreferentially annotated corpora for Spanish and Catalan. Lang. Resour. Eval. **44**, 315–345 (2010)
70. Rodriguez, K.J., Delogu, F., Versley, Y., Stemle, E., Poesio, M.: Anaphoric annotation of wikipedia and blogs in the live memories corpus. In: Proceedings of LREC (poster), Malta (2010)
71. Sgall, P., Hajicova, E., Panevova, J. (eds.): The Meaning of the Sentence in Its Semantic and Pragmatic Aspects. D. Reidel, Dordrecht/Boston (1986)
72. Sobha, L., Bandyopadhyay, S., Vijay Sundar Ram, R., Akilandeswari, A.: NLP tool contest @ICON2011 on anaphora resolution in Indian languages. In: Proceedings of ICON, Singapore (2011)
73. Sperberg-McQueen, C.M., Burnard, L. (eds.): Guidelines for Electronic Text Encoding and Interchange (TEI P3). Text Encoding Initiative, Oxford (1994)

74. Stede, M.: The Potsdam Commentary Corpus. In: ACL'04 Workshop on Discourse Annotation, Barcelona (2004)
75. Su, J., Yang, X., Hong, H., Tateisi, Y., Tsujii, J.: Coreference resolution in biomedical texts: a machine learning approach. Schloss Dagstuhl – Leibniz-Zentrum für Informatik, Dagstuhl Seminar Proceedings. 08131 – Ontologies and Text Mining for Life Sciences: Current Status and Future Perspectives (2008)
76. Taulé, M., Martí, M.A., Recasens, M.: AnCora: multilevel annotated corpora for Catalan and Spanish. In: Proceedings of LREC, Marrakech, pp. 96–101 (2008)
77. Tutin, A., Trouilleux, F., Clouzot, C., Gaussier, E., Zaenen, A., Rayot, S., Antoniadis, G.: Annotating a large corpus with anaphoric links. In: Proceedings of DAARC, Lancaster (2000)
78. Versley, Y.: Vagueness and referential ambiguity in a large-scale annotated corpus. Res. Lang. Comput. **6**(3–4), 333–353 (2008)
79. Wagner, A., Zeisler, B.: A syntactically annotated corpus of Tibetan. In: Proceedings of LREC, Lisbon (2004)
80. Walker, C., Strassel, S., Medero, J., Maeda, K.: ACE 2005 Multilingual Training Corpus. LDC2006T06. Linguistic Data Consortium, Philadelphia (2006)
81. Ward, G., Sproat, R., McKoon, G.: A pragmatic analysis of so-called anaphoric islands. Language **67**, 439–474 (1991)
82. Weischedel, R., Hovy, E., Marcus, M., Palmer, M., Belvin, R., Pradhan, S., Ramshaw, L., Xue, N.: OntoNotes: a large training corpus for enhanced processing. In: Olive, J., Christianson, C., McCary, J. (eds.) Handbook of Natural Language Processing and Machine Translation: DARPA Global Autonomous Language Exploitation. Springer, New York (2011)
83. Weischedel, R., Pradhan, S., Ramshaw, L., Palmer, M., Xue, N., Marcus, M., Taylor, A., Greenberg, C., Hovy, E., Belvin, R., Houston, A.: Ontonotes Release 2.0. LDC2008T04. Linguistic Data Consortium, Philadelphia (2008)

Evaluation Metrics

Xiaoqiang Luo and Sameer Pradhan

Abstract This chapter discusses how to evaluate anaphora or coreference resolution systems. The problem is non-trivial in that it needs to deal with a multitude of sub-problems, such as: (1) What is the evaluation unit (entities or links); if entities, is entity-alignment needed? if links, how to handle single-mention entities? (2) How to deal with the fact that the response mention set may differ from that of the key mention set? We will review the prevailing metrics proposed in the last two decades, including MUC, B-cubed, CEAF and BLANC. We will give illustrative examples to show how they are computed, and the scenarios under which they are intended to be used. We will present their strengths and weaknesses, and clarify some misunderstandings of the metrics found in the recent literature.

Keywords Evaluation metrics NLP evaluation • Evaluation metrics • Shared tasks

1 Introduction

An important problem in anaphora or coreference resolution research is how to measure the quality of a resolution system. A good metric not only reflects the true quality of a resolution system, but also facilitates comparing research work across institutions and time. While there is a need for a good metric to evaluate systems for all natural language processing (NLP) problems, the coreference problem deserves special attention for several reasons. First, in the course of last two decades, multiple evaluation metrics [2, 8, 13, 19, 21] have been proposed, all of which aimed at solving the evaluation problem or improving one or multiple existing metrics. The existence of multiple metrics, compounded with sometimes misunderstandings of these metrics [5, 17, 20], makes it difficult to compare two systems. Therefore, it

X. Luo (✉)
LinkedIn Inc., New York, NY, USA
e-mail: Xiaoqiang.luo@gmail.com

S. Pradhan
Boulder Learning, Inc., Boulder, CO, USA
e-mail: pradhan@boulderlearning.com; pradhan@cemantix.org

M. Poesio et al. (eds.), *Anaphora Resolution*, Theory and Applications of Natural Language Processing, DOI 10.1007/978-3-662-47909-4_5

benefits the research community to have a chapter that puts prevailing evaluation metrics into a single place where pros and cons of these metrics are discussed.

Second, finding a good evaluation metric for anaphora or coreference resolution is difficult because there are many needs that are hard to satisfy simultaneously. For example, should a missing coreference link be penalized the same way as a spurious one? should an entity with 100 mentions be treated the same way as a single-mention entity? Subjectively, it is desirable that a metric ought to rank systems in a way agreeing with our intuitions, e.g., the homogeneity and completeness criterion laid out for the clustering problem in [1]. It was pointed out in [1] that many clustering metrics do not satisfy all these criteria. Therefore, the chapter provides the practitioners in the field with an opportunity to understand the technical difficulties of evaluating anaphora or coreference resolution systems.

The anaphora or coreference resolution problem is often (mistakenly) deemed equivalent to the clustering problem. They are related in that both aim at placing objects into clusters, but the anaphora or coreference resolution is not a pure clustering problem: one crucial difference is that objects in clustering problems are identical in the system output and the gold standard, while mentions in an anaphora or coreference system's output may or may not be the same as those found in the gold standard. Therefore, an evaluation metric needs to be able to handle false-alarm mentions (i.e., spurious mentions not found in the gold standard) and missing mentions (i.e., mentions found in the gold standard and but are missing in the system output). For this reason, metrics for evaluating clustering algorithms (e.g., [18]) cannot be used directly, though sometimes they can be adapted to the coreference resolution problem [19].

This chapter surveys existing evaluation metrics, including the background from which they were proposed, the mathematical formulae to calculate these metrics, and their strengths and weaknesses. In the course of the presentation, we will also rectify some misinformation [5, 20] about some metrics found in the literature.

The chapter is organized as follows. In Sect. 2, we define the terminology and notation used in the rest of the chapter. This is needed as not all authors use the same terminology or notation, and they will help present various metrics in Sect. 4. Some issues common to all evaluation metrics are discussed in Sect. 3. The concluding remarks are found in Sect. 5.

2 Terminology and Notation

To facilitate the presentation, we define terminologies and notations used in this chapter. Individual phrases participating in an anaphora or coreference relationship are called **mentions** and the collection of mentions referring to the same physical object is called an **entity**. In the following passage taken from ACE data [13–15], mentions are marked with an underline, and mentions referring to the same entity are marked with the same subscript number.

The American Medical Association$_1$ voted yesterday to install the heir apparent$_2$ as its$_1$ president-elect$_2$, rejecting a strong, upstart challenge by a district doctor$_3$ who argued that the nation's largest physicians' group$_1$ needs stronger ethics and new leadership.

For example, "American Medical Association", "heir apparent," and "its" are *mentions*; "American Medical Association", "its" and "largest physicians' group" refer to the same organization and all are marked with the subscript 1; similarly, "heir apparent" and "president-elect" refer to the same person and are marked with the subscript 2.

It is worth pointing out that the mention defined here was called "markable", while our entity was termed "coreference chain" or "equivalence class" in the Message Understanding Conference (MUC) task [10, 11]. On the other hand, mentions defined here were called "entities" and entities defined here were called "equivalent class" by Bagga and Baldwin [2].

In coreference resolution, we need to compare an annotated gold standard with the output of a system. We use **key** to refer to gold-standard mentions or entities, and **response** to refer to mentions or entities in an anaphora or coreference system. The collection of key entities is denoted by $\mathscr{K} = \{K_i\}_{i=1}^{|\mathscr{K}|}$, where K_i is the ith key entity; accordingly, $\mathscr{R} = \{R_j\}_{j=1}^{|\mathscr{R}|}$ is the set of response entities, and R_j is the jth response entity. Unless stated explicitly, we assume that mentions are unique on both the key side and response side. In other words, that there are no key entities K_k, K_l $(k \neq l)$ such that they have a common mention $m \in K_k$ and $m \in K_l$; neither are there response entities R_k, R_l $(k \neq l)$ such that they have a common mention $m \in R_k$ and $m \in R_l$.

We use $\mathscr{M}_k$ and $\mathscr{M}_r$ to denote the set of key mentions and response mentions. It is not required that $\mathscr{M}_k$ be identical to $\mathscr{M}_r$. In other words, the coreference evaluation metrics presented in this chapter all work on both gold mentions and system mentions. This is important since some of them were perceived [5, 17, 20] as only working under the condition that $\mathscr{M}_k = \mathscr{M}_r$, but, as to be shown shortly, this is not the case.

We also use $|\cdot|$ to denote the size of a set. For example, $|\mathscr{K}|$ is the number of key entities; $|\mathscr{M}_r|$ is the number of response mentions; $|K_i|$ is the number of mentions in the key entity K_i; and $|R_j|$ is the number of mentions in the response entity R_j, etc.

3 Desiderata for Anaphora Or Coreference Evaluation

Anaphora or coreference evaluation is closely related to clustering evaluation. Many of the principles of clustering evaluation in the overview of [1] are applicable. For example, "cluster homogeneity" corresponds to the preference of high entity precision, and "cluster completeness" corresponds to that of high entity recall. A full account of the criteria is out of the scope of the chapter, and we encourage readers to refer to [1] for additional background.

As pointed out earlier, anaphora or coreference resolution is not identical to clustering because the set of response mentions do not have to be identical to that of key mentions. Therefore, we highlight a few desiderata specific to the anaphora or coreference resolution before delving into each individual evaluation metric.

3.1 Tampering-Free Principle

While the scope of anaphora or coreference resolution is to find antecedents or coreference chains of a set of given mentions, in reality the set of response mentions is often the output of another system. Therefore, it cannot be assumed that response mentions are always the same as those of key mentions. An evaluation metric should be able to handle both gold mentions and imperfect response mentions.

Evaluating a system operating on gold mentions is considerably easier. For this reason, there are recent research work [5, 17, 20] that advocate an approach of modifying response or even key mentions or entities so the two are transformed into an identical set. This is undesirable for two reasons. First, adding a step of manipulating the response and/or key mentions/entities makes the evaluation process much less transparent and straightforward; second, and more importantly, changing key or response mentions/entities before evaluation undermines the integrity of the evaluation process.

For this reason, the evaluation metrics presented in the chapter adhere to the original response mentions, and they are all computed without changing key or response and without the assumption that key and response mentions are identical.

3.2 Mention Weighted vs. Entity Weighted

Many existing metrics, including MUC, B-cubed, and CEAF, compute the document-level metric by aggregating or averaging entity-level scores. This creates two possible ways of computing the document-level score: first, the entity-level *raw scores* (or *counts*) are added and then averaged at the document level. In this scheme, each mention is equally important (and hence an entity with more mentions carries a larger weight than that of a smaller one) and this kind of metric is called *mention-weighted*.

A second scheme is to normalize the entity-level scores to a number between 0 and 1, and then take simple arithmetic average over all entities to compute the document-level metric. Each entity has the same weight in this scheme, and we call this kind of coreference metrics *entity-weighted*.

Not all existing coreference metrics build the document-level score from entity-level ones. For instance, BLANC [9, 19] computes the document-level score directly from the contingency table of mention-pairs. In such cases, there is no need to differentiate the mention-weighted metric from the entity-weighted one.

After an entity-level similarity metric is defined, switching from mention-weighted to entity-weighted is straightforward. For this reason, we will concentrate on mention-weighted metrics most of the time, and touch entity-weighted metrics in some necessary places.

3.3 Partial Credit

All coreference evaluation metrics will eventually compare whether or not two mentions are identical, or to what degree they are similar. Accordingly, we can assign a 0 or 1 score to a pair of key and response mention, or allow partial credit when two mentions share some attributes but are not 100 % identical. In most cases, extending from integer counts to similarities measured in real numbers is straightforward. For this reason, we will use the set intersection notation in the following presentation most of the time, such as $|K_i \cap R_j|$ to denote the number of common mentions between the key entity K_i and response entity R_j. If partial credit is allowed, all one has to do is to deem $|K_i \cap R_j|$ as a (real-number) similarity between K_i and R_j and the metrics in this chapter carry over.

3.4 Anaphora Resolution

In the setup of anaphora resolution, sometimes we are interested in finding the antecedent of an anaphor, and are less interested in the full coreference chain. When both key and response entities are of the form (antecedent, anaphor) pairs, the evaluation becomes simpler: all metrics in the chapter can work without modification. Specifically, the MUC metric measures what percentage of (antecedent, anaphor) pairs are correct. B-cubed and CEAF will treat (antecedent, anaphor) pairs as entities and allow partial credits if only one of (antecedent, anaphor) is correct in a pair. As for BLANC, within-entity links coincides with the set of (antecedent, anaphor) pairs, and BLANC formulae carry over to this setup in a straightforward manner.

4 Evaluation Metrics

In this section, we will present the MUC-F, B-cubed, CEAF and BLANC, four metrics used widely in the research community. While their definitions can be found in the literature [2, 8, 9, 19, 21], they were presented using different notations; some of them gave only examples where the set of response mentions is assumed identical to that of key mentions, leading to misunderstandings that they only work for gold mentions. In reaction to this lack of explicit recommendations on dealing with mismatches between key and system mentions, ad-hoc manipulation schemes were proposed [5, 17, 20], which makes comparing coreference results even harder.

Therefore, we present the aforementioned four metrics with unified notations and precise mathematical formulae. We further illustrate how they are calculated with detailed examples. While we are still far from a solution for evaluating anaphora and coreference resolution that is perfect in any and all aspects, we hope that the precise definition of the metrics, along with the reference implementation[1] in [16] will facilitate comparing coreference research work, which will in turn help to push the frontier of this field.

4.1 MUC F-Measure

We first present the MUC F-Measure, first proposed by [21], using the notations defined in Sect. 2.

The MUC F-Measure is computed by measuring the common coreference links.[2] between the key and the response. For recall, it counts how many key links are missing in the response. Missing coreference links are defined as the links found in key entities, but not in the response. Reference [21] observed that this can be computed by partitioning each key entity K_i with respect to response entities $\mathscr{R}$, which is defined as:

$$\mathscr{P}(K_i; \mathscr{R}) = \{K_i \cap R_j : j = 1, \cdots, |\mathscr{R}|\} \cup \bigcup_{m \in (K_i - \mathscr{R})} \{\{m\}\}, \tag{1}$$

where $(K_i - \mathscr{R})$ is understood as the set of mentions in K_i, but missing in $\mathscr{R}$. In other words, the partition is the collection of all subsets resulted from intersecting K_i with response entities, $\{R_j\}$, and the singleton sets formed by key mentions in K_i, but missing in the response $\mathscr{R}$. Notice that since the number of missing links needed to connect subsets in $\mathscr{P}(K_i; \mathscr{R})$ to form K_i is $|\mathscr{P}(K_i; \mathscr{R})| - 1$, and since the minimal number of links to connect all mention in K_i is just one less the number of mentions in K_i, or $|K_i| - 1$, the number of correct links is thus

$$\begin{aligned} N_c &= \sum_{i=1}^{|\mathscr{K}|} \big(|K_i| - 1) - (|\mathscr{P}(K_i; \mathscr{R})| - 1\big) \\ &= \sum_{i=1}^{|\mathscr{K}|} \big(|K_i| - |\mathscr{P}(K_i; \mathscr{R})|\big), \end{aligned} \tag{2}$$

where $|\mathscr{P}(K_i; \mathscr{R})|$ is the number of sets in the partition $\mathscr{P}(K_i; \mathscr{R})$.

[1] http://conll.github.io/reference-coreference-scorers

[2] Links for computing MUC-F are the minimum set of links needed to connect mentions in entities. Therefore, if an entity has n mentions, the number of links is $n - 1$. This contrasts with how links are counted in BLANC, where all pairs of mentions within an entity are counted.

Thus, the recall of the system, r, which is the ratio of the number of correct links, N_c, over the number of key links, can be computed as follows:

$$r = \frac{\sum_{i=1}^{|\mathscr{K}|}\left(|K_i| - |\mathscr{P}(K_i;\mathscr{R})|\right)}{\sum_{i=1}^{|\mathscr{K}|}\left(|K_i| - 1\right)}. \tag{3}$$

Computing the precision p of the system can be done by reversing the roles of the key and response entities, where the partition of a response entity R_j with respect to key entities $\mathscr{K}$ is:

$$\mathscr{P}(R_j;\mathscr{K}) = \{K_i \cap R_j : i = 1, \cdots, |\mathscr{K}|\} \cup \bigcup_{m \in (R_j - \mathscr{K})} \{\{m\}\} \tag{4}$$

and the precision is

$$p = \frac{\sum_{j=1}^{|\mathscr{R}|}\left(|R_j| - |\mathscr{P}(R_j;\mathscr{K})|\right)}{\sum_{j=1}^{|\mathscr{R}|}\left(|R_j| - 1\right)}. \tag{5}$$

Finally, the MUC F-measure is the harmonic mean of r and p:

$$F = \frac{2pr}{p+r}. \tag{6}$$

A Concrete Example Equations (1), (2), (3), (4), and (5) may seem overly complicated, but they are pretty easy to count. We will illustrate how MUC F-measure is calculated using the examples in Fig. 1, which contains a document with 12 key mentions in 3 entities: $\{1, 2, 3, 4, 5\}, \{6, 7\}, \{8, 9, A, B, C\}$. Sub-figure (b) to

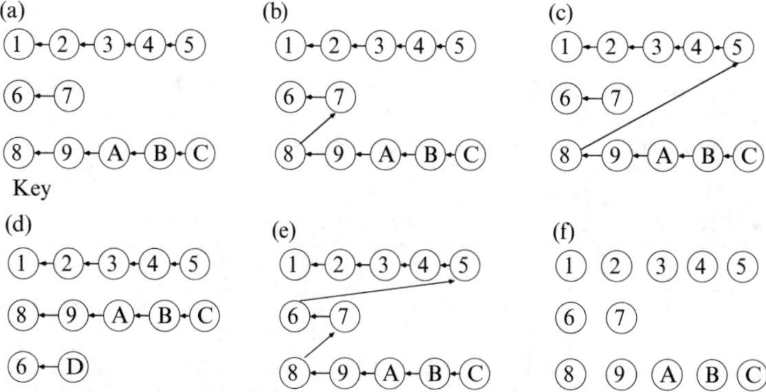

Fig. 1 Key entities (sub-figure (**a**)) and 5 responses (sub-figure (**b**)–(**f**))

(f) are 5 responses. Note that Response (d) contains a spurious mention D and a missing mention 7.

To compute the recall, we need to partition every key entity with respect to response entities. For instance, the partition for the key entity $\{1, 2, 3, 4, 5\}$ with respect to Response (b) is $\{\{1, 2, 3, 4, 5\}\}$; the partition for $\{6, 7\}$ is $\{\{6, 7\}\}$; the partition for $\{8, 9, A, B, C\}$ is $\{\{8, 9, A, B, C\}\}$. Therefore, the recall is

$$\frac{(5-1)+(2-1)+(5-1)}{(5-1)+(2-1)+(5-1)} = 1.$$

To compute the precision, all is needed to reverse the role of Response (b) and the key: the partition for the response entity $\{1, 2, 3, 4, 5\}$ with respect to the key is $\{\{1, 2, 3, 4, 5\}\}$; the partition for the response entity $\{6, 7, 8, 9, A, B, C\}$ with respect to the key is $\{\{6, 7\}, \{8, 9, A, B, C\}\}$. Thus the precision is:

$$\frac{(5-1)+(7-2)}{(5-1)+(7-1)} = \frac{9}{10}.$$

The MUC F-measure is then computed by taking the harmonic mean of the recall and the precision:

$$\frac{2 \times 1 \times \frac{9}{10}}{1 + \frac{9}{10}} = \frac{18}{19}.$$

The MUC recall, precision and F-measure for the other systems are computed similarly and are tabulated under the column "MUC" of Table 1, which also gives results for B-cubed (see Sect. 4.2), CEAF (see Sect. 4.3) and BLANC (see Sect. 4.4).

Response (d) deserves special attention as it contains a missing and a spurious mention: intersecting the key entity $\{6, 7\}$ with Response (d) results in two sets: $\{6\}$ and $\{7\}$. According to Equation (3), the contribution of the entity $\{6, 7\}$ is 0, since $|\{6, 7\}| = 2$, and $|\mathscr{P}(\{6, 7\}; \mathscr{R})| = 2$. Similarly, the contribution of the response

Table 1 MUC, B-cubed, $CEAF_m$, $CEAF_e$ and BLANC scores for Response (b)–(f) in Fig. 1. BLANC scores are approximate in decimal because the denominators are too large if expressed as fractions. Note that BLANC score is not the harmonic mean of recall and precision by definition

	MUC			B-cubed			$CEAF_m$			$CEAF_e$			BLANC		
Response	Rec.	Prec.	F	Rec.	Prec.	F	Rec.	Prec.	F	Rec.	Prec.	F	Rec.	Prec.	F
(b)	1	$\frac{9}{10}$	$\frac{18}{19}$	1	$\frac{16}{21}$	$\frac{32}{37}$	$\frac{5}{6}$	$\frac{5}{6}$	$\frac{5}{6}$	$\frac{11}{18}$	$\frac{11}{12}$	$\frac{11}{15}$	0.889	0.838	0.841
(c)	1	$\frac{9}{10}$	$\frac{18}{19}$	1	$\frac{7}{12}$	$\frac{14}{19}$	$\frac{7}{12}$	$\frac{7}{12}$	$\frac{7}{12}$	$\frac{5}{9}$	$\frac{5}{6}$	$\frac{2}{3}$	0.722	0.728	0.621
(d)	$\frac{8}{9}$	$\frac{8}{9}$	$\frac{8}{9}$	$\frac{7}{8}$	$\frac{7}{8}$	$\frac{7}{8}$	$\frac{11}{12}$	$\frac{11}{12}$	$\frac{11}{12}$	$\frac{5}{6}$	$\frac{5}{6}$	$\frac{5}{6}$	0.865	0.865	0.865
(e)	1	$\frac{9}{11}$	$\frac{9}{10}$	1	$\frac{3}{8}$	$\frac{6}{11}$	$\frac{5}{12}$	$\frac{5}{12}$	$\frac{5}{12}$	$\frac{10}{51}$	$\frac{10}{51}$	$\frac{10}{51}$	0.500	0.159	0.241
(f)	0	0	0	$\frac{1}{4}$	1	$\frac{2}{5}$	$\frac{1}{4}$	$\frac{1}{4}$	$\frac{1}{4}$	$\frac{4}{9}$	$\frac{1}{9}$	$\frac{8}{45}$	0.500	0.341	0.405

entity $\{6, D\}$ to the precision is also 0. Note that missing mentions hurt the recall and spurious mentions hurt the precision.

Observe that the MUC F-measure is not well defined for singleton entities, as exemplified by Response (f) (the precision is really 0/0). Since MUC F-measure is link-based, it is sometimes not sensitive to certain configurations. For instance, Response (b) is arguably better than (c) since the latter mixes two "big" entities while the former mixes a small entity with a big one, but two systems receive the identical score.

Another consequence of link-based scoring is that the metric under-penalizes the type of error where two distinctive entities are merged since it takes only one wrong link to merge 2 key entities. This is demonstrated by Response (d) vs. (e): Response (d) contains an extraneous mention D and a missing mention 7, and its MUC F-measure is $\frac{8}{9}$; Response (e) lumps all mentions into one entity and its F-measure is $\frac{9}{10}$, a score higher than that of Response (d). This is against one's intuition that Response (d) is much better since it outputs two correct entities and the third entity is half right, while Response (e) mixes 3 different entities.

Some of the shortcomings of the MUC F-measure were quickly discovered shortly after it was published. which prompted [2] to propose the B-cubed, a mention-based metric [2] that aimed to fix the drawbacks of the MUC F-measure. Before we move to discuss the B-cubed metric, it is worth pointing out that MUC F-measure is well-suited for evaluating anaphora resolution. If key and response entities are always pairs of mentions, partitioning a key (or a response) entity with respect to response (or key) amounts to essentially counting which links are correct.

4.2 B-Cubed F-Measure

Definition Like the MUC F-measure, the B-cubed metric also computes a recall and a precision between key entities and response entities; but unlike the MUC F-measure, B-cubed is based on mentions instead of links.

We first present how B-cubed recall is calculated. To that end, we again need to partition a key entity K_i with respect to the response entities $\mathscr{R}$, which is defined as:

$$\mathscr{B}(K_i; \mathscr{R}) = \{K_i \cap R_j : j = 1, \cdots, |\mathscr{R}|\} \quad (7)$$

$\mathscr{B}(K_i; \mathscr{R})$ is the set of subsets of intersecting K_i with every response entity $\{R_j\}$. $|K_i \cap R_j|$ is the number of mentions common to K_i and R_j; if partial credit is allowed, $|K_i \cap R_j|$ ought to be understood as the score measuring the commonality between K_i and R_j.

For each key mention $m \in K_i \cap R_j$, its contribution to recall is:

$$r(m) = \frac{|K_i \cap R_j|}{|K_i|} \quad (8)$$

Note that if a key mention is missing in response $\mathscr{R}$, its contribution to recall is 0. The total contribution from all mentions in $K_i \cap R_j$ to recall is thus:

$$r(i,j) = \sum_{m \in K_i \cap R_j} r(m) = \frac{|K_i \cap R_j|^2}{|K_i|} \tag{9}$$

The mention-weighted overall recall is just the sum of $r(i,j)$ normalized by the number of key mentions:

$$r = \sum_{i,j} \frac{|K_i \cap R_j|^2}{|K_i||\mathscr{M}_k|}. \tag{10}$$

Computing B-cubed precision is done by reversing the roles of key entities and response entities. In particular, the partition of a response entity R_j with respect to the key $\mathscr{K}$ is:

$$\mathscr{B}(R_j; \mathscr{K}) = \{K_i \cap R_j : i = 1, \cdots, |\mathscr{K}|\}. \tag{11}$$

The contribution to precision of all mentions in the response entity R_j with respect to K_i is:

$$p(i,j) = \frac{|K_i \cap R_j|^2}{|R_j|}. \tag{12}$$

The precision is the sum of $p(i,j)$ normalized by the number of response mentions:

$$p = \sum_{i,j} \frac{|K_i \cap R_j|^2}{|R_j||\mathscr{M}_r|}. \tag{13}$$

Finally, the B-cubed F-measure is the harmonic mean of r and p:

$$F = \frac{2pr}{p+r}. \tag{14}$$

If mentions in response entities are disjoint (in other words, no duplicate response mentions), then $\left(K_i \cap (\cup_j R_j)\right) \subset K_i$, or $\sum_j |K_i \cap R_j| \leq |K_i|$. Since $\sum_j |K_i \cap R_j|^2 \leq (\sum_j |K_i \cap R_j|)^2 \leq |K_i|^2$, we can conclude that

$$r = \sum_i \frac{1}{|K_i|} \sum_j \frac{|K_i \cap R_j|^2}{|\mathscr{M}_k|} \leq \sum_i \frac{1}{|K_i|} \frac{|K_i|^2}{|\mathscr{M}_k|} = 1, \tag{15}$$

and equality holds if and only if, for all i, $K_i \subset R_r$ for some r and $K_i \cap R_j = \emptyset$ ($j \neq r$). Similarly, it can be proven that, if key entities are disjoint, $p \leq 1$.

There is no such guarantee, however, for cases where key mentions are—perhaps inadvertently—repeated in the response. To see this, suppose that the key consists of one entity $\{a, b, c\}$ and the response three entities: $\{a, b\}$, $\{a, c\}$, $\{b, c\}$. Partitioning the key entity with respect to the first response entity $\{a, b\}$ creates two subsets, so both a and b will receive a credit $\frac{2}{3}$ from this partition. Repeating this process, the key mention a will also receive a credit $\frac{2}{3}$ from partitioning the key entity with respect to the second response entity. In total, the key mention a is assigned a credit of $\frac{4}{3}$; similarly, the key mention b and c are both assigned a total credit $\frac{4}{3}$. This leads to a recall $\frac{\frac{4}{3}+\frac{4}{3}+\frac{4}{3}}{3} = \frac{4}{3}$, which is greater than 1!

In fact, the recall can be driven to an arbitrarily large number by repeating key mentions in response! The issue of duplicate response mentions is not imaginary and is not a pathetic corner case. It can happen, for example, when a coreference system reads all noun-phrases and pronouns from a parse tree, and a mention is spanned both by an NP and a pronoun part-of-speech tag. In practice, this means that one has to make sure that mentions in responses are unique before applying the B-cubed metric, which violates the tampering-free principle.

The numerical difficulty of B-cubed recall stems from the fact that it allows a key entity to intersect with all response entities, which has probably unintended consequence that a correct key mention could be credited multiple times. That is the primary reason why CEAF, to be covered next, insists on 1-to-1 alignment between the key and the response.

B-cubed precision would exhibit similar problems in the case of duplicate key mentions, but does not in practice since key mentions and entities are normally created manually, and the data creator has full control of the problem.

B-cubed Examples We walk through the steps to calculate B-cubed metric for responses in Fig. 1.

For Response (b), intersecting the 3 key entities with response entities results in identical sets of entities, so the overall recall is 1. For precision, partitioning the response entity $\{1, 2, 3, 4, 5\}$ with respect to the key entities results in a single set—$\{1, 2, 3, 4, 5\}$, so the contribution to the precision from this entity is 5; partitioning the response entity $\{6, 7, 8, 9, A, B, C\}$ with respect to the key entities leads to two subsets: $\{6, 7\}$ and $\{8, 9, A, B, C\}$, so the precision for this entity is: $\frac{2^2+5^2}{7} = \frac{29}{7}$. The overall precision is then:

$$p = \frac{5 + \frac{29}{7}}{12} = \frac{16}{21}. \tag{16}$$

The mention-weighted B-cubed F-measure is $2 \times \frac{1\times\frac{16}{21}}{1+\frac{16}{21}} = \frac{32}{37}$.

B-cubed metrics can be computed similarly for other systems, and the results are tabulated in the column of Table 1 under "B-cubed." We can observe from these results that:

- The B-cubed metric measures common mentions between key and response entities, and therefore single-mention entities are no longer a problem. For

instance, Response (f) consists of all singletons and the B-cubed metric is well-defined.
- The B-cubed metric is sensitive to the sizes of response entities. For example, the MUC F-measure are identical for Response (b) and (c), but B-cubed assigns a better score to (b) than (c), which agrees with our intuition. It also ranks Response (b) better than (e), as a human would do.
- The B-cubed metric still assigns relatively high scores to "dummy" systems. For example, Response (e) lumps all mentions into one entity and receives a 100 % recall, while Response (f) gets 100 % precision.

4.3 Constrained Entity-Aligned F-Measure (CEAF)

B-cubed fixes several drawbacks of the MUC F-measure: responses with all singleton mentions can be evaluated without having numerical difficulty in B-cubed. However, B-cubed still exhibits unintuitive behaviors in some configuration.

For example, if all key entities are merged into one in response, the B-cubed recall is 1, even not all key entities are present and correct in response; more seriously, B-cubed's recall could be potentially unbounded if correct mentions are repeated in response. The latter means that the B-cubed score can be manipulated if one allows systems to create responses with duplicated mentions.

The root cause of unbounded B-cubed scores is that it allows a key (or response) entity to be credited multiple times against response (or key) entities. The Constrained Entity-Aligned F-Measure (CEAF) was originally proposed in [8] to solve this problem by insisting on the one-to-one entity alignment, and only entities that are aligned contribute to the final score. We cover CEAF in this section.

Entity Alignments Let

$$m = \min\{|\mathscr{K}|, |\mathscr{R}|\}$$
$$M = \max\{|\mathscr{K}|, |\mathscr{R}|\},$$

be the number of minimal and maximal number of entities, respectively, and let $\mathscr{K}_m \subset \mathscr{K}$ and $\mathscr{R}_m \subset \mathscr{R}$ be any subsets with m key and m response entities, respectively. That is, $|\mathscr{K}_m| = m$ and $|\mathscr{R}_m| = m$. Note that $\mathscr{K}_m$ and $\mathscr{R}_m$ may contain the empty set.

Let $G(\mathscr{K}_m, \mathscr{R}_m)$ be the set of one-to-one entity maps from $\mathscr{K}_m$ to $\mathscr{R}_m$, and G_m be the set of all possible one-to-one maps between the size-m subsets of $\mathscr{K}$ and $\mathscr{R}$, or

$$G(\mathscr{K}_m, \mathscr{R}_m) = \{g : \mathscr{K}_m \mapsto \mathscr{R}_m\},$$
$$G_m = \cup_{(\mathscr{K}_m, \mathscr{R}_m)} G(\mathscr{K}_m, \mathscr{R}_m),$$

where $\mathscr{K}_m \mapsto \mathscr{R}_m$ denotes one-to-one map.

The requirement of one-to-one map means that for any $g \in G(\mathcal{K}_m, \mathcal{R}_m)$, and any $R \in \mathcal{K}_m$ and $R' \in \mathcal{K}_m$, we have that $R \neq R'$ implies that $g(R) \neq g(R')$, which in turn implies that $R \neq R'$. Clearly, there are $m!$ one-to-one maps from $\mathcal{K}_m$ to $\mathcal{R}_m$ (or $|G(\mathcal{K}_m, \mathcal{R}_m)| = m!$), and $|G_m| = \binom{M}{m} m!$.

Let $\phi(K, R)$ be a measure of the similarity between a key entity K and a response entity R. Let us assume that $\phi(K, R)$ takes non-negative value: zero value means that K and R have nothing in common. For example, $\phi(K, R)$ could be the number of common mentions shared by K and R, in which case $\phi(R, R)$ simply denotes the number of mentions in entity R.

It is also assumed that the entity similarity is additive: for any $g \in G_m$, the total similarity $\Phi(g)$ for a map g is the sum of similarities between the aligned entity pairs: $\Phi(g) = \sum_{K \in \mathcal{K}_m} \phi(K, g(K))$. Given a document d, and its key entities $\mathcal{K}$ and response entities $\mathcal{R}$, we can find the "best" alignment that maximizes the total similarity:

$$
\begin{aligned}
g^* &= \arg\max_{g \in G_m} \Phi(g) \\
&= \arg\max_{g \in G_m} \sum_{K \in \mathcal{K}_m} \phi(K, g(K)).
\end{aligned}
\tag{17}
$$

Let $\mathcal{K}_m^*$ and $\mathcal{R}_m^* = g^*(\mathcal{K}_m^*)$ denote the key and response entity subsets where g^* is attained, respectively. Then the maximal total similarity is

$$
\Phi(g^*) = \sum_{K \in \mathcal{K}_m^*} \phi(K, g^*(K)). \tag{18}
$$

If we insist that $\phi(K, R) = 0$ whenever K or R is empty, then the non-negativity requirement of $\phi(K, R)$ makes it unnecessary to consider the possibility of mapping one entity to an empty entity since the one-to-one map maximizing $\Phi(g)$ must be in G_m.

Since we can compute the entity self-similarity $\phi(K, K)$ and $\phi(R, R)$ for any $K \in \mathcal{K}$ and $R \in \mathcal{R}$ (i.e., using the identity map), we are now ready to define the Constrained Entity-Aligned precision, recall, and F-measure (CEAF) as follows:

$$
r = \frac{\Phi(g^*)}{\sum_i \phi(K_i, K_i)} \tag{19}
$$

$$
p = \frac{\Phi(g^*)}{\sum_i \phi(R_i, R_i)} \tag{20}
$$

$$
F = \frac{2pr}{p + r}. \tag{21}
$$

The optimal alignment g^* involves only $m = \min\{|\mathcal{K}|, |\mathcal{R}|\}$ key and response entities, and entities not aligned do not get credit. Thus the F-measure (21) penalizes a coreference system that proposes too many (i.e., lower precision) or too few entities (i.e., lower recall), which is a desired property.

In the above discussion, it is assumed that the similarity measure $\phi(K, R)$ is computed for all entity pair (K, R). In practice, computation of $\phi(K, R)$ can be avoided if it is clear that K and R have nothing in common (e.g., if no mention in K and R overlaps, then $\phi(K, R) = 0$). These entity pairs will not be considered when searching for the optimal alignment. Consequently the optimal alignment could involve less than m key and response entities. This can speed up considerably the F-measure computation when the majority of entity pairs have zero similarity. Nevertheless, summing over m entity pairs in the general formulae (18) does not change the optimal total similarity between $\mathscr{K}$ and $\mathscr{R}$ and hence the F-measure.

In Equations (19), (20), and (21), there is only one document in the test corpus. Extension to corpus with multiple test documents is trivial: just accumulate statistics on the per-document basis for both denominators and numerators in (19) and (20), and find the ratio of the two.

So far, we have tacitly kept abstract the similarity measure $\phi(K, R)$ for entity pair K and R. We will defer the discussion of this metric to the following Subsection. Instead, we first present the algorithm computing the F-measure in Equation (21).

Optimal Alignment and F-measure From Equations (19) and (20), it is clear that the optimal alignment g^* is central to the computation of CEAF, but a naïve implementation of (17) would enumerate all the possible one-to-one maps (or alignments) between size-m (recall that $m = \min\{|\mathscr{K}|, |\mathscr{R}|\}$) subsets of $\mathscr{K}$ and size-m subsets of $\mathscr{R}$, and find the best alignment maximizing the similarity. Since this requires computing the similarities between mM entity pairs and there are $|G_m| = \binom{M}{m}m!$ possible one-to-one maps, the complexity of this implementation is $O(Mm + \binom{M}{m}m!)$. This is not satisfactory even for a document with a moderate number of entities: it will have about 3.6 million operations for $M = m = 10$, a document with only 10 key and 10 response entities.

Fortunately, the entity alignment problem under the one-to-one map constraint is the classical maximal bipartite matching problem and there exists an algorithm [7, 12] (henceforth Kuhn-Munkres Algorithm) that can find the optimal solution in polynomial time. Casting the entity alignment problem as the maximal bipartite matching is trivial: each entity in $\mathscr{K}$ and $\mathscr{R}$ is a vertex and a node pair (K, R), where $K \in \mathscr{K}, R \in \mathscr{R}$, is connected by an edge with the weight $\phi(K, R)$. Thus the problem (17) is exactly the maximal bipartite matching.

With the Kuhn-Munkres algorithm, the procedure to compute the F-measure (21) can be described as Algorithm 4.

The input to the algorithm are key entities $\mathscr{K}$ and response entities $\mathscr{R}$. The algorithm returns the best one-to-one map g^* and F-measure in equation (21). Loop from line 2–4 computes the similarity between all the possible key and response entity pairs. The complexity of this loop is $O(Mm)$. Line 5 calls the Kuhn-Munkres algorithm, which takes as input the entity-pair scores $\{\phi(K, R)\}$ and outputs the best map g^* and the corresponding total similarity $\Phi(g^*)$. The worst case (i.e., when all entries in $\{\phi(K, R)\}$ are non-zeros) complexity of the Kuhn-Algorithm

Algorithm 4 Computing the F-measure (21).

Input: key entities: $\mathscr{K}$; response entities: $\mathscr{R}$
Output: optimal alignment g^*; F-measure (21).
1:Initialize: $g^* = \emptyset$; $\Phi(g^*) = 0$.
2:**For** $i = 1$ **to** $|\mathscr{K}|$
3: **For** $j = 1$ **to** $|\mathscr{R}|$
4: **Compute** $\phi(K_i, R_j)$.
5:$[g^*, \Phi(g^*)]$=**KM**$(\{\phi(K,R) : K \in \mathscr{K}, R \in \mathscr{R}\})$.
6:$\Phi(\mathscr{K}) = \sum_{K \in \mathscr{K}} \phi(K, K)$; $\Phi(\mathscr{R}) = \sum_{R \in \mathscr{R}} \phi(R, R)$.
7:$r = \frac{\Phi(g^*)}{\Phi(\mathscr{K})}$; $p = \frac{\Phi(g^*)}{\Phi(\mathscr{R})}$; $F = \frac{2pr}{p+r}$.
8:**return** g^* and F.

is $O(Mm^2 \log m)$. Line 6 computes "self-similarity" $\Phi(\mathscr{K})$ and $\Phi(\mathscr{R})$ needed in the F-measure computation at Line 7.

The core of the F-measure computation is the Kuhn-Munkres algorithm at line 5. The algorithm is initially discovered by [7] and [12] to solve the matching (a.k.a assignment) problem for square matrices. Since then, it has been extended to rectangular matrices [4] and parallelized [3]. A recent review can be found in [6], which also details the techniques of fast implementation. A sketch of the algorithm can also be found in the appendix of [8].

Entity Similarity Metric We still need a concrete way to measure the similarity between a key entity K and a response entity R. In [8], Luo proposes two ways: one is to count how many common mentions K and R share (or if partial credit is allowed, a real number reflecting the similarity between the 2 sets of mentions); the other is the F-measure between the two entities[3]:

$$\phi_3(K, R) = |K \cap R| \tag{22}$$

$$\phi_4(K, R) = \frac{2|K \cap R|}{|K| + |R|}. \tag{23}$$

If $\phi_3(\cdot, \cdot)$ is adopted in Algorithm 4, $\Phi(g^*)$ is the number of total common mentions corresponding to the best one-to-one map g^* while the denominators of (19) and (20) are the number of key mentions and the number of response mentions, respectively. The F-measure in (21) can be interpreted as the ratio of mentions that are in the "right" entities. Similarly, if $\phi_4(\cdot, \cdot)$ is adopted in Algorithm 4, the denominators of (20) and (19) are the number of proposed entities and the number of response entities, respectively, and the F-measure in (21) can be understood as the ratio of correct entities. Therefore, (21) is called mention-based CEAF ($CEAF_m$ henceforth) and entity-based CEAF ($CEAF_e$ henceforth) when (22) and (23) are used, respectively.

[3]We use the same symbols $\phi_3(\cdot)$ and $\phi_4(\cdot)$ as in [8].

$\phi_3(\cdot,\cdot)$ and $\phi_4(\cdot,\cdot)$ are two reasonable entity similarity measures, but by no means the only choices. At mention level, partial credit could be assigned to two mentions with different but overlapping spans; or when mention type is available, weights defined on the type confusion matrix can be incorporated. At entity level, entity attributes, if available, can be weighted in the similarity measure as well.

The procedure of computing CEAF does not make any assumption about key and response mentions being identical: it works for both golden mentions and system mentions.

Illustrating Examples We illustrate how $CEAF_m$ and $CEAF_e$ are calculated with response (d) in Fig. 1.

First, we establish the optimal entity alignment. For both flavors of CEAF, the optimal alignment is:

$$\{1,2,3,4,5\} \leftrightarrow \{1,2,3,4,5\},$$
$$\{6,7\} \leftrightarrow \{6,D\},$$
$$\{8,9,A,B,C\} \leftrightarrow \{8,9,A,B,C\}.$$

The 3 pairs of aligned entities have 5, 1, 5 common mentions, respectively. Thus the $CEAF_m$ recall is $\frac{11}{12}$, precision is $\frac{11}{12}$, and $CEAF_m$ F-measure is $\frac{11}{12}$. The 3 aligned pairs' local F-measures are: 1, $\frac{1}{2}$, 1, respectively, thus the $CEAF_e$ recall is $\frac{1\frac{1}{2}+1}{3} = \frac{5}{6}$; the precision is also $\frac{5}{6}$; and $CEAF_e$ F-measure is $\frac{5}{6}$ as well.

Response (f) is an extreme in that all mentions are singletons. So one optimal entity alignment (the optimal alignment is clearly not unique in this case) is: $\{1,2,3,4,5\} \leftrightarrow \{1\}$, $\{6,7\} \leftrightarrow \{6\}$, $\{8,9,A,B,C\} \leftrightarrow \{8\}$. $CEAF_m$ recall, precision and F-measure are all $\frac{3}{12} = \frac{1}{4}$. For $CEAF_e$, 3 aligned entities' local F-measures are $\frac{2}{6} = \frac{1}{3}$, $\frac{2}{3}$, $\frac{1}{3}$, respectively. Thus $CEAF_e$ recall is $\frac{\frac{1}{3}+\frac{2}{3}+\frac{1}{3}}{3} = \frac{4}{9}$; precision is $\frac{\frac{1}{3}+\frac{2}{3}+\frac{1}{3}}{12} = \frac{1}{9}$; and F-measure is $\frac{8}{45}$.

Calculating $CEAF_m$ and $CEAF_e$ for other responses can be done in a similar fashion, hence we only tabulate the results in Table 1.

4.4 BLANC

The MUC F-measure considers only links within entities, while links across entities do not participate explicitly in calculating the metric. This leads to its difficulty of evaluating single-mention entities. BLANC, which stands for "BiLateral Assessment of Noun-phrase Coreference", solves the problem by considering both within-entity and cross-entity links. BLANC was initially proposed in [19] with the assumption that response mentions are identical to key mentions. This means that the metric is not applicable when response mentions are generated by machine, which is almost always the case in practice. The restriction was lifted in [9] where the authors extended BLANC to imperfect response mentions. Since the extended BLANC subsumes the original one, we will present it in this section.

Link Notations BLANC is defined on links formed by within-entity mentions and cross-entity mentions, and we will need a few extra notations.

Let $C_k(i)$ and $C_r(j)$ be the set of *coreference* links formed by mentions in K_i and R_j:

$$C_k(i) = \{(m_1, m_2) : m_1 \in K_i, m_2 \in K_i, m_1 \neq m_2\}$$
$$C_r(j) = \{(m_1, m_2) : m_1 \in R_j, m_2 \in R_j, m_1 \neq m_2\}$$

As can be seen, a link is an undirected edge between two mentions, and it can be equivalently represented by a pair of mentions. Note that when an entity consists of a single mention, its coreference link set is empty.

Let $N_k(i,j)$ $(i \neq j)$ be key *non-coreference* links formed between mentions in k_i and those in k_j, and let $N_r(i,j)$ $(i \neq j)$ be response *non-coreference* links formed between mentions in r_i and those in R_j, respectively:

$$N_k(i,j) = \{(m_1, m_2) : m_1 \in K_i, m_2 \in K_j\}$$
$$N_r(i,j) = \{(m_1, m_2) : m_1 \in R_i, m_2 \in R_j\}$$

Note that the non-coreference link set is empty when all mentions are in the same entity.

We use the same letter and subscription without the index in parentheses to denote the union of sets, e.g.,

$$C_k = \cup_i C_k(i), \quad N_k = \cup_{i \neq j} N_k(i,j)$$
$$C_r = \cup_j C_r(j), \quad N_r = \cup_{i \neq j} N_r(i,j)$$

We use $T_k = C_k \cup N_k$ and $T_r = C_r \cup N_r$ to denote the total set of key links and total set of response links, respectively. Clearly, C_k and N_k form a partition of T_k since $C_k \cap N_k = \emptyset$, $T_k = C_k \cup N_k$. Likewise, C_r and N_r form a partition of T_r.

We say that a key link $l_1 \in T_k$ equals a response link $l_2 \in T_r$ if and only if the pair of mentions from which the links are formed are identical. We write $l_1 = l_2$ if two links are equal. It is easy to see that the gold mention assumption—same set of response mentions as the set of key mentions—can be equivalently stated as $T_k = T_r$ (this does not necessarily mean that $C_k = C_r$ or $N_k = N_r$).

RAND Index and BLANC for Gold Mentions BLANC is adapted from the Rand Index [18], a metric for clustering objects. The Rand Index is defined as the ratio between the number of correct within-cluster links plus the number of correct cross-cluster links, and the total number of links.

When $T_k = T_r$, the Rand Index can be applied directly since coreference resolution reduces to a clustering problem where mentions are partitioned into clusters (entities):

$$\text{Rand Index} = \frac{|C_k \cap C_r| + |N_k \cap N_r|}{\frac{1}{2}\big(|T_k|(|T_k| - 1)\big)} \tag{24}$$

In practice, though, the simple-minded adoption of the Rand Index is not satisfactory since the number of non-coreference links often overwhelms that of coreference links [19], or, $|N_k| \gg |C_k|$ and $|N_r| \gg |C_r|$. The Rand Index, if used without modification, would not be sensitive to changes of coreference links.

BLANC solves this problem by averaging the F-measure computed over coreference links and the F-measure over non-coreference links. Using the notations in Sect. 2, the recall, precision, and F-measure on coreference links are:

$$R_c^{(g)} = \frac{|C_k \cap C_r|}{|C_k \cap C_r| + |C_k \cap N_r|} \tag{25}$$

$$P_c^{(g)} = \frac{|C_k \cap C_r|}{|C_r \cap C_k| + |C_r \cap N_k|} \tag{26}$$

$$F_c^{(g)} = \frac{2R_c^{(g)}P_c^{(g)}}{R_c^{(g)} + P_c^{(g)}}; \tag{27}$$

Similarly, the recall, precision, and F-measure on non-coreference links are computed as:

$$R_n^{(g)} = \frac{|N_k \cap N_r|}{|N_k \cap C_r| + |N_k \cap N_r|} \tag{28}$$

$$P_n^{(g)} = \frac{|N_k \cap N_r|}{|N_r \cap C_k| + |N_r \cap N_k|} \tag{29}$$

$$F_n^{(g)} = \frac{2R_n^{(g)}P_n^{(g)}}{R_n^{(g)} + P_n^{(g)}}. \tag{30}$$

Finally, the BLANC metric is the arithmetic average of $F_c^{(g)}$ and $F_n^{(g)}$:

$$\text{BLANC}^{(g)} = \frac{F_c^{(g)} + F_n^{(g)}}{2}. \tag{31}$$

Superscript ^{g} in these equations highlights the fact that they are meant for coreference systems with gold mentions.

Equation (31) indicates that BLANC assigns equal weight to $F_c^{(g)}$, the F-measure from coreference links, and $F_n^{(g)}$, the F-measure from non-coreference links. This avoids the problem that $|N_k| \gg |C_k|$ and $|N_r| \gg |C_r|$, should the original Rand Index be used.

BLANC Metric for Imperfect Response Mentions When response mentions are not identical to key mentions, a key coreference link may not appear in either C_r or N_r, so Equations (25), (26), (27), (28), (29), and (30) cannot be applied directly to systems with imperfect mentions. For instance, if the key entities are `{a,b,c}` `{d,e}`; and the response entities are `{b,c}` `{e,f,g}`, then the key coreference link `(a,b)` is not seen on the response side; similarly, it is possible that a response link does not appear on the key side either: `(c,f)` and `(f,g)` are not in the key in the above example.

To account for missing or spurious links, we observe that

- $C_k \setminus T_r$ are key coreference links missing in the response;
- $N_k \setminus T_r$ are key non-coreference links missing in the response;
- $C_r \setminus T_k$ are response coreference links missing in the key;
- $N_r \setminus T_k$ are response non-coreference links missing in the key.

The coreference F-measure and non-coreference F-measure can be extended as follows. Coreference recall, precision and F-measure are adapted as:

$$R_c = \frac{|C_k \cap C_r|}{|C_k \cap C_r| + |C_k \cap N_r| + |C_k \setminus T_r|} \tag{32}$$

$$P_c = \frac{|C_k \cap C_r|}{|C_r \cap C_k| + |C_r \cap N_k| + |C_r \setminus T_k|} \tag{33}$$

$$F_c = \frac{2R_c P_c}{R_c + P_c} \tag{34}$$

Non-coreference recall, precision and F-measure are as follows:

$$R_n = \frac{|N_k \cap N_r|}{|N_k \cap C_r| + |N_k \cap N_r| + |N_k \setminus T_r|} \tag{35}$$

$$P_n = \frac{|N_k \cap N_r|}{|N_r \cap C_k| + |N_r \cap N_k| + |N_r \setminus T_k|} \tag{36}$$

$$F_n = \frac{2R_n P_n}{R_n + P_n}. \tag{37}$$

The extended BLANC continues to be the arithmetic average of F_c and F_n:

$$\text{BLANC} = \frac{F_c + F_n}{2}. \tag{38}$$

We observe that the definition of the extended BLANC, Equations (32), (33), (34), (35), (36), and (37) subsume the BLANC-gold (25), (26), (27), (28), (29), and (30) due to the following proposition: If $T_k = T_r$, then $BLANC = BLANC^{(g)}$.

Proof We only need to show that $R_c = R_c^{(g)}$, $P_c = P_c^{(g)}$, $R_n = R_n^{(g)}$, and $P_n = P_n^{(g)}$. We prove the first one (the other proofs are similar and elided due to space limitations). Since $T_k = T_r$ and $C_k \subset T_k$, we have $C_k \subset T_r$; thus $C_k \setminus T_r = \emptyset$, and $|C_k \cap T_r| = 0$. This establishes that $R_c = R_c^{(g)}$.

Indeed, since C_k is a union of three disjoint subsets: $C_k = (C_k \cap C_r) \cup (C_k \cap N_r) \cup (C_k \setminus T_r)$, $R_c^{(g)}$ and R_c can be unified as $\frac{|C_k \cap C_r|}{|C_K|}$. Unification for other component recalls and precisions can be done similarly. So the final definition of BLANC can be succinctly stated as:

$$R_c = \frac{|C_k \cap C_r|}{|C_k|}, \quad P_c = \frac{|C_k \cap C_r|}{|C_r|} \tag{39}$$

$$R_n = \frac{|N_k \cap N_r|}{|N_k|}, \quad P_n = \frac{|N_k \cap N_r|}{|N_r|} \tag{40}$$

$$F_c = \frac{2|C_k \cap C_r|}{|C_k| + |C_r|}, \quad F_n = \frac{2|N_k \cap N_r|}{|N_k| + |N_r|} \tag{41}$$

$$\text{BLANC} = \frac{F_c + F_n}{2} \tag{42}$$

Boundary Cases Care has to be taken when counts in the BLANC definition are 0. This can happen when all key (or response) mentions are in one cluster or are all singletons: the former case will lead to $N_k = \emptyset$ (or, $N_r = \emptyset$); the latter will lead to $C_k = \emptyset$ (or $C_r = \emptyset$). Observe that as long as $|C_k| + |C_r| > 0$, F_c in (41) is well-defined; as long as $|N_k| + |N_r| > 0$, F_n in (41) is well-defined.

So we only need to augment the BLANC definition for the following cases:

(1) If $C_k = C_r = \emptyset$ and $N_k = N_r = \emptyset$, then BLANC $= I(\mathcal{M}_k = \mathcal{M}_r)$, where $I(\cdot)$ is an indicator function whose value is 1 if its argument is true, and 0 otherwise. $\mathcal{M}_k$ and $\mathcal{M}_r$ are the key and response mention set. This can happen when a document has no more than one mention and there is no link.
(2) If $C_k = C_r = \emptyset$ and $|N_k| + |N_r| > 0$, then BLANC $= F_n$. This is the case where the key and response side has only entities consisting of singleton mentions. Since there is no coreference link, BLANC reduces to the non-coreference F-measure F_n.
(3) If $N_k = N_r = \emptyset$ and $|C_k| + |C_r| > 0$, then BLANC $= F_c$. This is the case where all mentions in the key and response are in one entity. Since there is no non-coreference link, BLANC reduces to the coreference F-measure F_c.

Illustrating Examples We walk through a few extra examples and show how BLANC is calculated in detail. In all the examples below, each lower-case letter represents a mention; mentions in an entity are closed in {}; two letters in () represent a link. These examples are small, so they are easy to verify manually. For examples in Fig. 1, we include their BLANC scores in Table 1, which are represented in decimal numbers to avoid large denominators if fraction numbers are used.

Example 1 Key entities are $\{abc\}$ and $\{d\}$; response entities are $\{bc\}$ and $\{de\}$. Obviously,

$C_k = \{(ab), (bc), (ac)\}$;
$N_k = \{(ad), (bd), (cd)\}$;
$C_r = \{(bc), (de)\}$;
$N_r = \{(bd), (be), (cd), (ce)\}$.

Therefore, $C_k \cap C_r = \{(bc)\}, N_k \cap N_r = \{(bd), (cd)\}$, and $R_c = \frac{1}{3}, P_c = \frac{1}{2}, F_c = \frac{2}{5}$; $R_n = \frac{2}{3}, P_n = \frac{2}{4}, F_n = \frac{4}{7}$. Finally, BLANC $= \frac{17}{35}$.

Example 2 Key entity is $\{a\}$; response entity is $\{b\}$. This is boundary case (1): BLANC $= 0$.

Example 3 Key entities are $\{a\}\{b\}\{c\}$; response entities are $\{a\}\{b\}\{d\}$. This is boundary case (2): there are no coreference links. Since

$N_k = \{(ab), (bc), (ca)\}$,
$N_r = \{(ab), (bd), (ad)\}$,
we have
$N_k \cap N_r = \{(ab)\}$, and $R_n = \frac{1}{3}, P_n = \frac{1}{3}$. So BLANC $= F_n = \frac{1}{3}$.

Example 4 Key entity is $\{abc\}$; response entity is $\{bc\}$. This is boundary case (3): there are no non-coreference links. Since

$C_k = \{(ab), (bc), (ca)\}$, and $C_r = \{(bc)\}$,
we have
$C_k \cap C_r = \{(bc)\}$, and $R_c = \frac{1}{3}, P_c = 1$,
So BLANC $= F_c = \frac{2}{4} = \frac{1}{2}$.

5 Conclusion

In this chapter, we reviewed four major coreference evaluation metrics commonly used in the research community: MUC, B-cubed, CEAF, and BLANC. We discussed the merits and drawbacks of these metrics. We covered the latest advances in these metrics, for instance, the extension of the original BLANC to system mentions [9]. In addition, we have clarified misunderstandings about the metrics in recent literature and their use in scoring system mentions as opposed to gold mentions. We have documented the mathematical formula used to calculate the metrics and presented them using a uniform set of notations and concrete examples.

Furthermore, the four metrics have been implemented as open-source software freely available to research community [16] along with a suite of test cases. The issues related to the misunderstanding and incorrect use of these metrics for scoring predicted mentions affected three coreference evaluations—SemEval-2010, CoNLL-2011 and CoNLL-2012. Chapter "Evaluation Campaigns" goes over various aspects of designing and conducting such evaluations and the organizers of these evaluations have retrospectively revised the scores for the original submissions using the revised, reference implementation mentioned above.

While we have made significant progresses in coreference evaluation, the problem is still under active research, and we anticipate further improvements of existing metrics and possibly new metrics.

References

1. Amigó, E., Gonzalo, J., Artiles, J., Verdejo, F.: A comparison of extrinsic clustering evaluation metrics based on formal constraints. Inf. Retr. J. (2008). http://link.springer.com/journal/10791
2. Bagga, A., Baldwin, B.: Algorithms for scoring coreference chains. In: Proceedings of the Linguistic Coreference Workshop at The First International Conference on Language Resources and Evaluation (LREC'98), Granada, pp. 563–566 (1998)
3. Balas, E., Miller, D., Pekny, J., Toth, P.: A parallel shortest augmenting path algorithm for the assignment problem. J. ACM (JACM) **38**(4), 985–1007 (1991)
4. Bourgeois, F., Lassalle, J.C.: An extension of the Munkres algorithm for the assignment problem to rectangular matrices. Commun. ACM **14**(12), 802–804 (1971)
5. Cai, J., Strube, M.: Evaluation metrics for end-to-end coreference resolution systems. In: Proceedings of SIGDIAL, Tokyo, pp. 28–36 (2010)
6. Gupta, A., Ying, L.: Algorithms for finding maximum matchings in bipartite graphs. Technical report, RC 21576 (97320), IBM T.J. Watson Research Center (1999)
7. Kuhn, H.: The Hungarian method for the assignment problem. Nav. Res. Logist. Q. **2**(83), 83–97 (1955)
8. Luo, X.: On coreference resolution performance metrics. In: Proceedings of Human Language Technology (HLT)/Empirical Methods in Natural Language Processing (EMNLP), Vancouver (2005)
9. Luo, X., Pradhan, S., Recasens, M., Hovy, E.: An extension of BLANC to system mentions. In: Proceedings of the 52nd Annual Meeting of the Association for Computational Linguistics, vol. 2, Short Papers, pp. 24–29. Association for Computational Linguistics, Baltimore (2014). http://www.aclweb.org/anthology/P14-2005
10. MUC-6: Proceedings of the Sixth Message Understanding Conference(MUC-6). Morgan Kaufmann, San Francisco (1995)
11. MUC-7: Proceedings of the Seventh Message Understanding Conference(MUC-7), Fairfax (1998)
12. Munkres, J.: Algorithms for the assignment and transportation problems. J. SIAM **5**, 32–38 (1957)
13. NIST: The ACE evaluation plan. www.nist.gov/speech/tests/ace/index.htm (2003)
14. NIST: ACE 2005 evaluation. www.nist.gov/speech/tests/ace/ace05/index.htm (2005)
15. NIST: ACE 2008 evaluation. http://www.itl.nist.gov/iad/mig//tests/ace/2008 (2008)
16. Pradhan, S., Luo, X., Recasens, M., Hovy, E., Ng, V., Strube, M.: Scoring coreference partitions of predicted mentions: a reference implementation. In: Proceedings of the 52nd Annual Meeting of the Association for Computational Linguistics, vol. 2, Short Papers, pp. 30–35. Association for Computational Linguistics, Baltimore (2014). http://www.aclweb.org/anthology/P14-2006
17. Rahman, A., Ng, V.: Supervised models for coreference resolution. In: Proceedings of the 2009 Conference on Empirical Methods in Natural Language Processing, pp. 968–977. Association for Computational Linguistics, Singapore (2009). http://www.aclweb.org/anthology/D/D09/D09-1101
18. Rand, W.M.: Objective criteria for the evaluation of clustering methods. J. Am. Stat. Assoc. **66**(336), 846–850 (1971)
19. Recasens, M., Hovy, E.: BLANC: implementing the Rand index for coreference evaluation. Nat. Lang. Eng. **17**, 485–510 (2011). doi:10.1017/S135132491000029X. http://journals.cambridge.org/article_S135132491000029X

20. Stoyanov, V., Gilbert, N., Cardie, C., Riloff, E.: Conundrums in noun phrase coreference resolution: making sense of the state-of-the-art. In: Proceedings of the Joint Conference of the 47th Annual Meeting of the ACL and the 4th International Joint Conference on Natural Language Processing of the AFNLP, ACL'09, vol. 2, pp. 656–664. Association for Computational Linguistics, Stroudsburg (2009). http://dl.acm.org/citation.cfm?id=1690219.1690238
21. Vilain, M., Burger, J., Aberdeen, J., Connolly, D., Hirschman, L.: A model-theoretic coreference scoring scheme. In: Proceedings of MUC6, Columbia, pp. 45–52 (1995)

Evaluation Campaigns

Marta Recasens and Sameer Pradhan

Abstract In this chapter, we overview the major efforts in evaluation campaigns (shared tasks) for coreference resolution, where multiple participants are given the same datasets and annotations, and are evaluated on the same test set and using the same scoring software, thus making it possible to compare the different participating systems. More specifically, we overview the Message Understanding Conference (MUC), the Automatic Content Extraction program (ACE), the SemEval-2010 Task 1, the i2b2-2011 shared task, and the CoNLL-2011 and 2012 shared tasks. We discuss the critical issues behind the practice of coreference resolution evaluation, such as the range of mentions defined in the annotation guidelines, the use of gold vs. predicted mentions, the layers of preprocessing information that are provided, and the multiple coreference evaluation measures.

Keywords Evaluation campaigns Linguistic resources • Shared tasks • Linguistically annotated corpora

1 Introduction

The difficulty of evaluating the performance of coreference resolution systems is well illustrated by the evaluation campaigns that have been undertaken in the past two decades, from MUC-6 in 1995 to the CoNLL shared task in 2012. Despite close to a two-decade history of evaluations on coreference tasks, variation in their evaluation criteria and training data have made it difficult for researchers to have a clear idea about the state of the art or to determine which particular areas require further attention. There are many different parameters involved in defining a coreference task. Looking at the numbers reported in the literature can greatly affect the perceived difficulty of the task. It may seem like a very hard problem [89] or a

M. Recasens (✉)
Google Inc., Mountain Vew, CA, USA
e-mail: recasens@google.com

S. Pradhan
Boulder Learning, Inc., Boulder, CO, USA
e-mail: pradhan@boulderlearning.com; pradhan@cemantix.org

M. Poesio et al. (eds.), *Anaphora Resolution*, Theory and Applications of Natural Language Processing, DOI 10.1007/978-3-662-47909-4_6

relatively easy one [23]. Limitations in the size and scope of the available datasets have also constrained the progress of research. The MUC and ACE corpora are the most widely used datasets for reporting comparative results, but they differ in the entity types and coreference relations that are annotated. Furthermore, the ACE corpus evolved over a period of almost five years, with different incarnations of the task definition, and performance numbers being reported on different cross-sections, making it hard to disentangle and interpret the results.

The benefits and drawbacks of the different evaluation measures discussed in chapter "Evaluation Metrics" become apparent when the measures are put to practice in evaluation scenarios that vary in terms of dataset (and so annotation scheme) and task definition [92]. Critical issues include the use of gold or predicted mentions, the accuracy of morphological and parsing preprocessing tools in the correctness/stringency of predicted mention spans, the definition/scope of coreference in terms of the range of named entities, the inclusion or exclusion of singletons, which noun phrases are considered to be non-referential, the limitation to entity coreference or the inclusion of event coreference, the availability of gold information for some layers, and the restricted or unrestricted use of external resources.

A large number of possible setting combinations result from crossing these several dimensions, and the evaluation measures behave differently depending on the setting, sometimes with contradictory results [75]. As a result, it has been—and still is—hard to assess a system's 'true' performance as well as to compare systems. In order to illustrate the wide range of factors that come into play in the practice of coreference evaluation and how they influence the scores of the measures, this chapter covers the main evaluation campaigns that have been carried out in the field of coreference resolution: MUC-6 [38], MUC-7 [21], the multiple ACE programs [28], SemEval-2010 Task 1 [78], the i2b2-2011 shared task [96], and the CoNLL-2011 and 2012 shared tasks [72, 73]. The discussion reveals the lack of consistent reporting in the earlier years, and therefore the lack of availability of gold standards for various standard evaluation settings, and the lack of a generally accepted standard measure for coreference resolution evaluation. Both of these issues have been addressed by the more recent evaluations, which set out to establish a reliable benchmark.

2 The Coreference Resolution Task

Although the implementation details of key concepts of the task differ across the evaluation campaigns (as we discuss in the following subsections), the core definition of the coreference resolution task that is kept constant states that, given a test set, participating systems are required to automatically detect the coreference relations in a text. Namely, the mentions in the text that refer to the same entity, as defined in the annotation guidelines. For instance, for the text in (1), a system should output that *Major League Baseball*, *its* and *the league* are coreferent, etc.

(1) [Major League Baseball] sent [its] head of security to Chicago to review the second incident of an on-field fan attack in the last 7 months. [The league] is reviewing security at all ballparks to crack down on spectator violence.

The major disagreements between evaluation campaigns revolve around what a *mention* is and which mentions corefer, whether mentions are provided or automatically detected, what kind of preprocessing information systems are given or allowed to use, what languages are targeted, and what evaluation measure is used to assess the performance of the participating systems. This section provides an overview of each of these dimensions, and the next section goes into the details of each evaluation campaign.

2.1 Range of Mentions

In coreference resolution, a **mention** is defined as each of the units in a text referring to an entity. It is a term closely related to a *referring expression* in linguistics. In (1), the units *Major League Baseball* and *its head of security* are two examples of mentions. An entity can be referred to multiple times throughout a text—in which case we talk of **coreferent mentions**—or just once—in which case we talk of a **singleton mention** or a **singleton**. The set of mentions in a text largely overlaps with the set of NPs, but not all NPs are referential (e.g., expletive pronouns) and mentions can be syntactic units other than NPs (e.g., verbs). Just as coding schemes disagree in the definition of mention or markable (chapter "Annotated Corpora and Annotation Tools"), evaluation campaigns differ in the range of mentions they include, depending on the dataset they use.

On the one hand, the mention definitions of MUC and ACE were determined by the needs of the actual campaign, as the corpora were specifically developed to serve as training and test data for the respective evaluations. On the other hand, the datasets that were used in the SemEval and CoNLL shared tasks came from already existing corpora that had been annotated following more general linguistic criteria: CoNLL used the OntoNotes corpus [99], and SemEval included data from AnCora [79], OntoNotes [99], COREA [42], LiveMemories [81], and Tüba/DZ [44].

The task-oriented nature of ACE is especially evidenced by the fact that it only contains coreference annotations for NPs headed by named entities of seven semantic types: facilities, geopolitical entities, locations, organizations, persons, vehicles, and weapons.[1] These are the types that the ACE program considered to be the most relevant. In contrast, the other tasks make no distinction with respect to semantic types.

This semantic distinction aside, the four campaigns treat as a mention any NP—whether pronominal or headed by a common or pronoun noun—that is

[1]The first ACE editions focused on five classes, and later editions added vehicles and weapons.

referential. However, they differ in two major respects: whether singletons are or not annotated (see Sect. 2.1), and what NPs fall into the non-referential category, the largest disagreement concerning nominal predicates and appositive constructions (see Sect. 2.1). Additionally, the CoNLL shared task goes beyond NPs and includes verbal mentions as well (see later section on the CoNLL shared task).

Although there are a few other aspects in which the annotation schemes differ, such as the annotation of coordinated NPs, we limit our discussion to those issues that play a key role in characterizing the different evaluation campaigns. Chapter "Annotated Corpora and Annotation Tools" provides a detailed description of the syntactic and semantic factors involved in defining a markable. In fact, although some of the original corpora upon which the SemEval and CoNLL datasets built upon are annotated at a fine level of linguistic detail, the SemEval and CoNLL datasets simplified many of these aspects. The CoNLL dataset, for example, removed disfluencies and subtoken mentions (i.e., mentions that span only a part of a token), and used manual transcriptions of the conversational data as well as correct segmentation for Chinese and Arabic, including gold lemmas.

Singletons As per the above definition, **singletons** are entities that are referred to one single time in the text. A mention is a singleton if it does not corefer with any other mention in the text. Assuming that the text in (1) is complete, then singleton mentions include *its head of security*, *Chicago*, and so on. While the MUC and CoNLL datasets did not include singletons, i.e., they only annotated mentions of entities that are mentioned more than once, the ACE and SemEval datasets did include them.[2]

Given that singletons represent between 60 % and 70 % of all entities (see the SINGLETONS baseline in Sect. 3.3), this difference is not negligible. Whether singletons are or not included impacts the behavior of the evaluation measures—the larger the number of singletons, the higher B^3 and CEAF-ϕ_3 scores (see Sect. 2.5)—as well as the way systems approach the mention detection step. Some systems start by running a discourse-new detector to select only the mentions that are coreferent and so need to be clustered, ignoring the rest of mentions; while other systems treat all mentions as potentially coreferent.

On the other hand, if the task does not include singletons, there is a large difference in performance scores depending on whether mention detection is given or automatic (see Sect. 2.2): if systems are expected to detect mentions automatically, then singletons are often filtered out in a postprocessing step, whereas if the provided mentions are only those that need to be clustered into coreference classes, then the task becomes significantly easier and higher scores are thus to be expected.

[2]Although OntoNotes was not originally annotated with singletons, they were identified heuristically and added in the dataset used in SemEval so as to make the different datasets as similar as possible. A few non-referential NPs that could not be automatically detected (e.g., expletive pronouns) were unavoidably annotated as singletons in this process. In the Dutch dataset, only singletons for named entities are annotated.

The set of singletons can include both referential and non-referential mentions, or only the former. Since the starting point of most coreference resolution systems is to take all NPs as possible mentions, the distinction between referential and non-referential mentions at the singleton level only matters depending on the annotation scheme. For example, the Spanish data at SemEval (from the AnCora corpus) only includes referential singletons, but the English data at CoNLL (from OntoNotes) does not include any singleton, thus making the referential/non-referential distinction for singletons irrelevant in practice [77]. The topic of non-referentiality is discussed in the next section.

Singletons are one of the factors that interrelate with several aspects of the coreference task, requiring systems to be tuned accordingly, and account for major differences between the scores of different evaluation campaigns, making it impossible to compare system results across different evaluation parameters.

Non-Referential NPs A focal point of disagreement over the NP–mention intersection (namely, which NPs are referential mentions) concerns nominal predicates and appositive phrases on the one hand, and embedded NPs in premodifier position on the other hand.

Nominal Predicates and Appositive Phrases Since NPs in nominal predicates (2), also known as *copula constructions*, and appositive phrases (3) function as predicates rather than as referential arguments, the MUC coding scheme, and the MUC evaluation campaign by extension, have been criticized for including them in the mention set [25].

(2) Moscow is [the capital of Russia].

(3) Barbie, [the plastic princess], doesn't look the same way she used to.

Following MUC, we would get that in (4), *sales director of Sudsy Soaps* and *president of Dreamy Detergents* corefer.

(4) Henry Higgins, who was formerly [sales director of Sudsy Soaps], became [president of Dreamy Detergents].

ACE adopted the same practice as MUC, but the most recent evaluation campaigns, SemEval and CoNLL, reversed the trend by not considering nominal predicates and appositive NPs as referential mentions.

The implications of this for performance scores—and thus for the comparability across tasks—is that the MUC and ACE task definitions make it easier for systems to obtain higher scores regardless of whether their coreference resolution module is better or not. This is so for two reasons. First, these constructions occur frequently in any domain. Second, the subjects and complements of copular verbs, as well as appositives, can be detected automatically with relative ease based on a state-of-the-art parser, or straightforward from gold syntactic annotations.

Nominal Premodifiers The other major area of disagreement between annotation schemes are nominal premodifiers (5).

(5) A fire in a Bangladeshi [garment] factory has left at least 37 people dead.

The options are multiple here. The MUC dataset includes nominal premodifiers if they are coreferent with an NP that is not a modifier. Thus, *drug* is marked in (6-a), but *contract drilling* is not in (6-b).

(6) a. He was accused of money laundering and [drug] trafficking. However, the trade in [drugs] ...
b. Ocean Drilling and Exploration Co. will sell its contract drilling business. ... Ocean Drilling said it will offer 15–20 % of the contract drilling business through an initial public offering in the near future.

ACE annotates nominal premodifiers, including demonyms, as long as they fall into one of the NE types that are the focus of the task (see Sect. 3.2). Thus, neither *drug* nor *contract drilling* would be annotated under ACE. The general SemEval premise was that only referential NPs were annotated as mentions, thus theoretically excluding non-referential premodifiers in Germanic languages and bare postmodifiers in Romance languages (e.g., *sistema de [educación]* '[education] system'). However, although an effort was made to make the datasets of the different languages as consistent as possible, it was not feasible to manually revise all the annotations that failed to meet this criterion. As a result, they still show differences. The SemEval effort is a good example of the difficulty in achieving consistency between different coreference annotation schemes.

Finally, CoNLL used the OntoNotes dataset as it had been originally annotated. The decision taken in OntoNotes regarding nominal premodifiers was to only annotate proper nouns, thus *Army Corps* is annotated in (7-a), but *wheat* in *wheat fields* is not in (7-b).

(7) a. But the Army Corps of Engineers expects the river level to continue falling this month. "The flow of the Missouri River is slowed," an [Army Corps] spokesman said.
b. Wheat is an important part of the economy in the Midwest. In Kansas, [wheat fields] stretch as far as the eye can see.

Again, the consequence of these different decisions for evaluation campaigns is the variation in performance scores that is not the product of better or worse coreference resolution modules, but of the range of mentions that is present in the gold standard [75]. As we have pointed out, the gold dictates a system's approach to both mention detection (if automatic) and coreference resolution. Clearly, coreference resolution is easier or harder depending on the range of mentions that are included in the mention set.

Non-NP Mentions: Events So far we have mostly talked of mentions as a subset of the NPs in a text. However, we can make reference to objects other than entities, such as events or states of affairs, and these can be referred to with nouns or verbs (8).

(8) Sales of passenger cars [grew] 22 %. [The strong growth] followed year-to-year increases.

Although the majority of evaluation campaigns (namely, MUC, ACE and SemEval[3]) avoided this complexity by restricting the coreference task to entities (i.e., NPs), the CoNLL shared tasks defined their task as "unrestricted coreference" to highlight the fact that they included **verbal mentions** in addition to nominal mentions. For convenience, only the verbal head is marked, but it is intended to represent the VP. This avoids a common source of inter-annotator disagreement. Previous annotation efforts addressing abstract objects have reported high levels of inter-annotator disagreement in delimiting the span of non-NP mentions, since it is not always clear whether the verb, the clause or a larger discourse segment needs to be marked.

It turned out that most of the systems that participated in CoNLL chose to completely ignore verbs and focus exclusively on NPs, since only about 9 % of the mentions were verbs and detecting these would have added an additional layer of complexity. This aside, the fact that the CoNLL shared task, unlike the other campaigns, decided to include events is a factor to keep in mind when analyzing the CoNLL scores and another reason not to establish direct comparisons across campaigns.

2.2 Mention Detection

Apart from the range of mention types that are targeted, different campaigns also differ in the way participants are required to detect mentions. The options are evaluating either on **gold mentions** (i.e., systems are provided with the mentions manually annotated in the gold standard) or on **predicted** or **system mentions** (i.e., the mentions annotated in the gold standard need to be automatically detected by the systems, in addition to solving coreference links). The former lets systems focus on the coreference resolution step, and evaluation scores do not mix the quality of the coreference resolution algorithm with the quality of the preprocessing modules (e.g., detecting the exact boundaries of mentions, selecting the correct mentions types); however, the latter is closer to real scenarios where only an end-to-end system that first detects the mentions will be able to solve the coreference links [92].

In the gold scenario, corpora that do not include singletons make it much easier for systems to achieve high scores, as the coreference task comes down to classifying (or clustering) each mention into the right entity, the singleton class not

[3]Some of the original corpora from which the SemEval datasets were extracted contain coreference annotations for non-NP mentions, but verbal mentions were removed to keep the evaluation campaign simpler.

being an option.[4] On the other hand, if singletons are included, systems have to deal with the fact that the majority of mentions are singletons. There has been a fruitful line of research on anaphoricity and discourse-new classifiers [26, 62, 69]. The advantage of working on gold mentions is that each mention in the system output has its counterpart in the gold.

In contrast, in a system mention scenario, the difficulty of automatically detecting mentions varies according to the way coreference is annotated in the gold (see Sect. 2.1), from detecting a specific set of NE types to detecting the correct NP parses. Systems need to be tuned accordingly, and evaluation strategies as well. Given this variety, multiple subtypes of the system mention scenario have been used throughout the different campaigns.

Both the MUC and ACE tasks evaluated on system mentions[5] but, to bypass the parsing difficulty, the alignment between system and gold mentions was based on the mention head. A mention was considered to be correct if its span contained the head (marked in the corpora as the MIN attribute) and was within the gold mention boundaries. Given the gold mention in (9a), both (9b) and (9c) would be considered to be correct, but not (9d), which misses the mention head, or (9e), which includes words outside the mention boundaries.

(9) a. the skills he has amassed
    b. skills
    c. the skills
    d. he has amassed
    e. and the skill

SemEval offered both a gold setting, where gold mentions were provided, and a regular setting, where non-exact matches that included the mention's head word, like (9b) and (9c) were still used for evaluating the coreference output. Finally, the official CoNLL test was very strict and only aligned gold and system mentions that matched *exactly*, so a system outputting any of the (9b)–(9e) mentions was considered to fail to detect the gold mention in (9a). The CoNLL evaluation also included a second and third optional tracks where NP boundaries (i.e., all NPs) and gold mentions (i.e., only NPs and verbs participating in a coreference relation) were provided, respectively, at test time, thus separating the two dimensions of the mention detection problem, i.e., parsing and coreference membership.

Apart from the standard coreference evaluation measures, SemEval and CoNLL measured the mention detection subtask in terms of recall, precision, and F1. In SemEval, mentions were rewarded with 1 point if their boundaries coincided with those of the gold mention (9a), with 0.5 points if they included the head word

[4]Even though the gold scenario at the CoNLL-2011 and 2012 evaluations provided coreferent mentions only, not all participants exploited this hint to corefer every given mention, and left some mentions unlinked, thus not achieving 100 % recall for mention detection.

[5]ACE also had "diagnostic" tasks where gold mentions were provided.

and were subsumed within the gold mention's boundaries (9b) and (9c), and with 0 points otherwise (9d) and (9e). As mentioned above, CoNLL's and i2b2's policy was stricter and scored with 1 point system mentions that exactly matched those in the gold, and 0 points otherwise. However, the head-word-based mention scoring was used as a supplementary setting. Given that there are no singletons in the CoNLL data, the mention detection score for CoNLL cannot be considered in isolation, unlike SemEval.

In the case of the SemEval systems, relaxing the coreference scorer to head words resulted in improvements ranging from 0 to about 20 points across all the coreference measures. The difference was not so pronounced for the systems at i2b2 with respect to the strict scorer. A possible reason for this might be the frequency of one-token mentions and singletons. It is unclear how it affects the CoNLL evaluations since the head-word-based rescoring using the updated scorer has not been performed yet. Given the variety of languages and domains at SemEval, it does seem likely that having to detect the exact boundaries of mentions makes coreference resolution a harder task.

Whether gold or predicted mentions are used needs to be taken into account by coreference evaluation algorithms (Sect. 2.5) given that they cannot assume that a gold link, mention or entity necessarily has a counterpart in the system output. Consequently, they need to consider how to reward/penalize the mentions and links that are missing or spuriously added in the system output. Because evaluating on gold mentions was the tendency for several years, the original papers describing B^3 [4] and CEAF [61] did not specifically address how to tackle the alignment between gold and system entities [71]. More recently, multiple variations on manipulating gold and system outputs were proposed.[6] However, as argued by Pradhan et al. [71], the assumption that the gold and system output include the same set of mentions was never a requirement for any of the measures.[7]

Evaluating on gold mentions allows to isolate the task of coreference resolution itself from the pipeline of preprocessing tools, and thus it allows to focus on optimizing the strategies of coreference resolution proper. On the other hand, evaluating the complete pipeline of modules, including a less-than-perfect mention extraction module, yields results that are expressive from an application perspective. In the

[6] To summarize some of the variations that have been proposed:

- Bengtson and Roth [8] discard the predicted mentions that have no counterpart in the gold.
- Stoyanov et al. [92] use B^3_{all}, which retains all predicted mentions, and B^3_0, which discards all predicted mentions with no counterpart in the gold.
- Rahman and Ng [74] only discard the predicted mentions that have no counterpart in the gold and that are singletons.
- Cai and Strube [15] adjust a system output in three ways: gold mentions with no system counterpart are added as predicted singleton mentions, predicted singleton mentions with no counterpart are removed, and to compute precision, predicted coreferent mentions with no gold counterpart are added as gold singleton mentions.

[7] This assumption used to hold for BLANC [76], but not anymore since Luo et al.'s extension [64].

field of anaphora resolution, these two perspectives correspond to the distinction drawn by [67] between evaluation of anaphora resolution *algorithms* and evaluation of anaphora resolution *systems*. Published results are not very consistent in keeping this distinction clear. As a result, systems using predicted mentions [22, 89] have coexisted with systems using gold mentions [41, 63]. A turning point came with Stoyanov et al.'s [92] paper, which made a case for end-to-end coreference systems. The tendency for evaluating on predicted mentions has increased since then.

By conducting two separate evaluations on gold and predicted mentions, the SemEval and CoNLL tasks cast light on the decrease in performance when predicted mentions are used. Whether systems are evaluated on gold or predicted mentions—and with or without singletons, and on heads or on strict boundaries—has a noticeable impact on coreference scores and is thus another factor to take into account when looking at coreference scores and comparing evaluation campaigns.

2.3 Preprocessing Information

As described in chapter "Preprocessing Technology", coreference resolution requires linguistic information at different levels and therefore coreference resolution systems typically run an internal or external set of preprocessing modules that annotate the target documents with linguistic information useful for coreference. The typical preprocessing information assumed by most coreference systems includes tokenization, sentence breaks, POS tags, parse trees, mention chunks, and NEs. Since multiple taggers, parsers, and so on exist, preprocessing information takes one form or another depending on the preprocessing tools that are used. For example, while syntactic information for SemEval was provided in dependency form, CoNLL used constituents. Also, the quality of NLP tools is not the same across languages, nor their formats and guidelines.

Preprocessing modules have a direct effect on the coreference decisions made by coreference systems, and the extent to which their preprocessing quality affects the final performance of coreference systems is a question that recent shared tasks have tried to shed light on. This raises several interesting questions for a shared task to analyze: How do participating systems compare when given the exact same preprocessing information? What is the upper bound performance of a coreference system when gold preprocessing information is used? What other types of information can be used to help coreference resolution? To provide answers to these questions, recent shared tasks like SemEval and CoNLL have split the evaluation into the following tracks.

Gold Versus Predicted Tracks In the **gold track**, participants are provided with preprocessing information that was manually annotated, whereas in the **predicted track** preprocessing information is automatically predicted by NLP tools. The gold track represents the ideal scenario in which a coreference system does not need to deal with noisy annotations that could be misleading. For example, a typical feature of a coreference system compares the heads of two mentions (i.e., the heads of their NPs), but a parse tree error could result in the wrong head being detected in the predicted track.

Mention detection (Sect. 2.2) usually relies on the parse tree and is thus largely affected by the preprocessing quality: mentions derived from gold parse trees are much more reliable than those derived from a parse tree output by an automatic parser. To separate general preprocessing quality from mention-detection quality, the CoNLL shared tasks included two additional evaluation scenarios that provided gold mentions and gold mention boundaries, respectively, independently of whether the preprocessing information was gold or predicted. In the context of CoNLL, which used OntoNotes data, **gold mentions** include all the mentions that are manually annotated as coreferent, which do not include singletons. **Gold mention boundaries**, on the other hand, include both coreferent and singleton mentions (based on an NP, thus excluding verbal mentions). As a result, providing gold mentions was a greater help in CoNLL than in SemEval as the mention set had already filtered non-coreferent mentions, i.e., mentions that should not participate in a coreference relation. SemEval gold mentions find their counterpart in CoNLL gold mention boundaries.

Closed Versus Open Tracks Given that the purpose of a shared task is to compare multiple systems in a *controlled* scenario to make comparisons as direct as possible, the **closed track** does not allow participants to use any other information than the one that is provided. For the closed predicted track, state-of-the-art NLP tools are used to preprocess the datasets and provide the same predicted levels of information to all participants, including POS tags, parse trees, predicate arguments, and NE types. In the CoNLL shared tasks, the closed track also permitted the use of WordNet[8] as well as the table with number and gender predictions generated by Bergsma and Lin [9].

To explore the *unlimited* power of a coreference resolution system when no constraint is imposed, some shared tasks include an **open track** in which participants are allowed to bring in any kind of external information—as long as it does not explicitly use information from the test set—that they think could help coreference resolution, including running their own preprocessing tools. This made it possible for mature systems that run their own, not-easily-detachable preprocessing modules to participate. Open tracks though can make it harder to pinpoint why a system is better than another one. The level of participation in the open vs. closed tracks indicates that participants generally favor the closed scenario over the open one.

[8] Word senses in OntoNotes have a direct one-to-many mapping to WordNet senses.

2.4 Languages

Although English has dominated and was the only language included in the MUC and CoNLL-2011 shared tasks, other languages have been added as more resources have become available. ACE had tracks for Arabic, Chinese, and Spanish. One of the motivating factors behind SemEval was the multilingual aspect and it included five languages in addition to English, i.e., Catalan, Dutch, German, Italian, and Spanish. The CoNLL-2012 shared task extended its previous edition by adding Arabic and Chinese datasets to the English one.

Language introduces one more dimension of variation. Not only due to differences in the annotation schemes (e.g., annotation of relative pronouns), but also due to inherent differences between languages. For example, most Romance languages are pro-drop, thus showing a smaller number of explicit personal pronouns.

A relevant difference between Germanic and Romance languages, as attested by [65], is that the former tend to use more repetitions of previous coreferent mentions, whereas the latter make a greater use of synonyms, hypernyms, etc., to avoid repetitions. If we acknowledge the fact that same-head or same-string coreferent mentions are generally easier to resolve than their non-matching counterparts, then this clearly has an effect on the baseline scores for each language, English being "easier" than Spanish and Catalan in this respect.

In conclusion, coreference scores across languages should not be directly compared [75]. Most systems are tuned for English, which contributes to their lower scores on other languages if no language-specific training is used.

2.5 Evaluation Measures

One last distinguishing feature of an evaluation campaign—and a source of variation between campaigns for that matter—comes from the quantitative measure that is employed for assessing the performance of participating systems. This is even more relevant in light of the fact that there has been no general agreement on a unique evaluation measure for the coreference resolution task. The sister task, namely anaphora resolution, employed a basic accuracy measure corresponding to the ratio of correctly resolved pronouns to the total number of pronouns. As the task shifted from anaphora to coreference resolution, evaluation issues became more complex: rather than simply assessing whether the antecedent of every pronoun had been identified, there was a need to assess whether the system had successfully identified the different **coreference classes** or **coreference clusters**, that is, the sets of mentions that refer to the same entity.

It is hard for coreference-oriented metrics to capture in a single number all the criteria that a correct coreference output should meet: the number of correct coreference links, the number of correct mentions, and the number of classes or entities. As a result, each measure focuses on one aspect: MUC [97] and BLANC

[4, 64] are link-based measures (BLANC additionally measuring the balance between coreferent mentions and singletons), B^3 [4] and CEAF-ϕ_3 [61] are mention-based measures (unlike B^3, CEAF-ϕ_3 is based on a one-to-one entity alignment that counts every mention only once), and CEAF-ϕ_4 [61] is an entity-based measure. We refer the reader to chapter "Evaluation Metrics" for a full description of these measures and their formulas.

Because of the diversity of foci, the measures deliver different patterns of scores and it is not uncommon for them to disagree when ranking different systems [75], which makes it problematic for a shared task to compare participants. The measures tend to agree on the extremes, i.e., the best/worse outputs are usually ranked first/last by all the measures, but there is a good amount of variation in the range in between.

The history behind these multiple metrics is that starting from the MUC measure, which was the first coreference-specific measure and introduced on the occasion of the MUC shared task, new measures have repeatedly been proposed to overcome the shortcomings of the ones existing at the time. So MUC was followed by B^3, which was in turn followed by CEAF-ϕ_3 and CEAF-ϕ_4, and BLANC has been the latest addition.

For the purposes of an evaluation campaign, where an official ranking of the participating systems is desired, the most inclusive option seems to be taking the average of a link-based measure, a mention-based measure, and an entity-based measure, thus taking into account the different aspects. This is the MELA metric by Denis and Baldridge [27]: Mention Entity and Link Average score. It was adopted by the CoNLL-2011 and 2012 shared tasks and is known as the **CONLL average**, where $M = B^3$, $E =$ CEAF-ϕ_4, and $L =$ MUC. SemEval reported four of the measures, namely MUC, B^3, CEAF-ϕ_3, and BLANC. In contrast, the ACE evaluation campaigns developed their own measure, the ACE value [28], to fit the specifics of the task definition, which makes it hard to use on corpora annotated following more general coreference guidelines.

The use of these coreference measures on predicted mentions brought about several variations and buggy implementations due to the misunderstanding mentioned in Sect. 2.2 that B^3 and CEAF require the same set of gold and system mentions. This led to multiple proposals on how to manipulate the mentions in the gold standard and/or system outputs to be able to apply the scoring algorithms. See [71] for an in-depth discussion and a strong argument against mention manipulation, which is not only unnecessary, but potentially harmful as it can produce unintuitive results. Pradhan et al. [71] illustrate the application of all the coreference measures to scoring predicted mentions, including the recent extension of BLANC to handle predicted mentions [64].

As part of [71], an open-source and fully tested implementation of the main coreference evaluation measures (i.e., MUC, B^3, CEAF-ϕ_3, CEAF-ϕ_4, BLANC) was made available to the community.[9] This is the scoring package (v8.1) that we use in the next sections to report the results from the SemEval and CoNLL shared tasks,

[9]http://conll.github.io/reference-coreference-scorers/

whose official scorer at the time of evaluation was a previous version of this scorer that contained bugs.[10] We will see the measures at play in the next section.

3 Evaluation Campaigns

The purpose of an evaluation campaign, or shared task, is to evaluate different systems on the same task, on the same data, and using the same evaluation measure, to provide a fair, competition-like setting. This is especially useful for coreference resolution given the multiple dimensions and implementation options of the task, as discussed in the previous section. This section provides a broad overview of the major evaluation campaigns that have taken place to the present day. Table 1 summarizes where each campaign stands in relation with the characteristics presented in Sect. 2.

As Table 1 makes clear, no two campaigns have followed the same task definition. In an effort to better address the coreference resolution task, each evaluation campaign has explored different paths and taken different decisions, thus invalidating direct comparisons between the results obtained from different campaigns. Alongside the overview of evaluation campaigns, this section explores how different definitions of the coreference task affect the different evaluation scores, and which dimensions pose a greater challenge to coreference resolution systems.

3.1 Message Understanding Conference (MUC)

The Message Understanding Conferences (MUC) [39] were a series of evaluation campaigns designed to assess and to foster research on information extraction systems, with a special emphasis on military and news reports, as they were organized and financed by DARPA (Defense Advanced Research Projects Agency). The MUC program initiated the tradition of shared tasks in information extraction and largely shaped the research program in this field along its seven editions, from 1987 to 1997, each edition adding a greater level of complexity and improving upon the previous one. The early MUC editions basically consisted of slot filling tasks in which systems had to fill a template with information about specific events in a text. MUC-6 (1995) was a turning point in that an effort was made to move from ad hoc domain-dependent tasks, in which systems tended to use shallow understanding techniques, towards domain-independent subtasks that would be of practical use and

[10]The scorer used at SemEval-2010 was not the same version as the one used at the CoNLL-2011 and CoNLL-2012 shared tasks, as the latter incorporated a (buggy) implementation of Cai and Strube's [15] variations.

Table 1 Comparison of coreference resolution evaluation campaigns

	MUC	ACE	SEMEVAL	CONLL
#Editions	2	9	1	2
Datasets	MUC	ACE	ANCORA	ONTONOTES
			KNACK	
			ONTONOTES	
			TÜBA-D/Z	
			LIVEMEMORIES	
Languages	English	English	Catalan	English
		Arabic	Dutch	Chinese
		Chinese	English	Arabic
		Spanish	German	
			Italian	
			Spanish	
Singletons	N	Y	Y	N
NE types	Any	Facility	Any	Any
		GPE		
		Location		
		Organization		
		Person		
		Vehicle		
		Weapon		
Predicates	Y	Y	N	N
Events	N	N	N	Y
Measures	MUC	ACE-value	MUC	MUC
			B^3	B^3
			CEAF-ϕ_3	CEAF-ϕ_3
			BLANC	CEAF-ϕ_4
				BLANC
				CONLL
#Participants	7–7	10–16	6	21–16

performed automatically with high accuracy. To this end, the task of coreference resolution was first introduced in MUC-6, and it was kept in the evaluation task list of MUC-7 (1997).

The MUC-6 coreference dataset consists of Wall Street Journal articles totaling 30,000 words, and the MUC-7 dataset is a collection of New York Times articles totaling 25,000 words. Contrary to expectations, but in accordance with the long-standing philosophical debate, it turned out that defining coreference and formulating consistent annotation guidelines was not a trivial job (see discussion in chapter “Annotated Corpora and Annotation Tools”). As a result, the MUC-6 organizers decided to limit themselves to identity relations,[11] which was also the approached followed by MUC-7, after considering the inclusion of part-whole and set-subset relations. Still, the MUC annotation has been criticized for its inconsistencies and contradictions [25].

Apart from developing the first coreferentially annotated corpus, the MUC program created the first measure for evaluating coreference resolution, the MUC metric (chapter “Evaluation Metrics”), which has also been subject to severe criticisms, and alternative measures have been proposed [4, 61]. Consequently, subsequent evaluation campaigns have aimed at enhancing the task definition by providing more consistently annotated datasets and more reliable evaluation measures, as we discuss below. Nonetheless, both the MUC corpora and the MUC metric have remained extremely influential for having inaugurated the coreference resolution task, and they have been widely used for comparison with previous systems. MUC-7 is still listed among LDC’s top ten corpora and a new system is hardly ever presented without its MUC score.

The official test scores of the systems that participated in MUC-6 and MUC-7 are presented in Tables 2 and 3, respectively.

Table 2 Coreference performance scores of the MUC-6 systems

	MUC		
SYSTEM	R	P	F
Morgan et al. [68]	35.7	44.2	39.5
Lin [59]	**62.8**	63.4	63.1
Fisher et al. [30]	44.2	50.7	47.2
Grishman [37]	53.0	61.6	57.0
Baldwin et al. [6]	55.5	63.0	59.0
Gaizauskas et al. [32]	50.5	70.8	59.0
Appelt et al. [2]	58.8	**71.9**	**64.7**

Table 3 Coreference performance scores of the MUC-7 systems

	MUC		
SYSTEM	R	P	F
Fukumoto et al. [31]	28.4	60.6	38.6
Garigliano et al. [33]	46.9	57.0	51.5
Lin [60]	**58.2**	64.2	61.1
Baldwin et al. [5]	46.8	**78.0**	58.5
Humphreys et al. [46]	56.1	68.8	**61.8**

[11]Nominal predicates and appositive phrases fell under the Identity type in the MUC annotation scheme.

3.2 *Automatic Content Extraction Program (ACE)*

Continuing the tradition started by MUC of fostering research through evaluations, DARPA funded a follow-up program called Automatic Content Extraction (ACE) [28]. The focus of the program was to develop technology to identify and track *entities, relations* and *events* as they are mentioned in a text. The program began with the definition of the core task of Entity Detection and Tracking (EDT), which is an umbrella term under which the phenomenon of coreference plays a key role. EDT goes beyond coreference because it requires identifying specific types of entities in the source text, and extracting as well as unifying the specified attributes to form a unified representation of each entity.

The main goal of the evaluation was to promote building broader, more accurate information extraction engines that would be able to extract content from a source text. This could be in its original state, the result of the automatic transcription of audio, or extracted from an image using optical character recognition. Thus, the source could be text from various media (text, audio and image), languages (English, Chinese, Arabic and Spanish), and domains (newswire, broadcast conversations, weblogs, newsgroups, conversational telephone speech, etc.).

The evaluations were organized by NIST,[12] which maintains a record of the evaluation plans, lists of participants and their scores, and the scoring software. LDC[13] was the primary producer of the annotations used for training and evaluation, and maintains details about the datasets, annotation guidelines, as well as various tools. The scope of the evaluation was slowly broadened over the nine iterations, from 1999 to 2008, starting with a single language (English) and gradually spanning multiple domains and languages. Other tasks such as Relation Extraction, Event Detection and Tracking were gradually added. However, Entity Detection and Tracking remained the foundation on which these tasks were established. As explained in chapter "Linguistic and Cognitive Evidence About Anaphora", the phenomenon of coreference is not limited to within a document, but can occur across documents as well. At an early phase (2002), a cross-document task was evaluated using just the person entity type (PER). It was not until 2008, the last iteration of the evaluation, when the task became evaluated more thoroughly and was named "*global* EDT," as opposed to the default "*local* EDT" or within-document coreference.

Table 4 shows the matrix summarizing the various dimensions and tasks that were part of this program. We only focus on the aspect of ACE that is directly relevant to coreference, namely the EDT task. This was a composite of two primary

[12]http://www.itl.nist.gov/iad/mig/tests/ace/

[13]http://projects.ldc.upenn.edu/ace/data/

Table 4 ACE evaluation matrix on the different editions. All editions included English, the editions from 2004 to 2008 also included Chinese and Arabic, and the 2007 edition included Spanish too

	1999	2000	2001	2002	2003	2004	2005	2007	2008
Primary evaluation tasks									
Entity detection and recognition (EDR)		✓	✓	✓	✓	✓	✓	✓	✓
Entity mention detection (EMD)		✓	✓	✓	✓	✓	✓	✓	✓
Diagnostic tasks									
EDR coreference (gold mentions)						✓	✓	✓	✓
Entity attributes									
Type		✓	✓	✓	✓	✓	✓	✓	✓
Subtype						✓	✓	✓	✓
Class						✓	✓	✓	✓
Mention attributes									
Type (name/nominal/pronominal/pre)				✓	✓	✓	✓	✓	✓
Processing mode									
Document level		✓	✓	✓	✓	✓	✓	✓	✓
Cross document				✓[a]					✓[b]
Database reconciled				✓[a]					
Sources									
Newspaper (ground truth)		✓	✓	✓					
Newswire				✓	✓	✓	✓	✓	✓
Broadcast news (ground truth)		✓	✓	✓	✓	✓	✓	✓	✓
Broadcast news (ASR output)				✓		✓			
Broadcast conversation							✓	✓	✓
Weblogs							✓	✓	✓
Usenet newsgroups/discussion forums							✓	✓	✓
Conversational telephone speech							✓	✓	✓

[a]Only entities of type person
[b]Entities of type person and organization

tasks (the first half) and two secondary tasks (the second half):

1. Entity Detection (EDR)
2. Entity Attribute Recognition
3. Mention Detection (EMD)
4. Mention Extent Recognition

A new scoring strategy known as the ACE-score or ACE-value was designed for this program. The ACE-value ranges from a perfect score of 100 % (for a perfect output) down to 0 (for no output) or even down to negative scores (for systems that make costly errors). It was customized to give different weights to the different categories that were evaluated (e.g., entity types, their attributes, etc.). The upside of this strategy was that it was possible to tune a system's performance for a specific application; however, such a cost-based model can be non-intuitive, and hinder overall progress since participants tend to focus on the highly-weighted phenomena.

While the MUC program had made available about 50k annotated tokens, this program created about 16k annotated tokens. This certainly fueled machine-learning research for the coreference problem. One downside though was that the data was restricted to a subset of entity types (either five or seven types[14]), so for example, in (10), no mention is annotated for either *price* or *college degree* because they do not fall under any of the ACE entity types.

(10) The price of a college degree continues to rise.

Various factors such as the evolving task definition, the changing nature of the scores owing to the tuning of the scoring algorithm, and the variability of training and test data over the years, make a performance comparison between systems across the years not very meaningful. Since the goal of this chapter is not to analyze every single edition of ACE but to get an idea of the campaign and participating systems, we present the system results of the 2007 campaign, which contained the most languages—English, Chinese, Arabic and Spanish—on the EDT task. There were a total of 10 systems that participated: 6 sent results for English, 7 for Chinese, 2 for Arabic, and 1 for Spanish. Table 5 shows the performance of the participants that submitted results and attended the workshop as well.

The test sets for English, Chinese and Arabic comprised about 70k words,[15] and about 50k for Spanish. Most of the 2007 test data was the same as the 2005 evaluation, with the addition of roughly 10k Arabic data from the 2005 evaluation that was translated into Chinese and English, and annotated with entities.

3.3 SemEval-2010 Task 1

The 2010 edition of the SemEval Workshop (Evaluation Exercises on Semantic Evaluation) included a task on multilingual coreference resolution [78], organized by the University of Barcelona, Technical University of Catalonia, University College Ghent, University of Trento, and University of Tübingen. The task placed emphasis on multilinguality, the amount and quality of preprocessing information, and the comparison of different evaluation measures. To these ends, the task provided datasets in six languages (Catalan, Dutch, English, German, Italian, and Spanish) that contained gold and automatic annotations on several linguistic layers (e.g., PoS, parsing, NEs, etc.), and measured performance using the MUC score, B^3,

[14]The full list of seven ACE entity types includes: person (e.g., *the President of the U.S.*), organization (e.g., *University of Tennessee*), geopolitical entity (e.g., *the people of France*), location (e.g., *Germany*), facility (e.g., *the oil refinery*), vehicle (e.g., *the train*), and weapon (e.g., *knife*).

[15]In Chinese, the word count is approximated by multiplying the number of characters by 1.5.

Table 5 Coreference performance scores of the ACE-2007 participants in the evaluation for English, Chinese, Arabic and Spanish languages on the ACE domains—Broadcast Conversation (BC), Broadcast News (BN), Newswire (NW), Telephone conversation (TC), Usenet (UN) and Weblogs (WB)—along with the OVERALL score

	ACE-VALUE						
SYSTEM	OVERALL	BC	BN	NW	TC	UN	WB
ENGLISH							
BBN technologies	56.3	44.7	65.4	58.1	49.2	39.2	52.7
IBM	52.7	48.7	65.9	52.8	45.4	44.0	45.8
Lockheed Martin	46.1	50.5	50.0	46.8	39.5	39.7	42.1
Fudan University	24.2	21.0	34.7	22.9	34.9	14.6	20.7
Language computer corporation[a]	35.8	25.2	47.6	39.3	8.7	19.7	27.3
CHINESE							
Language computer corporation	45.0		49.7	46.9			35.0
Fudan University	28.8		35.6	30.2			18.4
Lockheed Martin	26.9		30.3	26.1			25.7
ARABIC							
BBN technologies	48.8		51.9	49.4			42.1
IBM	45.4		49.4	46.6			34.6
SPANISH							
IBM	51.0			51.0			

[a]Revised submission after fixing a bug that caused invalid byte offsets in the original submission

CEAF-ϕ_3, and BLANC (see chapter "Evaluation Metrics" for a description of the formulas).

The datasets followed the same tabular format as the CoNLL shared tasks (see chapter "Annotated Corpora and Annotation Tools" for a detailed description), and they were extracted from the following corpora, all of them consisting of newspaper articles: AnCora (345k words for Catalan, and 380k words for Spanish), OntoNotes (120k words for English), COREA (104k words for Dutch), LiveMemories (140k words for Italian), and Tüba/DZ (455k words for German). Unlike MUC, these corpora were not developed for a specific campaign but with a broader linguistic goal in mind, trying to overcome the limitations of the MUC annotation. In the same vein, systems were evaluated according to different scores in order to take into account the shortcomings of early measures such as MUC and B^3.

Additionally, the evaluation was split into four scenarios, depending on whether systems used the gold—including gold mentions—or automatic preprocessing information (i.e., gold and regular settings), and whether systems employed only the linguistic information provided in the datasets or made use of any additional tool or resource (i.e., closed and open settings). See Sect. 2.3 for the specifics of each scenario. This rich, but complex, evaluation layout turned out not to be as successful as initially conceived given that the six participating systems did not submit results for all the evaluation scenarios or languages, permitting only a partial comparison between the systems. The CoNLL-2012 task (Sect. 3.4) tried to remedy this.

A total of 24 participants registered for the task and downloaded the training materials. From these, 16 downloaded the test set, but only 6 submitted valid results. The performance scores for the four evaluation settings are summarized in Tables 6, 7, 8, 9, 10 and 11, one per each language. Some of these results differ from the ones provided in the task paper [78] because we rescored the system outputs using the latest version 8.1 of the coreference scorer, which fixes the problems of earlier versions of the scorer [71].[16]

The participation of systems across languages and settings was quite irregular, making it difficult to draw firm conclusions about the goals initially pursued by the task. English concentrated the most participants, followed by German, Catalan and Spanish, Italian, and Dutch. The number of languages addressed by each system ranged from one [93] to six [51, 108]. The best overall results were those for English, followed by German, then Catalan, Spanish and Italian, and finally Dutch. Apart from differences between corpora, there are other factors that might explain this ranking: (i) the fact that most of the systems were originally developed for English, and (ii) differences in corpus size (German having the largest corpus, and Dutch the smallest).

In general, the closed track attracted more participants than the open track, and comparing the results of the only system that participated in both, results only showed a slight improvement. Comparing the gold and predicted scenarios, performance was significantly higher when gold layers and gold mentions (including singletons) were given. However, it is not possible to separate how much of this is due to mention detection vs. gold preprocessing. The CoNLL-2011 task (Sect. 3.4) tried to remedy this by splitting the two dimensions.

Finally, the SemEval task brought to the fore that the best scoring systems did not surpass by much the scores obtained by two naive baselines:

SINGLETONS Baseline that clusters each mention into its own separate entity.
ONE ENTITY Baseline that clusters all the mentions of a document into a single entity.

They are shown in the last rows of Tables 6, 7, 8, 9, 10 and 11, using gold mentions. The SINGLETONS baseline is especially high for B^3 and CEAF, whereas the ONE ENTITY baseline is especially high for MUC. However, note that a score averaging MUC, B^3 and CEAF in the style of the CONLL average would always suffer from at least one of the scores.

3.4 CoNLL-2011 and 2012 Shared Tasks

The CoNLL-2011 and CoNLL-2012 shared tasks involved predicting coreference on the OntoNotes corpus [45, 70, 99] given predicted information for the other

[16]We ran the scorer using the head-word relaxed flag, as the original SemEval task did.

Table 6 Coreference performance scores of the SemEval systems on English

	MD			MUC			B^3			CEAF-ϕ_3			BLANC		
SYSTEM	R	P	F	R	P	F	R	P	F	R	P	F	R	P	B
CLOSED TRACK; GOLD LAYERS; GOLD MENTIONS															
Sapena et al. [83]	100	100	100	21.9	72.4	33.7	74.8	97.0	84.5	75.6	75.6	75.6	57.0	83.4	61.3
Kobdani and Schütze [51]	100	100	100	68.1	54.9	60.8	86.7	78.5	82.4	74.3	74.3	74.3	77.3	67.0	70.8
Attardi et al. [3]	99.8	81.7	89.8	23.7	24.4	24.0	74.6	72.1	73.4	75.0	61.4	67.6	55.8	48.1	48.9
Zhekova and Kübler [108]	92.5	99.5	95.9	17.2	25.5	20.5	67.8	83.5	74.8	63.4	68.3	65.8	45.3	60.4	49.7
Baseline (SINGLETONS)	100	100	100	0.0	0.0	0.0	71.2	100	83.2	71.2	71.2	71.2	50.0	49.2	49.6
Baseline (ONE ENTITY)	100	100	100	100	29.2	45.2	100	3.5	6.7	10.5	10.5	10.5	50.0	0.8	1.6
CLOSED TRACK; PREDICTED LAYERS; PREDICTED MENTIONS															
Kobdani and Schütze [51]	78.4	83.0	80.7	57.7	48.1	52.5	68.3	65.9	67.1	61.0	64.5	62.7	54.1	52.4	52.7
Attardi et al. [3]	79.6	68.9	73.9	23.8	25.5	24.6	62.1	60.5	61.3	61.7	53.4	57.3	41.2	41.6	38.7
Zhekova and Kübler [108]	66.7	83.6	74.2	11.6	18.4	14.2	50.9	69.2	58.7	48.2	60.4	53.6	25.2	44.5	31.4
OPEN TRACK; GOLD LAYERS; GOLD MENTIONS															
Uryupina [93][a]	100	100	100	56.1	57.5	56.8	82.6	85.7	84.1	77.5	77.5	77.5	69.3	75.3	71.8
Sapena et al. [83]	100	100	100	22.6	70.5	34.2	75.2	96.7	84.6	75.8	75.8	75.8	58.0	83.8	62.7
Baseline (SINGLETONS)	100	100	100	0.0	0.0	0.0	71.2	100	83.2	71.2	71.2	71.2	50.0	49.2	49.6
Baseline (ONE ENTITY)	100	100	100	100	29.2	45.2	100	3.5	6.7	10.5	10.5	10.5	50.0	0.8	1.6
OPEN TRACK; PREDICTED LAYERS; PREDICTED MENTIONS															
Broscheit et al. [12]	76.1	69.8	72.8	62.8	52.4	57.1	74.9	67.7	71.1	70.1	64.3	67.1	63.2	55.3	58.9
Uryupina [93][a]	79.8	76.4	78.1	55.0	54.2	54.6	73.7	74.1	73.9	70.4	67.4	68.9	59.8	62.3	60.7

[a]Scores from the Corry-B run

Table 7 Coreference performance scores of the SemEval systems on Dutch

SYSTEM	MD			MUC			B^3			CEAF-ϕ_3			BLANC		
	R	P	F	R	P	F	R	P	F	R	P	F	R	P	B
CLOSED TRACK; GOLD LAYERS; GOLD MENTIONS															
Kobdani and Schütze [51]	100	100	100	65.7	74.4	69.8	65.0	69.2	67.0	58.8	58.8	58.8	69.5	62.9	65.3
Baseline (SINGLETONS)	100	100	100	0.0	0.0	0.0	34.5	100	51.3	34.5	34.5	34.5	50.0	46.7	48.3
Baseline (ONE ENTITY)	100	100	100	100	66.4	79.8	100	8.1	14.9	19.7	19.7	19.7	50.0	3.3	6.1
CLOSED TRACK; PREDICTED LAYERS; PREDICTED MENTIONS															
Kobdani and Schütze [51]	77.2	28.7	41.8	60.5	19.0	29.0	57.4	6.4	11.5	29.1	10.8	15.8	40.9	3.6	5.9
Zhekova and Kübler [108]	42.8	30.8	35.8	7.1	11.8	8.8	14.4	24.4	18.1	22.0	15.7	18.3	10.4	9.8	7.5

Table 8 Coreference performance scores of the SemEval systems on Catalan

	MD			MUC			B^3			CEAF-ϕ_3			BLANC		
SYSTEM	R	P	F	R	P	F	R	P	F	R	P	F	R	P	B
CLOSED TRACK; GOLD LAYERS; GOLD MENTIONS															
Sapena et al. [83]	100	100	100	29.9	77.3	42.5	68.6	95.8	79.9	70.5	70.5	70.5	56.0	81.8	59.7
Kobdani and Schütze [51]	100	100	100	54.1	58.4	56.2	76.6	77.4	77.0	68.7	68.7	68.7	72.4	60.2	63.6
Attardi et al. [3]	100	96.8	98.4	17.2	57.7	26.5	64.4	93.3	76.2	66.0	63.9	64.9	53.1	75.6	53.6
Zhekova and Kübler [108]	75.1	96.3	84.4	8.7	17.0	11.5	47.7	76.3	58.7	46.6	59.7	52.3	33.6	52.6	39.8
Baseline (SINGLETONS)	100	100	100	0.0	0.0	0.0	61.2	100	75.9	61.2	61.2	61.2	50.0	48.7	49.3
Baseline (ONE ENTITY)	100	100	100	100	39.3	56.4	100	4.0	7.7	11.8	11.8	11.8	50.0	1.3	2.6
CLOSED TRACK; PREDICTED LAYERS; PREDICTED MENTIONS															
Kobdani and Schütze [51]	75.9	64.5	69.7	44.1	32.3	37.3	59.6	44.7	51.1	51.3	43.6	47.2	46.3	26.0	31.0
Attardi et al. [3]	83.3	82.0	82.7	15.2	46.9	22.9	55.8	76.6	64.6	57.5	56.6	57.1	36.7	59.6	38.6
Zhekova and Kübler [108]	51.4	70.9	59.6	6.5	12.6	8.6	32.3	55.6	40.9	33.2	45.7	38.4	17.2	31.8	21.7

Table 9 Coreference performance scores of the SemEval systems on Spanish

SYSTEM	MD			MUC			B^3			CEAF-ϕ_3			BLANC		
	R	P	F	R	P	F	R	P	F	R	P	F	R	P	B
CLOSED TRACK; GOLD LAYERS; GOLD MENTIONS															
Sapena et al. [83]	100	100	100	14.8	73.8	24.7	65.3	97.5	78.2	66.6	66.6	66.6	53.4	81.8	55.6
Kobdani and Schütze [51]	100	100	100	52.7	58.3	55.3	75.8	79.0	77.4	69.8	69.8	69.8	67.3	62.5	64.5
Attardi et al. [3]	100	96.8	98.4	16.6	56.5	25.7	65.2	93.4	76.8	66.9	64.7	65.8	52.9	74.3	53.2
Zhekova and Kübler [108]	73.8	96.4	83.6	9.6	18.8	12.7	46.8	77.1	58.2	45.7	59.7	51.7	32.3	52.4	39.0
Baseline (SINGLETONS)	100	100	100	0.0	0.0	0.0	62.2	100	76.7	62.2	62.2	62.2	50.0	48.8	49.4
Baseline (ONE ENTITY)	100	100	100	100	38.3	55.4	100	4.0	7.6	11.9	11.9	11.9	50.0	1.2	2.4
CLOSED TRACK; PREDICTED LAYERS; PREDICTED MENTIONS															
Kobdani and Schütze [51]	74.9	66.3	70.3	35.8	36.8	36.3	56.6	54.6	55.6	56.3	49.9	52.9	41.2	33.0	36.6
Attardi et al. [3]	82.2	84.1	83.1	14.0	48.4	21.7	56.6	79.0	66.0	58.6	60.0	59.3	36.4	60.1	39.0
Zhekova and Kübler [108]	51.1	72.7	60.0	7.6	14.4	10.0	32.7	57.1	41.6	33.6	47.7	39.4	17.4	34.0	22.4

Table 10 Coreference performance scores of the SemEval systems on German

	MD			MUC			B^3			CEAF-ϕ_3			BLANC		
SYSTEM	R	P	F	R	P	F	R	P	F	R	P	F	R	P	B
CLOSED TRACK; GOLD LAYERS; GOLD MENTIONS															
Kobdani and Schütze [51]	100	100	100	74.4	48.1	58.4	90.4	73.6	81.1	72.9	72.9	72.9	78.2	61.8	66.4
Attardi et al. [3]	100	100	100	16.4	60.6	25.9	77.2	96.7	85.9	77.7	77.7	77.7	54.4	75.1	57.4
Zhekova and Kübler [108]	92.6	95.5	94.0	22.1	21.8	22.0	73.4	77.9	75.6	67.4	69.1	68.2	45.6	49.3	47.1
Baseline (SINGLETONS)	100	100	100	0.0	0.0	0.0	75.5	100	86.0	75.5	75.5	75.5	50.0	49.4	49.7
Baseline (ONE ENTITY)	100	100	100	100	24.8	39.7	100	2.4	4.7	8.2	8.2	8.2	50.0	0.6	1.1
CLOSED TRACK; PREDICTED LAYERS; PREDICTED MENTIONS															
Kobdani and Schütze [51]	79.3	77.5	78.4	49.3	35.0	40.9	69.1	60.1	64.3	60.6	59.2	59.9	45.1	40.1	42.3
Attardi et al. [3]	60.9	57.7	59.2	10.2	31.5	15.4	47.2	54.9	50.7	50.9	48.2	49.5	20.6	29.8	21.4
Zhekova and Kübler [108]	50.6	66.8	57.6	9.5	11.4	10.4	41.2	53.7	46.6	39.4	51.9	44.8	15.0	28.2	19.4
OPEN TRACK; GOLD LAYERS; GOLD MENTIONS															
Broscheit et al. [12]	94.3	93.7	94.0	70.5	40.1	51.1	85.3	64.4	73.4	67.1	66.7	66.9	66.8	54.4	58.4
Baseline (SINGLETONS)	100	100	100	0.0	0.0	0.0	75.5	100	86.0	75.5	75.5	75.5	50.0	49.4	49.7
Baseline (ONE ENTITY)	100	100	100	100	24.8	39.7	100	2.4	4.7	8.2	8.2	8.2	50.0	0.6	1.1
OPEN TRACK; PREDICTED LAYERS; PREDICTED MENTIONS															
Broscheit et al. [12]	82.5	82.3	82.4	61.4	36.1	45.5	75.3	58.3	65.7	61.4	61.2	61.3	54.4	46.1	49.1

Table 11 Coreference performance scores of the SemEval systems on Italian

	MD			MUC			B^3			CEAF-ϕ_3			BLANC		
SYSTEM	R	P	F	R	P	F	R	P	F	R	P	F	R	P	B
CLOSED TRACK; GOLD LAYERS; GOLD MENTIONS															
Kobdani and Schütze [51]	98.5	98.5	98.5	48.1	42.3	45.0	76.7	76.9	76.8	66.0	66.0	66.0	56.8	62.0	58.7
Baseline (SINGLETONS)	100	100	100	0.0	0.0	0.0	71.1	100	83.1	71.1	71.1	71.1	50.0	49.2	49.6
Baseline (ONE ENTITY)	100	100	100	100	29.0	45.0	100	2.1	4.1	11.4	11.4	11.4	50.0	0.8	1.5
CLOSED TRACK; PREDICTED LAYERS; PREDICTED MENTIONS															
Kobdani and Schütze [51]	84.6	98.1	90.9	50.1	50.7	50.4	63.6	79.3	70.6	57.2	66.3	61.4	44.4	67.1	52.9
Zhekova and Kübler [108]	46.2	35.4	40.1	2.9	4.6	3.6	37.3	30.9	33.8	36.7	28.1	31.8	12.6	9.1	9.4
OPEN TRACK; PREDICTED LAYERS; PREDICTED MENTIONS															
Broscheit et al. [12]	42.9	80.9	56.0	35.4	54.2	42.8	34.7	70.9	46.6	35.2	66.4	46.0	17.5	55.3	26.4
Attardi et al. [3]	90.4	73.7	81.2	37.2	28.3	32.1	66.6	56.4	61.1	62.2	50.7	55.8	49.7	50.5	45.2

layers (i.e., parse information, entity types, etc.). The CoNLL-2011 shared task focused on the English language portion of OntoNotes v4.0 and, given its enthusiastic reception, an extended version was held in 2012 on all three languages of OntoNotes—English, Chinese and Arabic—and using its final release v5.0.

As is customary with CoNLL tasks, there were two tracks, *closed* and *open* (Sect. 2.3). Participants were provided a development set for tuning the models and were allowed to use it in addition to the training set for the final models. As described in chapter "Annotated Corpora and Annotation Tools", OntoNotes tags appositive and copular phrases separately from identity coreference. The shared tasks only included identity coreference. In the broadcast conversation, weblogs, and telephone conversation domains, documents can be very long. Thus, long documents were split into smaller parts and each part was annotated and treated as a separate document.

As explained in Sect. 2.5, given the multiple perspectives from which a coreference output can be evaluated and following the SemEval-2010 approach, CoNLL included all the SemEval-2010 metrics—MUC, B^3, CEAF-ϕ_3, BLANC—plus CEAF-ϕ_4 and the CONLL average, a MELA-like average of the metrics $\text{M} = \text{B}^3$, $\text{E} =$ CEAF-ϕ_4, and $\text{L} =$ MUC. For the 2011 evaluation, systems were ranked, and the winning system was determined according to the CONLL average. In the CoNLL-2012 evaluation, the winning system was selected based on the average of CONLL scores across all three languages.

In the 2011 evaluation, out of the 65 groups that showed interest in the task by registering online, 23 submitted results during the official evaluation week. Of these, 16 submitted only closed track results, 3 submitted only open track results, and 2 submitted both closed and open track results. The results for the 18 systems that participated in the closed track and the 5 systems that participated in the open track are shown in Table 12. As we did with the SemEval results in Sect. 3.3, we present the CoNLL results according to the latest version 8.1 of the scorer (Sect. 2.5), which accounts for the differences with respect to the official scores that were published.

The official track was the closed track using predicted preprocessing information and predicted mentions. Systems were provided with the predictions from state-of-the-art automatic systems (parse trees, semantic roles, word senses, and named entities), as well as the raw source text. Because the coreference annotations on OntoNotes do not contain singleton entities, the data contained only entities that had at least two mentions. Table 12 shows the scores of the closed and open tracks using predicted information. To make comparisons between the multiple measures easier, we only show the F-scores.

The official CoNLL average tops out in the low 50s. While this is lower than the figures reported by previous coreference evaluations, it was expected for several reasons: (i) mentions had to be predicted, (ii) only mentions that exactly matched the gold were counted as correct, and (iii) appositive and copular constructions, which can be relatively easily detected based on the parse tree, were not considered as coreference. The top-performing system (Lee et al. [55]) scored 51.5, which is 1.5 points higher than the second system (Sapena et al. [84]) and the third one (Björkelund and Nugues [11]), which scored 50.0 and 47.9, respectively. After

Table 12 Coreference performance scores of the CoNLL-2011 systems on English, using predicted mentions

SYSTEM	MD	MUC	B^3	CEAF-ϕ_3	CEAF-ϕ_4	BLANC	CONLL	FINAL MODEL	
	F	F^1	F^2	F	F^3		$\frac{F^1+F^2+F^3}{3}$	TRAIN	DEV
CLOSED TRACK; PREDICTED LAYERS; PREDICTED MENTIONS									
Lee et al. [55]	70.7	59.6	48.9	53.0	46.1	48.8	51.5	×	×
Sapena et al. [84]	68.4	59.5	46.5	51.3	44.0	44.5	50.0	√	√
Björkelund and Nugues [11]	69.0	58.6	45.0	48.4	40.0	46.0	47.9	√	√
Chang et al. [16]	64.9	57.1	46.0	50.7	40.0	45.5	47.7	√	√
Stoyanov et al. [91]	67.8	58.4	40.1	43.3	36.9	34.6	45.1	–	–
Santos and Carvalho [82]	65.5	56.6	42.9	45.1	35.5	41.3	45.0	√	√
Song et al. [88]	67.3	60.0	41.4	41.0	33.1	30.9	44.8	√	–
Devi et al. [87]	64.8	50.5	39.5	44.2	39.4	36.3	43.1	√	–
Yang et al. [105]	63.9	52.3	39.4	43.2	35.5	36.1	42.4	√	√
Charton and Gagnon [18]	64.3	52.5	38.0	42.6	34.5	35.6	41.6	√	–
Xiong et al. [101]	64.3	54.5	37.7	41.9	31.6	37.0	41.2	√	√
Zhou et al. [111]	62.3	49.0	37.0	40.6	35.0	35.0	40.3	√	√
Kobdani and Schütze [52]	61.0	47.0	34.8	38.0	34.1	32.6	38.6	√	–
Li et al. [58]	61.9	46.6	34.9	37.7	31.7	35.0	37.7	–	–
Kummerfeld et al. [49]	62.7	42.7	34.2	38.8	35.5	31.0	37.5	–	–
Chen et al. [20]	61.1	47.9	34.4	37.8	29.2	35.7	37.2	–	–
Zhekova and Kübler [109]	48.3	24.1	23.7	23.4	20.5	15.4	22.8	√	√
Irwin et al. [47]	26.7	20.0	11.7	18.5	14.7	6.3	15.5	–	–
OPEN TRACK; PREDICTED LAYERS; PREDICTED MENTIONS									
Lee et al. [55]	70.9	61.0	49.9	54.0	46.4	50.1	52.5	×	×
Cai et al. [14]	67.4	57.8	46.1	50.4	42.1	45.3	48.7	–	–
Uryupina et al. [95]	68.4	57.6	44.0	48.1	40.7	43.0	47.5	√	√
Klenner and Tuggener [50]	62.3	49.9	39.0	43.9	35.7	39.9	41.5	–	–
Irwin et al. [47]	35.3	27.2	16.0	22.8	17.8	9.8	20.3	–	–

fixing the issues with the scorer, systems at ranks 3 and 4 swapped their positions. This is understandable given that their CoNLL averages are so close.

Of the five systems that participated in the open track, three did not participate in the closed track not because they wanted to use more external tools or resources, but because they were already using tools that were hard to retrain, or were trained on non-OntoNotes data. Lee et al. [55] showed one point improvement when using external resources.

The CoNLL organizers were so fearful of fragmented participation across the various evaluation scenarios that they did not originally plan any additional track. However, after the main evaluation was over, participants were encouraged to submit results on two supplementary settings:

1. Predicted information and gold mention boundaries (Sect. 2.3): participants were provided the boundaries of all (non-verbal) mentions, including singletons.
2. Predicted information and gold mentions (Sect. 2.3): participants were provided the manually annotated spans of the mentions in the gold coreference chains.

Table 13 shows the performance of the systems that participated in the supplementary settings. It becomes apparent that having gold mentions (excluding singletons) significantly improves system performance; however, providing gold mention boundaries does not impact scores very significantly.

As mentioned earlier, the CoNLL-2012 shared task comprised three languages—English, Chinese and Arabic. Participants were not required to submit results on all three languages, but they were penalized if they did not as the final ranking was computed according to the macro average of the CoNLL averages across all three languages. Out of the approximately 60 participants that expressed interest, 16 submitted official results. Almost all the systems that participated in English also participated in Chinese, but only about half of the participants submitted outputs for all three languages.

Table 14 shows the results per language of the participating systems in the closed (official) track and the open track, using predicted information. Most of the systems also included the development test when training their final model. The top systems performed in the high 50s for English, improving significantly with respect to CoNLL-2011. The only difference was that the test set included one additional domain (namely, the New Testament). For a more detailed comparison with CoNLL-2011, see the task overview paper [72].

The performance on Chinese and Arabic was lower than on English, especially for Arabic. This was also the case in SemEval. One possible reason is the fact that most feature engineering to date has focused on English. Some systems did use a few Chinese-specific features, but no system exploited the specifics of Arabic. Another possible reason is the smaller size of the Arabic dataset as well as the lower performance of preprocessing tools for Arabic, especially the parser.

Table 14 also shows that, similarly to 2011, not many systems participated in the open track. This might indicate that participants have a preference for tracks that allow a fairer comparison across systems, or tracks that do not require running your systems for every preprocessing layer.

Table 13 Coreference performance scores of the CoNLL-2011 systems on English, using gold mention boundaries or gold mentions

SYSTEM	MD	MUC	B^3	CEAF-ϕ_3	CEAF-ϕ_4	BLANC	CONLL	FINAL MODEL	
	F	F^1	F^2	F	F^3		$\frac{F^1+F^2+F^3}{3}$	TRAIN	DEV
CLOSED TRACK; PREDICTED LAYERS; GOLD BOUNDARIES									
Lee et al. [55]	75.2	63.9	53.9	56.8	50.7	53.8	56.1	×	×
Björkelund and Nugues [11]	72.4	62.1	48.6	51.2	43.5	48.7	51.4	√	√
Chang et al. [16]	67.9	59.8	48.4	53.3	44.2	48.1	50.8	√	√
Stoyanov et al. [91]	70.3	61.5	43.7	46.4	40.1	38.4	48.4	–	–
Santos and Carvalho [82]	67.8	59.5	45.9	47.4	37.3	45.7	47.6	√	√
Song et al. [88]	66.7	55.5	40.6	41.2	33.2	31.8	43.1	√	–
Kobdani and Schütze [52]	66.1	51.9	39.0	41.1	37.5	36.9	42.8	√	–
Chen et al. [20]	64.9	51.6	38.0	41.0	32.5	39.0	40.7	–	–
Zhekova and Kübler [109]	62.7	35.2	31.5	31.4	28.1	25.8	31.6	√	√
Baseline (ONE ENTITY)	48.5	39.3	3.0	12.2	2.5	1.3	14.9	–	–
OPEN TRACK; PREDICTED LAYERS; GOLD BOUNDARIES									
Lee et al. [55]	75.4	65.4	55.0	57.9	51.1	55.2	57.2	×	×
Baseline (ONE ENTITY)	48.5	39.3	3.0	12.2	2.5	1.3	14.9	–	–
CLOSED TRACK; PREDICTED LAYERS; GOLD MENTIONS									
Chang et al. [16]	100	82.5	73.7	69.7	65.2	77.3	73.8	√	√
Baseline (ONE ENTITY)	100	87.3	24.1	25.2	7.1	9.7	39.5	–	–
OPEN TRACK; PREDICTED LAYERS; GOLD MENTIONS									
Lee et al. [55]	90.9	81.6	71.1	71.1	68.1	72.2	73.6	×	×
Baseline (ONE ENTITY)	100	87.3	24.1	25.2	7.1	9.7	39.5	–	–

Table 14 Coreference performance scores of the CoNLL-2012 systems on Chinese, Arabic and English, including the CONLL score on each language and the official macro average across all three languages

	OPEN			CLOSED			OFFICIAL	FINAL MODEL	
SYSTEM	ENGLISH CONLL	CHINESE CONLL	ARABIC CONLL	ENGLISH CONLL^{c1}	CHINESE CONLL^{c2}	ARABIC CONLL^{c3}	AVERAGE $\frac{c1+c2+c3}{3}$	TRAIN	DEV
PREDICTED LAYERS; PREDICTED MENTIONS									
Fernandes et al. [29]				60.6	51.5	45.2	52.4	√	√
Björkelund and Farkas [10]				57.4	52.5	43.5	51.1	√	√
Chen and Ng [19]		59.8		54.5	57.6	32.4	48.2	√	×
Stamborg et al. [90]				54.2	49.0	36.7	46.6	√	√
Uryupina et al. [94]				50.0	44.1	37.5	43.9	√	√
Yuan et al. [106]		54.8		52.9	54.3		35.7	√	√
Xu et al. [103]				52.6	51.4		34.6	√	×
Martschat et al. [66]				57.7	43.8		33.8	√	×
Zhekova et al. [110]				40.5	29.9	26.2	32.2	√	√
Zhang et al. [107]				54.2	42.2		32.1	–	–
Chang et al. [17]				56.1	32.1		29.4	√	×
Li [56]				36.1	33.8	16.2	28.7	√	√
Li et al. [57]				38.6	40.5		26.4	√	√
Shou and Zhao [86]				53.0			17.7	√	×
Yang[a]				49.4			16.4	√	×
Xiong and Liu [100]	54.2	31.0	29.4				0.0	√	√

[a]Participant that did not submit a system description paper

Table 15 shows the performance in the supplementary open and closed tracks when gold mention boundaries and gold mentions were provided. It is noteworthy that Chang et al. [17] ranked considerably higher in the supplementary track of English as compared to the overall best performing system (Fernandes et al. [29]). This captures how different approaches benefit from different levels of partially disclosed information and can explain discrepancies reported by previous research in coreference resolution. The CoNLL and SemEval results for English cannot be compared since SemEval used a smaller portion of OntoNotes with heuristically detected singleton entities and without verbal mentions.

Figure 1 shows the performance of the top system on each domain of OntoNotes, using predicted mentions or gold mentions. The latter results in higher performance, especially for the newswire domain (nw) in Arabic and Chinese. The results show that the gap across domains is not as wide as that in ACE. A likely reason, apart from the fact that the ACE corpus also included singletons, is the additional gold standard metadata that CoNLL provided. In particular, the spoken domain consisted of manually transcribed texts instead of the output of a speech recognizer.

3.5 i2b2-2011 Shared Task

In the interim between the CoNLL-2011 and 2012 shared tasks, the fifth i2b2 (Informatics for Integrating Biology and the Bedside) Workshop on Natural Language Processing Challenges for Clinical Records organized a shared task on coreference resolution in medical records [96],[17] in collaboration with the Veterans Affairs (VA) Consortium for Healthcare Informatics Research (CHIR). The goal was to evaluate the state of the art of coreference resolution in the clinical narrative of a patient, i.e., the unstructured portion of a patient's Electronic Medical Record (EMR).

The i2b2 organizers received advice from the CoNLL-2011 organizers and decided to follow the same scoring strategy and use the CoNLL average, but also to compute the average over MUC, B^3 and CEAF-ϕ_4 for R and P. However, they used their own implementation. Like CoNLL, they followed Cai and Strube's [15] variations to allow B^3 and CEAF to handle predicted mentions. This was still a misunderstanding at the time.

Two coreferentially annotated datasets were used: the ODIE corpus [85] and the i2b2/VA corpus [96]. The annotation schemes in both corpora followed closely the MUC-7 guidelines.[18] Mentions in the ODIE corpus included named entities, nominal and pronominal mentions of the following types: People, Anatomical Site, Disease/Syndrome, Sign/Symptoms, Procedure, Lab or Test Result, Indicator, Reagent, Diagnostic Aid, Organ or Tissue Function, Other, None. Mentions between

[17]https://www.i2b2.org/NLP/

[18]The corpus guidelines are given as an appendix to the main JAMIA publication [96].

Table 15 Coreference performance scores of the CoNLL-2012 systems on Chinese, Arabic and English, including the CONLL score on each language and the official macro average across all three languages, using gold mention boundaries and gold mentions

SYSTEM	OPEN			CLOSED			OFFICIAL	FINAL MODEL	
	ENGLISH CONLL	CHINESE CONLL	ARABIC CONLL	ENGLISH CONLL^{c1}	CHINESE CONLL^{c2}	ARABIC CONLL^{c3}	AVERAGE $\frac{c1+c2+c3}{3}$	TRAIN	DEV
PREDICTED LAYERS; GOLD MENTION BOUNDARIES									
Fernandes et al. [29]				60.8	55.6	44.8	53.7	√	√
Björkelund and Farkas [10]				57.0	57.1	43.4	52.5	√	√
Chen and Ng [19]		69.2		55.8	66.9	32.3	51.6	√	×
Stamborg et al. [90]				52.1	46.0	37.2	45.1	√	√
Yuan et al. [106]				54.2	60.8		38.3	√	√
Xu et al. [103]				51.1	59.7		36.9	√	×
Zhekova et al. [110]				41.5	31.2	25.5	32.7	√	√
Li [56]				29.1	32.8	12.9	25.0	√	√
Chang et al. [17]				57.6			19.2	√	√
Baseline (ONE ENTITY)	15.4	15.4	8.1	15.4	15.4	8.1	13.0	–	–
PREDICTED LAYERS; GOLD MENTIONS									
Fernandes et al. [29]				69.3	66.4	63.5	66.4	√	√
Chen and Ng [19]		80.4		71.3	79.2	43.2	64.6	√	×
Björkelund and Farkas [10]				68.0	70.2	54.9	64.3	√	√
Stamborg et al. [90]				68.0	64.2	45.9	59.4	√	√
Zhekova et al. [110]				54.9	42.7	54.8	50.8	√	√
Yuan et al. [106]				70.5	77.2		49.2	√	√
Xu et al. [103]				61.0	71.1		44.0	√	×
Li [56]				46.1	56.0	29.5	43.9	√	√
Baseline (ONE ENTITY)	39.5	36.2	32.9	39.5	36.2	32.9	36.2	–	–
Chang et al. [17]				77.2			25.7	√	√

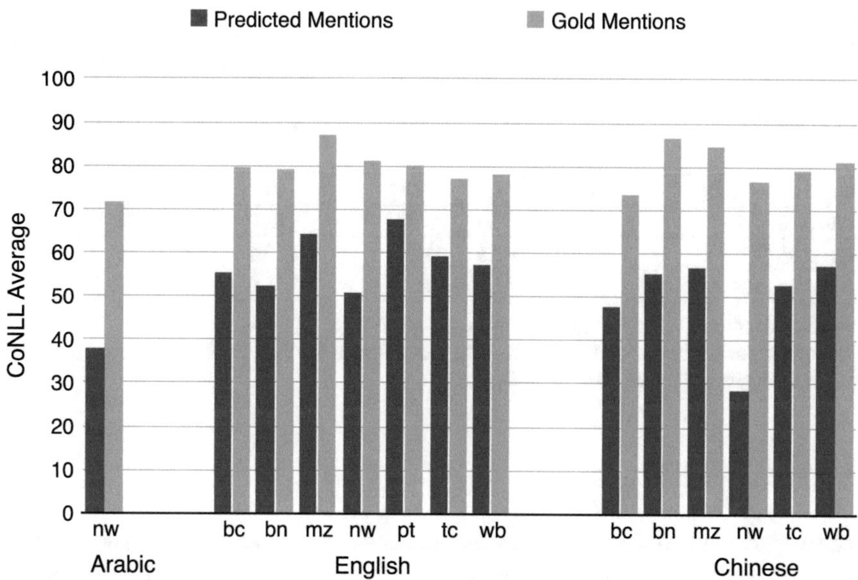

Fig. 1 Fernandes et al.'s [29] scores per domain, using predicted or gold mentions, and across all three languages

the system and gold were matched in two ways, inheriting SemEval's partial mention overlap (head-word mention match) and CoNLL's strict mention overlap.

In the i2b2/VA corpus, mentions were pre-annotated concepts from the i2b2/VA-2010 Challenge, i.e., Problem, Treatment, Test. In addition, references (pronouns and proper names) to people were added. As in the case of MUC, appositives and nominal predicates were annotated as coreference. Singleton entities were also annotated. The i2b2 2011 challenge comprised three tasks:

Task 1A: Mention detection and coreference resolution in the ODIE corpus.
Task 1B: Coreference resolution in the ODIE corpus using gold mentions.
Task 1C: Coreference resolution in the i2b2/VA corpus using gold mentions.

Table 16 shows performance in Task 1A , which is similar to the predicted tracks of SemEval and CoNLL, but of course the different datasets and annotation schemes make results incommensurable. In contrast, performance in Tasks 1B and 1C (Table 17) appears to be easier because gold mentions were provided. Also, many person mentions referred to the same patient.

Table 16 Performance of the i2b2 systems in Task 1A (predicted mentions)

	PARTIAL MENTION OVERLAP			STRICT MENTION OVERLAP		
	AVERAGE[a]			AVERAGE[a]		
SYSTEM	R	P	CONLL	R	P	CONLL
	TASK 1A					
Grouin et al. [40]	81.4	64.2	69.9	84.8	66.2	71.9
Lan et al. [54]	76.5	62.0	66.5	79.0	63.0	67.8
Cai et al. [13][b]	50.6	42.5	41.6	50.6	42.5	41.7
Baseline (SINGLETONS)	50.6	42.5	41.7	50.6	42.5	41.7

[a]Average over the R and P values, respectively, of MUC, B^3 and CEAF-ϕ_4
[b]We report the results as published at the i2b2 proceedings, but there might be an error given that they are the same as the baseline in the next row

4 Conclusions

The organization of shared tasks on coreference resolution has significantly pushed progress in this task, and the participating systems at CoNLL-2012 have come a long way since the early systems that were built for MUC-6. In addition to the participating systems, shared tasks create annotated datasets and set benchmarks that become extensively used in subsequent years by the community at large. As this chapter has shown, defining a shared task on coreference resolution requires making a decision on a few—sometimes contentious—issues, which we summarize now and provide practical guidelines that will hopefully be useful to organizers of future evaluation campaigns. The more consistent shared tasks are, the easier it will be draw comparisons between them.

Regarding the choice of dataset and, by extension, the choice of mentions, there is wide agreement that (1) nominal predicates and appositions should be treated as non-referential NPs, and thus not considered as (coreferent) mentions (Sect. 2.1), and that (2) singleton mentions should be annotated as part of the gold coreference annotation (Sect. 2.1).

On the issue of mention detection, our opinion is that both gold mentions and system mentions provide useful insights on the performance of a coreference resolution system and thus participants should be evaluated on both. The former allows to isolate the task of coreference resolution, while the latter evaluates the complete pipeline of preprocessing modules and the robustness of coreference systems to recover from or cope with errors in earlier stages. The head-word-based relaxed scorer is a good option to make the system mention scenario less dependent on syntactic and corpus-specific decisions regarding mention boundaries. On the other hand, the strict scorer might be a better choice for tasks in which incorrect mention boundaries negatively affect downstream components.

As for the preprocessing information, previous studies like [75] and the results of the CoNLL shared tasks show that using automatic preprocessing does not lead to major losses in coreference performance as compared to using gold

Table 17 Performance of the i2b2 systems in Tasks 1B and 1C (gold mentions) in terms of the CoNLL average

SYSTEM	AVERAGE[a] R	AVERAGE[a] P	CONLL
TASK 1B			
Glinos [35]	84.2	81.4	82.7
Rink et al. [80]	84.5	80.2	82.1
Cai et al. [13]	85.0	77.3	80.6
Grouin et al. [40]	84.8	76.9	80.2
Hinote et al. [43]	85.5	75.8	79.8
Lan et al. [54]	80.5	75.3	77.7
Gooch [36]	70.1	58.2	62.0
Benajiba et al. [7]	50.6	42.5	41.7
Baseline (SINGLETONS)	50.6	42.5	41.7
TASK 1C			
Xu et al. [102]	92.5	90.6	91.5
Rink et al. [80]	91.8	89.5	90.6
Yang et al. [104]	91.1	89.2	90.1
Hinote et al. [43]	89.8	89.5	89.6
Cai et al. [13]	89.4	88.2	88.8
Anick et al. [1]	91.5	85.7	88.3
Gooch [36]	85.8	89.5	87.5
Jindal et al. [48]	83.0	90.1	86.1
Grouin et al. [40]	86.2	85.0	85.6
Ware et al. [98]	84.6	85.0	84.8
Baseline (SINGLETONS)	59.7	51.7	54.1
TASK 1C (without UPMC data)			
Xu et al. [102]	92.0	90.5	91.3
Rink et al. [80]	91.3	89.5	90.4
Yang et al. [104]	90.5	89.0	89.7
Hinote et al. [43]	89.1	90.0	89.5
Cai et al. [13]	88.5	88.1	88.3
Gooch [36]	85.9	89.8	87.8
Anick et al. [1]	91.1	84.8	87.7
Dai et al. [24]	89.6	84.9	87.1
Jindal et al. [48]	82.0	90.5	85.7
Grouin et al. [40]	85.0	86.2	85.6
Baseline (SINGLETONS)	60.2	52.3	54.8

[a]Average over the R and P values, respectively, of MUC, B^3 and CEAF-ϕ_4

preprocessing. In addition, it is a more realistic scenario and we thus argue that the predicted track should be the official track in a shared task, optionally but not necessarily supplemented by a gold track. Regarding the closed versus open track distinction, both SemEval and CoNLL revealed a preference for closed tracks, which participants probably prefer given that they can focus on their coreference system and do not need to worry about all the preprocessing layers. Closed tracks also make it easier to compare directly between systems. Even though open tracks might be preferred by systems that include their own external modules, it seems that focusing organization efforts and participants in just the closed track is the way to go for future evaluation campaigns.

In terms of languages, English has dominated most of the shared tasks, but the last editions of ACE, SemEval-2010 as well as CoNLL-2012 reflect the growing interest in moving towards a more international scenario, and we thus encourage task organizers to include languages other than English.

Finally, coreference evaluation has been one of the most confusing parts in evaluation campaigns. As we have argued, the multiple measures that are available provide different ways of looking at a coreference output, and averaging a link-, mention- and entity-based measure as done by the CONLL average is a good compromise that has succeeded in capturing the strengths of a system at these different levels. We consider that using such an average for ranking the participating systems is the best option for a shared task. The results of each individual score should still be provided as they shed light on what aspects every system is stronger/weaker at. The long-standing bug in the scorer package used at SemEval and OntoNotes has been fixed after thorough discussions [71] and we strongly recommend that future researchers and shared tasks take this publicly available implementation[19] rather than reimplementing their own, which comes at the risk of introducing bugs and misinterpretations.

Numerical results are useful as a quick measure of a system's performance, but numbers alone can sometimes obscure the real quality of an output, consistent errors, etc. Recently, there have been several efforts at building error analysis tools [34, 53] that support a more qualitative analysis of coreference outputs, as we strive to build better and better coreference resolution systems.

Acknowledgements We would like to thank our co-organizers of SemEval-2010 Task 1 (Lluís Màrquez, Emili Sapena, M. Antònia Martí, Mariona Taulé, Véronique Hoste, Massimo Poesio, and Yannick Versley) and the CoNLL-2011/2012 Shared Tasks (Lance Ramshaw, Mitchell Marcus, Martha Palmer, Ralph Weischedel, Alessandro Moschitti, Nianwen Xue, Olga Uryupina, and Yuchen Zhang), as well as the organizers of the MUC, ACE and i2b2 evaluation campaigns.

We would also like to thank all the participants. Without their hard work, patience and perseverance, these evaluations would not have happened.

The second author gratefully acknowledges the support of the Defense Advanced Research Projects Agency (DARPA/IPTO) under the GALE program, DARPA/CMO Contract No. HR0011-06-C-0022, grants R01LM10090 from the National Library of Medicine, and IIS-1219142 from the National Science Foundation and the European Community's Seventh Framework Programme (FP7/2007-2013) under grant number 288024 (LiMoSINe).

[19]http://conll.github.io/reference-coreference-scorers

References

1. Anick, P., Hong, P., Xue, N., et al.: Coreference resolution for electronic medical records. In: Proceedings of the 2011 i2b2/VA/Cincinnati Workshop on Challenges in Natural Language Processing for Clinical Data, Boston (2011)
2. Appelt, D.E., Hobbs, J.R., Bear, J., Israel, D., Kameyama, M., Kehler, A., Martin, D., Myers, K., Tyson, M.: SRI international FASTUS system MUC-6 test results and analysis. In: Proceedings of MUC-6, Columbia, pp. 237–248 (1995)
3. Attardi, G., Rossi, S.D., Simi, M.: TANL-1: coreference resolution by parse analysis and similarity clustering. In: Proceedings of SemEval-2, Uppsala, pp. 108–111 (2010)
4. Bagga, A., Baldwin, B.: Algorithms for scoring coreference chains. In: Proceedings of the LREC Workshop on Linguistic Coreference, Granada, pp. 563–566 (1998)
5. Baldwin, B., Morton, T., Bagga, A., Baldridge, J., Chandraseker, R., Dimitriadis, A., Snyder, K., Wolska, M.: Description of the UPenn CAMP system as used for coreference. In: Proceedings of MUC-7, Fairfax (1998)
6. Baldwin, B., Reynar, J., Collins, M., Eisner, J., Ratnaparkhi, A., Rosenzweig, J., Sarkar, A., Srinivas: University of Pennsylvania: description of the University of Pennsylvania system used for MUC-6. In: Proceedings of MUC-6, Columbia, pp. 177–191 (1995)
7. Benajiba, Y., Shaw, J.: An SVM-based coreference resolution system based on philips information extraction. In: Proceedings of the 2011 i2b2/VA/Cincinnati Workshop on Challenges in Natural Language Processing for Clinical Data, Boston (2011)
8. Bengtson, E., Roth, D.: Understanding the value of features for coreference resolution. In: Proceedings of EMNLP 2008, Honolulu, pp. 294–303 (2008)
9. Bergsma, S., Lin, D.: Bootstrapping path-based pronoun resolution. In: Proceedings of the 21st International Conference on Computational Linguistics and 44th Annual Meeting of the Association for Computational Linguistics, Sydney, pp. 33–40 (2006)
10. Björkelund, A., Farkas, R.: Data-driven multilingual coreference resolution using resolver stacking. In: Proceedings of CoNLL-2012: Shared Task, Jeju Island, pp. 49–55 (2012)
11. Björkelund, A., Nugues, P.: Exploring lexicalized features for coreference resolution. In: Proceedings of CoNLL-2011: Shared Task, Portland, pp. 45–50 (2011)
12. Broscheit, S., Poesio, M., Ponzetto, S.P., Rodríguez, K.J., Romano, L., Uryupina, O., Versley, Y., Zanoli, R.: BART: a multilingual anaphora resolution system. In: Proceedings of SemEval-2, Uppsala, pp. 104–107 (2010)
13. Cai, J., Mujdricza, E., Hou, Y., Strube, M.: Weakly supervised graph-based coreference resolution for clinical texts. In: Proceedings of the 2011 i2b2/VA/Cincinnati Workshop on Challenges in Natural Language Processing for Clinical Data, Boston (2011)
14. Cai, J., Mujdricza-Maydt, E., Strube, M.: Unrestricted coreference resolution via global hypergraph partitioning. In: Proceedings of CoNLL-2011: Shared Task, Portland, pp. 56–60 (2011)
15. Cai, J., Strube, M.: Evaluation metrics for end-to-end coreference resolution systems. In: Proceedings of SIGDIAL, University of Tokyo, Tokyo, pp. 28–36 (2010)
16. Chang, K.W., Samdani, R., Rozovskaya, A., Rizzolo, N., Sammons, M., Roth, D.: Inference protocols for coreference resolution. In: Proceedings of CoNLL-2011: Shared Task, Portland, pp. 40–44 (2011)
17. Chang, K.W., Samdani, R., Rozovskaya, A., Sammons, M., Roth, D.: Illinois-coref: the UI system in the CoNLL-2012 shared task. In: Proceedings of CoNLL-2012: Shared Task, Jeju Island, pp. 113–117 (2012)
18. Charton, E., Gagnon, M.: Poly-co: a multilayer perceptron approach for coreference detection. In: Proceedings of CoNLL-2011: Shared Task, Portland, pp. 97–101 (2011)
19. Chen, C., Ng, V.: Combining the best of two worlds: a hybrid approach to multilingual coreference resolution. In: Proceedings of CoNLL-2012: Shared Task, Jeju Island, pp. 56–63 (2012)

20. Chen, W., Zhang, M., Qin, B.: Coreference resolution system using maximum entropy classifier. In: Proceedings of CoNLL-2011: Shared Task, Portland, pp. 127–130 (2011)
21. Chinchor, N.A.: Overview of MUC-7/MET-2. In: Proceedings of the Seventh Message Understanding Conference (MUC-7), Fairfax (1998)
22. Choi, Y., Cardie, C.: Structured local training and biased potential functions for conditional random fields with application to coreference resolution. In: Proceedings of HLT-NAACL, Rochester, pp. 65–72 (2007)
23. Culotta, A., Wick, M., Hall, R., McCallum, A.: First-order probabilistic models for coreference resolution. In: HLT/NAACL, Rochester, pp. 81–88 (2007)
24. Dai, H., Wu, C., Chen, C., et al.: Co-reference resolution of the medical concepts in the patient discharge summaries. In: Proceedings of the 2011 i2b2/VA/Cincinnati Workshop on Challenges in Natural Language Processing for Clinical Data, Boston (2011)
25. van Deemter, K., Kibble, R.: On coreferring: coreference in MUC and related annotation schemes. Comput. Linguist. **26**(4), 629–637 (2000). Squib
26. Denis, P., Baldridge, J.: Joint determination of anaphoricity and coreference resolution using integer programming. In: Proceedings of NAACL-HLT 2007, Rochester (2007)
27. Denis, P., Baldridge, J.: Global joint models for coreference resolution and named entity classification. Procesamiento del Lenguaje Natural **42**, 87–96 (2009)
28. Doddington, G., Mitchell, A., Przybocki, M., Ramshaw, L., Strassel, S., Weischedel, R.: The automatic content extraction (ACE) program – tasks, data, and evaluation. In: Proceedings of LREC 2004, Lisbon, pp. 837–840 (2004)
29. Fernandes, E., dos Santos, C., Milidiú, R.: Latent structure perceptron with feature induction for unrestricted coreference resolution. In: Proceedings of CoNLL-2012: Shared Task, Jeju Island, pp. 41–48 (2012)
30. Fisher, D., Soderland, S., McCarthy, J., Feng, F., Lehnert, W.: Description of the UMass system as used for MUC-6. In: Proceedings of MUC-6, Columbia, pp. 127–140 (1995)
31. Fukumoto, J., Masui, F., Shimohata, M., Sasaki, M.: Oki electric industry: description of the Oki system as used for MUC-7. In: Proceedings of MUC-7, Fairfax (1998)
32. Gaizauskas, R., Wakao, T., Humphreys, K., Cunningham, H., Wilks, Y.: University of Sheffield: description of the LaSIE system as used for MUC-6. In: Proceedings of MUC-6, Columbia, pp. 207–220 (1995)
33. Garigliano, R., Urbanowicz, A., Nettleton, D.J.: University of Durham: description of the LOLITA system as used in MUC-7. In: Proceedings of MUC-7, Fairfax (1998)
34. Gärtner, M., Björkelund, A., Thiele, G., Seeker, W., Kuhn, J.: Visualization, search, and error analysis for coreference annotations. In: Proceedings of ACL: System Demonstrations, Baltimore, pp. 7–12 (2014)
35. Glinos, D.: A search based method for clinical text coreference resolution. In: Proceedings of the 2011 i2b2/VA/Cincinnati Workshop on Challenges in Natural Language Processing for Clinical Data, Boston (2011)
36. Gooch, P.: Coreference resolution in clinical discharge summaries, progress notes, surgical and pathology reports: a unified lexical approach. In: Proceedings of the 2011 i2b2/VA/Cincinnati Workshop on Challenges in Natural Language Processing for Clinical Data, Boston (2011)
37. Grishman, R.: The NYU system for MUC-6 or where's the syntax? In: Proceedings of MUC-6, Columbia, pp. 167–175 (1995)
38. Grishman, R., Sundheim, B.: Design of the MUC-6 evaluation. In: Proceedings of the Sixth Message Understanding Conference (MUC-6), Columbia (1995)
39. Grishman, R., Sundheim, B.: Message understanding conference-6: a brief history. In: Proceedings of COLING, Copenhagen, pp. 466–471 (1996)
40. Grouin, C., Dinarelli, M., Rosset, S.: Coreference resolution in clinical reports – the limsi participation in the i2b2/va 2011 challenge. In: Proceedings of the 2011 i2b2/VA/Cincinnati Workshop on Challenges in Natural Language Processing for Clinical Data, Boston (2011)
41. Haghighi, A., Klein, D.: Unsupervised coreference resolution in a nonparametric Bayesian model. In: Proceedings of ACL, Prague, pp. 848–855 (2007)

42. Hendrickx, I., Bouma, G., Coppens, F., Daelemans, W., Hoste, V., Kloosterman, G., Mineur, A.M., Van Der Vloet, J., Verschelde, J.L.: A coreference corpus and resolution system for Dutch. In: Proceedings of LREC, Marrakech (2008)
43. Hinote, D., Ramirez, C., Chen, P.: A comparative study of co-refernece resolution in clinical text. In: Proceedings of the 2011 i2b2/VA/Cincinnati Workshop on Challenges in Natural Language Processing for Clinical Data, Boston (2011)
44. Hinrichs, E., Kübler, S., Naumann, K.: A unified representation for morphological, syntactic, semantic and referential annotations. In: ACL Workshop on Frontiers in Corpus Annotation II: Pie in the Sky, Ann Arbor (2005)
45. Hovy, E., Marcus, M., Palmer, M., Ramshaw, L., Weischedel, R.: OntoNotes: the 90 % solution. In: Proceedings of HLT/NAACL, pp. 57–60. Association for Computational Linguistics, New York City (2006)
46. Humphreys, K., Gaizauskas, R., Azzam, S., Huyck, C., Mitchell, B., Cunningham, H., Wilks, Y.: University of Sheffield: description of the LaSIE-II system as used for MUC-7. In: Proceedings of MUC-7, Fairfax (1998)
47. Irwin, J., Komachi, M., Matsumoto, Y.: Narrative schema as world knowledge for coreference resolution. In: Proceedings of CoNLL-2011: Shared Task, Portland, pp. 86–92 (2011)
48. Jindal, P., Roth, D.: Using domain knowledge and domain-inspired discourse model for coreference resolution for clinical narratives. In: Proceedings of the 2011 i2b2/VA/Cincinnati Workshop on Challenges in Natural Language Processing for Clinical Data, Boston (2011)
49. Klein, D., Kummerfeld, J.K., Bansal, M., Burkett, D.: Mention detection: heuristics for the OntoNotes annotations. In: Proceedings of CoNLL-2011: Shared Task, Portland, pp. 102–106 (2011)
50. Klenner, M., Tuggener, D.: An incremental model for coreference resolution with restrictive antecedent accessibility. In: Proceedings of CoNLL-2011: Shared Task, Portland, pp. 81–85 (2011)
51. Kobdani, H., Schütze, H.: SUCRE: a modular system for coreference resolution. In: Proceedings of SemEval-2, Uppsala, pp. 92–95 (2010)
52. Kobdani, H., Schütze, H.: Supervised coreference resolution with SUCRE. In: Proceedings of CoNLL-2011: Shared Task, Portland, pp. 71–75 (2011)
53. Kummerfeld, J.K., Klein, D.: Error-driven analysis of challenges in coreference resolution. In: Proceedings of EMNLP, Seattle, pp. 265–277 (2013)
54. Lan, M., Zhao, J., Zhang, K., et al.: Comparative investigation on learning-based and rule-based approaches to coreference resolution in clinic domain: a case study in i2b2 challenge 2011 Task 1. In: Proceedings of the 2011 i2b2/VA/Cincinnati Workshop on Challenges in Natural Language Processing for Clinical Data, Boston (2011)
55. Lee, H., Peirsman, Y., Chang, A., Chambers, N., Surdeanu, M., Jurafsky, D.: Stanford's multi-pass sieve coreference resolution system at the CoNLL-2011 shared task. In: Proceedings of CoNLL-2011: Shared Task, Portland, pp. 28–34 (2011)
56. Li, B.: Learning to model multilingual unrestricted coreference in OntoNotes. In: Proceedings of CoNLL-2012: Shared Task, Jeju Island, pp. 129–135 (2012)
57. Li, X., Wang, X., Liao, X.: Simple maximum entropy models for multilingual coreference resolution. In: Proceedings of CoNLL-2012: Shared Task, Jeju Island, pp. 83–87 (2012)
58. Li, X., Wang, X., Qi, S.: Coreference resolution with loose transitivity constraints. In: Proceedings of CoNLL-2011: Shared Task, Portland, pp. 107–111 (2011)
59. Lin, D.: University of Manitoba: description of the PIE system used for MUC-6. In: Proceedings of MUC-6, Columbia, pp. 114–126 (1995)
60. Lin, D.: Using collocation statistics in information extraction. In: Proceedings of MUC-7, Fairfax (1998)
61. Luo, X.: On coreference resolution performance metrics. In: Proceedings of HLT-EMNLP, Vancouver, pp. 25–32 (2005)
62. Luo, X.: Coreference or not: a twin model for coreference resolution. In: Proceedings of HLT-NAACL 2007, Rochester, pp. 73–80 (2007)

63. Luo, X., Ittycheriah, A., Jing, H., Kambhatla, N., Roukos, S.: A mention-synchronous coreference resolution algorithm based on the Bell tree. In: Proceedings of ACL, Barcelona, pp. 21–26 (2004)
64. Luo, X., Pradhan, S., Recasens, M., Hovy, E.: An extension of BLANC to system mentions. In: Proceedings of ACL, Baltimore, pp. 24–29 (2014)
65. Màrquez, L., Recasens, M., Sapena, E.: Coreference resolution: an empirical study based on SemEval-2010 shared Task 1. Lang. Resour. Eval. **47**(3), 661–694 (2012)
66. Martschat, S., Cai, J., Broscheit, S., Mújdricza-Maydt, É., Strube, M.: A multigraph model for coreference resolution. In: Proceedings of CoNLL-2012: Shared Task, Jeju Island, pp. 100–106 (2012)
67. Mitkov, R.: Towards a more consistent and comprehensive evaluation of anaphora resolution algorithms and systems. In: Proceedings of the Discourse Anaphora and Anaphora Resolution Colloquium (DAARC 2000), Lancaster, pp. 96–107 (2010)
68. Morgan, R., Garigliano, R., Callaghan, P., Poria, S., Smith, M., Urbanowicz, A., Collingham, R., Costantino, M., Cooper, C., the LOLITA Group: University of Durham: description of the LOLITA system as used in MUC-6. In: Proceedings of MUC-6, Columbia, pp. 71–85 (1995)
69. Ng, V.: Graph-cut-based anaphoricity determination for coreference resolution. In: Proceedings of NAACL-HLT 2009, Boulder, pp. 575–583 (2009)
70. Pradhan, S., Hovy, E., Marcus, M., Palmer, M., Ramshaw, L., Weischedel, R.: OntoNotes: a unified relational semantic representation. Int. J. Semant. Comput. **1**(4), 405–419 (2007)
71. Pradhan, S., Luo, X., Recasens, M., Hovy, E., Ng, V., Strube, M.: Scoring coreference partitions of predicted mentions: a reference implementation. In: Proceedings of ACL, Baltimore, pp. 30–35 (2014)
72. Pradhan, S., Moschitti, A., Xue, N., Uryupina, O., Zhang, Y.: CoNLL-2012 shared task: modeling multilingual unrestricted coreference in OntoNotes. In: Proceedings of CoNLL-2012: Shared Task, Jeju Island, pp. 1–40 (2012)
73. Pradhan, S., Ramshaw, L., Marcus, M., Palmer, M., Weischedel, R., Xue, N.: CoNLL-2011 shared task: modeling unrestricted coreference in OntoNotes. In: Proceedings of CoNLL-2011: Shared Task, Portland, pp. 1–27 (2011)
74. Rahman, A., Ng, V.: Supervised models for coreference resolution. In: Proceedings of EMNLP 2009, Suntec, pp. 968–977 (2009)
75. Recasens, M., Hovy, E.: Coreference resolution across corpora: languages, coding schemes, and preprocessing information. In: Proceedings of ACL, Uppsala, pp. 1423–1432 (2010)
76. Recasens, M., Hovy, E.: BLANC: implementing the rand index for coreference evaluation. Nat. Lang. Eng. **17**(4), 485–510 (2011)
77. Recasens, M., de Marneffe, M.C., Potts, C.: The life and death of discourse entities: identifying singleton mentions. In: Proceedings of NAACL-2013, Atlanta, pp. 627–633 (2013)
78. Recasens, M., Màrquez, L., Sapena, E., Martí, M.A., Taulé, M., Hoste, V., Poesio, M., Versley, Y.: SemEval-2010 Task 1: coreference resolution in multiple languages. In: Proceedings of SemEval-2, Uppsala, pp. 1–8 (2010)
79. Recasens, M., Martí, M.A.: AnCora-CO: coreferentially annotated corpora for Spanish and Catalan. Lang. Resour. Eval. **44**(4), 315–345 (2010)
80. Rink, B., Harabagiu, S.: A supervised multi-pass sieve approach for resolving coreference in clinical records. In: Proceedings of the 2011 i2b2/VA/Cincinnati Workshop on Challenges in Natural Language Processing for Clinical Data, Boston (2011)
81. Rodríguez, K.J., Delogu, F., Versley, Y., Stemle, E., Poesio, M.: Anaphoric annotation of Wikipedia and blogs in the live memories corpus. In: Proceedings LREC, Valletta (poster) (2010)
82. dos Santos, C.N., Carvalho, D.L.: Rule and tree ensembles for unrestricted coreference resolution. In: Proceedings of CoNLL-2011: Shared Task, Portland, pp. 51–55 (2011)
83. Sapena, E., Padró, L., Turmo, J.: RelaxCor: a global relaxation labeling approach to coreference resolution for the SemEval-2 coreference task. In: Proceedings of SemEval-2, Uppsala, pp. 88–91 (2010)

84. Sapena, E., Padró, L., Turmo, J.: RelaxCor participation in CoNLL shared task on coreference resolution. In: Proceedings of CoNLL-2011: Shared Task, Portland, pp. 35–39 (2011)
85. Savova, G.K., Chapman, W.W., Zheng, J., Crowley, R.S.: Anaphoric relations in the clinical narrative: corpus creation. J. Am. Med. Inform. Assoc. **18**(4), 459–465 (2011)
86. Shou, H., Zhao, H.: System paper for CoNLL-2012 shared task: hybrid rule-based algorithm for coreference resolution. In: Proceedings of CoNLL-2012: Shared Task, Jeju Island, pp. 118–121 (2012)
87. Sobha, L.D., Pattabhi, R.K.R., Vijay Sundar Ram, R., Malarkodi, C.S., Akilandeswari, A.: Hybrid approach for coreference resolution. In: Proceedings of CoNLL-2011: Shared Task, Portland (2011)
88. Song, Y., Wang, H., Jiang, J.: Link type based pre-cluster pair model for coreference resolution. In: Proceedings of CoNLL-2011: Shared Task, Portland, pp. 131–315 (2011)
89. Soon, W.M., Ng, H.T., Lim, D.C.Y.: A machine learning approach to coreference resolution of noun phrases. Comput. Linguist. **27**(4), 521–544 (2001)
90. Stamborg, M., Medved, D., Exner, P., Nugues, P.: Using syntactic dependencies to solve coreferences. In: Proceedings of CoNLL-2012: Shared Task, Jeju Island, pp. 64–70 (2012)
91. Stoyanov, V., Babbar, U., Gupta, P., Cardie, C.: Reconciling OntoNotes: unrestricted coreference resolution in OntoNotes with reconcile. In: Proceedings of CoNLL-2011: Shared Task, Portland, pp. 122–126 (2011)
92. Stoyanov, V., Gilbert, N., Cardie, C., Riloff, E.: Conundrums in noun phrase coreference resolution: making sense of the state-of-the-art. In: Proceedings of ACL-IJCNLP, Singapore, pp. 656–664 (2009)
93. Uryupina, O.: Corry: a system for coreference resolution. In: Proceedings of SemEval-2, Uppsala, pp. 100–103 (2010)
94. Uryupina, O., Moschitti, A., Poesio, M.: BART goes multilingual: the UniTN/Essex submission to the CoNLL-2012 shared task. In: Proceedings of CoNLL-2012: Shared Task, Jeju Island, pp. 122–128 (2012)
95. Uryupina, O., Saha, S., Ekbal, A., Poesio, M.: Multi-metric optimization for coreference: the UniTN/IITP/Essex submission to the 2011 CONLL shared task. In: Proceedings of CoNLL-2011: Shared Task, Portland, pp. 61–65 (2011)
96. Uzuner, O., Bodnari, A., Shen, S., Forbush, T., Pestian, J., South, B.R.: Evaluating the state of the art in coreference resolution for electronic medical records. J. Am. Med. Inform. Assoc. **19**(5), 786–791 (2012)
97. Vilain, M., Burger, J., Aberdeen, J., Connolly, D., Hirschman, L.: A model-theoretic coreference scoring scheme. In: Proceedings of MUC-6, Columbia, pp. 45–52 (1995)
98. Ware, H., Mullet, C., Jagannathan, V., El-Rawas, O.: Machine learning-based coreference resolution of concepts in clinical documents. In: Proceedings of the 2011 i2b2/VA/Cincinnati Workshop on Challenges in Natural Language Processing for Clinical Data, Boston (2011)
99. Weischedel, R., Hovy, E., Palmer, M., Marcus, M., Belvin, R., Pradhan, S., Ramshaw, L., Xue, N.: OntoNotes: a large training corpus for enhanced processing. In: Olive, J., Christianson, C., McCary, J. (eds.) Handbook of Natural Language Processing and Machine Translation. Springer, New York (2011)
100. Xiong, H., Liu, Q.: ICT: system description for CoNLL-2012. In: Proceedings of CoNLL-2012: Shared Task, Jeju Island, pp. 71–75 (2012)
101. Xiong, H., Song, L., Meng, F., Liu, Y., Liu, Q., Lv, Y.: ETS: an error tolerable system for coreference resolution. In: Proceedings of CoNLL-2011: Shared Task, Portland, pp. 76–80 (2011)
102. Xu, Y., Liu, J., Wu, J., Wang, Y., Chang, E.: EHUATUO: a mention-pair coreference system by exploiting document intrinsic latent structures and world knowledge in discharge summaries (Rank 1). In: Proceedings of the 2011 i2b2/VA/Cincinnati Workshop on Challenges in Natural Language Processing for Clinical Data, Boston (2011)
103. Xu, R., Xu, J., Liu, J., Liu, C., Zou, C., Gui, L., Zheng, Y., Qu, P.: Incorporating rule-based and statistic-based techniques for coreference resolution. In: Proceedings of CoNLL-2012: Shared Task, Jeju Island, pp. 107–112 (2012)

104. Yang, H., Willis, A., De Roeck, A., Nuseibeh, B.: A system for coreference resolution in clinical documents. In: Proceedings of the 2011 i2b2/VA/Cincinnati Workshop on Challenges in Natural Language Processing for Clinical Data, Boston (2011)
105. Yang, Y., Xue, N., Anick, P.: A machine learning-based coreference detection system for OntoNotes. In: Proceedings of CoNLL-2011: Shared Task, Portland, pp. 117–121 (2011)
106. Yuan, B., Chen, Q., Xiang, Y., Wang, X., Ge, L., Liu, Z., Liao, M., Si, X.: A mixed deterministic model for coreference resolution. In: Proceedings of CoNLL-2012: Shared Task, Jeju Island, pp. 76–82 (2012)
107. Zhang, X., Wu, C., Zhao, H.: Chinese coreference resolution via ordered filtering. In: Proceedings of CoNLL-2012: Shared Task, Jeju Island, pp. 95–99 (2012)
108. Zhekova, D., Kübler, S.: UBIU: a language-independent system for coreference resolution. In: Proceedings of SemEval-2, Uppsala, pp. 96–99 (2010)
109. Zhekova, D., Kübler, S.: UBIU: a robust system for resolving unrestricted coreference. In: Proceedings of CoNLL-2011: Shared Task, Portland, pp. 112–116 (2011)
110. Zhekova, D., Kübler, S., Bonner, J., Ragheb, M., Hsu, Y.Y.: UBIU for multilingual coreference resolution in ontonotes. In: Proceedings of CoNLL-2012: Shared Task, Jeju Island, pp. 88–94 (2012)
111. Zhou, H., Li, Y., Huang, D., Zhang, Y., Wu, C., Yang, Y.: Combining syntactic and semantic features by SVM for unrestricted coreference resolution. In: Proceedings of CoNLL-2011: Shared Task, Portland, pp. 66–70 (2011)

Preprocessing Technology

Olga Uryupina and Roberto Zanoli

Abstract Coreference is a complex phenomenon involving a variety of linguistic factors: from surface similarity to morphological agreement, specific syntactic constraints, semantics, salience and encyclopedic knowledge. It is therefore essential for any coreference resolution system to rely on a rich linguistic representation of a document to be analyzed. This chapter focuses on the preprocessing technology, taking into consideration a variety of external tools needed to create such representations, and shows how to combine them in a *Preprocessing Pipeline*, in order to extract mentions of entities in a given document, describing their linguistic properties.

Keywords Preprocessing technology NLP pipelines • NLP tools • Chunking

1 Introduction

Accurate interpretation of anaphoric links within a document relies on a variety of linguistic clues. State-of-the-art coreference resolution systems incorporate, therefore, a number of external Natural Language Processing (NLP) modules. Even the most knowledge-poor algorithms [26] need an NP-chunker to generate mentions (and a sentence splitter to provide input for the chunker). Additional knowledge may be gained from an NE-tagger and a parser, semantic role labeling tools and encyclopedic resources. All these external modules are typically combined in a *Preprocessing Pipeline* (cf. Fig. 1) that takes a document as an input and provides a list of mentions with their relevant linguistic properties.

Consider the following commonly used example[1]:

[1]In all the examples in this chapter we use square brackets to indicate correct (gold) mention boundaries.

O. Uryupina (✉)
DISI University of Trento, Trento, Italy
e-mail: uryupina@gmail.com

R. Zanoli
Fondazione Bruno Kessler, Trento, Italy
e-mail: zanoli@fbk.eu

M. Poesio et al. (eds.), *Anaphora Resolution*, Theory and Applications of Natural Language Processing, DOI 10.1007/978-3-662-47909-4_7

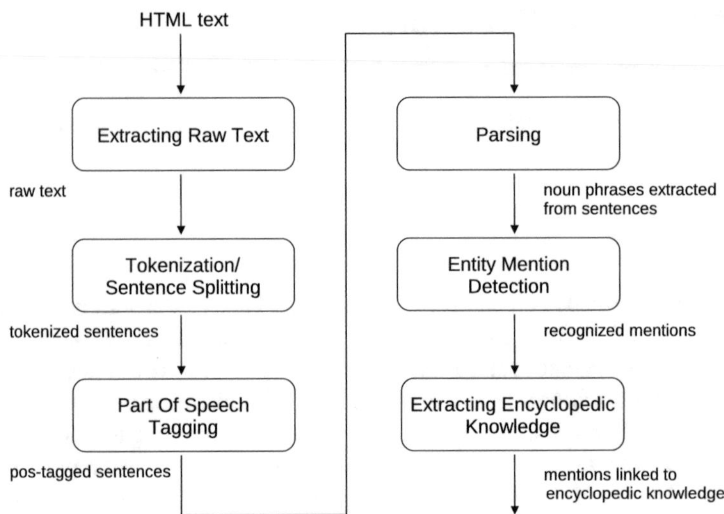

Fig. 1 A typical preprocessing pipeline for a coreference resolution system

(11) [Sophia Loren] says [she] will always be grateful to [Bono]. [The actress] revealed that [the [U2] singer] helped [her] calm down when [she] became scared by [a thunderstorm] while traveling on a plane.

To correctly analyze this snippet, a typical anaphora resolution system relies on a combination of general purpose and coreference-specific components. The former help extract the text body and split it into sentences and tokens, as well as provide their syntactic and semantic interpretation (cf. Table 1). The latter uses this information to create a list of *mentions*—basic units to be processed by the main coreference resolution module. This can be seen as a separate task, *Entity Mention Detection* (EMD).

Each mention is characterized with its extension (the sequence of tokens belonging to the given mention) and its properties. Table 2 shows a list of mentions for our example 11. Note that some properties might be unspecified: for example, the gender value for the mention "the U2 singer" cannot be reliably determined from the provided textual information.

Deficiencies at the preprocessing step may affect the overall coreference resolution quality to a very large extent. Thus, a previous study [46] shows that up to 35 % of precision errors and up to 18 % of recall errors made by a corpus-based coreference resolution system on the MUC data can be traced back to preprocessing inadequacies.

Thus, if our preprocessing pipeline is unable to provide correct mention properties, feature vectors extracted by the main coreference resolution component become either spurious or non-informative. For example, if our system is unable to detect the correct semantic class (PERSON) and gender (FEMALE) labels for "Sophia Loren", we can hardly expect it to find the correct antecedent for

Table 1 General-purpose preprocessing information for the first sentence of example (11)

Token	Sentence	Lemma	POS	NE
Sophia	–	sophia	NNP	B-PERSON
Loren	–	loren	NNP	I-PERSON
says	–	say	VBZ	O
she	–	she	PRP	O
will	–	will	MD	O
always	–	always	RB	O
be	–	be	VB	O
grateful	–	grateful	JJ	O
to	–	to	TO	O
Bono	–	bono	NNP	B-PERSON
.	END	.	.	O

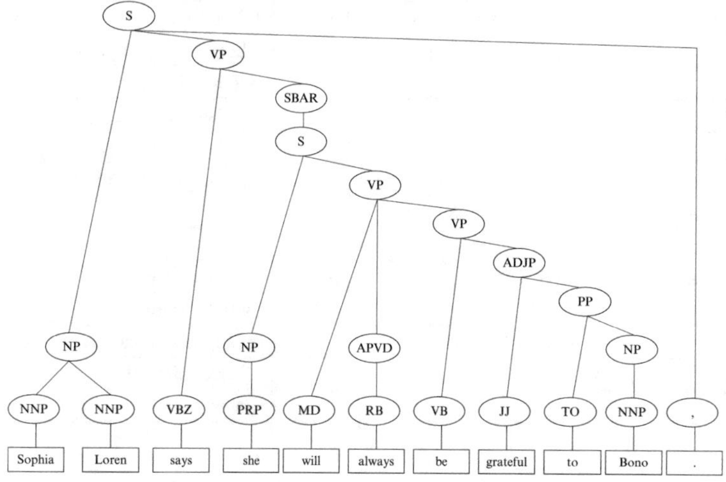

the pronoun "she", simply because the relevant feature vector does not contain enough information. Similarly, if our system provides no fine-grained semantic or encyclopedic knowledge and is thus unable to classify "Sophia Loren" as "actress", we cannot find the correct antecedent for our mention "the actress".

If the preprocessing pipeline cannot reliably detect mention boundaries, the coreference component could encounter problems, both at the testing and training phase. While testing, it provides incorrect output: for example, if the pipeline erroneously splits "Sophia Loren" into two different PERSON mentions, "Sophia" and "Loren", the coreference resolver is not able to resolve the pronoun "she", since the related name has not been correctly detected. While training, the coreference component starts with aligning gold mentions to the automatically extracted ones. When the alignment fails, the corresponding gold mentions do not generate any training instances and thus the valuable gold information becomes partially unavailable to the system.

Table 2 Mention Detection for example (11)

Mention	Head	Type	Sem. class	Number	Gender	Encyclopedic
Sophia Loren	Sophia Loren	NAM	PERSON	SG	F	category: entertainment
						subtype: actress
						name: Sofia Villani Scicolone
she	she	PRO	PERSON	SG	F	
Bono	Bono	NAM	PERSON	SG	M	category: music
						subtype: singer
						subtype: songwriter
						subtype: philanthropist
						name: Paul David Hewson
The actress	actress	NOM	PERSON	SG	F	category: entertainment
the U2 singer	singer	NOM	PERSON	SG	–	category: music
U2	U2	NAM	ORG	–	N	category: music
						subtype: musical group
						member: Bono
						member: Adam Clayton
						member: The Edge
						member: Larry Mullen
her	she	PRO	PERSON	SG	F	
she	she	PRO	PERSON	SG	F	
a thunderstorm	thunderstorm	NOM	OBJECT	SG	N	category: weather
						subtype: storm
a plane	plane	NOM	OBJECT	SG	N	category: aeronautics
						subtype: aircraft
						subtype: artifact

If one of general-purpose components makes an error, it might not affect our coreference resolver directly. For example, if the part-of-speech tagger classifies the adjective "scared" as a finite verb, it probably remains unnoticed by any coreference resolution system we are aware of. However, some errors may propagate to the coreference-specific part of the pipeline. For example, if the parser detects "that" as a noun phrase, the EMD component might propose "that" as a mention, and the coreference resolver might then create a spurious link from it to an arbitrary antecedent.

This example illustrates the importance of a high-quality preprocessing pipeline: even the most advanced model of coreference cannot cope with spurious mentions with noisy properties.

In this chapter we discuss preprocessing pipelines used in the state-of-the-art studies on coreference. In Sect. 2, we focus on general-purpose off-the-shelf components. In Sect. 3, we discuss state-of-the-art approaches to the EMD task. Systems may vary in the amount of external tools they use, as well as in their particular choices. We provide a brief summary on the preprocessing pipelines of publicly available systems in Sect. 5.

2 Off-the-Shelf Preprocessing

Several coreferentially annotated corpora have been made available in the past 15 years: MUC, ACE, ARRAU, OntoNotes and many others, see chapters "Annotated Corpora and Annotation Tools" and "Evaluation Campaigns" for details. These dataset come in different formats and therefore require varying amounts of preprocessing. Some corpora provide token-based standoff annotation in, for example, the MMAX2 XML (ARRAU) or CoNLL tabular (OntoNotes) formats. They typically contain some preprocessing information and therefore do not require most of the steps described in this section. Below we discuss the amount of preprocessing needed for either raw texts or corpora annotated with character-based standoff or inline schemes (ACE, MUC).

2.1 Extracting Raw Text

The first step of any pipeline involves interpreting the input format of the corpus to be processed to extract fragments of textual information. To our knowledge, no coreferentially annotated corpora contain documents with a complex HTML structure. No advanced HTML parsing and cleaning techniques (cf., for example, [1] for an overview of related approaches) are therefore necessary. Most research groups rely on in-house heuristical tools for extracting raw texts from the input data.

Several issues should be kept in mind at this preprocessing step. First, a raw text is required by other components of the pipeline, for example, by a parser or an NE-tagger. Errors or oversimplifications at this stage may propagate to further components of the pipeline thus decreasing their accuracy. Consider the following snippet, showing the first lines of a MUC-7 document:

(12) <DOCID> nyt960126.0277 </DOCID>
<STORYID cat=f pri=r> A4097 </STORYID>
<SLUG fv=tia-z> BC-[AEROSPATIALE]-[FORUM]-BL </SLUG>
<DATE> [01-26] </DATE>
<NWORDS> 0450 </NWORDS>
<PREAMBLE>
BC-[AEROSPATIALE]-[FORUM]-BLOOM
[BLOOMBERG FORUM]:
[[AEROSPATIALE]'S GALLOIS] SAYS [EUROPE] 'TOO SLOW'
(For use by New York Times News Service clients)
By Andrea Rothman
c.1996 [Bloomberg Business News]
</PREAMBLE>
<TEXT>

<p>
Paris, [Jan. 26] ([Bloomberg])—[Louis Gallois, [chief executive of [Aerospatiale]],] is unequivocal about how [Europe] compares to the [U.S.] in consolidating the aerospace and defense industries:

If we follow a naive approach and extract the raw text by simply eliminating all the SGML markup, the pipeline considers "1996 Paris, Jan.26 ..." to be a single sentence, yielding further errors at the parsing and chunking stages.[2] The correct solution involves identifying distinct document fragments and submitting them to further pipeline components separately.

Second, it might be beneficial to keep the HTML/SGML mark-up and incorporate it into the coreference resolution algorithm, for example, by designing markup-specific features. Not many state-of-the-art tools use HTML/SGML structure of their input documents, partially because at least some of the available corpora are stripped of this information. Several studies, however, show that HTML/SGML markup encodes valuable information relevant for the task. Thus, Uryupina [46] investigates correlations between the structure of MUC documents and anaphoricity. Luo et al. [31] show that ACE SGML markup helps improve the performance of their system.

At least some coreferentially annotated corpora contain automatically created transcripts of spoken language. Such documents may suffer from spelling and capitalization errors:

(13) George W. bush has an impressive victory. Before the night was out, some republicans were practically anointing him as their presidential candidate two years from now. ABC's dean Reynolds reports from Texas.

In this snippet, the names "Bush" and "Dean" are incorrectly lower-cased. These errors may propagate further to decrease the performance level of the mention detection component. A preprocessing pipeline for such documents should ideally include spelling correction [10, 36] and true-casing [30] modules. We are, however, unaware of any coreference resolution algorithm making use of such techniques.

2.2 *Tokenization and Sentence Splitting*

Prior to more sophisticated processing, the character stream produced at the previous step has to be broken up into significant constituents, that is words and sentences. Breaking the text into words is called *tokenization*, whereas splitting the text into sentences is referred to as *sentence splitting*. In spite of its presumed simplicity, no standard solution for character stream tokenization exists; in many

[2]The MUC guidelines require annotation of the SLUG, DATE, NWORDS, PREAMBLE and TEXT parts of a document.

languages, such as English, one of the main clues used to identify a word is the occurrence of white spaces: a space, a tab or a new line between words. However, these markers are not necessarily reliable: frequently, punctuation marks (commas, semicolons and periods) are attached to words and deciding whether or not they are part of a word could be problematic. In addition, periods are used in abbreviations and acronyms (e.g. “Mr.”, “U.S.”) and they should stay on with the word. For other languages that do not use white spaces as word separators, (e.g. Chinese and Japanese) the task becomes even more challenging.

The step of sentence splitting, or determining sentence boundaries in an unrestricted text, is often combined with tokenization, but it can also be performed separately. For English, most state-of-the-art NLP tools and libraries [20, 27] have built-in sentence splitting facilities. Still, some algorithms, for example, Charniak’s parser [13] rely on external sentence segmentation modules. A robust sentence splitter for English has been created by Reynar and Ratnaparkhi [42], who report the accuracy level of 98.5–99 % on the Wall Street Journal.

Nevertheless, if a particular corpus assumes annotation not only of the text body, but also of auxiliary and technical parts of a document (headers, preamble etc.), the best solution to the tokenization and sentence splitting problems involves a combination of an off-the-shelf tool with heuristical algorithms designed specifically for the data.

2.3 Part-Of-Speech Tagging

Part-Of-Speech (POS) tagging is the problem of determining the correct part of speech labels (e.g. noun, verb or adjective) of a sequence of words as identified at the previous phase. It plays an important role for the further higher-level preprocessing, such as recognizing noun phrases. For example, a possible analysis of the sentence:

(14) All human beings are born free and equal in dignity and rights.

is:

(15) $\mathit{All}_{[\mathit{determiner}]}$ $\mathit{human}_{[\mathit{adjective}]}$ $\mathit{beings}_{[\mathit{noun}]}$ $\mathit{are}_{[\mathit{verb}]}$ $\mathit{born}_{[\mathit{verb}]}$ $\mathit{free}_{[\mathit{adjective}]}$ $\mathit{and}_{[\mathit{conjunction}]}$ $\mathit{equal}_{[\mathit{adjective}]}$ $\mathit{in}_{[\mathit{preposition}]}$ $\mathit{dignity}_{[\mathit{noun}]}$ $\mathit{and}_{[\mathit{conjunction}]}$ $\mathit{rights}_{[\mathit{noun}]}$ $._{[\mathit{punctuation}]}$

The task is not trivial since many words are ambiguous: for example, the English word “tag” can be a noun (“the tag of a word”) or a verb (“to tag a word”). More often than not, POS taggers also perform morphological analysis of words, adding to the output a sequence of stems (lemmata) of the input words.

A number of approaches have been proposed for POS tagging. Rule-based taggers [23] assign a tag to each word by using a set of hand-written rules. In contrast to this, probabilistic approaches [17, 45] rely on a training corpus to get the most probable tag for a word. Finally, transformation-based approaches [9] combine rule-based and statistical modeling. Although the reported accuracy for most of the systems is around 97 %, these results are generally obtained under idealistic assumptions, when the taggers are applied to highly standardized text [22].

As far as publicly available taggers are concerned, TnT and Decision Tree Tagger are probably the most commonly used ones. According to the results reported by their developers [8, 45] the two taggers are in the same range of performance, showing an accuracy of 96.36–96.70 %, with Decision Tree Tagger being able to provide morphological analysis.

TnT TnT [8] is an efficient statistical part-of-speech tagger trainable on different languages and tagsets. English and German models are available from the distribution. On the Penn Treebank, the tagger shows the accuracy level of 96.7 %.

The tagger provides two commands for training and tagging: `tnt-para` and `tnt`. For our example (14), the output of the tagger trained on the Wall Street Journal, as provided in the original distribution, is shown in Table 3.

Decision Tree Tagger TreeTagger [45] is a tool for annotating textual documents with part-of-speech and lemma information. The TreeTagger has been successfully used for a number of languages (e.g. German, English, French, Italian) and is adaptable to other languages when a lexicon and a manually annotated training corpus are available.

TreeTagger provides modules for training and tagging: `train-tree-tagger` and `tree-tagger`. In addition, it includes a tokenizer and a sentence splitter.

For our example (14), the output of the tagger with the distributed model is shown in Table 4.

Table 3 The output of the TnT tagger on example (14)

All	DT
human	JJ
beings	NNS
are	VBP
born	VBN
free	JJ
and	CC
equal	JJ
in	IN
dignity	NN
and	CC
rights	NNS
.	.

Table 4 The output of the Decision Tree Tagger on example (14)

All	DT	all
human	JJ	human
beings	NNS	being
are	VBP	be
born	VVN	bear
free	JJ	free
and	CC	and
equal	JJ	equal
in	IN	in
dignity	NN	dignity
and	CC	and
rights	NNS	right
.	SENT	.

2.4 *Parsing*

After identifying POS tags, we move to the syntactic analysis of sentences according to a certain grammar theory. The basic division is between constituency and dependency grammars: constituency grammars describe the syntactic structure as sequences of syntactically grouped elements (e.g. noun phrases, verb phrases, etc.), whereas dependency grammars focus on the direct relations among words (e.g. a subject and its object depending on the main verb).

Parsing modules (for example, [13, 16, 27, 37]) determine syntactic structures, providing parse trees. As input, a typical state-of-the-art parser assumes a text, possibly split into sentences. It is also possible to run parsers on pre-tokenized data or even specify POS tags for all the words. The parser's output might be used for generating mentions (Sect. 3.1) and for extracting values for syntactic features.

Parsing errors may thus result in incorrect mention boundaries and spurious syntactic clues for coreference:

(16) A [mesmerizing set].

(17) Those materials, in turn, were encased in [Kevlar, [a synthetic fiber],] and Nomex to achieve a test strength of 400 pounds.

The parse trees suggested for these examples by Charniak's parser [13] are shown on Fig. 2. The parser considers "set" (example 16) to be a verb (labeled VBD—verb, past tense) and, thus, the mention detection module fails to recognize "a mesmerizing set". Complex appositive-coordinate constructions (example 17) are intrinsically problematic for parsing: a typical state-of-the-art parser has no knowledge that helps prefer the 2-entities interpretation ([Kevlar]$_1$, [a synthetic fiber]$_1$, and [Nomex]2) over the 3-entities interpretation ([Kevlar]$_1$, [a synthetic fiber]$_2$, and [Nomex]$_3$). Note that even if the syntactic structure is grasped correctly, we still need additional knowledge to account for a possible 1-entity interpretation ([Dr. C. Richard Tracy]$_1$, [director of the Biological Resources Research Center at

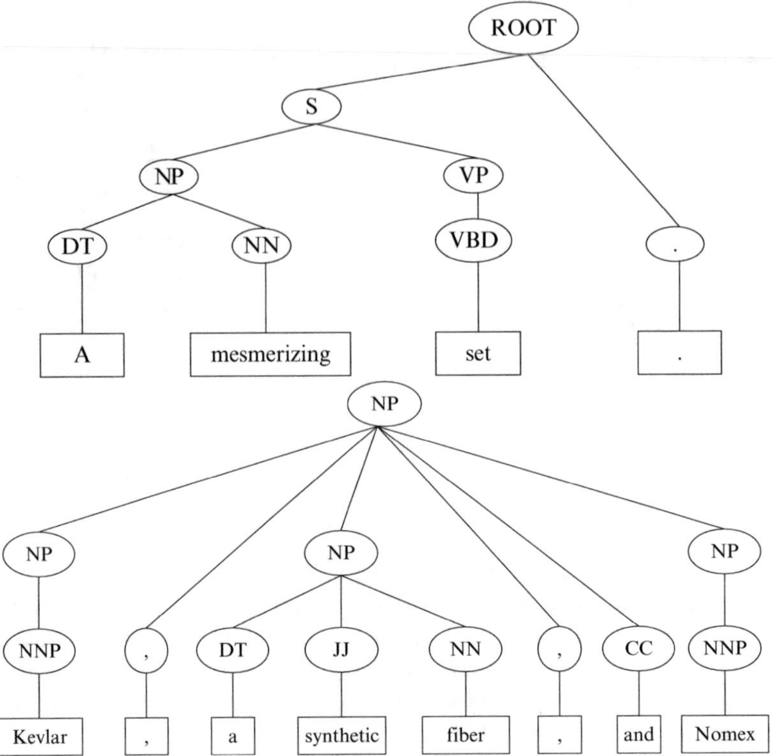

Fig. 2 Examples of parsing errors affecting coreference resolution

the University of Nevada at Reno]$_1$ and [a member of the Desert Tortoise Recovery Team]$_1$).

Below we provide a brief overview of some publicly available parsers. All of them show performance values of 87–91 % (F-score) at the standard evaluation on the Wall Street Journal dataset.

Collins' parser [16] uses a head-lexicalized model that relies on a very small amount of horizontal context, with local thresholding.

Charniak's original parser [13] uses a coarse-to-fine approach in conjunction with a best-first heuristic, where first a rough, unlexicalized step is carried out to have an efficient filter and then the full model (including large horizontal context and lexicalization) follows. The Charniak and Johnson parser [14] uses a reranking step, where the *n* most likely trees are taken, and a model with a larger context (including global features).

The Berkeley parser [37] starts out with a 0th order markovization but adds latent variables. It uses effective smoothing techniques in the EM steps and max-rule decoding instead of Viterbi decoding.

The Stanford parser [27] works with an enriched version of the grammar, which is a PCFG with head lexicalization (i.e., no smoothing is used), and the parser itself uses the A* approach to decoding.

There exist no studies on selecting the best parser for the full-scale coreference resolution task. Preiss [40] compares the performance of a heuristical pronominal anaphora resolution algorithm [29] with a number of publicly available parsers [11, 13, 16]. This study has revealed no significant differences between the parsers. However, its test set is fairly small, so, we believe that larger scale experiments are needed to make any conclusions.

2.5 Extracting Encyclopedic Knowledge

Several state-of-the-art coreference resolution systems rely on complex semantic representations of noun phrases, trying to capture possible sense variations between different occurrences of the same word. These approaches include a preprocessing step that links mentions to specific nodes in some knowledge base, such as WordNet or Wikipedia. Such techniques are discussed in details in chapter "Using Lexical and Encyclopedic Knowledge", below we only briefly focus on the preprocessing issues.

Many systems rely on the WordNet ontology [34] to obtain values for semantic features. WordNet is a large IS-A forest of atomary word sense units, or *synsets*. The mapping between synsets and words is a many-to-many correspondence. Most coreference resolution systems do not attempt any sophisticated word sense disambiguation and always choose the first synset for each nominal mention. This allows the organization of nouns in an IS-A hierarchy and thus for the computation of hyperonyms (for example, "repetition" is a hyperonym of "anaphora") and superconcepts, or semantic classes ("anaphora" is ABSTRACTION) for the head nouns of our mentions. The WordNet ontology also shows additional relations between synsets (for example, "syllable" is a *meronym* of "word"). This information, however, is not typically used: it would require functions for extensive sub-graph search and significantly slow down a system.

Some studies (Ponzetto and Poesio, State-of-the-art NLP approaches to coreference resolution: theory and practical recipes, ACL-09 tutorial, unpublished manuscript, 2009; [38]) make use of Web Knowledge bases, mainly Wikipedia. Again, the most common linking technique involves selecting the first Wikipedia page matching the head noun of a given mention. Bryl et al. [12], however, propose an advanced system for disambiguating mentions into Wikipedia senses. It has been shown [49] that these techniques may help improve coreference resolution.

3 Entity Mention Detection

The ultimate goal of any coreference resolution algorithm is to partition nominal descriptions, or *mentions*, in an arbitrary document into classes (*chains*), corresponding to discourse *entities*. Entities are objects or sets of objects in the real world. They might be indicated by their names, common nouns or noun phrases, or represented by pronouns. In our example (11), the following mentions could refer to the same entity:

Name Mention:	Sophia Loren
Nominal Mention:	the actress
Pronominal Mentions:	she, her, she

The *Entity Mention Detection* (EMD) task consists in detecting mentions, which involves identifying their extensions, and the location of the heads within the extensions. For example, in "the hurricane destroyed [the new glass-clad skyscraper]", the extension is the entire nominal phrase "the new glass-clad skyscraper" and the head is "skyscraper". The *mention type* (e.g. Name, Nominal or Pronoun) and the *semantic*, or *entity*, *type* (e.g., PERSON, ORGANIZATION, LOCATION) are often additional properties to be extracted. Eventually, mentions could be nested; that is, they could contain mentions of other entities, e.g. "the president of Ford", is a mention of type PERSON, containing "Ford"—another mention of type ORGANIZATION. Therefore, EMD is a more general and complex task than *Named Entity Recognition* (NER) aiming at identifying and classifying Name Mentions only.

Spurred on by the Message Understanding Conferences (MUC-6, 1995; MUC-7, 1997), a considerable amount of work has been undertaken on NER [2, 4, 7, 21], whereas EMD has become a topic of interest since ACE 2003.[3] In ACE, all mentions of each entity are to be detected and the attributes to be identified include mention and entity types and corresponding subtypes (a more specific type depending upon the main type; e.g. ADDRESS or WATER-BODY are possible subtypes of LOCATION).

Tasks such ACE, where there are inter-dependencies among different annotation levels (e.g. type and subtypes), introduce further levels of difficulty: assigning labels without taking into account these aspects could make the annotation inconsistent. For instance, in ACE, neither POPULATION-CENTER nor WATER-BODY can be subtypes of PERSON.

Several studies (cf. [24, 25] among many others) rely on manually annotated, or *gold* mentions. This allows to quickly build a coreference resolution system with virtually no preprocessing and thus helps focus on the task itself. More importantly, it enables straightforward comparison across systems: with the same (gold) set of mentions, the evaluation scores should better reflect the advantages

[3]http://projects.ldc.upenn.edu/ace/

and disadvantages of the coreference components. However, this is not always the case. For example, experiments of Ng [35] on gold mentions confirm that the most recent unsupervised approaches to coreference may rival supervised methods. At the same time, Ng shows that on system mentions the supervised algorithms are still significantly better than the unsupervised ones.

With the reference implementation of the coreference scorer made available recently [39], we believe that there remains no methodologically sound reason for simplifying the task through eliminating the EMD step and relying on gold mentions. This issue is discussed in more details in chapter "Evaluation Metrics".

Below we describe rule-based (3.1) and machine learning (3.2) approaches to the Entity Mention Detection Task.

3.1 Rule-Based Entity Mention Detection

For datasets with ACE-style annotation guidelines, focusing on specific semantic types, rule-based approaches aim at creating a large number of hand-crafted rules—typically, regular expressions exploiting the context around the mention to identify both the boundary and type. POS tags, syntactic features, and orthographic features, such as capitalization, are some of the most common features. Such systems often have a simple structure, they are generally easy to understand, yet difficult to design (rules must be correctly written and optimized by human experts), and to port on different domains (new rules need to be written). A similar system, exploiting the WordNet taxonomy [34], was proposed by Magnini [32]. Below we show some examples or regular expressions for PERSON mentions that are used by a typical Mention Detection system:

- @Honorific CapitalizedWord CapitalizedWord
  - @Honorific is a list of honorific titles such as Dr., Prof, Mr., etc.
  - Example: Mr. John
- FirstNames CapitalizedWord
  - @FirstNames is a list of common first names
  - Example: Bill Clinton
- CapitalizedWord lemma = "be" POS = "determiner" @PersonProfessionalCategories
  - @PersonProfessionalCategories is a list of common professional categories associated with persons, e.g poet, lawyer, etc.
  - Example: Hansteen was an astronomer

If the annotation guidelines assume that all the noun phrases in a document (and sometimes even other chunks) are considered mentions, the mention extraction modules rely on a combination of parsing trees and lists of Named Entities.

Unfortunately, not many studies go into details on this technique; below we describe a parsing-based mention detection algorithm implemented for Corry [47]:

1. Named entities are considered mentions if and only if they correspond to sequences of parsing constituents. Any partial overlap between NEs and parsing units is prohibited: for example, the sentence "For use by New York Times News Service clients" has been misanalyzed by the parser as "[For use by New York Times] [News Service clients]" and the system therefore discards the NE candidate mention "New York Times News Service".
2. Possessive pronouns are mentions if they are not parts of named entities.
3. Noun phrases (including non-possessive pronouns) are *candidate mentions* if they are not parts of named entities. The set of candidate mentions is filtered to eliminate pairs of NPs with the same head noun—embedding NPs are discarded. The remaining NPs are added to the set of mentions. For example, "the British trio that was an offshoot of the early 1980s goth band Bauhaus and was last glimpsed on the charts in 1989" and "the British trio" are both represented by the embedded description "the British trio". The selected NP-mentions are additionally aligned with the (already extracted) named entities if they share the same last word. For example, "guitarist Daniel Ash" and "Daniel Ash" get aligned and become one mention.

This procedure results in a pool of basic units: a mention can be embedded in another mention only if they have different head nouns, for example, in possessive constructions ("[[David Essex]'s granddad]") and coordinations ("[[the glam-rock suggestiveness], [the anguish] and [the angst]]"). It is essential for a coreference resolution system to operate on such basic descriptions, as they are less sensible to parsing errors than full NPs and can therefore be reliably extracted and quickly compared to each other. It is nevertheless important to pay attention to the context of a mention (including embedding noun phrases). This can be achieved by climbing up the parse tree from the basic NP node.

A similar procedure can be implemented for languages with no reliable parsing resources available: in such cases, we would need an NP-chunker to provide basic units.

Coreference resolution studies relying on such techniques do not report the evaluation results for their mention extraction component alone. The only figures available so far come from the SemEval-2010 Task 1 and CoNLL-2011/2012 evaluation campaigns. At SemEval-2010, the algorithm described above achieved an F-score of 78.1 % on the English data for the mention detection subtask. At CoNLL-2011, most systems relied on parsing-based mention detection techniques, showing EMD F-scores of 65–75 %.

3.2 Statistical Entity Mention Detection

A number of EMD approaches are based on machine learning. Almost all of them recast the task as a sequence labeling problem.[4] Different algorithms have been proposed recently: Hidden Markov Models [5], Maximum Entropy classifiers [6], Support Vector Machines [50, 52], and Conditional Random Fields [28, 33]. They do not use sets of hand-written rules, but need annotated corpora to derive them. These systems appeal to a trainable classifier to decide for each word whether or not it is part of a mention.

The trivial strategy adopts a different class for each mention type and an additional "O" class for all other words. However, this causes problems for contiguous mentions of the same type. In such a case, both mentions would be collapsed into a single mention. To solve the problem, a variety of annotation schemes have been proposed. The two variations of the *IOB* [41, 43] annotation format are probably the most common: according to *IOB2*, a label is assigned to each word in the text showing whether the word is at the beginning of a mention (*B*), inside a mention (*I*), or outside any mentions (*O*). The *IOB1* strategy differs from *IOB2* in using (*B*) only if necessary to avoid ambiguity (i.e. when two mentions of the same type follow each other); otherwise (*I*) is used even at the beginning of a mention. While the trivial strategy uses only n+1 classes for n mention types, *IOB* tagging requires 2n+1 classes. In Table 5, the *IOB2* annotation is used to indicate both the extension and the type of a mention:

This method, involving recognizing both the mention extension and its type at the same time, is referred to as the *all-in-one method*. In the CoNLL-2003 shared

Table 5 Mention boundaries in the IOB format

the	B-NOM
president	I-NOM
of	I-NOM
the	I-NOM
United	I-NOM
States	I-NOM
will	O
be	O
taking	O
a	O
trip	O
over	O
to	O
India	B-NAM

[4]An exception is the TK-EMD module of BART [48] that uses tree kernels to identify relevant parse nodes and classify them as ±mentions.

task on Named Entity Recognition, the best system based on the all-in-one approach achieved an F-score of 88.3 % [15].

In contrast to the all-in-one method, the *cascade method* is organized as a pipeline of processors wherein each stage accepts data from an initial input or from an output of a previous stage, executes a specific task, and sends the resulting data to the next stage, or to the output of the pipeline; for example, it could first recognize the mention boundaries, then assign the entity type, subtype, and mention type information. Table 6 shows how the IOB annotation could be used to represent different annotation layers: the mention extension on the second column, the head on the third column and the mention level on the last one.

In the CoNLL-2003 shared task, the best system based on this approach achieved an F-score of 88.77 % [21]. According to [44], the difference between the best two systems, implementing the cascade and all-in-one algorithms respectively, is not significant.

State-of-the-art EMD systems include a variety of features, representing different sources of information. The most commonly used features include:

- Lexical features, derived directly from tokens, e.g. the word itself, prefixes and suffixes (the first n characters at the start/end of the word), capitalization information, etc.
- Features derived by using other NLP techniques, e.g. sentence splitting, POS tagging, lemmatization, text chunking, parser, etc.
- External information given by gazetteers (lists of proper names of persons, locations, organizations), WordNet, Wikipedia, etc.
- Features obtained by running other EMD classifiers trained on different corpora.

Features are extracted within a context window of the target word (i.e. some words preceding and following the target word). In Fig. 3, for example, the words in a context windows of 5, their suffixes, PoS tags and lemmata are the

Table 6 Representing mention properties in the IOB format

the	B-EXT	O	B-NOM
president	I-EXT	B-HEAD	I-NOM
of	I-EXT	O	I-NOM
the	I-EXT	O	I-NOM
United	I-EXT	O	I-NOM
States	I-EXT	O	I-NOM
will	O	O	O
be	O	O	O
taking	O	O	O
a	O	O	O
trip	O	O	O
over	O	O	O
to	O	O	O
India	B-EXT	B-HEAD	B-NAM

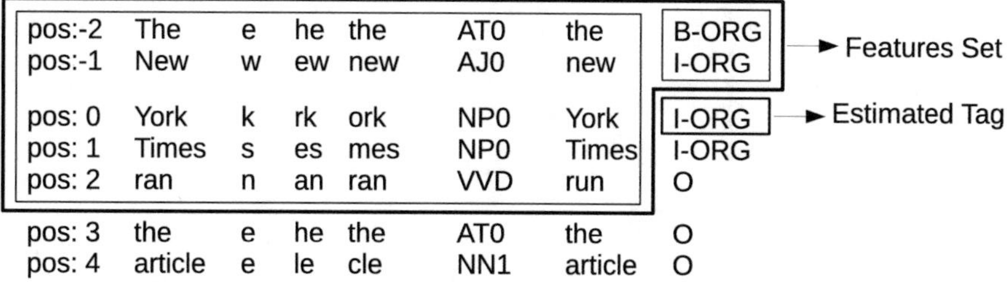

pos:-2 The e he the AT0 the B-ORG
pos:-1 New w ew new AJ0 new I-ORG
Features Set
pos: 0 York k rk ork NP0 York I-ORG
Estimated Tag
pos: 1 Times s es mes NP0 Times I-ORG
pos: 2 ran n an ran VVD run O
pos: 3 the e he the AT0 the O
pos: 4 article e le cle NN1 article O

Fig. 3 Feature selection: static and dynamic features are used during the training phase to learn the tag whereas, in the test phase, they are used to guess the correct tag

selected features (they are often called static features). In addition the tags assigned dynamically to the two words before the word to be annotated, are considered as features as well (dynamic features).

3.3 A Case Study

This section presents a case study based on Typhoon [3]—a system for Entity Mention Detection. Typhoon uses YamCha (i.e. a SVM-based machine learning environment) and it can exploit a rich set of linguistic features (e.g. part-of-speech) to recognize mentions. Despite its simplicity, the system has shown comparable accuracy with the state-of-the-art when tested at the Evalita 2009 evaluation campaign.[5] Figure 5 summarizes the architecture of Typhoon. This is a simplified view of the system given that the purpose of this section is to introduce the reader to the practical aspects of mentions detection by means of a fairly simple example. The rest of the section is organized as follows. We first briefly describe some background on YamCha, then move on to the system architecture and the experiments done to build Typhoon and finally we will see the results that the system obtained at Evalita 2009 and a real application where the system is being used. At the end of this section the readers should have understood the general architecture of a system for EMD and have some insights into implementation details.

SVM and YamCha The system presented in this section relies on Support Vector Machines (SVMs). Below, a brief overview of relevant technical details has been provided in order to help the reader implement a simple EMD system.

Support Vector Machines were developed by Vapnik [50] for binary classification. The algorithm looks for the optimal separating hyperplane which maximizes the margin between the two classes (see Fig. 4) in such a way that cases belonging to a category are on one side of the plane and cases with the other category are on

[5] http://www.evalita.it/2009/tasks/entity

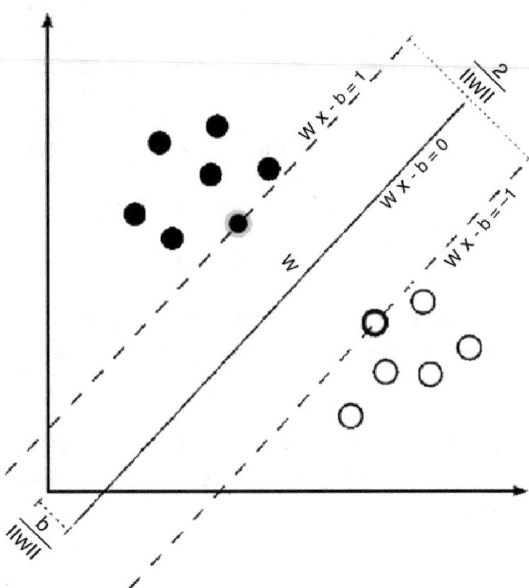

Fig. 4 The optimal separating hyperplane

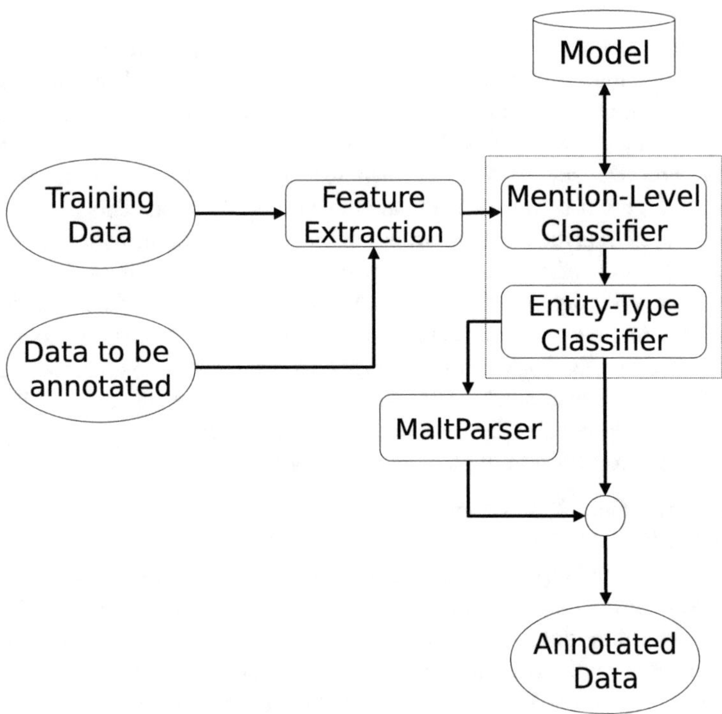

Fig. 5 Typhoon architecture

the other size of the plane. The points lying on the boundaries are called support vectors, and the middle of the margin is the optimal separating hyperplane.

YamCha [6] is an open source text chunker based on SVMs for handling both static and dynamic features, and for defining a number of parameters such as window-size, parsing-direction (forward/backward) and algorithms for multi-class problems (pairwise and one vs. rest).

Yamcha's input format (cf. Table 7) is compatible with the tabular format used in the previous section. The last column represents the true answer tag to be learned by SVMs.

The first step in using YamCha is to train it on a manually annotated dataset. For the above-mentioned example, the following YamCha command could be used to learn the mention level information:

```
make -f $YAMCHA_HOME/training/Makefile CORPUS=tr.data
MULTICLASS=2 MODEL=ex1 YAMCHA=$YAMCHA_HOME/usr/local/bin/yamcha
FEATURE="F:-1..1:0.. T:-1" SVMPARAM="-t 1 -d 2 -c 1"
TOOLDIR=$YAMCHA_HOME/libexec train
```

where:

- CORPUS is the location of the training file.
- MODEL is the name of the model the system builds.
- FEATURE is used to change the feature sets (window-size).
- SVMPARAM is used to change the training parameters of SVMs.

In the example above, CORPUS is set to `tr.data` and MODEL is set to `ex1`. FEATURE is set to `F:-1..1:0..`: YamCha is going to use all the features in the 1-token window, whereas the setting for SVMPARAM implies that the 2nd degree of polynomial kernel and one slack variable are used. Once the model has been learned, the following file are generated:

- ex1.log: log of training
- ex1.model: model file (binary, architecture dependent)
- ex1.txtmodel.gz: model file (text, architecture independent)
- ex1.se: support examples
- ex1.svmdata: training data for SVMs

Table 7 Yamcha input format

China	a	na	ina	NP0	China	GPE	B-NAM
export	t	rt	ort	NN1	export	null	O
growth	h	th	wth	NN1	growth	null	O
dips	s	ps	ips	VVZ	dip	null	O
as	s	as	null	CJS	as	null	O
EU	u	eu	null	NP0	EU	null	O
slows	s	ws	ows	VVZ	slow	null	O

[6]http://chasen.org/~taku/software/yamcha/

Classification costs of SVMs could be much larger than those of other algorithms. To increase the annotation speed, two algorithms, PKI and PKE, are available with YamCha. PKI and PKE are about 3–12 and 10–300 times faster than the original SVMs respectively. By default, PKI is used. To enable PKE, it is sufficient to recompile model files with -e option:

```
yamcha-mkmodel -e ex1.txtmodel.gz ex1.model
```

If -e is not given, PKI is employed.

By using the created model, the following command is available to identify mentions in the text to be processed:

```
yamcha -m ex1.model < tst.data
```

where:

- tst.data is the text to be annotated.

System Architecture Typhoon implements the *cascade-method* as described in Sect. 3.2 and consists of a combination of two classifiers in a cascade: (i) a *Mention-Level Classifier*, which identifies both the head of a mention and its mention level (NAM, NOM or PRO), and (ii) an *Entity-Type Classifier* which receives in input the output of the first classifier and for each annotated mention recognizes its type (PERSON, ORGANIZATION etc.). Both the classifiers are based on YamCha. In addition, to recognize the mention extensions, a parsing module based on MaltParser can be used in cascade to Typhoon. The Typhoon architecture in conjunction to MaltParser is summarized on Fig. 5.

In the first phase the system reads the training data and uses the *Feature Extraction* module so as to extract a variety of features for each word (e.g. suffixes, POS tag, lemma, and gazetteer information). Then the two classifiers based on YamCha use the produced features to build their models. Subsequently these models will be used by the same classifiers to label mentions in the data to be annotated. At the next step, for each annotated mention the parser accepts its head as an input and identifies the corresponding extension.

The outputs of the two classifier and MaltParser are combined to produce the final annotation: the output of the parser follows the CoNLL-X shared task format (i.e. tabular format) and as a result it is easy to add it to those produced by the classifiers.

Experiments The I-Cab data set, annotated for the Evalita-2009 competition, was used to build Typhoon. The training and development set are composed by 525 news stories taken from the local newspaper "L'Adige" belonging to four different days: September 7th, 2004; September 8th, 2004; October 7th, 2004 and October 8th, 2004; grouped in five categories: News stories, Cultural news, Economic news, Sport news and Local news. The test set, instead, is composed by new data taken from the same newspaper.

With respect to the format of the data, two types of files are available:

- UTF-8 text files: Files which contain the text of the document.
- ACE Program Format Files: Files which contain the annotation of the document using XML format. For each entity, it is indicated all its attributes (e.g. type) as well as all its mentions, specifying for each of them its head and its extent.

To make this data set compatible with Typhoon, it was first converted into the tabular format.

Then for each word a rich set of features was extracted by using the *Feature Extraction* module as depicted in Fig. 5: the word itself, both unchanged and lower-cased; its part-of-speech, prefixes and suffixes (1, 2, 3, or 4 characters at the start/end of the word); orthographic information (e.g. capitalisation and hyphenation) and gazetteers of generic proper nouns extracted from the Italian phone-book and from Wikipedia (154,000 proper names), from various sites about Italian cities, (12,000), Italian and American stock market (5,000 organisations) and Wikipedia geographical locations (3,200); moreover a list of 4,000 proper nouns extracted from a sport newspaper (Gazzetta dello Sport, year 2004). These features were extracted in a window of up to two words to the left/right to the target. Using the definition introduced in the previous section, we refer to these features as static, as opposed to dynamic features, which are decided dynamically during tagging. For the latter, we used the tag of the two tokens preceding the current token. Tables 8 and 9 show the features set used to build the Mention-Level Classifier and the Entity-Type Classifier.

It should be noted that the mention-level information (the label to be learned by the Mention-Level Classifier) appears as a feature for the Entity-Type Classifier. That is the Entity-Type Classifier uses the output of the Mention-Level Classifier as a feature to perform its annotation.

Table 8 Feature set for the Mention-Level Classifier

the	e	he	the	AT0	the	null	O
New	w	ew	new	AJ0	new	ORG	B-NAM
York	k	rk	ork	NP0	York	ORG	I-NAM
Times	s	es	mes	NP0	Times	ORG	I-NAM
ran	n	an	ran	VVD	run	null	O
the	e	he	the	AT0	the	null	O
article	e	le	cle	NN1	null	article	O

Table 9 Feature set for the Entity-Type Classifier

the	e	he	the	AT0	the	null	O	O
New	w	ew	new	AJ0	new	ORG	B-NAM	B-ORG
York	k	rk	ork	NP0	York	ORG	I-NAM	I-ORG
Times	s	es	mes	NP0	Times	ORG	I-NAM	I-ORG
ran	n	an	ran	VVD	run	null	O	O
the	e	he	the	AT0	the	null	O	O
article	e	le	cle	NN1	null	article	O	O

Finally, MaltParser is used to recognize mention extension. Table 10 shows the dependency parser analysis (following the CoNLL-X shared task format) for the mention "medical and health group"; considering "group" as the head, the extension will then be the whole mention "medical and health group".

Table 11 presents the result of a large number of experiments done to evaluate the relevance of the features to the final performance. Each feature is added one at the time to a default configuration obtained by using tokens only (on the 2nd column in the table). Since there were not many examples of pronouns (PRO) that refer to Geopolitical Entities (GPE), Locations (LOC) and Organizations (ORG), the results of these categories have not been reported.

Typhoon at Evalita 2009 Typhoon was evaluated in the EVALITA 2009 EMD task, a subtask of the Local Entity Detection and Recognition (LEDR) task.

The LEDR task at Evalita 2009 was designed to measure a system ability to detect a set of specified entities (i.e. persons, organizations, geo-political entities and geographical locations) mentioned in source texts, to recognize selected information about these entities (e.g. type), and to cluster the mentions for each entity together into a unique entity ID. LEDR systems have also been scored for Entity Mention Detection (EMD) accuracy. The goal of this evaluation was to assess the system's ability to detect entity mentions and output them along with their attributes. More precisely, the output for each entity mention includes the mention head, its level and type and the mention extension (optional).

Table 12 reports the results obtained by the system at Evalita; results are in terms of Precision (Pr), Recall (Re), F1 measure and annotation speed when the two different algorithms provided by YamCha, PKI and PKE, were tested:

Table 10 Dependency parsing for "medical and health group"

1	medical	_	JJ	JJ	_	4	amod	_	_
2	and	_	CC	CC	_	1	cc	_	_
3	health	_	NN	NN	_	1	conj	_	_
4	group	_	NN	NN	_	0	null	_	_

Table 11 Experimental results on the I-Cab data: contribution of different features to the performance of Typhoon

	Token	Pos	Affix	Ortho	Gazetteers
All	59.81	63.58	59.51	65.26	69.82
NAM_GPE	66.96	67.40	65.94	71.94	75.72
NAM_LOC	63.55	61.82	67.26	66.10	69.35
NAM_ORG	46.11	52.39	43.00	52.98	60.72
NAM_PER	55.66	72.54	59.91	72.96	82.02
NOM_GPE	48.33	47.06	46.43	49.61	49.23
NOM_LOC	44.19	34.67	36.36	57.14	47.31
NOM_ORG	58.65	51.33	52.31	58.40	60.40
NOM_PER	70.18	68.95	70.36	72.65	75.48
PRO_PER	66.33	68.06	65.71	64.64	65.57

Table 12 Evalita 2009 evaluation scores for Typhoon

Algorithm	Pr	Re	F1	Annotation speed
PKI	78.1	74.1	76.1	1,400
PKE	77.2	73.3	75.2	4,200

Applications Typhoon is being used in a number of applications. Among these it is worth mentioning the annotation of Italian Wikipedia as well as a corpus consisting of about 300 millions of words within the LiveMemories project.[7] It has also been used for labeling the SwiiT (Semantic WIkipedia for Italian) dataset: the Italian Wikipedia annotated at different levels, e.g.: basic NLP processing, entity mentions, and entity coreference.

4 Joint Mention Extraction and Coreference Resolution

Most state-of-the-art systems combine mention detection and coreference resolution in a pipeline architecture: first, a set of mentions is created for a document and each item of this set is assigned various linguistic properties; second, the set is partitioned into equivalence classes, or entities. Such architecture, however, suffers from the lack of interaction between two subprocesses: the former component cannot take advantage of the information provided by the latter. Consider the following example from [18]:

(18) Bill Clinton gave a speech today to [the Senate]$_1$. The president outlined his plan for budget reforms to [them]$_{2,ante=1}$.

The EMD component has identified, among others, two mentions, "the Senate" (name, organization) and "them" (pronoun, person). The coreference component in a pipeline system has a low chance of resolving "them" to "the Senate", due to the semantic class disagreement. This happens because the EMD component has prematurely assigned an incorrect label to an ambiguous mention. The error could have been avoided if a system was able to postpone such decisions, making use of the information provided by the coreference component at the later stage.

Several recent studies [18, 19] propose solutions to this problem by advocating joint inference for mention detection/classification and coreference resolution.

Denis and Baldridge [19] use the *Integer Linear Programming* framework to provide a joint model or coreference and mention classification. They do not attempt to learn mention boundaries (in practice, they evaluate their algorithm on gold boundaries). However, they learn semantic types (PERSON, ORGANIZATION, LOCATION etc.) for the predefined mentions from the ACE data.

Two classifiers, one for coreference and another for determining semantic types, are trained independently. At the testing stage, their outputs are combined in an

[7] http://www.livememories.org/

ILP problem, with a constraint enforcing semantic type consistency among different mentions of the same entity.

Denis and Baldridge show that their model yields superior performance for both coreference resolution and semantic type determination, compared to the respective modules in a pipeline architecture.

Daume and Marcu [18] propose another joint model for entity detection and coreference resolution. Their approach involves joint inference at both testing and training steps. Unlike Denis and Baldridge, they do not restrict the scope of their study to mention classification, but aim at the full-scale mention detection task.

Daume and Marcu formulate their problem in the *Learning as Search Optimization (LaSO)* framework. LaSO extends a standard search algorithm to incorporate learning by keeping and updating the weights vector w, where the weights correspond to the features. They search a space of hypotheses until it becomes impossible to reach the correct solution, at which point they update the weights vector in a corrective fashion. Each hypothesis corresponds to a complete analysis (both mention detection and coreference) of the initial segment of the document. By processing the document in the left-to-right manner and expanding the set of hypotheses, the system arrives at a joint solution for both tasks for the whole input.

Daume and Marcu show that their approach outperforms a pipeline system on the ACE-2004 dataset.

5 Preprocessing Pipelines for Publicly Available State-of-the-Art Coreference Resolution Systems

The coreference resolution task has received much research attention, but only very few system provide end-to-end processing and thus can be used to annotate raw texts with anaphoric links. Most state-of-the-art coreference resolution systems expect instead their input to be already preprocessed. This can facilitate the evaluation of such systems: when a dataset is preprocessed with the same set of tools and then passed as input to several coreference resolution platforms, the observed performance differences can be attributed only to their EMD and coreference components. Thus, at the recent CoNLL-2011/2012 and SemEval-2010 Task 1 evaluation campaigns, most systems participated in the *closed* track, where no external preprocessing modules were required or even allowed to be used.

Such systems, however, cannot be run on a raw text, which limits their practical applicability. Only very few publicly available coreference platforms support full-scale resolution from the raw text, accessing various preprocessing modules on the run.

Table 13 gives an overview of off-the-shelf components used by best-known publicly available end-to-end coreference resolution toolkits for English. It also contains information on the CherryPicker platform, that assumes as its input a sentence-delimited text, but otherwise provides all the preprocessing components.

Table 13 Preprocessing pipelines for publicly available coreference resolution systems

	BART	Cherry Picker	OpenNLP	Reconcile	Stanford Coref
sentence splitting tokenization	OpenNLP+Stanford	–	OpenNLP	OpenNLP, UIUC	Stanford
POS-tagging	from parser	Stanford	OpenNLP	OpenNLP, from parser	Stanford
parsing	Berkeley, (Charniak), (Stanford)	MINIPAR, Charniak	OpenNLP OpenNLP OpenNLP	Stanford, Berkeley	Stanford Stanford Stanford
EMD	parse-based	parse-based	OpenNLP	corpus-specific	parse-based

Modules that are supported but not used in the distributed default configuration are shown in brackets. Note that end-to-end systems for pronominal anaphora resolution (such as JavaRAP) are out of scope of our study.

6 Conclusion

In this chapter we have discussed preprocessing technology typically used by state-of-the-art coreference resolution systems. Coreference is a complex phenomenon and every resolver needs a number of external tools to obtain linguistic knowledge relevant for the task. Such modules are usually organized in a *Preprocessing pipeline*.

The *preprocessing pipeline* of an anaphora resolution system combines general-purpose modules with a coreference-specific *Entity Mention Detection* component. For the former, a number of off-the-shelf tools are publicly available for English. For the latter, no ready-to-use solution can be provided, as the mention detection algorithm depends crucially on the annotation guidelines for the data being processed.

State-of-the-art coreference resolution platforms, for example, BART [51] allow the user to choose between different tools or incorporate their own modules. Such choices should take into account the specifics of the input data (its format and annotation guidelines) and the quality of the available resources for a given language.

Possible direction for future research in this area include optimizing preprocessing pipelines in order to improve the overall performance level of a coreference resolution system. This may range from selecting appropriate modules and fine-tuning their parameters using optimization techniques, to retraining existing tools to provide better coverage for linguistic phenomena relevant for coreference.

A high-quality preprocessing pipeline is a vital prerequisite for a number of techniques discussed in the following chapters. For example, reliable evaluation figures (chapter “Evaluation Metrics”) can only be obtained with robust mention boundary detection. Accurate parse trees are essential for computing values of syntactic features, that become crucial, especially for pronominal anaphora resolution. Inconsistent semantic types and lack of sense disambiguation may decrease the usefulness of lexical and encyclopedic knowledge (chapter "Using Lexical and Encyclopedic Knowledge").

References

1. Baroni, M., Chantree, F., Kilgarriff, A., Sharoff, S.: CleanEval: a competition for cleaning web pages. In: Proceedings of the 6th International Conference on Language Resources and Evaluation (LREC 2008), Marrakech (2008)
2. Benajiba, Y., Diab, M., Rosso, P.: Arabic named entity recognition: a feature-driven study. IEEE Trans. Audio Speech Lang. Process. **15**(5), 926–934 (2009)
3. Biggio, S.M.B., Speranza, M., Zanoli, R.: Entity mention detection using a combination of redundancy-driven classifiers. In: Proceedings of the Seventh conference on International Language Resources and Evaluation, Valletta (2010)
4. Bikel, D.M., Miller, S., Schwartz, R., Weischedel, R.: A high-performance learning namefinder. In: Proceedings of ANLP-97, Washington, DC, pp. 194–201 (1997)
5. Bikel, D.M., Miller, S., Schwartz, R., Weischedel, R.: An algorithm that learns what's in a name. Mach. Learn. **34**(1), 211–231 (1999)
6. Borthwick, A.: A maximum entropy approach to named entity recognition. Ph.D. thesis, New York University (1999)
7. Borthwick, A., Sterling, J., Agichtein, E., Grishman, R.: Exploiting diverse knowledge sources via maximum entropy in named entity recognition. In: Proceedings of the Sixth ACL Workshop on Very Large Corpora, Montreal (1998)
8. Brants, T.: TnT – a statistical part-of-speech tagger. In: Proceedings of the Sixth Conference on Applied Natural Language Processing, Washington, DC (2000)
9. Brill, E.: Transformation-based error-driven parsing. In: Proceedings of the Third International Workshop on Parsing Technologies, Tilburg/Durbuy (1993)
10. Brill, E., Moore, R.C.: An improved error model for noisy channel spelling correction. In: Proceedings of the 38th Annual Meeting on Association for Computational Linguistics, Hong Kong, pp. 286–293 (2000)
11. Briscoe, E.J., Caroll, J.: Generalised probabilistic LR parsing of natural language (corpora) with unification-based grammars. Comput. Linguist. **19**(1), 25–59 (1993)
12. Bryl, V., Giuliano, C., Serafini, L., Tymoshenko, K.: Supporting natural language processing with background knowledge: coreference resolution case. In: Proceedings of the 9th International Semantic Web Conference, Shanghai (2010)
13. Charniak, E.: A maximum-entropy-inspired parser. In: Proceedings of the 1st Meeting of the North American Chapter of the Association for Computational Linguistics, Seattle, pp. 132–139 (2000)
14. Charniak, E., Johnson, M.: Coarse-to-fine n-best parsing and maxent discriminative reranking. In: Proceedings of the 43rd Annual Meeting of the Association for Computational Linguistics, Ann Arbor (2005)
15. Chieu, H.L., Ng, H.T.: Named entity recognition with a maximum entropy approach. In: Proceedings of CoNLL-2003, Edmonton, pp. 160–163 (2003)
16. Collins, M.: Head-driven statistical models for natural language parsing. Ph.D. thesis, University of Pennsylvania (1999)
17. Cutting, D., Kupiec, J., Pederson, J., Sibun, P.: A practical part-of-speech tagger. In: Proceedings of the Third Conference on Applied Natural Language Processing, Trento, pp. 133–140 (1997)

18. Daume III, H., Marcu, D.: A large-scale exploration of effective global featuresn for a joint entity detection and tracking model. In: Proceedings of the 2005 Conference on Empirical Methods in Natural Language Processing, Vancouver (2005)
19. Denis, P., Baldridge, J.: Global joint models for coreference resolution and named entity classification. In: Procesamiento del Lenguaje Natural 42. SEPLN, Barcelona (2009)
20. Finkel, J.R., Grenager, T., Manning, C.: Incorporating non-local information into information extraction systems by Gibbs sampling. In: Proceedings of the 43rd Annual Meeting of the Association for Computational Linguistics, Ann Arbor, pp. 363–370 (2005)
21. Florian, R., Ittycheriah, A., Jing, H., Zhang, T.: Named entity recognition through classifier combination. In: Proceedings of CoNLL-2003, Edmonton, pp. 168–171 (2003)
22. Giesbrecht, E., Evert, S.: Is part-of-speech tagging a solved task? an evaluation of POS taggers for the German Web as corpus. In: Proceedings of the 5th Web as Corpus Workshop, San Sebastian (2009)
23. Greene, B., Rubin, G.: Grammatical tagging of English. Technical report, Department of Linguistics, Brown University, Providence (1971)
24. Haghighi, A., Klein, D.: Unsupervised coreference resolution in a nonparametric Bayesian model. In: Proceedings of the 45th Annual Meeting of the Association for Computational Linguistics, Prague (2007)
25. Harabagiu, S., Maiorano, S.: Multilingual coreference resolution. In: Proceedings of the Language Technology Joint Conference on Applied Natural Language Processing and the North American Chapter of the Association for Computational Linguistics (ANLP-NAACL2000), Seattle, pp. 142–149 (2000)
26. Kennedy, C., Boguraev, B.: Anaphora for everyone: pronominal anaphora resolution without a parser. In: Proceedings of the 16th International Conference on Computational Linguistics, Copenhagen, pp. 113–118 (1996)
27. Klein, D., Manning, C.: Accurate unlexicalized parsing. In: Proceedings of the 41st Annual Meeting of the Association for Computational Linguistics, Sapporo, pp. 423–430 (2003)
28. Lafferty, J.D., McCallum, A., Pereira, F.C.N.: Conditional random fields: probabilistic models for segmenting and labeling sequence data. In: Proceedings of the 18th International Conference on Machine Learning, Williamstown, pp. 282–289 (2001)
29. Lappin, S., Leass, H.: An algorithm for pronominal anaphora resolution. Comput. Linguist. **20**(4), 535–561 (1994)
30. Lita, L.V., Ittycheriah, A., Roukos, S., Kambhatla, N.: tRuEcasIng. In: Proceedings of the 41st Annual Meeting of the Association for Computational Linguistics, Sapporo (2003)
31. Luo, X., Florian, R., Ward, T.: Improving coreference resolution by using conversational metadata. In: Proceedings of The 2009 Annual Conference of the North American Chapter of the Association for Computational Linguistics, Companion Volume: Short Papers, Boulder (2009)
32. Magnini, B., Negri, M., Prevete, R., Tanev, H.: A Wordnet-based approach to named-entities recognition. In: Proceedings of the COLING02 Workshop on SEMANET, Taipei (2002)
33. McCallum, A., Li, W.: Early results for named entity recognition with conditional random fields, feature induction and web-enhanced lexicons. In: Proceedings of Conference on Computational Natural Language Learning, Edmonton, pp. 188–191 (2003)
34. Miller, G.: Wordnet: an on-line lexical database. Int. J. Lexicogr. **3**(4), 235–312 (Winter 1990)
35. Ng, V.: Unsupervised models for coreference resolution. In: Proceedings of the 2008 Conference on Empirical Methods in Natural Language Processing, Honolulu, pp. 640–649 (2008)
36. Norvig, P.: How to write a spelling corrector (2007). http://norvig.com/spell-correct.html
37. Petrov, S., Barett, L., Thibaux, R., Klein, D.: Learning accurate, compact, and interpretable tree annotation. In: Proceedings of the 21st International Conference on Computational Linguistics and 44th Annual Meeting of the Association for Computational Linguistics, Sydney, 17–21 July 2006

38. Ponzetto, S.P., Strube, M.: Exploiting semantic role labeling, WordNet and Wikipedia for coreference resolution. In: Proceedings of the Human Language Technology Conference of the North American Chapter of the Association of Computational Linguistics, Morristown, pp. 192–199 (2006)
39. Pradhan, S., Luo, X., Recasens, M., Hovy, E.H., Ng, V., Strube, M.: Scoring coreference partitions of predicted mentions: a reference implementation. In: Proceedings of the 52nd Annual Meeting of the Association for Computational Linguistics (ACL 2014), Baltimore, 22–27 June 2014, vol. 2, Short Papers, pp. 30–35 (2014)
40. Preiss, J.: Choosing a parser for anaphora resolution. In: Proceedings of the 4th Discourse Anaphora and Anaphor Resolution Colloquium, Lisbon, pp. 175–180 (2002)
41. Ramshaw, L.A., Marcus, M.P.: Text chunking using transformation-based learning. In: Proceedings of the Third ACL Workshop on Very Large Corpora, Cambridge, MA (1995)
42. Reynar, J.C., Ratnaparkhi, A.: A maximum entropy approach to identifying sentence boundaries. In: Proceedings of the Fifth Conference on Applied Natural Language Processing, Washington, DC (1997)
43. Sang, E., Tjong, E.F., Sang, K., Veenstra, J.: Representing text chunks. In: Proceedings of EACL'99, Bergen (1999)
44. Sang, E.F.T.K., Meulder, F.D.: Introduction to the CoNLL-2003 shared task: language-independent named entity recognition. In: Proceedings of CoNLL-2003, Edmonton, pp. 142–147 (2003)
45. Schmid, H.: Probabilistic part-of-speech tagging using decision trees. In: Proceedings of the International Conference on New Methods in Language Processing, Manchester, pp. 44–49 (1994)
46. Uryupina, O.: Knowledge acquisition for coreference resolution. Ph.D. thesis, Saarland University (2007)
47. Uryupina, O.: Corry: a system for coreference resolution. In: Proceedings of the 5th International Workshop on Semantic Evaluation (SemEval'10), Uppsala (2010)
48. Uryupina, O., Moschitti, A.: Multilingual mention detection for coreference resolution. In: Proceedings of the International Joint Conference on Natural Language Processing (IJCNLP'13), Nagoya (2013)
49. Uryupina, O., Poesio, M., Giuliano, C., Tymoshenko, K.: Disambiguation and filtering methods in using Web knowledge for coreference resolution. In: Proceedings of The 24th Florida Artificial Intelligence Research Society Conference (FLAIRS-24), Palm Beach (2011)
50. Vapnik, V.N.: The Nature of Statistical Learning Theory. Springer, New York (1995)
51. Versley, Y., Ponzetto, S.P., Poesio, M., Eidelman, V., Jern, A., Smith, J., Yang, X., Moschitti, A.: BART: a modular toolkit for coreference resolution. In: Proceedings of the 46th Annual Meeting of the Association for Computational Linguistics on Human Language Technologies, Prague, pp. 9–12 (2008)
52. Yamada, H., Kudoh, T., Matsumoto, Y.: Japanese named entity extraction using support vector machines. Information Processing Society of Japan, SIG Notes NL 142-17 (2001)

Off-the-Shelf Tools

Yannick Versley and Anders Björkelund

Abstract Off-the-shelf coreference tools can be a useful ingredient for downstream applications in machine translation, information extraction or sentiment recognition. In this chapter, we will present the properties that are most important for the integration of coreference systems into a larger context, then describe the BART system, the dCoref system that is part of Stanford's CoreNLP suite, as well as IMSCoref and HOTCoref as examples of state-of-the-art systems that are purely based on machine learning. We finish the chapter by outlining a checklist-based approach on choosing, integrating and adapting a coreference system for a putative new application context.

Keywords Off-the-shelf tools NLP pipelines • Coreference resolution

1 Introduction

In order to reap the benefits of coreference systems in applications, we have to be able to embed them in a larger NLP workflow, either in order to test the potential impact that they have, or in order to set up one. To do that, users do not necessarily want to create their own annotated corpus or implement a coreference system from scratch. This applies in an evaluative setting question where the question is whether coreference information is useful at all, and whether it is close to being "good enough", but it is also true in many cases where a coreference resolver is part of a larger system. Work in a new language can also benefit from the existence of algorithm implementations whenever it is feasible to adapt the language-dependent part of the system to a new language.

Off-the-shelf tools, in the sense that we use in this chapter, are coreference resolution systems that are constructed in a way that makes them suitable for people

Y. Versley (✉)
ICL Universität Heidelberg, Heidelberg, Germany
e-mail: versley@cl.uni-heidelberg.de

A. Björkelund
IMS Universität Stuttgart, Stuttgart, Germany
e-mail: anders@ims.uni-stuttgart.de

M. Poesio et al. (eds.), *Anaphora Resolution*, Theory and Applications of Natural Language Processing, DOI 10.1007/978-3-662-47909-4_8

outside the original context to install them, and where additional effort went into presenting an understandable interface to the resolver. Because of the nature of coreference resolution, even such a system can be more difficult to use than a named entity recognizer: in most cases, coreference resolvers make use of syntax and additional layers of annotation, which are part of the system output and often make a suitable output format necessary.

In the rest of this chapter, we will present three multilingual coreference resolution systems that would commonly be considered off-the-shelf systems: BART (Beautiful Anaphora Resolution Toolkit), a toolkit for knowledge-rich coreference resolution which was originally developed for English and subsequently extended to cover Italian [2] and German [8] as well as Chinese and Arabic [53] and Polish [29]; The purely rule-based "Coreference Sieve" resolver which is part of the Stanford CoreNLP suite of tools for natural language processing for English; and IMSCoref [4] and HOTCoref [6], which are systems for machine-learning-based coreference resolution that have been applied to English, Chinese and Arabic. Section 6 provides a guide and checklist for choosing and adapting a coreference system based on properties of the domain and available data.

Users and Users of Coreference Systems There are many settings in which an off-the-shelf coreference resolver can be fruitfully employed. The BART system, which is the oldest of the three, has been incorporated in a system for textual entailment [60] machine translation [25, 26]. The Stanford system has been used in the context of information extraction [23] and the induction of verbose labels for semantic roles [54]. In contrast, authors of systems for more specialized purposes, such as the detection of subsequent mentions of cited work [1], or the highly specialized matching of names in nineteenth century novels [18] seem to be special cases where the task of anaphora and coreference resolution is too far away from the standard task applied to newspaper text (in one case, *Cutting* and *the Xerox tagger* could refer to the same published work, whereas in the other case, *Miss Bennett* and *Miss Elizabeth Bennett* would be two different people).

In many cases, researchers have extended coreference toolkits, or reused parts of the mention extraction and feature identification pipeline, for the development of other advanced coreference resolution techniques. For example, the BART framework has been used for the investigation of instance reweighting using Maximum Metric Score Training [65], as well as feature set optimization based on genetic algorithms [49, 52]. Cai and Strube and a subsequent CoNLL'2012 shared task entry by Martschat et al. [9, 34] have used BART as a platform for a global model using graph partitioning with hypergraph features.

2 General Considerations

The promise of an off-the-shelf tool is usually that the entry barrier to using it is relatively low, and that it can be fruitfully used as part of a larger linguistic pipeline.

The first success stories in the realm of "off-the-shelf" components have been part-of-speech tagging and chunking/parsing, for several reasons: the input format (space-separated tokens) is relatively easy, the structures of the output are comparatively easy to use, and the quality of chunks, and later parses, was sufficient to be useful in almost all cases. For English and many other languages, the recognition of named entities is another example that fulfills these criteria. As a counterexample, consider systems for word sense disambiguation (WSD), where the output (synsets in a lexicalized ontology) is too fine-grained to be reliable or useful, and supersense tagging, which solves a coarser-grained version of the same problem and has found more uses.

To make this more explicit, we could formulate a number of criteria for a coreference system (or any NLP component) to be a useful off-the-shelf tool:

- It should be possible to install the tool and get it running without requiring exotic hardware or software, or language resources that are generally unavailable to the user.
- It should be easy to get the texts to be processed into a format understood by the tool; This usually means that this format should be standardized[1] and/or easy to understand (e.g. space separated tokens in the case of POS tagging or parsing).
- The output of the tool should be such that it is easy to make use of it in a downstream application, which ideally would also be standardized or at least easily understandable.
- The quality of the output of the tool should high enough, or at least predictable enough, to be used at least for a proof-of-concept implementation. In the case of part-of-speech tagging and parsing, quality on out-of-domain texts deteriorates, but for many typical applications stays useful.

In this fashion, looking at the properties for typical off-the-shelf tools give us an idea for criteria that can be used to predict common stumbling stones in using an off-the-shelf coreference system.

2.1 Preprocessing

As seen in chapter "Preprocessing Technology", coreference systems use a complex preprocessing chain typically involving parsing, the identification of mention spans, and the identification of semantic classes and spans for names and nominals (entity mention detection).

[1] In the context of this discussion, *standardized* amounts to being described well enough that it is possible to write interoperable programs that solve edge cases in the same way, and that it is possible to get stakeholders to agree on one particular interpretation of that description. Formal endorsement by a government or standards body are not relevant to the descriptions in this chapter, although these do improve the feasibility for institutional users to buy or commission such components.

The author, as well as potentially the user, of an off-the-shelf coreference system, will be faced with a choice regarding the preprocessing pipeline: Some tools, such as BART or Stanford's dcoref package, bring their own preprocessing pipeline, which means that they can work from raw text, but that it is also harder to adapt them to a different preprocessing pipeline.

For those other components of the overall system that require input that is part of the preprocessing pipeline for coreference (parsing, named entity recognition, morphological processing and lemmatization), the usual solution will be to make other components use the results of coreference preprocessing. As a result, the output format will have to include not just the coreference information itself but also the results of the preprocessing.

Conversely, tools such as IMSCoref use a standardized format for the input, but do not prescribe or suggest which preprocessing the user should use. This means that it is up to the user to assemble and use the 'standard' preprocessing pipeline that was used to train the coreference model(s), but also that it is reasonably easy to switch components in this pipeline. From the point of view of system input, a more complex input format becomes necessary that can also represent the preprocessing results; conversely, there is no additional difficulty in re-using processing results that were computed for the coreference input in other components of an overall system.

2.2 *Input and Output*

Most systems complex enough to benefit from coreference resolution also use other components, such as syntactic information or named entity recognition. Thus, it is often necessary to integrate coreference tools as part of a larger linguistic pipeline: Either one wants to use separate components, and pass them into the coreference system so that it can use the information, or use a pipeline that has been tailored for that coreference system and use its preprocessing information in other modules of the overall system; in the first case, the input to the coreference system becomes more complex, in the second case, we have greater complexity at least on the output side of the coreference resolver.

As a result of the preprocessing involved, the input and/or output of coreference system quite often consists in a complex format involving multiple annotation layers for token annotations (part-of-speech, morphology, lemmas), syntactic structure (dependency parses or constituents) or markables (including the semantic type).

Within the group of multi-layer annotation formats, we can distinguish open formats which in principle allow other annotation layers (such as the MMAX2 format used by BART) from fixed formats such as the CoNLL-2011 format that is used by IMSCoref, and the CoreNLP XML format used by Stanford's dcoref system. These fixed formats are, by their nature, less flexible than generic multilayer format, but also more convenient since they are adapted to the exact task at hand. Moreover, they are usually the result of some (informal) standardization effort: across coreference systems in the case of the CoNLL-2011 format, and across different processing subsystems that are part of the CoreNLP architecture in the case of dcoref.

In terms of their nature, MMAX2, CoNLL-2011 and CoreNLP also represent three different approaches to the serialization of linguistic data:

- MMAX2 is an example of a **span-based standoff format**, which means that it has a relatively flexible but generic way of representing linguistic objects. Every noun phrase, and every markable, are represented as an XML tag that has a span extent (an amount of text such as "*US President*"); the way of representing text extents, or links between markables, is standardized between different annotation levels.
- CoreNLP's XML format is an example of a **layer-wise object serialization** format, where the format for each layer is specific to the particular annotation la and the representations that are used internally.
- The CoNLL-2011 format is an example of a **tabular text format**, where the linguistic annotation is represented in a text document with one row per token, and where layers of linguistic annotation occupy one or more column in the output format. For token-wise annotation, tabular text formats are a very straightforward choice (see part-of-speech tagging), but more complex annotations for attributed spans lead into less-intuitive methods of serializing more complex levels of annotation.

The complexity of multilayer annotations in general, and especially of standoff formats, leads not only to increased flexibility but also to greater frustration for non-specialist users: a student trying out BART in a course assignment [3] notes that adding annotations to corpora in MMAX2 files is relatively tedious.

2.3 *Internals and Adaptability*

In many cases, off-the-shelf systems are useful in exactly this capacity: using such a system, unmodified, as part of a larger system. In other cases, the user wants to adapt the coreference system to a different type of text, a different language, or make use of a different preprocessing toolchain than was used by the original authors.

Almost all of these use cases require the user to re-train the coreference model, i.e., convert the hand-annotated training data in a format suitable for the coreference resolver (possibly adding preprocessing information). Some of then, such as adding a different language, require the creation of a new preprocessing pipeline, and possibly changing internal parameters or rulesets for parametrizable or rule-based components that are tuned to a particular annotation scheme (for syntax or other components) or finding replacements for external resources used (such as gazetteers or wordnets).

In coreference systems that deal with multilinguality, such as BART or IMS-Coref, internal data structures are often already general enough that the immediate focus can lie on implementing an appropriate preprocessing pipeline, whereas other systems sometimes hard-code assumptions that do not hold cross-lingually. Conversely, the particularities of each language are often quite important to capture in a coreference system, which entails that language-dependent functionality and tuning is useful for both monolingual and multilingual coreference systems.

3 BART

BART, the "Baltimore Anaphora Resolution Toolkit" (later: "Beautiful Anaphora Resolution Toolkit") began its life at the Johns Hopkins Summer Workshop 2007 as a platform for integrating different state-of-the-art approaches to coreference resolution including the use of external knowledge sources such as Wikipedia or wordnets [43, 55], or evidence from corpus search and search engine queries [32, 41, 56], the use of tree kernels [62] or inference beyond mention-pair models, such as ranking-based selection of antecedents [55] or models based on scoring clusters [15].

BART was constructed to be very modular, aiming at integrating different preprocessing methods (chunking or parsing, different methods of integrating named entity tagging or ACE mention tagging), different kinds of features, as well as support for detailed error analysis using the MMAX2 annotation tool [37] and other tools based on this file format. As a result, BART has been successfully adapted to many different corpora and feature sets, but is also less straightforward to use than monolithic systems.

3.1 Framework and Architecture

A basic insight behind BART is that machine-learning based coreference systems, independently of language or the exact mechanism for coreference resolution, consist of a number of basic building blocks that are often changed or varied, and which can be recombined in various ways. As a result, BART offers standardized interfaces and implementations for these problems, and a solution for putting them together in a flexible manner, while also allowing a user to swap out parts of the architecture.

The first of these building blocks is a mechanism to store the input to the coreference resolver, including the detected mentions, as well as receive the output of the coreference resolver for the evaluation, in the form of the *MMAX2* file format and the *MiniDiscourse* library for handling this file format. The input to the coreference resolver is provided by a preprocessing toolchain that is distributed as a part of BART for the English version, but which exists as a separate mention detection tool for, e.g., the Italian and German versions; all the preprocessing toolchains create appropriate annotation layers in the MMAX2 format. For training and evaluation, the system has access to a layer containing the gold-standard clustering of coreference spans (*coref*), while the coreference resolver as such writes its output in the *response* layer.

The second building block are trainer and resolver components, which use the *Mention* objects that form the output of mention detection. In the case of a coreference trainer component, the input corpus contains mentions as well as the coreference information from the *coref* layer, and possibly additional linguistic information that is derived from MMAX2 layers or from external data. A trainer component extracts positive and negative examples that allow to build one or multiple classifiers. Its counterpart, the resolver component, takes these classifiers and uses their decisions on examples from the document to be annotated in order to create a *clustering* of the mentions in a document. In both cases, BART's infrastructure takes care of mapping between mentions and MMAX2 markables, and between the clustered objects and the coreference representation in the output format.

A third building block consists in a standardized representation for examples (i.e., things that can be fed to a machine learning classifier), and for feature extractors, which turn examples into descriptions that can be used in normal machine learning, as well as an interface to actual machine learning toolkits such as *WEKA*, *SVMlight*, or BART's own maximum entropy classifier. In this case, infrastructure support serves to ensure that (within reason) any feature extractor can be used with any classifier.

Because the interfaces both for feature extractors, and for machine learners is standardized, a coreference resolver realized in BART can use a declarative mechanism for specifying learners and the feature extractors to be used in a declarative fashion, via an XML configuration file. This declarative mechanism for parametrizing the coreference resolver, together with the possibility to automate resolution and evaluation, makes it possible to wrap learning and testing/evaluation in order to do automatic feature selection and parameter optimization (see subsection 3.5, infra).

3.2 The MMAX2 File Format

The MMAX2 file format, named after the annotation tool MMAX2 [37], is a token-based multilayer standoff format: It supports multiple annotation levels (allowing, say, for chunk and named entity levels with overlapping boundaries of both), but no sub-token annotations (which would be required to annotate the subtoken "*Sino*" in "*Sino*-American relations"). Each annotation level is contained in a separate file, which means that moving or renaming documents consists in the transfer or rename of several related files, while renaming or removing annotation layers can be done purely using file manipulation.

In terms of file system organization, an MMAX2 document consists of a sequence of words with IDs (the **word file**) and, for each markable layer, a

markable file containing descriptions of the annotated spans for this layer with their attributes.

A **markable** in MMAX2 parlance is an annotated span which contains information in attributes pertaining to that span. As an example, a *named entity* markable would span the text corresponding to that named entity (e.g. "*Bill Clinton*") and carry attributes describing the type of that named entity (e.g., type=PER).

Differences between MiniDiscourse and MMAX2 In comparison to the MMAX2 annotation tool, the MiniDiscourse library used by BART makes several simplifying assumptions.

On the file system level, MMAX2 allows (nearly) arbitrary file names and locations for word and markable files, which are then specified in a *.mmax2* file for each document. MiniDiscourse implements a unified convention where, all documents of one corpus (or subcorpus) have the same base directory, and where files belonging to each of these documents are organized into common subdirectories below that base directory.

Within a corpus, all *words* files are stored in the `Basedata` subdirectory of the base directory, as `(docid)_words.xml`, and all *markable* files are stored in the `markables` directora as `(docid)_(level)_level.xml`.

The MMAX2 format in general allows complex attributes such as pointers to other markables, or markable sets. MiniDiscourse is able to read these files, but does not treat these attributes specially – it internally represents all attributes as strings. In the case of coreference sets, BART performs conversions between partitions of markables on one hand and string-valued set attributes when storing the output of the coreference resolution and in the quantitative evaluation provided by BART.

However, BART's use of the MMAX2 file format is focused on a subset of the file format: the MiniDiscourse library used by BART for supporting the MMAX2 file format internally represents all attributes as strings, including those that would be pointers or sets in the MMAX2 annotation tool. Discontinuous markables are supported by the MiniDiscourse library, but many components of BART, including feature extractors and diagnostic tools, assume continuous markables and fail in the presence of discontinuities.

A Technical Overview of MiniDiscourse MiniDiscourse, BART's library for handling the MMAX2 format, is the lowest level of abstraction for dealing with corpora, which in turns serves more high-level abstractions such as the *Mention* interface discussed later. Thus, porting or extending BART would be possible by only accessing *Mention* objects and not much else. However, for more complicated corpus conversion purposes (where the tools from the *elkfed.mmax.tabular* package are not sufficient anymore) or when dealing with additional custom annotations that go beyond the information that *Mention* objects contain, *MiniDiscourse* offers a way to manipulate corpora in MMAX2 format more directly.

In the *MiniDiscourse* library, each document is represented by an object of the type `elkfed.mmax.minidisc.MiniDiscourse`. Existing documents can be loaded with the *load(corpus_dir, doc_id)* static method, whereas a new document can be created from a token sequence via the method *createFromTokens(corpus_dir,*

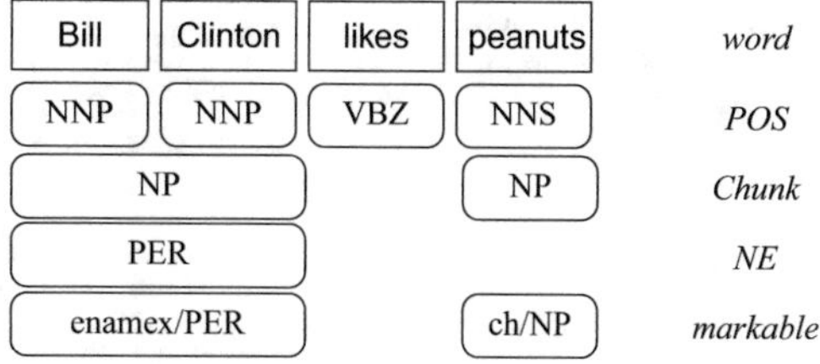

Fig. 1 Markable spans in MMAX2 format (labels in the image correspond to the *tag* attribute (pos/chunk/ne) or to a summary of attributes (markable)

doc_id, tokens). Existing markable levels are loaded on demand (or created as a new empty markable level) when accessed via the *getMarkableLevelByName* method of *MiniDiscourse*.

A markable level itself offers the possibility to get all markables (*getMarkables*), all markables overlapping a certain word (*getMarkablesAtDiscoursePosition*) or starting within a certain range of words (*getMarkablesAtSpan*).

Markables themselves offer methods to access their text span (*getLeftmostDiscoursePosition*, *getRightmostDiscoursePosition*), or their attributes (*getAttribute*, *setAttributes*).

In addition to dealing directly with markables, the *MiniDiscourse* API also offers an approach to deal with common tabular data formats as they are commonly produced by tools for POS or named entity tagging. The approach of the `elkfed.mmax.tabular` interface is thus to construct a list of *Column* objects which describe the columns in the tabular format used, and which can then be used to import or export data with the classes *TabularImport* and *TabularExport*.

For the simplest cases, the *Column* class represents single word-level markables which contain one tag (e.g. POS or lemma level). The most common case for named entities – having spans that are represented by B/I/O tags (giving "*Bill/B-PER Clinton/I-PER likes/O peanuts/O*" for the named entity layer of Fig. 1) – is supported by the class *BIOColumn*.

3.3 Preprocessing and Mention Creation

A *Preprocessing Pipeline* in BART parlance is a component that starts from a corpus with only tokens (and optionally gold-standard coreference information) and adds linguistic annotations to this corpus up to identifying mentions and creating markables for them on the *markable* layer.

Preprocessing pipelines can be BART-internal (as is the case of the English pipeline), or they can be BART-external (as is the case with the Italian and German pipelines). In the former case, most of the work is done by *PipelineComponent* subclasses in *elkfed.mmax.pipeline*, through the MiniDiscourse API for storing the information in MMAX2 format. In the latter case, preprocessing results are created in tabular form (see the *Preprocessing* chapter by Uryupina and Zanoli, this volume) and imported using the *elkfed.mmax.tabular* package, or are directly written in MMAX2 format by external tools.

Table 1 Markable schema for the English mention identification

Attribute	Description
markable-type	Source of the markable (*chunk,enamex*)
markable-label	*NP* for chunk markables or semantic class for named entities (*PER/LOC/ORG/EVT/TMP*)
sentenceid	Number of the enclosing sentence
lemmata	Word lemmas for the markable span
pos	Part-of-speech sequence for the markable span
isprenominal	Whether the markable is prenominal (the *aluminium* price, *US* trade representatives)

In either fashion, the preprocessing pipeline first identifies the basic linguistic structure of the document including part of speech, morphology and lemma information, and possibly parses and/or named entities. A subsequent step extracts more specific information into markables on the *markable* level, which are then interpreted by BART's *LanguagePlugin* to create *Mention* objects for the actual coreference processing (Table 1).

English Preprocessing The current recommended default for the English processing pipeline of BART uses only Java-based components and can be invoked via the entry point *elkfed.main.PreProcess*, which consults BART's configuration file to find out (i) which corpus (train and test part) is to be processed, and (ii) which components are to be invoked.

Based on the *pipeline* and *parser* settings in the *config.properties*, *elkfed.main.PreProcess* runs an appropriate pipeline for parsing, named entity recognition, and mention identification.

The *ParserPipeline* uses a syntactic parser, from which it extracts base-level noun phrases and part-of-speech tags (in addition to the parses, which are used in some features). For the Java-based components, the Berkeley parser [39] is used, with wrappers around the Stanford [27] and BLLIP parsers [13] being available as alternatives.

Named entity detection is performed using the Stanford Named Entity recognizer [21]. Subsequently, BaseNP spans and NE spans are used to construct markable spans in the fashion described by Soon et al [50] in a class named *elkfed.mmax.MarkableCreator*. Lemmas for the mentions are provided by the *MorphoAnalyzer* pipeline component, which uses the Stanford JavaNLP implementation of lemmatization as described by Minnen et al. [35].

German Preprocessing The German preprocessing pipeline differs from the English one in two important respects: the first one is that German, like Italian and unlike English, is a morphologically-rich language, and syntactic gender and number are marked. The second difference is that the pipeline mostly resides outside of BART, but is realized as a series of Python scripts that deal with parsing the input and the conversion from parse trees into actual markables.

In German as well as in the other languages supported by BART, constituent trees are the preferred form of syntactic information, as the relation between syntax nodes and markables or their spans is more direct. In the case of [8], parse trees were directly derived from the gold-standard syntax trees in the TüBa-D/Z treebank [51]. In the case of the SemEval-2010 shared task, the official data contained only dependency syntax (either as gold-standard dependencies converted from the original constituency trees of the treebank, or as automatic parses from MALTParser). For this reason, the SemEval contribution for German [7] used an intermediary step of dependency-to-constituency conversion. For the most common other use cases, it would be recommended to use a state-of-the-art constituent parser such as the Berkeley Parser, with a model that allows the reconstruction of grammatical function labels. The grammatical function labels would allow high-quality assignment of morphological tags and lemmas following the approach of [59], which uses syntactic structure to disambiguate morphology.

In a second step, a separate program (*export2coref.py/tiger2coref.py*) uses the syntactic, morphological, and lemma information from the parses by first identifying all maximal noun phrases with their minimal (Base noun phrase) span, their head(s). In the case of named entities, all name parts are included in the head span, as in the following example:

Example 0 (spans) [$_{\text{full}}$ [$_{\text{min}}$ der tapfere [$_{\text{head}}$ Peter Müller]], von dem alle reden]
[$_{\text{full}}$ [$_{\text{min}}$ *the courageous* [$_{\text{head}}$ *Peter Müller*]], *of whom everyone speaks*]

The script uses the morphological properties of the head to determine number and gender of the mention, and other criteria in determining the *mention type* (reflexive or personal pronoun, name, or definite or indefinite noun phrase). The semantic class for a markable is determined using the method of [55], considering information from gazetteers and GermaNet (Table 2).

Table 2 Markable schema for language-independent mention identification

Attribute	Description
markable-type	Syntactic category of the markable (*np,np.coord,poss, v.clitic,v.clitic2,v.zero*)
mention-type	Morphosemantic category of the markable (*pro.per1/2/3,pro.refl,nom.def/indef,nam*)
gend	Gender
num	Number
sem-type	Semantic type
head-pos	Head position (span(s) of word-ids)
sentenceid	Number of the enclosing sentence
pos	Part-of-speech tag sequence for the chunk part of the markable
min-ids	Span(s) of the chunk part of the markable
srole	Tuple of (unnormalized/normalized) grammatical function and governing head

3.4 The Baseline System

The *Soon* baseline system is a system based on the features and inference approach used by Soon et al. [50]. As such, it is easier to configure and use than many of the more advanced models, but is recommended for its simplicity rather than for its good (or even state-of-the-art) performance.

The implementation of the Soon baseline is split into multiple parts:

- The general infrastructure for entity-pair models (*PairInstance*, *PairFeatureExtractor*).
- Encoding and inference for the closest-first strategy of coreference resolution using an entity-pair classifier (*SoonEncoder*, *SoonDecoder*).
- The feature set of Soon et al. (encoded as *idc0_maxent.xml* configuration file).

This baseline-specific modules sit on BART's common infrastructure, which provides the interface between the corpus files and internal representations such as *Mention* objects or coreference sets, but which also provides common functionality for an interface to machine learning packages. Specifically,

- The subclasses of *MentionFactory* in *elkfed.coref.mentions* (with help of the subclasses of *LanguagePlugin* in *elkfed.lang*) create *Mention* objects based on the information in the *markable* level of the MMAX2 document.
- *InstanceWriter* and *RankerSink* (in *elkfed.ml*) offer a generic interface for the training part of machine learning tasks, which can be used to build models that in turn can be used using the *OfflineClassifier* and *Ranker* interfaces.
- The *SoonEncoder* takes a document, with its list of *Mention* objects, to generate training data for an *InstanceWriter*, which in turn extracts features using multiple *FeatureExtractor* objects.
- The *SoonDecoder* in turn takes a document, with its list of *Mention* objects, together with the models learned in the last step and the same list of *FeatureExtractor* objects.
- The classes *XMLTrainer*, *XMLClassifierBuilder* and *XMLAnnotator*, finally use XML configuration files to compose feature extractors, coreference encoders or decoders, and machine learning components, into the training or testing part of one coreference resolver.

Feature extractors are objects that take an example instance (be it for training or testing) and extract feature values (which can be boolean, string-valued, or, when dealing with tree-kernel support vector machines, tree-structured).

3.5 Advanced Models

The added complexity of multilayer standoff annotation and a modular architecture would certainly be overkill for a system that were limited to the baseline classifier. While some of the following variations on BART are either difficult to install or have not been published, they should nicely illustrate the axes of variation that BART's flexibility allows.

The JHU system – Wikipedia and Tree Kernels One goal of the JHU workshop on Exploiting Lexical and Encyclopedic Resources for Entity Disambiguation (ELERFED) was to bring together innovative approaches in coreference resolution, in particular the use of external resources to incorporate semantic knowledge [43, 55] (see also chapter 'Using Lexical and Encyclopedic Knowledge', this volume) as well as better use of syntactic structure with the aid of tree kernels [63].

The experiments described in the 2008 paper describing BART [58] evaluate BART development on the MUC-6 and ACE-02 corpora, based on results from the workshop. On ACE-02, the system uses the *Carafembic* mention tagger [61] to identify the mentions belonging to the semantic classes targeted by the ACE evaluation, and uses an extended feature set including a component for detection of name aliases derived from Wikipedia, and the use of tree kernels for improving the identification of (especially) intra-sentential coreference relations.

Subsequent work [57] presents the work on using kernels in coreference – the intra-sentential mentions but also specialized components for name matching and for detection of non-referring pronouns – in more detail.

Evalita 2009/SemEval 2010 – Multilingual BART A version of BART adapted for Italian – the first using the new *LanguagePlugin* extension described above – was used for the Evalita 2009 shared task on Local Entity Detection and Recognition [2]. For this, an adaptation of the baseline features to Italian was created, including an adapted *Alias* feature detecting name variants and abbreviations typical for Italian. In the preprocessing step of mention detection, the Typhoon system (see Uryupina and Zanoli, this volume). Section 6.3 provides additional commentary on this under the light of the first steps of *adapting* a coreference system to a new language (Table 3).

The German coreference system uses the generic set of features but also some additional features that include a lemma-matching heuristic that can deal with synthetic compounds, or a relatedness metric that works using the German wordnet GermaNet [30].

UniTN/IITP/Essex at CoNLL 2011 – Multi-Metric Optimization The CoNLL-2011 shared task submission by Uryupina et al. [52] uses BART together with an approach that performs supervised feature selection and parameter tuning.

Like in most complex systems based on machine learning, deciding for or against the inclusion of 42 features for each of two classifiers (pronouns and non-pronouns) is both computationally expensive and relatively important, especially since Soon et al.'s [50] approach to encode coreference decisions induces a nontrivial relationship between the decisions that a classifier makes and the quality of the coreference chains produced.

Table 3 Features used in the Italian and the German systems used in Evalita-2009 and SemEval-2010

German and Italian	
MentionType(M_i)	Linguistic category of M_i
MentionType(M_j)	Linguistic category of M_j
SemanticClass(M_i)	Semantic class of M_i
SemanticClass(M_j)	Semantic class of M_j
FirstMention(M_i)	M_i Is the first mention in the sentence
GenderAgreement(M_i,M_j)	Agreement (gender)
NumberAgreement(M_i,M_j)	Agreement (number)
AnimacyAgreement(M_i,M_j)	Agreement (animacy)
Alias(M_i,M_j)[a]	Specialized alias feature
Apposition(M_i,M_j)	Apposition detection
StringMatch(M_i,M_j)	String matching
Distance(M_i,M_j)	Distance in sentences
Only German	
InQuotedSpeech(M_i)	M_i Is within a quoted span of text
InQuotedSpeech(M_j)	M_j Is within a quoted span of text
NodeDistance(M_i,M_j)	Number of clause nodes and PPs
PartialMorphMatch(M_i,M_j)	String match of noun stem lemmas (without composition)
GermanetRelatedness(M_i,M_j)	Discretized distance in GermaNet

[a] The Italian system has a specially adapted alias feature

For the processing of OntoNotes, Uryupina et al. start from BART's default method of mention identification, but apply an additional filter that removes non-referring and indefinite pronouns ("*there*", "*nobody*", "*somebody*") as well as multi-word expressions, expletive "*it*" occurrences.

For the optimization of the feature set, Uryupina et al. use a multi-objective variant of genetic algorithm (nondominated sorting genetic algorithm II, [16], using the MUC, CEAF and Bcubed evaluation metrics as objective values.

UniTN/Essex at CoNLL 2012 – Learning-based Mention Detection In the CoNLL-2012 task, Uryupina et al. [53] extended BART to two languages where no previous expertise, infrastructure, or in-depth methods for extracting linguistic information were available: Arabic and Chinese. As BART was originally constructed to be a system for knowledge-rich coreference resolution (i.e., using linguistic information wherever possible), this approach is telling in the sense that it shows that meaningful work in a knowledge-poor setting is indeed feasible.

Uryupina's adaptations for Arabic and Chinese are centered on building mention detection and extractors for linguistic information based on the information in the coreference corpus.

Like older approaches for sequence modeling using SVMs (the Typhoon system detailed in Uryupina and Zanoli's section 3.31 in chapter 'Preprocessing Tools', this volume) or the system of [28] for selection markable spans based on a dependency tree, Uryupina's approach in [53] uses the training data to learn good cues for NPs that are good candidates (or not) for mentions. In this case, Uryupina uses a node-filtering model that is based on convolutional tree kernels, using a part of the tree including the NP that is a markable candidate, some context above, and some context below, pruned using tunable parameters for limiting the context above/below. Because the goal is to extract markables for the coreference system, Uryupina et al. learn a *biased* classifier, where the cost factor for false positives/false negatives is tuned to optimize the results of the coreference system.

Uryupina et al. also use several heuristics to extract linguistic information on mentions: coordinations (i.e., noun phrases containing a conjunction) are treated as plurals, some head finding rules yield the heads of noun phrases, which in turn helps the identification of pronouns, nominals, or names.

For Arabic, Uryupina et al. create a list of affixes that may correspond to gender and number properties, as well as falling back to lookup in an external dictionary. They also use affixes and syntactic structure to identify definite noun phrases (which are realized as affixes to the noun rather than with a separate article).

Uryupina et al.'s tree kernel-based approach to mention detection yields an improvement of 1.5–2 % over just using all noun phrases, which is quite substantial (even considering that having gold mentions – an unrealistic setting espoused by many coreference systems before 2008 – would give a six-fold improvement). The improved features – adding features that match lemmas instead of full forms) as well as the language-specific optimizations mentioned earlier – yield another improvement of 2 % (Arabic) or 0.4 % (Chinese).

HITS at CoNLL 2011/2012 – Hypergraph-based coreference A team at the *Heidelberg Institute of Theoretical Studies* (formerly: *European Media Lab*) participated at the CoNLL shared tasks with a system that used the general framework of BART but replaced the pairwise link classification with a system based on the idea of decomposing coreference chains into a number of hyperedges in a hypergraph/multigraph [10, 34].

While the original approach uses a spectral clustering approach for performing inference, subsequent research by Martschat [33] confirms that a simpler model that performs the clustering deterministically works even better for English.

While this approach shows that you can replace virtually every part of BART's framework – both the procedure for mention extraction and the actual inference mechanism used, it also drives home that good performance in mention extraction and careful feature engineering are the most important ingredients for a well-performing coreference system. (The system of Martschat [33], which is an open-source reimplementation of the graph-based approach, uses the CoNLL-2011 tabular format for input and output.)

4 Stanford's dcoref System

The dCoref coreference resolver from the Stanford NLP group [31] is interesting in the context of this chapter for two reasons: On the one hand, it comes with its own, integrated preprocessing pipeline, which means that it is easy for non-expert users to get to first results. On the other hand, the Stanford system is based on deterministic rules that declare mentions (or entities as partial coreference chains built from these mentions) to be coreferent or incompatible. This means that in domains with conventions that differ systematically from newspaper text, it may be possible to adapt the system for these domains by only modifying the system, rather than annotating significant amounts of coreference data and using a domain adaptation scheme.

4.1 CoreNLP Data Structures

The dCoref deterministic coreference resolver is part of a larger infrastructure called CoreNLP which aims at providing flexible enough underpinning for a number of NLP tasks including parsing, named entity recognition, coreference, and compositional sentiment recognition.

The pipeline architecture of Stanford's CoreNLP system is based on a *Map* data structure which uses the *typesafe map* pattern: for each attribute that a particular object can have, the key used to retrieve it must implement a tag interface `TypesafeMap.Key<VALUE>` that also specifies the type of the data stored under that key (which must have the a type matching `VALUE`). In this way, an open set of annotations can be stored in an object in a way that makes it easy to preserve typing information.

A pipeline in CoreNLP's parlance is a sequence of `Annotator` objects which can add information on tokenization, part-of-speec tagging, parsing and other steps of the pipeline. This is done by instantiating a `StanfordCoreNLP` object with a list of the steps performed (which means that CoreNLP follows a *catholic* approach in the sense of having a hand-curated list of components that can be used, in contrast to other approaches which allow an open list of pipeline components). Then, the user of the library instantiates an `Annotation` object with the text to be annotated and the annotation information is added by calling the `pipeline.annotate` method (Fig. 2).

It is possible to access the output of the CoreNLP pipeline by accessing the CorefChain objects (which are the coreference chain objects that the coreference resolver also uses internally).

The CoreNLP library also supports output in an XML format that is, in line with the 'catholic' approach pursued in its pipeline architecture, a simple XML serialization of the data structures of the system. In particular, each `CoreferenceChain`

```
Properties props = new Properties();
props.put("annotators", "tokenize, ssplit, pos, "+
  "lemma, ner, parse, dcoref");

String text = "This is an example sentence.";

Annotation document = new Annotation(text);
pipeline.annotate(document);

Map<Integer, CorefChain> graph = document.get(
    CorefChainAnnotation.class);
```

Fig. 2 Instantiating and using a pipeline with CoreNLP

object is transformed into a `<coreference>` tag that contains the mentions and part of the information contained in them.

4.2 The Coreference Sieve

The Stanford Sieve approach essentially consists of three components:

- Exact and approximate string matching
- Precise constructs such as appositions and copula constructions
- Pronoun resolution

Each of these components is integrated in the system as one or multiple *sieve* steps which can, for a given pair of partial coreference chains, decide that these are coreferent (and should be merged) or not coreferent (in which case a marker is added which forbids them from ever being merged). In case of multiple mentions/entities being candidates for being coreferent with a mention in a coreference chain, salience heuristics are used to select the one that is in the closest sentence, or in the most prominent position of the current sentence (see also chapter "Early Approaches to Anaphora Resolution: Theoretically Inspired and Heuristic-Based" on rule-based coreference resolution).

Improvements to the Sieve approach The current release of Stanford's dCoref approach incorporates two improvements: One is a machine learning model that predicts whether a detected mention should stay a singleton and not corefer with anything else [47], using information such as being a pronoun or proper noun, animacy, sentence position and grammatical role. With an adapted threshold, they succeed in pre-identifying about half of all singleton mentions at a precision close to 90 %.

In order to extend the coverage of the Stanford resolver to cases where coreference is not indicated by string similarity (see also chapter "Using Lexical and

Encyclopedic Knowledge" on using common-sense knowledge), Recasens et al. [46] extract an alias list from a comparable corpus of news stories based on techmeme.com, a site that provides clusters of related news stories. As a result of applying various filters and thresholds, they put the alias-pair candidates into four lists that can be applied (together with basic constraints such as number/animacy and NE-type agreement) in additional sieve steps.

5 IMSCoref and HOTCoref

IMSCoref [4] and HOTCoref [6] are systems that rely on structured machine learning and a language-agnostic and reasonably flexible way of defining features. Similar to the Stanford approach, HOTCoref also uses an entity-based scheme for keeping track of the partial coreference chains built so far, but in contrast to the Stanford approach of using hand-crafted rules to determine which mentions should or should not belong together, IMSCoref and HOTCoref focus on making effective use of the large training corpora that are available today for many languages.

5.1 IMSCoref

Contrary to BART and the Stanford dcoref system, the IMSCoref system [4] does not constitute a full processing pipeline, but only a coreference resolver. The resolver was developed for the CoNLL 2012 Shared Task [44], where it obtained the second best overall rank. It therefore reads and writes the CoNLL shared task format, and the necessary preprocessing (e.g., parse trees and named entities) is up to the user to provide.

The IMSCoref system revolves around a *mention-pair model*, where a binary classifier is trained to discriminate whether a pair of mentions is coreferent or not. A key aspect that differentiates the system from other mention-pair systems is its rich and configurable feature set.

The core machinery of IMSCoref is language-agnostic and the system makes few assumptions about the language it is operating on. However for the CoNLL 2012 Shared Task, the authors tuned the feature sets individually for each language (Arabic, Chinese, and English). Additionally, IMSCoref applies language-specific rules for mention extraction. Internally the system also includes head-percolation rules for the three languages that, given a phrase-structe parse of a sentence, extracts a head work for every constituent.

Table 4 Mention extraction rules in the IMSCoref system

Language	Extracted nodes
Arabic	NP, PRP, PRP$
Chinese	NP, PN, NR
English	NP, PRP, PRP$, NEs

5.2 *Mention Extraction*

The mention extraction component of IMSCoref is composed of a number of rules that operate on phrase-structure trees. Generally, the system extracts all noun phrases, as well as pronouns and named entities. Since the phrase-structure annotation schemes of the three languages from the 2012 Shared Task are language specific, so are the extraction rules. Additionally, the English mention extraction also extractes all named entities (NEs). The categories that extracted for each language are listed in Table 4.

Non-referential classifier The English version of IMSCoref also includes a separate classifier that targets non-referential (pleonastic) pronouns. This classifier operates as a filter that follows the mention extraction rules, and removes non-referential instances of the pronouns *it*, *we*, and *you*.

5.3 *Learning and Decoding*

Learning The IMSCoref system learns a binary classifier which is used to classify a pair of mentions as coreferent or disreferent. The system implements the training instance creation scheme of [50]. The classifier is a logistic regression classifier learned using LIBLINEAR [19].

Features IMSCoref includes customized feature sets for each language. The feature sets are specified in external files that are provided during training. The ability to configure the feature set in an external file makes it easy to experiment with other feature sets. Since IMSCoref uses a linear classifier, conjunctions of basic feature templates make up an important part of a feature set. Feature conjunctions are supported in an additive manner in the feature configuration file, thus allowing the user to experiment with any kind of conjunctions of basic templates.

Decoders The two most popular decoders (or inference algorithms) for pair-wise coreference resolvers include the *closest first* (CF) decoder [50] and the *best first* (BF) decoder [38]. The closest first decoder selects the closest coreferent mention for every mention, whereas the best first decoder selects the *most confident* preceding mention, where confidence is determined by the classification score of the classifier.

In addition to the above decoders, IMSCoref also includes variants where different decoders are used depending on whether the active mention is a pronoun or not. Moreover, IMSCoref implements an additional decoder, the *average max probability* (AMP) decoder. This decoder makes clustering decisions not only based on a pair of mentions, but considers, for an active mention, all links to each (partially) built cluster. The score of merging an active mention into a cluster is determined by the (geometric) average of the scores of all classification decisions between an active mention and an antecedent cluster.

Decoder stacking The authors of IMSCoref found that the AMP decoder was rather conservative and produced consistent clusters, but with low recall. The BF and CF decoders on the other hand are more prolific and had a tendency to merge clusters. In order to combine the strengths of both types of decoders, IMSCoref implements a *stacking* scheme, where the output of one resolver is fed as the input to another. The second resolver utilizes the output of the first as features.

5.4 Extension to Additional Languages

Extending IMSCoref to additional languages is fairly straightforward. Although the system relies on some language-specific rules and parameters, it is straightforward to change these or simply to start from a given language configuration when adaptating the resolver to a new language.

While IMSCoref relies on phrase-structure syntax for the mention extraction step, a modified version which can also rely on dependency syntax has been created [5].

5.5 HOTCoref

HOTCoref [6] builds on the same codebase as IMSCoref and is therefore similar in several respects (such as mention extraction, language-specific feature sets, and so on). The system, however, addresses three major drawbacks previously observed in mention-pair models:

- The training instance creation strategy of Soon et al. [50] sometimes selects unintuitive antecedents during training.
- The first mention of a cluster does not receive any meaningful treatment during training (and thus also not during inference).
- Mention-pair models are flawed since they only consider a pair of mentions in isolation, not taking entire clusters into consideration.

Training instance creation Selection of more meaningful antecedents goes back to the work of [38] who, contrary to [50], selected the closest non-pronominal mention as an antecedent when creating positive examples. Recently, this problem has been tackled by the use of *latent antecedents*, which is a more general approach to this problem [11, 12, 17, 20]. Instead of statically assigning one correct antecedent for every mention, the machine-learning algorithm is also used to deduce antecedents during training. Specifically, at every iteration, the current the weight vector is applied to find the optimal antecedent for every mention. This favors the assignment of antecedents that are easy to learn and generalize across documents.

Classification of discourse-first Since the training instance creation strategy of [50] does not handle the first mention of a cluster, standard mention-pair models do not directly learn how to handle these. In effect, a mention becomes the first of its cluster only if it was not clustered with anything on its left. It has therefore been proposed to include a dummy mention that can be used as the antecedent of discourse-first mentions [20, 36]. Mention pairs are thus created between every discourse-first mention and this dummy mention, enabling the machine-learning algorithm to pick up on regularities of discourse-first mentions.

Introducing cluster-level features HOTCoref also extends its feature representation to allow for features of (partial) clusters. The authors demonstrate that the inclusion of cluster-level features in a principled and effective manner needs to be done with great care, but show that when the machine-learning algorithm is tailored to the task, such features can contribute further to improved clustering accuracy.

Learning and Search HOTCoref is trained using a variant of the structured perceptron [14]. Therefore the minimal unit during training is a document, rather than a single mention-pair link. Structured perceptrons generally require the inference problem to be solved optimally. Without cluster-level features, this can be done straightforwardly using a best-first decoder. However, with cluster-level features this guarantee breaks down, and approximate inference remains the only viable option. With cluster-level features, HOTCoref applies beam search as the approximate search strategy, both during learning and testing.

6 Common Scenarios: Analysis and Summary

After we saw in some detail how different coreference systems are structured, we are in a better position to see how they can fit into the grander scheme of things, and how one could go at adapting them.

6.1 Selecting a Coreference System

As mentioned in the introduction, coreference systems are more complex systems than, say, named entity recognizers are, but even the latter ones can yield complex tradeoffs when used in a different domain or a different language than the one originally used to develop them.

In that sense, one should know the answer to several questions:

Do I have my own preprocessing pipeline? Many coreference systems either have their own adapted pipeline (for example, BART, CherryPicker, or Stanford's dCoref), or they expect input in a standardized format (IMSCoref).

Quite arguably, systems with tight integration, such as Stanford's tools, make it easy, or easier, to apply the complete pipeline to some text and use the outputs of the whole tool collection including parser and named entity recognition.

The Stanford approach also illustrates a different tradeoff, since its integrated pipeline makes it relatively easy to use the included Stanford parser, but less easy to use more sophisticated models such as the PCFG-LA parser of [39] or the BLLIP reranking parser of [13]. Since coreference resolution depends on the ability of the parser to identify good noun phrases, this means that easier upfront integration comes at a cost of more difficulty in integrating more specialized components.

A closed-source component such as CherryPicker is even a greater problem in this respect, even though it employs state-of-the-art tools, since that makes it relatively hard to change even minor things in the preprocessing pipeline.

Does my text match the genre of a pre-existing pipeline? Using an **existing pipeline**, as it is possible with dCoref or BART is highly recommended if the text is close to the material it was trained on – in most cases, that means texts that are close to the newspaper or newswire genre.

In many **new genres** that are at the center of interest today, though, tools that were trained on newspaper text perform poorly: Giesbrecht and Evert [24] found that part-of-speech taggers that perform highly in newspaper text in the domain they were trained on suffer a large reduction in accuracy when used on texts from a Web corpus. Foster et al. [22] found that syntactic parsers do not perform well out of the box, even though steps can be taken to re-train a parser using semi-supervised learning techniques to make it work better on the targeted domain. Young et al. [64] found that even for simple descriptions of images that they collected through crowdsourcing, using heuristics-based improvement of parses was the key to getting meaningful syntactic structures.

Is English my target language? When it comes to **languages other than English**, different things need to be kept in mind. To name one aspect, no off-the-shelf system offers a simple integrated pipeline such as the Stanford CoreNLP suite does for English. The second aspect is that notions such as subject, direct object, clauses etc. are differently expressed in each language and annotation scheme, which means that many coreference systems that have been developed for English and the Penn Treebank/OntoNotes annotation scheme only will need to be changed substantially. Systems that work for multiple languages, such as BART, offer the necessary underpinnings to work productively with a larger number of languages, but do so with a number of optimizations that are language specific, including access to ontological resources or specialized matching algorithms for that particular language.

The case where one applies coreference resolution to a new language can further be divided into two cases, the first being that one has language resources (dictionaries, taggers, parsers) for that language, but no corpus that would allow a statistical system, and the second would be that one has a large-enough corpus with (syntactic/morphological and) coreference information.

In the first case (language resources but no referentially annotated corpus), it is probably best to start with hand-written rules for mention detection and adapt one of the existing **rule-based resolvers** (such as the Stanford Sieve) to the structures found in that language. While this will only yield a first approximation of a working coreference resolver, it is also better than anything that one could hope to learn from a smaller coreference corpus. (The reason that such approaches do not figure prominently in the literature is that meaningful evaluation already requires a small-to-medium corpus with referential annotations.)

In the second case, where one has a large referentially annotated corpus, but not necessarily all the language resources, the most reasonable approach is to use **language-agnostic** methods for the learning-based construction of coreference systems, such as the methods for mention detection developed by [53] or Uryupina and Zanoli, this volume.

6.2 Integrating a Coreference System

The trivial case, where we have a coreference system with an associated linguistic processing pipeline that matches our target genre and domain, and where we can just apply this coreference system (and associated pipeline) and use its output, is not always typical of applications in the real world, even though it is arguably the case for which current coreference systems are optimized.

Then, the question would be, given that one typically does not have any in-domain evaluation data, what would be the issues in an off-the-shelf system where users can have a maximal impact for the effort they invest in testing or in improving auxiliary data used by the off-the-shelf system.

If the genre is substantially different, it may make sense to factor out the fit (or lack thereof) between preprocessing pipeline and coreference system, and look whether the following shallow heuristics give usable results, independent of the coreference system to be used:

Named Entities For **named entities**, exact and approximate string matching on the spans returned by a named entity recognizer is one of the major source of correct links in newspaper text, and may also be the most important factor in linking named entities in new text genres.

For this to work, several issues can be checked:

- Does the named entity recognizer find most of the instances of named entities you care about, with the correct spans? (This is usually not an issue in English or Romance-language newspaper text, since names are capitalized, but may be an issue with German-language text or text genres where it is common for authors to write in all-caps or all-small letters.)
- Does the set of possible suffixes and/or transformations – usually, subsequent mentions of company names or places leave out suffixes such as *Ltd.* or *GmbH*, or abbreviate a company name to initial letters – *General Motors* simply becomes *GM* resemble that of newspaper text? (The question may be moot if such transformations never occur because writers always use the short form.)

Third-person pronouns For **third-person pronouns**, many text genres show a high occurrence of anaphoric references where the antecedent is either very local (same or previous sentence) or corresponds to some globally salient entity (e.g., in a Wikipedia article or a biography).

In this case, the following issues are worth considering:

- Is there some kind of morphological tagger (for morphologically rich languages) that allows to assign number and grammatical gender, which allow to filter out incompatible antecedents in most cases?
  In English, for example, the `NN` and `NNS` tags distinguish singular and plural nouns, whereas grammatical gender coincides with more general ontological distinctions.
- Is there some kind of semantic tagger that allows to distinguish between animate and inanimate noun phrases?
  In the case of English, such a list is required to distinguish whether a noun phrase would be referenced as *he*, *she* or *it*. In the case of other languages, it is often still the case that animate entities are more likely to recur as a pronominal reference, whereas inanimate entities may recur with a gender-neutral *they* (for organizations), or with a designator such as *the company* or *the city*.
  While it seems commonsensical that knowledge-rich coreference resolvers such as BART depend on this kind of information, it is also the case that the Coreference Sieve approach as well as pure machine learning approaches such as IMSCoref/HOTCoref depend on resources that give animacy information for nouns. Quite fortunately, such resources can be induced from unannotated text with only moderate effort (see Bergsma, this volume).
- Does the syntactic analysis identify at least the kernels (chunks) of noun phrases reliably? Does it identify clause boundaries with good accuracy, if more complex sentence structures are commonplace? Is the syntactic annotation rich enough to distinguish subjects from non-subjects?

Speech pronouns The use of first and second person pronouns is one of the phenomena that varies the most across different genres. As an example, the OntoNotes corpus features interview transcripts where *I* or *you* refer to the speaker of the respective segment and its interlocutor, respectively. In newspaper text such as in the TüBa-D/Z corpus, *I* usually refers to the author and *you* to the reader, except for direct speech where, again *I* refers to the speaker of that bit of reported speech, and *you* refers to the person spoken to.

The off-the-shelf coreference systems presented in this chapter take this into account by being able to use explicit speaker annotations (in the case of English interview transcripts) as well as, for most cases, incorporating heuristics for quoted speech. However, these may not work, or not work as well, when such material is under-represented in the training material, or behaves very differently the what has been seen in training.

Given the assessment of the issues above, and the role that the coreference output will be playing in the intended application, it should become clear, what work is necessary, firstly, to get usable results from any coreference resolution system in the given domain, and, secondly, which strategy, respectively, would give most impact for a purely rule-based system, for a machine learning system which heavily depends on knowledge sources such as BART, or for a pure-breed machine learning system such as IMSCoref or HOTCoref.

6.3 Adapting a Coreference System

Bernaola-Biggio et al. [2] and Poesio et al. [42] report on the adaptation of BART for Italian. In addition to the more general infrastructure of the LanguagePlugin architecture explained earlier, which makes BART suitable for processing non-English language, additional work was necessary for ensuring good performance: On one hand, the creation of preprocessing pipelines for Italian, both for the AnaphoraBank corpus, where all maximal noun phrases are mentions, and for the iCab corpus which was used in the Evalita competition, which only treats mentions of certain semantic types (persons, organizations, locations, geopolitical entities). In the first case, identification of maximal noun phrases presupposes accurate parsing, and in the second case, additional semantic information is the key to good performance (see Uryupina and Zanoli, this volume).

Outside preprocessing, the adaptation that had the greatest impact was the adaptation of alias (approximate string matching and acronym recognition) to phenomena that are typical for Italian texts, in particular matching "*Provincia di Verona*" against "*Verona*", as well as adding company and person designators ("S.p.a.", or "D.ssa"), as well as allowing lower-case characters in abbreviation (which only rarely occur in English). The modifications for Italian also include the addition of a list of Italian demonyms (people vs. country names: *calabrese* vs. *Calabria*). The addition of these Italian-specific features yielded large improvements both in MUC F-score (47.9 for the language-independent system versus 56.4 for the adapted one) as well as in CEAF F-score (63.6 for the language-independent version versus 66.3 for the adapted one).

Reiter et al. [48] applied a processing chain, including coreference resolution with BART, on English descriptions of Indian rituals. This text type of ritual descriptions deviates significantly from newspaper text in that it contains many vocabulary items that are unseen in newspaper (including substantial amounts of indological terminology), as well as syntactic structures that are uncommon in newspaper texts.

To be able to process these ritual descriptions, Reiter et al. started by adapting the tokenizer to deal with the non-ASCII letters which occur in the non-English words, and proceeded to use domain adaptation techniques to ensure that part-of-speech annotation can be performed reliably. In addition to the standard Penn Treebank training set, they utilized a small amount (350 sentences) of POS-annotated text from the target domain. The combination of these two samples led to useful performance on their texts, whereas a part-of-speech tagger trained only on the Wall Street Journal domain would have suffered from rather low accuracy. In a second step, they trained a chunker based both on data from standard newspaper text, but also the small annotated corpus of ritual descriptions, which drastically improved performance from the performance only using newspaper text.

Using the adapted preprocessing, Reiter et al. used BART, JavaRAP [45] and GuiTaR [40] together with the stock models (in the case of JavaRAP and BART), on a small testing sample from the ritual descriptions corpus (about 295 sentences, containing 18 anaphoric expressions) which allowed to reach tentative conclusions about the usefulness of the approach. Reiter et al. found that the systems reach state-of-the-art performance on their text type (65 % MUC F-measure), but suffered from poor precision which was unsuitable for the task envisaged in their project (computing event chains).

In summary, one could say that the most immediate gains in the case of adapting a coreference system (and this applies both to Stanford's dCoref system and BART, partially also to IMSCoref/HOTCoref) can be seen from having a preprocessing pipeline that is well-adapted to the genre at hand, which can often be gained through even a limited amount of annotated in-domain data. In a next step, if annotated coreference data is available, one may want to check whether assumptions on name variation – which are usually derived from typical variations found in English or other language newspaper text – hold in that particular domain and which phenomena should be taken into account additionally.

7 Conclusion

In this chapter, we have outlined the inner workings of two multilingual coreference systems – BART, IMSCoref/HOTCoref – and Stanford's dCoref system as a monolingual example, and have pointed out common issues in integrating these systems in a larger pipeline. We have also shown existing evidence that, between the minimal amount necessary for interfacing an off-the-shelf component to developing a nearly-new coreference system, adapting an existing off-the-shelf system can be useful in new languages or domains, sometimes even when in-domain training data is unavailable or very sparse.

References

1. Athar, A., Teufel, S.: Context-enhanced citation sentiment detection. In: Proceedings of the 2012 Conference of the NAACL: HLT, Association for Computational Linguistics, Montréal, pp. 597–601 (2012). http://www.aclweb.org/anthology/N12-1073
2. Bernaola Biggio, S.M., Giuliano, C., Poesio, M., Versley, Y., Uryupina, O., Zanoli, R.: Local entity detection and recognition task. In: Proceedings of Evalita-2009, Reggio Emilia (2009)
3. Berndtsson, J.: Coreference resolution in BART: essay assignment for *Semantic Analysis in Language Technology*. http://stp.lingfil.uu.se/~santinim/sais/Ass1_Essays_FinalVersion/Berntsson_Jakob_essay_final.pdf (2014)
4. Björkelund, A., Farkas, R.: Data-driven multilingual coreference resolution using resolver stacking. In: Joint Conference on EMNLP and CoNLL – Shared Task, Jeju Island, pp. 49–55. Association for Computational Linguistics (2012). http://www.aclweb.org/anthology/W12-4503
5. Björkelund, A., Kuhn, J.: Phrase structures and dependencies for end-to-end coreference resolution. In: Proceedings of COLING 2012: Posters, The COLING 2012 Organizing Committee, Mumbai, pp. 145–154 (2012). http://www.aclweb.org/anthology/C12-2015
6. Björkelund, A., Kuhn, J.: Learning structured perceptrons for coreference resolution with latent antecedents and non-local features. In: Proceedings of the 52nd Annual Meeting of the Association for Computational Linguistics. Volume 1: Long Papers. Association for Computational Linguistics, Baltimore, pp. 47–57 (2014). http://www.aclweb.org/anthology/P14-1005
7. Broscheit, S., Poesio, M., POnzetto, S., Rodriguez, K.J., Romano, L., Uryupina, O., Versley, Y., Zanoli, R.: BART: A multilingual anaphora resolution system. In: Proceedings of SemEval-2010, Uppsala (2010)
8. Broscheit, S., Ponzetto, S.P., Versley, Y., Poesio, M.: Extending BART to provide a coreference resolution system for German. In: Proceedings of the 7th International Conference on Language Resources and Evaluation, Valletta (2010)
9. Cai, J., Strube, M.: End-to-end coreference resolution via hypergraph partitioning. In: Proceedings of Coling 2010, Beijing (2010)
10. Cai, J., Mujdricza-Maydt, E., Strube, M.: Unrestricted coreference resolution via global hypergraph partitioning. In: Proceedings of the 15th Conference on Computational Natural Language Learning: Shared Task, Portland (2011)
11. Chang, K.W., Samdani, R., Rozovskaya, A., Sammons, M., Roth, D.: Illinois-coref: the ui system in the conll-2012 shared task. In: Joint Conference on EMNLP and CoNLL – Shared Task, pp. 113–117. Association for Computational Linguistics, Jeju Island (2012). http://www.aclweb.org/anthology/W12-4513
12. Chang, K.W., Samdani, R., Roth, D.: A constrained latent variable model for coreference resolution. In: Proceedings of the 2013 Conference on Empirical Methods in Natural Language Processing, pp. 601–612. Association for Computational Linguistics, Seattle (2013). http://www.aclweb.org/anthology/D13-1057
13. Charniak, E., Johnson, M.: Coarse-to-fine n-best parsing and maxent discriminative reranking. In: Proceedings of the ACL 2005, Ann Arbor (2005)
14. Collins, M.: Discriminative training methods for hidden markov models: theory and experiments with perceptron algorithms. In: Proceedings of the 2002 Conference on Empirical Methods in Natural Language Processing, pp. 1–8. Association for Computational Linguistics (2002). doi:10.3115/1118693.1118694. http://www.aclweb.org/anthology/W02-1001
15. Culotta, A., Wick, M., McCallum, A.: First-order probabilistic models for coreference resolution. In: Proceedings of the HLT/NAACL 2007, Rochester (2007)
16. Deb, K., Pratap, A., Agarwal, S., Meyarivan, T.: A fast and elitist multiobjective genetic algorithm: NSGA-II. IEEE Trans. Evolut. Comput. **6**(2), 181–197 (2002)

17. Durrett, G., Klein, D.: Easy victories and uphill battles in coreference resolution. In: Proceedings of the 2013 Conference on Empirical Methods in Natural Language Processing, pp. 1971–1982. Association for Computational Linguistics, Seattle (2013). http://www.aclweb.org/anthology/D13-1203
18. Elsner, M.: Character-based kernels for novelistic plot structure. In: Proceedings of the 13th Conference of the European Chapter of the Association for Computational Linguistics, pp. 634–644. Association for Computational Linguistics, Avignon (2012). http://www.aclweb.org/anthology/E12-1065
19. Fan, R.E., Chang, K.W., Hsieh, C.J., Wang, X.R., Lin, C.J.: LIBLINEAR: a library for large linear classification. J. Mach. Learn. Res. **9**, 1871–1874 (2008)
20. Fernandes, E., dos Santos, C., Milidiú, R.: Latent structure perceptron with feature induction for unrestricted coreference resolution. In: Joint Conference on EMNLP and CoNLL – Shared Task, pp. 41–48. Association for Computational Linguistics, Jeju Island (2012). http://www.aclweb.org/anthology/W12-4502
21. Finkel, J.R., Grenager, T., Manning, C.: Incorporating non-local information into information extraction systems by gibbs sampling. In: Proceedings of the 43rd Annual Meeting of the Association for Computational Linguistics, University of Michigan (2005)
22. Foster, J., Cetinooglu, O., Wagner, J., Le Roux, J., Nivre, J., Hogan, D., van Genabith, J.: From news to comment: resources and benchmarks for parsing the language of Web 2.0. In: Proceedings of IJCNLP, Chiang Mai (2011)
23. Garrido, G., Cabaleiro, B., Penas, A., Rodrigo, A., Spina, D.: A distant supervised learning system for the tac-kbp slot filling and temporal slot filling tasks. In: Proceedings of Text Analysis Conference (TAC), Gaithersburg (2011)
24. Giesbrecht, E., Evert, S.: Part-of-speech tagging – a solved task? An evaluation of POS taggers for the Web as corpus. In: Proceedings of the 5th Web as Corpus Workshop (WaC 5), San Sebastian (2009)
25. Hardmeier, C.: Discourse in statistical machine translation: a survey and a case study. Discours **11** (2012). [online]. doi:10.4000/discours.8726
26. Hardmeier, C., Federico, M.: Modelling pronominal anaphora in statistical machine translation. In: Proceedings of the 7th International Workshop on Spoken Language Translation (IWSLT 2010), Paris (2010)
27. Klein, D., Manning, C.D.: Fast exact inference with a factored model for natural language parsing. In: NIPS 2002, Vancouver (2003)
28. Kobdani, H., Schütze, H.: Supervised coreference resolution with SUCRE. In: Proceedings of the 15th Conference on Natural Language Learning: Shared Task, Portland, pp. 71–75 (2011)
29. Kopeć, M., Ogrodniczuk, M.: Creating a coreference resolution system for polish. In: Proceedings of LREC 2010, Valletta (2010)
30. Kunze, C., Lemnitzer, L.: GermaNet – representation, visualization, application. In: Proceedings of LREC 2002, Las Palmas (2002)
31. Lee, H., Chang, A., Peirsman, Y., Chambers, N., Surdeanu, M., Jurafsky, D.: Deterministic coreference resolution based on entity-centric, precision-ranked rules. Comput. Linguist. **39**(4), 885–916 (2013)
32. Markert, K., Nissim, M.: Comparing knowledge sources for nominal anaphora resolution. Comput. Linguist. **31**(3), 367–402 (2005)
33. Martschat, S.: Multigraph clustering for unsupervised coreference resolution. In: Proceedings of the ACL Student Research Workshop, Sofia (2013)
34. Martschat, S., Cai, J., Broscheit, S., Mujdricza-Maydt, E., Strube, M.: A multigraph model for coreference resolution. In: Proceedings of the Shared Task of the 16th Conference on Computational Natural Language Learning, Jeju Island (2012)
35. Minnen, G., Caroll, J., Pearce, D.: Applied morphological processing of English. Nat. Lang. Eng. **7**(3), 207–223 (2001)
36. Morton, T.S.: Coreference for NLP Applications. In: Proceedings of the 38th Meeting of the Association for Computational Linguistics, Hong Kong (2000). http://aclweb.org/anthology-new/P/P00/P00-1023.pdf

37. Müller, C., Strube, M.: Multi-level annotation of linguistic data with MMAX2. In: Braun, S., Kohn, K., Mukherjee, J. (eds.) Corpus Technology and Language Pedagogy: New Resources, New Tools, New Methods, Peter Lang, Frankfurt a,M. (2006)
38. Ng, V., Cardie, C.: Improving machine learning approaches to coreference resolution. In: Proceedings of 40th Annual Meeting of the Association for Computational Linguistics, pp. 104–111. Association for Computational Linguistics, Philadelphia (2002). doi:10.3115/1073083.1073102. http://www.aclweb.org/anthology/P02-1014
39. Petrov, S., Barett, L., Thibaux, R., Klein, D.: Learning accurate, compact, and interpretable tree annotation. In: COLING-ACL 2006, Sydney (2006)
40. Poesio, M., Kabadjov, M.A.: A general-purpose, off-the-shelf anaphora resolution module: implementation and preliminary evaluation. In: LREC'2004, Lisbon (2004)
41. Poesio, M., Mehta, R., Maroudas, A., Hitzeman, J.: Learning to resolve bridging references. In: ACL-2004 (2004). http://cswww.essex.ac.uk/staff/poesio/publications/ACL04.pdf
42. Poesio, M., Uryupina, O., Versley, Y.: Creating a coreference resolution system for italian. In: Proceedings of the Seventh International Conference on Language Resources and Evaluation (LREC 2010), Valletta (2010)
43. Ponzetto, S.P., Strube, M.: Exploiting semantic role labeling, WordNet and Wikipedia for coreference resolution. In: Proceedings of HLT/NAACL 2006, New York (2006)
44. Pradhan, S., Moschitti, A., Xue, N., Uryupina, O., Zhang, Y.: Conll-2012 shared task: modeling multilingual unrestricted coreference in ontonotes. In: Joint Conference on EMNLP and CoNLL – Shared Task, pp. 1–40. Association for Computational Linguistics, Jeju Island (2012). http://www.aclweb.org/anthology/W12-4501
45. Qiu, L., Kan, M.Y., Chua, T.S.: A public reference implementation of the RAP anaphora resolution algorithm. In: Proceedings of LREC 2004, Lisbon (2004)
46. Recasens, M., Can, M., Jurafsky, D.: Same referent, different words: unsupervised mining of opaque coreferent mentions. In: Proceedings of NAACL-HLT 2013, Atlanta (2013)
47. Recasens, M., de Marneffe, M.C., Potts, C.: The life and death of discourse entities: identifying singleton mentions. In: Proceedings of HLT-NAACL 2013, Atlanta (2013)
48. Reiter, N., Hellwig, O., Mishra, A., Gossmann, I., Larios, B.M., Rodrigues, J., Zeller, B., Frank, A.: Adapting standard NLP tools and resources to the processing of ritual descriptions. In: Proceedings of the ECAI 2010 Workshop on Language Technology for Cultural Heritage, Social Sciences, and Humanities (LaTeCH), Lisbon (2010)
49. Sikdar, U.K., Ekbal, A., Saha, S., Uryupina, O., Poesio, M.: Differential evolution-based feature selection technique for anaphora resolution. Soft Comput. **19**(8), 2149–2161 (2015)
50. Soon, W.M., Ng, H.T., Lim, D.C.Y.: A machine learning approach to coreference resolution of noun phrases. Comput. Linguist. **27**(4), 521–544 (2001). http://acl.eldoc.ub.rug.nl/mirror/J/J01/J01-4004.pdf
51. Telljohann, H., Hinrichs, E.W., Kübler, S., Zinsmeister, H., Beck, K.: Stylebook for the Tübingen Treebank of Written German (TüBa-D/Z). Tech. rep., Seminar für Sprachwissenschaft, Universität Tübingen (2009)
52. Uryupina, O., Saha, S., Ekbal, A., Poesio, M.: Multi-metric optimization for coreference: the unitn / iitp / essex submission to the CoNLL shared task. In: Proceedings of CoNLL-2011, Portland (2011)
53. Uryupina, O., Moschitti, A., Poesio, M.: BART goes multilingual: the UniTN/Essex submission to the CoNLL-2012 shared task. In: Proceedings of the Joint Conference on EMNLP and CoNLL: Shared Task, Jeju Island (2012)
54. Vadlapudi, R.: Verbose labels for semantic roles. Master's thesis, Simon Fraser University (2013)
55. Versley, Y.: A constraint-based approach to noun phrase coreference resolution in German newspaper text. In: Konferenz zur Verarbeitung Natürlicher Sprache (KONVENS 2006), Konstanz (2006)
56. Versley, Y.: Antecedent selection techniques for high-recall coreference resolution. In: EMNLP 2007, Prague (2007)

57. Versley, Y., Moschitti, A., Poesio, M., Yang, X.: Coreference systems based on kernel methods. In: Proceedings of the 22nd International Conference on Computational Linguistics (Coling 2008), Manchster (2008)
58. Versley, Y., Ponzetto, S., Poesio, M., Eidelman, V., Jern, A., Smith, J., Yang, X., Moschitti, A.: BART: a modular toolkit for coreference resolution. In: ACL 2008 System Demonstrations, Baltimore (2008)
59. Versley, Y., Beck, A.K., Hinrichs, E., Telljohann, H.: A syntax-first approach to high-quality morphological analysis and lemma disambiguation for the TüBa-D/Z treebank. In: Proceedings of the 9th Conference on Treebanks and Linguistic Theories (TLT9), Tartu (2010)
60. Wang, R., Zhang, Y., Neumann, G.: A joint syntactic-semantic representation for recognizing textual relatedness. In: Text Analysis Conference TAC 2009 Notebook Papers and Results, Gaithersburg (2009)
61. Wellner, B., Vilain, M.: Leveraging machine readable dictionaries in discriminative sequence models. In: Proceedings of LREC 2006, Genoa (2006)
62. Yang, X., Su, J., Tan, C.L.: Kernel-based pronoun resolution with structured syntactic knowledge. In: Proceedings of the 21st International Conference on Computational Linguistics and the 44th Annual Meeting of the Association for Computational Linguistics, ACL-44, pp. 41–48 (2006). doi:10.3115/1220175.1220181. http://dx.doi.org/10.3115/1220175.1220181
63. Yang, X., Su, J., Tan, C.L.: Kernel-based pronoun resolution with structured syntactic knowledge. In: Proceedings of CoLing/ACL-2006 (2006). http://www.aclweb.org/anthology/P/P06/P06-1006
64. Young, P., Lai, A., Hodosh, M., Hockenmaier, J.: From image descriptions to visual denotations: New similarity metrics for semantic inference over event descriptions. Trans. Assoc. Comput. Linguist. **3**, 67–78 (2014)
65. Zhao, S., Ng, H.T.: Maximum metric score training for coreference resolution. In: Proceedings of Coling 2010, Beijing (2010)

Part III
Algorithms

The Mention-Pair Model

Veronique Hoste

Abstract This chapter introduces one of the early and most influential machine learning approaches to coreference resolution, the mention-pair model. Initiated in the mid-1990s and further developed into a more generic resolver by Soon et al. in 2001 and many others, the simple model still remains a popular benchmark in the learning-based resolution research. The mention-pair model recasts the coreference resolution problem as a classification task in which a classifier is trained to decide for a given pair of noun phrases whether they corefer or not. In a second step, full coreference chains are built by clustering these pairwise decisions. This chapter reviews the main building blocks of the mention-pair model: the construction of positive and negative instances and the related problem of data set skewness, the selection of informative features, and the choice of machine learner and clustering mechanism.

Keywords The mention-pair model mention-pair model • Coreference resolution

1 Introduction

In the last decade of the twentieth century, corpus-based techniques have become increasingly popular for the resolution of coreference relations.[1] At that time, they had already become the norm for many other natural language processing tasks such as part-of-speech tagging, parsing, grapheme-to-phoneme conversion, etc. Through the advent of corpora annotated with coreferential relations which were created in the framework of the Message Understanding Conferences MUC-6 and MUC-7, the base material was in place for the domain of coreference resolution to also shift towards a corpus-based perspective. These annotated corpora were used to derive

[1] In this chapter, no distinction will be made between the terms "anaphor" and "coreference". For a definition focusing on the differences between coreferences and anaphors, we refer to [1] and [2]

V. Hoste (✉)
University College Ghent, Groot-Brittanniëlaan 45, Ghent, Belgium
e-mail: veronique.hoste@hogent.be

M. Poesio et al. (eds.), *Anaphora Resolution*, Theory and Applications of Natural Language Processing, DOI 10.1007/978-3-662-47909-4_9

collocation patterns for filtering out unlikely antecedent candidates [3], to learn an ordered set of heuristics [4], to determine probabilities for the *n* candidates proposed by the Hobbs [5] algorithm [6], etc.

In the wake of these corpus-based approaches to coreference resolution, machine learning techniques also gained increasing popularity (e.g. [7]). One of the early approaches to coreference resolution was the so-called **mention-pair model**. It was first proposed by Aone and Bennet [8] and by McCarthy and Lehnert [9]; Soon et al. [10] and Ng and Cardie [11] turned it into one of the most influential learning-based coreference models. Whereas Aone and Bennet [8] focused on organizations in Japanese text and McCarthy [9] focused on the joint venture domain through the inclusion of domain-specific features, Soon et al. [10] were the first to define a generic set of features which was applicable across domains and they also evaluated their system on all types of noun phrases. Their algorithms – their choice of features, their training and decoding methods – have become the standard baseline for coreference resolution in the '00s, the new Hobbs algorithm.

The mention-pair model recasts the coreference resolution problem as a classification task: a classifier is trained to decide whether a pair of NPs or mentions is coreferential or not. In other words, resolving anaphor m_j can be viewed as the task of finding the mention m_i that maximizes the probability of the random variable L:

$$argmax_{m_i} P(L|m_j, m_i)$$

As exemplified in (19), the resolution involves finding the correct antecedent among many possibilities. This is done by using different types of knowledge: morphological and lexical knowledge such as number agreement and knowledge about the type of noun phrase, syntactic knowledge such as information about the syntactic function of anaphor and antecedent, semantic knowledge which allows for recognizing synonyms and hypernyms or which allows distinctions to be made between person, organization or location names, discourse knowledge, world knowledge, etc. In the mention-pair model, each pair of NPs is represented by a feature vector containing distance, morphological, lexical, syntactic and semantic information on both NPs and the relation between them. The goal of the feature information is to enable the machine learner to distinguish between coreferential and non-coreferential relations, to resolve that *we* in (19) are not *fruit flies*, but *humans*. After this binary classification, a second step, a separate clustering mechanism is used to coordinate the pairwise classification decisions and to build so-called 'coreference chains'.

(19) Fruit flies are for many reasons more successful than humans. And *we* help *them* with the things *they* are not able to do.

The remainder of this chapter is structured as follows. Section 2 deals with the problem of instance construction by starting with the preprocessing steps to be taken before instance creation; it continues with a discussion on the selection of positive and negative instances. In Sect. 3, an overview is given of the different information sources which are encoded in the feature vectors of the mention-pair approach to coreference resolution. Section 4 continues with a short overview of the full experimental set-up of a mention-pair coreference resolver, including the choice of machine learner for the binary classification and the clustering of these pairwise classifications. Section 5 concludes this chapter.

2 Instance Construction

The mention-pair model approach uses a typical supervised learning set-up. A training set containing labeled instances, which consist of attribute/value pairs with possibly disambiguating information for the classifier, is created and presented as learning material to a classifier. The task of the classifier, then, is to accurately predict the class of previously unseen instances. A general goal of classifier learning is to learn a model on the basis of training data which makes as few errors as possible when classifying previously unseen test data. The learner typically requires instances from at least two classes. In the case of coreference resolution, this implies that the training instances are feature vectors representing two mentions (m_i and m_j) and a label ("coreferent" or "non-coreferent") which allows the classifier to predict for a new pair of mentions, whether they do or do not corefer.

2.1 Preprocessing the Data

The focus in the mention-pair approaches is on resolving coreference relations between noun phrases. Soon et al. [10] were the first to focus on *all* noun phrases, including definite and demonstrative noun phrases, pronouns, proper nouns, embedded noun phrases, etc. In order to allow for instance construction between pairs of noun phrases, some preprocessing steps are required, such as tokenization, sentence segmentation, part-of-speech tagging, noun phrase identification, named entity recognition, nested noun phrase extraction, etc. Other natural language processing modules, such as parsing, semantic class determination, morphological processing, etc. are primarily useful for enabling the classifier to predict for a given pair of NPs whether they do or do not corefer. In all learning-based approaches to coreference resolution, the majority of these NLP modules is learning-based. For the modules aiming at the detection of the noun phrases in a text, a high performance is crucial, since not recognizing or only partially recognizing a given NP will lead to not creating any or to creating a false instance. Soon et al. [10] performed a quantitative and qualitative error analysis which explicitly addresses the influence of the different preprocessing modules and showed that their system was able to correctly identify about 85 % of the noun phrases appearing in coreference chains in a 100-document subset of the MUC-6 data set.

2.2 Positive and Negative Instances

The coreferential links in the annotated data set serve as the basis for the construction of the positive instances. When no sampling at all is used, these **positive instances** will be made by combining each anaphoric NP with each preceding element in the coreference chain. The **negative or non-referential instances** are then built by combining each anaphor with each preceding NP which is not part of any coreference chain and by combining each anaphor with each preceding NP which is part of another coreference chain. Such a procedure inevitably leads to a highly imbalanced or skewed class distribution caused by a small number of positive instances and a large number of negative instances. This is clearly exemplified in Table 1 for the anaphoric NP *He*. When trained on such imbalanced data sets, classifiers can exhibit a good performance on the majority class instances but a high error rate on the minority class instances. Always assigning the non-coreferent class will lead to a highly 'accurate' classifier, which cannot find any coreferent chain in a text. In order to cope with this imbalance, Soon et al. [10], for example, only create positive training instances between anaphoric NPs and their immediately preceding antecedent. The NPs occurring between the two members of each antecedent-anaphor pair are used for the creation of the negative training examples. In case of the example depicted in Table 1, this implies that only one instance, a positive one, will be created between *his* and *O'Brien*.

In addition to restricting the scope of instance selection on the basis of the annotations, other filtering approaches can be applied to the data. These filters split the basic set of instances in two parts: one part gets a label automatically assigned

Table 1 The construction of positive and negative instances in case of no filtering for the sentences. (The head of (the Catholic Church in (Phoenix, Arizona)$_1$)$_2$, Bishop Thomas O'Brien)$_3$ has resigned, (just one day)$_4$ after being charged with (a felony)$_5$. (He)$_3$ is accused of leaving (the scene of a fatal accident)$_6$. (Earlier this month)$_7$ (O'Brien)$_3$ narrowly escaped (prosecution over ((his)$_3$ handling of (sexual abuse allegations against (priests)$_{11}$)$_{10}$)$_9$)$_8$ (The sentences are taken from the trial data released for the SemEval Task 1 on Coreference Resolution in Multiple Languages. The trial data are extracted from the OntoNotes Corpus Release 2.0 (see http://www.bbn.com/ontonotes))

Anaphoric NP (m_1)	Candidate antecedent (m_2)	Classification	Soon et al. [10]
His	The head (...) Thomas O'Brien	POS	–
His	The Catholic Church in Phoenix, Arizona	NEG	–
His	Phoenix, Arizona	NEG	–
His	Just one day	NEG	–
His	A felony	NEG	–
His	He	POS	–
His	The scene of a fatal accident	NEG	–
His	A fatal accident	NEG	–
His	Earlier this month	NEG	–
His	O'Brien	POS	POS

by the filter, the other part is classified by a classifier. There are several ways to look at this approach. It can be regarded as a language engineering approach, or even as a preprocessing trick, but it can also be made into a principled approach to creating hybrid knowledge-based and machine learning-based systems where both approaches solve the problems they are best at.

Some of the filters proposed in literature aim exclusively at the reduction of negative instances, reducing the positive class skewness. Strube, Rapp and Müller [12] use the same methodology as Soon et al. [10] for the creation of positive and negative instances, but they also first apply a number of filters, which reduce up to 50 % of the negative instances. These filters are all linguistically motivated, e.g. discard an antecedent-anaphor pair (i) if the anaphor is an indefinite NP, (ii) if one entity is embedded into the other, e.g. if the potential anaphor is the head of the potential antecedent NP, (iii) if either pronominal entity has a value other than third person singular or plural in its agreement feature. Yang et al. [13] use the following filtering algorithm to reduce the number of instances in the training set: (i) add the NPs in the current and previous two sentences and remove the NPs that disagree in number, gender and person in case of pronominal anaphors, (ii) add all the non-pronominal antecedents to the initial candidate set in case of non-pronominal anaphors. Ng and Cardie [11] propose both negative sample selection (the reduction of the number of negative instances) and positive sample selection (the reduction of the number of positive instances), both under-sampling strategies aiming to create a better coreference resolution system. They use a technique for negative instance selection, similar to that proposed in [10] and they create negative instances for the NPs occurring between an anaphor and its farthest antecedent. Furthermore, they try to avoid the inclusion of hard training instances. Given the observation that one antecedent is sufficient to resolve an anaphor, they present a corpus-based method for the selection of easy positive instances, which is inspired by the example selection algorithm introduced by Harabagiu, Bunescu and Maiorano [4]. They show that system performance improves dramatically with positive sample selection. The application of both negative and positive sample selection leads to an even better performance. Uryupina [14] distinguishes between four types of markables (pronouns, definites, named entities, and all the other NPs) and proposes different sample selection mechanisms, reflecting the different linguistic behavior of these anaphors. In cross-comparative results with and without instance selection she shows an increase on both speed and performance. Hendrickx, Hoste and Daelemans [15] show on a Dutch corpus that a hybrid approach which combines five simple filter rules leads to a large instance reduction of up to 92 %, and produces a better F-score for the two learners (`Maxent` [53] and `TiMBL` [51]) they experimented with.

Hoste [16] rebalances the data without any a priori (linguistic) knowledge about the task to be solved and links it to the specific learning behaviour of a lazy learner (`TiMBL`) and an eager learner (`Ripper` [55]). She investigates the effect of random down-sampling (in slices of 10 % until reaching an equal number of positive and negative instances) and a more focused downsampling of the true negatives which are determined in a leave-one-out experiment on the different training folds. This work also shows that both learning approaches behave quite differently in case of skewness of the classes, and they also react differently to a change in class distribution: the lazy learner, which performs better on the minority class than the eager learner in case of a largely imbalanced class distribution, mainly suffers from a rebalancing of the data set. These results are confirmed for Spanish by Recasens and Hovy [17].

3 Selection of Informative Features

A good set of features is crucial for the success of the resolution systems. An ideal feature vector consists of features which are all highly informative and which can lead the classifier to optimal performance. In order to reach this optimal performance, the existing classification-based coreference resolvers all use a combination of distance, string-matching, grammatical, syntactic and semantic features. Since a wide variety of possibly interesting information sources has been proposed in the framework of coreference resolution, we will mainly restrict ourselves to the features used in the mention-pair coreference systems.

Distance features give information on the location of the candidate anaphoric NP and the candidate antecedent and also inform on the distance between both noun phrases.

String-matching features check for full or partial overlap between both NPs under consideration. In addition to checking for full or partial overlap at the word level, more sophisticated approaches have been explored. Strube, Rapp and Müller [12], for example, compute the minimum edit distance (MED) [18, 19] between two NPs, i.e. the minimum number of deletions, insertions, and substitutions required to transform one NP into the other. They show that the use of this feature leads to a significant performance improvement for the definite NPs and proper names. Yang et al. [20] add cluster features to the feature vector of a given anaphor. These cluster features describe the relationship (such as number and gender agreement, string similarity, etc.) between the candidate anaphor and a cluster of possibly referring NPs. In an analysis of the decision trees produced with and without cluster information, they show that string matching is crucial in both systems.

Grammatical features encode the grammatical properties of one or of both noun phrases involved in an instance, e.g. NP type, gender and number agreement between the NPs, etc.

Syntactic features inform on the function (e.g. subject, object, appositive, etc.) of the anaphoric or antecedent noun phrase in the sentence. We can observe that many systems use some form of shallow syntactic features such as [10, 21]. Some systems also look at deeper syntactic information sources. Yang, Su and Tan [22], for example, successfully explore the use of parse trees as a structural feature in a kernel-based method for pronoun resolution. Hendrickx, Hoste and Daelemans [23] investigate whether the syntactic information as predicted by a memory-based shallow parser can be enhanced with the richer syntactic information derived from a dependency parser. They show that adding these features leads to marginal improvements.

Semantic features inform on the animacy of the NPs or indicate whether a given noun phrase is male or female, whether it denotes an organization or a date, etc. There has been an increased interest in the use of semantic resources for coreference resolution. Especially WordNet [24] remains a very useful information source for coreference resolution (e.g. [21, 25–27]). Ponzetto and Strube [25], for example, study the effect of three semantic sources, namely WordNet, taxonomies extracted from Wikipedia and semantic role labeling, and show that these semantic features improve their system. Also additional resources have been explored. [28] encode semantic information as semantic relations based on the ACE 2004 relation ontology relations, 7 main types and 23 subtypes, and show its beneficial effect on coreference resolution. Ng [29, 30] explores the usefulness of adding semantic knowledge such as the 5 ACE semantic classes and of adding semantic similarity values as provided by Lin's [31] dependency-based thesaurus. Yang and Su [32] investigate the extraction of automatically discovered patterns which express semantic relatedness information for coreference resolution. Hendrickx et al. [15] investigate the usefulness of integrating automatically generated semantic clusters of [33] to model the semantic classes of noun phrases and compare its effect to the use of two other semantic features based on the Dutch EuroWordNet [34].

In addition to these core information sources, other types of features have also been explored. Iida et al. [35], for example, integrate discourse features extracted from Centering Theory. Bengtson and Roth [36] integrate a so-called memorization feature in their feature vector , which treats the presence or absence of each pair of final head nouns. Since only part of the noun phrases is anaphoric, various systems also include information on the anaphoricity of a given noun phrase (e.g. [36–39]).

The size of the feature vector differs considerably between the different systems. The anaphora resolution system for Japanese of Aone and Bennet [8], one of the first machine learning approaches to anaphora resolution, for example, uses 66 features, whereas the RESOLVE system of McCarthy [40] makes its predictions based on 8 features. Uryupina [41] experimented with a large feature vector of 351 nominal (1096 boolean/continuous) features. Furthermore, all systems distinguish between *'unary' features*, describing characteristics from a single anaphor or from its (candidate) antecedent and *'binary' or pairwise comparison features*, describing the characteristics of the relation between an anaphor and its (candidate) antecedent.

3.1 The Core Soon et al. Feature Vector and Its Successors

As Soon et al. [10] were the first to propose a full learning-based coreference resolution pipeline, we will first focus on their selection of features. Their system takes as input vectors consisting of 12 features, all of which had previously been used (by [9, 42] or [43]). The majority of the features, a combination of distance, string-matching, grammatical, syntactic and semantic features, is obtained on the basis of a shallow preprocessing of the text including tokenization, sentence segmentation, morphological processing, part-of-speech tagging, noun phrase identification, named entity recognition, nested noun phrase extraction and semantic class determination. This feature set, listed in full in Table 2, could be considered the core feature set for all subsequent coreference resolution systems. Soon et al. [10] show that even with a limited set of three features (viz. string match, alias and appositive), their decision tree learning system results are near to approaching the highest scores reported on the MUC-6 and MUC-7 data sets. They report an F-score of 62.6 on MUC-6, and of 60.4 on MUC-7 (using the MUC scorer).

Ng and Cardie [21] explore the effect of including 41 additional lexical, semantic and grammatical potentially useful knowledge sources on top of the features used by Soon et al. [10] for their coreference resolution classifier. When experimenting with a decision tree learner and a rule induction system, they show that the expansion of the feature set leads to a decrease in precision, especially for the common nouns, mainly caused by the application of low-precision rules. They suggest that data fragmentation has contributed to the drop in performance. In order to improve precision scores, they perform manual feature selection, discarding features used primarily to induce low-precision rules for common noun resolution and they retrain the classifier using the reduced feature set. This selection leads to a restricted feature set of 18 additional features to those proposed by Soon et al.. The resulting system developed by Ng and Cardie achieves an F-score of 70.4 on MUC6 and of 63.4 on MUC7 (using the MUC scorer).

Other work explicitly focused on evaluating the impact of different information sources has been proposed by a.o. [17, 36, 41]. Uryupina [41], for example, constructs a feature vector of 122 lexicographic, 64 syntactic, 29 semantic and

Table 2 Feature set as used by [10]

Type	Description	Value
Distance	Distance between m_i and m_j in terms of the number of sentences	Integer
String-matching	Is m_j an alias of m_i?	Boolean
	Do m_i and m_j match after stripping of articles and demonstrative pronouns?	Boolean
Grammatical	Does m_j start with an definite article?	Boolean
	Does m_j start with a demonstrative pronoun?	Boolean
	Is m_i pronominal?	Boolean
	Is m_j pronominal?	Boolean
	Do m_i and m_j agree in number?	Boolean
	Do m_i and m_j agree in gender?	Boolean
	Do m_i and m_j both contain a proper name?	Boolean
Syntactic	Is m_j an apposition?	Boolean
Semantic	Do m_i and m_j agree in semantic class	Boolean

136 discourse/salience-related features and compares different learners trained on these 351 features with a re-implementation of the Soon et al. system. She shows a moderate, but consistent, improvement in the system's performance and suggests that various possibilities for feature selection and ensemble learning with different feature splits could boost performance. Bengtson and Roth [36] focus on the implementation of a small set of high-quality features and show on the ACE data set that a simple pairwise model trained on these features can outperform more sophisticated models. Recasens and Hovy [17] reports experiments with a set of 47 features, many of them derived from the gold standard annotations in the Spanish AnCora corpus [44].

3.2 Assessing Feature Informativeness

Whereas in the early machine learning work (e.g. [8]) the usefulness of the different features was not evaluated, we can observe a tendency in more recent work (starting with Soon et al. [10], Ng and Cardie [21] and Yang et al. [20]), to also assess the informativeness of the features. Finding a good subset of features requires searching the whole space of feature subsets. Since an exhaustive search of this space is practically impossible, because this implies searching 2^n possible subsets for n attributes, different heuristic approaches to feature selection have been proposed.

Soon et al. [10], for example, study the contribution of the features by training their system only taking into account one single feature and some combinations of features. They observe a small number of features leading to a nonzero F-score for both the MUC-6 and MUC-7 data sets they experimented with and identify the string matching features as the most informative ones. Ng and Cardie [21] determine feature relevance by manually omitting the features leading to low-precision rules. Strube and Müller [45] use an iterative feature selection procedure in a spoken dialogue corpus. Hoste [16] experiments with backward elimination (see for example [46]) and bidirectional hill-climbing [47] for the selection of the relevant features. She confirms on different data sets that the string matching features are the most informative and shows that the different learners (viz. `TiMBL` and `Ripper`) she experimented with greatly differ in their sensitivity to feature selection. These results are confirmed in genetic algorithm experiments in which she performs joint feature selection and parameter optimization. Recasens and Hovy [17] also investigate the impact of feature selection on the Spanish AnCora corpus by carrying out a one-by-one elimination and hill-climbing forward selection.

Based on the assumption that feature informativeness might depend on the NP type under consideration, several researchers (e.g. [11, 12, 16]) evaluate the performance of their systems on different NP types, viz. pronouns, named entities and common noun NPs. Ng and Cardie [11], for example, observe a low precision on common noun resolution (antecedents were searched for many non-anaphoric common nouns) and a high precision on pronoun and proper noun resolution. A similar conclusion has been drawn by Strube, Rapp and Müller[12] on a corpus of German texts. Motivated by these findings, Hoste [16] has constructed three coreference resolvers, one for each NP type and compares their joint performance with a coreference resolver trained on a mixed data set. Her results show that no convincing evidence can be found for the initial hypothesis that three more specialized classifiers, each trained on the coreferential relations of a specific NP type, would perform better than one single classifier covering all coreferential relations. However, this idea of training separate systems for different types of NPs has also been explored by others (e.g. [48, 49]) outside the framework of the mention-pair model.

4 The Mention-Pair Coreference Resolver

As set out in the introduction, the mention-pair approach necessitates a two-step procedure. In a first step, pairs of noun phrases are classified as being coreferential or not. In a second step, one or more coreference chains or NP partitions are built on the basis of the positively classified instances.

4.1 Pairwise Classification

Having built the feature vectors for the coreference resolver, a selection can be made of one or several off-the-shelf learning algorithms. In the early machine learning approaches to coreference resolution, there was a predominant use of the C4.5 (C5.0) decision tree learner [50], which was for example used by [8, 9] and [10]. But nowadays, the performance of various different learners is often evaluated, including memory-based learners [51] (e.g. by [16, 17]), maximum entropy learners [52, 53] (as in [13, 15, 54]), the RIPPER rule learner [55] (as in [11, 16, 21, 37, 41]), voted perceptrons [56] (as in [36]) or an implementation of Support Vector Machines [57] (as in [41, 58]).

4.2 Generating Coreference Chains

In order to reconcile the independent pairwise classifications, some kind of clustering is needed to build chains of coreferent entities. In the so-called **closest-first clustering** approach proposed by Soon et al. [10], the algorithm starts from the immediately preceding NP and proceeds backwards in the reverse order of the NPs in the document until there is no remaining NP to test or until an antecedent (positively classified instance) is found. Based on the hypothesis that better coreference chains could be found by searching left-to-right for *a highly likely* antecedent instead of the *first* coreferent NP, Ng and Cardie [21] proposed the **best-first clustering** approach. They select as antecedent the noun phrase with the highest coreference likelihood value among the preceding NPs with coreference class values above 0.5. This approach in which the antecedent closest to the anaphor is preferred among those with the highest confidence, was already proposed earlier by Aone and Bennet [8]. In case of **aggressive merge** clustering [40, 59], each NP is merged with all of its preceding coreferent NPs, which can lead to higher recall scores. However, errors in both steps can lead to incorrect coreference chains: errors in the first step (e.g. an NP pair which is erroneously classified as negative) are not taken into account, thus irreparable by the second, and percolate to the end result, and errors in the second step immediately lead to mispredicted or missed equivalence classes. In order to identify errors in the resulting chains, Hoste and van den Bosch [60] proposed a post-correction of the coreference chains based on Levenshtein distance and show a modest increase in precision.

However, the mention-pair approaches have some well-known weaknesses. The two steps are not applied in an interleaved manner: the systems do not optimize for clustering-level accuracy. The coreference classifier is trained and optimized independently of the clustering algorithm to be used. Furthermore, since the candidate antecedents for a given anaphor are considered independently of one another, it is impossible to determine how good a candidate antecedent is compared to the other antecedents. Ng [61] also mentions the problem of the lack of expressiveness: the information extracted from the two noun phrases alone may not be sufficient to make an informed coreference decision, for example when the candidate antecedent is a pronoun. In order to cope with these weaknesses, various new models and approaches to NP coreference are developed, e.g. a mention-ranking model (e.g. [49]), an entity-mention model (e.g. [62, 63]). For a description of these models, we refer to the following chapters.

5 Conclusion

In this chapter, we introduced the "mention-pair model", a classification-based approach to coreference resolution, one of the most influential models among the machine learning approaches to the task. We first described the main system components, viz. the construction of the instance base, the selection of information sources and the choice of learner. In the description of the system architecture, a two-step architecture in which a clustering step follows a pairwise classification step, we also briefly focused on the weaknesses of this model.

References

1. Kibble, R.: Coreference annotation: Whither? In: Proceedings of the Second International Conference on Language Resources and Evaluation (LREC-2000), Athens, pp. 1281–1286 (2000)
2. van Deemter, K., Kibble, R.: On coreferring: coreference in muc and related annotation schemes. Comput. Linguist. **26**(4), 629–637 (2000)
3. Dagan, I., Itai, A.: Automatic processing of large corpora for the resolution of anaphora references. In: Proceedings of the 13th International Conference on Computational Linguistics (COLING-1990), Helsinki, pp. 330–332 (1990)
4. Harabagiu, S., Bunescu, R., Maiorano, S.: Text and knowledge mining for coreference resolution. In: Proceedings of the 2nd Meeting of the North American Chapter of the Association of Computational Linguistics (NAACL-2001), Pittsburgh, pp. 55–62 (2001)
5. Hobbs, J.: Resolving pronoun references. Lingua **44**, 311–338 (1978)
6. Ge, N., Hale, J., Charniak, E.: A statistical approach to anaphora resolution. In: Proceedings of the Sixth Workshop on Very Large Corpora, Montreal, pp. 161–170 (1998)
7. Kehler, A.: Probabilistic coreference in information extraction. In: Providence, R.I. (ed.) Proceedings of the Second Conference on Empirical Methods in Natural Language Processing (EMNLP-97), Providence, pp. 163–173 (1997)
8. Aone, C., Bennett, S.: Evaluating automated and manual acquisition of anaphora resolution strategies. In: Proceedings of the 33rd Annual Meeting of the Association for Computational Linguistics (ACL-1995), Cambridge, pp. 122–129 (1995)
9. McCarthy, J.: A trainable approach to coreference resolution for information extraction. PhD thesis, Department of Computer Science, University of Massachusetts, Amherst (1996)
10. Soon, W., Ng, H., Lim, D.: A machine learning approach to coreference resolution of noun phrases. Comput. Linguist. **27**(4), 521–544 (2001)
11. Ng, V., Cardie, C.: Combining sample selection and error-driven pruning for machine learning of coreference rules. In: Proceedings of the 2002 Conference on Empirical Methods in Natural Language Processing (EMNLP-2002), Philadelphia, pp. 55–62 (2002)
12. Strube, M., Rapp, S., Müller, C.: The influence of minimum edit distance on reference resolution. In: Proceedings of the 2002 Conference on Empirical Methods in Natural Language Processing (EMNLP-2002), Philadelphia, pp. 312–319 (2002)
13. Yang, X., Zhou, G., Su, S., Tan, C.: Coreference resolution using competition learning approach. In: Proceedings of the 41th Annual Meeting of the Association for Compuatiational Linguistics (ACL-03), Sapporo, pp. 176–183 (2003)
14. Uryupina, O.: Linguistically motivated sample selection for coreference resolution. In: Proceedings of DAARC-2004 Azores, (2004)
15. Hendrickx, I., Hoste, V., Daelemans, W.: Evaluating hybrid versus data-driven coreference resolution. In: Anaphora: Analysis, Algorithms and Application. Lecture Notes in Artificial Intelligence, vol. 4410, pp. 137–150. Springer, Berlin/New York (2007)
16. Hoste, V.: Optimization Issues in Machine Learning of Coreference Resolution. PhD thesis, Antwerp University (2005)
17. Recasens, M., Hovy, E.: A deeper look into features for coreference resolution. In: Proceedings of the 7th Discourse Anaphora and Anaphor Resolution Colloquium, Goa, pp. 29–42 (2009)
18. Levenshtein, V.: Binary codes capable of correcting deletions, insertions and reversals. Sov. Phys. Daklady **10**, 707–710 (1966)
19. Wagner, R., Fisher, M.: The string-to-string correction problem. J. ACM **21**(1), 168–173 (1974)
20. Yang, X., Su, S., Zhou, G., Tan, C.: A np-cluster approach to coreference resolution. In: Proceedings of the 20th International Conference on Computational Linguistics (COLING-2004), Geneva (2004)
21. Ng, V., Cardie, C.: Improving machine learning approaches to coreference resolution. In: Proceedings of the 40th Annual Meeting of the Association for Computational Linguistics (ACL-2002), Philadalphia, pp. 104–111 (2002)

22. Yang, X., Su, J., Tan, C.L.: Kernel based pronoun resolution with structured syntactic knowledge. In: Proceedings of the 21st International Conference on Computational Linguistics and the 44th Annual Meeting of the Association for Computational Linguistics, Sydney, pp. 41–48 (2006)
23. Hendrickx, I., Hoste, V., Daelemans, W.: Semantic and syntactic features for anaphora resolution for dutch. In: Proceedings of the CICLing-2008 conference. Lecture Notes in Computer Science, vol. 4919, pp. 351–361. Springer, Berlin (2008)
24. Fellbaum, C.: WordNet: An Electronic Lexical Database. MIT, Cambridge (1998)
25. Ponzetto, S., Strube, M.: Exploiting semantic role labeling, wordnet and wikipedia for coreference resolution. In: Proceedings of the Human Language Technology Conference of the NAACL, New York, pp. 192–199 (2006)
26. Markert, K., Nissim, M.: Comparing knowledge sources for nominal anaphora resolution. Comput. Linguist. **31**(3), 367–401 (2005)
27. Huang, Z., Zeng, G., Xu, W., Celikyilmaz, A.: Accurate semantic class classifier for coreference resolution. In: EMNLP '09: Proceedings of the 2009 Conference on Empirical Methods in Natural Language Processing, Singapore, pp. 1232–1240 (2009)
28. Ji, H., Westbrook, D., Grishman, R.: Using semantic relations to refine coreference decisions. In: Proceedings of Human Language Technology Conference and Conference on Empirical Methods in Natural Language Processing, Vancouver, pp. 17–24 (2005)
29. Ng, V.: Semantic class induction and coreference resolution. In: Proceedings of the 45th Annual Meeting of the Association of Computational Linguistics, Prague, pp. 536–543 (2007)
30. Ng, V.: Shallow semantics for coreference resolution. In: Proceedings of the Twentieth International Joint Conference on Artificial Intelligence, Hyderabad, pp. 1689–1694 (2007)
31. Lin, D.: Automatic retrieval and clustering of similar words. In: Proceedings of Coling-ACL, Montreal, pp. 768–774 (1998)
32. Yang, X., Su, J.: Coreference resolution using semantic relatedness information from automatically discovered patterns. In: Proceedings of the 45th Annual Meeting of the Association of Computational Linguistics, Prague, pp. 528–535 (2007)
33. Van de Cruys, T.: Semantic clustering in dutch. In: Proceedings of the Sixteenth Computational Linguistics in the Netherlands (CLIN), Amsterdam, pp. 17–32 (2005)
34. Vossen, P. (ed.): EuroWordNet: A Multilingual Database with Lexical Semantic Networks. Kluwer Academic, Norwell, (1998)
35. Iida, R., Inui, K., Takamura, H., Matsumoto, Y.: Incorporating contextual cues in trainable models for coreference resolution. In: Proceedings of the EACL 2003 Workshop on The Computational Treatment of Anaphora Budapest, (2003)
36. Bengtson, E., Roth, D.: Understanding the value of feaures for coreference resolution. In: Proceedings of the International Conference on Empirical Methods Conference in Natural Language Processing, Waikiki, pp. 294–303 (2008)
37. Ng, V., Cardie, C.: Identifying anaphoric and non-anaphoric noun phrases to improve coreference resolution. In: Proceedings of the 19th International Conference on Computational Linguistics (COLING-2002), Taipei (2002)
38. Uryupina, O.: High-precision identification of discourse new and unique noun phrases. In: Proceedings of the ACL Student Research Workshop, Sapporo, pp. 80–86 (2003)
39. Poesio, M., Uryupina, O., Vieira, R., Alexandrov-Kabadjov, M., Goulart, R.: Discourse-new detectors for definite description resolution: a survey and a preliminary proposal. In: Proceedings of the ACL Workshop on Reference Resolution, Barcelona (2004)
40. McCarthy, J., Lehnert, W.: Using decision trees for coreference resolution. In: Proceedings of the Fourteenth International Conference on Artificial Intelligence, Montreal, pp. 1050–1055 (1995)
41. Uryupina, O.: Coreference resolution with and without linguistic knowledge. In: Proceedings of the 5th International Conference on Language Resources and Evaluation, Genoa (2006)
42. Fisher, F., Soderland, S., Mccarthy, J., Feng, F., Lehnert, W.: Description of the umass system as used for muc-6. In: Proceedings of the Sixth Message Understanding Conference (MUC-6), pp. 127–140. Morgan Kaufman, San Francisco (1995)

43. Cardie, C., Wagstaff, K.: Noun phrase coreference as clustering. In: Proceedings of the 1999 joint SIGDAT Conference on Empirical Methods in Natural Language Processing and Very Large Corpora, College Park, pp. 82–89 (1999)
44. Taule, M., Marti, M.A., Recasens, M.: AnCora: multilevel annotated corpora for Catalan and Spanish. In: Proceedings of LREC-2008, Marrakesh (2008)
45. Strube, M., Müller, C.: A machine learning approach to pronoun resolution in spoken dialogue. In: Proceedings of the 41th Annual Meeting of the Association for Computational Linguistics (ACL-2003), Sapporo, pp. 168–175 (2003)
46. John, G., Kohavi, R., Pfleger, K.: Irrelevant features and the subset selection problem. In: International Conference on Machine Learning, New Brunswick, pp. 121–129 (1994)
47. Caruana, R., Freitag, D.: Greedy attribute selection. In: Proceedings of the International Conference on Machine Learning (ICML-1994), New Brunswick, pp. 28–36 (1994)
48. Ng, V.: Supervised ranking for pronoun resolution: some recent improvements. In: Proceedings of the Twentieth National Conference on Artificial Intelligence (AAAI), Pittsburgh, pp. 1081–1086 (2005)
49. Denis, P., Baldridge, J.: Specialized models and ranking for coreference resolution. In: Proceedings of the 2008 Conference on Empirical Methods in Natural Language Processing, Honolulu, pp. 660–669 (2008)
50. Quinlan, J.: C4.5: Programs for Machine Learning. Morgan Kaufmann, San Mateo (1993)
51. Daelemans, W., van den Bosch, A.: Memory-Based Language Processing. Cambridge University Press, Cambridge (2005)
52. Berger, A., Della Pietra, S., Della Pietra, V.: Maximum entropy approach to natural language processing. Comput. Linguist. **22**(1), 39–71 (1996)
53. Le, Z.: Maximum Entropy Modeling Toolkit for Python and C++ (version 20041229). Natural Language Processing Lab, Northeastern University (2004)
54. Kehler, A., Appelt, D., Taylor, L., Simma, A.: The (non)utility of predicate-argument frequencies for pronoun interpretation. In: Proceedings of 2004 North American Chapter of the Association for Computational Linguistics Annual Meeting, Boston, pp. 289–296 (2004)
55. Cohen, W.W.: Fast effective rule induction. In: Proceedings of the 12th International Conference on Machine Learning (ICML-1995), Tahoe, pp. 115–123 (1995)
56. Freund, Y., Shapire, R.E.: Large margin classification using the perceptron algorithm. Mach. Learn. **37**(3), 277–296 (1999)
57. Vapnik, V.N.: The Nature of Statistical Learning Theory. Springer, New York (1995)
58. Versley, Y., Moschitti, A., Poesio, M., Yang, X.: Coreference systems based on kernel methods. In: Proceedings of the 22nd International Conference on Computational Linguistics, Manchester, pp. 961–968 (2008)
59. Ng, V.: Machine learning for coreference resolution: from local classification to global ranking. In: Proceedings of the 43rd Annual Meeting of the ACL, Ann Arbor, pp. 157–164 (2005)
60. Hoste, V., van den Bosch, A.: A modular approach to learning dutch co-reference. In: Proceedings from the First Bergen Workshop on Anaphora Resolution, Bergen, pp. 51–75 (2007)
61. Ng, V.: Supervised noun phrase coreference research: the first fifteen years. In: Proceedings of the 48th Annual Meeting of the Association for Computational Linguistics, Los Angeles, pp. 1396–1411 (2010)
62. Luo, X., Ittycheriah, A., Jing, H., Kambhatla, N., Roukos, S.: A mention-synchronous coreference resolution algorithm based on the bell tree. In: Barcelona, S. (ed.) Proceedings of the 42nd Annual Meeting of the Association for Computational Linguistics (ACL-2004), Barcelona, pp. 136–143 (2004)
63. Yang, X., Su, S., Zhou, G., Tan, C.: Improving pronoun resolution by incorporating coreferential information of candidates. In: Proceedings of the 42nd Annual Meeting of the Association for Computational Linguistics (ACL-04), Barcelona, pp. 128–135 (2004)

Advanced Machine Learning Models for Coreference Resolution

Vincent Ng

Abstract Despite being the most influential learning-based coreference model, the mention-pair model is unsatisfactory from both a linguistic perspective and a modeling perspective: its focus on making local coreference decisions involving only two mentions and their contexts makes it even less expressive than the coreference systems developed in the pre-statistical NLP era. Realizing its weaknesses, researchers have developed many advanced coreference models over the years. In particular, there is a gradual shift from local models towards global models, which seek to address the weaknesses of local models by exploiting additional information beyond that of the local context. In this chapter, we will discuss these advanced models for coreference resolution.

Keywords Advanced Machine Learning Models mention-pair model • Mention-ranking model • Cluster-ranking model • Global models

1 Introduction

Broadly speaking, learning-based coreference models can be divided into two categories. *Supervised* models require coreference-annotated data during the training process, whereas *unsupervised* models do not. While the fact that unsupervised models do not require annotated data is certainly one of their appealing aspects, the most successful learning-based coreference models to date are arguably supervised models. In the previous chapter, we saw one of the simplest yet most influential coreference models, the mention-pair model. In this chapter, we will examine some advanced supervised models for coreference resolution.

Virtually all the advanced coreference models are motivated by the weaknesses of the mention-pair model. Hence, to facilitate the discussion of these models, let us begin by briefly revisiting the mention-pair model. As a binary classifier trained to determine whether two mentions are co-referring or not, the mention-

V. Ng (✉)
University of Texas at Dallas, 800 West Campbell Road, Mail Station EC31, Richardson, TX, 75080-3021, USA
e-mail: vince@hlt.utdallas.edu

M. Poesio et al. (eds.), *Anaphora Resolution*, Theory and Applications of Natural Language Processing, DOI 10.1007/978-3-662-47909-4_10

pair model makes local coreference decisions based on only the two mentions under consideration and their contexts. Being a *local* model, the mention-pair model has at least two major weaknesses. First, the model has limitations in expressiveness: the information extracted from two mentions and their local contexts may not be sufficient for making an informed coreference decision, especially if the candidate antecedent is semantically empty (e.g., a pronoun) or lacks descriptive information such as gender (e.g., *Clinton*). Second, since each candidate antecedent for a mention to be resolved (henceforth an *active mention*) is considered independently of the others, the model only determines how good a candidate antecedent is relative to the active mention, but not how good a candidate antecedent is relative to other candidates. In other words, they fail to answer the critical question of which candidate antecedent is most probable.

In the years since the mention-pair model was proposed, researchers have developed models of the coreference task that incorporate a more sophisticated view of coreference resolution than that adopted by the mention-pair model. In particular, there is a shift towards global models, which seek to address the aforementioned weaknesses of the mention-pair model by exploiting additional information beyond that of the local context. In this chapter, we will examine these advanced models for coreference resolution.

2 Improving Expressiveness

Somewhat interestingly, the aforementioned weaknesses of the mention-pair model make it even less expressive than the coreference models developed in the pre-statistical NLP era. Recall from chapter "Linguistic and Cognitive Evidence About Anaphora" that virtually all computational systems for coreference proposed before the mention-pair model were based on the "discourse entity" or "file card" model of anaphoric interpretation, which was originally formulated by Karttunen [28] and was made more formal by Heim [22] and Kamp [27] in theoretical linguistics and Webber [59] in computational linguistics. These discourse models are built up dynamically while processing a discourse: not only do they include the objects that have been mentioned, but they also provide interpretations of the context-dependent expressions. Hence, when interpreting a referring expression with respect to a discourse model, we have access to the interpretations of all the referring expressions processed so far. As discussed in chapter "Early Approaches to Anaphora Resolution: Theoretically Inspired and Heuristic-Based", systems based on the discourse entity or file card model include not only 'toy' systems like the ones discussed in Sidner [51], Carter [5] and Luperfoy [34], but also systems that are able to process large amounts of data like SRI's Core Language Engine [1], the systems that participated in the MUC-6 [37] and MUC-7 [38] competitions (e.g., the LASIE system [18] developed by the University of Sheffield), and Vieira and Poesio's system [57]. The same architecture has also been implemented in systems like GUITAR [43], BART [56], and more recently Recasens' [50] CISTELL system.

The *entity-mention* coreference model, which was proposed in 2004 to address the expressiveness problem of the mention-pair model, turns out to be conceptually similar to the aforementioned discourse entity or file card model of anaphoric interpretation. As we will see in more detail, by making later coreference decisions depend on earlier ones, the entity-mention model resolves anaphoric mentions by *incrementally* processing a discourse. It is this notion of incrementality that makes it conceptually similar to the earlier discourse models. Hence, what is genuinely new in recent work on the entity-mention model is (1) the development of algorithms for *training* the model, and (2) the attempt to empirically evaluate whether this model in fact leads to improved results.

To motivate the entity-mention model, consider an example taken from McCallum and Wellner [35]. Assume that a document consists of three mentions, "Mr. Clinton," "Clinton," and "she." The mention-pair model may determine that "Mr. Clinton" and "Clinton" are coreferent using string-matching features, and that "Clinton" and "she" are coreferent based on proximity and lack of evidence for gender and number disagreement. However, these two pairwise decisions together with transitivity imply that "Mr. Clinton" and "she" will end up in the same cluster, which represents an incorrect merge due to gender mismatch between the two mentions.

The entity-mention model can potentially avoid this kind of error by making the later coreference decisions depend on the earlier ones. Returning to our example, when resolving "she," the model takes into consideration that "Mr. Clinton" and "Clinton" are already in the same cluster, specifically by determining whether "she" belongs to the cluster containing "Mr. Clinton" and "Clinton." Hence, the focus of the entity-mention model is to enforce *global consistency* across coreference chains.

More generally, the entity-mention model determines whether an active mention belongs to a preceding, possibly partially-formed, coreference cluster. Hence, when training the model, each training instance corresponds to an active mention and a preceding cluster, and the class value is true if and only if the active mention is coreferent with the mentions defining the preceding cluster. A feature representing the instance can therefore be defined between the active mention and one or more of the mentions in the preceding cluster. In other words, unlike the mention-pair model, where the features are computed over two mentions, the features in the entity-mention model are computed between the active mention and the mentions in the preceding cluster. The ability to employ these *cluster-level* features makes the entity-mention model more expressive than the mention-pair model.

2.1 Implementing the Entity-Mention Model

So far, we have discussed at a high level the idea behind the entity-mention model: it aims to address the expressiveness problem of the mention-pair model by employing cluster-level features. To gain a better understanding of the entity-mention model, we will discuss in this subsection how it is implemented in practice. Like the implementation of the mention-pair model, we have to address four questions when implementing the entity-mention model. First, which learning algorithm should be used? Second, how should training instances be created? Third, what features should be used to represent an instance? Finally, which clustering algorithm should be used in combination with the learned entity-mention model to impose a partition on a given set of mentions in a test document?

Learning algorithms In principle, any existing classification-based learning algorithm can be used. For instance, Yang et al. [63] train a decision tree to classify whether an active mention and a preceding cluster are coreferent, and Luo et al. [33] train a maximum entropy model to determine the probability that an active mention belongs to a preceding cluster.

Training instance creation To train the model, a training instance can in principle be created between an active mention m_k and each of its preceding clusters. However, this instance creation method can yield a skewed class distribution where the negative instances significantly outnumber its positive counterparts, since m_k belongs to only one of its preceding clusters. To reduce class imbalance, Luo et al. and Yang et al. employ a training instance creation scheme that reduces the number of negative training instances as follows. If m_k does not have any antecedent, no training instances will be created from m_k. Otherwise, a negative instance is created between m_k and a preceding cluster c if (1) m_k does not belong to c and (2) c contains a mention that lies between m_k and m_j, where m_j is the closest antecedent of m_k. In essence, this training instance creation scheme retains only the negative instances in which the preceding cluster is "close enough" to the active mention, and can be viewed as a natural generalization of Soon et al.'s [52] training instance creation method developed for the mention-pair model (see the previous chapter). To better understand this training instance creation scheme, let us apply it to the sentence segment shown in Fig. 1, which we will refer to as the *Obama* example.

In this example, each mention m is annotated as $[m]^{cid}_{mid}$, where *mid* is the mention id and *cid* is the id of the cluster to which m belongs. As we can see, the six mentions are partitioned into four coreference clusters, with *Barack Obama*, *his*, and *he* in one cluster, and each of the remaining mentions in its own cluster.

Using the above training instance creation scheme, we can generate three training instances for *He*: ***i***({*Monday*}, *He*), ***i***({*secretary of state*}, *He*), and ***i***({*Barack Obama*, *his*}, *He*). The first two of these instances will be labeled as negative, and the last one will be labeled as positive.

Features Recall that in the mention-pair model, the features representing an instance belong to one of three types: features computed based on the active mention m (F_m); features computed based on the candidate antecedent a (F_a); and relational

[Barack Obama]$^1_1$ *nominated [Hillary Rodham Clinton]*$^2_2$ *as [[his]*$^1_3$ *secretary of state]*$^3_4$ *on [Monday]*$^4_5$. *[He]*$^1_6$ ...

Fig. 1 An illustrative example

features, which capture the relationship between m and a (F_{am}). The features employed by the entity-mention model can also be divided into three groups: features computed based on the active mention m (F_m); features computed based on the preceding cluster c (F_c); and features that capture the relationship between m and c (F_{cm}). Since the features in F_c and F_{cm} are computed based on a preceding cluster of mentions, they are sometimes referred to as *cluster-level* features.

As we can see, both models employ the features in F_m, whereas the features in F_c and F_{cm} are a generalization of those in F_a and F_{am}, respectively. Such generalization is typically achieved by applying a logical predicate. For example, consider NUMBER AGREEMENT, a feature in F_{am} that determines whether two mentions agree in number. By applying the ALL predicate to NUMBER AGREEMENT, we can create a cluster-level feature in F_{cm} that has the value true if and only if the active mention m_k agrees in number with *all* of the mentions in the preceding cluster c. Other commonly-used logical predicates for creating cluster-level features include relaxed versions of the ALL predicate, such as MOST, which is true if m_k agrees in number with more than half of the mentions in c; ANY, which is true as long as m_k agrees in number with just one of the mentions in c; and NONE, which is true if m_k does not agree in number with any of the mentions in c. Logical predicates can be similarly applied to the features in F_a to create the cluster-level features in F_c. For instance, given NUMBER, a feature in F_a that determines whether a candidate antecedent is singular or plural in number, we can apply the *All* predicate to create a cluster-level feature that determines whether all of the mentions in c are singular, whether all of them are plural, or whether all of them agree in number.

Clustering algorithm After training the entity-mention model, we have to employ a clustering algorithm in combination with the learned model to impose a partitioning on the mentions in a test text. The coreference clustering algorithms that are typically used in combination with the mention-pair model, such as single-link clustering and best-first clustering, can also be used in combination with the entity-mention model. One of the reasons for their ubiquity in coreference research is that they resemble the way humans perform coreference: like a human, these two clustering algorithms process the mentions in a text in a left-to-right manner. For each mention encountered, single-link clustering links it to the closest preceding cluster that is classified as coreferent with it by the entity-mention model, whereas best-first clustering links it to the preceding cluster that has the highest probability of being coreferent with it according to the entity-mention model.

Note that the preceding clusters are formed incrementally. For instance, when resolving active mention m_k, the clusters preceding m_k are formed based on the predictions of the entity-mention model for the first $k-1$ mentions. Hence, in the ith iteration of these clustering algorithms, a coreference decision has to be made as to which preceding cluster mention m_i should be linked to, and at the end of the ith iteration, we obtain what we call an ith-order partial partition, which is a partition of the first i mentions in the test text.

Some researchers are concerned that single-link clustering and best-first clustering are too greedy. Recall that in each iteration, these clustering algorithms extend the partial partition produced in the previous iteration by processing the currently active mention. Since these algorithms only keep track of one partial partition, any erroneous coreference decisions made in the earlier iterations cannot be undone in the later iterations. At first glance, one could address this problem by keeping track of *all* possible partial partitions in each iteration rather than just the best one. In practice, keeping track of all possible partial partitions is computationally intractable, as the number of partial partitions is exponential in the number of mentions in a document.

Consequently, Luo et al. [33] propose a "less greedy" version of best-first clustering, which we call k-best-first clustering: instead of keeping track of only the best partial partition at the end of each clustering iteration, k-best-first clustering keeps track of the k-best partial partitions, where the score of a partial partition is computed based on the probabilities or confidence values of the coreference decisions used to construct it. More specifically, Luo et al. organize the space of partial partitions as a Bell tree, in which (1) each node corresponds to an ith-order partial partition and (2) the ith level contains all possible ith-order partial partitions. Given a Bell tree, k-best-first clustering amounts to performing a beam search starting from the root of the tree and using a beam size of k. To expedite the identification of the k-best partial partitions in each iteration, Luo et al. employ a number of heuristics to prune improbable partitions.

Despite its improved expressiveness, the entity-mention model has not yielded particularly encouraging results. For example, Luo et al. [33] report that in an evaluation on the ACE 2002 and 2003 coreference corpora, their entity-mention model does not perform as well as their mention-pair model, and Yang et al.'s [63] entity-mention model produces results that are only marginally better than those of the mention-pair model when evaluated on the a set of coreference-annotated MEDLINE abstracts selected from the GENIA corpus. At first glance, these results may seem somewhat counter-intuitive. However, it is important to note that any results involving the comparison between two coreference models need to be interpreted in context. Specifically, all these authors have shown is that the entity-mention model has not yielded particularly encouraging results compared to the mention-pair model when using the feature set, the learning algorithm, and the clustering algorithm of their choices. It is entirely possible that the results of the comparison will change with these parameters.

Nevertheless, Luo et al. made the important finding that the entity-mention model successfully enforces global consistency while using only $\frac{1}{20}$ as many features as the mention-pair model. Thus it avoids errors made by the mention-pair model that involve clustering a male pronoun and a female pronoun into the same entity, for example.

2.2 Improving the Expressiveness of the Entity-Mention Model

In the previous subsection, we saw that the entity-mention models in Luo et al. [33] and Yang et al. [63] did not perform as well as one would expect. In an attempt to improve their entity-mention model, Yang et al. [60] put forward a hypothesis: while cluster-level features attempt to summarize the information extracted from the mentions in a preceding cluster, they may not be doing so *adequately*. In other words, Yang et al. hypothesize that some essential information about the mentions in a preceding cluster may be lost when summarized by the cluster-level features. More specifically, cluster-level features do not allow us to easily refer to the individual mentions in a preceding cluster. Consider, for instance, a coreference rule learned by Yang et al.'s entity-mention model, which determines whether an active mention B is coreferential with a preceding cluster A:

coref(A,B) :– pronoun(B), has_mention(A,C), nameNP(C), has_mention(A,D), indefNP(D), subject(D).

This rule classifies B as coreferential with A if (1) B is a pronoun; (2) there exists a mention C in A such that C is a named entity; and (3) there exists another mention D in A such that D is an indefinite NP appearing as a clausal subject. Note that cluster-level features do not enable us to learn coreference rules like this, because these features encode information about a preceding cluster rather than information about individual mentions in the cluster (e.g., C and D in the above rule). At first glance, it may seem that one can fix this problem simply by introducing features that encode information about the individual mentions in a preceding cluster. However, this solution is unlikely to work in practice. Recall that virtually all off-the-shelf machine learning algorithms assume fixed-length feature vectors as input. However, since the number of mentions in a preceding cluster is different for different clusters, adding features that encode information about each mention in a preceding cluster to the feature set will result in variable-length feature vectors.

Yang et al. [60] propose to address this problem by learning such coreference rules using the Inductive Logic Programming (ILP) learning algorithm. Informally, the goal of ILP is to learn *first-order* rules such as the one shown above, where the variables on the left side of a rule are universally quantified and those that appear only on the right side are existentially quantified. Hence, in our example, A and B are universally quantified, and C and D are existentially quantified. ILP assumes as input a set of positive and negative training examples, $E = E^+ \cup E^-$, and a set of background knowledge K of the domain, and attempts to induce rules that cover as many examples in E^+ and as few examples in E^- as possible. As demonstrated in the example rule above, the advantage of using ILP for coreference resolution stems from its *relational* nature: it makes it possible to explicitly represent relations between an entity and the mentions it contains.

To better understand how ILP works, consider again the *Obama* example. For convenience, let us use m_j to denote the jth mention, c_i to denote the ith coreference cluster, and c_{i_j} to denote the subset of c_i preceding m_j. Using this notation for our example, m_3 refers to *his*; c_1 refers to the set { *Barack Obama, his, He* }; and e_{1_3} refers to the subset of c_1 preceding m_3, namely, { *Barack Obama* }.

Training instances can be created using the same method as described in the preceding subsection. Each instance is represented using a predicate $link(c_{i\_j}, m_j)$, where m_j is an active mention and c_{i_j} is a partial cluster. For example, three training instances are created for *He*:

link(c_{1_6}, m_6).
link(c_{3_6}, m_6).
link(c_{4_6}, m_6).

The first predicate corresponds to a positive training instance and is stored in E^+, whereas the last two correspond to negative training instances and are stored in E^-. In essence, E^+ and E^- contain the predicates that encode the "class values" of the training instances. The "features" for each instance are encoded as predicates and stored in the background knowledge base K. Recall that in the entity-mention model, we have three types of features, namely F_m, F_c, and F_{cm}. These three feature types are represented in ILP as three different types of predicates, as described below.

A feature f in F_m, which encodes knowledge about an active mention m, is represented using a predicate $f(m, v)$, where v is a binary value indicating whether m is true with respect to f. For example, the pronoun *He* in the *Obama* example can be described by predicates such as:

defNP$(m_6,0)$.
indefNP$(m_6,0)$.
nameNP$(m_6,0)$.
pronoun$(m_6,1)$.

As the names of these predicates suggest, they assert the facts that *He* is a pronoun, and is neither a named entity nor a definite or indefinite NP.

A feature f in F_c, which encodes knowledge about a preceding cluster c, is represented using a predicate $f(c, v)$, where v is a binary value indicating whether c is true with respect to f. For example, to encode the facts that all the mentions in c_{1_6} in the *Obama* example agree in gender and number, we employ the following predicates:

AllNumAgree$(c_{1\_6},1)$.
AllGenderAgree$(c_{1\_6},1)$.

A feature f in F_{cm}, which encodes the relationship between an active mention m and a preceding cluster c, is represented using a predicate $f(c, m, v)$, where v is a binary value indicating whether c and m are compatible with respect to f. For example, to encode the facts that *He* is compatible with c_{1_6} with respect to gender and number in the *Obama* example, we employ the following predicates:

AllEMNumAgree$(c_{1\_6},m_6,1)$.
AllEMGenderAgree$(c_{1\_6},m_6,1)$.

To enable easy reference of individual mentions in a preceding cluster, which is one of the motivations behind employing ILP for coreference resolution, we can employ the predicate *has_mention*(c,m) to describe whether preceding cluster c contains mention m. Specifically, we create one *has_mention*(c,m) predicate for each preceding cluster c and each mention m in c. For example, for preceding cluster c_1 in the *Obama* example, Yang et al. [60] create the following *has_mention* predicates:

has_mention(c_{1_6}, m_1).
has_mention(c_{1_6}, m_3).

Now that we have a means to refer to individual mentions in a preceding cluster, we can encode information about each mention m_i in preceding cluster c as well as its relationship with active mention m_j. Returning to the *Obama* example, we can encode information about m_1, which belongs to c_{1_6}, and its relationship with m_6, by introducing the following predicates:

nameNP(m_1,1).
pronoun(m_1,0).
...
nameAlias(m_1,m_6,0).
genderAgree(m_1,m_6,1).
...

These predicates encode the facts that *Barack Obama* is a named entity but not a pronoun, and it agrees in gender with but is not a name alias of *He*.[1]

As noted by Yang et al. [60], the predicate *has_mention* serves as a bridge to integrate entity-mention knowledge and mention-pair knowledge, so that we can exploit the global information about a preceding cluster and the individual mentions in the cluster when determining whether there exists a coreference relation between an active mention and a preceding cluster.

After constructing E^+, E^-, and K, we can employ ILP to induce first-order coreference rules, each of which determines the conditions under which a mention belongs to a preceding cluster. Yang et al. evaluate the resulting ruleset on the ACE 2003 corpus. In comparison with a mention-pair model learned using ILP, the ILP-based entity-mention model yields a small but statistically significant improvement.

2.3 A Variant of the Entity-Mention Model

Several variants of the entity-mention model have been investigated. In this subsection, we examine one such model proposed by Culotta et al. [10], which they refer to as a first-order probabilistic model.

Culotta et al.'s model resembles the entity-mention model in that it aims to improve the expressiveness of the mention-pair model by computing features over a cluster of mentions. However, it is not an entity-mention model: it determines the probability that a given set of mentions is coreferent, rather than the probability that an active mention belongs to a preceding cluster. To gain a better understanding of

[1]In many existing coreference resolvers, a mention is typically considered a name alias of another mention if one is an abbreviation or an acronym of the other.

this model, let us specify for it the four elements needed to implement a coreference model: the choice of the learning algorithm, the choice of the clustering algorithm, the training instance creation method, and the features used to represent an instance.

Learning algorithm Culotta et al. employ maximum entropy modeling to train their first-order probabilistic model. Unlike the entity-mention model described in the previous subsection, their probabilistic model is trained in an error-driven fashion, which we will describe in more detail shortly. Since the model is a maximum entropy model, its parameters are the feature weights.

Clustering algorithm A bottom-up agglomerative clustering algorithm is used to cluster the mentions. This greedy iterative algorithm operates as follows. Initially, each mention is in its own cluster. In each iteration, the algorithm identifies the two clusters that have the highest similarity, which in their case is computed using the first-order probabilistic model, and merges them into a single cluster. This iterative process continues until additional merging does not improve the probability of the clustering.

Features Recall that in the entity-mention model, we can employ three types of features: features computed based on the active mention m (F_m), features computed based on the preceding cluster c (F_c), and features that encode the relationship between m and c (F_{cm}). Since the first-order model determines the probability that a given set of mentions is coreferent, there is no notion of an active mention. Consequently, only F_c is applicable. Culotta et al. employ first-order predicates such as ALL, MOST, and ANY, as described previously, to construct features for encoding information extracted from a cluster of mentions, hence the name *first-order probabilistic model*.

Training instance creation Since the model computes the probability that a set of mentions is coreferent, each training instance corresponds to a set of mentions. The label of an instance is positive if these mentions are coreferent; otherwise, it is negative. Hence, one can in principle generate one training instance from each possible subset of mentions in a training text, but since the number of subsets is exponential in the number of mentions, this naive training instance creation method is computationally infeasible. To address this problem, one can employ sampling, where we generate a training instance by randomly sampling a set of mentions from a training set and assign a label to the resulting instance based on whether the subset of mentions is coreferent or not.

To further improve the sampling method, Culotta et al. employ error-driven sampling, where the training instances are created from the errors the model makes on the training documents. Their error-driven training procedure works as follows. First, they randomly initialize the parameters (i.e., the feature weights) of the first-order probabilistic model. Given these initial parameters, they process each training document one after the other. For each document, they perform bottom-up agglomerative clustering on the document until an incorrect clustering decision is made. They then update the feature weights in response to this mistake, and repeat this process for the next training document. Like other online learning algorithms, this training procedure makes a fixed number of passes over the training documents.

The question, then, is: how should training instances be created in response to the mistake? When the clustering algorithm erroneously merges two clusters, the training procedure generates one positive training instance and one negative training instance. The negative training instance is created based on the cluster resulting from the erroneous merge, and the "nearby" positive instance is created via merging two existing clusters that are coreferent with each other.

Since we are employing online learning, the next question is: how should the feature weights be updated given the newly generated positive and negative instances? One way would be to perform *classification-based* updates, as is typically done in the classical perceptron learning algorithm. Specifically, all the weights associated with the negative instance are decreased, while all the weights associated with the positive instance are increased. However, Culotta et al. make a good case that it is undesirable to perform classification-based updates. Consider a training instance where not all mentions in the corresponding cluster are coreferent (i.e., it is a negative instance) but a subset of them are. Since it is a negative instance, a classification-based update will penalize all the features associated with the corresponding cluster. In particular, it will unjustly penalize those features associated with the positive subset of the cluster.

To address this problem, Culotta et al. propose to modify the optimization criterion of training to perform *ranking* rather than *classification* of the training instances. Recall that in response to a mistake, two training instances, one positive and one negative, will be generated. The goal of ranking, then, is to adjust the feature weights so that the positive instance is assigned a higher score than its negative counterpart. This approach allows the learner to focus on penalizing the *difference* between the feature vectors associated with the two training instances, thereby not penalizing those features representing overlapping coreference clusters. This update can be done using MIRA, a relaxed online maximum-margin training algorithm [9]. Details can be found in Culotta et al. [10].

When evaluating on the ACE 2004 coreference corpus using gold mentions, Culotta et al. report that their first-order probabilistic coreference model manages to learn what a good intermediate clustering is, as evidenced by the difference in system performance they find between purely batch learning and their online update method. In addition, their model achieves a B^3 F-measure of 79.3 %, significantly outperforming their implementation of the mention-pair model by an absolute B^3 F-measure of 6.8 %. As mentioned before, these results should not be taken to imply that the entity-mention model is superior to the mention-pair model in general: they only suggest that the entity-mention model is superior to the mention-pair model given the particular combination of the feature set, the learning algorithm, and the clustering algorithm that the authors employ.

3 Identifying the Most Probable Candidate Antecedent

While the entity-mention model and its variants address the expressiveness problem associated with the mention-pair model, it does not address the other problem: failure to identify the most probable candidate antecedent for an active mention. To address the latter problem, researchers have examined the *mention-ranking* model, whose goal is to impose a ranking on the candidate antecedents for an active mention so that the most probable candidate antecedent has the highest rank. Ranking is arguably a more natural formulation of coreference resolution than classification, as a ranker allows all candidate antecedents to be considered *simultaneously* and therefore directly captures the competition among them. Another desirable consequence is that there exists a natural resolution strategy for a ranking approach: an anaphoric mention is resolved to the candidate antecedent that has the highest rank. This contrasts with classification-based approaches, where many clustering algorithms have been employed to coordinate the potentially contradictory pairwise classification decisions and it is still not clear which of them is the best.

Note, however, that the idea of ranking candidate antecedents goes much further back than Connolly et al. [7, 8], who proposed the first learning-based coreference model that employs the notion of ranking in the mid-1990s. Recall from chapter "Early Approaches to Anaphora Resolution: Theoretically Inspired and Heuristic-Based" that many rule-based anaphora resolution algorithms adopted the so-called *generate-filter-rank* strategy: to resolve an anaphoric mention, they (1) *generate* a set of candidate antecedents for it; (2) *filter* those candidates that violate the hard constraints on coreference with the anaphor (e.g., binding constraints, gender and number agreement); and (3) *rank* the remaining ones by salience so that the anaphor is resolved to the most salient candidate antecedent. For example, Hobbs [23] implicitly imposes a ranking on the candidate antecedents by visiting them in the given syntactic parse tree in a particular order. Carter [5] employs Hobbs' antecedent-ranking method for inter-sentential anaphora resolution. Ranking is also commonly used in centering algorithms. For example, in the BFP algorithm [4], the forward-looking centers are ranked by grammatical function (e.g., subjects are ranked higher than objects, which are then ranked higher than adjuncts). In contrast, Strube and Hahn's [54] centering algorithm employs functional ranking (i.e., ranking based on Prince's [45] taxonomy of given-new information): old entities are ranked higher than mediated entities, which are in turn ranked higher than new entities. Finally, ranking has been implemented by assigning a score to each candidate antecedent that reflects how salient a candidate is. For example, in Lappin and Leass' [30] RAP algorithm, the salience of a candidate antecedent is computed as the sum of the weights of the *factors* it satisfies. Some factors are based on sentence recency and grammatical function, while others are based on whether a mention occurs in dispreferred syntactic positions.

Given the extensive use of ranking in anaphora resolution in the pre-statistical NLP era, what is genuinely new in recent work on the mention-ranking model is (1) the development of algorithms for *training* the model, and (2) the attempt to empirically evaluate whether this model in fact leads to improved results. In the rest of this section, we will examine this model more closely.

3.1 Implementing the Mention-Ranking Model

So far we have discussed at a high level the idea behind the mention-ranking model. The question, then, is: how can we train a ranker to rank an arbitrary number of candidate antecedents for an active mention? An idea put forth by Connolly et al. [7, 8] is to convert this problem of ranking an arbitrary number of candidate antecedents into a set of *pairwise ranking* problems, each of which involves ranking exactly two candidates. To rank two candidates, a *classifier* can be trained using a training set where each instance corresponds to the active mention as well as two candidate antecedents and possesses a class value that indicates which of the two candidates is better. This idea was certainly ahead of its time, as it is embodied in many of the advanced ranking algorithms developed in the machine learning and information retrieval communities in the past few years. Later, Yang et al. [62, 64] and Iida et al. [24] independently reinvented the technique, calling it the *twin-candidate* model and the *tournament* model, respectively. The name *twin-candidate model* is motivated by the fact that the model considers two candidates at a time, whereas the name *tournament model* was assigned because each ranking of two candidates can be viewed as a tournament (with the higher-ranked candidate winning the tournament) and the candidate that wins the largest number of tournaments is chosen as the antecedent for the active mention.

To gain a better understanding of the mention-ranking model, let us discuss how it can be implemented by specifying the four elements needed to implement a coreference model: the choice of the learning algorithm, the choice of the clustering algorithm, the training instance creation method, and the features used to represent an instance.

Training instance creation As mentioned above, given the problem of ranking an arbitrary number of candidate antecedents for an active mention, the typical approach is to recast it as a set of pairwise ranking problems. To learn a model for pairwise ranking, each training instance should be composed of an active mention, m, two of its candidate antecedents, $c1$ and $c2$, and a (binary) class value indicating which candidate is the correct antecedent. A natural question is: can we also create training instances where both candidate antecedents are correct or neither of them is correct, and assign to these instances a class value that indicates that the two candidates should have the same rank? The answer is yes, although previous work has decided not to accommodate this possibility [7, 24, 62, 64]. One reason could be that these "same-rank" instances significantly outnumber their "different-rank" counterparts, creating a skewed class distribution that could pose a problem for learning algorithms.

Using the above training instance creation scheme, we can generate six training instances for *He*: ***i***(*his*, *Monday*, *He*), ***i***(*his*, *secretary of state*, *He*), ***i***(*Barack Obama*, *Monday*, *He*), ***i***(*Barack Obama*, *secretary of state*, *He*), ***i***(*Barack Obama*, *Hillary Rodham Clinton*, *He*), and ***i***(*Hillary Rodham Clinton*, *his*, *He*). The first five of these instances will be labeled as positive (to indicate that the first of the two candidate antecedents is correct), and the last one will be labeled as negative (to indicate that the second of the two candidate antecedents is correct). The three "same-rank" training instances, namely ***i***(*Hillary Rodham Clinton*, *Monday*, *He*), ***i***(*Hillary Rodham Clinton*, *secretary of state*, *He*), and ***i***(*Barack Obama*, *his*, *He*), will not be created.

While not creating "same-rank" training instances addresses class imbalance, we still have another problem: the size of the training set is potentially large, since the number of training instances grows cubically with the number of mentions in a document. To address this problem, a commonly-used solution is to include only a subset of the "different-rank" instances into the training set. Yang et al. [62, 64], for example, employ the following instance selection scheme. If the active mention is a pronoun, they include only those instances where both candidates (1) agree with the anaphor in number, gender, and person, and (2) appear in either the same sentence as the anaphor or in one of the preceding two sentences. On the other hand, if the anaphor is non-pronominal, they include only those instances where both candidates are non-pronominal and are at most one sentence apart from each other.

Features Given an active mention m and two candidate antecedents $c1$ and $c2$, five types of features are typically employed: features computed based on $c1$, features computed based on $c2$, features computed based on m, features that capture the relationship between m and $c1$, and features that capture the relationship between m and $c2$. Unlike in the entity-mention model, no cluster-level features are employed in the mention-ranking model.

Learning algorithm While Connolly et al. [7], Iida et al. [24], and Yang et al. [62, 64], all employ the decision tree learner [46], any off-the-shelf learning algorithm can be used in principle.

Clustering algorithm There are two common ways to resolve an active mention during testing. In Connolly et al.'s single-elimination tournament model, the learned pairwise ranking model is applied to exactly one pair of its candidate antecedents in each round, processing the candidates based on the farthest-to-closest order. The losing candidate is discarded, and the winning candidate is used to construct the test instance for the next round. The last winner is chosen as the active mention's antecedent. In regular tournament ranking [64], the learned model is applied to each pair of its candidate antecedents, and the candidate that is classified as better the largest number of times is selected as its antecedent. To break ties, the candidate that is closer in distance to the active mention is preferred.

Thus far we have avoided discussing how the mention-ranking model addresses the problem of identifying *non-anaphoric* or *discourse-new* mentions. A non-anaphoric or discourse-new mention is a mention that is *not* coreferent with any preceding mention in the associated text (e.g., a singleton or the first mention in a coreference chain), and therefore should not be resolved. Note, however, that the mention-ranking model cannot distinguish between anaphoric and non-anaphoric mentions, and will therefore attempt to resolve *every* mention to its highest-ranked candidate antecedent. Perhaps not surprisingly, the resolution of non-anaphoric mentions could harm the precision of a coreference resolver.

To address this problem, researchers have proposed two approaches to identify anaphoric mentions. In the *pipeline* approach [14, 26], a separate component commonly known as an *anaphoricity determination* system is employed to determine whether a mention is anaphoric or non-anaphoric prior to coreference resolution, and the mention-ranking model will resolve only those mentions that are determined to be anaphoric. One potential weakness of the pipeline approach is that the errors made by the anaphoricity determination component may propagate to the coreference resolver.

In light of this weakness, researchers have investigated a *joint* approach [39, 61], where the mention-ranking model is enhanced with the capability to jointly perform anaphoricity determination and coreference resolution. For example, Yang et al. [61] extend their pairwise ranking model [64] as follows. During training, they augment their training set with additional training instances. Specifically, they create a new training instance by pairing a non-anaphoric mention with randomly selected candidate antecedents, assigning it a class value that indicates that none of the two candidate antecedents is preferred. To avoid class imbalance, only a subset of these training instances are used to augment the training set. During testing, they first create the test instances for an active mention in the same way as the training instances and then score each of the active mention's candidate antecedents. To score a candidate antecedent, they (1) initialize its score to 0; and (2) for each test instance in which the candidate antecedent appears, increase its score by 1 if it is the preferred antecedent but decrease its score otherwise. After scoring, if none of the candidates has a positive score, the active mention will be posited as non-anaphoric. Otherwise, it will be resolved to the candidate that has the highest score.

Ng [39] puts forward a different proposal to jointly perform anaphoricity determination and coreference resolution. The idea is to first augment the set of candidate antecedents for each active mention with a *null* candidate antecedent, and then train the model to "resolve" a non-anaphoric mention to the *null* antecedent by creating additional training instances involving the *null* antecedent as follows. If the active mention is non-anaphoric, we create additional training instances by pairing the *null* candidate antecedent with each non-*null* candidate antecedent, assigning a higher rank to the *null* candidate antecedent. On the other hand, if the active mention is anaphoric, we create only one additional training instance by pairing the *null* candidate antecedent with the correct (non-*null*) antecedent of the active mention, assigning a higher rank to the non-*null* antecedent.

We conclude this section by mentioning an alternative implementation of the mention-ranking model. Denis and Baldridge [13, 14] have trained a mention ranker using maximum entropy. This maximum entropy mention ranker aims to distribute probability mass over the candidate antecedents of an active mention such that the correct antecedent is the most probable. Hence, each training "instance" corresponds to an active mention and all of its candidate antecedents, where a non-zero probability mass is distributed over each of its correct antecedents.

4 Combining the Best of Both Worlds

While the entity-mention model and the mention-ranking model are conceptually simple extensions of the mention-pair model, their contributions should not be under-estimated: they revive some of the important ideas developed prior to the advent of the statistical NLP era and represent a significant departure from their mention-pair counterpart, which for many years was *the* learning-based coreference model for NLP researchers. The proposal of these two models was facilitated in part by advances in statistical modeling of natural languages: statistical NLP models have evolved from capturing local information to global information, and from employing classification-based models to ranking-based models. In the context of coreference resolution, the entity-mention model enables us to compute features based on a *variable* number of mentions, and the mention-ranking model enables us to *rank* a *variable* number of candidate antecedents. Nevertheless, neither of these models addresses both weaknesses of the mention-pair model satisfactorily: while the mention-ranking model allows all candidate antecedents to be ranked and compared simultaneously, it does not enable the use of cluster-level features; on the other hand, while the entity-mention model can employ cluster-level features, it does not allow all candidates to be considered simultaneously.

Motivated in part by this observation, Rahman and Ng [48] propose a learning-based approach to coreference resolution that is theoretically more appealing than both the mention-ranking model and the entity-mention model: the *cluster-ranking* approach. Specifically, they recast coreference as the problem of determining which of a set of preceding coreference *clusters* is the best to link to an active mention using a learned *cluster-ranking model*. In essence, the cluster-ranking model combines the strengths of the mention-ranking model and the entity-mention model, and addresses *both* weaknesses associated with the mention-pair model. Note that the cluster-ranking model is conceptually similar to Lappin and Leass' [30] heuristic pronoun resolver, which resolves an anaphoric pronoun to the most salient preceding cluster.

In the rest of this section, we will describe Rahman and Ng's implementation of the cluster-ranking model.

4.1 Training and Applying the Cluster-Ranking Model

For ease of exposition, we will describe in this subsection how to train and apply the cluster-ranking model when it is used in a pipeline architecture, where anaphoricity determination is performed prior to coreference resolution. In the next subsection, we will show how the two tasks can be learned jointly.

Recall that the cluster-ranking model ranks a set of preceding clusters for an active mention m_k. Since a cluster ranker is a hybrid of the mention-ranking model and the entity-mention model, the way it is trained and applied is also a hybrid of the two.

In particular, the training instances are created in the same way as in the mention-ranking model, except that each training instance corresponds to an active mention, m_k, and two of its preceding clusters, c_i and c_j. More specifically, the training set consists of ordered pairs (x_{ik}, x_{jk}), where x_{ik} and x_{jk} are vectors composed of cluster-level features describing the relationship between m_k and c_i and the relationship between m_k and c_j respectively, c_i is the preceding cluster containing mentions that are coreferent with m_k, and c_j is a preceding cluster containing mentions that are not coreferent with m_k. Consider again our running example in Fig. 1. The training set consists of three ordered pairs generated for *He*. For the first pair, c_i = {*Barack Obama, his*} and c_j = {*Monday*}. For the second pair, c_i = {*Barack Obama, his*} and c_j = {*secretary of state*}. For the third pair, c_i = {*Barack Obama, his*} and c_j = {*Hillary Rodham Clinton*}.

Rahman and Ng use the ranker-learning algorithm in the SVM^{light} software package [25] to train cluster rankers. The goal of this learner is to find a parameter vector $\overrightarrow{w}$ that yields a "ranking score" function $\overrightarrow{w} \cdot \Phi(x_{ik})$ that minimizes the number of violations of pairwise rankings provided in the training set.

As mentioned above, cluster rankers, like the entity-mention model, employ cluster-level features. Given a training instance representing an anaphoric mention m_k and two of its preceding clusters c_i and c_j, Rahman and Ng employ cluster-level features that describe (1) the relationship between m_k and c_j and (2) the relationship between m_k and c_i. They derive their cluster-level features from a subset of the 39 features shown in Table 1, which they use to train their baseline mention-pair model. Specifically, the cluster-level features are created using four predicates: NONE, MOST-FALSE, MOST-TRUE, and ALL. For each feature F that describes the relationship between an active mention and its candidate antecedent in Table 1 (i.e., features 11–39), they first convert F into an equivalent set of binary-valued features if it is multi-valued. Then, for each resulting binary-valued feature F_b, they create four binary-valued cluster-level features: (1) NONE-F_b is true when F_b is false between m_k and each mention in c_j; (2) MOST-FALSE-F_b is true when F_b is true between m_k and less than half (but at least one) of the mentions in c_j; (3) MOST-TRUE-F_b is true when F_b is true between m_k and at least half (but not all) of the mentions in c_j; and (4) ALL-F_b is true when F_b is true between m_k and each mention in c_j. Hence, for each F_b, exactly one of these four cluster-level features evaluates to true.

Applying the learned cluster-ranking model to a test text is similar to applying the mention-ranking model. Specifically, the mentions are processed in a left-to-right manner. For each active mention m_k, Rahman and Ng first apply a classifier independently trained on the features described in Ng and Cardie [41] on SVM^{light} to determine if m_k is non-anaphoric. If so, m_k will not be resolved. Otherwise, they create test instances for m_k by pairing it with each of its preceding clusters. The

Table 1 Features used by Rahman and Ng [48] to train their baseline mention-pair model. Non-relational features describe a mention and in most cases take on a value of **Y**ES or **N**O. Relational features describe the relationship between the two mentions and indicate whether they are **C**OMPATIBLE, **I**NCOMPATIBLE or **N**OT **A**PPLICABLE

Features describing m_j, a candidate antecedent		
1	PRONOUN_1	Y if m_j is a pronoun; else N
2	SUBJECT_1	Y if m_j is a subject; else N
3	NESTED_1	Y if m_j is a nested NP; else N
Features describing m_k, the active mention		
4	NUMBER_2	SINGULAR or PLURAL, determined using a lexicon
5	GENDER_2	MALE, FEMALE, NEUTER, or UNKNOWN, determined using a list of common first names
6	PRONOUN_2	Y if m_k is a pronoun; else N
7	NESTED_2	Y if m_k is a nested NP; else N
8	SEMCLASS_2	The semantic class of m_k; can be one of PERSON, LOCATION, ORGANIZATION, DATE, TIME, MONEY, PERCENT, OBJECT, OTHERS, determined using WordNet [15] and the Stanford NE recognizer [16]
9	ANIMACY_2	Y if m_k is determined as HUMAN or ANIMAL by WordNet and an NE recognizer; else N
10	PRO_TYPE_2	The nominative case of m_k if it is a pronoun; else NA. E.g., the feature value for *him* is HE
Features describing the relationship between m_j, a candidate antecedent and m_k, the active mention		
11	HEAD_MATCH	C if the mentions have the same head noun; else I
12	STR_MATCH	C if the mentions are the same string; else I
13	SUBSTR_MATCH	C if one mention is a substring of the other; else I
14	PRO_STR_MATCH	C if both mentions are pronominal and are the same string; else I
15	PN_STR_MATCH	C if both mentions are proper names and are the same string; else I
16	NONPRO_STR_MATCH	C if the two mentions are both non-pronominal and are the same string; else I
17	MODIFIER_MATCH	C if the mentions have the same modifiers; NA if one of both of them don't have a modifier; else I
18	PRO_TYPE_MATCH	C if both mentions are pronominal and are either the same pronoun or different only with respect to case; NA if at least one of them is not pronominal; else I
19	NUMBER	C if the mentions agree in number; I if they disagree; NA if the number for one or both mentions cannot be determined
20	GENDER	C if the mentions agree in gender; I if they disagree; NA if the gender for one or both mentions cannot be determined
21	AGREEMENT	C if the mentions agree in both gender and number; I if they disagree in both number and gender; else NA
22	ANIMACY	C if the mentions match in animacy; I if they don't; NA if the animacy for one or both mentions cannot be determined

(continued)

Table 1 (continued)

Features describing m_j, a candidate antecedent		
23	BOTH_PRONOUNS	C if both mentions are pronouns; I if neither are pronouns; else NA
24	BOTH_PROPER_NOUNS	C if both mentions are proper nouns; I if neither are proper nouns; else NA
25	MAXIMALNP	C if the two mentions does not have the same maximial NP projection; else I
26	SPAN	C if neither mention spans the other; else I
27	INDEFINITE	C if m_k is an indefinite NP and is not in an appositive relationship; else I
28	APPOSITIVE	C if the mentions are in an appositive relationship; else I
29	COPULAR	C if the mentions are in a copular construction; else I
Features describing the relationship between m_j, a candidate antecedent and m_k, the active mention (continued from the previous page)		
30	SEMCLASS	C if the mentions have the same semantic class (where the set of semantic classes considered here is enumerated in the description of the SEMCLASS_2 feature); I if they don't; NA if the semantic class information for one or both mentions cannot be determined
31	ALIAS	C if one mention is an abbreviation or an acronym of the other; else I
32	DISTANCE	Binned values for sentence distance between the mentions
Additional features describing the relationship between m_j, a candidate antecedent and m_k, the mention to be resolved		
33	NUMBER'	The concatenation of the NUMBER_2 feature values of m_j and m_k. E.g., if m_j is *Clinton* and m_k is *they*, the feature value is SINGULAR-PLURAL, since m_j is singular and m_k is plural
34	GENDER'	The concatenation of the GENDER_2 feature values of m_j and m_k
35	PRONOUN'	The concatenation of the PRONOUN_2 feature values of m_j and m_k
36	NESTED'	The concatenation of the NESTED_2 feature values of m_j and m_k
37	SEMCLASS'	The concatenation of the SEMCLASS_2 feature values of m_j and m_k
38	ANIMACY'	The concatenation of the ANIMACY_2 feature values of m_j and m_k
39	PRO_TYPE'	The concatenation of the PRO_TYPE_2 feature values of m_j and m_k

test instances are then presented to the ranker, and m_k is linked to the cluster c_i that has the highest ranking score (i.e., $\overrightarrow{w} \cdot \Phi(x_{ik})$ is the highest among the preceding clusters). Note that these partial clusters preceding m_k are formed incrementally based on the predictions of the ranker for the first $k-1$ mentions.

4.2 Joint Anaphoricity Determination and Coreference Resolution

The cluster-ranking model described above can be used to determine which preceding cluster an anaphoric mention should be linked to, but it cannot be used to determine whether a mention is anaphoric or not. The reason is simple: all the training instances are generated from anaphoric mentions. Hence, to jointly learn anaphoricity determination and coreference resolution, the ranker must be trained using instances generated from *both* anaphoric and non-anaphoric mentions.

Specifically, when training the ranker, Rahman and Ng provide each active mention with the option to start a new cluster by creating an additional instance that (1) contains features that solely describe the active mention (i.e., features 4–10 in Table 1), and (2) has the highest rank value among competing clusters if it is non-anaphoric and the lowest rank value otherwise. The main advantage of jointly learning the two tasks is that it allows the ranking model to evaluate *all* possible options for an active mention (i.e., whether to resolve it, and if so, which preceding cluster is the best) *simultaneously*.

After training, the resulting cluster ranker processes the mentions in a test text in a left-to-right manner. For each active mention m_k, Rahman and Ng create test instances for it by pairing it with each of its preceding clusters. To allow for the possibility that m_k is non-anaphoric, they create an additional test instance that contains features that solely describe the active mention (similar to what we did in the training step above). All these test instances are then presented to the ranker. If the additional test instance is assigned the highest rank value by the ranker, then m_k is classified as non-anaphoric and will not be resolved. Otherwise, m_k is linked to the cluster that has the highest rank. As before, all partial clusters preceding m_k are formed incrementally based on the predictions of the ranker for the first $k - 1$ mentions.

4.3 Evaluating the Cluster-Ranking Model

Rahman and Ng provided a comprehensive evaluation of their cluster-ranking model, using the mention-pair model, the entity-mention model, and the mention-ranking model as baselines. In this subsection, we present their empirical results.

4.3.1 Experimental Setup

Corpus Rahman and Ng used the ACE 2005 coreference corpus as released by the Linguistic Data Consortium,[2] which consists of the 599 training documents used in the official ACE evaluation. To ensure diversity, the corpus was created by selecting documents from six different sources: Broadcast News, Broadcast Conversations, Newswire, Webblog, Usenet, and conversational telephone speech. For evaluation, they partitioned the 599 documents into a training set and a test set following a 80/20 ratio, ensuring that the two sets had the same proportion of documents from the six sources.

Mention extraction Rahman and Ng evaluated the four coreference models (the mention-pair model, the entity-mention model, the mention-ranking model, and the cluster-ranking model) using both *true mentions* (i.e., gold standard mentions[3]) and *system mentions* (i.e., automatically identified mentions). To extract system mentions from a test text, they trained a mention extractor on the training texts. They recast mention extraction as a sequence labeling task, where they assigned to each token in a test text a label that indicated whether it **b**egan a mention, was **i**nside a mention, or was **o**utside a mention. Hence, to learn the extractor, they created one training instance for each token in a training text and derived its class value (one of **b**, **i**, and **o**) from the annotated data. Each instance represented w_i, the token under consideration, and consisted of 29 linguistic features:

Lexical (7): Tokens in a window of seven: $\{w_{i-3}, \ldots, w_{i+3}\}$.

Capitalization (4): whether w_i `IsAllCap`, `IsInitCap`, `IsCapPeriod`, and `IsAllLower` (see Bikel et al. [3]).

Morphological (8): w_i's prefixes and suffixes of length one, two, three, and four.

Grammatical (1): The part-of-speech (POS) tag of w_i obtained using the Stanford log-linear POS tagger [55].

Semantic (1): The named entity (NE) tag of w_i obtained using the Stanford CRF-based NE recognizer [16].

Gazetteers (8): Eight dictionaries containing pronouns (77 entries), common words and words that are not names (399.6k), person names (83.6k), person titles and honorifics (761), vehicle words (226), location names (1.8k), company names (77.6k), and nouns extracted from WordNet that are hyponyms of PERSON (6.3k).

Rahman and Ng employed CRF++,[4] a C++ implementation of conditional random fields, for training the mention detector, which achieved an F-score of 86.7

[2]www.ldc.upenn.edu

[3]Note that only mention *boundaries* are used.

[4]Available from http://crfpp.sourceforge.net

(86.1 recall, 87.2 precision) on the test set. These extracted mentions were used as system mentions in their coreference experiments.

Scoring programs To score the output of a coreference model, Rahman and Ng employed three scoring programs: MUC [58], B^3 [2], and ϕ_3-CEAF [32].

A complication arises when B^3 is used to score a response partition containing system mentions. B^3 constructs a mapping between the mentions in the response and those in the key. Hence, if the response is generated using gold-standard mentions, then every mention in the response is mapped to some mention in the key and vice versa. In other words, there are no twinless (i.e., unmapped) mentions [53]. This is not the case when system mentions are used, but the original description of B^3 does not specify how twinless mentions should be scored [2]. To address this problem, Rahman and Ng set the recall and precision of a twinless mention to zero, regardless of whether the mention appears in the key or the response.

Additionally, in order not to over-penalize a response partition, Rahman and Ng removed all the twinless mentions in the response that are singletons. The rationale is simple: since the resolver has successfully identified these mentions as singletons, it should not be penalized, and removing them avoids such penalty.

4.3.2 Results and Discussion

The mention-pair baseline Rahman and Ng trained their first baseline, the mention-pair coreference classifier, on the 39 features described in Table 1 using the SVM learning algorithm as implemented in the SVM^{light} package.[5] Results of this baseline using true mentions and system mentions, shown in row 1 of Tables 2 and 3, are reported in terms of recall (R), precision (P), and F-score (F) provided by the three scoring programs. As can be seen, this baseline achieves F-scores of 54.3–70.0 and 53.4–62.5 for true mentions and system mentions, respectively.

The entity-mention baseline To train their second baseline, the entity-mention coreference classifier, Rahman and Ng employed the SVM learner, representing each instance with the cluster-level features used by their cluster-ranking model. Results of this baseline are shown in row 2 of Tables 2 and 3. For true mentions, this baseline achieves an F-score of 54.8–70.7. In comparison to the mention-pair baseline, F-score rises insignificantly according to all three scorers.[6] Similar trends can be observed for system mentions, where the F-scores between the two models are statistically indistinguishable across the board.

The mention-ranking baseline Rahman and Ng's third baseline was the mention-ranking coreference model, trained using the ranker-learning algorithm in SVM^{light}.

[5]For this and subsequent uses of the SVM learner in their experiments, Rahman and Ng set all the learning parameters to their default values.

[6]Rahman and Ng used Approximate Randomization [42] for testing statistical significance, with p set to 0.05.

Table 2 MUC, CEAF, and B^3 coreference results using true mentions

		MUC			CEAF			B^3		
	Coreference model	R	P	F	R	P	F	R	P	F
1	Mention-pair model	71.7	69.2	70.4	54.3	54.3	54.3	53.3	63.6	58.0
2	Entity-mention model	71.7	69.7	70.7	54.8	54.8	54.8	53.2	65.1	58.5
3	Mention-ranking model (Pipeline)	68.7	73.9	71.2	57.8	57.8	57.8	55.8	63.9	59.6
4	Mention-ranking model (Joint)	69.4	77.8	73.4	61.6	61.6	61.6	57.0	70.1	62.9
5	Cluster-ranking model (Pipeline)	71.7	78.2	74.8	61.8	61.8	61.8	58.2	69.1	63.2
6	Cluster-ranking model (Joint)	69.9	83.3	**76.0**	63.3	63.3	**63.3**	56.0	74.6	**64.0**

Table 3 MUC, CEAF, and B^3 coreference results using system mentions

		MUC			CEAF			B^3		
	Coreference model	R	P	F	R	P	F	R	P	F
1	Mention-pair model	70.0	56.4	62.5	56.1	51.0	53.4	50.8	57.9	54.1
2	Entity-mention model	68.5	57.2	62.3	56.3	50.2	53.1	51.2	57.8	54.3
3	Mention-ranking model (Pipeline)	62.2	68.9	65.4	51.6	56.7	54.1	52.3	61.8	56.6
4	Mention-ranking model (Joint)	62.1	73.0	67.1	53.0	58.5	55.6	50.4	65.5	56.9
5	Cluster-ranking model (Pipeline)	65.3	72.3	68.7	54.1	59.3	56.6	55.3	63.7	59.2
6	Cluster-ranking model (Joint)	64.1	75.4	**69.3**	56.7	62.6	**59.5**	54.4	70.5	**61.4**

Each instance was represented using the 39 features shown in Table 1. To identify non-anaphoric mentions, they employed two methods. In the first method, they adopted a pipeline architecture, where they trained an SVM classifier for anaphoricity determination independently of the mention ranker on the training set. They then applied the resulting classifier to each test text to filter non-anaphoric mentions prior to coreference resolution. Results of the mention ranker are shown in row 3 of Tables 2 and 3. As can be seen, the ranker achieves F-scores of 57.8–71.2 and 54.1–65.4 for true mentions and system mentions, respectively, yielding a significant improvement over the entity-mention baseline in all but one case (MUC/true mentions).

In the second method, they performed anaphoricity determination jointly with coreference resolution using the method described in the previous subsection. While we discussed this joint learning method in the context of cluster ranking, it should be easy to see that the method is equally applicable to the mention-ranking model. Results of the mention ranker using this joint architecture are shown in row 4 of Tables 2 and 3. As can be seen, the ranker achieves F-scores of 61.6–73.4 and 55.6–67.1 for true mentions and system mentions, respectively. For both types of mentions, the improvements over the corresponding results for the entity-mention baseline are significant, and suggest that mention ranking is a precision-enhancing device. Moreover, in comparison to the pipeline architecture in row 3, F-score rises significantly by 2.2–3.8 % for true mentions, and improves by a smaller margin of 0.3–1.7 % for system mentions. These results demonstrate the benefits of joint modeling.

The cluster-ranking model As in the mention-ranking baseline, Rahman and Ng employed both the pipeline architecture and the joint architecture for anaphoricity determination when evaluating their cluster-ranking model. Results are shown in rows 5 and 6 of Tables 2 and 3, respectively, for the two architectures. When true mentions are used, the pipeline architecture yields an F-score of 61.8–74.8, which represents a significant improvement over the mention ranker adopting the pipeline architecture. With the joint architecture, the cluster ranker achieves an F-score of 63.3–76.0. This also represents a significant improvement over the mention ranker adopting the joint architecture, the best of the baselines, and suggests that cluster ranking is a better precision-enhancing model than mention ranking. Moreover, comparing the results in these two rows reveals the superiority of the joint architecture over the pipeline architecture, particularly in terms of its ability to enhance system precision. Similar performance trends can be observed when system mentions are used.

5 Other Advanced Learning-Based Coreference Models

So far we have discussed several instantiations of the entity-mention model, the mention-ranking model, and the cluster-ranking model, showing how they address one or more of the weaknesses of the mention-pair model. These coreference models are by no means the only advanced supervised models that researchers have investigated. While it is not possible for us to enumerate all of the existing supervised coreference models, we will introduce three additional advanced coreference models that we believe are worth examining. Unlike in the previous sections, we will only provide a high-level overview of these three models, and refer the reader to the original papers for details.

5.1 Finley and Joachims' Coreference Model

We argued in the previous section that ranking loss is a more appropriate objective function to minimize than classification loss for supervised coreference resolution. Motivated in part by this observation, Finley and Joachims [17] propose a ranking-based coreference model, but rather than ranking candidate antecedents (as in the mention-ranking model) or preceding clusters (as in the cluster-ranking model), their model ranks coreference partitions. Specifically, they propose a ranking-based objective function that allows an SVM to be trained to rank two coreference partitions. Another major innovation of their work is the incorporation of the information provided by a coreference scoring program into the training process, so that the SVM ranker can be optimized with respect to *any* coreference scoring program of interest.

To see how the information provided by the coreference scorer can be profitably used during the training process, let us briefly review how SVM ranking is done. When given two partitions to rank (during testing), a learned SVM ranker first assigns a score to each partition and then determines the ranks based on these scores. Ideally, not only do we want the ranker to assign a higher score to the better partition, but we also desire the *difference* between the two scores to reflect the difference in quality between these partitions. For instance, if the two partitions are similar in quality, the difference in the two scores should be smaller than that if one partition has a substantially higher quality than the other.

Intuitively, taking this difference into account during the *training* process would enable us to acquire a better SVM ranker. Hence, during the training process, where each training instance is composed of a correct partition and an incorrect partition, we first score the two partitions associated with each training instance using the coreference scorer of interest,[7] and then train the SVM ranker such that the *margin of separation* (i.e., the difference) between the correct partition and the incorrect partition for each training instance is no less than the difference between their scores. The constraints on the margin of separation can be easily enforced by modifying the linear constraints associated with the constrained optimization problem to be solved by the SVM learner. We refer the reader to Finley and Joachims' work for details.

Since the SVM ranker is trained to rank partitions, it is natural to define cluster-level features for characterizing a partition. However, Finley and Joachims choose to characterize a partition using features that are defined on a pair of mentions rather than a cluster of mentions. In other words, the learned coreference model is not an entity-mention model.

It is worth mentioning that one challenge associated with their approach is the choice of incorrect partitions for generating training examples: since the number of incorrect partitions is exponential in the number of mentions to be clustered, it is computationally infeasible to generate one training example from each incorrect partition. To address this problem, Finely and Joachims present a heuristic procedure for intelligently selecting "informative" incorrect partitions for providing training examples.

5.2 McCallum and Wellner's Coreference Model

Another coreference model that operates at the partition level is McCallum and Wellner's [36] probabilistic model, which is designed to score a coreference partition. Their goal is to train the model in such a way that the probability assigned to the correct partition will be the highest among those of the competing partitions. The model they employ is a conditional random field [29], where each feature

[7]The correct partition will receive a perfect score, of course.

function is defined on two mentions, m_j and m_k, as well as a binary label, y_{jk}, which indicates whether the two mentions are coreferent or not. Hence, this model is to some extent similar in spirit to Finley and Joachims' model, since both of them are concerned with scoring coreference partitions rather than mentions. Moreover, like Finley and Joachims' model, this model employs feature functions that are defined on two mentions. In particular, it does not exploit cluster-level features and therefore is not an entity-mention model either.

To optimize the feature weights with respect to the aforementioned objective function, they employ gradient descent. However, computing the expectation term in the gradient is computationally expensive given the exponential number of possible partitions for a given set of mentions. To address this problem, they employ Collins' [6] voted perceptron algorithm, where they approximate the gradient in each training iteration using only the candidate partition that has the highest score under the current parameter setting. Unlike Finley and Joachims' approach, this CRF approach cannot optimize clusters with respect to the desired coreference scoring program.

5.3 *Daumé III and Marcu's Coreference Model*

Daumé III and Marcu [11] employ the Learning as Search Optimization (LaSO) framework [12] to learn in an online fashion a linear function for scoring a preceding coreference cluster. The LaSO framework is a generic framework for addressing learning tasks with structured output, and is therefore applicable to coreference resolution since the output of a coreference model is a partition.

Given our discussion in this chapter, we can introduce Daumé III and Marcu's coreference model without introducing the LaSO framework. Specifically, we will discuss this model in terms of how it is related to some of the models we have seen so far, in hopes of giving the reader a different perspective of this model.

Specifically, Daumé III and Marcu's coreference model bears some resemblance to the cluster-ranking model in that the training instances for their model are created in the same way as those for the cluster-ranking model.[8] They employ a large-margin update rule to train the feature weights of a linear function in an online fashion. In other words, given the current weight parameters, the linear function is applied to score the instance corresponding to each partial partition formed with respect to the active mention under consideration, and the feature weights are updated if (1) the function makes a mistake (i.e., the score of the correct partial partition is not the highest among those of the competing partial partitions) or (2) the function is close to making a mistake (i.e., the score of the correct partial partition

[8]Note that the model proposed by Daumé III and Marcu is a model for jointly performing mention detection and coreference resolution. In our discussion, we focus on the portion of their model that is relevant to learning a coreference partition. See their paper [11] for details.

is only minimally higher than that of the partial partition with the second highest score).

Daumé III and Marcu's model also bears some resemblance to Culotta et al.'s [10] model. Both of these models are trained in an online fashion. While this may not seem like a crucial point, it is worth mentioning that training models in an error-driven fashion may make them more adaptive to the way they are being used. In addition, both of them employ cluster-level features and can therefore be viewed as variants of the entity-mention model.

6 Summary

In this chapter, we have discussed a number of advanced supervised models for coreference resolution that aim to address the weaknesses of the mention-pair model. While we have centered our discussion on *discriminative* coreference models, there have been several recent attempts on designing *generative* coreference models. Despite the fact that these two types of models have represented two quite independent branches of research in coreference resolution, there is in fact an interesting connection between them. Recall that generative models try to capture the true conditional probability of some event. In the context of coreference resolution, this will be the probability of a mention having a particular antecedent or of it referring to a particular preceding cluster. Since these probabilities have to normalize, this is similar to a ranking objective: the system is trying to raise the probability that a mention refers to the correct antecedent or preceding cluster at the expense of the probabilities that it refers to any other. Thus, the antecedent version of the generative coreference model as proposed by Ge et al. [19] resembles the mention-ranking model, while the cluster version as proposed by Haghighi and Klein [21] is similar in spirit to the cluster-ranking model.

While the cluster-ranking model performs better than many existing supervised coreference models, an interesting question is: does it perform better than all of these models with respect to every type of anaphor? To answer this question, Rahman and Ng [49] create an ensemble of supervised coreference models that comprise different versions of the mention-pair model, the entity-mention model, the mention-ranking model, and the cluster-ranking model by training them on different feature sets, and show that the resulting ensemble performs better than any of the individual models. This implies that these models complement each other's strengths and weaknesses, and that no single model performs better on all types of anaphors. Given that unsupervised models [20, 40, 44] and heuristic models [31, 47] have rivaled their supervised counterparts in performance, an interesting research direction would be to examine whether we can further improve coreference resolution accuracy by combining supervised models with unsupervised and heuristic models of coreference.

References

1. Alshawi, H., Carter, D., van Eijck, J., Moore, R., Moran, D., Pulman, S.: Overivew of the Core Language Engine. In: Proceedings of the International Conference on Fifth Generation Computer Systems, Tokyo, pp. 1108–1115 (1988)
2. Bagga, A., Baldwin, B.: Entity-based cross-document coreferencing using the vector space model. In: Proceedings of the 36th Annual Meeting of the Assocation for Computational Linguistics and the 17th International Conference on Computational Linguistics, Montreal, pp. 79–85 (1998)
3. Bikel, D.M., Schwartz, R., Weischedel, R.M.: An algorithm that learns what's in a name. Mach. Learn.: Spec. Issue Nat. Lang. Learn. **34**(1–3), 211–231 (1999)
4. Brennan, S.E., Friedman, M.W., Pollard, C.J.: A centering approach to pronouns. In: Proceedings of the 25th Annual Meeting of the Association for Computational Linguistics, Stanford, pp. 155–162 (1987)
5. Carter, D.M.: Interpreting Anaphors in Natural Language Texts. Ellis Horwood, Chichester (1987)
6. Collins, M.: Discriminative training methods for Hidden Markov Models: theory and experiments with perceptron algorithms. In: Proceedings of the 2002 Empirical Methods in Natural Language Processing, Prague, pp. 1–8 (2002)
7. Connolly, D., Burger, J.D., Day, D.S.: A machine learning approach to anaphoric reference. In: Proceedings of International Conference on New Methods in Language Processing, New Brunswick, pp. 255–261 (1994)
8. Connolly, D., Burger, J.D., Day, D.S.: A machine learning approach to anaphoric reference. In: New Methods in Language Processing, pp. 133–144. UCL Press, London (1997)
9. Crammer, K., Singer, Y.: Ultraconservative online algorithms for multiclass problems. J. Mach. Learn. Res. **3**, 951–991 (2003)
10. Culotta, A., Wick, M., McCallum, A.: First-order probabilistic models for coreference resolution. In: Human Language Technologies 2007: The Conference of the North American Chapter of the Association for Computational Linguistics; Proceedings of the Main Conference, Rochester, pp. 81–88 (2007)
11. Daumé III, H., Marcu, D.: A large-scale exploration of effective global features for a joint entity detection and tracking model. In: Proceedings of Human Language Technology Conference and Conference on Empirical Methods in Natural Language Processing, Vancouver, pp. 97–104 (2005)
12. Daumé III, H., Marcu, D.: Learning as search optimization: approximate large margin methods for structured prediction. In: Proceedings of the 22nd International Conference on Machine Learning, Bonn, pp. 169–176 (2005)
13. Denis, P., Baldridge, J.: A ranking approach to pronoun resolution. In: Proceedings of the Twentieth International Conference on Artificial Intelligence, Hyderabad, pp. 1588–1593 (2007)
14. Denis, P., Baldridge, J.: Specialized models and ranking for coreference resolution. In: Proceedings of the 2008 Conference on Empirical Methods in Natural Language Processing, Honolulu, pp. 660–669 (2008)
15. Fellbaum, C.: WordNet: An Electronic Lexical Database. MIT, Cambridge, MA (1998)
16. Finkel, J.R., Grenager, T., Manning, C.: Incorporating non-local information into information extraction systems by gibbs sampling. In: Proceedings of the 43rd Annual Meeting of the Association for Computational Linguistics, Ann Arbor, pp. 363–370 (2005)
17. Finley, T., Joachims, T.: Supervised clustering with support vector machines. In: Proceedings of the 22nd International Conference on Machine Learning, Bonn, pp. 217–224 (2005)
18. Gaizauskas, R., Wakao, T., Humphreys, K., Cunningham, H., Wilks, Y.: Description of the LaSIE ystem as used for MUC-6. In: Proceedings of the Sixth Message Understanding Conference (MUC-6), pp. 207–220. Morgan Kaufmann, Columbia (1995)

19. Ge, N., Hale, J., Charniak, E.: A statistical approach to anaphora resolution. In: Proceedings of the Sixth Workshop on Very Large Corpora, Montreal, pp. 161–170 (1998)
20. Haghighi, A., Klein, D.: Unsupervised coreference resolution in a nonparametric bayesian model. In: Proceedings of the 45th Annual Meeting of the Association of Computational Linguistics, Prague, pp. 848–855 (2007)
21. Haghighi, A., Klein, D.: Coreference resolution in a modular, entity-centered model. In: Proceedings of Human Language Technologies: The 2010 Annual Conference of the North American Chapter of the Association for Computational Linguistics, pp. 385–393 (2010)
22. Heim, I.: The semantics of definite and indefinite noun phrases. Ph.D. thesis, University of Massachusetts at Amherst, Amherst (1982)
23. Hobbs, J.: Resolving pronoun references. Lingua **44**, 311–338 (1978)
24. Iida, R., Inui, K., Takamura, H., Matsumoto, Y.: Incorporating contextual cues in trainable models for coreference resolution. In: Proceedings of the EACL Workshop on the Computational Treatment of Anaphora, Budapest (2003)
25. Joachims, T.: Optimizing search engines using clickthrough data. In: Proceedings of the Eighth ACM SIGKDD International Conference on Knowledge Discovery and Data Mining, Edmonton, pp. 133–142 (2002)
26. Kabadjov, M.A.: Task-oriented evaluation of anaphora resolution. Ph.D. thesis, University of Essex, Colchester (2007)
27. Kamp, H.: A theory of truth and semantic interpretation. In: Formal Methods in the Study of Language. Mathematical Centre, Amsterdam (1981)
28. Karttunen, L.: Discourse referents. In: Syntax and Semantics 7 – Notes from the Linguistic Underground, pp. 363–385. Academic, New York/London (1976)
29. Lafferty, J.D., McCallum, A., Pereira, F.C.N.: Conditional random fields: probabilistic models for segmenting and labeling sequence data. In: Proceedings of 18th International Conference on Machine Learning, Williamstown, pp. 282–289 (2001)
30. Lappin, S., Leass, H.: An algorithm for pronominal anaphora resolution. Comput. Linguist. **20**(4), 535–562 (1994)
31. Lee, H., Chang, A., Peirsman, Y., Chambers, N., Surdeanu, M., Jurafsky, D.: Deterministic coreference resolution based on entity-centric, precision-ranked rules. Comput. Linguist. **39**(4), 885–916 (2013)
32. Luo, X.: On coreference resolution performance metrics. In: Proceedings of Human Language Technology Conference and Conference on Empirical Methods in Natural Language Processing, Vancouver, pp. 25–32 (2005)
33. Luo, X., Ittycheriah, A., Jing, H., Kambhatla, N., Roukos, S.: A mention-synchronous coreference resolution algorithm based on the Bell tree. In: Proceedings of the 42nd Annual Meeting of the Association for Computational Linguistics, Barcelona, pp. 135–142 (2004)
34. LuperFoy, S.: The representation of multimodal user interface dialogues using discourse pegs. In: Proceedings of the 30th Annual Meeting of the Association for Computational Linguistics, Newark, pp. 22–31 (1992)
35. McCallum, A., Wellner, B.: Toward conditional models of identity uncertainty with application to proper noun coreference. In: Proceedings of the IJCAI Workshop on Information Integration on the Web Acapulco, (2003)
36. McCallum, A., Wellner, B.: Conditional models of identity uncertainty with application to noun coreference. In: Advances in Neural Information Proceesing Systems. MIT, Cambridge (2004)
37. MUC-6: Proceedings of the Sixth Message Understanding Conference. Morgan Kaufmann, San Francisco (1995)
38. MUC-7: Proceedings of the Seventh Message Understanding Conference. Morgan Kaufmann, San Francisco (1998)
39. Ng, V.: Supervised ranking for pronoun resolution: some recent improvements. In: Proceedings of the 20th National Conference on Artificial Intelligence, Edinburgh, pp. 1081–1086 (2005)
40. Ng, V.: Unsupervised models for coreference resolution. In: Proceedings of the 2008 Conference on Empirical Methods in Natural Language Processing, Honolulu, pp. 640–649 (2008)

41. Ng, V., Cardie, C.: Identifying anaphoric and non-anaphoric noun phrases to improve coreference resolution. In: Proceedings of the 19th International Conference on Computational Linguistics, Taipei, pp. 730–736 (2002)
42. Noreen, E.W.: Computer Intensive Methods for Testing Hypothesis: An Introduction. Wiley, New York (1989)
43. Poesio, M., Kabadjov, M.A.: A general-purpose, off-the-shelf anaphora resolution module: implementation and preliminary evaluation. In: Proceedings of the Fourth International Conference on Language Resources and Evaluation, Lisbon, pp. 663–666 (2004)
44. Poon, H., Domingos, P.: Joint unsupervised coreference resolution with Markov Logic. In: Proceedings of the 2008 Conference on Empirical Methods in Natural Language Processing, Honolulu, pp. 650–659 (2008)
45. Prince, E.: Toward a taxonomy of given-new information. In: Cole, P. (ed.) Radical Pragmatics, pp. 223–255. Academic, New York (1981)
46. Quinlan, J.R.: C4.5: Programs for Machine Learning. Morgan Kaufmann, San Mateo (1993)
47. Raghunathan, K., Lee, H., Rangarajan, S., Chambers, N., Surdeanu, M., Jurafsky, D., Manning, C.: A multi-pass sieve for coreference resolution. In: Proceedings of the 2010 Conference on Empirical Methods in Natural Language Processing, Boston, pp. 492–501 (2010)
48. Rahman, A., Ng, V.: Supervised models for coreference resolution. In: Proceedings of the 2009 Conference on Empirical Methods in Natural Language Processing, Singapore, pp. 968–977 (2009)
49. Rahman, A., Ng, V.: Ensemble-based coreference resolution. In: Proceedings of the 22nd International Joint Conference on Artificial Intelligence, Barcelona, pp. 1884–1889 (2011)
50. Recasens, M.: Coreference: Theory, annotation, resolution and evaluation. Ph.D. thesis, University of Barcelona, Barcelona (2010)
51. Sidner, C.: Towards a computational theory of definite anaphora comprehension in English discourse. Ph.D. thesis, Massachusetts Institute of Technology (1979)
52. Soon, W.M., Ng, H.T., Lim, D.C.Y.: A machine learning approach to coreference resolution of noun phrases. Comput. Linguist. **27**(4), 521–544 (2001)
53. Stoyanov, V., Gilbert, N., Cardie, C., Riloff, E.: Conundrums in noun phrase coreference resolution: making sense of the state-of-the-art. In: Proceedings of the Joint Conference of the 47th Annual Meeting of the ACL and the 4th International Joint Conference on Natural Language Processing of the AFNLP, Singapore, pp. 656–664 (2009)
54. Strube, M., Hahn, U.: Functional centering – grounding referential coherence in information structure. Comput. Linguist. **25**(3), 309–344 (1999)
55. Toutanova, K., Klein, D., Manning, C.D., Singer, Y.: Feature-rich part-of-speech tagging with a cyclic dependency network. In: Proceedings of the Human Language Technology Conference of the North American Chapter of the Association for Computational Linguistics, Edmonton, pp. 173–180 (2003)
56. Versley, Y., Ponzetto, S.P., Poesio, M., Eidelman, V., Jern, A., Smith, J., Yang, X., Moschitti, A.: BART: a modular toolkit for coreference resolution. In: Proceedings of the ACL-08: HLT Demo Session, Columbus, pp. 9–12 (2008)
57. Vieira, R., Poesio, M.: An empirically-based system for processing definite descriptions. Comput. Linguist. **26**(4), 539–593 (2000)
58. Vilain, M., Burger, J., Aberdeen, J., Connolly, D., Hirschman, L.: A model-theoretic coreference scoring scheme. In: Proceedings of the Sixth Message Understanding Conference, pp. 45–52. Morgan Kaufmann, San Francisco (1995)
59. Webber, B.L.: A Formal Approach to Discourse Anaphora. Garland Publishing, Inc., New York (1979)
60. Yang, X., Su, J., Lang, J., Tan, C.L., Li, S.: An entity-mention model for coreference resolution with inductive logic programming. In: Proceedings of the 46th Annual Meeting of the Association for Computational Linguistics: Human Language Technologies, Columbus, pp. 843–851 (2008)

61. Yang, X., Su, J., Tan, C.L.: Improving pronoun resolution using statistics-based semantic compatibility information. In: Proceedings of the 43rd Annual Meeting of the Association for Computational Linguistics, University of Michigan, pp. 165–172 (2005)
62. Yang, X., Su, J., Tan, C.L.: A twin-candidate model for learning-based anaphora resolution. Comput. Linguist. **34**(3), 327–356 (2008)
63. Yang, X., Su, J., Zhou, G., Tan, C.L.: An NP-cluster based approach to coreference resolution. In: Proceedings of the 20th International Conference on Computational Linguistics, Geneva, pp. 226–232 (2004)
64. Yang, X., Zhou, G., Su, J., Tan, C.L.: Coreference resolution using competitive learning approach. In: Proceedings of the 41st Annual Meeting of the Association for Computational Linguistics, Sapporo, pp. 176–183 (2003)

Integer Linear Programming for Coreference Resolution

Nick Rizzolo and Dan Roth

Abstract In this chapter, we introduce Integer Linear Programming (ILP) and review some of its best performing applications to coreference resolution in the literature. We develop some intuitions for how to pose ILPs based on learned models and to how expert knowledge can be encoded as constraints that the learned models must then respect. We describe some of the difficulties encountered during both the development of an ILP and its deployment as well as how to deal with them. Finally, we see how ILP can create an environment in which independently learned models share knowledge for their mutual benefit.

Most of the top results on coreference resolution over the last few years were achieved using an ILP formulation, and we provide a snapshot of these results. Conceptually, and from an engineering perspective, the ILP formulation is very simple and it provides system designers with a lot of flexibility in incorporating knowledge. Indeed, this is where we believe future research should focus.

Keywords Integer Linear Programming Approaches for Coreference Resolution global models • Integer linear programming • Coreference resolution

1 Introduction

As with many tasks in natural language processing, the task of coreference resolution can be formulated as a set of interdependent classification decisions. These decisions affect the interpretation of a document's content. An incorrect set of classifications will result in an incorrect interpretation at best or a logically inconsistent or incoherent interpretation at worst. Thus, it is natural to pose the coreference resolution problem as a constrained optimization problem. This formulation follows a body of work originated with [34] that provided a

N. Rizzolo (✉)
Google Inc., San Francisco, CA, USA
e-mail: rizzolo@google.com

D. Roth
University of Illinois at Urbana/Champaign, Champaign, IL, USA
e-mail: danr@illinois.edu

M. Poesio et al. (eds.), *Anaphora Resolution*, Theory and Applications of Natural Language Processing, DOI 10.1007/978-3-662-47909-4_11

way to study interdependent prediction problems as Integer Linear Programming problems. Formulating coreference problems this way we aim to maximize a scoring function that corresponds to the quality of the document level coreference decision–partitioning the set of mentions to entities–while satisfying structural and linguistic constraints that ensure a consistent interpretation.

The focus of this chapter will be a discussion of the issues encountered when posing coreference resolution as an integer linear program. First, we introduce the basic concepts behind Integer Linear Programming (ILP) in Sect. 3 and lay out an ILP framework for solving coreference resolution in Sect. 4. Next, in Sect. 5, we show that framework in action by applying it to a simple, ad-hoc model that performs very well in practice. Section 6 then introduces a class of constraints that enable the trivial incorporation of expert knowledge into a coreference resolution system: transitivity constraints. Section 7 discusses the use of ILP to combine multiple models such that their predictions are weighed against each other for their mutual benefit. Finally, Sect. 9 concludes and outlines directions for future research.

2 Integer Linear Programming Formulations of NLP Problems

Making decisions in natural language processing often involves assigning values to sets of interdependent variables where the expressive inter-dependencies among them influence, or even dictate, what assignments are possible. A general way to think about these problems is as those that depend on multiple models that are to be combined in ways that respect the models' suggestions along with domain and task specific constraints. In some cases, some or all the models, responsible for a subset of the output variables of interest, can be learned simultaneously but, in general, this may not be practical or even possible.

The general framework used here – Constrained Conditional Models (CCMs) [6, 9] augments the learning of conditional (probabilistic or discriminative) models with declarative constraints as a way to support decisions in an expressive output space while maintaining modularity and tractability of training and inference. Within this framework, the probabilistic output of the learned models is used as an objective function for a global constrained optimization problem. The outcome of this decision problem is an assignment of values to all output variables of interest; an assignment that takes into account the learned model as well as the global constraints. While incorporating expressive dependencies in a probabilistic model can lead to intractable training and inference, this framework allows one to learn a rather simple model (or multiple simple models), and make decisions with more expressive models that take into account also global declarative (hard or soft) constraints.

This type of model combination should be distinguished from so-called "pipeline" approaches in which models are evaluated in a predefined order with earlier models used as filters or features for later models. In a pipeline approach, the predictions made by each model are non-negotiable in later stages of the pipeline. In CCMs, however, no predictions are made until a consensus is reached among all models. Knowledge encoded in the constraints can thereby serve to improve every model's prediction quality. Indeed, the first example of this formulation was given in [34] in the context of an information extraction problem; a pipeline of a named entities model and an entity relations model was replaced by a constrained optimization problem that can support changing recommendations made earlier in the pipeline. Since then, formulating global decision problems in NLP as constrained optimization problems via CCMs has been used in a large number of problems, including coreference resolution [8, 10, 11] and these formulations will be discussed in details in the rest of this chapter.

3 Introduction to LP and ILP

Linear programming (LP) [4] is a specialized form of *mathematical programming* [17], in which a function over a set of variables called the *objective function* is optimized while satisfying a set of user-defined constraints over the same variables. The difference in LP as opposed to other types of mathematical programming is that the objective function and all of the constraints are linear in the variables. A linear program has the form

$$\begin{aligned} &\min\ \mathbf{c}^{\mathrm{T}} \cdot \mathbf{x} \\ &\text{s.t.}\ \ \mathbf{A} \cdot \mathbf{x} \geq \mathbf{b} \end{aligned}$$

where $\mathbf{x}$ is the set of n variables whose values may be manipulated and assigned during the optimization, $\mathbf{c}$ is an n-dimensional vector referred to as the *cost vector*, $\mathbf{A}$ is an $m \times n$ matrix known as the *constraint matrix*, and $\mathbf{b}$ is an m-dimensional vector which we will call the *bounds vector*. LP also supports the maximization of the objective function as well as upper-bounded and equality constraints. When any of these options are exercised, the problem can be restored to the form above via simple algebraic manipulations and the addition of auxiliary variables.

3.1 Linear Programming Intuitions

Example 0 Farmer Joe wants to plant soybeans and wheat on his 10 acre farm. Soybeans will make a \$375 profit per acre, and wheat makes \$550. While the start-up costs to plant soybeans are \$500 per acre, wheat only costs \$100. Joe has \$3300 total to make his initial investment. He'd also like to get all his planting done within 12 h. Planting an acre of soybeans takes 0.8 h, whereas wheat takes 1.5 h. How many acres of each commodity should Joe plant in order to maximize profit?

It's easy to see how the situation on Joe's farm can be posed as a linear program:

$$\begin{array}{lrl}
\max & 375x_1 + 550x_2 & \text{Profit} \\
\text{s.t.} & x_1 + x_2 \leq 10 & \text{Real estate} \\
& 500x_1 + 100x_2 \leq 3300 & \text{Start-up cost} \\
& 0.8x_1 + 1.5x_2 \leq 12 & \text{Time} \\
& x_1 \geq 0 & \\
& x_2 \geq 0 &
\end{array}$$

Let's first see if we can reason about this problem intuitively. We first notice that wheat is more profitable than soybeans. If real estate were our only constraint, it would make sense to cover Joe's farm with it. However, wheat takes more time to plant; so much so that we can only cover 8 acres in 12 h. Furthermore, the ratio of wheat to soybean planting time is greater than the ratio of wheat to soybean profit per acre. Therefore, if we save some time by not covering all 8 acres with wheat, we can use that time to fill real estate above and beyond 8 acres with soybeans, and the extra real estate utilization will more than make up for the lost wheat profit.

Of course, this strategy of sacrificing wheat for soybeans should only work until the point that all 10 acres are covered. After that, it no longer makes sense to sacrifice wheat. Plus, we haven't yet considered our start-up cost constraint. Fortunately, since we have realized the situation on Joe's farm as a linear program (and since it only has 2 free variables), we can thoroughly explore the space of all possible solutions geometrically. Figure 1 illustrates this space, in which the shaded region is known in the literature as the *feasible region* or *feasible set*. These are the solutions that satisfy all constraints. Note that the slope of the "Time" constraint is simply (the opposite of) the planting time ratio mentioned above.

In addition to the feasible region, Fig. 1 also plots unit vectors illustrating our objective function. These vectors are simply $\mathbf{c} = \langle 375, 550 \rangle$ normalized and translated repeatedly. Note that the resulting line is perpendicular to the line $\mathbf{c}^{\mathrm{T}} \cdot \langle x_1, x_2 \rangle = 0$ which has slope equal to (the opposite of) the profit ratio mentioned above. Let's call this the *zero-profit line* (not pictured). We now see that our task is to find a point in the feasible region as far from the zero-profit line as possible in the direction of $\mathbf{c}$. Moving perpendicularly to $\mathbf{c}$ (e.g. along the zero-profit line) will not change the value of the objective function, and moving along any vector with a component that opposes $\mathbf{c}$ will cause the objective function's value to decrease.

With these insights, it is not hard to confirm the intuitions given above. The intersection of the "Time" and "Real estate" constraints shows where the farm is completely covered and our wheat sacrificing strategy stops paying off. Interpreted geometrically, this strategy simply moves us from solution "A" to solution "B" along the feasible region boundary formed by the "Time" constraint. This direction of motion has a positive component in the direction of $\mathbf{c}$.

Now consider what would happen if the profit from wheat were to increase. Eventually, the "Profit" vector would become perpendicular with the "Time" constraint, at which point the planting time and profit ratios would be equal. Any

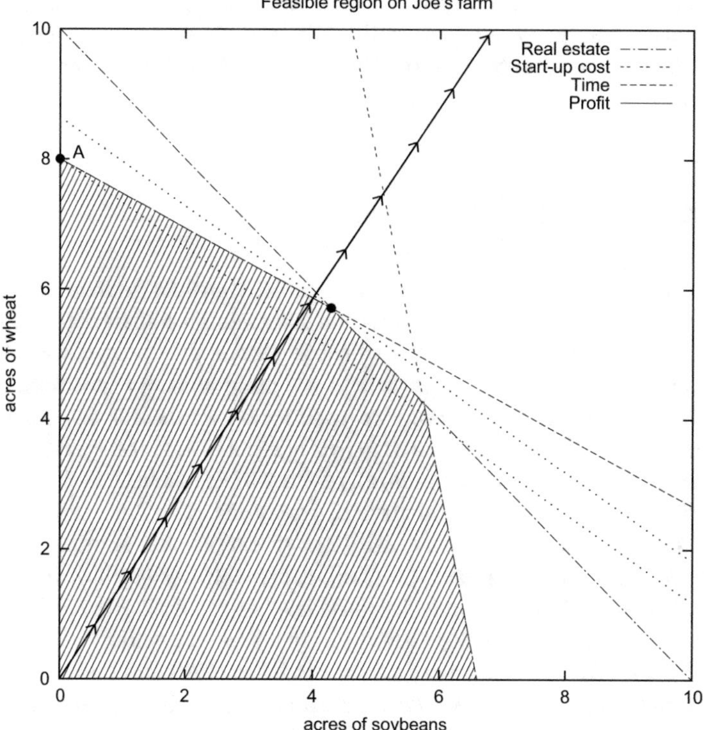

Fig. 1 The feasible region on farmer Joe's farm is shaded. Profit increases fastest in the direction of the arrows. It does not change when moving perpendicularly to them; e.g. along the *dotted lines* containing "A" and "B"

further increase would then make 8 acres of wheat and 2 unplanted acres the most profitable configuration. On the other hand, a decrease in wheat profit would eventually bring the "Start-up cost" constraint into play.

3.2 LP Algorithms

The first algorithm for solving linear programs is the famous Simplex method of Dantzig [25]. It is based on exactly the intuition above: simply travel from vertex to vertex on the feasible region's polytope until doing so would not improve the objective function. Since the feasible region must be convex (it is the intersection of half-spaces), we know we've found an optimal solution [5]. Unfortunately, while this algorithm works well in practice, it takes exponential time in the worst case.

More recently, polynomial time algorithms for solving linear programs have been discovered [14, 18]. These aptly named "interior point methods" take steps that improve the objective function within the interior of the feasible region and approach optimality asymptotically. While their worst case complexity is polynomial, they are not always faster than a finely tuned Simplex implementation in practice.

3.3 Integer Linear Programming

While Linear Programming is widely applicable, it cannot address an important subclass of problems in which objectives and constraints are also expressed linearly, where fractional solutions are not applicable. A company might want to know how many employees to hire or whether or not build a factory in several different locations. In coreference resolution, we wish to know whether or not to place a link indicating coreference between each pair of mentions. In these cases, fractional results will not suffice. In other words, all of our variables must take integral values for the solution to be feasible. Furthermore, simply rounding the results from an LP solver is not an option. First of all, there are an exponential number of rounding alternatives (up or down for each variable). Moreover, any or all of these choices may result in suboptimality or even infeasibility. In general, ILP is NP-hard [19].

Nevertheless, ILP has been successful in practice on a variety of tasks [2, 11, 22, 23, 30, 34, 35]. The popularity of the model comes from its modularity and expressiveness [9]. It can work with discriminative [30] and probabilistic models [35], allowing expressive and long range structural constraints without blowing up the size of the model. It can combine the strengths of multiple systems by constraining them to agree on the final decision [11, 22, 38]. It can even force a problem's output variables into an organized structure such as a rooted tree [23]. In addition, ILP constraints can be viewed as a mechanism for incorporating domain knowledge [7, 10, 30].

Another factor in the recent success of ILP is the observation that, while ILP is NP-hard in general, in practice relatively large problems can be solved quite efficiently. While the reason for it is not completely understood we can intuitively attribute it to two issues. First, propositional constraints often result in a *totally unimodular* constraint matrix (defined below). This property is very desirable, because it implies a feasible region whose vertices are all integral. Thus, no matter the objective function, a LP algorithm is sufficient to derive an integral solution [16].

Definition 1 (Unimodularity) A square, integer matrix is called *unimodular* if its determinant is either -1 or 1.

Definition 2 (Total unimodularity) An integer matrix is called *totally unimodular* (TUM) if each of its square, nonsingular submatrices is unimodular.

An equivalent way to state Definition 2 is to say that a matrix $\mathbf{A}$ is TUM if and only if $\det(\mathbf{S}) \in \{-1, 0, 1\}$ for every square submatrix $\mathbf{S}$ of $\mathbf{A}$, where det stands for determinant. We now prove a lemma that can help us recognize total unimodularity in the future.

Lemma 1 *If every entry in a matrix* **A** *is in* $\{-1, 0, 1\}$ *and every square submatrix* **S** *of* **A** *contains at least one row or column itself containing at most one non-zero entry, then* **A** *is TUM.*

While the total unimodularity condition is sufficient to guarantee that the ILP problem is easy (see [35] for a discussion in the context of other popular NLP models) it is not a necessary condition. However, there is a second reason many ILP formulation of NLP problem often result in problems that are not that difficult computationally. In many NLP applications the constraints are relatively sparse; that is, the number of target variables active in each constraint is relatively small. Experimentally, this often gives rise to problems that are easier. Unlike the TUM condition, this is often due to interaction with the objective function [36]. Of course, some ILP formulations of NLP problems can result in computationally difficult problems and many approximation inference algorithms have been studied in this context; this discussion of this is outside the scope of this chapter, but see [20] for new developments that address these difficulties.

The variables $\mathbf{x}$ in an ILP are almost always used to indicate the selection of a particular prediction value. For example, a variable may indicate that the third word in the sentence is a noun, or that the first two noun phrases in a sentence do not refer to the same entity. As such, we constrain these variables to take a value in $\{0, 1\}$. When all variables are constrained in this way, we say the problem is a *0–1 ILP*. In this case, the variables can be thought of as Boolean, and the constraints can be thought of as sentences in a propositional logic. In fact, any propositional logic statement can be efficiently converted to an equivalent set of linear inequalities for use in a 0–1 ILP, and automated systems have been developed for doing so [32, 33]. This ability can be quite useful since the formulation of a non-trivial constraint as a linear inequality can be less than obvious.

4 The Coreference Resolution Objective Function

The objective function in any mathematical programming problem is the metric by which the collective settings of the variables are measured. When applied in the context of machine learning and inference, the objective function corresponds directly to the learned model or models from which predictions are solicited. If we wish to maximize the likelihood of a document, our objective function should represent the likelihood of a document. If we wish to maximize the number of correct predictions offered by our model(s), our objective function should count correct predictions. These intuitive notions will be explored in this section.

In the literature, ILP formulations for coreference resolution always start with pairwise variables $x_{i,j} \in \{0, 1\}$, $1 \leq i < j \leq n$ indicating whether or not mentions m_i and m_j are coreferent. Formulations in which more mentions are directly related

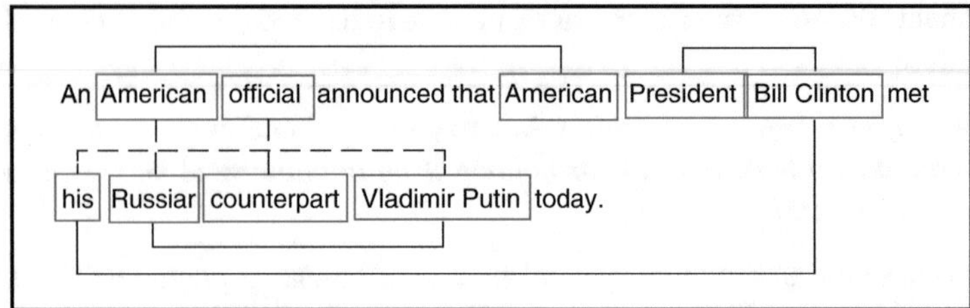

Fig. 2 Pairwise coreference variables depicted as a graph. The nodes (*boxes*) are mentions of real world entities. *Edges* between pairs of mentions represent the variables. A *solid, edge* indicates that the variable is turned on, whereas a *dashed edge* indicates the opposite (not all edges are shown)

by a single variable are also possible, but could greatly increase the total number of variables in the problem, which complicates things for the ILP solver. Fortunately, many of the advantages that these more complicated formulations might offer can be recovered by relating the pairwise variables to each other via constraints.

Figure 2 illustrates pairwise variables as edges in a graph where the nodes represent mentions. A solid edge indicates the variable is set to 1, while a dashed edge indicates the variable is set to 0. All of the solid edges are included, but some of the dashed edges have been omitted to reduce clutter. The figure happens to depict an appropriate assignment for our variables; it is this assignment which we hope our ILP solver will compute for us automatically.

Of course, a formulation with pairwise variables is directly amenable to the popular pairwise models in the literature. The most common type of model translated to the ILP setting decomposes the probability of a document over random variables $X_{i,j}$ representing the coreference of a mention pair. The probability of a document $\mathscr{D}$ is given as the product of the probabilities of all these variables taking their particular settings:

$$P(\mathscr{D}) = \prod_{j=2}^{n} \prod_{i=1}^{j-1} P(X_{i,j} = x_{i,j}) \quad (1)$$

Another option is to use the probability of a particular mention being coreferent as our model's estimate of the likelihood that such a prediction would be correct. We can then compute the expected number of correct predictions on a document as follows:

$$C(\mathscr{D}) = \sum_{j=2}^{n} \sum_{i=1}^{j-1} P(X_{i,j} = x_{i,j}) \quad (2)$$

The objective function must be linear for use in an ILP. Thus, Equation (2) is ready for use, but we must apply a transformation to Equation (1) if we prefer it.

Taking the log, we get

$$L(\mathscr{D}) = \sum_{j=2}^{n} \sum_{i=1}^{j-1} \log(P(X_{i,j} = x_{i,j})) \tag{3}$$

The log function is monotonic, meaning that for any $x_1 < x_2$, we have $\log(x_1) \leq \log(x_2)$. Therefore, if we rank assignments to the $X_{i,j}$ variables according to Equation (1), we get exactly the same ranking as when we use Equation (3) instead.

Finally, before getting involved with specific approaches in the following sections, lets see how models such as the above can be encoded as an ILP's objective function, using Equation (3) as an example. Let $p_{i,j}^{(x)} = \log(P(X_{i,j} = x))$.

$$\begin{aligned} \max \ & \sum_{j=2}^{n} \sum_{i=1}^{j-1} p_{i,j}^{(1)} x_{i,j} + p_{i,j}^{(0)}(1 - x_{i,j}) \\ \text{s.t.} \ & 0 \leq x_{i,j} \leq 1 \ \forall i,j | i < j \\ & x_{i,j} \text{ integer } \forall i,j | i < j \end{aligned}$$

In fact, this particular form is popular in the literature [11, 12, 27]. However, to see for practical purposes what this looks like when each ILP variable appears only once, we will do a little extra algebra and drop constants that do not affect the outcome of the variables' settings.

$$\begin{aligned} \max \ & \sum_{j=2}^{n} \sum_{i=1}^{j-1} \left(p_{i,j}^{(1)} - p_{i,j}^{(0)}\right) x_{i,j} \\ \text{s.t.} \ & 0 \leq x_{i,j} \leq 1 \ \forall i,j | i < j \\ & x_{i,j} \text{ integer } \forall i,j | i < j \end{aligned}$$

The coefficients of our variables now represent the log odds that the corresponding pair of mentions is coreferent. This is not a requirement, however, and a given learning algorithm that interprets its learned parameters differently has no a priori reason to perform better or worse. So, throughout this chapter, we will use the following generic form as a starting point for the ILP formulations we discuss:

ILP 1

$$\begin{aligned} \max \ & \sum_{j=2}^{n} \sum_{i=1}^{j-1} c(m_i, m_j) x_{i,j} \\ \text{s.t.} \ & 0 \leq x_{i,j} \leq 1 \ \forall i,j | i < j \\ & x_{i,j} \text{ integer } \forall i,j | i < j \end{aligned}$$

where $c : \mathscr{M} \times \mathscr{M} \rightarrow \mathbb{R}$ gives the coreference model's score when given a pair of mentions as input. Its only practical restriction is that it be positive if and only if the model prefers that the input mentions be coreferent.

5 Basic Formulation: Implicit Clustering

One of the best performing coreference systems available today is the simple, pairwise model of Bengtson and Roth [3]. This model uses a comprehensive feature set to produce a high precision, low recall prediction indicating whether a given pair of mentions is coreferent. It follows that the model is often wrong when it predicts that two mentions are *not* coreferent, and in turn that predictions are often inconsistent when taken collectively. For example, if mention pairs $\langle m_i, m_j \rangle$ and $\langle m_j, m_k \rangle$ are predicted coreferent, but mention pair $\langle m_i, m_k \rangle$ is predicted non-coreferent, how should we resolve the ambiguity?

Following prior work [26], Bengtson and Roth use the simple "Best-Link" clustering algorithm, which was found to outperform the "Closest-Link" clustering algorithm from the seminal work of Soon et al. [37]. In Best-Link clustering, we process the document from left to right, considering each mention m_j in turn. If there exists at least one mention m_i, $i < j$ such that the classifier produces a score on the pair $\langle m_i, m_j \rangle$ higher than some predetermined threshold θ, then a link is established between m_j and the particular m_i yielding the highest score from the classifier. This process results in a forest of links between mentions. Finally, we take the transitive closure over this forest to produce the final clustering.

Best-Link clustering is easy to implement in any programming language. However, if we encode the approach as an ILP, we may be able to add additional domain knowledge via constraints that would be difficult to incorporate in a procedural implementation.

Example 3 Assume we have a document $\mathscr{D}$ containing a set of mentions $\{m_i\}_{i=1}^n, m_i \in \mathscr{M}$, a pairwise scoring function $c : \mathscr{M} \times \mathscr{M} \rightarrow \mathbb{R}$, and the threshold θ described above. How can the Best-Link clustering algorithm be posed as an ILP whose output represents a forest of coreference links?

Bengtson and Roth used the regularized averaged perceptron learning algorithm [15] which produces an activation $\sigma(\langle m_i, m_j \rangle) = \mathbf{w} \cdot \Phi(\langle m_i, m_j \rangle)$ for each input pair, where $\Phi(\cdot)$ is a vector of feature values and $\mathbf{w}$ is a vector of learned parameters. With this in mind, we start with ILP 1 and choose $c(m_i, m_j) = \sigma(\langle m_i, m_j \rangle) - \theta$. Note that although the objective function will not be probabilistically motivated in this case, the ILP solver will only have an incentive to establish the link $\langle m_i, m_j \rangle$ when $\sigma(\langle m_i, m_j \rangle) > \theta$, exactly as intended.

Finally, we need constraints to ensure that at most one $x_{i,j} = 1$ for a given j. Here's the final ILP:

ILP 2

$$\begin{aligned}
\max \ & \sum_{j=2}^{n} \sum_{i=1}^{j-1} (\sigma(m_i, m_j) - \theta) x_{i,j} \\
\text{s.t.} \ & \sum_{i=1}^{j-1} x_{i,j} \leq 1 \ \forall j \\
& 0 \leq x_{i,j} \leq 1 \ \forall i, j | i < j \\
& x_{i,j} \ \text{integer} \ \forall i, j | i < j
\end{aligned}$$

Lemma 2 *The formulation of Best-Link clustering in ILP 2 is TUM.*

Proof We'd like to use Lemma 1 to prove the current lemma. Thus, letting **A** be the constraint matrix defined in ILP 2, we must show that all square, nonsingular submatrices of **A** contain at least one row or column which itself contains a single non-zero entry. Since we only care about square, *nonsingular* submatrices of **A**, we will not be concerned with any square submatrix containing a row or column of all zeros. Now consider the boundary constraints ensuring $x_{i,j} \in \{0, 1\}$. For each $x_{i,j}$, we have two boundary constraints each containing a single non-zero coefficient. Any non-singular submatrix of **A** containing such a row will therefore satisfy the lemma.

The only submatrices of **A** left to consider are now the non-singular submatrices that only contain constraints ensuring that at most one $x_{i,j} = 1$ for a given j. Since there is only one such constraint for each j, it is easy to confirm that every column in such a submatrix contains exactly one non-zero entry.

Thus, Best-Link decoding can be carried out efficiently in an optimization framework. This result is not surprising considering the simplistic structure of the Best-Link algorithm. The antecedent selection for each mention happens completely independently of the antecedent selection for every other mention. Certain kinds of constraints such as the one in [3] which prohibits a mention that is not a pronoun from selecting a mention which is a pronoun as its direct antecedent can also be incorporated easily. However, see Sect. 6 for a discussion of the limitations of this formulation in general.

We title this basic ILP formulation "implicit" since its output is a forest of mention links whose transitivity is implicit. A cluster emerges from each connected component of the forest, but we have not verified, by the classifier or any other means, the coreference of mentions not explicitly linked to each other in each component. Next, we move to formulations that can support this verification explicitly.

6 Explicit Clustering

While the inference regimen described in Sect. 5 is efficient and performs well, it may be viewed as leaving something to be desired in its linguistic motivations. Its output is a forest of mention links whose transitivity is merely implicit; simply take the transitive closure without verifying, by the classifier or any other means, the coreference of mentions not explicitly linked to each other. Thus, important information learned by the classifier about which mentions cannot be coreferent may be ignored. Additionally, it is difficult to enforce *as a constraint* the expert knowledge we may have about two mentions m_i and m_j that cannot be in the same cluster. Simply adding the constraint $x_{i,j} = 0$ will not suffice, since solutions involving $x_{k,i} = 1$ and $x_{k,j} = 1$ for some $k < i$ will still satisfy all constraints even though they violate our intentions.

Furthermore, when expert knowledge prescribes that mentions m_i and m_j must be coreferent, the constraint $x_{i,j} = 1$ may not have the desired effect. This constraint overrides the classifier's decision to link m_j to some other mention m_k, $k < j$. In general, the sets of mentions connected to m_i and m_k are different, and switching m_j's antecedent in this way may not have a positive overall effect on the document's clustering. We'd prefer an optimization scheme that reorganizes our clustering under these conditions, but since antecedent selections are completely independent in Best-Link clustering, no such reorganization will occur.

In this section, we will explore two possible ILP formulations for dealing with these issues. First, in Sect. 6.1, we try abandoning the Best-Link constraints for constraints that directly enforce transitivity over our original ILP variables. Then, in Sect. 6.2, we consider more complex formulations that preserve the spirit of Best-Link clustering while supporting additional constraints more effectively than the original Best-Link ILP on its own. Finally, Sect. 6.3 discusses options available when these ILPs become intractable.

6.1 Encoding Transitivity Directly

The idea to enforce transitivity directly over a pairwise classifier is inspired by the notion that both positive and negative coreference evidence discovered by that classifier should be taken into account when arranging the final clustering. Managing these types of competing concerns is exactly what ILP is intended for. We merely need to express as constraints the idea that whenever mention pairs $\langle m_i, m_j \rangle$ and $\langle m_j, m_k \rangle$ are deemed coreferent, mention pair $\langle m_i, m_k \rangle$ should be as well. That way, when there is strong evidence against the coreference of $\langle m_i, m_k \rangle$, the ILP solver will be forced to reconsider the other two mention pairs.

Example 3 Assume we have a document $\mathscr{D}$ containing a set of mentions $\{m_i\}_{i=1}^n, m_i \in \mathscr{M}$ and a pairwise scoring function $c : \mathscr{M} \times \mathscr{M} \to \mathbb{R}$. How can the transitivity of coreference links be enforced in an ILP whose output represents a set of mention clusters?

The aforementioned constraints need to be enforced over all triples of mentions $\langle m_i, m_j, m_k \rangle$. We accomplish this by adding constraints to ILP 1.

ILP 3

$$
\begin{aligned}
\max \sum_{j=2}^{n} \sum_{i=1}^{j-1} & c(m_i, m_j)\, x_{i,j} \\
\text{s.t.}\quad & x_{i,j} + x_{j,k} \leq x_{i,k} + 1 \;\; \forall i,j,k \\
& 0 \leq x_{i,j} \leq 1 \qquad \forall i,j \mid i<j \\
& x_{i,j} \text{ integer} \qquad \forall i,j \mid i<j
\end{aligned}
$$

The first constraint says that when both $x_{i,j}$ and $x_{j,k}$ are 1, $x_{i,k}$ will have to be 1 for the constraint to be satisfied. If either $x_{i,j}$ or $x_{j,k}$ is 0, then no requirement is enforced on the value of $x_{i,k}$. For a given triple of mentions, say $\langle m_1, m_2, m_3 \rangle$, we will have the constraints

$$x_{1,2} + x_{2,3} \leq x_{1,3} + 1 \tag{4a}$$

$$x_{1,2} + x_{1,3} \leq x_{2,3} + 1 \tag{4b}$$

$$x_{2,3} + x_{1,3} \leq x_{1,2} + 1 \tag{4c}$$

all of which are necessary to achieve the desired effect.

The alert reader will have noticed that ILP 3 actually includes many redundant variables and constraints. First, note that the objective function and the last constraint line are the same as in ILP 1. They each imply a single binary variable for every unique mention pair, since they always restrict *i* to be less than *j*. The first constraint, however, is not so careful. We could agree to take it as implied that *i*, *j*, and *k* are mutually exclusive and that the variable name $x_{i,j}$, $i > j$ is merely an alias for $x_{j,i}$, or we could make it explicit, like this:

ILP 4

$$
\begin{aligned}
\max \sum_{j=2}^{n} \sum_{i=1}^{j-1} & c(m_i, m_j)\, x_{i,j} \\
\text{s.t.}\quad & x_{i,j} + x_{j,k} \leq x_{i,k} + 1 \;\; \forall i,j,k \mid i<j<k \\
& x_{i,j} + x_{i,k} \leq x_{j,k} + 1 \;\; \forall i,j,k \mid i<j<k \\
& x_{j,k} + x_{i,k} \leq x_{i,j} + 1 \;\; \forall i,j,k \mid i<j<k \\
& 0 \leq x_{i,j} \leq 1 \qquad \forall i,j \mid i<j \\
& x_{i,j} \text{ integer} \qquad \forall i,j \mid i<j
\end{aligned}
$$

This formulation has $O(n^3)$ constraints, and it can incorporate additional constraints that force particular mention pairs to be coreferent or non-coreferent easily. Unfortunately, it won't always be efficient.

Lemma 3 *The constraint matrix in ILP 4 is not TUM for any* $n \geq 3$.

This lemma indicates that we have no guarantee that solving ILP 4 will be tractable in general. However, Finkel and Manning [12] found that the vast majority of the documents in the MUC-6 and ACE Phase 2 testing sets could be processed in a reasonable amount of time. They also showed an improvement (over tractable documents) in a variety of scoring metrics as a result of enforcing transitivity. It is important to note as well that their pairwise classifier was trained on all pairs of mentions. Because this procedure may take into account links between any mention pairs, this choice is likely more amenable to their inference regimen than, for instance, the more selective set of mention pairs sampled by Bengtson and Roth [3] at training time.

6.2 Applying Constraints to Best-Link Clustering

Best-Link clustering, while ad-hoc, does perform very well, so it is natural to attempt improving it by adding expert knowledge in the form of constraints. However, as discussed above, this will not be as straight forward as we might hope. We cannot simply add the transitivity constraints in ILP 4 to the Best-Link constraints in ILP 2 since they contradict each other. So, we will first create a set of auxiliary variables to keep track of which mentions are coreferent by implication given a Best-Link forest. The semantics of these variables must be enforced by a carefully designed set of constraints. Then we can enforce arbitrary constraints over the auxiliary variables.

We start with ILP 2, and then define auxiliary variables $t_{i,j} \in \{0, 1\}$, $1 \leq i < j \leq n$ such that $t_{i,j} = 1$ if and only if mentions m_i and m_j are connected via some path established by the x variables. Of course, the $t_{i,j}$ variables won't actually have this property unless we constrain them to have it. When designing the necessary constraints, it will be very useful to conceptualize them using First-Order Logic (FOL). The reader is then referred again to Rizzolo and Roth [32] for an algorithm that automatically translates from a logic form to linear inequalities.

A Recursive Definition For our first attempt, we design our constraints "recursively," like this:

$$
\begin{aligned}
t_{i,j} \Leftrightarrow\ & x_{i,j} \\
& \vee \exists k,\ k < i, \qquad x_{k,j} \wedge t_{k,i} \\
& \vee \exists k,\ i < k < j,\ x_{k,j} \wedge t_{i,k} \\
& \vee \exists k,\ j < k, \qquad x_{j,k} \wedge t_{i,k}
\end{aligned}
\tag{5}
$$

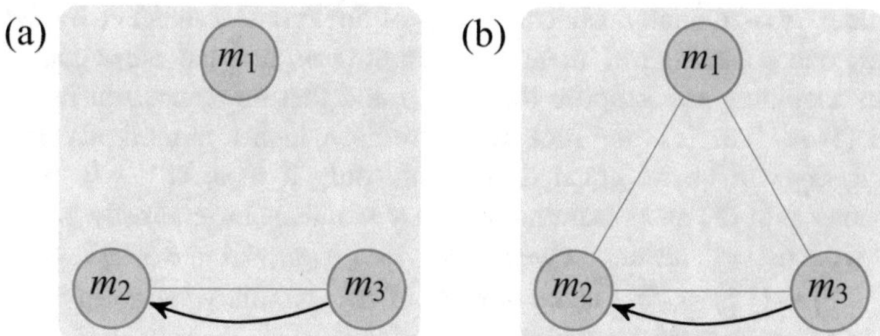

Fig. 3 A Best-Link forest (*black, curved arrows*) and auxiliary variables (*gray, straight edges*) intended to represent the transitive closure. Unfortunately, both instantiations of the auxiliary variables satisfy constraint (5). (**a**) Auxiliary variables yielding transitive closure satisfy constraint (5). (**b**) Auxiliary variables that merge the two Best-Link trees into one cluster satisfy constraint (5) as well

This constraint breaks up the definition of $t_{i,j}$ into four separate clauses. First, it is clear that $t_{i,j}$ should be 1 whenever $x_{i,j} = 1$. If $x_{i,j} \neq 1$, perhaps there is a mention m_k occurring elsewhere in the document such that (a) a Best-Link edge has been directly established between m_k and m_j, and (b) m_k is known to be connected to m_i through other Best-Link edges as indicated by our auxiliary variables (thus giving this constraint a "recursive feel"). The last three clauses are simply variations on this idea depending on the location of m_k relative to m_i and m_j. In total, the constraint will translate to $O(n^3)$ linear inequality constraints.

It should be clear that if the $t_{i,j}$ variables are given settings that correspond to the transitive closure of the Best-Link edges, then constraint (5) will be satisfied. However, this constraint also allows undesirable auxiliary variable settings. In particular, any Best-Link tree containing more than one mention can be merged into a single cluster with any other Best-Link tree via auxiliary variable settings without violating the constraint. Figure 3 illustrates this scenario, wherein the black, curved arrows represent Best-Link variables that have been set to 1, and the red, straight edges represent auxiliary variables that have been set to 1. In Fig. 3b, the auxiliary variables have merged the two Best-Link trees into a single cluster.

So why should constraint (5) allow $t_{1,2} = 1$ and $t_{1,3} = 1$? Considering $t_{1,2}$, the fourth clause of the constraint is invoked, relying on the illegitimate assignment $t_{1,3} = 1$ to make its case. Considering $t_{1,3}$, the third clause of the constraint is invoked, relying on the illegitimate assignment $t_{1,2} = 1$ to make its case. In this way, the two illegitimate assignments have reinforced each other. Neither one could exist alone, but with both in place, the constraint is satisfied.

One suggestion to fix this problem might be to include a penalty coefficient on each auxiliary variable in the objective function. Since the objective function in ILP 2 is being maximized, we would give each auxiliary variable a small, negative coefficient η. It is necessary for η to be small, since we don't want the optimal solution to be influenced by the fact that many auxiliary variables have been turned on.

Consider two mutually exclusive sets of mentions connected by Best-Link variables, one containing n_1 mentions including m_i and the other containing n_2 mentions including m_j. Suppose that $i < j$ and that no antecedent has yet been selected for m_j (i.e., it is the root of the tree in which it is currently contained). In ILP 2, $x_{i,j}$ will be set equal to 1 if and only if $\sigma(m_i, m_j) - \theta > 0$. After adding constraint (5) and assuming auxiliary variables have already been set to 1 for the two existing clusters, however, we need $\sigma(m_i, m_j) - \theta + \eta T > 0$, where $T = \binom{n_1+n_2}{2} - \left[\binom{n_1}{2} + \binom{n_2}{2}\right]$ is the number of new auxiliary variables that must be set to 1 in response to this new link.

With a little extra effort, we can determine a value for η generally for a document with n mentions. Let c_{min} be the smallest positive coefficient on a Best-Link variable:

$$c_{min} = \min_{\langle m_i, m_j \rangle \in \mathcal{M}^2} \begin{cases} \infty & \sigma(m_i, m_j) \leq \theta \\ \sigma(m_i, m_j) - \theta & \text{otherwise} \end{cases}$$

To ensure that η does not affect the Best-Link variables' settings, we must make sure that c_{min} outweighs $\eta\tau$, where τ is the largest amount of auxiliary variables that might need to be set to 1 as a result of setting a Best-Link variable to 1. τ can be maximized by assuming that the new Best-Link variable will merge all mentions in the document into a single cluster, and that before it does, the two existing clusters have an equal number of mentions (or just as equal as possible):

$$\tau = \binom{n}{2} - \left[\binom{\lceil n/2 \rceil}{2} + \binom{\lfloor n/2 \rfloor}{2}\right]$$

Now we just need $0 > \eta > -\frac{c_{min}}{\tau}$, so $\eta = -\frac{c_{min}}{2\tau}$ sounds reasonable.

An Inductive Definition While penalizing auxiliary variables can coerce constraint (5) to give us the correct clusters, this solution may not be flexible enough in general. The reason is that the final score given by the objective function to the complete assignment ends up penalizing larger clusters disproportionately more than smaller clusters. If we wish to combine our coreference model with another model, this may become problematic.[1]

We will now explore the possibility of designing our auxiliary variables so that they need not be penalized. They will be designed inductively, in a series of tiers, with each new tier representing a longer path length between all pairs of mentions. The variable named $t_{i,j}^{(l)}$ will indicate whether or not there exists a path of length exactly l along Best-Link edges (possibly containing repeated edges) between mentions m_i and m_j. We will also retain the variables $t_{i,j}$ with their originally intended semantics, and their definitions will be made possible by the observation

[1]On the other hand, there may be good linguistic motivation to penalize clusters in exactly this way, since most documents have many more small clusters than large ones.

that there can be no path between two mentions (without repeated edges) of length more than $n - 1$.

Below, we give the inductive definition of our auxiliary variables. Note that tier 2 serves as the base case, since tier 1 would be equivalent to the existing Best-Link variables.

$$\begin{aligned} t_{i,j}^{(2)} \Leftrightarrow\ & \exists k,\ k < i, \quad x_{k,j} \wedge x_{k,i} \\ & \vee \exists k,\ i < k < j,\ x_{k,j} \wedge x_{i,k} \\ & \vee \exists k,\ j < k, \quad x_{j,k} \wedge x_{i,k} \end{aligned} \tag{6}$$

$$\forall l,\ 2 < l < n, \quad \begin{aligned} t_{i,j}^{(l)} \Leftrightarrow\ & \exists k,\ k < i, \quad x_{k,j} \wedge t_{k,i}^{(l-1)} \\ & \vee \exists k,\ i < k < j,\ x_{k,j} \wedge t_{i,k}^{(l-1)} \\ & \vee \exists k,\ j < k, \quad x_{j,k} \wedge t_{i,k}^{(l-1)} \end{aligned} \tag{7}$$

$$t_{i,j} \Leftrightarrow x_{i,j} \vee \exists l,\ 2 \leq l < n,\ t_{i,j}^{l} \tag{8}$$

Under this formulation, the $t_{i,j}$ variables have the intended semantics without the need to give them non-zero coefficients in the objective function. However, it translates to $O(n^4)$ linear inequality constraints as opposed to $O(n^3)$ in the recursive formulation.

To reiterate, either the recursive or the inductive formulation will now support arbitrary constraints over the auxiliary variables. In particular, we can add constraints that force a particular pair of mentions either to be in the same cluster or not via $t_{i,j} = 1$ and $t_{i,j} = 0$, respectively. The ILP solver will then reorganize the Best-Link edges in accordance with these constraints.

6.3 Computational Troubleshooting

The explicit encoding of transitivity discussed in Sect. 6.1 and the implicit transitivity encoded over Best-Link clustering in Sect. 6.2 can both overwhelm an ILP solver on reasonably large documents. It is often necessary in these situations to discard some constraints, potentially sacrificing some correctness for processing speed. In this section, we discuss strategies for doing this.

Anti-Euclideanity First we consider the explicit encoding of transitivity. Denis and Baldridge [27] took a closer look at the constraints (4) (see ILP 4 for their more general form), naming them according to their function. Constraint (4a) inherits the name *transitivity*. Constraints (4b) and (4c) take the names *Euclideanity* and *anti-Euclideanity* respectively, as they complete the triangle.

The anti-Euclideanity constraint proved particularly interesting in their case, as it had a direct relation to the function of their independent anaphoricity model. In effect, this constraint says that if two antecedents m_i and m_j have been selected for a particular mention m_k, then m_i must also make sense as an antecedent for

m_j. However, this could be a linguistically appealing line of reasoning in general, since we generally like to think of the most cannonical mentions, those that are most likely to serve as antecedents, as occurring earlier in the document. Denis and Baldridge showed an improvement on ACE Phase II data when including only this constraint with their other models. We take a closer look at their approach including the anaphoricity model in Sect. 7.

Local Transitivity Another way to cut down the number of linear inequalities in our ILP is to restrict the transitive property to only those mentions which are "close enough" to each other. This strategy makes sense linguistically, since coreferent mentions that are closer to each other are more likely to be lexically dissimilar, and thus may benefit more from the additional evidence that transitivity constraints bring to bear. It also can be applied to any of the formulations discussed above. As an example, we show ILP 4 augmented for local transitivity below:

ILP 5

$$
\begin{array}{lll}
\max & \displaystyle\sum_{j=2}^{n}\sum_{i=1}^{j-1} c(m_i, m_j)\, x_{i,j} & \\
\text{s.t.} & x_{i,j} + x_{j,k} \leq x_{i,k} + 1 & \forall i,j,k \mid i < j < k \,\wedge\, \delta(m_i, m_k) \leq \Delta \\
 & x_{i,j} + x_{i,k} \leq x_{j,k} + 1 & \forall i,j,k \mid i < j < k \,\wedge\, \delta(m_i, m_k) \leq \Delta \\
 & x_{j,k} + x_{i,k} \leq x_{i,j} + 1 & \forall i,j,k \mid i < j < k \,\wedge\, \delta(m_i, m_k) \leq \Delta \\
 & 0 \leq x_{i,j} \leq 1 & \forall i,j \mid i < j \\
 & x_{i,j} \text{ integer} & \forall i,j \mid i < j
\end{array}
$$

In ILP 5, Δ is a constant, and $\delta : \mathscr{M} \times \mathscr{M} \rightarrow \mathbb{R}$ is a function measuring the distance between two mentions. All we need to do now is define the notion "close enough." Our distance function could measure the distance between two mentions in terms of the number of intervening mentions, or it could count the number of words or sentences between them, or anything else found to be appropriate.

Incremental Refinement The most general strategy we'll discuss is the incremental addition of violated constraints proposed by Riedel and Clarke [31]. The idea is based on the observation that although it is hard to solve an ILP, it is easy to determine if any constraints are violated when given a candidate solution. Initially, keep only the most easily satisfied constraints in the ILP. Then, after running the ILP solver, check to see if the full complement of constraints has been satisfied incidentally. If they have, we are finished. Otherwise, we add to the ILP only those specific constraints that were violated in the candidate solution. Then solve again and repeat as necessary. Needless to say, this idea can be applied on any ILP whatsoever. Riedel and Clarke evaluated their approach on dependency parsing and found it to be quite successful.

7 Combining Multiple Models

This section will explore the use of ILP to combine models under a single optimization framework in such a way that they all benefit from shared information. This type of model combination should be distinguished from so-called "pipeline" approaches in which models are evaluated in a predefined order with earlier models used as filters or features for later models. In a pipeline approach, the predictions made by each model are non-negotiable in later stages of the pipeline. In the combination approach discussed presently, however, no predictions are made until a consensus is reached among all models. Knowledge encoded in the constraints can thereby serve to improve every model's prediction quality.

The first works to combine a model of coreference with other models via ILP have been those of Denis and Baldridge [11, 27]. In this section, we discuss their approaches for combining their coreference model with a binary anaphoricity model and a multi-class named entity model. See also chapter "Detecting Non-reference and Non-anaphoricity" for further discussion of these issues.

7.1 Anaphoricity

A phrase is considered anaphoric (roughly) if it refers to some real world entity described more explicitly elsewhere in the discourse. Determining the anaphoricity of a mention differs from the coreference resolution task in two major ways. First, anaphoricity is a binary decision on a single mention; we are not interested in determining which entity is being referred to. Second, explicit references to the entity (e.g. proper names) are not considered anaphoric; instead, they are the mentions to which anaphoric mentions refer. That said, we will make the simplifying assumption that the only non-anaphoric mention in any cluster of coreferent mentions is the one occurring earliest in the document.

Given a model of anaphoricity, we'll need new ILP variables to represent its predictions. Let $y_i \in \{0, 1\}$, $1 \leq i \leq n$ indicate whether or not mention i is an anaphor. We'll also need a new scoring function $a : \mathscr{M} \rightarrow \mathbb{R}$ giving the learned anaphoricity model's score on a given mention. Next, we need to decide how our joint coreference-anaphoricity model decomposes the probability of a document, similarly to how we made the decision in Sect. 4. For the purposes of this exposition, let's define our joint model to simply multiply all the relevant coreference and anaphoricity probabilities together. Finally, we will constrain our two types of variables to agree with each other. Adding these ideas to ILP 1 results in:

ILP 6

$$
\begin{aligned}
\max \quad & \sum_{j=2}^{n} \sum_{i=1}^{j-1} c(m_i, m_j)\, x_{i,j} + \sum_{i=1}^{n} a(m_i)\, y_i \\
\text{s.t.} \quad & x_{i,j} \le y_j \ \forall i,j \mid i<j \\
& \sum_{i=1}^{j-1} x_{i,j} \ge y_j \ \forall j \\
& 0 \le x_{i,j} \le 1 \ \ \forall i,j \mid i<j \\
& 0 \le y_i \le 1 \ \ \forall i \\
& x_{i,j} \ \text{integer} \ \ \forall i,j \mid i<j \\
& y_i \ \text{integer} \ \ \forall i
\end{aligned}
$$

ILP 6 is the formulation proposed in [11]. Note that without transitivity constraints, an implicit transitive closure will need to be taken over the links in the solution. In fact, the coreference classifier is completely unconstrained other than with respect to the anaphoricity classifier. If not for those constraints, the ILP solver would simply turn on all and only those links for which $c(m_i, m_j) > 0$. With those constraints, however, the scores from the two models are weighed against each other. This causes the predictions of this joint formulation to differ from those of ILP 1 whenever and only when the two models disagree and the anaphoricity model "wins". There are exactly two such situations:

(i) $\exists j,\ a(m_j) > 0 > \max_{i<j} c(m_i, m_j)$ and $a(m_j) > -\max_{i<j} c(m_i, m_j)$; therefore it is beneficial to link the highest (albeit negative) scoring mention pair so that the anaphoricity reward can also be collected.

(ii) $\exists j,\ a(m_j) < 0,\ |\mathscr{I}^+(j)| > 0$, and $-a(m_j) > \sum_{i \in \mathscr{I}^+(j)} c(m_i, m_j)$, where $\mathscr{I}^+(j) = \{i \mid i < j \wedge c(m_i, m_j) > 0\}$; therefore it is beneficial to turn off all links in $\{\langle m_i, m_j \rangle \mid i \in \mathscr{I}^+(j)\}$ so that the anaphoricity penalty is not incurred.

Denis and Baldrige found that situation (i) was the more prevalent of the two, leading to an increase in the number of coreference links established by their model. This, in turn, lead to a performance boost as measured by the MUC scoring metric, which is known to favor larger clusters [21], and a performance degredation as measured by both B^3 and CEAF [27].

Now that we have more familiarity with the role of the anaphoricity model in this approach, we should be able to better appreciate the anti-Euclideanity constraint ((4c)) discussed in Sect. 6.3. It provides another opportunity, in addition to situation (ii) above, for the anaphoricity classifier to contribute knowledge about mention pairs that cannot be coreferent. Situation (ii) relies on the coreference and anaphoricity models to disagree, perhaps strongly, about whether or not mention m_j has any antecedents; the anaphoricity score must be low enough to counteract all of m_j's positive antecedent scores. Constraint (4c), on the other hand, enables the system to weigh evidence about the anaphoricity of two different mentions against each other. Using the specific constants mentioned in that constraint, a low anaphoricity score for m_2 need only counteract the positive coreference scores associated with $\langle m_1, m_3\rangle$ and $\langle m_2, m_3\rangle$.

7.2 *Named Entity Classification*

During coreference resolution, Denis and Baldrige assume that mention boundaries are given. Since it is a reasonable assumption that all named entities appearing in a document constitute separate mentions, the named entity recognition task becomes simply named entity classification. The ACE dataset on which they evaluated their approaches offers five named entity types: *person*, *organization*, *location*, *geo-political entity*, and *facility*.

To combine a named entity model with our existing models, we wish to follow the same line of reasoning that we used when combining the anaphoricity model with the coreference model. This time, for each mention m_i, we'll need five new ILP variables $z_{i,t} \in \{0,1\}$, $1 \le i \le n$, $t \in \mathscr{T}$, where $\mathscr{T}$ is the set of named entity types. Thus, in contrast to the binary models where a single ILP variable was sufficient, in this case we need one ILP variable for each possible prediction value. They must also be constrained so that only a single variable takes the value 1 for any given i.

Next, we'll define our joint model of the document to simply multiply all the relevant probabilities together. Using the notation of Sect. 4, the joint distribution is decomposed as:

$$P(\mathscr{D}) = \left(\prod_{j=2}^{n}\prod_{i=1}^{j-1} P(X_{i,j} = x_{i,j})\right)\prod_{i=1}^{n} P(Y_i = y_i)P(Z_i = z_i) \tag{9}$$

Note that our new ILP variables $z_{i,t}$ are not analogous to the random variables $Z_i \in \mathscr{T}$ in quite the same way that our ILP variables $x_{i,j}$ are analogous to the random variables $X_{i,j}$. However, when taken collectively with the constraint that exactly one of them will take the value 1, they serve their purpose exactly as intended.

We'll also need a new scoring function $v : \mathscr{M} \times \mathscr{T} \to \mathbb{R}$ giving the learned named entity model's score on a given mention and entity type. In light of the discussion above, the definition of this scoring function will be more straightforward than that of $c(\cdot,\cdot)$ or $a(\cdot)$. Specifically, it will represent directly a single log probability instead of the difference between two of them. As such, the ILP solver's preference for one named entity type over another will come from the comparison of all five values with each other as opposed to comparing a single coefficient's value with zero. That's why $P(Z_i = z_i)$ in Equation (9) corresponds to a summation in the objective function of ILP 7 below.

In addition, we must define the relationship between our new named entity model and the other two models. Denis and Baldrige impose the constraint that coreferential mentions must have the same named entity type. Finally, we'll complete the picture with the addition of the anti-Euclideanity constraint. Adding all of these ideas to ILP 6, we get:

ILP 7

$$
\begin{aligned}
\max \; & \sum_{j=2}^{n} \sum_{i=1}^{j-1} c(m_i, m_j)\, x_{i,j} + \sum_{i=1}^{n} \left(a(m_i)\, y_i + \sum_{t \in \mathcal{T}} v(m_i, t)\, z_{i,t} \right) \\
\text{s.t.} \; & x_{j,k} + x_{i,k} \le x_{i,j} + 1 \quad \forall i,j,k \mid i < j < k \quad \Big\} \text{ Anti-Euclideanity} \\
& \left.\begin{aligned} & x_{i,j} \le y_j && \forall i,j \mid i < j \\ & \sum_{i=1}^{j-1} x_{i,j} \ge y_j && \forall j \end{aligned}\right\} \text{ Anaphoricity} \\
& \left.\begin{aligned} & 1 - x_{i,j} \ge z_{i,t} - z_{j,t} && \forall i,j,t \mid i < j \wedge t \in \mathcal{T} \\ & 1 - x_{i,j} \ge z_{j,t} - z_{i,t} && \forall i,j,t \mid i < j \wedge t \in \mathcal{T} \\ & \sum_{t \in \mathcal{T}} z_{i,t} = 1 && \forall i \end{aligned}\right\} \text{ Named entities} \\
& \left.\begin{aligned} & 0 \le x_{i,j} \le 1 && \forall i,j \mid i < j \\ & 0 \le y_i \le 1 && \forall i \\ & 0 \le z_{i,t} \le 1 && \forall i,t \mid t \in \mathcal{T} \\ & x_{i,j} \text{ integer} && \forall i,j \mid i < j \\ & y_i \text{ integer} && \forall i \\ & z_{i,t} \text{ integer} && \forall i,t \mid t \in \mathcal{T} \end{aligned}\right\} \text{ Binary variables}
\end{aligned}
$$

Take a look at the first two named entity constraints. They are identical, except that the variables on the right hand side of the inequality switch places. In either case, the right hand side will always evaluate to a value in $\{-1, 0, 1\}$. Thus, these constraints have no effect when $x_{i,j} = 0$. However, when $x_{i,j} = 1$, we now require both versions to take a value less than or equal to 0. Since the two versions are opposites of each other, the only option is 0. In that case, for all t, $z_{i,t} = z_{j,t}$.

We should expect the incorporation of these named entity constraints to increase the precision of our coreference model, and we hope they'd improve the accuracy of our named entity classifications as well. The precision of the coreference model would increase because of cases where it believes two mentions are coreferent, but the named entity model more strongly believes their entity types are different and disallows the link. Named entity classifications would see an improvement in accuracy if there are mentions whose classification is unclear, but which are resolved by strong coreference links. Denis and Baldrige [27] confirm these intuitions about coreference precision, even when the anaphoricty and anti-Euclideanity constraints are not present, although the boost is not quite as great as simply using Closest-Link clustering with no other constraints. Unfortunately, named entity classification accuracy was not reported.

The full, three model combination in ILP 7 including all constraints resulted in big improvements in all evaluated metrics when compared to either ILP 1 alone or their pairwise classifier with Closest-Link clustering. It is interesting to note, though, that the biggest improvement in the B^3 and CEAF metrics came when finally adding in the anti-Euclideanity constraint.

8 Experiments with an ILP Based Coreference Resolution System

This section briefly presents recent experimental results with an ILP based Coreference Resolution system. The models experimented with below are slight variations of some of the models described in details earlier in this chapter and are based on a recent CoNLL shared task [29] where an ILP based system [8] was ranked first in two of the four scoring metrics (B^3 and BLANC), and ranked third in average score.

The system presented below, *Illinois-Coref* [8], closely follows the earlier discussion in the chapter. Its key inference method is the *Best-Link* method which we compare with an explicit clustering, *All-Link* method. We briefly present below the ILP formulations used, the learning protocols, and the overall architecture that was designed to incorporate linguistically-motivated constraints, several of which were developed and integrated into the system. The data set used in the experiments is the CoNLL-11 shared task data, OntoNotes-4.0.

8.1 System Architecture

Illinois-Coref follows the architecture used in Bengtson and Roth [3]. First, candidate mentions are detected. Next, a pairwise classifier is applied to each pair of mentions, generating a score that indicates their compatibility. Next, at inference stage, a coreference decoder, formulated as an ILP, aggregates these scores into mention clusters. This flexible decoder architecture allows linguistic or knowledge-based constraints to be easily added to the system: constraints may force mentions to be coreferent or non-coreferent and can be used in either of the inference protocols, the Best-Link and the All-Link. We note for completeness that, since mentions that are in singleton clusters are not annotated in the OntoNotes-4.0 data set, we remove those as a post-processing step.

Given a document, a mention detector generates a set of mention candidates that are used by the subsequent components of the system. A robust mention detector is crucial, as detection errors will propagate to the coreference stage. As we show below, the system that uses gold mentions outperforms the system that uses predicted mentions by a large margin, from 15 % to 18 % absolute difference. See [8] for more details on the mention detection.

The basic input to the inference algorithm is a pairwise mention score, which indicates the compatibility score of a pair of mentions. For any two mentions u and v, the compatibility score w_{uv} is produced by a pairwise scoring component that uses extracted features $\phi(u, v)$ and linguistic constraints c:

$$w_{uv} = \mathbf{w} \cdot \phi(u, v) + c(u, v) + t, \tag{10}$$

where $\mathbf{w}$ is a weight vector learned from training data, $c(u, v)$ is a compatibility score given by the constraints, and t is a threshold parameter (to be tuned). The features used are the same as in Bengtson and Roth [3], with the knowledge extracted from the OntoNotes-4.0 annotation. The exact use of the scores and the procedure for learning weights $\mathbf{w}$ varies and depends on the inference algorithms described next.

The first inference method studied experimentally is the Best-Link approach described earlier. Given a pairwise scorer $\mathbf{w}$, we compute the compatibility scores — w_{uv} from Equation (10) — for all mention pairs u and v. Let y_{uv} be a binary variable, such that $y_{uv} = 1$ *only if* u and v are in the same cluster. For a document d, *Best-Link* solves the following ILP formulation:

$$\begin{aligned} \max \ & \sum\nolimits_{u,v} w_{uv} y_{uv} \\ \text{s.t.} \ & \sum\nolimits_{u<v} y_{uv} \leq 1 \ \forall v, \\ & y_{uw} \in \{0, 1\}. \end{aligned} \tag{11}$$

Equation (11) generates a set of connected components and all the mentions in each connected component constitute an entity.

In order to support the *Best-Link* inference, the pairwise scoring function $\mathbf{w}$ needs to be trained in a way that is compatible with it. Namely:

- Positive examples: for each mention u, we construct a positive example (u, v), where v is the closest preceding mention in u's equivalence class.
- Negative examples: all mention pairs (u, v), where v is a preceding mention of u and u, v are not in the same class.

As a result of the singleton mentions not being annotated in the current data set, there is an inconsistency in the sample distributions in the training and inference phases. Therefore, we apply the mention detector to the training set, and train the classifier using the union set of gold and predicted mentions.

We compare the *Best-Link* method with an explicit clustering approach, the *All-Link* approach. *All-Link* scores a cluster of mentions by including all possible pairwise links in the score. It is also known as correlational clustering [1] and has been applied to coreference resolution in the form of supervised clustering [13, 24] before. The ILP formulation of *All-Link* is given below.

$$\begin{aligned} \max \ & \sum\nolimits_{u,v} w_{uv} y_{uv} \\ \text{s.t.} \ & y_{uw} \geq y_{uv} + y_{vw} - 1 \ \forall u, w, v, \\ & y_{uw} \in \{0, 1\}. \end{aligned} \tag{12}$$

The inequality constraints in Equation (12) enforce the transitive closure of the clustering. The solution of Equation (12) is a set of cliques, and the mentions in the same cliques corefer, as in ILP 3. Note that an explicit enumeration of the transitivity constraints as given in ILP 4 may be too constrained. In practice, it was found that dropping one of the three transitivity constraints for each triple of mention variables performs better, and this is the version used in the experiments (a similar observation was made in [27]). Training the scoring function **w** needs to be somewhat different in this case, since all pairwise edges could take part in a decision. A a structured perceptron algorithm is used in this case, and the details can be found in [8].

Both inference methods compared here allow an incorporation of constraints. The constraints used in this experimental study are based on an analysis of mistakes made on a development set. See [8] for some more discussion of the constraints. It is worth noting that, as shown in the experimental results below, there is a lot of room for improvement by augmenting the system with more knowledge based constraints.

8.2 Experiments

The following experiments presents the performance of the system on the OntoNotes-4.0 data set. Table 1 shows the performance for the two inference protocols, *Best-Link* and *All-Link*, with and without constraints. *Best-Link* outperforms *All-Link* for both predicted and gold mentions. Adding constraints improves the performance slightly for *Best-Link* on predicted mentions. In the other configurations, the constraints either do not affect the performance or slightly degrade it. Table 2 shows the results obtained on the test data, using the best system configurations found on a development set. We report results on predicted mentions with predicted boundaries, predicted mentions with gold boundaries, and when using gold mentions. (Note that the *gold boundaries* results are different from the *gold mention* results; specifying gold mentions requires coreference resolution to exclude singleton mentions; gold boundaries were provided by the shared task organizers and also include singleton mentions.)

Table 1 The performance of the two inference protocols on gold and predicted mentions. The systems are trained on the OntoNotes training set and evaluated on a development set. We report the F1 scores (%) on mention detection (MD) and coreference metrics (MUC, BCUB, CEAF). The column AVG shows the averaged scores of the three metrics

	Pred. mentions w/pred. boundaries					Gold mentions			
Method	MD	MUC	BCUB	CEAF	AVG	MUC	BCUB	CEAF	AVG
Best-Link	64.70	55.67	69.21	43.78	56.22	80.58	75.68	64.69	**73.65**
Best-Link w/Const.	64.69	55.8	69.29	43.96	**56.35**	80.56	75.02	64.24	73.27
All-Link	63.30	54.56	68.50	42.15	55.07	77.72	73.65	59.17	70.18
All-Link w/Const.	63.39	54.56	68.46	42.20	55.07	77.94	73.43	59.47	70.28

Table 2 The results of our the system on the OntoNotes test set. The system uses *Best-Link* decoding with constraints on predicted mentions and *Best-Link* decoding without constraints on gold mentions. The systems are trained on the union of the training and development sets

Task	MD	MUC	BCUB	CEAF	AVG
Pred. mentions w/pred. boundaries	64.88	57.15	67.14	41.94	55.96
Pred. mentions w/gold boundaries	67.92	59.79	68.65	41.42	56.62
Gold mentions	–	82.55	73.70	65.24	73.83

8.3 *State of the Art*

The best published results on coreference resolution in time of the publication of this chapter are achieved by an ILP-based system, described in [10]. The approach presented there augments the methods described earlier in this chapter in two key ways. First, instead of first training the best-link pairwise function between mentions and then using it in the ILP inference, learning of the pairwise function is performed jointly with inference, making use of a novel latent structural SVM approach. Second, and more relevant from this chapter's perspective, the learned pairwise scoring function is augmented with knowledge-based constraints. Rather than making use of the learned pairwise function $s(d, w)$, a function of the document d parameterized using a weight vector w, this approach makes use of the scoring function

$$s(d, w) + \sum_{p=1}^{n} \rho_p \psi_p(d, C),$$

where the second term is the score contributed by domain specific constraints $\psi_1, \ldots, \psi_n$ with their respective scores $\rho_1, \ldots, \rho_n$. In particular, $\psi_p(d, C)$ measures the extent to which a given clustering C satisfies the pth constraint.

9 Conclusion

In this chapter, we introduced Integer Linear Programming and reviewed some of its best performing applications to coreference resolution in the literature. We developed some intuitions for how to pose ILPs based on learned models and to how expert knowledge can be encoded as constraints that the learned models must then respect. We also got a sense for some of the pitfalls encountered during both the development of an ILP and its deployment as well as how to deal with them. Finally, we saw how ILP can create an environment in which independently learned models share knowledge for their mutual benefit.

The experimental results reported are very promising. The ILP formulation is very simple and it provides system designers with a lot of flexibility in incorporating knowledge. Indeed, this is where we believe most of the research should focus. There is still a long way to go, since there is little success so far in figuring out what declarative–linguistics, background and structural knowledge–can contribute to better coreference resolution. In particular, the expert knowledge and additional constraints offered for use in ILPs thus far have, for the most part, concerned only pairs of mentions. While ILP gives these constraints a more global effect, the formulations could also provide ways to encode more expressive knowledge. We believe that knowledge about the coherence of entire clusters or the document as a whole could provide significant advancement. ILP gives us the potential to encode this information easily. Interestingly, the challenges so far were not those of tractability, but rather those of encoding the appropriate knowledge in a way that supports better coreference resolution.

Very recent work [28] makes a proposal for knowledge acquisition and representation required to address hard cases of coreference resolution (e.g., hard pronoun resolution cases); in particular, it shows how an ILP framework can be used to address these quite successfully, providing additional evidence and hope that more progress can be made within this framework,

References

1. Bansal, N., Blum, A., Chawla, S.: Correlation clustering. In: IEEE Symposium of Foundation of Computer Science, Vancouver (2002)
2. Barzilay, R., Lapata, M.: Aggregation via set partitioning for natural language generation. In: Proceedings of HLT/NAACL, New York, June 2006
3. Bengtson, E., Roth, D.: Understanding the value of features for coreference resolution. In: Proceedings of the Conference on Empirical Methods for Natural Language Processing (EMNLP), Honolulu, pp. 294–303, Oct 2008
4. Bertsimas, D., Tsitsiklis, J.N.: Introduction to Linear Optimization. Volume 6 of Athena Scientific Series in Optimization and Neural Computation. Athena Scientific, Nashua (1997)
5. Boyd, S., Vandenberghe, L.: Convex Optimization. Cambridge University Press, New York (2004)
6. Chang, M., Ratinov, L., Rizzolo, N., Roth, D.: Learning and inference with constraints. In: Proceedings of the National Conference on Artificial Intelligence (AAAI), Chicago, pp. 1513–1518, July 2008
7. Chang, M., Ratinov, L., Roth, D.: Constraints as prior knowledge. In: ICML Workshop on Prior Knowledge for Text and Language Processing, Helsinki, pp. 32–39, July 2008
8. Chang, K., Samdani, R., Rozovskaya, A., Rizzolo, N., Sammons, M., Roth, D.: Inference protocols for coreference resolution. In: Proceedings of the Annual Conference on Computational Natural Language Learning (CoNLL), Portland, pp. 40–44. Association for Computational Linguistics (2011)
9. Chang, M., Ratinov, L., Roth, D.: Structured learning with constrained conditional models. Mach. Learn. **88**(3), 399–431 (2012)
10. Chang, K.-W., Samdani, R., Roth, D.: A constrained latent variable model for coreference resolution. In: Proceedings of the Conference on Empirical Methods for Natural Language Processing (EMNLP), Seattle (2013)

11. Denis, P., Baldridge, J.: Joint determination of anaphoricity and coreference resolution using integer programming. In: Proceedings of the Annual Meeting of the North American Association of Computational Linguistics (NAACL), Rochester (2007)
12. Finkel, J.R., Manning, C.D.: The importance of syntactic parsing and inference in semantic role labeling. In: Proceedings of the Annual Meeting of the Association for Computational Linguistics – Human Language Technology Conference, Short Papers (ACL-HLT), Columbus (2008)
13. Finley, T., Joachims, T.: Supervised clustering with support vector machines. In: Proceedings of the International Conference on Machine Learning (ICML), Bonn (2005)
14. Freund, R., Mizuno, S.: Interior point methods: current status and future directions. In: Frenk, H., Roos, K., Terlaky, T., Zhang, S. (eds.) High Performance Optimization. Volume 33 of Applied Optimization, chapter 18, pp. 441–446. Springer, New York (2000)
15. Freund, Y., Schapire, R.E.: Large margin classification using the perceptron algorithm. Mach. Learn. **37**(3), 277–296 (1999)
16. Hoffman, A., Kruskal, J.: Integral boundary points of convex polyhedra. In: Kuhn, H., Tucker, A. (eds.) Annals of Mathematics Studies, vol. 38, pp. 223–246. Princeton University Press, Princeton (1956). Linear Inequalities and Related Systems
17. Jeter, M.W.: Mathematical Programming: An Introduction to Optimization. Volume 102 of Monographs and Textbooks in Pure and Applied Mathematics. Marcel Dekker, New York (1986)
18. Karmarkar, N.: A new polynomial-time algorithm for linear programming. In: Proceedings of the ACM Symposium on the Theory of Computing, New York, pp. 302–311. The Association for Computing Machinery (1984)
19. Karp, R.: Reducibility among combinatorial problems. In: Miller, R., Thatcher, J. (eds.) Complexity of Computer Computations, pp. 85–103. Plenum Press, New York (1972)
20. Kundu, G., Srikumar, V., Roth, D.: Margin-based decomposed amortized inference. In: Proceedings of the Annual Meeting of the Association for Computational Linguistics (ACL), Sofia, vol. 8 (2013)
21. Luo, X.: On coreference resolution performance metrics. In: Proceedings of the Conference on Empirical Methods for Natural Language Processing (EMNLP), Vancouver (2005)
22. Marciniak, T., Strube, M.: Beyond the pipeline: discrete optimization in NLP. In: Proceedings of the Annual Conference on Computational Natural Language Learning (CoNLL), Ann Arbor, pp. 136–143. Association for Computational Linguistics, June 2005
23. Martins, A., Smith, N., Xing, E.: Concise integer linear programming formulations for dependency parsing. In: Proceedings of the Annual Meeting of the Association for Computational Linguistics (ACL), pp. 342–350. Suntec, Singapore, Aug 2009. Association for Computational Linguistics
24. Mccallum, A., Wellner, B.: Toward conditional models of identity uncertainty with application to proper noun coreference. In: The Conference on Advances in Neural Information Processing Systems (NIPS), Vancouver (2003)
25. Nash, J.: The (Dantzig) simplex method for linear programming. Comput. Sci. Eng. **2**(1), 29–31 (2000)
26. Ng, V., Cardie, C.: Improving machine learning approaches to coreference resolution. In: Proceedings of the Annual Meeting of the Association for Computational Linguistics (ACL), Philadelphia (2002)
27. Pascal, D., Baldridge, J.: Global joint models for coreference resolution and named entity classification. In: Procesamiento del Lenguaje Natural. Sociedad Española para el Procesamiento del Lenguaje Natural (SEPLN), Spain (2009)
28. Peng, H., Khashabi, D., Roth, D.: Solving hard coreference problems. In: Proceedings of the Annual Meeting of the North American Association of Computational Linguistics (NAACL), Denver, vol. 5 (2015)
29. Pradhan, S., Ramshaw, L., Marcus, M., Palmer, M., Weischedel, R., Xue, N.: Conll-2011 shared task: modeling unrestricted coreference in ontonotes. In: Proceedings of the Annual Conference on Computational Natural Language Learning (CoNLL), Portland (2011)

30. Punyakanok, V., Roth, D., Yih, W.: The importance of syntactic parsing and inference in semantic role labeling. Comput. Linguist. **34**(2), 257–287 (2008)
31. Riedel, S., Clarke, J.: Incremental integer linear programming for non-projective dependency parsing. In: Proceedings of the Conference on Empirical Methods for Natural Language Processing (EMNLP), Sydney, pp. 129–137 (2006)
32. Rizzolo, N., Roth, D.: Modeling discriminative global inference. In: Proceedings of the First International Conference on Semantic Computing (ICSC), Irvine, pp. 597–604. IEEE, Sept 2007
33. Rizzolo, N., Roth, D.: Learning based Java for rapid development of NLP systems. In: Proceedings of the International Conference on Language Resources and Evaluation, Valletta, May 2010
34. Roth, D., Yih, W.: A linear programming formulation for global inference in natural language tasks. In: Ng, H.T., Riloff, E. (eds.) Proceedings of the Annual Conference on Computational Natural Language Learning (CoNLL), Boston, pp. 1–8. Association for Computational Linguistics (2004)
35. Roth, D., Yih, W.: Integer linear programming inference for conditional random fields. In: Proceedings of the International Conference on Machine Learning (ICML), Bonn, pp. 737–744 (2005)
36. Roth, D., Yih, W.: Global inference for entity and relation identification via a linear programming formulation. In: Getoor, L., Taskar, B. (eds.) Introduction to Statistical Relational Learning. MIT, Cambridge (2007)
37. Soon, W.M., Ng, H.T., Lim, D.C.Y.: A machine learning approach to coreference resolution of noun phrases. Comput. Linguist. **27**(4), 521-544 (2001)
38. Srikumar, V., Roth, D.: A joint model for extended semantic role labeling. In: Proceedings of the Conference on Empirical Methods for Natural Language Processing (EMNLP), Edinburgh (2011)

Extracting Anaphoric Agreement Properties from Corpora

Shane Bergsma

Abstract Anaphora resolution algorithms have long made use of the reliable agreement between pronouns and their antecedents in properties such as gender and number. To apply constraints or preferences for anaphoric agreement, real systems need ways to automatically determine these properties for arbitrary noun phrases, in context. This chapter describes a variety of algorithms for extracting noun gender and number, ranging from simple heuristics to large-scale machine learning approaches. We describe the drawbacks and advantages of the different algorithms, focusing mostly on English anaphora resolution. We pay special attention to recent methods for extracting agreement information directly from large volumes of raw text.

Keywords Extracting Anaphoric Agreement Properties from corpora corpus-derived approaches • Agreement properties • Linguistic resources

1 Introduction

In human communication, the form of a pronoun gives a listener some clues about which specific entity is being referred to. For example, consider two possible forms for the third-person pronoun in (1):

1. My uncle introduced me to backgammon. I still love to play {him, it}.

When the pronoun *him* is used, we know the referent is masculine, and we identify the antecedent as the likewise-masculine *uncle*. When the pronoun *it* is used, the antecedent is interpreted as the neutral noun *backgammon*.

In English, pronouns reliably reflect the semantic gender, number, and person of their referent. In other natural languages, a pronoun may also reflect its referent's age, animacy, proximity, divinity, social familiarity, and many other things. When a pronoun reflects various semantic or grammatical properties of its antecedent, as *him*

S. Bergsma (✉)
Department of Computer Science, University of Saskatchewan, JHU Center of Excellence, Baltimore, Saskatoon, SK, Canada S7N 5C9
e-mail: shane.a.bergsma@gmail.com

M. Poesio et al. (eds.), *Anaphora Resolution*, Theory and Applications of Natural Language Processing, DOI 10.1007/978-3-662-47909-4_12

does with *uncle*, we say the pronoun *agrees* with its antecedent in these properties. Eye-tracking studies have shown that agreement information is used rapidly when humans resolve pronouns [2].[1]

In addition to providing information about its referent, a pronoun may also provide information about its syntactic role in the sentence. For example, *he* inflects to become *him* as an object, *his* as a possessive, etc. In some languages, a possessive pronoun may also reflect the gender of the noun it *modifies*. For example, in French the first-person possessive pronoun *mon* is used with masculine nouns, as in *mon livre* (*livre* is masculine), while *ma* is used with feminine ones, as in *ma soeur*. In both cases we nevertheless know the pronoun has a first-person, singular referent.

It seems inconceivable that a computer program could automatically and reliably resolve anaphora to their antecedents without exploiting agreement information. Indeed, anaphora resolution algorithms have long made use of such knowledge. For example, Hobbs' algorithm traverses the parse tree of a sentence "in a particular order looking for noun phrases of the correct gender and number" [31]. In Brennan et al.'s centering approach, a list of discourse entities is created for each pronoun, "which match [the pronoun's] agreement features" [10]. Lappin and Leass use a gender/number filter to remove candidates from later scoring [34]. Mitkov's knowledge-poor approach considers as potential candidates only those noun phrases "which agree in gender and number with the pronominal anaphor" [41]. In fact, this author knows of no proposed anaphora resolution system that does not exploit agreement information in some way. The question then, is how?

Using agreement in anaphora resolution involves three steps: (a) determining the relevant semantic properties of the pronoun, (b) determining the relevant semantic properties of each candidate antecedent, and (c) exploiting the agreement or disagreement between these properties when making resolution decisions. The first step is straightforward; since the number of unique pronouns in most languages is limited, we can simply manually encode the semantic properties of the different pronoun forms, and provide this information as prior knowledge to our system. For example, Table 1 gives the semantic properties of English pronouns. The second

Table 1 Semantic properties of English pronouns

Pronoun group	Person	Number	Gender
He, his, him, himself	Third	Singular	Masculine
She, her, hers, herself	Third	Singular	Feminine
It, its, itself	Third	Singular	Neutral
They, their, them, themselves	Third	Plural	Masculine/feminine/neutral
I, my, me, myself, mine	First	Singular	Masculine/feminine
We, our, us, ourselves, ours	First	Plural	Masculine/feminine
You, your, yourself, yours	Second	Singular	Masculine/feminine
You, your, yourselves, yours	Second	Plural	masculine/feminine

[1]See chapter "Linguistic and Cognitive Evidence About Anaphora" of this book for further discussion on the role of agreement information in human anaphora interpretation.

step is usually the tricky part. We need the knowledge that *uncle* is masculine while *backgammon* is neutral. The manner in which we acquire and encode this knowledge affects how the agreement properties are exploited in the third step. This chapter focuses on practical approaches for acquiring the needed semantic knowledge, and effective ways to use this knowledge in real pronoun resolution systems.

Our focus, like that of the community, is mainly on resolving English pronouns. The agreement properties we are concerned with are the gender and number of English noun phrases (NPs). We also discuss work that focuses on distinguishing masculine/feminine NPs from those that are neutral. This work is sometimes referred to as *animacy identification* [45], although see Zaenen et al. [53] for a related definition of animacy (in work unrelated to anaphora resolution).

We first discuss how the usage of anaphoric agreement properties has evolved over time. This leads to a discussion of the two dominant trends of the modern era: (a) leveraging existing tools and resources (such as word lists, taggers, named-entity recognition software, etc.), and (b) learning agreement properties directly from text. The latter trend is the main focus of this chapter. Finally, we conclude by making some observations on how we can make and measure progress in the future.

2 The Evolving Use of Anaphoric Agreement Properties

In early anaphora resolution systems, candidate antecedents that did not match in gender and number were often filtered by hand during the manual evaluation of the algorithms. Unfortunately, this meant that early anaphora resolution systems could not be applied automatically to unrestricted text.

Over time, a greater emphasis was placed on "deliverables and evaluation" in all areas of computational linguistics [15]. In particular, the inclusion of coreference resolution as a task in the Message Understanding Conferences (MUC) [42, 43] helped spur fully-automatic anaphora resolution algorithms. Some of these algorithms included mechanisms for applying anaphoric agreement properties. We discuss the dominant approaches in Sect. 3.

Early automatic pronoun-resolution systems often focused on technical manuals [34, 41]. Aside from being "particularly well behaved text" [33], manuals include few masculine or feminine entities. Semantic agreement is thus less important, as morphological cues alone provide good indicators for distinguishing singular from plural NPs. Systems that were applied to news text, where agreement information is more valuable, continued to use manual involvement [11, 52]. For example, Byron and Tetreault [11] provide, for each discourse entity, "the referent's animacy and gender from a hand-coded agreement-feature database."

Kennedy and Boguraev [33] applied their automatic anaphora resolution algorithm to a variety of text genres, but report that gender mismatch accounts for 35 % of their system's errors. They note that using a "lexical database which includes more detailed gender information will result in improved accuracy."

Similarly, Stuckardt [51] reports that "30 % of [his pronoun resolution system's] precision errors are due to the assignment of incorrect gender attributes," and these "may be eliminated if additional lexical information becomes available."

One notable exception to these early, gender-poor approaches was the influential work of Ge et al. [23], which we return to in Sect. 4.3. They give the first approach to automatically extracting noun gender and number information from corpora.

3 Extracting Agreement Properties from Existing Resources

In this section, we describe approaches to determining NP gender/number that are not based on learning from corpora. Here we focus on approaches that assign gender using simple heuristics or existing lexical resources.

3.1 Obvious Disagreement

When resolving pronouns, we often encounter candidate antecedents that are themselves pronouns. Anaphora systems should prevent resolving a pronoun from one semantic class (like neutral) to pronouns of another (like plural). In English, we prohibit coreference between pairs of pronouns from different rows of Table 1.

There are some exceptions that arise due to the transitivity of the coreference relation. Generally, if A refers to B and B refers to C, then A and C must also be considered coreferent. This can lead to problems as in the following example:

> The law requires the lower-earning partner to choose between taking *his* or *her* own earned benefit or one-half of the partner's benefit.

In this case, both *his* and *her* refer to "the lower-earning partner," and thus they must also be coreferent with one another. Fortunately many such gender-neutral constructions can be easily identified and specially handled. More difficult cases arise in data where entities such as *China* and *the Chinese* can be marked as coreferent (as in MUC annotations). Both neutral and plural pronouns might therefore end up in the same coreference chain. Note that applying a disagreement filter would not prevent us from finding at least one correct antecedent; problems only arise if we require the final sets of coreferent entities (formed by transitive closure) to be consistent in their semantic properties.

Gender information is also apparent for nouns prefaced by a gender-specific honorific such as *Mr* or *Mrs*. Whenever a form like *Mr. Diller* is observed in text, Soon et al. [50] propagate the appropriate gender to other nouns in the document with a matching final string, e.g. to an earlier occurrence of the full name *Peter H. Diller*.

3.2 Named Entity Recognition

Named entity recognition (NER) is the process of identifying and classifying proper nouns. Named-entities are mapped into pre-defined categories, such as PERSON, ORGANIZATION, or LOCATION. These categories are known as the named-entity *types*. NER can be performed with very high accuracy (e.g. an F-measure of 93.4 in [37]). Since each named entity type can generally only be referred to by a subset of the pronoun groups (e.g., *it* is used for LOCATIONs), NER can be used as a preprocessing step for anaphora resolution in order to provide semantic information for proper nouns [26, 50]. For this reason, some previous work in the anaphora resolution community has focused solely on acquiring gender information for *common* nouns, assuming NER will handle the proper noun cases [45].

However, there are compelling reasons to also extract agreement information for proper nouns. First of all, NER systems usually only assign categories to a subset of the proper nouns in text, and would not be able to provide the semantic properties for named entities like *Lassie* or *Cabernet Sauvignon*. Secondly, NER makes no distinction between feminine and masculine entities, so knowledge of named-entity type alone does not prevent resolving *he* to *Margaret Thatcher*. Finally, it has recently been shown that knowledge of noun gender and number can improve the accuracy of NER itself [19, 32], and is thus useful in its own right. Systems that perform anaphora resolution and named-entity recognition jointly also implicitly exploit gender information when performing NER [17, 25]; Daumé and Marcu show that a joint NER/coreference model performs better than a pipelined approach [17].

3.3 Parsing and Tagging

In English, number information can be determined using standard parsers or part-of-speech taggers; these tools associate number information with tagged nouns [20]. For example, the widely-used tag set from the Penn Treebank includes tags specifically for plural common (NNS) and plural proper (NNPS) nouns. Such information is exploited in most anaphora resolution systems. English parsers and taggers mark number, but not gender, because number agreement can be used to resolve syntactic ambiguity [20].

In languages having grammatical gender (as opposed to the natural or semantic gender of English), there are often gender-specific tags in standard tag sets. Supervised tagging techniques can therefore assign gender to words [28]. These taggers pay attention to gender-indicating features of both the word's context and its form, and often require large amounts of gold standard data to train. An approach to determining grammatical gender using minimal resources was proposed in [16], and achieves very high accuracy on five European test languages.

Past research has observed that it can sometimes be harmful to rely directly on tags for number agreement properties [4]. For example, Mitkov [40] reports an error where the correct antecedent *data* is filtered as a candidate for the pronoun *it* because *data* is interpreted as a plural noun while *it* is singular. Another disagreement arises when singular, collective nouns like *team* are referred to by plural pronouns. To handle these cases, Mitkov [41] created a comprehensive list of number agreement exceptions and provides this information to his anaphora resolution system. Daumé and Marcu [17] attempted to automatically collect such cases by looking for fillers of the pattern "members of the ..." in a large corpus.

3.4 WordNet

Many anaphora resolution systems acquire agreement properties using WordNet [5, 12, 18, 20, 30, 44, 45, 50]. WordNet is a large-scale, widely-used and richly-annotated lexical resource [21]. WordNet arranges words into sets of synonyms (synsets), and links the synsets via semantic relations. A word may occur in multiple synsets if it has multiple senses. A particularly useful WordNet relation is hyponymy, also known as the *is-a* relation. For example, *ostrich* is a hyponym of *bird*. Hypernymy is the inverse relation of hyponymy; *bird* is a hypernym of *ostrich*. Hyponym/hypernym relations between the WordNet synsets form a hierarchy of lexical relations. For examples, an *ostrich* is a *bird*, which is a *vertebrate*, which is a *chordate*, which is an *animal*, which is an *organism*, etc. Noun synsets in WordNet are partitioned into separate hierarchies; each noun synset in WordNet is related, via a chain of hypernyms, to one of twenty-five *unique beginners* [21, Sec. 1.2]. A unique beginner "can be regarded as a primitive semantic component of all words in its hierarchically structured semantic field" [38]. The unique beginners in WordNet include *animal*, *person*, *event*, and *relation*.

If we assign gender (or any other semantic property) to a unique beginner, we can infer the gender of all nouns in its hierarchy, since all nouns in the hierarchy should share the semantic properties of the most primitive element. For example, Harabagiu et al. [30] declare all synsets in the *person* hierarchy to be compatible with both masculine and feminine pronouns. Harabagiu et al. also exploit two other heuristics for assigning gender information using WordNet: (1) gender information is propagated to a synset if one of the first four words in the gloss of that synset has already been assigned gender information, and (2) the appropriate gender is propagated to all the nouns in a synset if any element of the synset is a phrase containing the words *male*, *female*, or *woman* (e.g. *cleaning lady* will inherit the feminine gender since it is in the same synset as *cleaning woman*). Whenever gender is assigned to a synset, all the hyponyms of that synset also inherit the gender properties.

In earlier work using WordNet, Denber [18] makes all synsets that are hyponyms of the synset *male* masculine, all hyponyms of *female* feminine, all hyponyms of *object* neutral, and all hyponyms of *creature* animate (masculine or feminine).

The WordNet-based procedures output a gender assignment (potentially with the value *unknown*) for each synset in WordNet. Of course, for a given noun in text, it may not be clear which synset the noun belongs to, since nouns may belong to multiple synsets. Soon et al. [50] simply use the first sense of the head noun of each noun phrase (which corresponds to the most frequent sense of that noun), while Evans and Orăsan [20] compute an average score over all senses. Harabagiu et al. [30] assign a noun's gender via the disjunction of the properties of all the noun's senses. It is not clear how often nouns have distinct synsets with conflicting genders, nor has it been determined which of the above procedures works best.

Regardless of how information from the different senses are combined, we still have the issue that these approaches provide gender/number for noun *types*, but we ultimately need to assign gender/number to noun *tokens*, in context. A token has one sense (and gender), a type may have many. We will revisit this issue later.

Since WordNet is a manually-constructed database, it also suffers from both low coverage (especially for proper nouns) and the inclusion of very rare senses. For example, the nouns *computer* and *company* both have a WordNet sense that is a hyponym of *person* [47]. Some of the above algorithms would thus falsely indicate these nouns are compatible with masculine and feminine pronouns.

3.5 List Data

Another way to assign gender information is to check whether the noun, or part of the noun, occurs on lists of entities with known genders. For example, Cardie and Wagstaff [12] and Soon et al. [50] make use of lists of common human first names. Denber [18] and Bengtson and Roth [5] uses lists of male, female, and place names. Daumé and Marcu [17] use about 40 lists of human names (from censuses and baby name books), countries, cities, islands, ports, provinces, states, airports (from the FAA), company names (from NASDAQ/NYSE web pages), etc. They also use the output of an existing NER system, creating lists of named entities from names that were tagged at least 100 times in a large corpus. Similarly, Bergsma et al. [9] use lists of first names, family names, cities, provinces, countries, corporations, languages, etc. In the latter two approaches, rather than assigning gender directly to the various lists, the presence of a noun on a list is used as a feature in a classifier. The association between each list and a gender/number is learned from training data.

Applying list data can be problematic because some entries inevitably correspond to very rare senses of a word. For example, the nouns *London*, *Paris*, *America*, and *India* are all among the top 1000 female baby names of 2009 in the United States (www.ssa.gov/OACT/babynames/). Of course, in a typical document, it would almost always be harmful to allow feminine pronouns to resolve to these words.

4 Learning Agreement Properties from Corpora

There are many advantages to using existing resources. Chiefly, it allows anaphora resolution researchers to focus on applying knowledge rather than acquiring it from scratch. However, previous work suggests that knowledge from existing resources may be insufficient for robust anaphora resolution. Several previous studies have shown that when applying such knowledge in real systems, gender/number mistakes remain a significant source of anaphora resolution errors [4, 18, 33, 51]. Unfortunately, it is also difficult to say which of the above methods is most reliable. The problem is that methods for establishing anaphoric agreement are usually only subcomponents of larger systems; thus targeted evaluations, and empirical comparisons of different approaches, are usually omitted from published papers.

In the absence of this information, however, we can still sketch the obvious drawbacks of the above approaches. First of all, each approach only covers a subset of the noun phrases for which we need information. While most focus on proper nouns, WordNet-based methods only have good coverage for common nouns. Secondly, some approaches only provide a subset of the properties we need. For example, NER does not distinguish between masculine and feminine, and English taggers do not distinguish between masculine, feminine, and neutral. Finally, when using lists and lexical databases, we do not know whether a particular entry is widely applicable or if it only represents a rare usage (like a *computer* or *America* being a person). Essentially, existing resources are inadequate because they have not been specifically designed with the objective of supporting anaphora resolution.

One possible solution, which has received growing attention in recent years, is to collect the agreement properties directly from raw text. By adopting this solution, we could ensure that we collect all the properties we need (i.e., both gender and number) for all the types of nouns in text (i.e., both proper and common nouns). This section investigates a range of such solutions.

Many of these approaches are based on a common process. We first locate instances in text where NPs and pronouns are likely coreferent. We then count how often each NP co-occurs in these instances with pronouns of masculine, feminine, neutral, and plural gender/number. Since a noun like *computer* often co-occurs with neutral pronouns, *computer* will be interpreted as neutral.

The output of the process is sometimes called a *gender/number model*. The model gives the gender/number likelihoods for a wide range of noun phrases. For example, Table 2 provides some sample gender information from the gender model of Bergsma and Lin [8] (where the counts have been converted to percentages). In this data the collective noun *team* is mostly neutral, but plural reference is very possible. Thus unlike other approaches, special handling of collective nouns is not needed. Note also that, as desired, *company* and *computer* are unambiguously neutral. Finally, note that reasonable scores are assigned to both proper and common nouns, and to those that may be both, like *rivers*; e.g., *Doc Rivers*, *Joan Rivers*, *subterranean rivers*, etc. Of course, like the WordNet and list-based approaches, this is a model of noun *types*, rather than a predictor for noun *tokens*, in context.

Table 2 Example noun gender/number proportions (%)

Word	Masculine	Feminine	Neutral	Plural
Company	0.6	0.1	98.1	1.2
Computer	1.4	0.5	96.3	1.7
Condoleeza rice	4.0	92.7	0.0	3.2
Mosquitos	0.6	0.0	1.3	98.1
Pat	58.3	30.6	6.2	4.9
President	94.1	3.0	1.5	1.4
Rivers	73.8	6.1	3.9	16.1
Team	4.0	0.5	75.4	20.1
Wife	9.9	83.3	0.8	6.1

We can use this information probabilistically in an anaphora resolver. For example, since *president* is usually referred to by masculine pronouns (but sometimes also by feminine ones) we incorporate this bias as a preference in the resolution system, rather than as a hard constraint. The philosophy is to keep all the information we acquired, and let the later stages determine how best to apply it. We now describe a range of corpus-based approaches that collect similar kinds of information.

4.1 Supervised Approaches

Imagine someone has labeled tens of millions of noun phrases, in context, with gender information. If MASC, FEM, NEUT, and PLUR are the tags for masculine, feminine, neutral and plural gender/number, then a segment of such hypothetical data might look like (ignoring the marking of the NP boundaries):

> Sportswriters/PLUR complain that baseball/NEUT's owners/PLUR are corrupting the game/NEUT. The owners/PLUR gripe that players/PLUR are destroying it/NEUT from within by demanding too much money/NEUT. Recent developments/PLUR have escalated the doomsaying/NEUT... Last week/NEUT, the Atlanta Braves/PLUR superstar pitcher/MASC Greg Maddux/MASC accepted a five-year contract/NEUT worth $57.5 million/NEUT, the biggest ever.

If we had such data, we could extract a gender model directly from the annotations. We would just count how often each NP is labeled as each gender/number. Our example provides instances of *superstar pitcher* and *Greg Maddux* being masculine, *sportswriters, owners, players, developments* and *Atlanta Braves* being plural, and a variety of nouns being neutral. Unfortunately, no such data exists at a scale that would allow us to extract a comprehensive gender/number database.

We also have some labeled *anaphora resolution* data. Such data indirectly provides gender/number information. Consider the following annotation:

> Sportswriters complain that Major League Baseball's greedy owners are corrupting the game. The owners gripe that players are destroying it<ANTECEDENT="game"> from within by demanding too much money.

Since the antecedent of *it* is *game*, we know that *game* is a semantically neutral noun in this context. It is clear that if we had a sufficiently-large set of labeled anaphora resolutions, we could also extract a comprehensive gender/number database. While again no such data exists, this idea forms the basis of many of the other approaches described later in this section.

While existing anaphora annotations are not large enough to directly provide comprehensive gender/number data, these annotations have been exploited in other ways. Bergsma et al. [7, 9] uses anaphora annotations to extract evaluation data for gender/number models. Anaphora annotations can also provide labeled examples for training supervised gender/number predictors. Supervised learning gives us a way to combine the predictions of multiple approaches into a single gender/number prediction. We simply build a classifier with a separate feature for the prediction score of each approach, and then use standard learning techniques (e.g. SVM or decision trees) to derive the mapping from these features to a single output prediction. Such a combination is desirable since many of the resources presented in Sect. 3 provide complementary information. Bergsma [7] uses anaphora annotation-derived gender/number data as training examples to weight the contribution of the counts from different predictors. Bergsma et al. [9] use such data to combine the features in their "semi-supervised extension." Daumé and Marcu [17] also use such data to train a gender/number classifier. Their classifier uses a variety of lexical and list-derived features to predict the gender and number of NPs. Note, however, this classifier forms only a small part of the overall system and its accuracy is not given.

4.2 Orăsan and Evans' Approach

Orăsan and Evans [45] propose two algorithms for animacy prediction, one rule-based and one using a supervised classifier. For training and evaluation of their system, they manually annotated 19,701 NPs for animacy in the SEMCOR corpus (a corpus that includes WordNet synset-annotations), and 3,124 NPs in a corpus of Amnesty International articles. The NPs are annotated in context (tokens rather than types). A baseline system predicting *inanimate* in all cases would achieve 83 % and 88 % accuracy on the two test sets.

The rule-based algorithm (originally in [20]), is similar to other approaches that exploit the hyponym hierarchy and unique beginners of WordNet (Sect. 3.4). Synsets that are hyponyms of the *animal*, *person*, and *relation* unique beginners are considered animate. Furthermore, for NPs that are the subject of verb phrases, the synset of the verb is also used to determine animacy. Verbs that are hyponyms of the unique beginners *cognition*, *communication*, *emotion*, and *social* are considered to take animate subjects. For a given NP, the algorithm predicts the NP's animacy from the animacy of its synsets, exploiting contextual features and the animacy properties of the governing verb if the NP is a subject. This approach only performs marginally better than the baseline on test data.

This poor accuracy relative to the baseline is especially significant since so many previous systems have used a similar technique without evaluating the effectiveness (Sect. 3.4). Orăsan and Evans [45] attribute the problem to the unique beginners not truly being reflective of the animacy of all the beginner's hyponyms, i.e., the higher-level concepts are too general.

They therefore propose an approach that assigns animacy to individual synsets. The overlap between the SEMCOR animacy annotations and the SEMCOR synset annotations is exploited to label the animacy of those WordNet synsets which occur in SEMCOR. Then, animacy is propagated up the WordNet hierarchy from specific synsets (like *girlfriend*) to more general synsets (like *woman*). This is opposite to the direction that gender was propagated in Harabagiu et al. [30] (see Sect. 3.4). Animacy (or inanimacy) propagates up to a new synset if there is sufficient consistency in the animacy of the synsets's hyponyms (where consistency is measured according to a chi-squared test). That is, *woman* would be labeled animate if its hyponyms *debutante*, *heroine*, and *girlfriend* were all labeled animate. If there is sufficient ambiguity in the hyponym animacy, the animacy of the noun itself is classified as *undecided*. Ultimately, 94 % of synsets in WordNet are labeled animate or inanimate, while 6 % are left undecided.

The animacy of NPs, in context, is then assigned using a supervised classifier, trained on the SEMCOR animacy data. The classifier uses both lexical/contextual features and features derived from the WordNet animacy decisions. This classifier is found to perform much better than the rule-based approach, and actually above the level of human annotator agreement. When the supervised predictor was used in conjunction with a pronoun resolution system, pronoun resolution accuracy was very close to the levels achieved using oracle animacy identification.

4.3 Ge, Hale, and Charniak's Approach

Ge, Hale, and Charniak [23, 29] proposed the first method for automatically extracting agreement properties from raw text. They investigated whether it was feasible to learn noun gender from a large corpus of automatically-resolved anaphora (they do not apply the method to determine plurals). Of course, the automatic resolver makes mistakes. However, if the errors are random and we annotate sufficient examples, the true gender/number distribution should dominate.

Ge et al. try two pronoun resolution strategies on the 21-million-word Wall Street Journal corpus and collect the gender statistics directly from the annotated data. The first strategy is to use the *previous noun heuristic*: pronouns are resolved to the most recent NP occurring before the pronoun (this strategy was found to resolve pronouns correctly 43 % of the time in their other experiments). The second strategy is to apply a gender-unaware version of the Hobb's algorithm [31] (this had an accuracy of 65.3 % for pronoun resolution). Unsurprisingly, the second strategy is found to extract better gender information, achieving 70.3 % gender-assignment accuracy on a set of NPs with gendered honorifics. More importantly, the gender information was found to improve the accuracy of the pronoun resolver, from 82.9 % to 84.2 %.

An analysis of the gender system's errors indicates that the two pronoun resolution strategies do not err randomly, but repeatedly make stereotypical mistakes. For example, *wife* and *husband* are assigned the incorrect, opposite genders, since they tend to co-occur with pronouns of the opposite gender in text.

4.4 Pattern-Based Approaches

While Ge et al. [23]'s approach extracts gender information by resolving every pronoun that occurs in a text, *pattern-based* approaches only use instances where noun-pronoun coreference is more reliable; that is, instances matching a predefined coreference pattern. This section explores three pattern-based approaches.

While these approaches acquire gender and number for English nouns, similar strategies have been used for predicting the animacy of nouns in Norwegian [46]. In that work, the counts of various animacy-indicating patterns are combined in a supervised decision-tree classifier.

Bergsma's Approach Bergsma [7] notes that there are many instances in text where a pronoun can be resolved to an antecedent without ambiguity. For example, principle A of binding theory requires a reflexive pronoun (like *himself*) to have its antecedent in its governing category [24]. If we see the headline in text, "criminal photoshops himself into charity photos," we know *himself* refers to *criminal* and hence we can add a count of *criminal* being masculine to our gender/number model. In other words, we could potentially determine the gender of any particular noun by counting how often it binds with masculine, feminine, neutral and plural reflexives in a large corpus.

Bergsma [7] expands on this intuition by defining a small set of lexico-syntactic patterns that tend to co-occur with coreferent noun/pronoun pairs. The patterns were derived from intuition, unlike the automatically-derived Bergsma and Lin [8] patterns we will see below. The Bergsma patterns differ from Baldwin [3]'s rules for high-precision anaphora resolution in that the Bergsma patterns only look at a fragment of the text as opposed to using previous sentences in the discourse. Noun/pronoun fillers of the patterns are collected from a large parsed corpus (from roughly 6 GB of news text). For example, one pattern captures instances where a possessive pronoun (pos) and preceding NP (N) are linked as follows:

E.g. *Barack Obama* defended *his* jeans yesterday on the Today show.

Collecting counts from such patterns is found to provide fairly precise gender statistics, even with "parser errors, ungrammatical text and false bindings" polluting the statistics [7]. With enough data, false evidence (e.g. *Barack Obama defended her…*) is washed out by counts from true anaphor/antecedent fillers. Therefore, both the coverage and robustness of the model depend on how much text can be parsed.

To exploit a much larger volume of data, another set of statistics is collected from flat patterns using text from the entire web. E.g., patterns such as "Barack Obama * his," "Barack Obama * her," "Barack Obama * its," and "Barack Obama * their" are submitted to a search engine, where '*' is the wildcard operator for the Google API. Quotation marks are included around the query to ensure an exact phrase match. The search engine returns the number of pages available for each query, which is taken as an approximation for the number of times the NP (here, *Barack Obama*) and each possessive pronoun (*his/her/its/their*) co-occur in the pattern. These counts are used to build the gender/number model of the NP. Counts for patterns using nominative (subject) and reflexive pronouns are also collected.

The corpus and web pattern counts are then used to assign gender/number properties to nouns. The counts are converted to features for a classifier, and a supervised gender predictor is trained. The task is to predict the gender of a noun phrase, out of context. A classifier using only corpus counts achieves an F-Score of 85.4 %; a classifier with only web counts achieves 90.4 %; and a classifier using both achieves 92.2 % on the held-out test nouns.

Perhaps surprisingly, this exceeds the 88.8 % average F-Score of three native English speakers who also guessed gender for the same noun list. Humans performed worse on unfamiliar NPs and they were also more likely to interpret a noun phrase as one of its less frequent senses. Since humans can nevertheless resolve anaphora reliably in real text, this suggests that *context* is very useful for correctly interpreting noun gender, and we return to this issue later in the chapter.

Bergsma [7] also incorporates the statistical gender agreement features into a supervised anaphora resolution system. The system was evaluated on 1381 annotated pronouns in the American National Corpus. Adding the statistical gender information was found to improve resolution accuracy from 63.2 % to 73.3 %.

Ji and Lin's Approach Despite the excellent performance, there are several drawbacks to relying on search engines for the gender information. First of all, the Google API used in [7] is no longer active (although others exist). Second, the semantics of the '*' operator have changed for the worse; while '*' previously matched only single words, it now can span multiple words (even across sentences). Most importantly, it is simply too inefficient to query a search engine for counts in a practical anaphora resolution system.

Fortunately, a good alternative exists; rather than using a search engine, we can collect counts from a web-scale N-gram corpus. Ji and Lin [32] duplicate Bergsma [7]'s web patterns using a corpus with 4.1 billion N-grams [36], and also add counts for some effective new patterns. The new patterns include seeing how often each NP was followed by the words *who*, *which*, *where*, or *when*; these counts provide excellent indicators of an NP's animacy. The N-gram-derived information was applied to the task of unsupervised mention detection, and the results compared favourably to those achieved by supervised approaches.

Ji and Lin [32]'s collected data is "freely available for research purposes" at http://nlp.cs.qc.cuny.edu/ngram_genderanimacy.zip.

4.5 Bergsma and Lin's Approach

One key issue with the pattern-based approaches is that they rely on human intuition to define the coreference-indicating patterns. Of course, there may be many other good patterns that reliably link a coreferent pronoun to its antecedent; if we knew about these patterns, we could potentially extract a lot more (and hence better coverage) gender/number information from the same amount of text. Also, some of the above patterns are very coarse. A pattern like, "Barack Obama * his/her/its/their" may match cases like, "Barack Obama needs their support," which would erroneously contribute to the counts of *Barack Obama* being a plural entity.

Bergsma and Lin [8] address this by automatically deriving a set of fine-grained lexico-syntactic patterns that reliably link a pronoun and its antecedent. The patterns are then used to extract gender/number information.

The Bergsma and Lin patterns are defined over dependency parse trees. Each pattern is a *dependency path*: a sequence of dependency links connecting an NP and a pronoun in the tree. Figure 1 gives the dependency tree for the phrase, "John needs his support." For convenience, we write the dependency path for this tree as "*Noun* needs *pronoun*'s support." Note that a path does not include the terminal NP and pronoun; for example, "John needs his support" and "He needs their support" have the same dependency path.

The objective is to determine which dependency paths reliably connect coreferent NP-pronoun pairs, and which paths do not. Ultimately, the Bergsma and Lin algorithm can determine that the dependency path "*Noun* needs *pronoun*'s friend" is likely to connect coreferent NP-pronoun pairs (e.g, *John*=*his* in *John needs his friend*). On the other hand, the algorithm learns that "*Noun* needs *pronoun*'s support" rarely connects coreferent pairs (e.g, *John*≠*his* in *John needs his support*).

How does it learn this? Once again, first imagine that we had billions of pronouns annotated with their antecedents (perhaps annotated along the lines of the example in Sect. 4.1). If we had such data, then for every NP and pronoun that are connected by a depedency path, we could see whether or not the NP and the pronoun are annotated as being coreferent. For a particular dependency path, like "*Noun* needs *pronoun*'s support," we can count how often this path links *coreferent* NP-pronoun

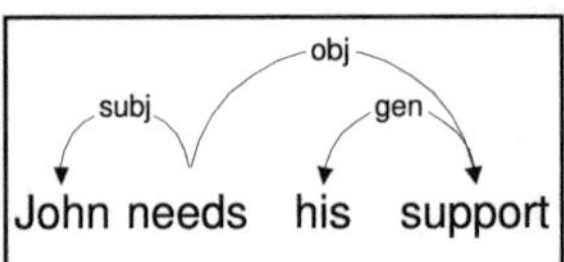

Fig. 1 Example dependency tree from Bergsma and Lin [8]

pairs (relatively rarely for this example) and how often it links *non-coreferent* pairs (relatively often).

Let $Y(p)$ be the number of times the NP-pronoun pair of a path, p, are coreferent, and let $N(p)$ be the number of times they are not-coreferent. We define the *coreference* of a path p as:

$$C(p) = \frac{Y(p)}{Y(p) + N(p)} \tag{1}$$

A high $C(p)$ value indicates that the path reliably connects coreferent NP-pronoun pairs. A low $C(p)$ value, as is learned for "*Noun* needs *pronoun*'s support," indicates that the path usually does not connect coreferent entities.

Of course, we don't actually have billions of gold standard anaphora annotations. However, there are many cases in text where coreference is unambiguous. For example, for the phrase, "we need our friends" it is clear that *we* and *our* co-refer. In this instance, the dependency path connects coreferent terminals, and we can add to our $Y(p)$ count for this path. On the other hand, if we see, "I need his support," then it is also clear that *I* and *his* are *not* coreferent; the two pronouns are from different pronoun classes. We would instead increment $N(p)$ for this path.

So, the key insight of Bergsma and Lin [8] is to count how often a dependency path occurs with two *pronouns* that agree ($Y(p)$) or disagree ($N(p)$) in their semantic properties. This agreement is used as a substitute for actual coreference annotations, and is obviously only available for those paths connecting two pronouns. Nevertheless, Bergsma and Lin obtain $C(p)$ values for "millions of paths" in a 85 GB corpus of parsed news articles.

$C(p)$ knowledge is useful for helping to resolve pronouns, as we can prevent (resp. encourage) resolving a pronoun to a candidate antecedent if the pronoun and candidate are connected by a path with a low (resp. high) $C(p)$ score.

For learning gender/number, on the other hand, we can select a subset of paths with high $C(p)$ scores, and use these as the patterns for pattern-based gender-mining (Sect. 4.4). Table 3 gives some example paths with high $C(p)$ values. Whenever we

Table 3 Example coreferent paths from Bergsma and Lin [8]: *Italicized* entities generally corefer

	Pattern	Example
1.	*Noun* left ... to *pronoun*'s wife	*Buffett* will leave the stock to *his* wife
2.	*Noun* says *pronoun* intends...	*The newspaper* says *it* intends to file a lawsuit
3.	*Noun* was punished for *pronoun*'s crime	*The criminal* was punished for *his* crime
4.	... left *Noun* to fend for *pronoun-self*	They left *Jane* to fend for *herself*
5.	*Noun* lost *pronoun*'s job	*Dick* lost *his* job
6.	... created *Noun* and populated *pronoun*	Nzame created *the earth* and populated *it*
7.	*Noun* consolidated *pronoun*'s power	*The revolutionaries* consolidated *their* power
8.	*Noun* suffered ... in *pronoun*'s knee ligament	*The leopard* suffered pain in *its* knee ligament

Table 4 Gender classification performance from Bergsma and Lin [8] (%)

Classifier	F-Score
Original Bergsma [7] pattern-based approach using 6 GB corpus	85.4
Duplicated Bergsma [7] pattern-based approach using 85 GB corpus	88.0
Original Bergsma [7] search-engine-based	90.4
Bergsma and Lin [8] path-based gender/number (85 GB corpus)	90.3

see such paths connecting an NP and pronoun in a corpus (e.g. "Dick lost his job" in Table 3, Num. 5), we would count this as an instance of the NP co-occurring with the pronoun's gender (*Dick* is masculine). After collecting these counts over a very large corpus, we can build a high-coverage gender/number model. Bergsma and Lin [8] collected coreference-path-based gender information for several million noun phrases in their 85 GB corpus of news articles.

How well does the acquired data actually work? Table 4 gives some results comparing the gender/number classification performance of the path-based model to the original Bergsma [7] approach (see Sect. 4.4). First of all, notice the pattern-based approach improves in accuracy with a much larger corpus: from 85.4 % F1 when trained on 6 GB to 88.0 % F1 when trained on 85 GB. Also, note that using the same large corpus, the path-based approach is better: 90.3 % F1. This is slightly below the level of the Bergsma system using search engines, but avoids the impracticalities of using a search engine within an anaphora resolution system [8].

The Bergsma and Lin data is publicly available at http://webdocs.cs.ualberta.ca/~bergsma/Gender/. To our knowledge, this remains the most comprehensive gender/number database available. It has been used in a wide range of anaphora and coreference resolution systems, and was a standard resource allowed in the closed track at the CoNLL-2011 shared task on "Modeling Unrestricted Coreference in OntoNotes" [48]. In particular, it was used by the Stanford system that won the competition [35] (note the Stanford system is also available for download at http://www-nlp.stanford.edu/software/dcoref.shtml). For researchers looking to quickly get an anaphora resolution system off the ground, we recommend downloading and using the Bergsma and Lin dataset.

4.6 Unsupervised Approaches

Perhaps the most elegant method for learning gender and number is to derive a gender/number model as an integrated component of a fully unsupervised, generative anaphora resolution model [13, 14, 25, 27].

Gender/Number via Unsupervised Pronoun Resolution Cherry and Bergsma [14] proposed the first unsupervised generative model for pronoun resolution. For each pronoun p in a corpus, a single preceding NP is assumed to be the pronoun's antecedent. This antecedent is also assumed to occur on a fixed list of NPs preceding the pronoun in the discourse. Like the early statistical approaches [23], a probability model provides the probability of each of these candidates being the antecedent. At test time, pronouns are simply resolved to their most likely antecedents according to the model. Unlike the early probabilistic approaches, however, labeled training data is not used to collect the statistics for the model parameters. In the Cherry and Bergsma approach [14], the identity of the antecedent is treated as a hidden (*unobserved* or *latent*) variable; the model parameters are learned from unlabeled text using the EM algorithm.

First let us consider the probability model. Cherry and Bergsma [14] more or less define the joint probability of a pronoun, p, and an antecedent candidate, c, as:

$$P(p,c) = P(p|c)P(p_{gov}|c)P(c)P(dist[c,p]) \tag{2}$$

Where p_{gov} is the governor of the pronoun, and $dist[c,p]$ is the distance between c and p in terms of the number of intervening NPs. Cherry and Bergsma collapse all pronouns from the same semantic group (i.e., each row of Table 1) into a single category label as the possible p values (i.e., MASC, FEM, NEUT, PLUR). The term $P(p|c)$ is therefore the gender/number model. For a given candidate c, there are four conditional probabilities, one for each pronoun category being generated by the candidate. These conditional probabilities thus look a lot like the rows of Table 2.

Let us return to the issue of assigning actual values to these models for particular p, c combinations. Unfortunately, we don't have labeled data to collect the statistics. If we did – if everything was *observed* – we would just count how often we saw various events and then normalize the counts of these events to produce the probabilities. In our corpus we only see the pronouns and the candidates, not the identity of the antecedents. A standard approach to such problems is to use the EM algorithm to "fill in" the hidden variables so that the likelihood of the data we do observe is maximized. That is, EM iteratively adjusts the probabilities of what we don't see (the identity of the hidden antecedent) so that the probabilities of what we do see (the pronouns) have high scores under our model.

Informally, applying EM amounts to: (a) initializing the model probabilities in Equation (2), (b) finding the likelihood of each antecedent candidate ($P(c|p)$) using the model probabilities (E-Step), and (c) taking these likelihoods as fractional co-occurrence counts for recomputing the model probabilities (M-Step), and then iterating through (b) and (c) for some number of iterations. Like Ge et al. [23]'s approach, every pronoun in text is resolved before gender is extracted. We can think of EM as iteratively refining the initially-poor resolutions, and thus also iteratively learning better gender (and context/distance) models. At the end of the EM process, we can resolve a pronoun by determining which antecedent candidate, c, has the maximum probability under our model, given the current pronoun we wish to resolve: $\hat{c} = \text{argmax}_c P(c|p) = \text{argmax}_c P(p,c)$.

Charniak and Elsner [13] also learn a pronoun resolution system using EM. They expand on the simple Cherry and Bergsma [14] model by including new model parameters. These include modeling the likelihood of coreference depending on the syntactic position of the candidate (e.g., subject vs. object), the type of pronoun (reflexive, subject, object, possessive) and the type of antecedent (common, proper, or pronominal). They also resolve first and second person pronouns, and jointly identify non-anaphoric pronouns. In generative approaches, improvements in all aspects of the model should lead to improvements in the gender/number component, as better models should resolve pronouns better, leading to better antecedent/gender co-occurrence statistics.

The Charniak and Elsner [13] system correctly resolved 68.6 % of pronouns, evaluating on the same data used by Ge et al. [23]. This level of performance exceeded the accuracy of several publicly-available supervised and rule-based pronoun resolution systems on the same data. These comparison systems achieved 52.9 %, 53.4 % and 59.3 %. Note that on different data (but also from the news domain), the simpler Cherry and Bergsma [14] system achieved 63.2 % accuracy. This suggests that the Charniak and Elsner enhancements result in improved performance.

The Charniak and Elsner system (and their gender model) is publicly available.[2]

Gender/Number via Unsupervised Coreference Resolution Unlike the above pronoun-specific approaches, the unsupervised approaches of Haghighi and Klein [25, 27] are generative models for resolving *all* NPs. They thus handle pronoun resolution as a sub-task. The Haghighi and Klein models implicitly include gender/number components.

The recent Haghighi and Klein system [27] reports "the best results to date on the complete end-to-end coreference task." While the unsupervised pronoun resolution systems described above must determine the antecedent for each pronoun as a latent variable, the Haghighi and Klein model is rather more complex. There are many more unobserved connections (hidden variables) in the model. Each mention in text (e.g. *Obama*, *he*, *the president*) is probabilistically generated by a variable representing a real-world entity (e.g. an entity representing "Barack Obama") and these entities are in turn generated by variables representing abstract entity *types*, (e.g. *Person* or *Organization*).

Like in the unsupervised pronoun resolution approaches, the model parameters in Haghighi and Klein [27] (and the assignments to the unobserved variables) are chosen in order to maximize the likelihood of the observed data under the model. They adopt a variational, staged approach to learning the parameters; the model is sufficiently complex that using EM "would be very difficult" [27]. After all the parameters are learned, partitions of NPs are generated by assigning mentions to their most likely entities. Anaphors are thus resolved to antecedents by virtue of being in the same partition.

In terms of gender/number statistics, the system in [27] is unique in that it shares pronoun co-occurrence statistics at the entity-level. That is, it might learn that the type *Person* is, in general, referred to by third-person masculine and feminine pronouns (and first and second-person pronouns). Gender is ultimately associated

[2] http://bllip.cs.brown.edu/download/emPronoun.tar.gz

with a specific name only implicitly through the name's entity assignment. This is similar to the early approaches that applied named-entity recognition as a preprocessing step (Sect. 3.2), but in Haghighi and Klein's work, the entity types and assignments are both learned without labeled training data.

Another interesting aspect of the implementation of [27] is the inclusion of specific Wikipedia abstracts in the training data. These abstracts were selected "to have subjects amongst the frequent proper nouns in the evaluation datasets" [27]. Including such abstracts would therefore greatly enrich the gender models with respect to the evaluation NPs. This is because of the topic-specific nature of Wikipedia articles, where "many anaphoric references [in the article bodies] have the article title as their referent" [1]. This has been exploited to automatically resolve Wikipedia pronouns, for question answering and other applications, at least as far back as Filippova and Strube [22]. By adding Wikipedia abstracts to their training corpus, Haghighi and Klein [27] are therefore also adding many instances where pronouns fairly unambiguously resolve to their correct proper noun antecedents.[3] Since the learned gender/number (and other) model parameters are partly based on these easy pronoun-proper noun resolutions, the proper nouns in question will have more accurate gender/number statistics. The system can rely on these more-accurate statistics at test time to resolve ambiguities involving the same proper nouns on different data.

4.7 Semi-supervised Approaches

The above approaches go a long way to providing robust gender/number information for pronoun resolution. Since they learn from raw text, they can provide gender for a wide variety of nouns. On the other hand, one weakness of the above models, like earlier WordNet and list-based approaches, is that they are *type*-based: they learn corpus-wide probabilities for word forms, rather than a noun/gender assignment for a specific noun token, in context (which is what we really need for pronoun resolution). The Ge et al. [23] system, for example, knows that *Ford* is usually neutral (the gender model gives it a 94 % probability of being so). It does not, however, say anything different if the phrase is, "Ford stars alongside Cate Blanchett and Shia LaBeouf," and even if *Harrison Ford* was mentioned earlier in the document.

A related issue is what happens if the gender/number model is used on new data, where previously-unseen nouns may occur? In the absence of NP-pronoun co-occurrence information, we would still like to make an educated guess for an unseen

[3]Their model's complexity only allowed training on a very small fraction of the total number of articles in Wikipedia. It would be interesting to assess the feasibility of using the *resolution-to-article-topic* heuristic on its own to learn a gender/number model from *all* of Wikipedia.

NP. For example, we would like to predict that the NP *Alina Kabayeva* is feminine based on gender-indicating features of the string (e.g., the gender-indicating suffix *-yeva*, the female given name *Alina*, etc.).

Theoretically, we could use a classifier to predict any noun's gender/number using features for its context, for its pronoun co-occurrence statistics, and for its substrings and list memberships (Sect. 4.1). Unfortunately, since such a classifier might have many hundreds of thousands or millions of features, there is simply not enough annotated data to train it effectively. However, is there an effective way to automatically annotate sufficient data for such a model?

Bergsma et al. [9] propose such an approach. The key insight is to use, as the model's supervision, gender probabilities obtained in an unsupervised manner. Bergsma et al. represent NPs, in context, using a rich set of features, and annotate these NPs automatically whenever they have highly-confident probabilities in the gender database of Bergsma and Lin [8]. The feature weights are determined by training over these automatically-generated examples. The predictions of this model are combined with the original Bergsma and Lin probabilities, in a second round of training, now using gold-standard labeled data. The overall system is thus *semi-supervised*, combining both large-scale unsupervised learning with some limited supervision.

The final semi-supervised system was shown to predict noun gender and number with 95.5 % accuracy on 2596 test nouns, well above the predictions using only the Bergsma and Lin gender/number counts. Also note that the baseline accuracy on this task is reported as 38.1 % for choosing the *neutral* class. Orăsan and Evans [45] also report very high accuracy, but only for the binary animate vs. non-animate distinction and only for common nouns. Recall that the baselines on their task (choosing inanimate) were 83 % and 88 % on the two datasets.

There is also some supervision in the recent Haghighi and Klein [27] model. They provide a set of *prototypes* for each entity type used by the model, and define which pronouns (and proper nouns and nominals) are associated with such types. For example, they might define *Bush*, *Gore*, and *Hussein* as proper noun prototypes of the PERSON type and restrict this type to co-occur with *president*, *minister*, and *official* common nouns and masculine/feminine pronouns. This was found to give "useful priming" to the system.

Finally, also note that while Cherry and Bergsma [14] report a semi-supervised maximum entropy extension to their EM system, this supervision does not affect the learning of the gender/number model. It is applied only after the model parameters have been learned using EM. An interesting future direction would be to incorporate the maximum entropy model into EM; in fact, recent research in other applications has shown this might be possible even without annotated data at all [6].

5 Conclusion

Applying agreement properties is an integral part of anaphora resolution. However, early anaphora resolution systems did not consider how to acquire the necessary world knowledge. Some later systems operated in domains where agreement properties were less important. Other systems used what information they could get from existing resources, such as WordNet, parsers, part-of-speech taggers, and named entity recognizers. However, no previous resource was found to comprehensively supply all the needed information. As a solution, the past decade has seen several proposals for acquiring agreement properties directly from labeled, unlabeled, or automatically-labeled corpora. Data acquired in this manner seems to provide a better gender/number model, and incorporating it leads to better pronoun resolution.

Looking at this research as a whole, we see some general trends. First of all, *more data is better data*: acquiring data from the whole web using coarse patterns works better than acquiring data from parsed corpora using precise patterns [7] (although combining both sources works even better). Secondly, systems that exploit context perform better: whether considering the governing verb of subject NPs [45], or including other features for the NP context [9], using context leads to better results. Finally, machine learning has proven very useful for this task. It allows both the combination of diverse sources of knowledge via supervised learning [7, 9, 45], and the acquisition of gender properties as latent information via an unsupervised generative process [13, 14, 25].

We also note that there is no reason to start from scratch in terms of building an agreement model for your own pronoun resolution system. We have noted several gender/number/animacy databases that are now available online.

Accuracy on animacy and gender/number prediction have reached very high levels [9, 45], in some cases above human agreement [7, 45]. In one instance, a pronoun resolution system using automatic animacy identification for common nouns performed similarly to one using an oracle animacy predictor [45]. One is left wondering whether this is a solved problem; at least, whether gender/number mistakes now contribute a very small number of errors relative to everything else that currently goes wrong in automatic anaphora resolution. Judging from more recent systems using corpus-derived gender/number information, however, gender/number inaccuracy is still a significant source of resolution errors [39, 49].

As better evaluations for pronoun resolution systems in general are developed, and as more resolution systems become publicly available and get applied to real problems, then progress in gathering agreement properties will also be easier to assess. Furthermore, there will be a growing need for gender/number models for other domains and languages. The solutions developed for general English text may need revision in new contexts, and new questions will arise. For example, is there a benefit in automatically distinguishing masculine and feminine proper names for Spanish, German, or French pronoun resolution? Would it be useful to learn which entities (like children and pets) are not usually addressed with formal second-person pronouns (in languages with such distinctions)?

Finally, gender and number properties are now being exploited in other areas beyond pronoun resolution, such as named-entity recognition [19, 32]. Various other syntactic and semantic problems in NLP could benefit from such information. For example, semantic role labeling and part-of-speech tagging often involve disambiguating between constructions like, "the team won yesterday," where *team* is the subject of the past-tense verb *won*, and phrases like, "the trophy won yesterday," where *trophy* is the semantic object of the verb participle *won*. When analyzing these constructions, it may be useful to know that *team* is more animate than *trophy*. In fact, compared to *trophy*, *team* is followed much more frequently by *who* than by *which* in text. While the approaches presented in this chapter generally treat both *trophy* and *team* as inanimate neutral nouns, a different definition of animacy could be useful for different tasks. Attacking new problems may give insight into solutions that will also help us apply agreement properties to resolve anaphora.

References

1. Amaral, C., Cassan, A., Figueira, H., Martins, A., Mendes, A., Mendes, P., Pinto, C., Vidal, D.: Priberam's question answering system in QA@CLEF 2007. In: Cross Language Evaluation Forum: Working Notes for the CLEF 2007 Workshop, Budapest (2007)
2. Arnold, J., Eisenband, J., Brown-Schmidt, S., Trueswell, J.: The rapid use of gender information: evidence of the time course of pronoun resolution from eyetracking. Cognition **76**(1), B13–B26 (2000)
3. Baldwin, B.: CogNIAC: high precision coreference with limited knowledge and linguistic resources. In: Proceedings of the ACL Workshop on Operational Factors in Practical, Robust Anaphora Resolution for Unrestricted Texts, Madrid (1997)
4. Barbu, C., Evans, R., Mitkov, R.: A corpus based investigation of morphological disagreement in anaphoric relations. In: LREC, Las Palmas (2002)
5. Bengtson, E., Roth, D.: Understanding the value of features for coreference resolution. In: EMNLP, Waikiki (2008)
6. Berg-Kirkpatrick, T., Bouchard-Côté, A., DeNero, J., Klein, D.: Painless unsupervised learning with features. In: NAACL, Los Angeles (2010)
7. Bergsma, S.: Automatic acquisition of gender information for anaphora resolution. In: Proceedings of the 18th Conference of the Canadian Society for Computational Studies of Intelligence (Canadian AI), Victoria (2005)
8. Bergsma, S., Lin, D.: Bootstrapping path-based pronoun resolution. In: COLING-ACL, Sydney (2006)
9. Bergsma, S., Lin, D., Goebel, R.: Glen, Glenda or Glendale: unsupervised and semi-supervised learning of English noun gender. In: CoNLL, Boulder (2009)
10. Brennan, S.E., Friedman, M.W., Pollard, C.J.: A centering approach to pronouns. In: ACL, Stanford (1987)
11. Byron, D.K., Tetreault, J.R.: A flexible architecture for reference resolution. In: EACL, Bergen (1999)
12. Cardie, C., Wagstaff, K.: Noun phrase coreference as clustering. In: EMNLP-VLC, College Park (1999)
13. Charniak, E., Elsner, M.: EM works for pronoun anaphora resolution. In: EACL, Athens (2009)
14. Cherry, C., Bergsma, S.: An Expectation Maximization approach to pronoun resolution. In: CoNLL, Ann Arbor (2005)

15. Church, K.W., Mercer, R.L.: Introduction to the special issue on computational linguistics using large corpora. Comput. Linguist. **19**(1), 1–24 (1993)
16. Cucerzan, S., Yarowsky, D.: Minimally supervised induction of grammatical gender. In: NAACL, Edmonton (2003)
17. Daumé III, H., Marcu, D.: A large-scale exploration of effective global features for a joint entity detection and tracking model. In: HLT-EMNLP, Vancouver (2005)
18. Denber, M.: Automatic resolution of anaphora in English. Technical report, Imaging Science Division, Eastman Kodak Co. (1998)
19. Elsner, M., Charniak, E., Johnson, M.: Structured generative models for unsupervised named-entity clustering. In: HLT-NAACL, Boulder (2009)
20. Evans, R., Orăsan, C.: Improving anaphora resolution by identifying animate entities in texts. In: DAARC, Lancaster (2000)
21. Fellbaum, C. (ed.): WordNet: An Electronic Lexical Database. MIT, Cambridge (1998)
22. Filippova, K., Strube, M.: Using linguistically motivated features for paragraph boundary detection. In: EMNLP, Sydney (2006)
23. Ge, N., Hale, J., Charniak, E.: A statistical approach to anaphora resolution. In: Proceedings of the Sixth Workshop on Very Large Corpora, Montreal (1998)
24. Haegeman, L.: Introduction to Government & Binding theory, 2nd edn. Basil Blackwell, Cambridge (1994)
25. Haghighi, A., Klein, D.: Unsupervised coreference resolution in a nonparametric Bayesian model. In: ACL, Prague (2007)
26. Haghighi, A., Klein, D.: Simple coreference resolution with rich syntactic and semantic features. In: EMNLP, Singapore (2009)
27. Haghighi, A., Klein, D.: Coreference resolution in a modular, entity-centered model. In: HLT-NAACL, Los Angeles (2010)
28. Hajič, J., Hladká, B.: Probabilistic and rule-based tagger of an inflective language: a comparison. In: ANLP, Washington DC (1997)
29. Hale, J., Charniak, E.: Getting useful gender statistics from English text. Technical report: CS-98-06, Brown University (1998)
30. Harabagiu, S., Bunescu, R., Maiorano, S.: Text and knowledge mining for coreference resolution. In: NAACL, Pittsburgh (2001)
31. Hobbs, J.: Resolving pronoun references. Lingua **44**(311), 311–338 (1978)
32. Ji, H., Lin, D.: Gender and animacy knowledge discovery from web-scale N-grams for unsupervised person mention detection. In: PACLIC, Hong Kong (2009)
33. Kennedy, C., Boguraev, B.: Anaphora for everyone: pronominal anaphora resolution without a parser. In: COLING, Copenhagen (1996)
34. Lappin, S., Leass, H.J.: An algorithm for pronominal anaphora resolution. Comput. Linguist. **20**(4), (1994)
35. Lee, H., Chang, A., Peirsman, Y., Chambers, N., Surdeanu, M., Jurafsky, D.: Deterministic coreference resolution based on entity-centric, precision-ranked rules. Comput. Linguist. **39**(4), 885–916 (2013)
36. Lin, D., Church, K., Ji, H., Sekine, S., Yarowsky, D., Bergsma, S., Patil, K., Pitler, E., Lathbury, R., Rao, V., Dalwani, K., Narsale, S.: New tools for web-scale N-grams. In: LREC, Valletta (2010)
37. Mikheev, A., Grover, C., Moens, M.: Description of the LTG system used for MUC-7. In: 7th Message Understanding Conference, Fairfax (1998)
38. Miller, G.A.: Nouns in WordNet: a lexical inheritance system. Int. J. Lexicogr. **3**(4), 245–264 (1990)
39. Miltsakaki, E.: Antelogue: pronoun resolution for text and dialogue. In: Coling 2010: Demonstrations, Beijing (2010)
40. Mitkov, R.: Factors in anaphora resolution: they are not the only things that matter. a case study based on two different approaches. In: ACL/EACL Workshop on Operational Factors in Practical, Robust Anaphora Resolution, Madrid (1997)

41. Mitkov, R.: Robust pronoun resolution with limited knowledge. In: ACL-COLING, Montreal (1998)
42. MUC-6: Coreference task definition (v2.3, 8 Sept 1995). In: Proceedings of the Sixth Message Understanding Conference (MUC-6), Columbia (1995)
43. MUC-7: Coreference task definition (v3.0, 13 July 1997). In: Proceedings of the Seventh Message Understanding Conference (MUC-7), New York (1997)
44. Ng, V., Cardie, C.: Improving machine learning approaches to coreference resolution. In: ACL, Philadephia (2002)
45. Orăsan, C., Evans, R.: NP animacy identification for anaphora resolution. JAIR **29**(1), 79–103 (2007)
46. Øvrelid, L.: Towards robust animacy classification using morphosyntactic distributional features. In: EACL Student Research Workshop, Trento (2006)
47. Pantel, P., Ravichandran, D.: Automatically labeling semantic classes. In: HLT-NAACL, Boston (2004)
48. Pradhan, S., Ramshaw, L., Marcus, M., Palmer, M., Weischedel, R., Xue, N.: Conll-2011 shared task: modeling unrestricted coreference in ontonotes. In: Proceedings of the Fifteenth Conference on Computational Natural Language Learning: Shared Task, Portland, pp. 1–27 (2011)
49. Raghunathan, K., Lee, H., Rangarajan, S., Chambers, N., Surdeanu, M., Jurafsky, D., Manning, C.: A multi-pass sieve for coreference resolution. In: EMNLP, Portland (2010)
50. Soon, W.M., Ng, H.T., Lim, D.C.Y.: A machine learning approach to coreference resolution of noun phrases. Comput. Linguist. **27**(4), 521–544 (2001)
51. Stuckardt, R.: Design and enhanced evaluation of a robust anaphor resolution algorithm. Comput. Linguist. **27**(4), 479–506 (2001)
52. Tetreault, J.R.: A corpus-based evaluation of centering and pronoun resolution. Comput. Linguist. **27**(4), 507–520 (2001)
53. Zaenen, A., Carletta, J., Garretson, G., Bresnan, J., Koontz-Garboden, A., Nikitina, T., O'Connor, M.C., Wasow, T.: Animacy encoding in English: why and how. In: ACL Workshop on Discourse Annotation, Barcelona (2004)

Detecting Non-reference and Non-anaphoricity

Olga Uryupina, Mijail Kabadjov, and Massimo Poesio

Abstract In this chapter we discuss proposals concerning the detection of non-referentiality and non-anaphoricity, and the integration of such methods in an anaphora resolution system. We first review in brief a number of proposals on the topics, also covering literature on detecting abstract anaphora and discussing available resources; we then discuss in detail the proposals by Bergsma on expletive detection, and by Poesio et al. and Kabadjov on discourse-new detection.

Keywords Detecting non-reference and non-anaphoricity coreference resolution • Non-reference • Non-anaphoricity

1 Introduction

As discussed in earlier chapters, anaphora (or coreference) resolution is the task of identifying the **(discourse) entity** a mention refers to – which in most modern systems, in which entities are represented in terms of **coreference chains** (equivalence sets of mentions referring to the same entity), boils down to partitioning the mentions in a text into these coreference chains. This simple picture is, however, complicated in number of ways. First of all, not all mentions refer. As discussed in chapter "Linguistic and Cognitive Evidence About Anaphora", some mentions are semantically vacuous; other mentions, while making a semantic contribution, are not referring. In addition, many referring mentions do not corefer with any other mention, i.e., the coreference chain to which they belong is in fact a singleton set.

Regarding the first point – English syntax requires the subjects of finite clauses to be explicitly realized. As a result, sentences such as *It rains*, which in languages such as Italian, Spanish or Japanese would not have a subject, have as a subject an *it*

O. Uryupina (✉)
DISI University of Trento, Trento, Italy
e-mail: uryupina@gmail.com

M. Kabadjov • M. Poesio
School of Computer Science and Electronic Engineering, University of Essex, Wivenhoe Park, Colchester CO4 3SQ, UK
e-mail: malexa@essex.ac.uk; poesio@essex.ac.uk

M. Poesio et al. (eds.), *Anaphora Resolution*, Theory and Applications of Natural Language Processing, DOI 10.1007/978-3-662-47909-4_13

which doesn't realize any argument of the verb; it's only there for syntactic reasons. Such proforms are called **expletives** or **pleonastic**. Being able to recognize such proforms could improve the performance of an anaphora resolution system, at least in principle.

The second complication is that even mentions which do contribute to the logical form of a sentence may not be **referring**. As discussed in chapter "Linguistic and Cognitive Evidence About Anaphora", noun phrases can play at least three types of semantic roles in the logical form of a sentence. First of all, noun phrases can refer to an entity: this is the case of noun phrase *John* in *John is a policeman*. Secondly, they can act as predicates: e.g., noun phrase *a policeman* in the example just given is not referring – it is used to express a property of the entity referred to by mention *John*. Thirdly, nominal phrases can act as **quantifiers**. For example, in *No self-respecting Italian likes pineapple on her pizza*, the nominal phrase *No self-respecting Italian* does not refer to any entity: according to modern linguistics, the sentence means that the intersection of the sets of self-respecting Italians and the set of people liking pineapple on their pizza is empty, and the determiner *No* specifies this. Note however that the quantifier *No self-respecting Italian* can nevertheless act as 'antecedent' for the anaphoric pronoun *her* (pronouns whose 'antecedent' is a quantifier, like *her*, are called **bound anaphors**).[1]

The third complexity to take in mind is that many, in fact most, properly referring mentions are **non-anaphoric** or at least do not corefer with entities previously introduced via nominal mentions. The great majority of mentions in most texts are **discourse new**: they introduce new entities in a discourse. And a great many referring mentions are referring to entities not directly introduced via nominal mentions – e.g., in associative anaphora and in reference to abstract objects (see chapter "Linguistic and Cognitive Evidence About Anaphora").

To appreciate the extent to which these complexities affect current anaphora resolution systems, consider the following example from the OntoNotes dataset [28, 50]:

(1) Why do [you]$_1$ think only [lowly soldiers]$_2$ and [no generals]$_3$ have been convicted? Because [generals]$_4$ have [the power]$_5$, [that]$_6$'s why!

The snippet in (1) contains six nominal expressions, that can potentially be partitioned into coreference chains in 203 ways. Some of the candidate partitions, however, can be reliably ruled out at an early stage, based on simple mention-level contextual clues. First, *no generals* (M_3) is a quantifier, thus non referring to any particular set of generals although it can bind pronominal expressions (but such

[1]And indeed, the clearest difference between 'anaphora resolution' as specified in theoretical linguistics/psycholinguistics and 'coreference resolution' as specified by the MUC annotation guidelines lies precisely in the treatment of predicative and quantificational NPs. In anaphora resolution predicative NPs have no antecedents, but bound pronouns do; conversely, in coreference resolution the links between bound pronouns and the quantifiers that bound them are not annotated, but those between predicative NPs and their 'antecedents' are. (See chapter "Annotated Corpora and Annotation Tools".)

binding relations are typically not annotated in anaphoric/coreference corpora, see chapter "Annotated Corpora and Annotation Tools"). Most importantly, *no generals* should not be deemed as coreferent with *generals* (M_4), even though they share very similar surface forms. Depending on the annotation guidelines, an anaphora resolution system should either classify this nominal as non-referring, or a belonging to a singleton chain. Second, the pronoun *that* (M_6) refers to an **abstract entity** (*generals have the power*) and should therefore not be part of any coreference chain including previously occurred nominal expressions. This is an important clue since most pronouns are anaphoric and therefore a typical coreference resolution system would tend to propose an antecedent for M_6, leading to a spurious link. Finally, *you* (M_1) is a **deictic** expression that refers to the hearer and not to any particle person mentioned in the snippet.

Many anaphoric resolvers do not include any special provision to recognize such cases. But in many cases, non-referring, non-anaphoric and discourse new expressions can be reliably identified using various linguistic cues. It might therefore be beneficial for a coreference resolver to incorporate submodules for these tasks. First, referentiality and anaphoricity detection can be modeled as simple binary classification problems allowing for straightforward implementation. This can help improve the precision level of our coreference resolver: for example, if our referentiality detector classifies with a high confidence *no generals* in (1) as non-referential, this mention can be assigned to a singleton chain in the final partition and the coreference system will not introduce such spurious links as {"no generals", "generals"}. Second, when used as pre-filters in a pipelined architecture, such modules might help significantly reduce the pool of candidate mentions and thus considerably increase the performance speed. Thus, by assigning M_1, M_3 and M_6 to singleton chains, we can reduce the total number of all the possible partitions in our example (1) from 203 to just 5. This is especially important in the context of state-of-the-art complex models of coreference that are very sensitive to the size of their input problems.

The rest of this chapter is organized as follows. In Sect. 2 we survey work on the different subtasks of anaphora resolution concerned with detecting non-referentiality and non-anaphoricity, and on integrating such work with anaphora resolution systems. In Sect. 3, we provide a detailed description of a state-of-the-art algorithm for expletive detection [6]. In Sect. 4, we discuss the in-depth investigation of non-anaphoricity in [29].

2 Non-referentiality, Non-anaphoricity, and Related Tasks

In this section we look in more detail at the subtasks of anaphora resolution concerned with referentiality and anaphoricity, and survey the solutions proposed, discussing also relevant work in corpus annotation.

2.1 Detecting (Non) Referentiality and (Non) Antecedenthood

Expletives As discussed in chapter "Linguistic and Cognitive Evidence About Anaphora", linguists have been distinguishing between anaphoric and expletive usages of pronouns for a very long time [26, 27, 54, 60, 61]. One of the most thoroughly covered topics in this context is the expletive usage of English *it*, and extensive analyses of the constructions in which such usages occur have been provided e.g., in [54, 60, 61]. Early computational approaches to pronominal anaphora resolution circumvented the problem by manually excluding expletives from their evaluation datasets (see e.g., [38] for a discussion). Lappin and Leass's algorithm [36], discussed in chapter "Early Approaches to Anaphora Resolution: Theoretically Inspired and Heuristic-Based", used expletive recognition heuristics such as rules for recognising modal adjectives (e.g., 'It is *good* to know') and cognitive verbs (e.g., 'It is *believed* that polar bears. . . '). In the past decade, several statistical algorithms for automatic identification of expletive *it* have been proposed [5, 6, 9, 22]. We briefly discuss here the proposals by Evans and by Versley et al., and Bergsma's algorithm in more detail in Sect. 3.

Evans [22] developed a classifier able to classify every occurrence of the pronoun *it* into one of the seven classes **nominal anaphoric**, **clause anaphoric**, **proaction**, **cataphoric**, **discourse topic**, **pleonastic** and **idiomatic/stereotypic**. Each occurrence of *it* is annotated with 35 features, that can be broadly grouped into the following six categories:

1. **Position** of the pronoun in text is recorded in terms of word position in sentence and sentence position in paragraph. (Pronouns at the beginning of paragraphs are unlikely to be anaphoric.)
2. **Surface features** extracted from the text surrounding the pronoun, such as whether the pronoun immediately follows a prepositional word (pleonastic pronouns seldom appear after a prepositional word) or whether the pronoun is followed by complementisers or adjectives (pleonastic pronouns often precede such expressions).
3. **Word lemmas** of preceding and subsequent text within the same sentence (in particular verbs). These are meant to bypass the need for compiling external lists of trigger words like 'weather adjectives' or 'cognitive verbs'.
4. **Part-of-speech** for a window of eight words centred around the pronoun.
5. Certain **grammatical patterns** like 'adjective + noun phrase' (for example, '*It* was obvious [the plan] would work') and 'complementiser + noun phrase' (for example, '*It* was obvious [that the plan] would work').
6. **Proximity** of the pronoun to complementisers, *-ing* verb forms, and prepositions, in terms of number of tokens in between.

Evans then trained an expletive classifier using the implementation of the k nearest neighbour (KNN) algorithm implemented in Tilburg University's Memory Based Learner (TiMBL) [17]. He used for training and testing a data set he created, formed by 77 texts from the SUSANNE and BNC corpora from a diverse set of genres such as politics, science, fiction and journalism. Their corpus consisted of 368, 830 words and contained 3171 occurrences of *it* broken down into the seven target classes as follows: 67.93 % to nominal anaphora, 0.82 % to clause anaphora, 0.06 % to proaction, 0.09 % to cataphora, 2.08 % to discourse topic, 26.77 % were pleonastic, and 2.24 % to idiomatic/stereotypic constructions.

Evans reports precision and recall figures for each of the seven classes as follows: $F = 77.12\,\%$ for nominal anaphora, $F = 0\,\%$ for clause anaphora, $F = 0\,\%$ for proaction, $F = 0\,\%$ for cataphora, $F = 2.85\,\%$ for discourse topic, $F = 71.26\,\%$ for pleonastic and $F = 1.37\,\%$ for idiomatic/stereotypic constructions. Evans' classifier has also been integrated with the MARS anaphora resolution system [38] discussed in chapter "Early Approaches to Anaphora Resolution: Theoretically Inspired and Heuristic-Based".

Versley et al. [66] argued that tree kernels are particularly suited for identifying expletives, as they are able automatically to identify generalizations about the lexical and structural context around a word such as those encoded in the features used by Evans. In their experiments, they used the BBN Pronoun corpus to train and test an expletive classifier using the Penn Treebank parse trees. On expletive classification Versley et al.'s best classifier achieved a performance of $F = 74.36\,\%$, compared to a result of $F = 49.6\,\%$ obtained using a baseline classifying all instances of *it* as expletive. They then integrated this classifier in the BART anaphora resolution system, using the output of the expletive detector as an additional feature into their pronoun resolution module. Their system achieved $F = 66.5\,\%$ for pronouns on the MUC-6 corpus, a small improvement over the performance of the version of BART they used of $F = 66\,\%$ but the upperbound with perfect expletive classification would be $F = 68.4\,\%$.

Non-referring nominals The fact that not all nominals are referring has been known in the semantics literature for several decades [31, 58, 70]. One of the best known references in this area is the work by Karttunen [31], who discussed examples such as (2):

(2) Bill doesn't have [a car].

Sentence (2) does not imply the existence of any specific "car". In Karttunen's terms, the NP *a car* does not *establish a discourse referent* and therefore it cannot participate in any coreference chain – none of the alternatives in (3) can follow (2):

(3) A. [It] is black.
B. [The car] is black.
C. [Bill's car] is black.

Karttunen identifies several factors affecting the referential status of NPs, including modality, negation, or non-factive verbs. He argues that an extensive analysis of the phenomenon requires a sophisticated semantic treatment; and indeed numerous theories of semantic representation were proposed to account for such constraints, most notably Discourse Representation Theory or DRT [30], discussed in chapter "Linguistic and Cognitive Evidence About Anaphora". Later linguistic studies further investigated what kind of entities are allowed to participate in coreferent chains, and identified some of the relevant factors: internal morphosyntax, interaction between negation, modality, quantification, attitude predicates among others [58, 70].

Quite a lot of anaphora resolution systems based on DRT, thus incorporating its treatment of non-referential NPs, were developed in computational linguistics in the 1980s [2], the most recent system of this type being the Boxer semantic interpreter [8]. An algorithm for identifying *nonlicensing* NPs based on Karttunen's theory of referentiality was proposed by Byron and Gegg-Harrison [12]. Their approach relies on a handcrafted heuristic, encoding some of Karttunen's factors and shows mixed results w.r.t. the impact of such a prefiltering on (pronominal) coreference resolution.

Pragmatic effects on antecedenthood Empirical analysis of the results of anaphora resolution has shown that besides the semantic constraints just discussed there are pragmatic restrictions on the likelihood that entities will serve as antecedents for subsequent reference. The term **antecedenthood detection** [63] has been used for the task of identifying mentions that are not likely to be antecedents. Further discussion of the degree of antecedenthood of entities can be found in [55]. A generalization of the antecedenthood and anaphoricity tasks, the **entity lifespan** detection problem, has been proposed recently [56]: the objective is, for a given nominal expression, to predict the size of its corresponding coreference chain. A binary classifier is trained based on contextual features to discriminate between singletons and longer chains. This is an important area of research, that needs further investigation.

2.2 Discourse-New Detection and Anaphora Resolution

Detecting discourse-new mentions The task of **discourse new detection** consists of classifying nominal mentions according to their **information status**: i.e., distinguishing between descriptions introducing new entities and those referring to already established ones. Numerous theories concerning the information status of nominals have been proposed in the literature [23, 24, 37, 52, 53]. We point the reader to [65] and [67] for extensive overviews and comparison of some of the main theoretical proposals in this regard. Of these, the best known is the theory developed by Prince [52, 53], who introduces a distinction between **discourse givenness** and **hearer givenness** that results in the following taxonomy:

- *brand new* NPs introduce entities that are both discourse and hearer new ("a bus"), some of them, *brand new anchored* NPs, contain explicit link to some given discourse entity ("a guy I work with"),
- *unused* NPs introduce discourse new, but hearer old entities ("Noam Chomsky"),
- *evoked* NPs introduce entities already present in the discourse model and thus discourse and hearer old: *textually evoked* NPs refer to entities which have

already been mentioned in the previous discourse ("he" in "A guy I worked with says he knows your sister"), whereas *situationally evoked* are known for situational reasons ("you" in "Would you have change of a quarter?"),
- *inferrables* are not discourse or hearer old, however, the speaker assumes the hearer can infer them via logical reasoning from evoked entities or other inferrables ("the driver" in "I got on a bus yesterday and the driver was drunk"), *containing inferrables* make this inference link explicit ("one of these eggs").

Many linguistic theories [23, 24, 37, 52] focus on anaphoric usages of definite descriptions (either evoked or inferrables). As a result, many of the early systems focused exclusively on the task of finding an antecedent for a given expression. Corpus studies have revealed, however, that more than 50 % of (definite) NPs in newswire texts are not anaphoric [23, 49]. These findings suggest that developing data-driven approaches for the automatic identification of discourse new NPs may improve the performance of anaphora resolution systems. A number of algorithms for identifying discourse-new mentions have therefore been proposed in the anaphora resolution literature, especially for definite descriptions. Vieira and Poesio use a wide range of hand-crafted heuristics [68] (these heuristics are discussed in some detail in chapter "Early Approaches to Anaphora Resolution: Theoretically Inspired and Heuristic-Based"). Bean and Riloff make use of syntactic heuristics, but also mine additional patterns for discourse-new description from corpus data [4]. Ng and Cardie develop a supervised algorithm, integrating a number of syntactic and lexical clues as features in a learning-based approach [41, 42]. Uryupina proposes a web-based algorithm for identifying discourse-new and unique NPs [62]. The approach helps overcome the data sparseness problem of [4]. By relying on Internet counts. Finally, Kabadjov provides an extensive evaluation of different features relevant for the discourse new detection task [29]. We will discuss the latter approach in Sect. 4 below. Anaphoricity detection algorithms have been also proposed for other languages, including Spanish [44] and Chinese [34]. We discuss below how these discourse-new detectors were integrated in anaphora resolution systems.

A corpus specific problem arose within the context of the recent CoNLL evaluation campaigns [50, 51]. The ONTONOTES dataset, as used for the CoNLL shared tasks, only provides annotations for non-singleton coreference chains. Most participants have therefore applied some form of rule-based prefiltering to identify nominal expressions that are extremely unlikely to participate in any coreference relations, such as named entities of certain types (for example, QUANTITY) or non-referential pronouns (for example, "nobody"). To our knowledge, only very few approaches have been proposed to tackle the problem of ONTONOTES *mention detection* in a more principled way. Thus, Björkelund and Farkas have trained three classifiers to filter out non-anaphoric instances of *it*, *you* and *we* [7]. Kummerfeld et al. investigated various post- and pre-filtering heuristics for adapting their mention detection algorithm to the ONTONOTES English data in a semi-automatic way, reporting mixed results [35]. Finally, Uryupina and Moschitti propose a tree kernel-based algorithms for learning ONTONOTES mentions directly from the data [64].

Integrating Anaphoricity and Referentiality Detectors into Coreference Resolution Systems Early studies reported mixed results with respect to the effectiveness of discourse-new and referentiality detectors for full-scale coreference resolution. When such a detector is integrated as a preprocessing filter, some types of errors might propagate to drastically deteriorate the performance level of the coreference resolver: if a (referring or anaphoric) nominal expression is incorrectly filtered out at an early step, the system excludes it from the pool of candidate anaphors and can therefore never recuperate proposing a correct antecedent; on the contrary, if a (non-referring or discourse new) nominal expression is missed by the filter, the system might still correctly assign it to a singleton chain at a later stage by suggesting no suitable links. One of the most commonly used coreference resolution evaluation metric, the MUC scorer [69], is particularly sensitive to the former type of errors. With the introduction of more varied evaluation metrics (see chapter "Evaluation Metrics" for details), however, the research on anaphoricty and referentiality detection received a considerable boost, leading to more advanced architectural solutions that, in turn, bring an improvement in the MUC score as well.

Ng and Cardie [41] propose a global optimization approach: they fine-tune learning parameters of their anaphoricity classifier to optimize the final performance level of the coreference resolver on the held-out data. Their experiments suggest that an anaphoricity pre-filter can improve the overall performance level of a coreference resolver, provided it is trained with an unbalanced precision-recall trade-off parameter. (See also chapter "The Mention-Pair Model".) A similar technique has been adopted by Uryupina and Moschitti, who use an oracle-based simulation experiment to limit the search space for several parameters to be optimized to reduce the amount of expensive re-training in global parameter optimization [64]. Kabadjov [29] advocates a post-filtering approach; this approach is discussed in detail in Sect. 4. Finally, Denis and Baldridge [18] propose a joint model for anaphoricity and antecedenthood detection. Their approach relies on integer linear programming (ILP) to find a solution that is consistent with anaphoricity constraints. This approach is discussed in detail in chapter "Integer Linear Programming for Coreference Resolution".

It must be noted that all these algorithms improve the overall performance of coreference resolution, but at the same time require much more computational resources than the simplistic pipelined architecture. Thus, the global optimization solution [41] relies on multiple learning iterations and is therefore slow at the training stage. The ILP solution, on the contrary, does not require extra training time, but assumes a computationally expensive joint inference technique at the testing stage.

2.3 Event Anaphora and Abstract Object Anaphora

Finally, all systems have to deal with expressions that although strictly speaking anaphoric, are beyond the scope of the system, or the annotated corpus used to train and test it, or both. Recall the demonstrative pronoun *that* (M_6) in example (1). Although this mention is a context-depending anaphoric expression, its antecedent is not an entity introduced by another nominal mention, but an **abstract object** introduced by the clause *generals have the power*. Such anaphoric expressions are known as **references to abstract objects** [1] or cases of **discourse deixis** [71].

Interpreting references to abstract objects is very hard, as we even lack an agreed upon theory of what type of abstract objects there are. Asher [1] proposes an ontology including objects of increasing abstractness, from events to situations to propositions to facts, but there is no widespread agreement on how to discriminate between these different types of abstract objects. (See [48] for an empirical analysis of the types of objects referred to by demonstrative *this*, and [32] for an analysis of references to abstract objects via demonstrative nominals with so-called **shell nouns**.) As a result, until recently there weren't either corpora annotated with this type of references, or anaphora resolution algorithms for resolving them – most anaphora resolution systems only try to recognize such references so as not to attempt interpreting them. But there have been some recent developments in this regard.

Hand-coded algorithms for resolving pronominal references to abstract objects in the most general case have been proposed by Eckert and Strube [21] and Byron [11]. Kolhatkar [32] proposed statistical algorithms for resolving shell nouns, using the corpus she annotated. Much more progress has been made on a specific type of abstract reference: **event coreference resolution**. This progress has been motivated by the appearance of the ONTONOTES corpus (see chapter "Annotated Corpora and Annotation Tools"), in which coreference links between anaphoric expressions (mainly pronouns) and events/situations are annotated. In the recent CoNLL evaluation campaigns (see chapter "Evaluation Campaigns" and [50, 51]) such links were included in the evaluation set, although given the complexity of the task, most participating systems opted for never proposing clause-level antecedents. A number of proposals were however published after the datasets were released, using rich syntactic representations to identify and resolve (pronominal) references to abstract events [15, 33].

2.4 Annotated Resources

The tasks of anaphoricity and referentiality detection have not received much attention from the computational linguistics community until recently. As a result, only very few manually annotated corpora support the development of supervised models for the tasks discussed in this section by including annotations for coreference, anaphoricity and referentiality of the same documents. We briefly review here the options available – see chapter "Annotated Corpora and Annotation Tools" for a more extensive discussion of the available corpora.

Anaphoricity Adopting a naive definition of discourse new mention as one that does not have any antecedent, we could straightforwardly induce the gold labels for anaphoricity from any coreference-annotated corpus: we mark the first mention in each chain as *discourse new*, whereas all the subsequent ones, if any, will be marked as *discourse old*. Such annotation scheme, however, only reflects a very simplistic definition of discourse novelty, covering only the mentions that Prince would classify as textually evoked descriptions. This situation is worsened by the fact that, as discussed in chapter "Annotated Corpora and Annotation Tools", in many of the most commonly used corpora singletons are not annotated: this is true, e.g., of MUC and ONTONOTES. Singletons are annotated in the ACE corpora, but only for the mentions referring to the restricted number of semantic types considered of interest. Clearly, such corpora do not provide very useful resources to train a discourse-new detector.

Three options are in principle available. First of all, a corpus in which all anaphoric relations are annotated could be used, including reference to abstract objects and associative anaphora. As far as we know there is only one medium-size corpus of this type, ARRAU [45] (see chapter "Annotated Corpora and Annotation Tools"). The second option is to use a corpus in which although not all anaphoric relations are annotated, all mentions are marked with their information status, as done, e.g., in [16, 39, 43]. Finally, one could use a corpus in which only the information status of nominals is marked. All of these solutions of course require all referring mentions to be annotated.

Referentiality Very few corpora label the referential status of noun phrases. The most commonly used datasets, MUC, ACE and ONTONOTES [20, 25, 50] do not include any annotation for non-referring NPs. According to the guidelines for these datasets, such NPs should be ignored by the coders and not treated as mentions to annotate. The problem is that one cannot assume that if an NP is not annotated it must be non-referential, since none of these corpora label all the referential expression: MUC and ONTONOTES do not mark singleton chains, whereas the ACE annotation is restricted to specific semantic types.

The already mentioned ARRAU corpus however does include an extensive annotation of non-referential descriptions. According to the ARRAU guidelines, all nominal expressions, regardless of their referentiality, should be treated as mentions. Each mention is then labelled as referential or non-referential. Referential expressions are then further marked as discourse-new or discourse-old, and discourse-old should then be linked to their coreference chains. Non-referential mentions are then further subcategorized into expletives (4); predicates, including appositions, copulas and other types of predicative nominals (5); coordinations (6); parts of multiword or idiomatic expressions (7); quantifiers (8) and incomplete descriptions (9):

(4) But [it] doesn't take much to get burned.
(5) The new ad plan from Newsweek, [a unit of the Washington Post Co.], is [the second incentive plan the magazine has offered advertisers in 3 years].
(6) [Both Newsweek and U.S. News] have been gaining circulation in recent years.
(7) Apple II owners, for [example], had to use their television sets as screens and stored data on audiocassettes.
(8) They also said that vendors were delivering goods more quickly in October than they had for [each of the five previous months].
(9) what about [the uh]

Some statistics about referentiality for the different ARRAU domains are summarized in Table 1.

On average, around 13–15 % of all the mentions in ARRAU are non-referential. This highlights the importance of the reference detection subtask for coreference resolution. Three ARRAU domains, however, exhibit different distributions of non-referential mentions. The news text from the WSJ portion of the Penn Treebank in the RST domain contain a large number of predicates and coordinations. Dialogue transcripts (Trains) and child fiction (PearStories), on the contrary, mostly contain very simple sentences with few nominal predicates. Expletive pronouns are very common in dialogues and fiction, but much more rare in news text. Finally, carefully edited RST documents contain virtually no incomplete mentions.

Other medium-to-large-scale corpora annotated with referentiality information include the ANCORA corpus for Spanish [57], the LiveMemories corpus for Italian [59] and the Tüba/DZ corpus of coreference in German.[2]

Discourse deixis A number of corpora are annotated with references to abstract objects of different type. Pronominal references to abstract objects are annotated in the annotation of the TRAINS corpus produced by Byron [10], in the DAD corpus of Danish and Italian produced by Navarretta [40] and in the annotation

Table 1 Referentiality in the ARRAU corpus

Status	RST	Trains	PearStories
Referential	62,461 (86.73 %)	14,646 (86.15 %)	3401 (84.85 %)
Non-referential: expletive	444 (0.61 %)	853 (5.01 %)	122 (3.04 %)
Non-referential: predicate	4387 (6.09 %)	147 (0.86 %)	84 (2.09 %)
Non-referential: coordination	2414 (3.35 %)	235 (1.38 %)	37 (0.92 %)
Non-referential: idiomatic	639 (0.88 %)	149 (0.87 %)	42 (1.04 %)
Non-referential: quantifier	1738 (2.41 %)	818 (4.81 %)	132 (3.29 %)
Non-referential: incomplete	2 (0 %)	149 (0.87 %)	36 (0.89 %)

[2]http://www.sfs.uni-tuebingen.de/en/ascl/resources/corpora/tueba-dz.html

of EuroParl by Dipper and Zinsmeister [19]. The corpus produced by Kolhatkar [32] contains annotated shell noun references. Among the general-purpose anaphora corpora, ARRAU and ANCORA are annotated for general reference to abstract objects, whereas in ONTONOTES, reference to events is annotated.

3 Detecting Non-referentiality: Bergsma et al.'s Algorithm

In this section we discuss in more detail one of the best-known proposal of this type, the approach developed by Bergsma et al. [5, 6] that combines supervised learning with lexical features extracted from a large unlabeled dataset to create a robust and efficient system for detecting non-referential *it*. The approach relies on a binary classifier encoding syntactic and semantic properties of pronominal contexts. In what follows, we describe the methodology, two types of features used in the system, and evaluation results.

3.1 Methodology

This algorithm models the non-referentiality detection task as a simple binary supervised classification problem. Each instance of *it* in the dataset is represented as a feature vector. The features encode various properties of the pronoun's context and are described in more details below. The classifier can be trained on any corpus annotated with referentiality. However, as we have seen in Sect. 2.4 above, such datasets are not common. To overcome the issue, referentiality labels can be induces from data annotated with coreferential links: if an instance of *it* is not linked to any other mention, one can assume that it is non-referential. Note that the same technique cannot be applied to other types of mentions: for example, referring nominal mentions can form singleton chains (consider mention "lowly soldiers" (M_2) in our example (1)). A referential usage of *it*, however, should be either anaphoric or cataphoric.

Bergsma et al. report their evaluation results on two corpora: the BBN Pronoun Coreference Corpus [72] and the ItBank [5]. Both dataset contain newswire documents, however, they represent different domains corresponding to several text sources (Wall Street Journal, Science News and Slate).

Any off-the-shelf machine learning tool can be used for this problem, since it is formulated as a straightforward supervised binary classification task. In practice, Bergsma et al. report their results using the logistic regression packages from Weka and LibLinear.

3.2 Lexical Features

Most traditional approaches to non-referential pronoun detection rely on syntactic heuristics to identify expletive usages of *it*. While syntactic patterns may provide important clues, they alone are not sufficient to discriminate between anaphoric and expletive pronouns. Consider the following example from [6]:

(10) A. [It] is able to maintain a stable price.
B. [It] is important to maintain a stable price.

Although these two sentences follow the same syntactic structure, in (10A), the pronoun refers to a specific object, whereas (10B) is a typical example of expletive *it*.

Following this observation, Bergsma et al. propose to focus on shallow context features. Provided sufficient training data are given to the model, it can be expected to learn the relevant patterns automatically without expensive manual syntactic feature engineering and, at the same time, making use of relevant lexical distinctions. To this end, each sentence containing *it* is first normalized: all the digits are replaced with 0, all the named entities are converted into a special "NE" token. The system then extracts lexical features encoding pronominal contexts, as summarized in Table 2.

3.3 Web Count Features

A supervised model trained with the lexical features presented in Table 2 shows a promising performance level for such a simple approach. Thus, it can successfully induce the information that the presence of additional third person neuter pronouns ("it" or "its") is a good indicator for referentiality. On the contrary, complementizers ("that", "to") often occur within expletive contexts.

However, on a conventional size corpus, the model suffers from the data sparsity problem, making it impossible to fully represent the relevant lexical information. To overcome the issue, Bergsma et al. rely on the information extracted from web counts. From the manually annotated data, they extract contexts containing the pronoun "it" and use them to generate templates, removing the pronoun itself. At

Table 2 Detecting referentiality: templates for lexical features from [6] and their instanciations for (10A)

Feature template	Window size	Examples
3, 4 and 5-grams containing `it`	−5,+5	it-is-able, it-is-able-to, it-is-able-to-maintain
Token + position	−2,+5	is_{+1}, $\text{able}_{+1}, \ldots,$ maintain_{+4}
Unigrams to the right	1,+20	is_{right}, able_{right}, to_{right}, maintain_{right}
Unigrams to the left	−10,−1	∅

Table 3 Detecting referentiality: filler types for web-count features, as reported in [5]

Filler type	String
3rd person singular pronoun	it/its
3rd person plural pronoun	they/them/their
Any other pronoun	I/me/my/...
Infrequent token	<UNK>
Any other token	*

the next stage, they query the Google N-gram corpus to obtain counts for different words filling the empty slot. This approach relies on the following intuition: in referential contexts, non-pronominal words can appear relatively often (for example, "China is able to maintain", generated from (10A) could be found multiple times in a large enough corpus); expletive contexts, on the contrary, generate patterns that are characteristic for non-referential pronouns and cannot be filled with other words ("China is important to maintain" would be rare even in a very large dataset).

Following a normalization step (stemming, applying heuristics for irregular verbs, replacing digits and named entities with special auxiliary tokens), Bergsma et al. extract web counts for different types of fillers, as summarized in Table 3. They encode obtained web counts as features, with each individual feature corresponding to the filler's type, the template length (4 or 5) and the position of the filler in the pattern.

In [6], a modification of this feature subset is proposed. The new features rely on a restricted set of patterns (only "it", "they" and "them" fillers and only 4-token templates are considered) and a more aggressive normalization strategy. This results in a minor performance drop, but at the same time allows for a very efficient implementation that can be stored in the memory together with all the models and thus allows for fast processing of large amounts of data.

3.4 Evaluation

Table 4 summarizes the evaluation results reported by Bergsma et al. for different parts of their system [6]. Note that the reported figures correspond to several test sets, with the train set remaining the same (roughly a half of the BBN corpus). Of the three test sets, two come from the same domain as BBN-train (BBN-test and WSJ-2), whereas ItBank contains out-of-domain data. The results show several important trends. First, only 67–75 % of "it" instances are referential. This highlights the importance of the task for accurate pronoun resolution and text understanding in general. Second, web counts outperform more traditional lexical features. Although web counts correspond to more shallow patterns and smaller contexts, they are extracted from a much larger text collection and thus suffer less from the data sparsity issue. This is especially crucial for the out-of-domain setting, where web counts outperform lexical features by almost 5 %. Most importantly, the

Table 4 Detecting referentiality: the system's accuracy (%) on different test sets, as reported in [6]

Features	BBN-test	WSJ-2	ItBank
Majority class	72.5	74.9	67.7
Lexical features	82.9	82.5	78.7
Web counts	83.3	85.6	83.1
Lexical + counts (NADA)	86.0	86.2	85.1

two groups of features can be combined effectively to further boost the performance. This combination is used by NADA – publicly available toolkit for detecting non-referential "it" instances.[3]

4 Discourse-New Detection

Virtually every modern anaphoric resolver includes some ability to detect discourse-new mentions, but relatively few studies have focused exclusively on the issue. In this section we describe in detail one example of in-depth investigation of discourse-new detection and its use in anaphora resolution, the analysis of discourse-new detection initiated by Poesio et al. [47] and continued in Kabadjov's doctoral thesis [29].

4.1 Features for Discourse New Detection

The objective of Poesio et al. was to assess the results of integrating a discourse-new detector with a definite description resolver, specifically the DD resolution module of GUITAR [46].[4] To begin with, Poesio et al. [47] analyzed the literature on discourse-new detection define their feature space as follows. Every definite description from the annotated corpus produces a training example in the form of $(\mathbf{x}_j, c)$. The target c is binary, the DD has an annotated antecedent or not (i.e., discourse-new). The input features $(\mathbf{x})$ attempt to capture various types of knowledge and are discussed next.

1. **Direct Anaphora.** A single feature, which is produced by running the *direct anaphora* algorithm proposed by Vieira and Poesio [68] and recording the distance in terms of utterances between the antecedent put forward by the algorithm and the anaphor (i.e., the definite description being resolved). The possible values for this features are $-1, 0, 1, 2, \ldots$, which respectively mean

[3]https://code.google.com/p/nada-nonref-pronoun-detector/

[4]GUITAR's DD resolution module is an implementation of the Vieira/Poesio algorithm, see chapter "Early Approaches to Anaphora Resolution: Theoretically Inspired and Heuristic-Based".

no antecedent was proposed, the antecedent is within the same utterance, one utterance apart, two utterances apart, and so on.

Predicative. Two features to detect *predicative noun phrases*:

2. **Apposition.** Value 1 if the DD appears in appositive position, 0 otherwise.
3. **Copular.** Value 0 if not in a copular sentence, 1 if the DD appears on the left-hand side of the copula, and 2 if it appears on the right-hand side.

Proper names. Two boolean features to capture *proper names*:

4. **C-head.** Value 1 if the DD head is capitalised, 0 otherwise.
5. **C-premod.** Value 1 if one of the premodifiers is capitalised, 0 otherwise.

Functionality. As for *funtional* definite descriptions, there are several features meant to approximate "definite probability" by making use of Internet counts. First, they compute Internet counts using Google's API for the following lexical level variations of each DD: "Det Y", "Det H" and "Det A", where `Y` is the phrase left after removing the DD determiner, `H` is the syntactic head of the DD, `A` is the first adjective premodifier (if any) and `Det` is either "the", "a" or "an". And then the following ratios are computed:

6. $\frac{\#\text{“}theH\text{”}}{\#\text{“}aH\text{”}}$
7. $\frac{\#\text{“}theH\text{”}}{\#H}$
8. $\frac{\#\text{“}theY\text{”}}{\#\text{“}aY\text{”}}$
9. $\frac{\#\text{“}theY\text{”}}{\#Y}$
10. $\frac{\#\text{“}theA\text{”}}{\#\text{“}aA\text{”}}$
11. $\frac{\#\text{“}theA\text{”}}{\#A}$
12. **Superlative.** Value 1 if one of the premodifiers is a superlative, 0 otherwise.
13. **Establishing Relative.** A single feature, whose value is 0 if the DD is not postmodified, 1 if postmodified by a prepositional phrase, 2 if postmodified by a relative clause, and 3 otherwise (i.e., some other type of postmodification).

Position. Three features to capture the *position* of the definite description within the text:

14. **Title.** Value 1 if the DD appears in the title (if markup available), 0 otherwise.
15. **FirstPar.** Value 1 if the DD appears in the first paragraph of the document (if markup available), 0 otherwise.
16. **FirstSent.** Value 1 if the DD appears in the first sentence of the document, otherwise.

Surface. A few features to capture *surface features* of the definite description:

17. **DDHasAttributes.** Value 1 if the set of attributes (i.e., premodifiers) is not empty, 0 otherwise.
18. **IsEmbedded.** Value 1 if the definite description is an embedded noun phrase (possibly postmodifying another NP).

19. **NumberOfWords.** The number of words composing the definite description.

V&P. Three features from the original *Vieira and Poesio's algorithm*[5]:

20. **DDAttributesIsSubset.** Value 1 if the set of attributes of DD is a subset of the set of attributes of the antecedent, 0 otherwise.
21. **AnteSubsequentMention.** Value 1 if the size of the equivalence class of the antecedent is greater than 1, 0 otherwise.
22. **AnteIdentical.** Value 1 if the proposed antecedent and the anaphor are identical definite descriptions, 0 otherwise.

Antecedent. Several features representing knowledge about the *proposed antecedent*[6]:

23. **AnteHasAttributes.** Value 1 if the set of attributes of the proposed antecedent is not empty, 0 otherwise.
24. **AnteIsEmbedded.** Value 1 if the proposed antecedent is an embedded noun phrase.
25. **AnteType.** This is a number from 0 to 19 uniquely identifying the type of NP that is the proposed antecedent (e.g., the-np, the-pn, pn).

4.2 *Integrating a Discourse-New Detector in a Definite Description Resolver*

As discussed in Sect. 2.2, four main approaches to integrating discourse-new detection into coreference resolution have been pursued in the literature:

1. Do not train a separate classifier for discourse-new detection, but allow the coreference classifier to use features such as those discussed in the previous section directly. This is arguably the approach most commonly adopted.
2. Train a separate discourse-new detector, and use it as a *pre-resolutionfilter* removing candidate mentions prior to coreference resolution. This is the approach followed by, for instance, Ng and Cardie [41]. (See also the discussion of their approach in chapter "The Mention-Pair Model".)
3. Use the discourse-new detector as a *post resolution* filter, either allowing an antecedent proposed by the coreference resolver to go through, or else precluding an anaphoric link. This is the approach followed by Kabadjov [29]; we discuss it in detail this section.

[5]In the case where no antecedent has been proposed, these features assume a value of -1.

[6]In the case where no antecedent has been proposed, these features assume a value of -1.

4. Use Integer Linear Programming (ILP) to integrate two separate classifiers, a coreference resolver and a discourse-new detector, as proposed by Denis and Balridge [18]. This approach is discussed in chapter "Integer Linear Programming for Coreference Resolution".

Kabadjov [29] carried out a number of experiments using the features discussed above to train a discourse-new detector, and integrating the detector as a post-resolution filter for the definite description resolver of GUITAR.

In [29] experiments with four machine learning methods are discussed: decision trees, maximum entropy (ME), support vector machines (SVMs) and neural networks. Here we focus only on their work with ME and SVM classifiers, since these were used in both of their main experiments (discussed below). For the SVM experiments, Kabadjov used the implementation of the SVM technique in the publicly available LIBSVM library [13] with radial basis function (RBF) kernel $K(x, y) = e^{-\gamma||x-y||^2}$ and the optimal parameters C and γ obtained by cross-validation within each fold. For the ME experiments, Kabadjov used the openNLP MAXENT package [3] which is a library for training and using maximum entropy models. The implemented training algorithm in the library is the *Generalised Iterative Scaling* algorithm using 100 iterations. ME models output a probability for a given class, which means a threshold must be used to produce an actual classification. Kabadjov [29] found an optimal threshold of 0.74 for the discourse-new class based on his cross validation experiment.

Kabadjov [29] ran two experiments: a ten fold cross validation experiment on hand-parsed data and an experiment on automatically parsed data. The GNOME and VPC corpora were used as datasets in both experiments. We summarise both below.

Experiment 1: Processing Hand-parsed Data

In order to evaluate separately the performance of the system at detecting Non-Anaphoricity (NA), Coreference Resolution (COREF), and overall, Kabadjov introduced separate P/R metrics, defined as follows. The definitions of P/R used for evaluating performance at NA are:

$$P_{NA} = \frac{NA_{corr}}{NA_{sys}} \tag{11}$$

$$R_{NA} = \frac{NA_{corr}}{NA} \tag{12}$$

where NA_{corr} is the number of markables correctly classified as non-anaphoric, NA_{sys} is the total number of markables classified as non-anaphoric and NA is the total number of targeted non-anaphoric markables.

For coreference resolution, he introduces the following versions of precision and recall:

$$P_{COREF} = \frac{COREF_{corr}}{COREF_{sys}} \tag{13}$$

$$R_{COREF} = \frac{COREF_{corr}}{COREF} \tag{14}$$

where $COREF_{corr}$ is the number of markables resolved correctly to their antecedent, $COREF_{sys}$ is the number of markables for which an antecedent was proposed by the system and COREF is the total number of markables that have an annotated antecedent.

Finally, Kabadjov introduces a combined measure of performance taking into account both non-anaphoricity classification and coreference resolution:

$$P = \frac{NA_{corr} + COREF_{corr}}{NA_{sys} + COREF_{sys}} \tag{15}$$

$$R = \frac{NA_{corr} + COREF_{corr}}{NA + COREF} \tag{16}$$

where NA_{corr}, $COREF_{corr}$, NA_{sys}, $COREF_{sys}$, NA and COREF are as defined above.

On discourse-new classification Kabadjov's ME and SVM classifiers attained $F_{NA} = 89\,\%$ and $F_{NA} = 90.2\,\%$, respectively, compared to $F_{NA} = 78.9\,\%$ obtained by the baseline of assigning all definite descriptions to the discourse-new class, and an upper bound of $F_{NA} = 100\,\%$.[7]

On definite description resolution Kabadjov's ME- and SVM-based modules achieved $F_{COREF} = 68.6\,\%$ and $F_{COREF} = 68.8\,\%$ respectively, whereas Vieira and Poesio's direct anaphora algorithm (henceforth, baseline$_1$) achieved $F_{COREF} = 67.9\,\%$ and a simple same-head match algorithm, which proposes as antecedent the last markable (if any) with the same head occurring before the definite description in the text (henceforth, baseline$_2$) achieved $F_{COREF} = 62.7\,\%$.The upper bound obtained if perfect DN classification (i.e., $100\,\%$) was available was $F_{COREF} = 74.2\,\%$. Both ME- and SVM-based modules were statistically significantly superior to both baselines according to the *t* and *sign* tests.

Finally, the overall performance of Kabadjov's ME- and SVM-based modules was $F = 83.6\,\%$ and $F = 83.5\,\%$, respectively, in the context of the same baselines as in the previous case, $F = 82.1\,\%$ and $F = 75.22\,\%$, for baseline$_1$ and baseline$_2$, respectively, and a ceiling of $F = 91.8\,\%$.[8]

[7]However, note that a ceiling of 100 % may be a bit too high based on earlier work by Poesio and Vieira [49] where inter-annotator agreement on the task was estimated at $K = 0.76$ (kappa value).

[8]The baselines and ceiling scores were computed with some additional assumptions such as considering discourse-new those definite descriptions for which no antecedent was proposed by the original resolution algorithm.

Kabadjov [29] carried out a sample complexity analysis to estimate the minimum size of training set for successful learning to happen. Based on the lack of performance peak over a gradual increase of performance by increasing the data set, he concluded that more data was needed to reach optimum performance, though, based on their experiments he noted that having a discourse-new detector even if not maximally accurate is better than having no discourse-new detection in place.

Additionally, Kabadjov also performed a feature analysis to gain an insight into what features are more important than others. For that purpose he analysed the induced decision trees. He found out that the most important feature was the *direct anaphora* feature, since it consistently appeared at the root of all the decision trees, followed by the length of the definite description (number of words) and whether there is a capitalised premodifier (cPremod). Kabadjov also noted that the two most common leaf nodes were the *AnteCat* feature capturing the type of the antecedent (e.g., proper name, definite description, pronoun, etc.) and the *Relative* feature, which captures the type of post-modification.

Experiment 2: Processing Automatically Parsed Data

In addition to the 10-cross-validation experiment on hand-parsed data, Kabadjov also ran an experiment on fully automatically processed texts. The purpose of this second experiment was to compare learned classifiers trained on 93 % of the data set from the 10-X-Validation experiment[9] (i.e., 93 % of GNOME and VPC combined) and tested on a different data set (the CAST corpus).

In order to carry out this experiment Kabadjov parsed the CAST corpus with Charniak's parser [14] and then automatically aligned the noun phrases (NPs) with the markables of human annotation. He also modified the way the *sign* test is applied by considering as test items the definite descriptions, for which the version of GUITAR without the DN classifier proposes an antecedent, and then within this set DD's positively affected by the DN classifier count as pluses, DD's negatively affected as minuses and DD's on which DN has made no difference are ignored.

The ME- and SVM-based modules of the system achieved resolution performance of $F_{COREF} = 58.9\,\%$ and $F_{COREF} = 59.3\,\%$, respectively, in the context of $F_{COREF} = 58.5\,\%$ as baseline[10] and $F_{COREF} = 65.4\,\%$ as ceiling.[11] In this second experiment only their SVM-based module achieved statistically significant improvement over the baseline.

In the light of the performance upper bounds presented above, Poesio et al.'s and Kabadjov's experimental results suggest that there is clearly still much room for improvement. On one hand Kabadjov claims that extending their experiments on a larger data set will produce more accurate DN classifiers which will in turn translate into improved definite description resolution. On the other hand extending the data representation model to include more features that are able to capture more

[9]The remaining 7 % were set aside for validation and parameter tuning.

[10]The baseline here is baseline_1 from the 10-X-Validation experiment (i.e., Vieira and Poesio's direct anaphora algorithm).

[11]Assuming perfect DN classification.

fine-grained aspects and subtleties of the discourse-new phenomenon as well as more accurate pre-processing for computing feature values would naturally raise the overall performance.

5 Conclusion

In this chapter we surveyed work on non-reference and non-anaphoricity detection, and discussed in detail the proposal for expletive detection by Bergsma et al. [5, 6] and by Poesio et al. and Kabadjov on discourse-new recognition [29, 47].

Acknowledgements This work was supported in part by the LIMOSINE project (Uryupina, Poesio), in part by the SENSEI project (Kabadjov, Poesio).

References

1. Asher, N.: Reference to Abstract Objects in English. D. Reidel, Dordrecht (1993)
2. Asher, N., Wada, H.: BUILDRS: an implementation of DR theory and of LFG. In: Proceedings of COLING-86, FRG, Bonn, pp. 540–545 (1986)
3. Baldridge, J., Morton, T.: The openNLP MAXENT package. Software available at http://maxent.sourceforge.net/
4. Bean, D.L., Riloff, E.: Corpus-based identification of non-anaphoric noun phrases. In: Proceedings of the Annual Meeting of the Association for Computational Linguistics (ACL), College Park (1999)
5. Bergsma, S., Lin, D., Goebel, R.: Distributional identification of non-referential pronouns. In: Proceedings of ACL-08: HLT, Columbus, pp. 10–18 (2008)
6. Bergsma, S., Yarowsky, D.: NADA: a robust system for non-referential pronoun detection. In: Proceedings of DAARC, Faro, pp. 12–23 (2011)
7. Björkelund, A., Farkas, R.: Data-driven multilingual coreference resolution using resolver stacking. In: Joint Conference on EMNLP and CoNLL – Shared Task, Association for Computational Linguistics, Jeju Island, pp. 49–55 (2012). http://www.aclweb.org/anthology/W12-4503
8. Bos, J.: Wide-coverage semantic analysis with BOXER. In: Bos, J., Delmonte, R. (eds.) Proceedings of Semantics in Text Processing (STEP), pp. 277–286. College Publications, London (2008)
9. Boyd, A., Gegg-Harrison, W., Byron, D.: Identifying nonreferential *it*: a machine learning approach incorporating linguistically motivated patterns. In: Proceedings of the ACL Workshop on Feature Engineering for Machine Learning in Natural Language Processing, Ann Arbor, pp. 40–47 (2005)
10. Byron, D.: Resolving pronominal reference to abstract entities. In: Proceedings of the Annual Meeting of the Association for Computational Linguistics (ACL) (2002)
11. Byron, D.K.: Resolving pronominal reference to abstract entities. In: Proceedings of the 40th Annual Meeting of the Association for Computational Linguistics (ACL '02), Philadelphia, pp. 80–87 (2002)
12. Byron, D.K., Gegg-Harrison, W.: Eliminating non-referring noun phrases from coreference resolution. In: Proceedings of the Discourse Anaphora and Reference Resolution Conference (DAARC2004), Lancaster, pp. 21–26 (2004)

13. Chang, C.C., Lin, C.J.: LIBSVM: a library for support vector machines (2001). Software available at http://www.csie.ntu.edu.tw/~cjlin/libsvm
14. Charniak, E.: A maximum-entropy-inspired parser. In: Proceedings of the Meeting of the North American Chapter of the Association for Computational Linguistics (NAACL), Seattle (2000)
15. Chen, B., Su, J., Pan, S.J., Tan, C.L.: A twin-candidate based approach for event pronoun resolution using composite kernel. In: Proceedings of the 23rd International Conference on Computational Linguistics (COLING), Beijing (2010)
16. Collovini, S., Vieira, R.: Learning discourse-new references in portuguese text. In: Proceedings of IFIP 19th World Computer Congress, Santiago, pp. 267–276. Springer (2006)
17. Daelemans, W.: TiMBL: Tilburg University memory based learner version 2 reference guide. Technical Report ILK99-01, Tilburg University (1999)
18. Denis, P., Baldridge, J.: Joint determination of anaphoricity and coreference resolution using integer programming. In: Human Language Technologies 2007: The Conference of the North American Chapter of the Association for Computational Linguistics, Rochester, pp. 236–243 (2007)
19. Dipper, S., Zinsmeister, H.: Annotating abstract anaphora. Lang. Res. Eval. **46**(1), 37–52 (2012)
20. Doddington, G., Mitchell, A., Przybocki, M., Ramshaw, L., Strassell, S., Weischedel, R.: The automatic content extraction (ACE) program–tasks, data, and evaluation. In: Proceedings of the Language Resources and Evaluation Conference, Lisbon (2004)
21. Eckert, M., Strube, M.: Dialogue acts, synchronising units and anaphora resolution. J. Semant. **17**, 51–89 (2001)
22. Evans, R.: Applying machine learning toward an automatic classification of *it*. Lit. Linguist. Comput. **16**(1), 45–57 (2001)
23. Fraurud, K.: Definiteness and the processing of NPs in natural discourse. J. Semant. **7**, 395–433 (1990)
24. Hawkins, J.A.: Definiteness and Indefiniteness. Croom Helm, London (1978)
25. Hirschman, L.: MUC-7 coreference task definition, version 3.0. In: Chinchor, N. (ed.) Proceedings of the 7th Message Understanding Conference. NIST (1998). Available online at http://www-nlpir.nist.gov/related_projects/muc/proceedings/muc_7_toc.html
26. Hirst, G.: Anaphora in Natural Language Understanding: A Survey. Springer, Berlin/New York (1981)
27. Hobbs, J.: Resolving pronoun references. Lingua **44**(311), 339–352 (1978)
28. Hovy, E., Marcus, M., Palmer, M., Ramshaw, L., Weischedel, R.: OntoNotes: the 90 % solution. In: Proceedings of HLT/NAACL, New York (2006)
29. Kabadjov, M.A.: A comprehensive evaluation of anaphora resolution and discourse-new recognition. Ph.D. thesis, Department of Computer Science, University of Essex (2007)
30. Kamp, H., Reyle, U.: From Discourse to Logic. D. Reidel, Dordrecht (1993)
31. Karttunen, L.: Discourse referents. In: McKawley, J. (ed.) Sytax and Semantics, vol. 7, pp. 361–385. Academic Press, New York (1976)
32. Kolhatkar, V.: Resolving shell nouns. Ph.D. thesis, University of Toronto (2014)
33. Kong, F., Zhou, G.: Improve tree kernel-based event pronoun resolution with competitive information. In: Proceedings of IJCAI, Barcelona (2011)
34. Kong, F., Zhu, Q., Zhou, G.: Anaphoricity determination for coreference resolution in English and Chinese languages. J. Comput. Res. Dev. **49**(5), 1072 (2012)
35. Kummerfeld, J.K., Bansal, M., Burkett, D., Klein, D.: Mention detection: heuristics for the OntoNotes annotations. In: Proceedings of the Fifteenth Conference on Computational Natural Language Learning: Shared Task, Association for Computational Linguistics, Portland, pp. 102–106 (2011). http://www.aclweb.org/anthology/W11-1916
36. Lappin, S., Leass, H.J.: An algorithm for pronominal anaphora resolution. Comput. Linguist. **20**(4), 535–562 (1994)
37. Loebner, S.: Natural language and generalised quantifier theory. In: Gärdenfors, P. (ed.) Generalized Quantifiers, pp. 93–108. D. Reidel, Dordrecht (1987)
38. Mitkov, R.: Anaphora Resolution. Longman, London/New York (2002)

39. Muzerelle, J., Lefeuvre, A., Schang, E., Antoine, J.Y., Pelletier, A., Maurel, D., Eshkol, I., Villaneau, J.: Ancor_centre, a large free spoken French coreference corpus. In: Proceedings of LREC, Reykjavik (2014)
40. Navarretta, C.: Pronominal types and abstract reference in the Danish and Italian dad corpora. In: Johansson, C. (ed.) Proceedings of the Second Workshop on Anaphora Resolution (WAR II), NEALT proceedings series, Bergen, pp. 63–71 (2008)
41. Ng, V.: Learning noun phrase anaphoricity to improve coreference resolution: issues in representation and optimization. In: Proceedings of the 42nd Annual Meeting of the Association for Computational Linguistics, Barcelona, pp. 152–159 (2004)
42. Ng, V., Cardie, C.: Identifying anaphoric and non-anaphoric noun phrases to improve coreference resolution. In: Proceedings of the 19th International Conference on Computational Linguistics, Taipei, pp. 730–736 (2002)
43. Nissim, M., Dingare, S., Carletta, J., Steedman, M.: An annotation scheme for information status in dialogue. In: Proceedings of LREC, Lisbon (2004)
44. Palomar, M., Muñoz, R.: Definite descriptions in an information extraction system. In: Monard, M., Sichman, J.S. (eds.) Advances in Artificial Intelligence. Lecture Notes in Computer Science, vol. 1952, pp. 320–328. Springer, Berlin/Heidelberg (2000)
45. Poesio, M., Artstein, R.: Anaphoric annotation in the ARRAU corpus. In: Proceedings of LREC, Marrakesh (2008)
46. Poesio, M., Kabadjov, M.A.: A general-purpose, off-the-shelf anaphora resolution module: implementation and preliminary evaluation. In: Proceedings of the International Conference on Language Resources and Evaluation (LREC), Lisbon (2004)
47. Poesio, M., Kabadjov, M.A., Vieira, R., Goulart, R., Uryupina, O.: Do discourse-new detectors help definite description resolution? In: Proceedings of the International Workshop on Computational Semantics (IWCS), Tilburg (2005)
48. Poesio, M., Modjeska, N.N.: Focus, activation, and this-noun phrases: an empirical study. In: Branco, A., McEnery, R., Mitkov, R. (eds.) Anaphora Processing, pp. 429–442. John Benjamins, Amsterdam/Philadelphi (2005)
49. Poesio, M., Renata, V.: A corpus-based investigation of definite description use. Computat. Linguist. **24**(2), 183–216 (1998)
50. Pradhan, S., Moschitti, A., Xue, N., Uryupina, O., Zhang, Y.: CoNLL-2012 shared task: modeling multilingual unrestricted coreference in OntoNotes. In: Proceedings of the Sixteenth Conference on Computational Natural Language Learning (CoNLL'12), Jeju (2012)
51. Pradhan, S., Ramshaw, L., Marcus, M., Palmer, M., Weischedel, R., Xue, N.: Conll-2011 shared task: modeling unrestricted coreference in ontonotes. In: Proceedings of the Fifteenth Conference on Computational Natural Language Learning (CoNLL 2011), Portland (2011)
52. Prince, E.F.: Toward a taxonomy of given-new information. In: Cole, P. (ed.) Radical Pragmatics, pp. 295–325. Academic Press, New York (1981)
53. Prince, E.F.: The ZPG letter: subjects, definiteness and information status. In: Thompson, S., Mann, W. (eds.) Discourse Description: Diverse Analyses of a Fund-Raising Text, pp. 295–325. John Benjamins, Amsterdam/Philadelphia (1992)
54. Quirk, R., Greenbaum, S., Leech, G., Svartvik, J.: A Comprehensive Grammar of the English Language. Longman, Harlow (1985)
55. Recasens, M.: Coreferència: Teoria, anotació, resolució i avaluació. Ph.D. thesis, Universitat de Barcelona (2010)
56. Recasens, M., de Marneffe, M.C., Potts, C.: The life and death of discourse entities: identifying singleton mentions. In: HLT-NAACL, Atlanta, pp. 627–633 (2013)
57. Recasens, M., Martí, M.A.: Ancora-co: coreferentially annotated corpora for Spanish and Catalan. Lang. Res. Eval. (2009)
58. Roberts, C.: Modal Subordination, Anaphora and Distributivity. Garland, New York (1990)
59. Rodriguez, K.J., Delogu, F., Versley, Y., Stemle, E., Poesio, M.: Anaphoric annotation of Wikipedia and blogs in the live memories corpus. In: Proceedings of LREC (poster), Valletta (2010)
60. Sinclair, J. (ed.): Collins COBUILD English Grammar. Harper Collins, London (1995)

61. Swan, M.: Practical English Usage. Oxford University Press, Oxford/New York (1995)
62. Uryupina, O.: High-precision identification of discourse-new and unique noun phrases. In: Proceedings of the ACL'03 Student Workshop, Sapporo, pp. 80–86 (2003)
63. Uryupina, O.: Detecting anaphoricity and antecedenthood for coreference resolution. Procesamento del Lenguaje Natural **42**, 113–120 (2009)
64. Uryupina, O., Moschitti, A.: Multilingual mention detection for coreference resolution. In: Proceedings of the International Joint Conference on Natural Language Processing (IJCNLP'13), Nagoya (2013)
65. Vallduvi, E.: Information packaging: a survey. Research Paper RP-44, University of Edinburgh, HCRC (1993)
66. Versley, Y., Moschitti, A., Poesio, M., Yang, X.: Coreference systems based on kernels methods. In: Proceedings of the International Conference on Computational Linguistics (COLING), Manchester, pp. 961–968 (2008)
67. Vieira, R.: Definite description resolution in unrestricted texts. Ph.D. thesis, Centre for Cognitive Science, University of Edinburgh (1998)
68. Vieira, R., Poesio, M.: An empirically-based system for processing definite descriptions. Comput. Linguist. **26**(4), 539–593 (2000)
69. Vilain, M., Burger, J., Aberdeen, J., Connolly, D., Hirschman, L.: A model-theoretic coreference scoring scheme. In: Proceedings of the Sixth Message Understanding Conference (MUC-6), Columbia, pp. 45–52 (1995)
70. Ward, G., Birner, B.J.: Information structure. In: Horn, L.R., Ward, G. (eds.) Handbook of Pragmatics, pp. 153–174. Blackwell, Oxford/Basil (2004)
71. Webber, B.L.: Structure and ostension in the interpretation of discourse deixis. Lang. Cognit. Process. **6**(2), 107–135 (1991)
72. Weischedel, R., Brunstein, A.: BBN Pronoun Coreference and Entity Type Corpus. Linguistic Data Consortium, Philadelphia (2005). LDC2005T33

Using Lexical and Encyclopedic Knowledge

Yannick Versley, Massimo Poesio, and Simone Ponzetto

Abstract Semantic information is one of the indispensable ingredients that are necessary to raise the performance of anaphora resolution – both for pronominal anaphors and for anaphoric definite descriptions – beyond the baseline level. In contrast to hard criteria such as binding and agreement constraints, however, the question of semantic constraints and preferences and its operationalization in a system that performs anaphora resolution, is more complex and a larger variety of solutions can be found in practice.

Keywords Using lexical and encyclopedic knowledge lexical knowledge • Encyclopedic knowledge • Linguistic resources

1 Introduction

It is possible to construct a relatively well-performing coreference system that is purely based on the preprocessing results (syntax, named entity resolution) together with precise but ultimately shallow heuristics, e.g. the system of Lee et al. [40]. In this sense, distance and syntactic heuristics together with good animate/inanimate distinctions (see chapter "Extracting Anaphoric Agreement Properties from Corpora") for pronouns and string matching and string similarity heuristics give a system that performs quite respectably compared to simpler machine learning approaches such as that of Soon et al. [76]. Indeed, at the CoNLL-2011 shared task, Lee et al.'s Stanford Sieve system performed better than systems with more impressive inference and feature approaches.

Y. Versley (✉)
University of Heidelberg, Heidelberg, Germany
e-mail: versley@cl.uni-heidelberg.de

M. Poesio
University of Essex, Colchester, UK
e-mail: poesio@essex.ac.uk

S. Ponzetto
University of Mannheim, Mannheim, Germany
e-mail: simone@informatik.uni-mannheim.de

M. Poesio et al. (eds.), *Anaphora Resolution*, Theory and Applications of Natural Language Processing, DOI 10.1007/978-3-662-47909-4_14

This fact is only seemingly at odds with the often-stated claim that successful coreference resolution has to depend on world knowledge: Indeed, the most successful CoNLL-2012 entry, Fernandes et al. [19] and, to give a much earlier example, including features targeting more elaborate phenomena, Kameyama et al. [32], which performed best at the original MUC-6 competition, all successfully use more elaborate features. Simultaneously, though, we find work that finds absolutely no benefit to more elaborate features, such as Ng and Cardie [55], who explore a large number of features and achieved substantial gains over [76], but found lexical features based on WordNet to be non-helpful, or Kehler et al. [33], who claim that a well-performing coreference resolution (at least in their case) does not benefit from selectional preference information. Such work, in turn, coexisted with even earlier work such as Carter's SPAR [11] that emphasizes the importance of common-sense knowledge, or work such as Harabagiu et al. [27], who find large gains from doing extensive modeling of semantic relatedness using an extended version of WordNet.

One factor of this is the issue of evaluation, particular what we will call **non-realistic settings** that are less sensitive to low-precision resolution behaviour where actual usage in a component for coreference resolution would create (too) many false positives, whereas in realistic evaluation settings (as they are standard in most work done today), more cautious techniques allow more modest (but practically relevant) performance gains.

A second factor is that reductions of coreference to a classification problem, as found in early machine learning approaches such as [76] or [55] have to approximate the structured prediction task of finding coreference chains through binary decisions, making the addition of additional features to a system a non-trivial undertaking, whereas the most well-performing machine learning systems in use today [7, 17, 19] use approaches that are more closely modeling the actual resolution process, and by consequent can use a much larger and richer feature set than the older approaches.

A third factor is the development of **larger and better corpora** in the last 20 years and of **lexical and encyclopedic resources** in the last 10 years, which are all instrumental in the resolution for less trivial links with a precision that is high enough to benefit realistic coreference resolution.

Let us therefore first gain a clearer picture of the specific phenomena in anaphora and coreference resolution that can benefit from lexical and encyclopedic knowledge, and discuss the resources available for this task, before discussing work that integrates this kind of knowledge in more detail.

1.1 Phenomena Requiring Lexical and Encyclopedic Knowledge

In coreference resolution, lexical and encyclopedic knowledge could conceivably help the resolution of pronominal anaphora (*Clinton–she*), the resolution of nominals to either names (*Beijing–the city*) or other nominals (*the capital–the city*), as well as the resolution of names variations that are not detectable through string matching (*IBM–Big Blue*).

Pronoun anaphora Much early work on pronoun resolution that is still well-known today works completely using agreement constraints and factors such as recency and syntactic salience that do not need semantic information. Similarly, the single most effective heuristic for resolving non-pronouns, string matching, can work completely without any semantic information. This prevalence of knowledge-poor techniques, however, is not due to accident, or ignorance of the problem: Early works on reference resolution such as Charniak's 1972 PhD thesis [12] or later Carter's SPAR system [11] explicitly acknowledge the importance of commonsense knowledge to the interpretation of pronouns and non-pronouns alike, to the point of mentioning examples like the following (due to Charniak [12]) where correct resolution of the pronoun requires a full understanding of the text:

(20) Today was Jack's birthday. Penny and Janet went to the store. They were going to get presents. Janet decided to get a top. "Don't do that" said Penny. "Jack has a top. He will make you take it back".

In the example, it does not refer to the most recent top mentioned (the one Jack has), but the (hypothetical!) top that Janet wants to buy. While the full understanding of a text, which would be necessary to resolve such cases successfully, is still not within reach, verifying the fit of the antecedent with the context of the anaphor (e.g., *wear–shirt* being more likely than *wear–store*) or finding plausible progressions of contextual roles (when *A steals* something, and *B investigates*, *A* is more likely to be the one who *is arrested*, while *B* may be the one who *arrests*) seem to be in the range of an approach that uses sufficient lexical knowledge in an effective way.

To operationalize semantic constraints, we have at our disposition the anaphor and antecedent itself, but also their context (mostly, in the sense of the immediate syntactic context rather than a larger notion of discourse context, which would be much harder to model). For pronouns, the form of the anaphor itself (i.e., the pronoun) gives preciously few information beyond compatibility considerations. Therefore, most of the work on using semantic or world knowledge information in pronoun resolution has focused on using context elements, especially **selectional restrictions**. More ambitious approaches in this respect also try to exploit regularities in **event participants** in a discourse, for example the fact that an object of kidnap would occur later as an object (rather than the subject) of release, as in the following example (due to Bean and Riloff [3]):

(21) Jose Maria Martinez, Roberto Lisandy, and Dino Rossy, who were staying at a Tecun Uman hotel, were kidnapped by armed men who took them to an unknown place. After they were released…

However, such semantic preferences usually show **interaction with syntactic preferences**; for example, the following example is easy to misunderstand because a strong syntactic preference (unavailability of non-NP referents) works against the one plausible interpretation:

(22) After Windows 7 comes out in October, will Microsoft somehow force us XP users to stop using it?

The correct antecedent *XP* is dispreferred over the syntactically salient candidate *Windows 7*, requiring the reader to use world knowledge to infer that *it* in this case refers to Windows XP.

Definite Nominals In the case of definite descriptions (common noun-headed noun phrases with a definite article, also called nominals), the information from the head of the anaphoric noun phrase is more useful and can – in the ideal case – be as good a filter for possible antecedents as shallow string matching can be, and most of the approaches in Sect. 1.2 start from this idea. In the following example (cf. Versley [82]), for example, we can exploit **lexical relations** that are good indicators of compatibility in an antecedent, as (female) pedestrian is a hyponym of woman, and car is a synonym of automobile[1]:

(23) An 88-year-old (female) pedestrian has been gravely injured in a collision with a car. When crossing the Waller Heerstrasse, the woman had obviously overlooked the automobile. The driver could not brake in time.

In a similar vein, we often find nominal anaphora where a name antecedent describes an instance of the concept (as in *Berlin ... the city*)[2]:

(24) Even though Berlin ranks last when it comes to growth, the Senator for Economic Development already sees the city as a "Mekka for founders".

This neat connection between lexical relations and antecedence, however, does not mean that our problem is solved: on one hand, around half of the anaphoric definite descriptions do not have an antecedent with a clear[3] lexical relation.

On the other hand, a definite description can also designate a newly introduced entity which is either inferred from the general scenario or that has a non-identity anchor (see chapter "Detecting Non-reference and Non-anaphoricity").

A different set of lexical relations such as those betwee *car* and *driver* can also enable **non-coreferent (associative) bridging relations**, which link an anaphoric definite description to a non-coreferent antecedent.

In an investigation of both coreferent and non-coreferent bridging relations between definite descriptions and mentions in the previous text, Poesio and Vieira

[1]TüBa-D/Z corpus, sentence 190.

[2]Translated from TüBa-D/Z corpus, sentence 2015.

[3]Clear is meant in the sense that it holds up to lexicographic criteria, as opposed to the contents of both terms being incomparable logically.

[57] break up the bridging descriptions into six classes, motivated mostly by processing considerations:

- lexical relations between the heads: synonymy, hypernymy, meronymy (e.g.: *new album ... the record*)
- instance relations linking definite descriptions to proper names (e.g.: *Bach ... the composer*)
- modifiers in compound nouns (e.g.: *discount packages ... the discounts*)
- event entities introduced by VPs (Kadane Oil Co. is currently *drilling ... the activity*)
- associative bridging on a discourse topic (*the industry* in a text on oil companies)
- more complex inferential relations, including causal relations

In the 204 bridging definite descriptions from Poesio and Vieira's corpus,[4] 19 % of definite descriptions had a lexical relation between common noun heads and 24 % were definite descriptions referring to named entities.

Many of these *bridging descriptions* thus pertain to cases that are anaphoric, but which we do not want a system to annotate as coreferent. For example, given a house, we can talk about the door (without ever introducing it as a referent), which is acceptable even when a semantically similar antecedent would be available.

In addition to the difference between coreference, semantic compatibility, lexical relations and relatedness/association, we have to keep in mind that different corpora have annotation guidelines that, although well-motivated, may strike the cursory reader as counterintuitive: The TüBa-D/Z guidelines, for example, preclude **generic mentions** from annotation since their reference properties are not always clear-cut. Consider the following example (25):

(25) The pelage of the Siberian tiger is moderately thick, coarse and sparse [...] Generally, the coat of western populations was brighter and more uniform than that of the Far Eastern populations. [...] In the southeast Trans-Caucasus, the Siberian tiger's main prey was wild boar.

In this example,[5] the Siberian tiger refers generically to the whole subspecies and various subpopulations, which would make annotation potentially difficult.

To provide a different example,[6] consider metonymic mentions of a country such as Israel for either the country, its government, or its population, such as in the following example

(26) Israel will ask the United States to delay a military strike against Iraq until the Jewish state is fully prepared for a possible Iraqi attack with nonconventional weapons, the defense minister said in remarks published Friday. [...] Israel is equipping its residents with gas masks and preparing kits with

[4] A small subset of the Wall Street Journal section of the Penn Treebank.

[5] From http://en.wikipedia.org/wiki/Siberian_tiger

[6] ACE-2, document NWIRE/APW19980213.1305.

> antidotes. [. . .] Israel's armed forces chief, Lt. Gen. Amnon Lipkin-Shahak, appeared on national television Friday night in attempt to reassure a jittery public. "When events are concrete and actually unfolding, we will include the entire population in the measures we decide are appropriate to take," Shahak said in an interview with Channel Two Television.

In the example, Israel and the entire population are coreferent, as they pertain to different aspects (government, population) of the same named entity; as in the example, this sometimes leads to undesirable results, as Israel, its, and its residents violates several strong linguistic constraints (i-within-i, c-command).

In the OntoNotes corpus, a different treatment of metonymy is used, and the Jewish state and its residents would always be separate entities, with counterintuitive effects when considering metonymic mentions such as in "Israel is in fear", which would be non-coreferent to the mention in "Israel will ask the United States", and the underspecified "Israel's armed forces" would pose a problem in these guidelines.

Therefore, different kinds of semantic information would be needed for the ACE and OntoNotes corpora: For the former, one would need to find metonymous mentions such as *China–Beijing*, whereas for the latter, disambiguation would be needed to separate different uses of the same name *Israel*. Due to the fact that only a minority of definite descriptions is anaphoric, a successful resolver would integrate anaphoricity detection (see chapter "Detecting Non-reference and Non-anaphoricity") and the resolution proper. A corollary of this is that results for methods that improve the recall of coreference resolution through means of noisy features (for example, through unsupervised learning) often have to be taken with a large grain of salt, since many evaluation settings that are common in this area – either presupposing a perfect filter for discourse-new mentions or only considering antecedent candidates that are themselves part of a coreference chain – overestimate the utility of such features.

1.2 Lexical and Encyclopedic Information Sources

While earlier work such as Kameyama's MUC-6 system [32] relied on resources specifically built or compiled for the coreference system, and some resources such as gender information are specific to anaphora resolution (see Bergsma chapter), state-of-the-art systems that target lexical and encyclopedic knowledge heavily rely on general-purpose resources to provide lexical and encyclopedic information. Because this is partly independent of the approach for integrating the information into an anaphora or coreference system, we will briefly review the main contenders here.

Lexical resources One of the oldest resources for lexical knowledge is WordNet [50], born out of a desire to be able to find words according to semantic criteria, which has become one of the staples in English-language natural language processing. The backbone of WordNet consists of *synsets* which link synonymous word senses together, and which are in turn organized into a (mostly) taxonomic structure with a smaller number of non-taxonomic relations.

Using WordNet's structure, it is possible to find synonyms (*the suit...the lawsuit*) and hyperonymic relations (*the villa...the house*), but also some near-synonyms when looking at coordinate terms that have a direct hyperonym in common. It is possible to use these relations in a direct manner in order to detect antecedents for nominal mentions that have one of these well-known semantic relations, e.g. in Vieira and Poesio's [85] approach for resolving definite descriptions.

WordNet has been used in coreference resolution by defining semantic classes that encompass certain subtrees of the concept tree, as used in the system of Soon et al. [76], but it is also possible to use distance or similarity measures for coreference, as demonstrated by Lin's MUC-6 system [41], or in the experiments of Ponzetto and Strube [61].

In addition to taxonomic information, WordNet (and many non-English wordnets) offers non-taxonomic relations, which are often too sparse to be a reliable source of information, and glosses, which provide a natural-language explanation of the meaning of words and can be exploited for (low-precision) relatedness measures such as those used by Harabagiu et al. [27].

Another source of lexical (rather than encyclopedic) information can be found in the various resources that cover verbs in particular **FrameNet** [1] and **VerbNet** [34], which both help in generalizing over the grammatical role of one particular verb; because selectional preferences or co-occurrence of argument positions cannot be read off directly from FrameNet's or VerbNet's lexicon, they are most often used together to generalize verb-specific data rather than being used in isolation.

Semi-Structured and Structured Encyclopedic Knowledge Purely lexical resources such as WordNet purposely do not cover named entities, and thus have long excluded all encyclopedic knowledge. The goal of providing a complete sense repository for English common nouns has led to disregard of information about individuals (i.e., named entities), as is evidenced by the limited number of individuals it contains – only 9.4 % according to Miller and Hristea [51] – and by the fact that an individual-specific relation such as instantiation has been introduced with version 2.1 (i.e., in 2005).

As a consequence, earlier works such as Ng and Cardie [55] or Poesio et al.'s [59] investigation into this topic could only rely on the preprocessing results in addition to features extracted from raw text. However, this situation is changing with encyclopedic knowledge that is either extracted automatically or semi-automatically from Wikipedia, or (in the case of FreeBase) curated manually.

Wikipedia is a collaborative open source encyclopedia edited by volunteers and provides a very large domain-independent encyclopedic repository: the English version, as of December 2014, contains more than 4,675,000 articles with tens of millions of internal hyperlinks.

There are at least three main features which make Wikipedia attractive as a knowledge repository for AI and CL applications:

1. good **coverage** across many domains: it contains a large amount of information, in particular at the instance level
2. **multilingual**: it is available with a (mostly) uniform structure for hundreds of languages, even though the size of Wikipedias in different languages vary substantially: German, the second-largest edition of Wikipedia, still contains 1,789,000 articles and there are about 15 languages with more than 800,000 articles, and other languages such as Korean and Arabic, still have a sizeable number of articles (both around 300,000).
3. **up-to-date**: it includes continuously updated content, which provides current information.

Wikipedia exists only since 2001 and has been considered a reliable source of information for an even shorter amount of time [25], so researchers in CL have only later begun to exploit its content or use it as a resource. Since May 2004, Wikipedia contains a thematic categorization scheme by means of its categories: articles can be assigned to one or more categories, which are further categorized to provide a so-called "category tree". In practice, this "tree" is not designed as a strict hierarchy, but contains a coexistence of multiple categorization schemes. Ponzetto and Strube [62], for example, posit that the category of hierarchies, while not being a taxonomy, is generally organized according to specificity.

Wikipedia also contains **structured information** beyond the categories: in particular, the attributes of many salient entities (plants, cities, US presidents, etc.) are listed in a standardized fashion in so-called *Infoboxes*, and there are also many tables with useful data (e.g. a table mapping countries to capitals, or demonyms such as Chinese or German to the respective country names), together with list pages that contain all entries of one particular category (e.g., *seventeenth century composers*).

Thus, subsequent efforts to create resources such as **DBpedia** [49] worked on not just reshaping the category tree, but in extracting useful ontological information out of Wikipedia's data. Another undertaking, the **YAGO** knowledge base [79], sews together Wikipedia information with WordNet and the GeoNames gazetteer for place names. While not always meeting gold-quality standards (YAGO is based on an automatic extraction process, not manual annotation), YAGO yields a good combination of Wikipedia's good coverage for named entities and WordNet's taxonomical information.

YAGO includes about 80 relations (included LOCATEDIN for topological inclusion, or BORNIN for persons being born in a particular city), including a MEANS relation that relates names to their (potential) referent – the string "*Einstein*", for example, has MEANS relations to the concept nodes for Albert Einstein and the musicologist Alfred Einstein – and a TYPE relation which links a particular entitiy to classes they belong to (e.g., physicist). Through MEANS and TYPE relations, it is thus possible to get from a surface string to the corresponding entity concept as well as to attributes, or types, describing that entity.

The **FreeBase** database [8], which is partly based on data from Wikipedia but has since been enriched with data on many other entities in different domains; FreeBase is manually curated, and contains various properties and relations for each entity that are specific to each type of entity (i.e., persons have different properties than medical plants or rock bands).

Learning from Unannotated Text Approaches using manually built knowledge bases rely on high-quality knowledge manually encoded by human experts at the cost of a (necessarily) limited coverage. By consequent, unsupervised (or even semi-supervised) techniques to learn relevant information from unannotated text – which, at least for general-domain text, exists in large quantities even in language other than English – are potentially very attractive since they would allow it to cover even less-frequent words. However, the most popular approaches in distributional semantics all suffer from relatively low precision, which makes it necessary to consider techniques that offer more precision (and, conversely, may be more modest in the coverage and achievable recall that they allow to achieve).

The most well-known among the techniques offering higher precision than purely considering word co-occurrences in large corpora consists in the extraction (and possibly weighting) of **lexicosyntactic patterns** within large corpora.

The occurrence of such patterns is taken to be indicative of particular lexical relations, for example the patterns introduced by Hearst [28] for hypernymy (e.g., *Y*s such as *X*, *X* and other *Y*s) or by Berland and Charniak [5] for part-of relations (*Y*'s *X*, *X* of *Y*). These semantic relations can be then used to help identify strongly related mention pairs as coreferent.

Fleischman et al. [20] follow a similar approach, but extract a large number appositional patterns covering the following constructions based on POS patterns:

- Nominal/Noun constructions
  [*trainer*] [*Victor Valle*]
- syntactic appositions
  [*George McPeck*], [*an engineer from Peru*]

These patterns would individually have relatively low precision, which is why Fleischman et al. use the extracted patterns with a learning-based filter to improve the precision of the approach. To build the classifier-based filter, they use 5000 annotated pairs, together with features describing the surface form of nominal and noun, which allows them to filter the extracted apposition patterns using the learned classifier.

The **sources for unannotated text** that researchers have used for these purposes have varied with time: When, in the early 2000s, corpora such as the BNC counted as large, we soon saw both the coming of larger corpora – in particular, the *English Gigaword* corpus, which contains several billion words of newswire text, as well as Web corpora growing in size from one billion to several billions. Further, exploiting the Web through search engine queries was identified as a useful technique by, e.g., Markert and Nissim [45], but is rarely used in modern systems because of the difficulties in scaling to larger corpora, as well as changing (or simply disappearing)

APIs of search engines, which hinder both reproducibility and scalability of the approach. In contrast, some approaches that allow larger scale than normal Web corpora use the N-gram counts dataset published by Google,[7] or very large Web corpora extracted from the ClueWeb dataset,[8] which contains one complete Web crawl from 2009 and thus allows to construct large corpora in a more reproducible fashion.

Beyond using patterns found in a corpus, there is also the possibility to use standard approaches for **distributional similarity** or thematic relatedness, as used in some of the approaches in Sect. 2.1; However, *similarity* rather than *instance* relations between words tend to be less useful for at least the two following reasons:

- Most distributional "similarity" measures that are commonly used are actually *relatedness* measures that score highly on non-taxonomic pairs of words such as *house–door* or *currency–government*, which means that these measures will typically produce a large number of semantically dissimilar but thematically related spurious antecedents.
- In many cases, semantic similarity between noun phrases (such as between *US Software* and *Software from India*, or between a *goat* and a *sheep*) can still hold when the two mentions are incompatible, despite the fact that their context distributions are as similar as those of quasi-synonyms such as *home* and *house*.

Learning Semantic Information from Coreference Corpora The fact that it is possible to learn semantics constraints or preferences for coreference from coreferentially annotated corpora sounds self-evident enough that one may wonder why only fairly recent systems do this. Part of the answer lies in the available corpora with coreference annotation (cf. chapter "Annotated Corpora and Annotation Tools"): early coreference corpora were rather small (the MUC-6 and MUC-7 documents have below 100 documents together), which means that any such approach would run into data sparsity issues.

The second point that makes this an issue is the interaction between feature design and learning algorithm: the decision tree classifier used by, e.g. Soon et al. [76] or Ng and Cardie [55] works best when used with relatively few, informative, features, and the reduction of coreference to binary classification that was the dominant approach until recently does not necessarily benefit from large, sparse feature sets. Even classification approaches that work in a suitable machine learning framework and on large enough corpora, such as Daumé and Marcu's [16], or the ranking-based system for nominal and names of Versley [82], which could (or can) potentially benefit from this information were designed with data scarcity in mind.

[7]Brants, Thorsten, and Alex Franz. Web 1T 5-gram Version 1 LDC2006T13. Web Download. Philadelphia: Linguistic Data Consortium, 2006.

[8]http://lemurproject.org/clueweb09.php/

Modern corpora such as OntoNotes [63], TüBa-D/Z [80] or the Prague Dependency Treebank [53] offer as much as (or more than) one million words of coreferentially annotated text, which means that certain facts (such as that *the country* likes named entity mentions of the GPE class as antecedents) can be learned effectively from the training set (which in turn may limit the applicability to other domains; the issue of out-of-domain performance of coreference systems has not been investigated as systematically as, e.g., the out-of-domain performance of statistical parsers).

2 Early Approaches

Much of the research until early 2000s targeted specific linguistic phenomena, for the simple reason that the available annotated corpora lent themselves more to manual inspection and careful modeling than to the construction of machine learning-based approaches that rely purely on the annotated data. Subsequent research presents results for all kinds of mentions, but often suffers from the fact that evaluation algorithms were described but not always implemented in the same way, or applied on the same kind of output (see the discussion in chapter "Evaluation Metrics"). In particular, many researchers used the gold-standard mentions as system input, which leads to a severe overestimation of the system's precision, and has been widely criticized both informally and in the literature [44, 77]; as this kind of evaluation has only a weak relation to system performance in practice, quantitative results from such comparison have to be taken with a large grain of salt; however, we find the explorative part of the work may be interesting in its own right.

2.1 Approaches for Specific Phenomena

Using Semantic Compatibility Information for Pronoun Resolution One basic distinction that is necessary for resolving English pronoun anaphora is the male/female/inanimate distinction that corresponds to the *he/she/it* form of pronouns (and corresponds to a difference that is realized in the morphological properties of the antecedent noun phrase in morphologically richer languages). We refer the reader to chapter "Extracting Anaphoric Agreement Properties from Corpora" for a more extensive discussion of this, noting in passing that work such as Ge et al.'s generative model for pronoun anaphora [24] or Soon et al.'s distinction of semantic classes [76] have the important benefit of giving the system information about the he/she/it distinction.

The work of Dagan and Itai [13] similarly presents an approach where automatic parses from a 60 million word corpus are used to extract statistics about subject-verb and object-verb cooccurrences, which are then used as a model of **selectional preferences**. Using a hand-selected sample of it pronouns where the antecedent as well as one or more other candidates compatible in number, gender and syntactic position were in the same sentence, Dagan and Itai found that in 64 % of the cases, antecedent and candidates all occurred at least five times in the parsed corpus, and of these, 87 % had the correct antecedent allowed by their selectional preference model, and in about half of these cases, the antecedent was the only one that fits the selectional preferences.

While this approach clearly steers free of most problems that would hinder the use in a full coreference system – among others, noise in the determination of agreement features, classification of named entities, or treatment of infrequent words – it has certainly inspired further research that aims at using selectional preferences. For instance, Dagan et al. [14] present a post-processor for a rule-based pronoun resolver, which breaks ties in the system's coreference decisions based on predicate-argument cooccurrence statistics, i.e. how many times a pronoun occurs as the argument of a certain predicate. A model based on distributional methods is also presented in Klebanov and Wiemer-Hastings [35], which use Latent Semantic Analysis [38] to model world knowledge for pronoun resolution. Finally, Kehler et al. [33] discuss the integration of selectional preference features in a maximum-entropy based pronoun resolver; they find that in the absence of number or gender agreement features, selectional preference features give a very visible loss in accuracy, whereas otherwise they yield a small (but not statistically significant) improvement over a model with no selectional preferences.

Using Semantic Compatibility Information for Nominal Resolution In the resolution of nominal coreference, Vieira and Poesio's [85] on a subset of the Penn Treebank texts and subsequent work using the GNOME corpus of definite descriptions [59] is focused on the question of resolving definite descriptions (i.e., nominal mentions with a definite article). Among the anaphoric definite descriptions that have a different head from their antecedent (which Vieira and Poesio call *bridging* descriptions), they use synonymy/hypernymy/part-of and co-hyponym relations to successfully resolve 39 % of all such bridging descriptions (from under 10 % if just taking the closest noun phrase as an antecedent). Leaving aside precision errors, this shows that WordNet lacks coverage for many of the *bridging* relations found in the corpus; Work using distributional similarity as a ranking criterion [58] shows that this only results in appropriate antecedents for 23.6 % of such definite descriptions, perhaps underlining the importance of targeting specific relations instead of using a general relatedness measure.

Markert and Nissim [45] contend that some of this stems from relations that are asserted purely in the text and not holding globally: In example (27) (from [46]), the text constructs a relation of *age* being a *risk factor* that we would not expect to find in any realistic ontology.

(27) You either believe Symour can do it again or you don't. Beside *the designer's age*, other risk factors for Mr. Cray's company include the Cray-3's [...] chip technology.

Markert and Nissim's solution then, is to use pattern-based text mining to uncover hyponym relations that are asserted in a text, even when they would not hold in principle or globally. They compare the use of WordNet with (i) pattern mining on the British National Corpus [10], but also (ii) using a search engine to query patterns on the World Wide Web. They show that it is possible to increase recall from 56.2 % (for string matching only) to 64.9 % using WordNet, 59.7 % using the BNC, or 71.3 % using Web search when constrining antecedents to match in number, with precision that still reaches 62.7 % (BNC) or 71.3 % (Web) for resolving a definite description that is known to be discourse-old.

Gasperin and Vieira [22] use a word similarity measure (from [23], very similar to Lin's [42] measure). In contrast to Poesio, Schulte im Walde and Brew's [58] work, they do not resolve to the semantically closest noun, but instead build lists of globally most similar words (a so-called *distributional thesaurus*), and enable the resolution to antecedents that are in the most-similar list of the anaphoric definite, where the antecedent has the anaphoric definite in its most-similar list, or where the two lists overlap. Working on Portuguese data, Gasperin and Vieira find that they reach similar levels of resolution accuracy to the earlier results of Poesio, Schulte im Walde and Brew's with a window-based association metric.

The pattern-based approach requires large corpora to achieve a reasonable recall: this is because patterns occur rarely in corpora. Accordingly, researchers in CL turned in the last years to the Web as a very large resource of linguistic data and developed a variety of knowledge acquisition methodologies (typically using weakly supervised techniques) to mine this large repository of text.

In a similar fashion, Poesio et al. [59] use a multilayer perceptron with features including simple graph distance in WordNet (indicating the number of nodes between the anaphor and the potential antecedent) and a feature based on the raw count of matches for a search engine query using a meronymy pattern. To express salience, Poesio et al. include the sentence distance to the anaphor, but also whether it is in first-mention position, or if any preceding mention of the entity had been in first-mention position.

Bunescu [9] proposes to use discourse-based patterns in conjunction with web queries to resolve bridging anaphora: To resolve an associate definite description to an antecedent, he embeds anaphor and antecedent noun phrases in a pattern "*Y*. The *X verb*", where *verb* is subsequently filled with a list of auxiliary and modal verbs, and results are scored using pointwise mutual information. On a test set of associative bridging anaphora sampled from the Brown corpus section of the Penn Treebank, Bunescu's approach reaches a precision of 53 % at a recall of 22.7 %. A very similar approach is presented by Garera and Yarowsky [21], who investigate the use of an unsupervised model to extracts hypernym relations from cooccurrence statistics for resolving definite nominals. The method aims at exploiting association metric scores to find likely categories for named entities: using the English Gigaword corpus as source of textual data, they evaluate on a hand-selected sample and show that, when using the same corpus, their association measure can achieve greater recall than Hearst-style patterns.

Versley [83] tackles the question of more efficient combination of hand-annotated resources (such as GermaNet [37], a German wordnet) and unsupervised learning from corpora, more specifically the use of generic distributional similarity. He finds that for the problem of selecting an antecedent in the setting used by Markert and Nissim, or Garera and Yarowsky, syntax-based distributional similarity measures are more effective at improving recall when simply used in ranking (similar to Poesio, Schulte im Walde, and Brew's approach using a window-based association measure) than when using it via the intermediate of a distributional thesaurus. However, these measures offer a similarly low precision as semantic classes (which can be computed with high accuracy using GermaNet and other hand-crafted resources, but only offer very limited information). As distributional measures such as that of Padó and Lapata [56] are not strictly limited to semantic classes, however, it is possible to fruitfully combine filters for distributional similarity, distance, and model-assigned semantic class to reap large improvements in precision at a small cost in recall (yielding 80 % overall precision and 59 % overall recall, against 70 % precision and 64 % overall recall for the unmodified distributional similarity and 67 % overall precision and 62 % overall recall for semantic classes only). In combination with GermaNet and Web-based pattern search, it is thus possible to find a coreferent antecedent for definite descriptions with 79 % precision and 68 % recall, or 73 % overall F-measure. As these experiments (like those of Markert and Nissim, or Garera and Yarowsky) assume gold-standard information on the discourse-old/discourse-new distinction, the benefit of these recall-oriented resolution methods is likely to be less pronounced in a more realistic setting that takes into account discourse-new classification.

2.2 A Rush on Gold Mentions

Harabagiu et al. [27] make extensive use of WordNet, including non-taxonomic relations, for different coreference resolution subtasks in MUC-style coreference resolution. They go beyond synonymy and hypernymy and consider **more general paths in WordNet** that they find between anaphor-antecedent pairs found in the training data. To find candidate pairs, they filter out anaphoric expressions with an antecedent that can be found with knowledge-poor methods, such as string matching, appositions, name variation, or the most salient compatible antecedent. For the remaining anaphoric definite expressions, they look for anaphor-antecedent pairs that are related by at most five of the following relation types in the WordNet graph:

- SYNONYM, ISA/R-ISA and HAS-PART correspond to synonymy and hypernymy and meronymy relations.
- GLOSS/DEFINES connect a word in a synset to the word used to define it.
- IN-GLOSS/IN-DEFINITION connects an element of the synset with one of the first words in its definition.

- MORPHO-DERIVATION connects morphologically related words.
- COLLIDE-SENSE connects synsets of the same word (homonyms or polysemous senses).

Harabagiu et al. use three factors to measure the confidence of a WordNet path to predict a coreference relation. The first factor is a binary-valued flag that is set to 1 if another coreference chain contains mentions in the same nominal as the anaphor and the antecedent – e.g. given *Massimo's son* and *his bicycle*, if *son* and *his* have been previously found to be coreferent, the factor for the former pair is set to 1, else to 0.

The second factor prefers "stronger" relations where each WordNet relation type is assigned a weight ranging from 1.0 for SYNONYM over 0.9 for ISA and GLOSS (down to 0.3 for IN-GLOSS). The weight is averaged over the relation types occurring in the path, with multiple occurrences of a relation weighted down by a factor corresponding to their number of occurrences. Additionally, the total number of different relations is used to weight down longer paths.

As an example, a path with one HASPART edge (weight 0.7) and two ISA edges (weight 0.9) would receive a weight of $\frac{1}{2} \cdot \left(\frac{0.7}{1} + \frac{0.9}{2}\right) \approx 0.57$, whereas a path with two ISA edges would receive a score of $\frac{1}{1} \cdot \frac{0.9}{2}$.

Finally, the last factor is a semantic measure inspired by the tf-idf weighting scheme and it is determined by considering the search space built when considering at most five combinations of the semantic relations defined above, starting from either of the synset a nominal can be mapped to. The overall confidence of a path is given by a weighted harmonic mean of the three factors. Confidence scores are then used to iteratively select the paths with the highest confidence as rules of the system.

By exploiting lexical knowledge from WordNet in a flexible way, Harabagiu et al.'s proposal is able to achieve a very visible improvement in MUC F-measure from 72.3 % to a 81.9 %, albeit on gold-standard mentions together with the MUC F-measure, which favors low-precision, high-recall approaches. Later work by Luo et al. [44] points out that in this setting, putting all mentions of the test set into one coreference chain yields an impossibly high baseline of 88.2 % F-measure (with 100 % recall and 78.9 % precision).

Poor evaluation and the ad-hoc-ness of their weighting functions aside, Harabagiu et al.'s work is noteworthy in that they use WordNet to derive a general distance measure, including the definitions contained in the glosses, which yield a markedly different information source from Poesio et al.'s earlier approach (more focused on using the information in WordNet as it is and getting highly precise subsumption and synonymy predictions). They also use a global clustering-based model that can make use of more reliable decisions (e.g. for possessive pronouns) to influence other decisions (for the possessed NPs) where the coreference between the possessors provides additional information, something that would be nontrivial to incorporate into a machine learning approach.

Ponzetto and Strube: Relatedness in Wikipedia Incorporating semantic knowledge into a machine-learning based system for coreference resolution – in this case WordNet, the use of Wikipedia's category hierarchy, and the use of Semantic Role Labeling – is the main goal of presented in Ponzetto and Strube [61].

Ponzetto and Strube use the category tree from Wikipedia as an unlabeled semantic network and compute semantic relatedness scores by means of taxonomy-based semantic distance measures previously developed for WordNet [39, 66, 75, 86].

Starting from the baseline system from Soon et al. [76], they extend it with different knowledge sources, including semantic distance scores computed from WordNet and Wikipedia, and present experiments on the ACE 2003 dataset. The authors find a large improvement in terms of recall on the broadcast news section (whereas the results on the newswire section are modest), with Wikipedia-based scores performing on par with WordNet. WordNet and Wikipedia features tend to consistently increase performance on common nouns. However, semantic relatedness is found not to always improve the performance on proper names, where features such as string matching and alias seem to suffice.

Semantic similarity computed from the Wikipedia taxonomy is evaluated extrinsically by Ponzetto [60], who use them as features of a supervised coreference resolver in the same way as the previously used semantic relatedness scores. The evaluation on the ACE-2 data show that using relatedness works better than computing paths along the ISA hierarchy. Semantic relatedness always yields better results than using similarity scores: but while this is a counterintuitive result, the author argues that this behaviour is an artifact of the annotations in ACE. The use of the Geo-political entities (GPE) class in the ACE data allows for coreferential links such as *Beijing* … *China* and therefore mixes metonymy with coreference phenomena – cf. the discussion in the introduction to this chapter and the link between Israel and its residents in the example (26). To generate these coreference links one needs indeed a more permissive notion of semantic compatibility, i.e. semantic relatedness. Using ISA relations only is (rightfully) expected to work better for data modeling coreference as identity only, which is the case for OntoNotes and most non-English corpora.

Ji et al.: Relation detection and coreference An alternative to knowledge-lean approaches leveraging existing resources and unsupervised approaches extracting structured knowledge from unstructured textual resources is to learn semantic regularities directly from the same coreferentially annotated corpora used to train supervised coreference resolvers. Ji et al. [29] use heuristics integrate constraints from relations between mentions with a coreference resolver. The methodology consists of a two-stage approach where the probabilities output from a MaxEnt classifier are rescored by adding information about the semantic relations between the two candidate mentions. These relations are automatically output by a relation tagger, which is trained on a corpus annotated with the semantic relations from the ACE 2004 relation ontology. Given a candidate pair 1.B and 2.B and the respective mentions 1.A and 2.A they are related to in the same document, they identify three lightweight rules to identify configurations informative of coreference:

1. If the relation between 1.A and 1.B is the same as the relation between 2.A and 2.B, and 1A and 2A don't corefer, then 1.B and 2.B are less likely to corefer.
2. If the relation between 1.A and 1.B is different from the relation between 2.A and 2.B and 1.A is coreferent with 2.A, then 1.B and 2.B are less likely to corefer.
3. If the relation between 1.A and 1.B is the same as the relation between 2.A and 2.B and 1.A is coreferent with 2.A, then 1.B and 2.B are more likely to corefer.

While Ji et al. argue that the second rule usually has high accuracy independently of the particular relation, the accuracy of the other two rules depends on the particular relation. For example, the chairman of a company, which has a EMPORG/Employ-Executive relation, may be more likely to remain the same chairman across the text than a spokesperson of that company, which is in the EMPORG/Employ-Staff relation to it.

Accordingly, the system retain only those rule instantiated with a specific ACE relation which have a precision of 70 % or more, yielding 58 rule instances. For instances that still have lower precision, they try conjoining additional preconditions such as the absence of temporal modifiers such as "current" and "former", high confidence for the original coreference decisions, substring matching and/or head matching. In this way, they can recover 24 additional reliable rules that consist of one of the weaker rules plus combinations of at most 3 of the additional restrictions.

They evaluate the system, trained on the ACE 2002 and ACE 2003 training corpora, on the ACE 2004 evaluation data and provide two types of evaluation: the first uses Vilain et al.'s scoring scheme, but uses perfect mentions, whereas the second uses system mentions, but ignore in the evaluation any mention that is not both in the system and key response. Using these two evaluation methods, they get an improvement in F-measure of about 2 % in every case. In the main text of the paper, Ji et al. report an improvement in F-measure from 80.1 % to 82.4 %, largely due to a large gain in recall. These numbers are relatively high due to the fact that Ji et al. use a relaxed evaluation setting disregarding spurious links. A strict evaluation on exact mentions is able instead to yield an improvement in F-measure from 62.8 % to 64.2 % on the newswire section of the ACE corpus.

Ng: Semantic classes and similarity Ng [54] includes an ACE-specific semantic class feature that achieves superior results to Soon et al.'s method using WordNet by looking at apposition relations between named entities and common nouns in a large corpus to find better fitting semantic classes than using WordNet alone. In addition, he uses a semantic similarity feature similar to the one introduced by Gasperin et al. (indicating if one NP is among the 5 distributionally most-similar items of the other), and two features that are learnt from an held-out subset of the training data:

- a pattern-based feature, encoding the span between mentions by means of a variety of patterns, e.g. as sequences of NP chunk tokens;
- an anaphoricity feature which encodes how often an NP is seen as a discourseold noun phrase in the corpus;

- a coreferentiality feature modeling the probability that two noun phrases are coreferent, estimated by looking at pairs occurring in the corpus.

Training on the whole ACE-2 corpus, Ng is able to improve the MUC score from 62.0 % on the ACE-2 merged test set to 64.5 % using all the features except the pattern-based one.

Yang and Su: Selecting Extraction Patterns Yang and Su [87] present an approach to select patterns as features for a supervised coreference resolver. Starting from coreferent pairs found in the training data such as "Bill Clinton" and "President" (or, due to the annotation scheme of the ACE corpora, "Beijing" and "China", cf. the example 6), they extract patterns from Wikipedia where a pattern is defined as the context that occurs between the two mention candidates – e.g. "(*Bill Clinton*) is elected (*President*)".

To select those patterns that identify coreferent pairs with a high precision, the method filters out in a first step those that extracts more non-coreferent pairs than coreferent ones in the training data. In a subsequent step, patterns are ranked – based either on raw frequency or on a reliability score – and the 100 top-ranking patterns are kept. In the case of the frequency-based approach, a feature is created for each pattern that indicates the frequency of that particular word pair with the pattern in the Wikipedia data.

For the other approaches, they calculate a reliability metric for each pattern (determined by summing the pointwise mutual information values between a pair of noun phrases and the pattern, over all coreferent pairs from the training data). The score for a given pattern and a pair of fillers is then determined as the value of the reliability of that pattern multiplied by the positive mutual information between positive mention pairs. Yang and Su apply these features in a coreference resolution system similar to the one described by Ng and Cardie [55] on the ACE-2 corpus. Using the reliability-based single relatedness feature for proper names (the setting they found to work best) results in an improvement from 64.9 % F-measure to 67.1 % on the newswire portion, 64.9 % to 65.0 % on the newspaper portion, and from 62.0 % to 62.7 % on the broadcast news part.

Daumé and Marcu: WordNet and Patterns An integrated approach is presented in Daumé III and Marcu [16], who use several classes of features. Besides including WordNet graph distance and WordNet information for preceding/following verbs (in an attempt to let the coreference resolver learn approximate selectional preferences in a supervised way), they also use name-nominal instance lists mined by Fleischman et al. from a large newspaper corpus [20], as well as similar data mined from a huge (138 GB) web corpus [72]. They also used several large gazetteer lists of countries cities, islands, ports, provinces, states, airport locations and company names, as well as a list of group terms that may be referenced with a plural term.

3 Current Approaches

From the previous section, it should be clear that a large body of work exists that predates the recent shared-task evaluations in SemEval-2010 [73] as well as CoNLL-2011/2012 [64, 65], starting on small datasets created for the investigation of one particular problem, then ongoing with the MUC and ACE corpora; however, inconsistent evaluation practices make it somewhat difficult to compare approaches by different authors and/or to quantify the impact of techniques more precisely. This is compounded by the use of non-realistic settings using gold mentions that creates a picture of the usefulness of high-recall resolution techniques that does not correlate with performance in practice. Hence, the following investigation will try to gather a coherent picture of the problem based on work that uses a common corpus (usually the CoNLL version of the OntoNotes corpus) and on a standardized implementation of the evaluation metrics (as released in the CoNLL scorer).

3.1 Quantifying the Problem

If we want lexical/encyclopedic features to be effective, we should focus on the phenomena that have the most impact, possibly also on those where we can get the most precise description.

One of the most well-known papers comparing the behaviour of multiple coreference resolution systems is the one by Kummerfeld and Klein [36], who compares several open-source systems [4, 6, 17, 40, 67, 78, 84] as well as the participants of the CoNLL-11 shared task. In the context of this chapter, we see that their "*average of top ten systems*" data contains about as many extra as missing mentions for proper names, of which more than three quarters have matching text or matching head, whereas for nominals we see many more extra than missing text-matching mentions than missing ones; on the side of mentions without common text or common head, there are many more missing than extraneous ones. However, we need to look a bit further for a more detailed analysis.

The most detailed analysis of system coverage for coreference resolution on the OntoNotes/CoNLL dataset to this date has been performed by Martschat and Strube [48].[9] Their goal is to distinguish types of recall errors (i.e., links between mentions/entities that the coreference system should have made, but didn't make), and to this end they first transform the mention clusters of the original coreference dataset (where a set of mentions referring to one entity is annotated as belonging together) to a directed graph of antecedence relationships.

Based on a superset of directed edges linking all mentions to each other – Martschat and Strube assume that the introducing mention comes before the

[9]Both the error analysis code and the code for Martschat's CoRT system are publically available at https://github.com/smartschat/cort

subsequent one, excluding cataphoric relationships – they give priority to edges representing true positive links where the given coreference system and the gold standard agree.

Beyond that, they apply different heuristics to weight the edges that are aimed to uncover sensible antecedence relationships:

- antecedence links from an *uninformative preceding mention* to more informative following one are avoided, in particular where the preceding mention is a pronoun and the following one is a non-pronoun, or where the preceding mention is a nominal one and the following one is a name.
- antecedence links are *weighted by distance*, such that the closest link is chosen among several that are otherwise admissible.

Like Kummerfeld, Martschat considers the output of different systems, including the Stanford Sieve resolver [40], his own system [47], IMSCoref (see [6], or the description in chapter "Off-the-Shelf Tools") as well as the BerkeleyCoref system (see [17] or the description in Sect. 3.3). The Stanford system and Martschat's CoRT system are rule-based resolvers using heuristics for cannot-merge constraints and steps that create links among several mentions, whereas IMSCoref and Berkeley-Coref are based on machine learning classifiers (and consequently can use, e.g., a lexicalized feature model).

In his investigation, Martschat finds that the Stanford Sieve and IMSCoref make the most errors, whereas less of them occur with CoRT and BerkeleyCoref. He also investigates how of the recall errors are *common* to all the coreference systems: only half of the errors in coreference between names are common, while other categories show around 80 % overlap in the errors that each system makes.

Coreference relations among name mentions, presumably the most interesting as not all systems agree on them, could already benefit from better approximate string matching (where clearly the difficulty in approximate string matching is to cover more cases *while maintaining good precision*).

Among these 475 cases of missed links between **two names**, about 154 have a complete string match, which means that either annotation inconsistencies or errors in mention extraction would be responsible for them (e.g., a non-match between *China* and *China's*). A further 109 of these missing links have at least one token in common, pointing to approximate string matching that operated too cautiously. Then, about 104 cases remain where the two mentions share no token in common, which are in majority due to date matching, aliases (e.g., *Florida* and *the Sunshine State*), and acronyms, followed by a long tail of metonymy (e.g., using the capital city's name metonymously for a country), roles (such as *Al Gore... Vice President*), as well as names that are used with inconsistent spelling (especially foreign names).

Martschat found 371 links with a **nominal** having a **name antecedent**, which are often knowledge-dependent (for example, *Mr. Papandreou* being *the prime minister*). Of these, Martschat found that the ten most frequent heads make up 88 of the 371 errors.

Finally, there are a great many links **between nominals** that are missed. Of the 835 instances here, 174 are ones where the subsequent mention is an indefinite noun phrase, which one would normally exclude on linguistic grounds. 341 links in total are noun phrases with matching heads, which again drives home the fact that some problems in coreference resolution are difficult to do *with enough precision*.

Martschat also investigates a sample of 50 coreference links between two nominals with differing heads; of these 50 instances, 23 are hyponyms, 10 are synonyms. Comparing with the rest of these numbers, we see that "boring" problems such as name-nominal matches or same-head nominals, which were not necessarily the most prominent case for the phenomenon-oriented papers of the mid-2000s, are actually fairly important to achieve good coreference resolution performance overall.

Looking at the different systems individually, several facts become apparent; the first is that supervised learning systems can resolve a number of different-head links correctly when they are **frequently coreferent** in the training data (see also Sect. 3.3 for a discussion of this). In particular, the Berkeley Coreference system recovers some links not found by Martschat's CoRT system. On the other hand, both the Stanford system and Martschat's system can resolve some cases that the learning-based systems miss by using more sophisticated alias heuristics, but conversely they miss some cases by performing overly strict modifier agreement checks in cases with matching substrings.

In Martschat's comparison, matching between two names is easiest, but the number of precision errors varies substantially between the systems (where the BerkeleyCoref system shows about 24 % precision errors and the Stanford Sieve gives about 31 % precision errors). Matching name/nominal links (in either direction) is the least precise category among those investigated. Among the systems investigated, CoRT is the most precise in finding links between two nominals.

3.2 Using Lexical and Encyclopedic Resources

As one of the more modern papers using resources containing lexical and encyclopedic knowledge, let us look at the work of Rahman and Ng [68], who use the YAGO ontology, a pattern dictionary (linking named entities to probable words for their semantic type), as well as some resources for representing verbs using FrameNet and PropBank

Rahman and Ng start with a cluster-ranking coreference resolver, to which they add features that would specifically help in resolving cases where world knowledge would be helpful.

Like some or most of the work in Sect. 3.5 below, Rahman and Ng use features based on **YAGO**, including both aliases and hyperonymy-type links, which would allow to resolve "*Martha Stewart*" to the WordNet concept "*celebrity*" via the intermediary of "Television personalities" (the Wikipedia category that *Martha Steward* is found in, and linked to WordNet in YAGO's ontology).

For pronouns, where knowledge-poor systems can only use morphological agreement and salience/recency, governing verbs as well as the antecedent's governing verbs can give a better indication of antecedent plausibility than the pronoun alone.

Rahman and Ng, in this case, use features based on **FrameNet** and **PropBank** (mostly using PropBank for assigning semantic roles, which are then assumed to be consistent across the verbs of a FrameNet frame) and try to assess whether a pronoun and its (potential) antecedent would fit together.

Specifically, one feature considers whether both governing verbs could be part of the same FrameNet frame (yielding a value of yes, if they could be, no, if the possible frames fo not overlap, or the information that one or both verbs are not part of FrameNet).

The other feature for Rahman and Ng's way of integrating frame information into the coreference resolver is to look at the semantic roles assigned by the PropBank labeler, limiting the consideration to ARG0 (proto-subject) and ARG1 (proto-object) and leaving out all other roles to avoid sparse data. The feature using this information then indicates whether anaphor and antecedent are both ARG1, both ARG1, show a transition (ARG1 to ARG0, or ARG0 to ARG1), or that one or both of the noun phrases have a different role than ARG0 or ARG1.

Rahman and Ng combine both of these role-related features, yielding 15 binary-valued features. To apply these to cluster ranking, they add a feature whenever it is true for at least one of the mentions in the candidate's cluster.

Besides features based on specific resources such as YAGO or FrameNet, Rahman and Ng also use features that are based on a simpler, more direct representation of the mentions or their context, using, e.g., the heads themselves as features.

In their **noun pairs** feature, Rahman and Ng represent the mention and corresponding antecedent candidate as an ordered pair of heads, replacing named entities by a more general representation (either the label from the named entity recognizer itself, in the case when one is a common noun and one is a name, or the concatenation of both NE classes when both are names, replaced by "[*class*]-SAME" and "[*class*]-SUBSAME" features whenever two mentions have the same named entity class and either their strings match or there is an overlap in a subset of the tokens).

To improve the generalization capability for the fully lexicalized features, Rahman and Ng replace 10 % of the common nouns in training by a special UNSEEN label, meaning that the fully lexicalized features are not used, whereas "UNSEEN-SAME" and "UNSEEN-DIFFERENT" features are used based on whether the anaphor and the antecedent-candadate show string identity or not.

To extend coverage beyond that of FrameNet, Rahman and Ng also include a feature based on the PropBank roles together with just verb lemmas (instead of frames), which uses the **verb pair** together with the respective roles.

To further increase the coverage for noun phrase-name pairs, Rahman and Ng use existing repositories of NP pairs extracted through patterns [20, 54], covering, for example pairs such as "*Eastern Airlines*" and "*the carrier*", for a total of slightly over one million NP pairs. They use a binary-valued feature indicating whether the anaphor and any mention in the candidate cluster can be found in the extracted database.

In their evaluation, Rahman and Ng build the additional world knowledge features into a state-of-the art coreference resolver based on cluster ranking, and find that all of the proposed features give improvements (sometimes small, sometimes rather visible).

Among the features aimed at non-pronouns, their *YAGO-Types* feature (aimed at hyperonymy-like relations within YAGO) and the non-resource-using *word pairs* features perform at about the same level, with the resource-based YAGO-Types feature sometimes reaching better precision, and both features reaching better precision as well as recall than the pattern-based *Appositives* feature or the *YAGO-Means* feature, which only targets aliases and synonymy.

Among the verb-based features, which should make a difference mainly for pronouns and other not-as-informative noun phrases, Rahman and Ng report that the *verb pairs* feature performs better than the *FrameNet* feature on both precision and recall, yielding a consistent advantage over all evaluation measures, corpora, and system variants (mention-pair vs. cluster ranking).

Altogether, Rahman and Ng get a very large improvement of about 4 % from the combination of all features, across different corpora (ACE and OntoNotes) and evaluation metrics (Bcubed and CEAF). In particular, this is a difference about as large as that between cluster-ranking and the simpler mention pair model. They also show that, among the low-hanging fruits in terms of features that can be used with just a large training corpus and no additional lexical resources, the largest gains can be achieved using the noun-pairs features, followed by those using pairs of adjective phrases and then pairs of verbs.

Bansal and Klein [2] present another approach to use external resources – in this case, patterns extracted from Google's Web n-grams dataset covering both the case of name-noun patterns used in previous work but also more general co-occurrence statistics based on this data.

Bansal and Klein start from a mention-pair model similar to the Reconcile system of [77], but using a decision tree learner (which gave more precise results in their study, with a relatively small cost in terms of recall), and add additional features to capture more information on *general lexical affinities* (i.e., relatedness expressed through co-occurrence), *lexical relations* (i.e., relations expressed through patterns such as those used by Rahman and Ng, earlier this section), *similarity of entity-based context* (typical verbs or adjectives co-occurring in pre-defined patterns), as well as matches of the soft clustering from an existing dataset [43], as well as statistics about plausible fillers for a *pronoun context*.

In the simplest case, **co-occurrence of the head words** within a 5-gram window is counted, and normalized by the counts of each individual head word by itself, and using a binned log-value of this ratio as a feature (except for a normalizing overall count, this statistic is very similar to the *pointwise mutual information* statistic, and indicates the degree of first-order relatedness of the two items).

For the **patterns co-occurrence** feature, Bansal and Klein use Hearst-like co-occurrence patterns indicating isA-relations. In particular, they use patterns of the form

- h_1 BE DET? h_2
- h_1 (and|or) (other|the other|another) h_2
- h_1 (other than|such as|, including|, especially) DET? h_2
- h_1 of (the|all) h_2

(Where BE corresponds to the forms *is/are/was/where*, and DET corresponds to the forms *a/an/the*).

They use these patterns in the form of a quantized normalized count for all patterns together, using a binning strategy similar to the general co-occurrence feature.

For the **entity-based context** feature, Bansal and Klein look for copula or passive constructions linking one head to a descriptive word using the "*h* BE DET? *y*" pattern (finding not only nouns such as *head* for president, but also predicates such as *elected* or *responsible*), using the list of the frequent 30 matches to construct a descriptor for a head word, and turn these descriptor list for one feature that indicates whether there is a match within the top *k* items on both lists (leaving the *k* as a tuning parameter), and one whether both lists have the same dominant part of speech (for one of adjectives, nouns, adverbs or verbs), or *no-match* otherwise.

For the **cluster-based** similarity, Bansal and Klein look for the topmost-ranked cluster-id that is common to the (20 most salient) clusters for two heads, and use the rank sum as a feature in binned form.

Finally, their **pronoun context** feature is most useful for pronoun anaphors in that it also looks at the context of the mention: given a context "(pronoun) r r'", Bansal and Klein try to estimate how likely it is that the pronoun has an antecedent "h_1" that would fit this context by considering co-occurrences of h_1 with the first right context word either directly neighbouring (R1) or with a gap in-between (R1gap), or with both right context words directly neighbouring (R2).

As an example, if "*his*" in "*his* victory" is considered with a candidate "*Bush*" as h_1, the normalized count

$$\frac{\text{count}(\text{“}\textit{Bush's} \star \textit{ victory}\text{”})}{\text{count}(\text{“}\star \textit{ 's victory}\text{”})\,\text{count}(\text{“}\textit{Bush}\text{”})}$$

would be calculated for the R1gap feature. Counts for the different variations are binned and used as separate features.

In their experiments, which use the MUC metric and the B^3all variant of the Bcubed evaluation metric, they find that they get a large improvement (about 4 %) from switching from a linear classifier (averaged perceptron) to a decision tree learner, and another gain of about 1.1–1.8 % for all the web-based features together, with the largest improvement coming through the pronoun context feature (+0.6 % MUC, +0.4 % B3all), the Hearst patterns (+0.2 % MUC, +0.4 % B3all) as well as the headword similarity through context features (+0.4 % MUC, +0.1 % B3all).

Bansal and Klein report that, in comparison to their baseline system, the new system is more successful at resolving many name-noun coreference links such as finding "*the EPA*" as the antecedent of "*the agency*" or "*Barry Bonds*" as antecedent of "*the best baseball player*", and that strong general co-occurrence, as well as the absence of cluster-match and/or Hearst pattern matches, as well as the R2 pronoun context feature are strongly discriminative for the decision tree.

3.3 Lexicalized Modeling of Coreference

Two mostly recent innovations – namely the predominance of learning models that (like maximum entropy, support vector machines, or structured learning counterparts of these, but unlike decision trees) support high-dimensional feature spaces on the one hand, and the availability of relatively large coreferentially annotated corpora, makes the use of **lexicalized features** such as the *noun pair* or *verb pair* features used by Rahman and Ng in the previous section both possible and (as it turns out) quite attractive.

As examples of systems that can use more detailed information in a purely supervised learning scenario that does not involve external resources, we will have a look at two relatively modern systems (Durrett and Klein's *Easy Victories* system [17] as well as Björkelund's *HOTCoref* system [7], also described in Sect. 3.6 and chapter "Off-the-Shelf Tools", respectively). Durrett and Klein use the term *Easy Victories* to describe the fact that cluster ranking with an online learning approach (as used by Durrett and Klein, or by Björkelund's HOTCoref) allows it to make use of lexicalized features quite easily, and that these lexicalized features offer a straightforward way to improve the resolution of more difficult cases whenever the relevant information occurs frequently enough in a large corpus.

To start with the learning and inference part, Durrett and Klein use a mention-synchronous resolver similar to that of Luo et al. [44] or Daumé and Marcu [16], applying loss-scaled online updates whenever a wrong resolution decision in training occurs; this avoids the training set balance that plagued classical mention-pair systems such as [76] or [55]. By assigning different (local) losses to different types of wrong decisions (*false negatives*, *wrong links*, or *false anaphors*), Durrett and Klein can model the decisions for structure-building in coreference in a suitable way.

Durrett and Klein combine their individual features from general information (type of both mentions – names, nominals, or various types of pronouns), more specific features on the current mention, or more specific features on the antecedent candidate – in particular, *head word*, as well as *first*, *last*, *preceding* and *following* words as well as the length of that mention – or alternatively, features that fire based on the pair, namely string match of the heads or of the complete string, and distance in terms of sentences or mentions (capped at 10).

Durrett and Klein show that their surface lexicalized features successfully cover distinctions such as definiteness, number/gender/person matching for pronouns, as well as some information on the grammatical role of a mention. Using specialized features for these criteria, as well as WordNet-based hypernymy and synonymy, an existing number and gender dataset (see chapter "Extracting Anaphoric Agreement Properties from Corpora"), as well as named entity types and rough clusters of nominal heads and verbal roles, then, gives an additional gain leading from a CoNLL metric score of 60.06 to 60.42, which is substantially less impressive than the gains from the "generic" lexicalized features.

The reason for this rather small gain from more semantic features, according to Durrett and Klein (all while they achieve a substantially larger gain – from 75.08 to 76.68 – in the non-realistic setting with gold mentions) is the insufficient precision of the cues for non-same-head mentions.

For their *final* system, Durrett and Klein combine the surface features with additional features that do not necessarily target semantics but are proven to be helpful, in particular whether two mentions are nested, a dependencies feature including the parent and grandparent POS tags and arc direction, as well as a speaker identification feature, on top of the aforementioned gender/number data. Using all these features, Durrett and Klein's *final* system reaches a CoNLL score of 61.58, indicating that their framework, together with a simple homogeneous set of features together with a small set of (non-semantic!) specialized features yields relatively high performance.

3.4 Knowledge-Based Alias Resolution

An approach that is conceptually different is used by Recasens, Can and Jurafsky [74], who use a corpus of comparable documents to extract **aliases** (i.e. pairs of nouns or names that uniquely refer to the same thing, but which may not be similar on the surface level), such as *Google* and *the Mountain View search company*.

Recasens et al. start by downloading clusters of documents about the same events from the *Techmeme* news aggregation site, obtaining 25k story clusters totalling about 160 million words. Among the documents pertaining to the same story, they rank the verbs according to their tf-idf score (excluding light verbs and reporting verbs), to gather comparable mentions of events such as *Google crawls web pages* and *The search giant crawls sites*, and assuming that the subjects and the objects each are referring to the same thing unless one of a list of *filtering* criteria is fulfilled, which are added to exclude some spurious pairs (raising the precision from 53 % to 74 %): If both mentions are named entities, if at least one of them is a number or temporal NE, or the mention of the verb has a negator, the pair is filtered out.

In a second step, Recasens et al. remove determiners as well as clausal modification, yielding a core consisting of the head noun or name, adjectival or genitive premodifiers, and PP postmodifiers. They also generalize non-head named entities to their types, allowing to link "*the leadership change*" to "⟨*Person*⟩*'s departure*". Recasens et al. report that their method finds not only synonymy and instance relations such as *change* versus *update*, but also metonymic cases such as *content* versus *photo*, or *government* versus *chairman*.

Recasens et al. incorporate the extracted dictionaries in the rule-based *dcoref* resolver, and evaluate their system using gold mentions, a setting with which they achieve a gain of 0.7 % F1 score for the CoNLL metric.

3.5 Combining NE Linking and Coreference

While it has been a long-term goal of some work (e.g. Ponzetto and Strube [61]) to include knowledge based on names in coreference resolution, both the ambiguity resolution of names and the mechanisms to use knowledge about entities have improved in recent work: In particular, the current state of the art includes newer resources such as the YAGO ontology, as well as annotated data on general-purpose linking of names to Wikipedia, either in the form of data generated from Wikipedia itself or in the shared tasks of the Text Analytics Conference [30, 31]. In particular, neither Rahman and Ng nor Ponzetto and Strube make use of such a dataset or the taggers derived from that data to disambiguate mentions of entities.

Uryupina et al.: Name disambiguation and YAGO relations Among the first to use name disambiguation in a coreference systems were Uryupina et al. [81], who use a name disambiguation approach based on training data derived from Wikipedia based on a kernel capturing gappy n-gram, single-word and latent semantic information, and subsequently using YAGO MEANS and TYPE relations as features.

To improve the precision of their YAGO-based features, Uryupina et al. use several filters that exclude cases that often yield false positives:

The first one is **discourse-new detection** for potential hyperonyms: If a candidate for a hyperonym has a modifier indicating a non-anaphoric mention, such as *any other country* in

(28) [India]'s advantage, it simply has more skilled, English-speaking programmers than [any other country] outside the U.S.

where Uryupina et al. suppress the indication of a YAGO TYPE relation whenever the determiner of the subsequent noun phrase is incompatible with a coreference relation. The second covers **too common hypernyms**, which are terms at a very general level of the taxonomy such as *group* or *part* which frequently occur in false positives, based on a manual analysis. A third filter prohibits the feature from firing for nominal-name links (as opposed to name-nominal ones) since these are often part of wrong or inconsistent coreference decisions.

Uryupina et al. test their approach on the ACE-02 corpus, against two baselines: one using Soon et al.'s [76] features, and one additionally using a WIKI-ALIAS feature that detects mentions linking to the same concept in Wikipedia.

In Uryupina et al.'s work, improvements were not uniform across the sections of the ACE data, but they show that the disambiguation, as well as the features based on YAGO relations and the additional filters can improve performance quite a bit – 1.6 % CEAF and 2 % MUC for gold mentions on BNEWS, or 1.4 % and 1.8 % over the baseline with WIKI-ALIAS feature, whereas the improvements for the other parts of the ACE corpus are less drastic.

While Uryupina et al.'s improvements are not uniform across all parts of the ACE-02 corpus, it should be noted that they show both the use of disambiguating and linking named entities to external ontologies as well as the usefulness of having interpretable structure rather than just using super- and subcategories within Wikipedia.

Ratinov and Roth: Relatedness through attributes A number of subsequent approaches have used more elaborate learning approaches together with gold mentions, such as Ratinov et al. [70], who extract **attributes** from Wikipedia pages (such as *Redmond* for *Microsoft*), which they then use to further the recall in a system based on a hybrid of Lee et al.'s Sieve and a more standard mention-pair model, using the GLOW named entity linker of [71].

Ratinov and Roth use the attributes both for name-name and name-noun candidates, where they have different roles: two names of the same kind are very likely not to corefern, whereas a name and a matching noun often indicate an anaphoric relation.

Hajishirzi et al.: Comparibility/Incomparibility A similar idea underlies the NECo system of Hajishirzi et al. [26]: They start from the Stanford Sieve system (see chapter "Early Approaches to Anaphora Resolution: Theoretically Inspired and Heuristic-Based" for a discussion), but incorporate both the detected spans and the suggested linked entities in the mention clusters, and add to the sieve steps of the Stanford system two additional ones making use of the NEL information: one that is akin to the YAGO-MEANS relation which merges two coreference clusters if they link to the same entitiy, and one more akin to the YAGO-TYPE relation which merges common noun mentions with antecedents that have this noun as an attribute in Freebase (which covers descriptions such as *Donald Tsang* being a *president*, or *Disneyland* being a *park*).

Hjishirzi et al. use an ensemble from the named entity linkers GLOW [71] and WikipediaMiner [52] to extract high-confidence named entity link candidates, where mention spans from both the coreference system and the from the NEL are merged and those duplicates that differ only by a stop word.

- an *exact link* l_m if the entire span excluding stop words links to a known entity.
- a *head link* h_m if the head matches a known mention (e.g., *President Clinton* to *Bill Clinton* because of the head word *Clinton*)

Clusters correspondingly receive an exact link l_c and a head link h_c based on their most prominent mention (the *exemplar* in the parlance of the Stanford Sieve). Clusters are regarded as incompatible if they have incompatible (i.e., non-null and different) exact or head links.

Table 1 The most commonly used fine-grained attributes from Freebase and Wikipedia (out of over 500 total attributes) in [26]

Country	President	City	Area
Company	Starte	Region	Location
Place	Agenc	Power	Unit
Body	Market	Park	Province
Manager	Organization	Owner	Trial
Site	Prosecutor	Attorney	County
Senator	Stadium	Network	Building
Attraction	Government	Department	Person
Origin	Plant	Airport	Kingdom
Capital	Operation	Author	Period
Nominee	Candidate	Film	Venue

Additionally, the algorithm keeps track of lists of related entities:

- a list L_m of all entities with a direct link to the span's entity (including, for example, *Alabama* for *Bill Clinton*, or, for *The governor of Alaska Sarah Palin* references to *List of governors of Alaska*, *Alaska* and *Sarah Palin*).
- a list L'_m that additionally includes entities linked to sub-phrases
- A list L_c for each cluster that contains *all* linked entities found in a cluster

To be considered plausible merge candidates, two clusters must be *related* to each other in FreeBase; when merging, not only are the standard attributes of Sieve mentions are merged but also the union of the clusters' attributes is taken (Table 1).

Hajizhirzi et al. compare their system with the Standford system on both the ACE-2004 and CoNLL-2011 datasets, including a fully automatic setting using system mentions and automatic named entity linking. They can achieve significant increases in the MUC score and slight increases on the B^3 score, and achieve larger improvements on the ACE-2004 dataset with respect to the Stanford Sieve system. They also compare the results on ACE2004-NWIRE to a version that omits the non-linking constraints between mentions that have incompatible NE links, showing that a substantial part of the performance gains come from enforcing *in*compatibility between mentions sharing a common word (such as *Staples* the company and *Todd Staples* the politician).

3.6 *Joint Models of NEL and Coreference*

Also on gold mentions, Zheng et al. [88] extend the idea of Ratinov and Roth to use *Dynamic Linking*, meaning that the coreference decisions of a mention-pair model can influence the subsequent decisions of named entity linking, using a reranking of the candidates. To do this, they use an existing named entity linking system [15], but keep (ambiguous) lists of candidate links, which they subsequently merge and rerank during inference.

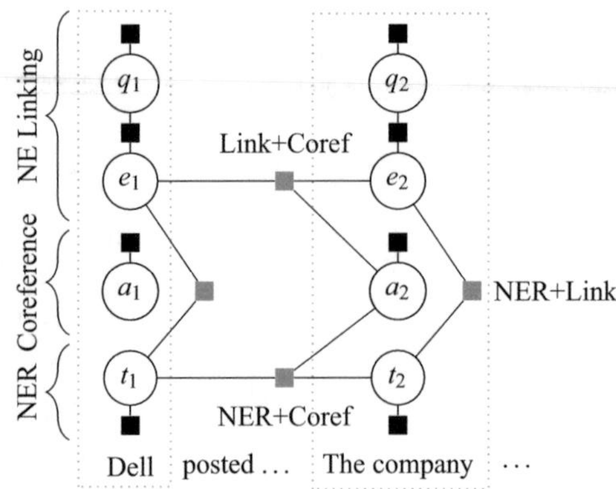

Fig. 1 Interaction between factors on different levels (from [18]): Consistency between Linking and NER is encouraged by NER+Link factors (e_1/t_1, e_2/t_2), Consistency between coreferent Link and NER mentions is ensured by Link+Coref ($e_1/e_2/a_2$) and NER+Coref ($t_1/t_2/a_2$) factors

A system with tighter integration between named entity recognition, entity linking and coreference in a **factor graph model for coreference and linking** was presented by Durrett and Klein [18], who model the decision in these tasks and the interactions across levels in a factor graph, using iterations of belief propagation in a pruned factor graph for inference in that model.

The intuition behind it all is simple: named entity recognition on ambiguous instances (e.g. shortened names) can profit from at least some kind of coreference information, and similarly can profit from Wikipedia knowledge, and similarly coreference can profit from better named entity information.

Features The *coreference* variables (a_1, a_2 in Fig. 1) in the model indicate, for each mention, whether it is new or should be resolved to some (previous-mention) antecedent, with the feature set of Durrett and Klein's earler lexicalized mention-ranking approach [17].

Named entity variables (t_1, t_2) specify, for each span, what semantic type (if any) they are, and consequently also describe the semantic type of their surrounding mention. They use state-of-the-art token-based features such as those used in earlier work on NER [69], including word clusters.

Finally, *entity linking* factors (e_1, e_2) link one mention to a particular Wikipedia title (or none); these are based on a query string that is supposed to be a latent variable (i.e., unobserved both in training and in testing) specifying which part of the mention string is queried for, as, e.g. *Chief Executive Michael Dell* has not been hyperlinked on Wikipedia whereas *Michael Dell* does. In addition, the relation between the "official" page title and the related text portion of the mention is modeled through a *query* variable (q_1, q_2).

Interaction factors Durrett and Klein then link the variables on each level by cross-task interaction factors that use information across different tasks:

- The simplest factors concern *entity linking and NER*, in particular evidence such as categories (e.g. *American financiers*) or infobox types (e.g. *Person*, *Company*), as well as the predicate occurring in a copula clause in the first sentence of a Wikipedia article.

- Other factors enforce consistency between *Coreference* and *NER*: in particular, the pair of semantic types for the current and antecedent mention, and combinations of semantic type and head of the current mention, and the semantic type and head of the antecedent mention containing exactly one lexicalized item.
- Finally, factors joining *Coreference and Entity Linking* have a similar structure to those between coreference and NER, but use indicators of relatedness (same title, shared links, or links to each other)

Inference To perform efficient inference with the joint factors, a first pass is carried out using only the within-level factors (which are substantially less complicated), to *prune* the possible variable settings, reducing both the size of the problem and the number of combinations that has to be considered for the joint factors.

Durrett and Klein use *Minimum Bayes Risk* decoding for the inference, meaning that they compute marginals over each variable (specifying how likely e.g. a given antecedence relation is) and compose the solution from most likely variable settings, instead of simply using the single highest-scoring solution. This kind of inference can be advantageous to provide some isolation between the levels when it comes to uncertain results, at the potential disadvantage that the solution returned by this kind of inference may not always respect the consistency of multiple variables against each other.

Results Durrett and Klein test their approach on a different test set for each task; for coreference in particular, they use the CoNLL-2012 and ACE-2005 test sets for the final evaluation of the coreference resolution performance of their system and compare their 2013 system (which does global coreference resolution based on a pipeline approach involving other components) to a version of their system without cross-task factors, and the complete, joint version of their system.

While the *independent* version of their system, presumably identical in approach to the 2013 version but with the better preprocessing that is part of the new system, Durrett and Klein achieve a score of 61.23 on the CoNLL-2012 test set, about 0.9 higher than the 2013 version. On top of this very competitive system, the interaction factors and joint decoding yields a further 0.5 improvement to 61.71, slightly higher than Björkelund's HOTCoref system (see [7] or chapter "Off-the-Shelf Tools").

4 Conclusion

In this chapter, we have discussed some of the issues around lexical and encyclopedic knowledge in more detail: from the problems that should be solved, to the lexical and encyclopedic knowledge that is available outside of annotated corpora to help in the decision, to the ways you can exploit both lexicalized models in large corpora and the incorporation of entity linking into corpora.

We saw that part of the confusion around using encyclopedic knowledge were works that perform evaluation in *non-realistic settings*, such as using gold mentions (i.e. using only mentions that are part of a coreference set in the gold standard, substantially simplifying the task) including early work by Harabagiu et al. [27]. Even more recent work such as Ponzetto and Strube [61] or even Ratinov and Roth [70] and Zheng et al. [88] that shows large gains from complex features does so in great part because these non-realistic settings are more forgiving of recall-heavy resolution strategies that sacrifice precision in order to find more coreference links.

Conversely, in realistic settings, where the loss in precision would be amplified by the additional (non-gold) mentions present, it is substantially harder to achieve gains by incorporate lexical and encyclopedic knowledge, but still possible and necessary, as demonstrated by most of the work discussed in the rest of this chapter, which uses more cautios techniques to achieve more modest (but practically relevant) performance gains.

According to the resources that were or are available, we see that there is a significant shift towards supervised *lexicalized* models for coreference that is fueled by the general availabilty of large corpora such as TüBa-D/Z or OntoNotes; in the direct comparison of Rahman and Ng, we see that lexicalized features are low-hanging fruits in the sense that they achieve larger improvements than unsupervised learning (in part because supervised learning yields task-specific information while unsupervised learning only yields more general, and often more noisy, distinctions).

To use encyclopedic knowledge fully, Uryupina et al. and subsequent research by Ratinov and Roth, Hajishirzhi and Zilles *inter alia* shows that it is beneficial to use named entity linking, or disambiguation of entity mentions, to make full benefit of the information in Wikipedia, and that, contrary to the more extensive relationships sought after by the early work of Ponzetto and Strube, synonymy-like alias relations (YAGO-MEANS) and hyperonymy-like instance relation (YAGO-TYPE) are key to achieving access to precise, reliable lexical and encyclopedic information.

References

1. Baker, C.F., Fillmore, C.J., Lowe, J.B.: The Berkeley FrameNet project. In: Proceedings of the 36th Annual Meeting of the Association for Computational Linguistics and 17th International Conference on Computational Linguistics, Montreal, pp. 86–90 (1998)
2. Bansal, M., Klein, D.: Coreference semantics from web features. In: Proceedings of the 50th Annual Meeting of the Association for Computational Linguistics (ACL 2012), Jeju Island, pp. 839–398 (2012)
3. Bean, D., Riloff, E.: Unsupervised learning of contextual role knowledge for coreference resolution. In: Proceedings of the Human Language Technology Conference of the North American Chapter of the Association for Computational Linguistics (HLT-NAACL 2004), Boston, pp. 297–304 (2004)
4. Bengtson, E., Roth, D.: Understanding the value of features for coreference resolution. In: Proceedings of the Conference on Empirical Methods in Natural Language Processing, Honolulu, pp. 294–303 (2008)

5. Berland, M., Charniak, E.: Finding parts in very large corpora. In: Proceedings of the 37th Annual Meeting of the Association for Computational Linguistics (ACL 1999), College Park, pp. 57–64 (1999)
6. Björkelund, A., Farkas, R.: Data-driven multilingual coreference resolution using resolver stacking. In: Joint Conference on EMNLP and CoNLL – Shared Task, Jeju Island, pp. 49–55 (2012)
7. Björkelund, A., Kuhn, J.: Learning structured perceptrons for coreference resolution with latent antecedents and non-local features. In: Proceedings of the 52nd Annual Meeting of the Association for Computational Linguistics (ACL 2014), Baltimore, pp. 47–57 (2014)
8. Bollacker, K., Evans, C., Paritosh, P., Sturge, T., Taylor, J.: Freebase: a collaboratively created graph database for structuring human knowledge. In: Proceedings of the 2008 ACM SIGMOD International Conference on Management of Data, SIGMOD '08. ACM, New York, pp. 1247–1250 (2008). doi:10.1145/1376616.1376746
9. Bunescu, R.: Associative anaphora resolution: a web-based approach. In: Proceedings of the EACL 2003 Workshop on the Computational Treatment of Anaphora, Budapest, pp. 47–52 (2003)
10. Burnard, L. (ed.): Users Reference Guide British National Corpus Version 1.0. Oxford University Computing Service, Oxford (1995)
11. Carter, D.M.: Common sense inference in a focus-guided anaphor resolver. J. Semant. **4**, 237–246 (1985)
12. Charniak, E.: Toward a model of children's story comprehension. Ph.D. thesis, MIT Computer Science and Artificial Intelligence Lab (CSAIL) (1972)
13. Dagan, I., Itai, A.: Automatic processing of large corpora for the resolution of anaphora references. Papers Presented to the 13th International Conference on Computational Linguistics, Helsinki (1990)
14. Dagan, I., Justeson, J., Lappin, S., Leass, H., Ribak, A.: Syntax and lexical statistics in anaphora resolution. Appl. Artif. Intell. **9**, 633–644 (1995)
15. Dalton, J., Dietz, L.: A neighborhood relevance model for entity linking. In: Proceedings of the 10th Conference on Open Research Areas in Information Retrieval, Lisbon, pp. 149–156 (2013)
16. Daumé III, H., Marcu, D.: A large-scale exploration of effective global features for a joint entity detection and tracking model. In: Proceedings of Human Language Technology Conference and Conference on Empirical Methods in Natural Language Processing (HLT/EMNLP 2005), Vancouver, pp 97–104 (2005)
17. Durrett, G., Klein, D.: Easy victories and uphill battles in coreference resolution. In: Proceedings of the 2013 Conference on Empirical Methods in Natural Language Processing (EMNLP 2013), Seattle, pp. 1971–1982 (2013)
18. Durrett, G., Klein, D.: A joint model for entity analysis: coreference, typing and linking. Trans. Assoc. Comput. Linguist. **2**, 477–490 (2014)
19. Fernandes, E.R., dos Santos, C.N., Milidiu, R.L.: Latent trees for coreference resolution. Comput. Linguist. **40**(4), 801–835 (2014)
20. Fleischman, M., Hovy, E., Echihabi, A.: Offline strategies for online question answering: answering questions before they are asked. In: Proceedings of the 41st Annual Meeting of the Association for Computational Linguistics (ACL 2003), Sapporo, pp. 1–7 (2003)
21. Garera, N., Yarowsky, D.: Resolving and generating definite anaphora by modeling hypernymy using unlabeled corpora. In: Proceedings of the Tenth Conference on Computational Natural Language Learning (CoNLL-X), New York, pp. 37–44 (2006)
22. Gasperin, C., Vieira, R.: Using word similarity lists for resolving indirect anaphora. In: ACL'04 Workshop on Reference Resolution and Its Applications, Barcelona, pp. 40–46 (2004)
23. Gasperin, C., Gamallo, P., Augustini, A., Lopes, G., de Lima, V.: Using syntactic contexts for measuring word similarity. In: Proceedings of the ESSLLI 2001 Workshop on Knowledge Acquisition and Categorization, Helsinki, pp. 18–23 (2001)
24. Ge, N., Hale, J., Charniak, E.: A statistical approach to anaphora resolution. In: Proceedings of the Sixth Workshop on Very Large Corpora (WVLC/EMNLP 1998), Montreal, pp. 161–171 (1998)

25. Giles, J.: Internet encyclopedias go head to head. Nature **438**(7070), 900–901 (2005)
26. Hajishirzi, H., Zilles, L., Weld, D.S., Zettlemoyer, L.: Joint coreference resolution and named-entity linking with mult-pass sieves. In: Proceedings of the 2013 Conference on Empirical Methods in Natural Language Processing (EMNLP 2013), Seattle, pp. 289–299 (2013)
27. Harabagiu, S., Bunescu, R., Maiorano, S.: Text and knowledge mining for coreference resolution. In: Proceedings of the 2nd Meeting of the North American Chapter of the Association of Computational Linguistics (NAACL-2001), Pittsburgh, pp. 55–62 (2001)
28. Hearst, M.: Automatic acquisition of hyponyms from large text corpora. In: Proceedings of the 14th International Conference on Computational Linguistics (COLING 92), Nantes, pp. 539–545 (1992)
29. Ji, H., Westbrook, D., Grishman, R.: Using semantic relations to refine coreference decisions. In: Proceedings of the Conference on Human Language Technology and Empirical Methods in Natural Language Processing (HLT-EMNLP 2005), Prague, pp. 17–24 (2005)
30. Ji, H., Grishman, R., Dang, H.T., Griffin, K., Ellis, J.: Overview of the TAC 2010 knowledge base population track. In: Text Analytics Conference (TAC 2010), Gaithersburg (2010)
31. Ji, H., Nothman, J., Hachey, B.: Overview of TAC-KBP2014 entity discovery and linking tasks. In: Proceedings of Text Analytics Conference (TAC 2014), Gaithersburg (2014)
32. Kameyama, M.: Recognizing referential links: an information extraction prespective. In: ACL Workshop on Operational Factors in Practical, Robust Anaphora Resolution for Unrestricted Texts, Madrid, pp 46–53 (1997)
33. Kehler, A., Appelt, D., Taylor, L., Simma, A.: The (non)utility of predicate-argument frequencies for pronoun interpretation. In: Proceedings of the Human Language Technology Conference of the North American Chapter of the Association for Computational Linguistics (HLT-NAACL 2004), Boston, pp 289–296 (2004)
34. Kipper, K., Dang, H.T., Palmer, M.: Class-based construction of a verb lexicon. In: Proceedings of the Seventeenth National Conference on Artificial Intelligence (AAAI 2000), Austin, pp 691–696 (2000)
35. Klebanov, B., Wiemer-Hastings, P.M.: Using LSA for pronominal anaphora resolution. In: Proeedings of the Computational Linguistics and Intelligent Text Processing, Third International Conference, (CICLing 2002), Mexico City, pp. 197–199 (2002)
36. Kummerfeld, J.K., Klein, D.: Error-driven analysis of challenges in coreference resolution. In: Proceedings of the 2013 Conference on Empirical Methods in Natural Language Processing (EMNLP 2013), Seattle, pp. 265–277 (2013)
37. Kunze, C., Lemnitzer, L.: GermaNet – representation, visualization, application. In: Proceedings of LREC 2002, Las Palmas (2002)
38. Landauer, T.K., Dumais, S.T.: A solution to Plato's problem: the latent semantic analysis theory of acquisition. Psychol. Rev. **104**(2), 211–240 (1997)
39. Leacock, C., Chodorow, M.: Combining local context and WordNet similarity for word sense identification. In: Fellbaum, C. (ed.) WordNet, an Electronic Lexical Database, pp. 265–283. MIT, Cambridge (1998)
40. Lee, H., Chang, A., Peirsman, Y., Chambers, N., Surdeanu, M., Jurafsky, D.: Deterministic coreference resolution based on entity-centric, precision-ranked rules. Comput. Linguist. **39**(4), 885–916 (2013)
41. Lin, D.: University of Manitoba: description of the PIE system used for MUC-6. In: Proceedings of the 6th Message Understanding Conference (MUC-6), Columbia, pp. 113–126 (1995)
42. Lin, D.: Automatic retrieval and clustering of similar words. In: 36th Annual Meeting of the Association for Computational Linguistics and 17th International Conference on Computational Linguistics (CoLing-ACL 1998), Montreal, pp. 768–774 (1998)
43. Lin, D., Church, K., Ji, H., Sekine, S., Yarowsky, D., Bergsma, S., Patil, K., Pitler, E., Lathbury, R., Rao, V., Dalwani, K., Narsale, S.: New tools for web-scale n-grams. In: Proceedings of the International Conference on Language Resources and Evaluation (LREC 2010), Valletta (2010)
44. Luo, X., Ittycheriah, A., Jing, H., Kambhatla, N., Roukos, S.: A mention-synchronous coreference resolution algorithm based on the Bell tree. In: Proceedings of the 42nd Annual

Meeting of the Association for Computational Linguistics (ACL 2004), Barcelona, pp. 135–142 (2004)

45. Markert, K., Nissim, M.: Comparing knowledge sources for nominal anaphora resolution. Comput. Linguist. **31**(3), 367–402 (2005)
46. Markert, K., Nissim, M., Modjeska, N.N.: Using the web for nominal anaphora resolution. In: Proceedings of the 2003 EACL Workshop on the Computational Treatment of Anaphora, Budapest (2003)
47. Martschat, S.: Multigraph clustering for unsupervised coreference resolution. In: Proceedings of the ACL Student Research Workshop, Sofia (2013)
48. Martschat, S., Strube, M.: Recall error analysis for coreference resolution. In: Proceedings of the 2014 Conference on Empirical Methods in Natural Language Processing (EMNLP 2014), Doha, pp. 2070–2081 (2014)
49. Mendes, P.N., Jakob, M., Bizer, C.: DBpedia: a multilingual cross-domain knowledge base. In: Proceedings of the Eighth International Conference on Language Resources and Evaluation (LREC-2012), Istanbul, pp. 1813–1817 (2012)
50. Miller, G.A., Fellbaum, C.: Semantic networks of English. Cognition **41**, 197–229 (1991)
51. Miller, G.A., Hristea, F.: WordNet nouns: classes and instances. Comput. Linguist. **32**(1), 1–3 (2006). doi:10.1162/coli.2006.32.1.1
52. Milne, D., Witten, I.H.: Learning to link with Wikipedia. In: Proceedings of the ACM Conference on Information and Knowledge Management (CIKM), Napa Valley, pp. 509–518 (2008)
53. Nedoluzhko, A., Mírovyskí, J.: How dependency trees and tectogrammatics help annotating coreference and bridging relations in Prague dependency treebank. In: Proceedings of the Second International Conference on Dependency Linguistics (DepLing 2013), Prague, pp 244–251 (2013)
54. Ng, V.: Shallow semantics for coreference resolution. In: Proceedings of the 20th International Joint Conference on Artificial Intelligence (IJCAI 2007), Hyderabad, pp. 1689–1694 (2007)
55. Ng, V., Cardie, C.: Improving machine learning approaches to coreference resolution. In: 40th Annual Meeting of the Asssociation for Computational Linguistics, Philadelphia, pp. 104–111 (2002)
56. Padó, S., Lapata, M.: Dependency-based construction of semantic space models. Comput. Linguist. **33**(2), 161–199 (2007)
57. Poesio, M., Vieira, R., Teufel, S.: Resolving bridging descriptions in unrestricted text. In: ACL-97 Workshop on Operational Factors in Practical, Robust, Anaphora Resolution for Unrestricted Texts, Madrid, pp. 1–6 (1997)
58. Poesio, M., Schulte im Walde, S., Brew, C.: Lexical clustering and definite description interpretation. In: AAAI Spring Symposium on Learning for Discourse, Stanford, pp. 82–89 (1998)
59. Poesio, M., Mehta, R., Maroudas, A., Hitzeman, J.: Learning to resolve bridging references. In: Proceedings of the 42nd Annual Meeting on Association for Computational Linguistics (ACL 2004), Barcelona, pp. 143–150 (2004)
60. Ponzetto, S.P.: Knowledge Acquisition from a Collaboratively Generated Encyclopedia, Dissertations in Artificial Intelligence, vol 327. IOS Press, Amsterdam (2010)
61. Ponzetto, S.P., Strube, M.: Exploiting semantic role labeling, WordNet and Wikipedia for coreference resolution. In: Human Language Technology Conference of the North American Chapter of the Association of Computational Linguistics (HLT-NAACL 2006), New York, pp. 192–199 (2006)
62. Ponzetto, S.P., Strube, M.: Deriving a large-scale taxonomy from wikipedia. In: Proceedings of the Twenty-Second AAAI Conference on Artificial Intelligence (AAAI 2007), pp. 1440–1445 (2007)
63. Pradhan, S., Ramshaw, L., Weischedel, R., MacBride, J., Micciulla, L.: Unrestricted coreference: identifying entities and events in ontonotes. In: Proceedings of the IEEE International Conference on Semantic Computing (ICSC), Irvine (2007)
64. Pradhan, S., Ramshaw, L., Marcus, M., Palmer, M., Weischedel, R., Xue, N.: CoNLL-2011 shared task: modeling unrestricted coreference in OntoNotes. In: Proceedings of the Fifteenth

Conference on Computational Natural Language Learning: Shared Task, Portland, pp. 1–27 (2011)

65. Pradhan, S., Moschitti, A., Xue, N., Uryupina, O., Zhang, Y.: CoNLL-2012 shared task: modeling multilingual unrestricted coreference in OntoNotes. In: Joint Conference on EMNLP and CoNLL – Shared Task, Jeju Island, pp. 1–40 (2012)
66. Rada, R., Mili, H., Bicknell, E., Blettner, M.: Development and application of a metric to semantic nets. IEEE Trans. Syst. Man Cybern. **19**(1), 17–30 (1989)
67. Rahman, A., Ng, V.: Supervised models for coreference resolution. In: Proceedings of the 2009 Conference on Empirical Methods in Natural Language Processing (EMNLP09), Singapore, pp. 968–977 (2009)
68. Rahman, A., Ng, V.: Coreference resolution with world knowledge. In: Proceedings of the 49th Annual Meeting of the Association for Computational Linguistics: Human Language Technologies (ACL 2011), Portland, pp. 814–824 (2011)
69. Ratinov, L., Roth, D.: Design challenges and misconceptions in named entity recognition. In: Proceedings of the Conference on Computational Natural Language Learning (CoNLL), Boulder, pp. 147–155 (2009)
70. Ratinov, L., Roth, D.: Learning-based multi-sieve coreference resolution with knowledge. In: Proceedings of the 2012 Joint Conference on Empirical Methods in Natural Language Processing and Computational Natural Language Learning (EMNLP-CoNLL 2012), Jeju Island, pp. 1234–1244 (2012)
71. Ratinov, L., Downey, D., Anderson, M., Roth, D.: Local and global algorithms for disambiguation to Wikipedia. In: Proceedings of the 49th Annual Meeting of the Association for Computational Linguistics: Human Language Technologies (ACL 2011), Portland, pp. 1375–1384 (2011)
72. Ravichandran, D., Pantel, P., Hovy, E.: Randomized algorithms and NLP: using locality sensitive hash function for high speed noun clustering. In: Proceedings of the 43rd Annual Meeting of the Association for Computational Linguistics (ACL 2005), Ann Arbor, pp. 622–629 (2005)
73. Recasens, M., Màrquez, L., Sapena, E., Martí, M.A., Taulé, M., Hoste, V., Poesio, M., Versley, Y.: Semeval task 1: coreference resolution in multiple languages. In: Proceedings of the 5th International Workshop on Semantic Evaluation (SemEval 2010), Los Angeles, pp. 1–8 (2010)
74. Recasens, M., Can, M., Jurafsky, D.: Same referent, different words: unsupervised mining of opaque coreferent mentions. In: Proceedings of NAACL-HLT 2013, Atlanta (2013)
75. Seco, N., Veale, T., Hayes, J.: An intrinsic information content metric for semantic similarity in WordNet. In: Proceedings of the 16th European Conference on Artificial Intelligence (ECAI 2004), Valencia, pp. 1089–1090 (2004)
76. Soon, W.M., Ng, H.T., Lim, D.C.Y.: A machine learning approach to coreference resolution of noun phrases. Comput. Linguist. **27**(4), 521–544 (2001)
77. Stoyanov, V., Gilbert, N., Cardie, C., Riloff, E.: Conundrums in noun phrase coreference resolution: making sense of the state of the art. In: Proceedings of the 47th Annual Meeting of the Association for Computational Linguistics and the 4th International Joint Conference on Natural Language Processing of the AFNLP (ACL/IJCNLP 2009), Singapore, pp. 656–664 (2009)
78. Stoyanov, V., Cardie, C., Gilbert, N., Riloff, E., Buttler, D., Hysom, D.: Coreference resolution with Reconcile. In: Proceedings of the 48th Annual Meeting of the Association for Computational Linguistics, Uppsala, pp. 156–161 (2010)
79. Suchanek, F.M., Kasneci, G., Weikum, G.: YAGO: a core of semantic knowledge unifying WordNet and Wikipedia. In: Proceedings of the 16th World Wide Web Conference (WWW 2007), Banff, pp. 697–706 (2007)
80. Telljohann, H., Hinrichs, E.W., Kübler, S., Zinsmeister, H., Beck, K.: Stylebook for the Tübingen Treebank of Written German (TüBa-D/Z). Technical Report, Seminar für Sprachwissenschaft, Universität Tübingen (2009)
81. Uryupina, O., Poesio, M., Giuliano, C., Tymoshenko, K.: Disambiguation and filtering methods in using Web knowledge for coreference resolution. In: Proceedings of the Twenty-Fourth International FLAIRS Conference (FLAIRS 2011), Palm Beach (2011)

82. Versley, Y.: A constraint-based approach to noun phrase coreference resolution in German newspaper text. In: Konferenz zur Verarbeitung Natürlicher Sprache (KONVENS 2006), Konstanz, pp. 143–150 (2006)
83. Versley, Y.: Antecedent selection techniques for high-recall coreference resolution. In: Proceedings of the 2007 Joint Conference on Empirical Methods in Natural Language Processing and Computational Natural Language Learning (EMNLP-CoNLL), Prague, pp. 496–505 (2007)
84. Versley, Y., Ponzetto, S., Poesio, M., Eidelman, V., Jern, A., Smith, J., Yang, X., Moschitti, A.: BART: a modular toolkit for coreference resolution. In: Proceedings of the 46th Annual Meeting of the Association for Computational Linguistics on Human Language Technologies: Demo Session (ACL 2008 Demo), Columbus, pp. 9–12 (2008)
85. Vieira, R., Poesio, M.: An empirically based system for processing definite descriptions. Comput. Linguist. **26**(4), 539–593 (2000)
86. Wu, Z., Palmer, M.: Verb semantics and lexical selections. In: Proceedings of the 32nd Annual Meeting of the Association for Computational Linguistics (ACL 1994), Las Cruces, pp. 133–138 (1994)
87. Yang, X., Su, J.: Coreference resolution using semantic relatedness information from automatically discovered patterns. In: Proceedings of the 45th Annual Meeting of the Association for Computational Linguistics (ACL 2007), Prague, pp. 528–535 (2007)
88. Zheng, J., Vilnis, L., Singh, S., Choi, J., McCallum, A.: Dynamic knowledge-base alignment for coreference resolution. In: Proceedings of the Seventeenth Conference on Computational Natural Language Learning (CoNLL 2013), Sofia, pp. 153–162 (2013)

Part IV
Applications

Coreference Applications to Summarization

Josef Steinberger, Mijail Kabadjov, and Massimo Poesio

Abstract In this chapter we discuss the connection between anaphora/coreference resolution and summarization. The discussion follows the summarization framework based on Latent Semantic Analysis (LSA), however, the ideas can be applied to any sentence-scoring approach. After describing the ways of combining basic (lexical) features of the summarizer with those received from the coreference resolution system we try to answer the question whether coreference resolution helps to improve the quality of selected content even if coreference resolution systems are still far from perfect. Both single-document and multi-document summarization branches are discussed. Then we focus on post-processing techniques to improve the referential clarity and coherence of extracted summaries.

Keywords Coreference applications to summarization • Applications of coreference • Latent semantic analysis

1 Introduction

Information about anaphoric relations could be beneficial for summarization which involves extracting (possibly very simplified) discourse models from text. We investigate exploiting automatically extracted information about the coreferring expressions in a text for two different aspects of the summarization task: firstly to enrich the representation of a text, from which a summary is then extracted; and secondly, to check that the anaphoric expressions contained in the summary thus extracted still have the same interpretation that they had in the original text.

In the following discussion we follow the latent semantic analysis (LSA [23]) summarization framework proposed in [14] and later improved in [46]. This

J. Steinberger
Faculty of Applied Sciences, Department of Computer Science and Engineering, NTIS Centre, University of West Bohemia, Univerzitni 8, Pilsen, 306 14, Czech Republic

M. Kabadjov (✉) • M. Poesio
School of Computer Science and Electronic Engineering, University of Essex, Wivenhoe Park, Colchester, CO4 3SQ, UK
e-mail: malexa@essex.ac.uk; poesio@essex.ac.uk

M. Poesio et al. (eds.), *Anaphora Resolution*, Theory and Applications of Natural Language Processing, DOI 10.1007/978-3-662-47909-4_15

approach follows what has been called a term-based approach [18]. In term-based summarization, the most important information in a document is found by identifying its main 'terms' (also sometimes called 'topics'), and then extracting from the document the most important information about these terms. Such approaches are usually classified as 'lexical' approaches or 'coreference- (or anaphora-) based' approaches. Lexical approaches to summarization use word similarity and other lexical relations to identify central terms [3]; we would include among these previous approaches based on LSA [14, 46]. Coreference- or anaphora-based approaches[1] [2, 6, 8, 51] identify these terms by running a coreference- or anaphoric resolver over the text. Using both lexical and anaphoric information to identify the main terms was discussed in [49].

Summarization by sentence extraction may produce summaries with 'dangling' anaphoric expressions – expressions whose antecedent has not been included in the summary, and therefore cannot be interpreted or are interpreted incorrectly. A method for using anaphoric information to check the entity coherence of a summary once this has been extracted has been proposed in [49]. The algorithm checks that the interpretation of anaphoric expressions in a summary is consistent with their interpretation in the original text.

Even if the discussion is strongly tied with the LSA-based framework the ideas of using coreference features in combination with basic summarizer's features to improve content selection can be used by any sentence-scoring approach. The post-processing entity-coherence checking can be used irrespective of the method the summary was produced with.

The chapter is organized as follows. Section 2 gives overview of the research in text summarization. Then we discuss the potential of using anaphora/coreference resolution in summarization together with the related work (Sect. 3). In Sect. 4 we discuss ways for incorporating coreference information into vector-space-based source representations. Then, in Sect. 5, the improvement in content selection when using coreference is discussed (the case of single-document summarization). We show both upper bound performance when manual coreference annotations are used and performance when automatic tools are involved. In Sect. 6 an algorithm for checking the entity-coherence of a summary is shown. Since Sect. 5 discusses the case of single-document summarization and intra-document coreference Sect. 7 goes further with mutli-document summarization and inter-document coreference. In the last Sects. 8 and 9 conclusions and pointers to further reading are given.

[1]We rather use the term 'coreference resolution' as a more general term to anaphora resolution. However, when we discuss single-document summarization the term refers to the task of identifying successive mentions of the same discourse entity (intra-document coreference resolution/anaphora resolution), as opposed to the task of 'inter-document coreference resolution' appropriate in the case of multi-document summarization which involves collecting all information about an entity, including information expressed by appositions and other predicative constructions.

2 Text Summarization

A basic processing model for Text Summarization, proposed by Sparck-Jones [45] comprises three main stages: source text interpretation to construct a source representation, source representation transformation to form a summary representation, and summary text generation. More practically-motivated approaches use shallow linguistic analysis and only partially cover the processing model. However, more ambitious ones attempting all three stages using deep semantic analysis have been proposed in the literature.

The first approaches were based on shallow linguistic analysis such as word frequencies [26], cue phrases (e.g., "in conclusion", "in summary") and location (e.g., title, section headings) [12]. Later, machine learning approaches that combine a number of surface features have been proposed [22]. There are also more sophisticated approaches, but still working at the surface level, exploiting cohesive relations like coreference [2, 8, 51] and lexical cohesion [3] to identify salience or purely lexical approaches trying to identify 'implicit topics' by conflating together words using methods inspired by Latent Semantic Analysis LSA [14, 46]. There are also approaches purely based on discourse structure (e.g., RST) [30]. And finally there are knowledge-rich approaches, where the source undergoes a substantial semantic analysis during the process of filling in a predefined template [32] or the source data is available in a more structured way (i.e., events have been identified already) [31].

Summarization evaluation, a closely related issue, is a particularly challenging problem. Manual evaluation gives more precise results, however, it is a subjective task and thus it needs to be done in a large scale and it is very expensive. On the other hand, automatic evaluation methods give just rough image of summary quality, however, they need usually just some reference documents, like human-written abstracts.

Summaries are usually scored from two different perspectives: linguistic quality (readability) and content quality. *Linguistic quality* is often assessed by human annotators. They assign a value from a predefined scale to each summary. The quality aspects contain: grammaticality, non-redundancy, reference clarity, coherence and structure.

Content quality is often measured by comparison with a model summary. For sentence extracts, it is often measured by *co-selection*. It finds out how many sentences overlap in a model and an automatic summary. It can be measured by simple precision/recall figures. The main problem with P&R is that human judges often disagree on what the top p% most important sentences are. With *Relative Utility* [43] the model summary represents all sentences of the input document with confidence values for their inclusion in the summary. For example, the confidence value of a sentence can correspond to the number of annotators who selected that sentence.

If the model summary is a free text written by a human or the system does not only extract the most important sentences the evaluation method has to work with smaller units (words, n-grams or phrases). The *ROUGE* (Recall-Oriented Understudy for Gisting Evaluation) family of measures, which are based on the similarity of n-grams, was firstly introduced in 2003 [24]. Suppose a number of annotators created reference summaries – reference summary set (*RSS*). The ROUGE-*n* score of a candidate summary is computed as follows:

$$\text{ROUGE-}n = \frac{\sum_{C \in RSS} \sum_{gram_n \in C} Count_{match}(gram_n)}{\sum_{C \in RSS} \sum_{gram_n \in C} Count(gram_n)}, \tag{1}$$

where $Count_{match}(gram_n)$ is the maximum number of n-grams co-occurring in a candidate summary and a reference summary and $Count(gram_n)$ is the number of n-grams in the reference summary. Notice that the average n-gram ROUGE score, ROUGE-*n*, is a recall metric. There are other ROUGE measures, such as ROUGE-L – a longest common subsequence measure – and ROUGE-SU4 – a bigram measure that enables up to 4 unigrams inside of bigram components to be skipped [25].

Imagine we have two reference summaries and two candidate summaries:

(2)
	ref1:	Eight killed in Finnish school massacre
	ref2:	Student kills eight in Finnish school shooting
	cand1:	Shooting in a Finnish school: eight dead
	cand2:	Finland: school gunman left suicide note

The first candidate summary is very similar to both reference summaries, the second is only partly relevant (*Finland school*). ROUGE-1 will simply count terms co-occurring in a candidate summary and reference summaries denominated by the number of terms in reference summaries (recall). For *cand1* $(4 + 5)/(6 + 7) = 0.615$, for *cand2* $(1 + 1)/(6 + 7) = 0.153$. ROUGE-2 works the same, but on the bigram level. In the case of *cand1* there is only one bigram (*Finnish school*) which is contained in both reference summaries: $(1 + 1)/(5 + 6) = 0.182$, *cand2* doesn't contain any bigram from reference. ROUGE-L is similar to ROUGE-1 but the terms have to be in the same order. ROUGE-L of *cand1* will be $(3+3)/(6+7) = 0.46154$ (*in Finnish school* matches in both reference summaries). ROUGE-L of *cand2* will be the same as its ROUGE-1. ROUGE-SU4 allows up to 4 unigrams between the bigram items, unigrams count also to give advantage to fragments that contain the reference words but not bigrams. ROUGE-SU4 of *cand1*is $(7 + 7)/(20 + 26) = 0.304$ (*[in], [in, finnish], [in, school], [finnish], [finnish, school], [school], [eight]*). The second candidate will match only *school*: $(1+1)/(20+26) = 0.043$. For more details see [25].

The Pyramid method is a semi-automatic evaluation method [35]. Its basic idea is to identify summarization content units (SCUs), which are not bigger than a clause. They are used for comparison of information in summaries. SCUs that appear in more model summaries will get greater weights, so a pyramid will be formed after SCU annotation of model summaries. At the top of the pyramid there are SCUs that appear in most of the summaries and thus they have the greatest weight. The lower in the pyramid the SCU appears, the lower its weight is because it is contained in fewer summaries. The SCUs in a peer summary are then compared against an existing pyramid to evaluate how much information is agreed between the peer and the model summaries. However, this promising method still requires some annotation work.

Another possibility to evaluate summaries is to use *extrinsic (task-based)* methods. They measure the performance of using the summaries for a certain task (e.g. document categorization [28], information retrieval [44] or question answering [33]).

In recent years DUC/TAC[2] took a leading role in the summarization roadmap. The tracks have been developing since DUC2000 until DUC2007, starting with single-document summarization and moving on to multi-document summarization [37]. The next step from multi-document summarization was update summarization[3] which piloted in DUC2007 and represented the main track in TAC2008 and TAC2009. Aspect summarization[4] in TAC2010 (and 2011) goes even one step further to understanding the text content by incorporating information extraction. Language-independence gives the picture another dimension, the new goals are multilingual summarization [13, 53] or cross-language summarization [54].

3 Coreference and Summarization

In [8] the following news article was used to illustrate why being able to recognize coreference chains may help in identifying the main topics of a document.

(3) PRIEST IS CHARGED WITH POPE ATTACK

A Spanish priest was charged here today with attempting to murder the Pope. *Juan Fernandez Krohn*, aged 32, was arrested after a man armed with a bayonet approached the Pope while he was saying prayers at Fatima on Wednesday night. According to the police, *Fernandez* told the investigators today that *he* trained for the past six months for the assault. ... If found guilty, *the Spaniard* faces a prison sentence of 15–20 years.

As Boguraev and Kennedy point out, the title of the article is an excellent summary of the content: an entity (*the priest*) did something to another entity (*the pope*). Intuitively, this is because understanding that *Fernandez* and *the pope* are

[2]The National Institute of Standards and Technology (NIST) initiated the Document Understanding Conference (DUC) series [11] to evaluate automatic text summarization. Its goal is to further progress in summarization and enable researchers to participate in large-scale experiments. Since 2008 DUC has moved to TAC (Text Analysis Conference) [52] that follows the summarization evaluation roadmap with new or upgraded tracks.

[3]When producing an update summary of a set of topic-related documents the summarizer assumes prior knowledge of the reader determined by a set of older documents of the same topic. The update summarizer thus must solve a novelty vs. redundancy problem.

[4]In the aspect summarization scenario a given list of core information aspects for different event types should be addressed in the automatic summaries.

the central characters is crucial to providing summaries of texts like these.[5] Among the clues that help us to identify such 'main characters,' the fact that an entity is repeatedly mentioned is clearly important.

Methods that only rely on lexical information to identify the main topics of a text, such as the lexical-based methods discussed in the previous section, can only capture part of the information about which entities are frequently repeated in the text. As example (3) shows, stylistic conventions forbid verbatim repetition, hence the six mentions of *Fernandez* in the text above contain only one lexical repetition, *'Fernandez'*. The main problem are pronouns, that tend to share the least lexical similarity with the form used to express the antecedent (and anyway are usually removed by stopword lists, therefore do not get included in the SVD matrix). The form of definite descriptions (*the Spaniard*) doesn't always overlap with that of their antecedent, either, especially when the antecedent was expressed with a proper name. The form of mention which more often overlaps to a degree with previous mentions is proper nouns, and even then at least some way of dealing with acronyms is necessary (cf. *European Union/E.U.*). On the other hand, it is well-known from the psychological literature that proper names often are used to indicate the main entities in a text. What coreference resolution can do for us is to identify which discourse entities are repeatedly mentioned, especially when different forms of mention are used. Instead of a summary, the approach in [8] extracted list of those linguistic expressions which refer to the most prominent objects mentioned in the discourse.

In [2] coreference-based summarization was used in an information retrieval scenario. Automatically generated document summaries were used to support relevance judgments of the IR user. Firstly, coreference is employed in retrieving referential relations between the terms of the original IR query and the terms of the documents that are considered to be relevant. Coreference is the main clue also in generation of the document summary when sentences containing entities of the query are identified. The system follows the coreference chains and, according to several heuristics, selects a subsequence of sentences of highest relevance. The approach further provides lexically informative substitute expressions for anaphors that may, out of their original context, become incomprehensible.[6]

The use of coreference resolution for the scenario of generic summarization is proposed in [1]. There is no user query that prescribes relevant entities on which the summary should focus. They try to find a single coreference chain which corresponds to the central entity the text is about. The subsequence of sentences in which this entity is salient is then extracted.

---

[5]In many non-educational texts only an 'entity-centered' structure can be clearly identified, as opposed to a 'relation-centered' structure of the type hypothesized in Rhetorical Structures Theory and which serves as the basis for discourse structure-based summarization methods [21, 40].

[6]The approach deals with object coreference and event coreference. They further consider the issue of referential relations beyond the identity relation covering a few domain-specific special cases.

According to the representative approaches, coreference information is employed in different processing stages. The first stage consists of relating some terms of the query to coreferring occurrences in the document pool over which the application runs. If there is no query the system first has to find the focus of the document pool (e.g. central entities/events). This may be considered as a special case of the cross-document coreference resolution problem. At the second processing stage, the system follows a coreference chain(s) in order to select a subsequence of sentences that would form a document summary. The last stage is to identifying coreferring antecedents for anaphoric occurrences in order to provide maximally informative substitute expressions.

4 Coreference Knowledge Representation

Purely lexical methods determine the main 'topics' of a document on the basis of the simplest possible notion of term, simple words, or n-grams. In this section we will see, however, that coreference information can be easily integrated in a mixed lexical/coreference representation by generalizing the notion of 'term' used to include as well, and counting a discourse entity *d* as occurring in sentence *s* whenever the coreference resolver identifies a noun phrase occurring in *s* as a mention of *d*.

Coreference Chain Elements Substitution The simplest way of using coreference information is to keep using only words as terms, and use anaphora resolution as a pre-processing step [49]. That is, after identifying the coreference chains within each text, replace all referring nominal expressions with the first element of their anaphoric chain. The modified text could then be used as an input for any summarization approach. However, in [49] it was shown that this simple approach does not lead to improved results.

Word Terms and Discourse Entities within the same Space A better approach, it turns out, is to generalize the notion of term, treating coreference chains as another type of term that may or may not occur in a sentence. The idea is illustrated in Table 1, where the summarizer's input matrix contains two types of terms: terms in the lexical sense (i.e., words/n-grams) and terms in the sense of discourse entities, represented by coreference chains. The representation of a sentence then specifies not only if that sentence contains a certain word, but also if it contains a mention of a discourse entity. With this representation, the chain terms may tie together sentences that mention the same entity even if they do not contain the same lexical item.

The resulting matrix is effectively an enriched vector-space representation entailing not only lexical, but also anaphoric information, which can then be used as input to summarizers.

Table 1 Aggregative source representation

	unit_1	unit_2	unit_3	...
ngram_1	Lexical info			
ngram_2				
...				
entity_1	Entity info			
entity_2				
...				

5 Using Coreference for Salient Content Selection

Next, we briefly introduce latent semantic analysis (LSA, [23]) and the summarization approach based on it. Then we summarize the single-document summarization experiments described in [49] to determine the upper bound performance and to show real performance when an automatic anaphora resolver is used.

5.1 LSA-Based Summarization

LSA is a fully automatic mathematical/statistical technique for extracting and inferring relations of expected contextual usage of words in passages of discourse.

It has been extensively used in NLP applications including information retrieval [7] and text segmentation [10], and also summarization [14], which was later extended by Steinberger and Ježek [46].

The approach first builds a term-by-sentence matrix from the source, then applies Singular Value Decomposition (SVD) which finds the latent (orthogonal) dimensions, which in simple terms correspond to the different topics discussed in the source, and finally uses the resulting matrices to identify and extract the most salient sentences.

More formally, firstly a term-by-sentence matrix $\mathbf{A}$ is created. Each element a_{ij} of $\mathbf{A}$ represents the weighted frequency of term i in sentence j and is defined as:

$$a_{ij} = L(i,j) \cdot G(i), \tag{4}$$

where $L(i,j)$ is the local weight of term i in sentence j and $G(i)$ is the global weight of term i in the text. The weighting scheme found to work best uses a binary local weight and an entropy-based global weight:

$$L(i,j) = 1 \text{ if term } i \text{ appears at least once in sentence } j; \quad \text{otherwise } L(i,j) = 0 \tag{5}$$

$$G(i) = 1 - \sum_j \frac{p_{ij} \log(p_{ij})}{log(n)}, p_{ij} = \frac{t_{ij}}{g_i}, \tag{6}$$

where t_{ij} is the frequency of term i in sentence j, g_i is the total number of times that term i occurs in the whole text and n is the total number of sentences.

Let's illustrate the approach by the following simplified example – summarizing these five article titles:

(7) s1: Cyclone smashes into Bangladesh coast
s2: Ferocious cyclone hits Bangladesh coast
s3: Thousands evacuate as cyclone approaches Bangladesh
s4: WFP offers emergency food to victims
s5: US offers help for cyclone victims

Basically, there are two topics: (1) *the cyclon hit* and (2) *help offered to victims.* The term-by-sentence matrix **A**:

$$
A = \begin{array}{|ccccc|l}
s1 & s2 & s3 & s4 & s5 & \\
1.86 & 1.86 & 1.86 & 0 & 1.86 & cyclone \\
1 & 0 & 0 & 0 & 0 & smashes \\
1.68 & 1.68 & 1.68 & 0 & 0 & bangladesh \\
1.43 & 1.43 & 0 & 0 & 0 & coast \\
0 & 1 & 0 & 0 & 0 & ferocious \\
0 & 1 & 0 & 0 & 0 & hits \\
0 & 0 & 1 & 0 & 0 & thousands \\
0 & 0 & 1 & 0 & 0 & evacuate \\
0 & 0 & 1 & 0 & 0 & approaches \\
0 & 0 & 0 & 1 & 0 & WFP \\
0 & 0 & 0 & 1.43 & 1.43 & offers \\
0 & 0 & 0 & 1 & 0 & emergency \\
0 & 0 & 0 & 1 & 0 & food \\
0 & 0 & 0 & 1.43 & 1.43 & victims \\
0 & 0 & 0 & 0 & 1 & us \\
0 & 0 & 0 & 0 & 1 & help
\end{array} \quad (8)
$$

The next step is to apply the Singular Value Decomposition (SVD) to matrix **A**. The SVD of an $m \times n$ matrix is defined as:

$$\mathbf{A} = \mathbf{U} \cdot \mathbf{S} \cdot \mathbf{V}^T, \quad (9)$$

where **U** ($m \times n$) is a column-orthonormal matrix, whose columns are called left singular vectors. The matrix contains representations of terms expressed in the newly created (latent) dimensions. **S** ($n \times n$) is a diagonal matrix, whose diagonal elements are non-negative singular values sorted in descending order. $\mathbf{V}^T$ ($n \times n$) is a row-orthonormal matrix which contains representations of sentences expressed in the latent dimensions. The dimensionality of the matrices is reduced to r most important dimensions and thus, we receive matrices **U'** ($m \times r$), **S'** ($r \times r$) a $\mathbf{V'}^T$ ($r \times n$).

From a mathematical point of view, SVD derives a mapping between the m-dimensional space specified by the weighted term-frequency vectors and the r-dimensional singular vector space.

From an NLP perspective, what SVD does is to derive the *latent semantic structure* of the document represented by matrix A: i.e. a breakdown of the original document into r linearly-independent base vectors which express the main 'topics' of the document.

The following numbers represent 2-dimensional SVD decomposition of our example term-by-sentence matrix **A**:

$$
\underset{\mathbf{U'}}{\begin{array}{r|cc|}
 & dim1 & dim2 \\
cyclone & 0.72 & 0.07 \\
smashes & 0.11 & -0.06 \\
bangladesh & 0.53 & -0.27 \\
coast & 0.31 & -0.17 \\
ferocious & 0.11 & -0.06 \\
hits & 0.11 & -0.06 \\
thousands & 0.10 & -0.04 \\
evacuate & 0.10 & -0.04 \\
approaches & 0.10 & -0.04 \\
WFP & 0.02 & 0.21 \\
offers & 0.12 & 0.58 \\
emergency & 0.02 & 0.21 \\
food & 0.02 & 0.21 \\
victims & 0.12 & 0.58 \\
us & 0.07 & 0.20 \\
help & 0.07 & 0.20
\end{array}}
\cdot
\underset{\mathbf{S'}}{\begin{array}{|cc|}
dim1 & dim2 \\
5.1 & 0.0 \\
0.0 & 3.32
\end{array}}
\cdot
\underset{\mathbf{V'}^T}{\begin{array}{|ccccc|l}
s1 & s2 & s3 & s4 & s5 & \\
0.55 & 0.57 & 0.50 & 0.08 & 0.36 & dim1 \\
-0.19 & -0.21 & -0.13 & 0.69 & 0.66 & dim2
\end{array}}
\tag{10}
$$

As $\mathbf{V'}^T$ contains sentences expressed by relative importance of the top topics they mention and **S'** contains topic importance, by multiplying these matrices we receive the latent space of matrix $\mathbf{V'}^T$ in which vector length of each dimension correspond to its importance. Let's call the final matrix $\mathbf{F} = \mathbf{S'} \cdot \mathbf{V'}^T$.

Sentence selection starts with the sentence that has the longest vector in matrix **F** (the vector, the column of **F**, is denoted as f_{best}). After placing it in the summary, the topic/sentence distribution in matrix **F** is changed by subtracting the information contained in that sentence:

$$\mathbf{F}_{(i+1)} = \mathbf{F}_{(i)} - \frac{\mathbf{f}_{best} \cdot \mathbf{f}_{best}^T}{|\mathbf{f}_{best}|^2} \cdot \mathbf{F}_{(i)} \tag{11}$$

The vector lengths of similar sentences are decreased, thus preventing inner summary redundancy. After the subtraction the process of selecting the sentence that has the longest vector in updated matrix $\mathbf{F}_{(i+1)}$ and subtracting its information from $\mathbf{F}_{(i)}$ is iteratively repeated until the required summary length is reached.

When we return to our example: $\mathbf{F}_{(0)}$ represents the multiplication of matrices **S'** and $\mathbf{V'}^T$. The longest vector in the matrix has sentence *s2*. This sentence will be selected to the summary and the previous equation will be used to recalculate the matrix $\mathbf{F} \rightarrow \mathbf{F}_{(1)}$. Notice that the values of sentences *s1* and *s3*, sentences similar to the selected one, are reduced. From the next iteration of the matrix, $\mathbf{F}_{(1)}$, *s5* will be selected.

$$\begin{array}{r|rrrrr|} \multicolumn{6}{c}{\mathbf{F}_{(0)}} \\ & s1 & \mathbf{s2} & s3 & s4 & s5 \\ dim1 & 2.784 & \mathbf{2.9} & 2.52 & 0.395 & 1.827 \\ dim2 & -0.627 & \mathbf{-0.696} & -0.445 & 2.276 & 2.183 \end{array}$$

$$\begin{array}{r|rrrrr|} \multicolumn{6}{c}{\mathbf{F}_{(1)}} \\ & s1 & s2 & s3 & s4 & \mathbf{s5} \\ dim1 & 0.0090 & 0.0 & 0.036 & 0.538 & \mathbf{0.595} \\ dim2 & 0.039 & 0.0 & 0.151 & 2.242 & \mathbf{2.478} \end{array} \quad (12)$$

5.2 *Performance Upper Bound*

In [49], in order to determine whether anaphoric information might help, and which method of adding anaphoric knowledge to the LSA summarizer is best, they annotated 37 documents from the CAST corpus using the annotation tool MMAX [34].

The CAST Corpus The CAST corpus [36] contains news articles taken from the Reuters Corpus and a few popular science texts from the British National Corpus. Summaries are specified by providing information about the importance of sentences [16]: sentences are marked as *essential* or *important* for the summary. The corpus also contains annotations for *linked* sentences, which are not significant enough to be marked as important/essential, but which have to be considered as they contain information essential for the understanding of the content of other sentences marked as essential/important.

For acquiring model summaries at specified lengths and getting the sentence scores (for relative utility evaluation) a score of 3 was assigned to the sentences marked as essential, a score of 2 to important sentences and a score of 1 to linked sentences.

Evaluation Measure As a main measure Relative Utility (see Sect. 2) was chosen because it could be computed automatically given the already existing annotations in the CAST corpus. RU allows model summaries to consist of sentences with variable ranking.

Table 2 Improvement over lexical-based LSA with manually annotated anaphoric information

Summarization ratio (%)	Lexical LSA	Manual – substitution	Manual – addition
15	0.595	0.573	**0.662**
30	0.645	0.662	**0.688**

Upper Bound Results Results for the 15 % (resp. 30 %) summarization ratio using a variety of summarization evaluation measures are presented in Table 2. The tables show that even with perfect knowledge of anaphoric links, the performance when using Substitution method does not change much. The problem that happened in some of the documents was that SVD deteriorated when a frequently used entity was substituted by its full nominal expression. As a result, the score of the sentence was extremely boosted when it contained the mention of the entity. And thus, sentences that contained the mention of this entity were all considered important, no matter what else they contained.

On the other hand, the addition method could potentially lead to substantial improvements.

5.3 *Using an Automatic Tool in Single-Document Summarization*

In [49] the question of whether using an automatic anaphora resolution tool can lead to an improved performance was also addressed. For this purpose they used GuiTAR [39],[7] described in the chapter on off-the-shelf tools. We next discuss the performance reported in [49] when the anaphora resolution is incorporated in the summarizer.

Does Automatic AR Improve Summarization? To use GuiTAR, [49] first parsed the texts using Charniak's parser [9]. The output of the parser was then converted into the MAS-XML format expected by GuiTAR by one of the preprocessors that come with the system.[8] Finally, GuiTAR was run to add anaphoric information to the files. The resulting files were then processed by the summarizer.

GuiTAR achieved a precision of 56 % and a recall of 51 % over the 37 documents; on definite description resolution, a precision of 69 % and a recall of 53 %; for possessive pronouns resolution, a precision of 53 %, recall 53 %; finally, for personal pronouns, precision of 44 %, recall 46 %. The figures are based on simple link-based scoring.

The results obtained by the summarizer using GuiTAR's output are presented in Table 3 (RU scores).

[7] Available as open source software at http://guitar-essex.sourceforge.net/.

[8] This step includes heuristic methods for guessing agreement features.

Table 3 Improvement over lexical-based LSA with GuiTAR

Summarization ratio (%)	Lexical LSA	GuiTAR – substitution	GuiTAR – addition
15	0.595	0.530	**0.640**
30	0.645	0.626	**0.678**

Table 3 clearly shows that using GuiTAR and the addition method leads to significant improvements over the baseline LSA summarizer. The improvement in Relative Utility measure was significant (95 % confidence by the *t*-test). On the other hand, the substitution method did not lead to significant improvements, as was to be expected given that no improvement was obtained with 'perfect' anaphora resolution (see previous section).

In conclusion, this study showed that (i) we could expect performance improvements over purely lexical LSA summarization using anaphoric information, (ii) significant improvements at least by the Relative Utility score could be achieved even if this anaphoric information was automatically extracted, and (iii) these results were only achieved, however, using the Addition method.

Comparison to State-of-the-art What Steinberger et al.'s work [49] did not show was how well are their results compared with the state-of-the-art, as measured by evaluation over a standard reference corpus such as DUC 2002, and using the standard ROUGE measure.

DUC 2002 included a single-document summarization task, in which 13 systems participated. 2002 is the last version of DUC that included single-document summarization evaluation of informative summaries. Later DUC editions (2003 and 2004) contained a single-document summarization task as well, however only very short summaries (75 Bytes) were analyzed. The DUC-2002 corpus used for the task contains 567 documents from different sources; 10 assessors were used to provide for each document two 100-word human summaries. In addition to the results of the 13 participating systems, the DUC organizers also distributed baseline summaries (the first 100 words of a document). The coverage of all the summaries was assessed by humans.

In DUC 2002, the SEE evaluation tool was used, but in later editions of the initiative the ROUGE measure (see Sect. 2) was introduced, which is now widely used.

As shown in Table 4, for this particular corpus there is a strong correlation between humans and ROUGE-1 (and ROUGE-L). Steinberger et al. [49] used all four main ROUGE scores to determine the significance of their results.

In Table 5 there are the ROUGE scores[9] of the purely lexical LSA summarizer; of the summarizer combining both lexical and anaphoric information (LSA+GuiTAR);

[9] All system summaries were truncated to 100 words as traditionally done in DUC. ROUGE version and settings:

```
ROUGEeval-1.4.2.pl -c 95 -m -n 2 -l 100 -s -2 4 -a duc.xml.
```

Table 4 Correlation between ROUGE scores and human assessments

Score	Correlation
ROUGE-1	0.92574
ROUGE-2	0.80090
ROUGE-SU4	0.78396
ROUGE-L	0.92561

Table 5 ROUGE scores

System	ROUGE-1	ROUGE-2	ROUGE-SU4	ROUGE-L
28	0.42776	0.21769	0.17315	0.38645
LSA+GuiTAR	**0.42280**	**0.20741**	**0.16612**	**0.39276**
21	0,41488	0.21038	0.16546	0.37543
DUC baseline	0.41132	0.21075	0.16604	0.37535
19	0.40823	0.20878	0.16377	0.37351
LSA	**0.40805**	**0.19722**	**0.15728**	**0.37878**
27	0.40522	0.20220	0.16000	0.36913
29	0.39925	0.20057	0.15761	0.36165
31	0.39457	0.19049	0.15085	0.35935
15	0.38884	0.18578	0.15002	0.35366
23	0.38079	0.19587	0.15445	0.34427
16	0.37147	0.17237	0.13774	0.33224
18	0.36816	0.17872	0.14048	0.33100
25	0.34297	0.15256	0.11797	0.31056
Random	0.29963	0.11095	0.09004	0.27951
17	0.13528	0.05690	0.04253	0.12193
30	0.07452	0.03745	0.02104	0.06985

and of the 13 systems which participated in DUC-2002. We also list a baseline and a random summarizer (the lowest baseline).

The performance of the ‘lexical only’ LSA summarizer is significantly worse only than that of the best system in DUC 2002, system 28, in ROUGE-1, ROUGE-2 and ROUGE-SU4, and significantly better than that of 9 in ROUGE-1, 7 in ROUGE-2, 7 in ROUGE-SU4 and 10 in ROUGE-L of the systems that participated in that competition. However, when anaphoric information is included (LSA+GuiTAR) the summarizer is even better: it is significantly better than 11 systems in ROUGE-1, 9 in ROUGE-2, 9 in ROUGE-SU4 and 13 in ROUGE-L, it is significantly better than the baseline in ROUGE-L at the 90 % confidence level, and it is not significantly worse than any of the systems.

6 Checking Entity Coherence in Summaries

Anaphoric expressions can only be understood with respect to a context. This means that summarization by sentence extraction can wreak havoc with their interpretation: there is no guarantee that they will have an interpretation in the context obtained by extracting sentences to form a summary, or that this interpretation will be the same as in the original text. Consider the following example.

(13) PRIME MINISTER CONDEMNS IRA FOR MUSIC SCHOOL EXPLOSION

(S1) [Prime Minister Margaret Thatcher]$_1$ said Monday [[the Irish Republican Army]$_2$ members who blew up [the Royal Marines School of Music]$_3$ and killed [10 bandsmen]$_4$ last week]$_5$ are monsters who will be found and punished.

(S2) "[The young men whom we lost]$_4$ were murdered by [common murderers who must be found and brought to justice and put behind bars for a very long time]$_5$," [she]$_1$ said following a tour of [[the school's]$_3$ wrecked barracks]$_6$ in Deal, southeast England.

...

(S3) [Gerry Adams, president of [Sinn Fein, the legal political arm of [the IRA]$_2$]$_8$]$_7$ issued a statement disputing [Mrs. Thatcher's]$_1$ remarks, saying "[she]$_1$ knows in [her]$_1$ heart of hearts the real nature of the conflict, its cause and the remedy".

...

(S4) "[We]$_8$ want an end to all violent deaths arising out of the present relationship between our two countries," [Adams]$_7$ said.

...

(S5) [The IRA]$_2$ claimed responsibility for the explosion, and police said they are looking for [three men with Irish accents who rented a house overlooking [the barracks]$_6$]$_5$.

If sentence S2 were to be extracted to be part of the summary, but S1 was not, the pronoun *she* would not be understandable as it would not have a matching antecedent anymore. The reference to *the school* would also be uninterpretable. The same would happen if S5 were extracted without also extracting S2; in this case, the problem would be that the antecedent for *the barracks* is missing.

Examples such as the one just shown suggest another use for anaphora resolution in summarization – correcting the references in the summary. Our idea was to replace anaphoric expressions with a full noun phrase in the cases where otherwise the anaphoric expression could be misinterpreted. We discuss this method in detail next.

6.1 Reference Correction Algorithm

The correction algorithm works as follows.

1. Run anaphora resolution over the source text, and create anaphoric chains.
2. Identify the sentences to be extracted using a summarization algorithm such as the one discussed in the previous sections.

3. For every anaphoric chain, replace the first occurrence of the chain in the summary with its first occurrence in the source text. After this step, all chains occurring in both source and summary start with the same lexical form.

   For example, in the text in (13), if sentence S4 is included in the summary, but S3 is not, the first occurrence of chain 7 in the summary, *Adams*, would be substituted by *Gerry Adams, president of Sinn Fein, the legal political arm of the IRA*.
4. Run the anaphoric resolver over the summary.
5. For all nominal expressions in the summary: if the expression is part of a chain in the source text and it is not resolved in the summary (the resolver was not able to find an antecedent), or if it is part of a different chain in the summary, then replace the anaphoric expression with the head of the first chain expression from the source text.

This method can be used in combination with the summarization system discussed in earlier sections, or with other systems; and becomes even more important when doing sentence compression, because intrasentential antecedents can be lost as well. However, automatic anaphora resolution can introduce new errors. We discuss our evaluation of the algorithm next.

6.2 Evaluation

To measure the recall of the reference checker algorithm we would need anaphoric annotations, that were not available for DUC data. The precision was manually measured as follows. To measure the precision of the step where the first occurrences of a chain in the summary were replaced by the first mention of that chain in the source text, a sample of 155 documents was taken and precision was measured by hand, obtaining the results shown in Table 6.

We can observe that full texts contained on average 19 anaphoric chains, whereas summaries about 7. In 66 % of the summary chains the sentence where the first chain occurrence appeared was selected for the summary, and in 9 % there was no need to replace the expression because it already had the same form as the first element of the chain. So overall the first chain occurrence was replaced in 25 % of the cases;

Table 6 Evaluation of step 3, the first chain occurrence replacement

Observed state	Overall	Per-doc.
Chains in full text	2906	18.8
Chains in summary	1086 (37.4 % of full text chains)	7.0
First chain occurrence in the summary	714 (65.7 % of summary chains)	4.6
First chains element with the same lexical form	101 (9.3 % of summary chains)	0.7
First chain occurrence replaced	271 (25 % of summary chains)	1.7
Correctly replaced	186 (**Precision: 68.6 %**)	1.2

Table 7 Evaluation of step 5, checking the comprehensibility of anaphors in the summary. (Replaced + means that the expressions were correctly replaced; replaced − that the replacement was incorrect). *S* = summary, *FT* = full text

Observed state	Correct	Incorrect
In a chain only in S	16 (67 %)	8 (33 %)
In a chain only in FT	32 (70 %) (replaced +)	14 (30 %) (replaced −)
In the same chain in FT and S	336 (83 %)	69 (17 %)
In a different chain in FT and S (correct in FT)	81 (72 %) (replaced +)	32 (28 %) (replaced +)
In a different chain in FT and S (incorrect in FT)	39 (77 %) (replaced −)	12 (23 %) (replaced −)
Replacements overall	145 (**69 %**)	65 (31 %)

the precision was 68.6 %. This suggests that the success in this task correlates with the quality of the anaphora resolver.

After performing anaphora resolution on the summary and computing its anaphoric chains, the anaphors without an antecedent are replaced. A sample of 86 documents was analyzed and again the precision was measured by hand. Overall, 145 correct replacements were made in this step and 65 incorrect, for a precision of 69 %. Table 7 analyzes the performance on this task in more detail.

The first row of the table lists the cases in which an expression was placed in a chain in the summary, but not in the source text. In these cases, our algorithm does not replace anything.

Our algorithm however does replace an expression when it finds that there is no chain assigned to the expression in the summary, but there is one in the source text; such cases are listed in the second row. We found that this replacement was correct in 32 cases; in 14 cases the algorithm replaced an incorrect expression.

The third row summarizes the most common case, in which the expression was inserted into the same chain in the source text and in the summary. That is, the first element of the chain in the summary is also the first element of the chain in the source text. When this happens, in 83 % of cases GuiTAR's interpretation is correct; no replacement is necessary.

Finally, there are two subcases in which different chains are found in the source text and in the summary (in this case the algorithm performs a replacement). The fourth row lists the case in which the original chain is correct; the last, cases in which the chain in the source text is incorrect. In the first column of this row are the cases in which the anaphor was correctly resolved in the summary but it was substituted by an incorrect expression because of a bad full text resolution; the second column shows the cases in which the anaphor was incorrectly resolved in both the full text and the summary, however, replacement was performed because the expression was placed in different chains.

6.3 A Summary Before and After Reference Checking

Examples (14) and (15) illustrate the difference between a summary before and after reference checking. A reader of (14) may not know who *the 71-year-old Walton* or *Sively* are, and what *store* is referred to in the text. In addition, the pronoun *he* in the last sentence is ambiguous between *Walton* and *Sively*. On the other hand, *the singer* in the last sentence can be easily resolved. This is because the chains *Walton*, *Sively* and *the store* do not start in the summary with the expression used for the first mention in the source text. These problems are fixed by step 3 of the reference checker. The ambiguous pronoun *he* in the last sentence of the summary is resolved to *Sively* in the summary and *Walton* in the source text.[10] Because the anaphor occurs in a different chain in the summary and in the full text, it has to be substituted by the head of the first chain occurrence noun phrase, *Walton*. *The singer* in the last sentence is resolved identically in the summary and in the full text: the chains are the same, so there is no need for replacement.

(14) WAL-MART FOUNDER PITCHES IN AT CHECK-OUT COUNTER (summary before reference checking)

> ***The 71-year-old Walton***, considered to be one of the world's richest people, grabbed a note pad Tuesday evening and started hand-writing merchandise prices for customers so their bills could be tallied on calculators quickly. *Walton*, known for his down-home style, made a surprise visit to ***the store*** that later Tuesday staged a concert by *country singer Jana Jea* in *its* parking lot. *Walton* often attends promotional events for *his* Arkansas-based chain, and ***Sively*** said *he* had suspected the boss might make an appearance. ***He*** also joined *the singer* on stage to sing a duet and led customers in the Wal-Mart cheer.

(15) WAL-MART FOUNDER PITCHES IN AT CHECK-OUT COUNTER (summary after reference checking)

> ***Wal-Mart founder Sam Walton***, considered to be one of the world's richest people, grabbed a note pad Tuesday evening and started hand-writing merchandise prices for customers so their bills could be tallied on calculators quickly. *Walton*, known for his down-home style, made a surprise visit to ***his store in this Florida Panhandle city*** that later Tuesday staged a concert by *country singer Jana Jea* in *its* parking lot. *Walton* often attends promotional events for *his* Arkansas-based chain, and ***store manager Paul Sively*** said *he* had suspected the boss might make an appearance. **Walton** also joined *the singer* on stage to sing a duet and led customers in the Wal-Mart cheer.

[10]The previous sentence in the source is: "*Walton* continued talking with customers during the concert."

7 Cross-Document Coreference and Multi-document Summarization

Multi-document summarization brings a cross-document dimension for coreference resolution. Even if instead of a coreference resolver a more general multilingual named entity disambiguator and geo tagger were used results confirmed the improvement [20].

7.1 Multilingual Entity Recognition and Disambiguation

The disambiguation of entities in free text consists of first recognizing a named entity in the text and then grounding it to an entity in the real world, say a location, a person or an organization. The EMM system includes modules for entity recognition and disambiguation in 19 languages [41, 42]. These modules are now being used as part of the summarization task to add normalized and disambiguated structural information as input for LSA. Next, we describe in more details two EMM modules for entity disambiguation: one for geographical locations and another one for persons and organizations.

Historically (e.g., MUC-7 [17]), place name recognition consisted of identifying references to locations in text and disambiguating them from homographic person names or from other homographic words. For instance, there are places called 'Javier' (Spain) and 'Solana' (Philippines), and there are places called 'And' (Iran), 'To' (Ghana) and 'Be' (India). Within the EMM framework, the recognition in [41] go beyond this MUC task by furthermore disambiguating between various homographic place names in order to identify precise latitude-longitude information and to put a dot on a map. For example, there are 15 different locations each with the names of 'Berlin', 'Paris' and 'Roma', and there are 205 places called 'San Antonio'. In their experiments Kabadjov et al. [20] make use of that EMM component to augment the term-by-sentence matrix (Table 1) with disambiguated and normalized location information.

They additionally make use of the multilingual person and organization recognition tools described in [42]. What distinguishes this tool from others is its high multilinguality and, most of all, the functionality to map name variants referring to the same entity. Name spelling variation is not only a multilingual phenomenon, but it is even very frequent within a single language. In [42] up to 170 ways of spelling the same name were identified. By recognizing and mapping existing name variants for the same entity and by feeding this normalized information to the LSA representation (as described in Sect. 4), additional useful cross-document links can be established.

Augmenting the initial matrix with information about disambiguated entities naturally does not only provide stronger inter-sentential cohesion (i.e., the LSA clusters sentences from different documents that make reference to the same entities), but also multilingual capabilities inherited by the multilingual entity disambiguation. Thus, this approach to summarization is not only multi-document, but also multilingual.[11]

7.2 Multi-document Summarization Results

Using a standard English corpus for Summarization research developed by the US National Institute for Standards and Technology (NIST) for the 2008 Text Analysis Conference (hereafter TAC-08), Kabadjov et al. [20] obtained promising, though not statistically significant, improvements over a lexical-only baseline ranked in the top 15–24 % across all evaluation metrics at the 2008 TAC competition. For the following experiments the popular ROUGE metric to evaluate the performance was used. The results are presented in Table 8.

On the standard multi-document summarization task (see Table 8), we include the official scores at TAC-08 of a lexical-only summarizer that was as a baseline for the experiments (cf. first row of the table) as well as an improved version of it referred to as 'lexical only' (cf. second row). The third row shows the performance when only entities (only coreference information) are used. The fourth row of Table 8 corresponds to the results obtained by combining the lexical and coreferring expressions.

From Table 8 can be seen that the performance of the 'lexical+entities' version of the system is higher than the 'lexical only' version, the baseline, but the improvement is not statistically significant. Using only entities for summarization is not sufficient.

Kabadjov et al. [20] note that the EMM entity disambiguation module used in their experiment was optimized for precision, since in the EMM's context the vast amounts of data (i.e., over 80K articles processed per day) makes up for the compromise on recall. However, in the TAC-08 context there is substantial room for improvement of the entity disambiguation recall by bringing in an intra-document coreference resolution system, such as GuiTAR [19]. In the light of

Table 8 Improvement with coreference information in multi-document summarization results

Approach	ROUGE-1	ROUGE-2	ROUGE-SU4
Lexical only TAC-08	0.355	0.088	0.123
Lexical only	0.359	0.087	0.125
Entities only	0.333	0.076	0.113
Lexical + entities	0.367	0.093	0.13

[11]The multilingual named entity disambiguator and geo-tagger developed at the JRC have already been used for cross-lingual linking of multilingual news clusters produced by the EMM system [50].

this, the performance of both ‘entity only’ and ‘lexical+entities’ approaches can be improved by working on the full coreference resolution systems.

8 Conclusion

As pointed out by the literature discussed throughout the chapter, using coreference information does lead to improved selection of salient content both in single-document and multi-document lexical-based extractive summarization. Naturally, however, the way in which coreference information is used matters. For instance, substitution did not result in significant improvements even with perfect coreference knowledge. The addition method, on the other hand, produced significant improvements in both cases when annotated coreference information and an automatic resolver were used.

Coreference resolution can be used as well as a post-processing step to correct entity mentions in the summary. Although, the overall performance is highly dependent on the quality of coreference resolution. Hence, a high-precision resolver is needed for this task. Automatic evaluation of linguistic quality of summaries could not be implemented without the use of coreference resolution either.

9 Further Reading

We recommend to start with the line of papers we followed in this chapter. The first approach that exploited cohesive relations like coreference to identify salience was proposed in [8].

Coreference-oriented text representation was also used in other works. In modeling local coherence as defined by the Centering theory [15], Barzilay and Lapata [4] put forward a similar document representation to the one discussed in the chapter, called ‘entity grid’ which was essentially an entity-by-sentence matrix. Though, as opposed to [47] they did not attempt to combine it with a purely lexical representation. Combining several sources of knowledge in the vector space model, among which key words and entities, was independently proposed by R. Steinberger et al. [50] while working on language-independent news cluster representation for cross-lingual news cluster linking. For that representation, they developed multilingual tools for geo-tagging and entity disambiguation [42].[12]

There has been increasing interest recently among text summarization researchers in post-processing techniques to improve the referential clarity and coherence of extractive summaries, and among natural language generation

[12]The use of the multilingual tools in higher-level applications can be seen at http://emm.newsexplorer.eu/.

researchers in generating referential expressions in context. The GREC tasks [5] are aimed at researchers in both of these groups, and the objective is the development of methods for generating chains of referential expressions for discourse entities in the context of a written discourse, as is useful for post-processing extractive summaries and repeatedly edited texts (such as Wikipedia articles).

ROUGE has been widely used for content quality evaluation so far. In [48] including entities to the n-gram based measure led to an improved performance measured in the AESOP TAC'09 task. One of the five aspects of linguistic quality evaluation in DUC/TAC has been referential clarity. Evaluation of this bit of linguistic quality was proposed in [38]. The approach yielded a satisfactory correlation with human-assigned linguistic quality.

Acknowledgements This work was supported by project "NTIS - New Technologies for Information Society", European Centre of Excellence, CZ.1.05/1.1.00/02.0090, and by project MediaGist, EU's FP7 People Programme (Marie Curie Actions), no. 630786.

References

1. Azzam, S., Humphreys, K., Gaizauskas, R.: Using coreference chains for text summarization. In: Proceedings of the ACL'99 Workshop on Conference and Its Applications, Baltimore. ACL (1999)
2. Baldwin, B., Morton, T.S.: Dynamic coreference-based summarization. In: Proceedings of EMNLP'98, Granada. ACL (1998)
3. Barzilay, R., Elhadad, M.: Using lexical chains for text summarization. In: Mani, I., Maybury, M. (eds.) Advances in Automated Text Summarization. MIT, Cambridge (1997)
4. Barzilay, R., Lapata, M.: Modeling local coherence: an entity-based approach. In: Proceedings of the 43rd Annual Meeting of the Association for Computational Linguistics, Ann Arbor. ACL (2005)
5. Belz, A., Kow, E., Viethen, J.: The GREC named entity generation challenge 2009: overview and evaluation results. In: Proceedings of ACL-IJCNLP'09 Workshop on Language Generation and Summarisation, Singapore. ACL (2009)
6. Bergler, S., Witte, R., Khalife, M., Li, Z., Rudzicz, F.: Using knowledge-poor coreference resolution for text summarization. In: Proceedings of DUC'03, Edmonton. NIST (2003)
7. Berry, M.W., Dumais, S.T., O'Brien, G.W.: Using linear algebra for intelligent IR. SIAM Rev. **37**(4), 573–595 (1995)
8. Boguraev, B., Kennedy, C.: Salience-based content characterisation of text documents. In: Mani, I., Maybury, M. (eds.) Advances in Automated Text Summarization. MIT, Cambridge (1997)
9. Charniak, E.: A maximum-entropy-inspired parser. In: Proceedings of NAACL'00, Philadelphia. ACL (2000)
10. Choi, F.Y.Y., Wiemer-Hastings, P., Moore, J.D.: Latent semantic analysis for text segmentation. In Proceedings of EMNLP, Pittsburgh. ACL (2001)
11. Document understanding conference: http://duc.nist.gov/
12. Edmundson, H.: New methods in automatic extracting. J. Assoc. Comput. Mach. **16**(2), 264–285 (1969). ACM
13. Giannakopoulos, G., El-Haj, M., Favre, B., Litvak, M., Steinberger, J., Varma, V.: TAC 2011 multiling pilot overview. In: Proceedings of the Text Analysis Conference 2011, Gaithersburg. NIST (2011)

14. Gong, Y., Liu, X.: Generic text summarization using relevance measure and latent semantic analysis. In: Proceedings of the 24th Annual International ACM SIGIR Conference on Research and Development in Information Retrieval, New Orleans, pp. 19–25. ACM (2001)
15. Grosz, B., Aravind, J., Scott, W.: Centering: a framework for modelling the local coherence of discourse. Comput. Linguist. **21**(2), 203–225. ACL (1995)
16. Hasler, L., Orasan, C., Mitkov, R.: Building better corpora for summarization. In: Proceedings of Corpus Linguistics, Lancaster. UCREL, Lancaster University (2003)
17. Hirschman, L.: MUC-7 coreference task definition, version 3.0. In: Proceedings of the 7th Message Understanding Conference, Fairfax. NIST (1998)
18. Hovy, E., Lin, C.: Automated text summarization in SUMMARIST. In: Mani, I., Maybury, M. (eds.) Advances in Automated Text Summarization. MIT, Cambridge (1997)
19. Kabadjov, M.: A comprehensive evaluation of anaphora resolution and discourse-new recognition. PhD thesis, University of Essex 2007
20. Kabadjov, M., Steinberger, J., Pouliquen, B., Steinberger, R., Poesio, M.: Multilingual statistical news summarisation: preliminary experiments with English. In: Proceedings of IAPWNC at the IEEE/WIC/ACM WI-IAT, Milano. IEEE Computer Society (2009)
21. Knott, A., Oberlander, J., O'Donnell, M., Mellish, C.: Beyond elaboration: the interaction of relations and focus in coherent text. In: Sanders, T., Schilperoord, J., Spooren, W. (eds.) Text Representation: Linguistic and Psycholinguistic Aspects. John Benjamins, Amsterdam/Philadelphia (2001)
22. Kupiec, J., Pedersen, J., Chen, F.: A trainable document summarizer. In: Proceedings of the 18th Annual International ACM SIGIR Conference on Research and Development in Information Retrieval, Seattle, pp. 68–73. ACM (1995)
23. Landauer, C.T., Dumais, S.: A solution to plato's problem: the latent semantic analysis theory of the acquisition, induction, and representation of knowledge. Psychol. Rev. **104**, 211–240 (1997). American Psychological Association
24. Lin, C., Hovy, E.: Automatic evaluation of summaries using n-gram co-occurrence statistics. In: Proceedings of HLT-NAACL, Edmonton. ACL (2003)
25. Lin, C.: ROUGE: a package for automatic evaluation of summaries. In: Proceedings of the Workshop on Text Summarization Branches Out, Barcelona. ACL (2004)
26. Luhn, H.: The automatic creation of literature abstracts. IBM J. Res. Dev. **2**(2), 159–165 (1958). IBM
27. Mani, I. (ed.): Proceedings of the Workshop on Intelligent and Scalable Text Summarization at the Annual Joint Meeting of the ACL/EACL, Madrid. ACL (1997)
28. Mani, I., Firmin, T., House, D., Klein, G., Sundheim, B., Hirschman, L.: The TIPSTER summac text summarization evaluation. In: Proceedings of the 9th Meeting of the European Chapter of the Association for Computational Linguistics, Bergen. ACL (1999)
29. Mani, I., Maybury, M. (eds.): Advances in Automatic Text Summarization. MIT, Cambridge (1999)
30. Marcu, D.: From discourse structures to text summaries. In: Mani [27]
31. Maybury, M.: Generating summaries from event data. In: Mani and Maybury [29]
32. McKeown, K., Radev, D.: Generating summaries of multiple news articles. In: Proceedings of the 18th Annual International ACM SIGIR Conference on Research and Development in Information Retrieval, Seattle, pp. 74–82. ACM (1995)
33. Morris, A., Kasper, G., Adams, D.: The effects and limitations of automatic text condensing on reading comprehension performance. Inf. Syst. Res. **3**(1), 17–35 (1992). INFORMS
34. Mueller, C., Strube, M.: MMAX: a tool for the annotation of multi-modal corpora. In: Proceedings of the 2nd IJCAI Workshop on Knowledge and Reasoning in Practical Dialogue Systems, Seattle. Morgan Kaufmann (2001)
35. Nenkova, A., Passonneau, R., McKeown, K.: The pyramid method: incorporating human content selection variation in summarization evaluation. ACM Trans. Speech Lang. Process. **4**(2), 1–23 (2007). ACM
36. Orasan, C., Mitkov, R., Hasler, L.: CAST: a computer-aided summarization tool. In: Proceedings of EACL'03, Budapest. ACL (2003)

37. Over, P., Dang, H., Harman, D.: DUC in context. Inf. Process. Manag. **43**(6), 1506–1520 (2007). Special Issue on Text Summarisation (Donna Harman, ed.). Elsevier.
38. Pitler, E., Louis, A., Nenkova, A.: Automatic evaluation of linguistic quality in multi-document summarization. In: Proceedings of the 48th Annual Meeting of the Association for Computational Linguistics, Uppsala, pp 544–554. ACL (2010)
39. Poesio, M., Kabadjov, M.: A general-purpose, off-the-shelf anaphora resolution module: implementation and preliminary evaluation. In: Proceedings of LREC, Lisbon. ELRA (2004)
40. Poesio, M., Stevenson, R., Di Eugenio, B., Hitzeman, J.: Centering: a parametric theory and its instantiations. Comput. Linguist. **30**(3), 309–363 (2004). ACL
41. Pouliquen, B., Kimler, M., Steinberger, R., Ignat, C., Oellinger, T., Blackler, K., Fuart, F., Zaghouani, W., Widiger, A., Forslund, A., Best, C.: Geocoding multilingual texts: recognition, disambiguation and visualisation. In: Proceedings of the 5th LREC, Genoa, pp. 53–58. ELRA (2006)
42. Pouliquen, B., Steinberger, R.: Automatic construction of multilingual name dictionaries. In: Goutte, C., Cancedda, N., Dymetman, M., Foster, G. (eds.) Learning Machine Translation. MIT, Cambridge (2009)
43. Radev, D., Jing, H., Budzikowska, M.: Centroid-based summarization of multiple documents. In: ANLP/NAACL Workshop on Automatic Summarization, Seattle. ACL (2000)
44. Radev, D., Teufel, S., Saggion, H., Lam, W., Blitzer, J., Qi, H., Celebi, A., Liu, D., Drabek, E.: Evaluation challenges in large-scale document summarization. In: Proceeding of the 41st meeting of the Association for Computational Linguistics, Sapporo. ACL (2003)
45. Sparck-Jones, K.: Automatic summarising: factors and directions. In: Mani and Maybury [29]
46. Steinberger, J., Ježek, K.: Text summarization and singular value decomposition. Lect. Notes Comput. Sci. **2457**, 245–254 (2004). Springer
47. Steinberger, J., Kabadjov, M., Poesio, M.: Improving LSA-based summarization with anaphora resolution. In: Proceedings of HLT/EMNLP'05, Vancouver, pp. 1–8. ACL (2005)
48. Steinberger, J., Kabadjov, M., Pouliquen, B., Steinberger, R., Poesio, M.: WB-JRC-UT's participation in TAC 2009: update summarization and AESOP tasks. In: Proceedings of TAC'09, Gaithersburg. NIST (2009)
49. Steinberger, J., Poesio, M., Kabadjov, M., Ježek, K.: Two uses of anaphora resolution in summarization. Inf. Process. Manag. **43**(6), 1663–1680 (2007). Elsevier
50. Steinberger, R., Pouliquen, B., Ignat, C.: Using language-independent rules to achieve high multilinguality in text mining. In: Fogelman-Soulié, F., Perrotta, D., Piskorski, J., Steinberger, R. (eds.) Mining Massive Data Sets for Security. IOS-Press, Amsterdam (2009)
51. Stuckardt, R.: Coreference-based summarization and question answering: a case for high precision anaphor resolution. In: International Symposium on Reference Resolution and Its Applications to Question Answering and Summarization, Venice (2003)
52. Text analysis conference: http://www.nist.gov/tac
53. Turchi, M., Steinberger, J., Kabadjov, M., Steinberger, R.: Using parallel corpora for multilingual (multi-document) summarisation evaluation. In: Proceedings of CLEF-10, pp. 52–63. Springer (2010)
54. Wan, X., Li, H., Xiao, J.: Cross-language document summarization based on machine translation quality prediction. In: Proceedings of the 48th Annual Meeting of the Association for Computational Linguistics, pp. 917–926. ACL (2010)

Towards a Procedure Model for Developing Anaphora Processing Applications

Roland Stuckardt

Abstract This chapter goes one step further towards real-world applications, providing a survey of particular cases in diverse highly relevant domains, among which are biomedicine, medicine, and legal domain. It is suggested that the design of an appropriate anaphora processing technology should be based on a detailed understanding of the particular application scenario that goes well beyond the mere recognition of the generic application type (information extraction, text summarization, etc.). As elucidated by the survey, supplementary resources such as corpora annotated with domain information and domain entity databases play an important role for case-specific anaphora processing. Summing up these insights, a procedure model will be distilled that is designed to assist the natural language engineer in systematically approaching novel application scenarios. It is suggested to employ this procedure model as well a framework for publicly documenting application-related anaphora processing work, fostering progress of the discipline by enhancing visibility and comparability of approaches, eventually enabling reuse of previous work related to similar scenarios.

Keywords Applications of anaphora resolution • Applications of coreference resolution • Natural language engineering • Off-the-shelf anaphora resolution systems • Biomedical texts • Pharmagenomic texts • Medical texts • Legal texts • Information extraction • Text summarization • Entity grounding • Domain-specific natural language processing • Gene databases • Proteinprotein interaction

R. Stuckardt (✉)
IT-Beratung, Sprachtechnologie, Medienanalyse, D-60433 Frankfurt am Main, Germany
e-mail: roland@stuckardt.de

M. Poesio et al. (eds.), *Anaphora Resolution*, Theory and Applications of Natural Language Processing, DOI 10.1007/978-3-662-47909-4_16

1 Introduction

In the last 10 years, increasingly complex successful practical applications of anaphora processing[1] have been developed. This work is highly relevant as it addresses the intricacy of particular application cases. It stands in contrast to earlier investigations, which were chiefly located at a generic level of consideration: standardized scenarios of coreference-based information extraction, text summarization, and question answering were looked at, focusing on fundamental feasibility issues, while neglecting the complexity of real-world application scenarios.

In this regard, when dealing with real-world applications of anaphora processing, it proves necessary to distinguish between four conceptual layers:

1. thematic application domain: e.g., biomedicine, possibly qualified by a microdomain, e.g., fruit fly genomics;
2. generic application type: e.g., information extraction (IE);
3. particular application scenario: e.g., intelligent user interface enabling content-oriented research paper browsing to enhance efficiency in genomic database curation;
4. anaphora processing required: e.g., resolution of third-person pronominal anaphora, resolution of associative anaphora, cross-document coreference resolution.

As will be substantiated below, designing an appropriate anaphora processing technology for a particular application case necessitates a detailed understanding of each of the above layers. The key aim of the subsequent considerations is to derive a **procedure model** that enables practitioners and natural language engineers to proceed systematically in the process of designing and developing a suitable technology that matches the specific requirements. Among the issues to be addressed are:

- developing a detailed understanding of the characteristics of the particular application scenario (item 3 above); this yields the proper base for
- selecting appropriate off-the-shelf technology (where feasible);
- designing custom-made approaches/algorithms (where required);
- selecting/building the required resources, including human expert knowledge (where required);
- properly dealing with the key methodological issues.

The aim of the procedure model is thus to raise awareness of the bandwidth of anaphora processing issues to be dealt with when approaching new application scenarios, that is, of the particular types of anaphora processing to be distinguished, of the resources to be employed, and the methodology to be followed for system-

[1] The term **anaphora processing** shall be understood to comprise all varieties of anaphor and (inter- as well as cross-document) coreference resolution, including entity grounding.

atically evaluating and optimizing the implemented solution. It shall incorporate a guidance to asking the relevant questions in the right order, and to keep an eye out for available linguistic, domain, and supplementary resources that have been successfully employed in similar predecessor applications of the same domain or generic type. Moreover, it provides a framework for systematically documenting one's own achievements, thus fostering visibility and reusability.

The chapter is organized as follows. Based on a survey of successful practical applications in the most important application domains (Sect. 2), a procedure model shall be distilled that supports the natural language engineer in systematically approaching new application scenarios (Sect. 3). Based on this, a proposal for the enhancement of visibility, comparability, and reusability of application work will be made, thus enabling consolidation of insights gained through recent anaphora processing research (Sect. 4).

As there has been a lot of respective recent work, space is too restricted to discuss all mentionable practical application cases in full detail. The selection of cases has been chiefly guided by the desiderata of covering the application domains currently considered most relevant, and of illustrating the bandwidth and potential intricacy of typical application scenarios. Supplementing references to further important application cases will be given; the reader is encouraged to refer to the literature for background information.

By its very nature, this chapter incorporates a point of confluence, underlining the importance of the algorithms, resources, and methodologies that have been thoroughly discussed in the first three parts of the book. Thus, there are numerous cross-references; in particular, this holds with respect to the issues covered by the Resources part, that is: annotated corpora and annotation tools, evaluation criteria and tools, preprocessing technology, off-the-shelf tools, and evaluation campaigns. In order to avoid fatiguing the reader, we'll thus commonly omit respective cross-references if it is obvious where to find additional information on a particular topic.

2 Successful Application Cases: A Survey

The comprehensive survey that will be presented in this section serves two principal purposes. (A) It gives a broad overview of successful anaphora processing applications in economically relevant domains, thus illustrating the high practical relevance of anaphora processing research and technology. (B) It develops an understanding of the topics to be covered, that is, the questions to be asked by the procedure model to be formulated below: in looking at diverse particular application scenarios and domains, we will inductively learn which types of anaphora processing to distinguish, which types of linguistic, domain and supplementary resources to look for, and which methodological issues to think about.

A study of recent publications describing concrete applications of anaphora processing reveals that important work has been done in the following thematic application domains:

- biomedicine (pharmacogenomics),
- medicine,
- legal domain,
- news domain,
- email communication,
- consumer test reports.

Fostered by a number of well-recognized dedicated conferences and workshops text mining in biomedicine and pharmacogenomics, the vast majority of practical application scenarios is located in the **biomedical** (or **pharmacogenomic**) **domain**, as it embodies an economically highly relevant application field that offers ample opportunities for the potentially gainful employment of state-of-the-art natural language processing technology. There are large collections of documents to be properly managed in order to achieve best possible accessibility for biomedical researchers; accessibility obviously benefits highly from proper syntactic standardization as well as from content-oriented structuring. As manual maintenance of respective knowledge structures is an extremely laborious and thus expensive task, it suggests itself to investigate which parts of this job can be subjected to the discretion of automatic or semiautomatic NLP support.

As will become clear below, anaphora processing plays a central role in this regard. Thus, three application cases in biomedicine shall be discussed in detail, elucidating the great bandwidth of different application scenarios within one and the same thematic domain. In addition, some further interesting conceptual and methodological contributions will be discussed, which have implications for other domains as well.

The **medical** (or **clinical**) **domain** is of high importance as well; it shall thus be looked at one particularly interesting application scenario in this area.

Moreover, a highly relevant case from the **legal domain** will be studied, signifying that there are as well very interesting applications outside the natural sciences.

Finally, some further interesting cases from diverse thematic domains or with generic (multi-domain) scope will be briefly described.

2.1 Applications in Biomedicine

The biomedical (or pharmacogenomic) application domain lies in the intersection of the three life science disciplines of biology, medicine, and pharmacology. It deals with diverse challenging problems such as identifying mentions of genes, proteins, diseases, and drugs as well as extracting sophisticated composite information, e.g., protein-protein, gene-disease, drug-protein, drug-disease, drug-drug, and even gene-disease-drug relations. These tasks are of unprecedented difficulty since, for instance, the surface forms of the entities and relations to be extracted are typically much more complex than in the classical application fields of information extraction and retrieval such as the news domain. Hahn et al. [15] give an excellent survey of the state of the art of biomedical text mining, focusing on recent approaches to extracting information from the pharmacogenomics literature. Another excellent source are the proceedings of the ACL BioNLP workshops—see, for instance, Cohen et al. [4].

Because of the inherent complexity of even some allegedly basic problems in this domain (such as tokenization, sentence boundary detection, etc.), many applications are just content with the mundane task of named entity extraction, possibly restricting considerations to abstracts of biomedical publications. If, however, one moves on to considering the full texts as well, then, at the latest, anaphoric relations become relevant. For some pertinent current research on biomedical anaphora resolution, see, e.g., Kilicoglu and Demner-Fushman [20], D'Souza and Ng [7], Nguyen et al. [28], and Segura-Bedmar [33].

We will now look at three particular biomedical text mining applications that employ anaphora resolution.

Supporting the Curation of Gene Databases **Gasperin** [10] describes an important application of anaphor resolution, contributing to an interactive tool that is designed to **support the curators of a database of genomic research** by identifying domain-relevant entities in scientific articles. Specifically, the genomic database FlyBase, which accumulates research articles about the fruit fly *Drosophila Melanogaster*, is considered. The work stands in the broader context of applying general NLP technology to implement an innovative user interface (the so-called PaperBrowser) with enhanced navigational functionalities in order to facilitate FlyBase curation (see Karamanis et al., [18]). This work is economically highly relevant, as gene database curation typically requires knowledge of domain experts trained to identify and index relevant entities; furthermore, the amount of documents to be processed is typically large.

The NLP components employed are named entity recognition and anaphor resolution. The goal is to automatically link all textual mentions that are referring to a particular gene or that are related to it. This can be regarded as an instance of the generic application type of information extraction, or, taking into account that the FlyBase curators still see whole documents rather than mere extracts, information retrieval. The essentials of this application scenario can thus be schematically rendered as follows:

application domain: biomedicine;
microdomain: fruit fly genomics;
generic application type: information extraction (IE), information retrieval (IR);
particular application scenario: providing enhanced (content-oriented) navigational functionalities as part of an intelligent user interface that improves efficiency in cura-

tion of a database containing articles on fruit fly genomics;

anaphora processing required: identification of mentions of genes and related entities, including identification of coreference and domain-relevant associative[2] (mainly *bio-type* and *set-member*) relations between these mentions.

In looking more closely at Gasperin's work, some key issues can be identified that should be dealt with when approaching an anaphora processing application case:

- identifying the types of anaphors to be dealt with: in case of the FlyBase curation scenario, a closer look at the documents to be processed revealed that a mere 3 % of all relevant mentions are by pronouns; thus, it was decided only to address non-pronominal NP (names, acronyms, definite descriptions), including instances of associative anaphora;
- identifying existing domain-specific resources that might be useful to accomplish the required anaphora processing functionality: in the considered case, the approach will be based on (i) preprocessing the documents with the **Gene Name Recognizer** of Vlachos et al. [42, 43] that is specific to the considered microdomain, and (ii) information from **Sequence Ontology (SO)** (Eilbeck et al. [8]) to perform domain-specific semantic typing as required for determining genomic relations among relevant entity mentions, which enables recognition of associative anaphora;
- delineating the basic parameters of the anaphora processing approach to be employed: as annotation is expensive in the fruit fly microdomain, it was decided to follow a semi-supervised approach that doesn't rely on manually annotated training data, instead referring to available domain resources, particularly SO.

Gasperin (ibid.) gives examples that illustrate the intricacy of anaphora processing in the genomics domain. In

> ...is composed of five proteins, encoded by the male-specific lethal genes. ...The MSL proteins colocalize to hundreds of sites ... male animals die when they are mutant for any one of the five msl genes.

the identical head nouns and SO **biotypes** of *five proteins* and *The MSL proteins* are taken as evidence that these mentions are coreferring; moreover, mention *the five msl genes* is interpreted to be associatively related with antecedent mention *The MSL proteins* as they're of different biotypes (gene vs. protein) while sharing an identical modifier (MSL). The last-mentioned associative case elucidates how the employed

[2]**Associative anaphora** is a particular case of definite NP anaphora in which a discourse entity can be referred to that has not been explicitly mentioned because it is associatively related to an entity that has been explicitly mentioned. Among the frequently observed associations are *part-whole* and *set-member* relations, which might have a domain-specific flavor. As biomedical entities (genes etc.) are typically discussed by referring to concepts rather than to individual instances, *part-whole* and *set-member* relations can be understood to conflate.

resolution approach combines general with domain-specific syntactic and semantic evidence.

The second highly relevant type of associative anaphora to be covered is **set-member relations** between anaphor and antecedent (in either direction), as in ... *ced-4 and ced-9* ... *the genes* ... (see Gasperin and Briscoe [12]). Again, the required evidence is contributed by SO, as it models some immediate *set-member* relationships between the considered entities, e.g.: *a transcript is part of a gene*; in addition, there are eight handcrafted rules specific to the genomics microdomain that enable the deduction of further *set-member* relations modeled indirectly (mainly transitively) by SO, e.g.: *mRNA is part-of-a gene*. Evidence of this type is then employed to recognize particular instances of associative anaphora.

This discussion illustrates the type of expertise and semantic knowledge engineering typically required to cope with the complexity of a particular domain. But even at the basic level of surface syntactic pattern matching, subtleties of the particular domain should be appropriately accounted for: according to writing conventions of the genomics domain, gene names are typically written with lower-cased italicized letters (*msl genes*) while protein names are typically written non-italicized and upper-cased (MSL proteins). Thus, on one hand, one has to take care of not being too case-sensitive during matching; on the other hand, this fact can be leveraged for selecting the right interpretation of otherwise ambiguous mentions.

According to formal evaluation results, the implemented semi-supervised (rule- and domain-resources-based) system achieves (P,R) tradeoffs of (0.59,0.81) for the coreferent cases, and (0.56,0.22) for the associative cases. Compared to some previous approaches, performance is regarded to be slightly worse. However, one should take into account that no expensive manually annotated training data have been employed.

There has been highly relevant follow-up work on the above application case by Gasperin and Briscoe [12] and Gasperin [11], employing the same domain-specific resources, but investigating what can be accomplished by resorting to a statistical (supervised) approach, thus dropping the demand of getting along without manually annotated reference data. This approach is regarded to be innovative as it is among the first investigations on probabilistic models dealing with coreference as well as with associative anaphora. Though based on a comparatively small corpus of 5 manually annotated biomedical full articles[3] (about 33,300 words), it achieves a performance that is regarded state-of-the-art[4]; but results indicate as well that further substantial research is required on identifying additional domain-specific sources of evidence to improve performance on associative anaphora.

Supporting Researchers to Keep Current with Work on Protein-Protein Interactions Sanchez et al. [31] investigate the potential contribution of automated

[3]As opposed to biomedical *abstracts*, which have been considered in most previous investigations.

[4]For coreference, (P,R) tradeoffs in the range between (0.56,0.55) and (0.69,0.67) are quoted, while performance on associative anaphora is shown to range between (0.29,0.35) (*biotype*) and (0.39,0.42) (*set-member*), depending upon the probabilistic model employed.

anaphora processing in another biomedical microdomain that is expected to gain from the application of automated natural language processing technology: protein-protein interactions. From a general perspective, the considered application case is to support scientific researchers to keep current with significant work in the field of biomedicine; see Cooper and Kershenbaum [5] for further information about the application case. In view of the steadily increasing number of papers published, the research community would gain enormously if there were NLP-based means to automatically identify and structure particularly relevant content. In other words, the generic application type is thus information extraction. While Sanchez et al. do not explicate full details of a particular application scenario, the key facts of this case can be summarized as follows:

application domain:	biomedicine;
microdomain:	protein-protein interactions;
generic application type:	information extraction; possibly (upon further elaboration) as well text summarization;
particular application scenario:	supporting scientific researchers to keep current with significant work in the considered microdomain, which is to be accomplished through automated discovery of protein-protein interaction relations in domain-relevant documents;
anaphora processing required:	restricted intra-document anaphor (coreference) resolution—resolving those anaphoric mentions of domain-relevant entities that occur in descriptions of protein-protein interaction relations.

That is, anaphora processing shall be employed as a preprocessing stage of relational information extraction in order to boost IE recall.

Given these general requirements, Sanchez et al. proceeded to explore the details of the application case as necessary for tackling the anaphor resolution task. A distribution study revealed that 90 % of the relevant anaphors are pronouns, while a mere 10 % are sortal.[5] Moreover, pleonastic, i.e., non-referential occurrences of *it* were identified to be as frequent as referential occurrences. A typical case containing a relevant it occurrence looks as follows (taken from the Journal of Biological Chemistry, cited by [31]):

> The same result was obtained for the dm-rabphilin: it specifically interacted with dm-Rab27, not with dm-Rab3 or dm-Rab8. . . .

Sanchez et al. thus restricted their considerations to the resolution of pronouns (those occurring in descriptions of protein-protein interactions). As they expected

[5]**Sortal anaphora** is defined as a particular case of definite NP anaphora in which a discourse entity referred to by mentioning its general concept (i.e., its *sort*) only, as it is the case in: *The same result was obtained for the dm-rabphilin. This protein specifically interacted . . . .*

that this problem can be adequately addressed by resorting to linguistic (i.e., domain-independent) syntactic and semantic evidence, Sanchez et al. decided to employ the off-the-shelf tool **GuiTAR** (Poesio et al., [29]), which includes a pronoun resolver. Preprocessing, however, comprises biomedicine-specific PoS tagging and named entity recognition, using the available component technology **GENIA PoS tagger** (Tsuruoka et al. [40]) and **ABNER** (Settles [34]). According to first evaluation results on a corpus of 23 relevant documents (considering full texts vs. abstracts), a small improvement in protein-protein interaction extraction is achieved, which thus indicates the usefulness of general-purpose anaphor resolvers in particular application cases.

One key point to take along is that the anaphora processing problem to be solved in this particular case differs considerably from the problem to be solved in the FlyBase curation scenario, although the domain is the same. This hints that each particular application scenario requires careful individual analysis in order to enable selection of the most appropriate anaphora processing technology. Section 3 below will further elaborate on this point, devising a systematic approach.

Information Extraction of Biomolecular Relations The seminal work of **Castaño et al.** [3] deals with an application case of anaphor resolution similar to the one discussed in the previous section: supporting information extraction of biomolecular relations in biomedical literature. However, a broader range of relevant relations (not confined to a special case such as protein-protein interactions) is considered. As they do not delineate a particular application scenario, their contribution can be conceived as of paradigmatic value for a broad range of particular IE applications in the biomedical domain. The approach targets the two fundamental anaphora processing tasks of (a) identifying anaphoric noun phrases and (b) resolving them by resorting to biomedical knowledge. Unlike some recent research, considerations are restricted to biomedical abstracts, which are taken from the **MEDLINE** and **PUBMED** databases.[6] Based on a general distributional analysis over the MEDLINE abstracts, Castaño et al. identified both pronominal and non-pronominal (sortal) object anaphora as prevalent and thus potentially relevant. Again, this indicates that additional information about the particular application scenario is of high potential value: it can help restricting the anaphora processing efforts to the really relevant type(s) of anaphora, as already seen in the above-discussed two cases.

[6]**MEDLINE** (Medical Literature Analysis and Retrieval System Online) is a publicly available database that provides bibliographic references of international research articles in medicine. For many articles, abstracts are made available. MEDLINE is a service of the US-American National Center for Biotechnology Information (NCBI). **PUBMED**, which is as well a service of NCBI, embodies a meta database of *bio*medical articles that includes MEDLINE (see http://www.ncbi.nlm.nih.gov/pubmed/).

Among the most important contributions of Castaño et al. are the investigations of how to use the semantic type of bio-entities derived from the **UMLS**[7] **Metathesaurus** for (a) identifying domain-relevant mentions (i.e., those that refer to bio-entities) and (b) resolving anaphoric mentions by resorting to domain-specific morphological and semantic preference factors. In particular, they found out that employing **domain-specific sortal information** beats resorting to the usual subject-object distinction that is employed by many classical (domain-unspecific) approaches (e.g., Lappin and Leass [24] and Kennedy and Boguraev [19]). According to formal evaluation on an annotated corpus, (P,R) results of (0.80,0.71) for pronouns and (0.74,0.75) for sortals are obtained when employing domain-specific preferences; for pronouns, this is a significant gain.

There has been follow-up work on domain-specific morphological factors by **Wellner et al.** [47], who further study respective string similarity metrics to be employed for mapping biomedical entity mentions to entries in the UMLS Metathesaurus. This is an instance of the anaphora processing task of **entity grounding**, which will be discussed in full detail below.

Conceptual and Methodological Work While not referring to generic and particular application scenarios, further relevant research in the biomedical domain deals with conceptual and methodological key issues of domain-specific anaphora processing.

Nguyen and Kim [27] systematically investigate the role that domain-specific characteristics play for the appropriate design of a machine-learning-based pronoun resolution system to be applied, having in view the biomedical domain. They consider texts of two domains, comparing anaphora processing of biomedical research papers (using the **GENIA corpus**)[8] and news texts (using the extensively studied MUC and ACE corpora). Corpus analyses and empirical experiments are conducted, indicating that domain characteristics should be taken into account for obtaining an optimal solution even when restricting considerations to pronouns. Basically and essentially, they confirm the above findings according to which a detailed understanding of the distributional properties of anaphoric expressions within the domain is key, strengthening this proposition by referring to microdistributions, i.e., by distinguishing between particular types of pronouns. Moreover, as expected, the contribution of a particular feature employed by the ML approach is found to differ from domain to domain, but even (within a particular domain) from corpus to corpus. This further substantiates the above claim that taking into account the

[7]Embodying a compendium of controlled vocabularies in the biomedical sciences, **UMLS (= Unified Medical Language System)** can be seen as a comprehensive thesaurus and ontology of biomedical concepts. It consists of various components (Metathesaurus, Semantic Network, SPECIALIST Lexicon) that are useful for developing medical NLP applications. (See http://www.nlm.nih.gov/research/umls/.)

[8]The **GENIA corpus** is a collection of MEDLINE abstracts manually annotated according to a biomedical data model (**GENIA Ontology**) that covers a subset of the substances and the biological locations involved in reactions of proteins. (See http://www-tsujii.is.s.u-tokyo.ac.jp/GENIA/home/wiki.cgi)

domain and scenario characteristics is key. As it is shown that this statement even applies to pronominal anaphora, it can be concluded that employing an off-the-shelf anaphor resolution system as Sanchez et al. ([31], see above) did might yield suboptimal results in many cases.

Bin et al. [1] study the resolution of a particular type of pronominal anaphora that has been identified to be relevant in the biomedical domain: ***other*-anaphora**. Working on 2,000 annotated MEDLINE abstracts taken from the **GENIA corpus**, they deal with cases like the following

> IL-10 inhibits nuclear stimulation of nuclear factor kappa B (NF kappa B).
> Several other transcription factors including NF-IL-6, AP-1, AP-2, GR, CREB, Oct-1, and Sp-1 are not affected by IL-10.

in which mention *Several other transcription factors* is referring to an entity indirectly introduced by the antecedent mention *nuclear factor kappa B*, viz., the set of all transcription factors, to which a *part-of* relation holds. The technique employed to resolve such instances of indirect anaphora is itself a highly relevant contribution: automatically mined domain-specific lexical patterns (modeling *part-of* relations) are shown to clearly outperform a set of manually designed generic patterns when referred to as a source of evidence in a machine learning approach to *other*-anaphora. Importantly, the results obtained are significant in two conceptual regards: (a) they further substantiate the potential value of employing domain-specific techniques even at the level of particular types of anaphoric expressions; (b) as the manually designed patterns perform considerably better in the news domain, this gives additional evidence that the most appropriate approach (in this case: automatically mined vs. manually designed patterns) might depend on the particular domain considered.

Su et al. [38] work as well on MEDLINE abstracts taken from the **GENIA corpus**, studying, however, general coreference resolution based on various knowledge sources specific to the biomedical domain. They conducted extensive annotation work, building a collection of 1,999 MEDLINE abstracts augmented with coreference information (the **MedCo corpus**[9]).

Gasperin et al. [13] develop a domain-specific annotation scheme suitable for capturing referential relations between biomedical entities relevant for training and evaluating anaphora processing approaches in this domain. As the available models of biomedical relations such as UMLS or the GENIA Ontology are regarded to be too coarse-grained, they devise respective refinements. Further observing that the lack of respective publicly available resources severely impedes progress of research, they initiated construction of an annotated corpus of full-text biomedical articles (rather than abstracts) to be made freely available to the research community.[10]

[9] see http://nlp.i2r.a-star.edu.sg/medco.html

[10] see http://www.wiki.cl.cam.ac.uk/rowiki/NaturalLanguage/FlySlip/Flyslip-resources

Watters et al. [46] consider two further methodological facets of the resources issue: (a) whether domain experts should be employed for annotating corpora, and (b) how the user interface for conducting annotation should be designed. The main criteria considered are simplicity of user interface implementation and quality (in particular, reliability) of obtained annotations. According to the results of a pilot study, for pronouns, resorting to layman knowledge and employing a simple user interface suffices. However, for non-pronominal anaphora (not considered in [46]), the situation might be different, as one expects a higher fraction of anaphoric mentions the resolution of which requires domain-specific rather than general linguistic knowledge.

2.2 *Applications in Medicine*

In the medical (or clinical) application domain, text mining considers documents related to anamnesis, treatment, and discharge of patients as gathered in hospitals. While there is definitely an overlap with the biomedical domain, it is important to understand that the texts to be processed are of a different genre. In a considerable number of cases, these documents are of a relatively informal type—e.g., consisting of free text that has been recorded on the fly during, or immediately after, patient treatment. One thus speaks as well about *clinical narratives* in this regard.

Anaphoric relations clearly play an important role in this domain. Correspondingly, this topic has found considerable attention in the last years—see, for instance, Savova et al. [32], Zheng et al. [48], and Wang et al. [45]. As this research has shown, there are particular methodological and distributional issues to be taken into account that render anaphora processing very domain- and genre-specific here.

We will now describe one particular application scenario in detail and briefly look at a second one.

Tracking Pertinent Findings in Radiology Free-Text Reports A highly relevant and relatively complex application scenario of anaphora processing is considered by **Son et al.** [35]: applying cross-document coreference resolution for tracking evolution of relevant indicator lesions (here: diagnostic findings related to lung cancer cases) in unstructured radiology reports. The context of this work is a system that performs intra-document information extraction over radiology reports, having in view various particular applications such as enhanced content-oriented information retrieval over the structured extracts, which might be relevant for case searching (in clinical environments), population studies (in research), and teaching—see Taira [39]. Son et al. follow up on this work, illustrating how to tailor available NLP technology for an essentially generic application type (viz., intra-document IE in medical free text reports) to a particular application scenario by augmenting it with enhanced anaphora processing custom-made for the scenario. Notably, it is a complex case of cross-document coreference resolution on entities beyond the object anaphora level.

Boiling this down to the essential characteristic yields the schematic description:

application domain: medicine;
microdomain: radiology/oncology;
generic application type: information extraction (IE), information retrieval (IR);
particular application scenario: tracking evolution over time of pertinent diagnostic findings in radiology free-text records in order to facilitate condition management in medical treatment and to provide feedback for treatment outcomes assessment;
anaphora processing required: cross-document coreference resolution to establish referential links between pertinent findings in temporally subsequent radiology documents, referring to the results of a preprocessing engine that identifies isolated findings employing intra-document relational information extraction (including intra-document coreference resolution).

Son et al. employ a probabilistic model to recognize inter-document coreference of related diagnostic findings, such as the development of tumor locations, sizes, etc. Since there may be more than one tumor in a given patient case, this is a non-trivial task, amounting to associate subsets of documents belonging to findings about particular medical entities (here: tumors), taking into account the boundary condition that associated documents belong to the health record of a particular patient. As the findings are represented as complex structured relational entities (frames, which are constructed by the upstream intra-document IE), the devised solution differs significantly from the above-discussed approaches, which tackle object anaphora only.

Being semantic entities of radiology, oncology, and general medicine, frames (= findings) are mapped to sets of respective microdomain-specific (rather than linguistic) features, among which are existence, location, quantity, size, severity, and trend of the relevant indicator lesions ([35], p1389); as the probabilistic engine works on pairs of frames to be classified as pertinent or non-pertinent, further features are employed to capture the relevant relational aspects, distinguishing between trend features (to model change of size etc.) and extrinsic features (those determined by referring to additional external evidence not represented in the frames). These extrinsic features embody an excellent example of how important an in-depth expertise of the thematic domain, including the available external resources, can be for tackling a particular anaphora processing task. In the considered case, further potentially relevant evidence is gathered from **health insurance claims data**, which contains information about the medical treatment applied, e.g. related surgical interventions. In this regard, identifying those particular interventions that are related to the radiology microdomain required a detailed understanding of the

CPT-4 codes[11] employed to specify medical interventions, which, in turn, required a detailed understanding of the **ICD-9-CM medical diagnostics code**[12] (ibid, p1390).

The approach has been implemented using standard maximum entropy technology, and evaluated on a set of about 250 computer tomography reports belonging to 50 lung cancer patients. Son et al. report a cross-document coreference resolution (P,R) performance of (0.72,0.63) employing the model-theoretic MUC scoring scheme (Vilain et al. [41]).

It would be beyond the scope of this chapter to get into more detail about the details of this rather sophisticated approach. The reader is encouraged to take a closer look at the paper [35], as this is a very illustrative case. The key point to take along is that coping with complex application scenarios might require deep expert knowledge of the microdomain and its available resources.

Coreference Resolution on Hospital Discharge Summaries **He** [16] describes another application of coreference resolution on a particular class of electronic medical records: **hospital discharge summaries**. While not focusing on a particular application scenario, the anaphora processing techniques investigated are regarded to be useful enhancements of medical information extraction as applicable for automatic patient-care quality monitoring and medical-assist question answering systems. The work focuses on five medical semantic categories that are of particular relevance in hospital discharge summaries.

2.3 Applications in the Legal Domain

Supporting Attorneys' Preparation for Litigation Another highly relevant application field is considered by **Dozier and Zielund** [6], who study cross-document coreference resolution of attorneys, judges, and expert witness name mentions in legal documents. Possibly combined with additional IE functionality to discover particular relations between such persons, this information is regarded to be useful to support attorneys in preparing for litigation. While not focusing on a particular application scenario, Dozier and Zielund mention some concrete ways to put such information to good use: first and foremost, it can be immediately applied to compile detailed profiles of people working in the legal domain; another concrete scenario is the detection of conflicts of interest among people that are working on a legal matter. A large number of heterogeneous text sources are considered, including news, case law, law reviews, and MEDLINE abstracts (for background information

[11]Maintained by the American Medical Association (AMA), **CPT** (= **Current Procedural Terminology**) standardizes communication of information about medical services, e.g., between physicians, patients, and health insurance providers.

[12]Published by the WHO, **ICD** (= **International Statistical Classification of Diseases and Related Health Problems**) is a code employed internationally for the uniform communication about diseases, injuries, etc., and its concomitant circumstances.

on medical expert witnesses). An important point to note about the cross-document anaphora processing task is that it is accomplished indirectly by linking person mentions in the documents to existing profile records, which can be understood as models of unique real world persons; cross-document coreference relations are thus recognized indirectly by collecting references to identical profile records. In this regard, we can thus speak of reference resolution proper rather than mere anaphor resolution. This task of linking textual mentions to standardized external representations is commonly called **entity grounding** in the literature (see below).

Putting this in our standard schema, we get:

application domain:	legal domain;
microdomain:	n. a.;
generic application type:	information extraction (IE), information retrieval (IR);
particular application scenario:	compiling detailed profiles of people working in the legal domain, identifying conflicts of interest among people working on related legal matters, and similar (not yet fixed);
anaphora processing required:	cross-document coreference resolution of person name mentions, involving entity grounding (i.e., reference resolution proper) by referring to existing person profile records.

Entity grounding of attorneys and judges is accomplished by referring to an existing commercially distributed resource (the **Westlaw Legal Dictionary**) that provides biographical records, while expert witness mentions are grounded by consulting a lexicon of respective entries that has been created during the project through text mining of 300,000 jury verdict and settlement documents; this involved referring to publicly available **professional license information**[13] and an **expertise taxonomy**,[14] extracting about 100,000 profiles. Again, this illustrates the importance of an excellent knowledge of publicly available domain-related resources.

Cross-document coreference resolution is implemented as a two step procedure: (1) finite-state techniques are employed for extracting mentions of attorneys, judges, and expert witnesses; (2) a Bayesian network is used for probabilistically matching extracted mentions with biographical profiles. Formal evaluation showed that entity grounding performance depends upon whether, in the particular document collection considered, a highly stereotypical syntax is employed to refer to persons; (P,R) results have been determined to respectively range between (0.98,0,96) and (0.95,0.6).

---

[13]Among the sources tapped are the US Drug Enforcement Agency, which license health care professionals, and other professional licensing agencies; Dozier and Zielund don't give full details here.

[14]Dozier and Zielund don't give details here

The work of Dozier and Zielund can be regarded key as it opened up another economically highly relevant sphere of activity for automatic anaphora processing: (a) in the legal domain, there are huge amounts of unstructured textual information to be coped with; (b) as legal expert workforce is particularly expensive, support by enhanced content-oriented NLP applications is more than welcome; (c) existing digital resources, such as the biographical profiles and the professional license records referred to above, can be readily employed to tackle new, challenging NLP tasks.

2.4 Further Applications in Miscellaneous Domains

There are various other interesting application cases in diverse domains that are worth to be briefly described. Some further entity grounding scenarios shall be discussed first.

Grounding of Spatial Named Entities Leidner et al. [25, 26] consider the problem of grounding spatial named entities, where *spatial* is to be understood in a general sense, comprising diverse cases such as geo-spatial and bio-spatial entities. The generic scenario of applications that employ spatial named entity grounding is to combine an initial step of entity extraction to identify the domain-relevant entities (e.g., country names (geo), parts of an organism (biomedicine)) with a subsequent step of mapping these entities to representations of real world objects, referring, for instance, to digital geographic resources or to digital atlases of organisms.[15] This output can then be used to generate visual surrogates of the text, i.e., graphical maps that depict the locations mentioned in and extracted from the text. This can be of immediate use in diverse generic application scenarios such as text summarization and question answering. Leidner et al. delineate some particular scenarios such as supporting crisis management by aiding analysts to trace trouble spots.

The entity grounding step includes resolution of ambiguous place names, which is accomplished by applying two so-called **minimality heuristics**: (a) *one referent per discourse*, which means that an ambiguous place name is interpreted to refer to the same location throughout a particular discourse; (b) *spatial minimality*, which amounts to interpreting all ambiguous place name mentioned in a particular discourse in a way that the spatial region covering all place names mentioned in this discourse becomes as small as possible. However, while this might yield correct results in many cases, it is obvious that there are many basic counter-examples. E.g., consider a text about negotiations between the governments of France and the United States which mentions Paris and Washington; in this case, it is unlikely that Paris refers to the so-named place in Texas. This gives evidence that the heuristics

[15] See Leidner et al. (ibid.), who enumerate some interesting geographical gazetteers and biomedical resources to be referred to as entity grounding models.

requires supplementation with further (micro)domain- and application-scenario-specific criteria.[16]

Grounding of Biomedical Entities In their BioAR approach, **Kim and Park** [21] investigate anaphor resolution followed by protein entity mention grounding in biomedical research papers . The intended generic application type is biomedical information extraction, addressing biological interactions of arbitrary types (Kim [22]). While no particular scenario is considered, possible applications are seen in the fields of information visualization for biomedical knowledge discovery and ontology development. The grounding task is accomplished by referring to the available **proteome database Swiss-Prot**.[17] Evaluation has been carried out on 1,505 MEDLINE abstracts on yeast, yielding (P,R) results of (0.6,0.41) for protein name grounding. This work is interesting as Kim and Park emphasize the key importance of domain-specific resolution strategies and resources for capturing the essence of the biomedical field, hypothesizing that its success might not immediately translate to other domains.

Hachey et al. [14] deal as well with biomedical reference resolution proper, but focus on gene mention grounding, referring to databases of organism gene identifiers. They consider the subdomain of fly, mouse, and yeast genes but neither refer to generic nor to particular application scenarios.

Grounding of Person Names Elsayed et al. [9] address the cross-document coreference resolution task of **grounding person mentions** that occur in email collections. This research is very interesting as the implemented solution makes extensive use of the particularities of the application case, exploiting, besides the email content, its **social context**, i.e., the thread an email belongs to, other emails with identical senders/recipients, etc. There are highly relevant application cases, e.g. supporting law enforcement agencies in analyzing confiscated computer data, or aiding historians in comparable tasks. Experimental evaluation is carried out on a subset of the **Enron email dataset**[18] made available by Carnegie-Mellon University, showing accuracy rates well above 0.8 for an implementation of person mention resolution based on a probabilistic model that exploits, in particular, social context.

Wang [44] explores another application case of cross-document person name resolution that involves entity grounding: deciding whether **transliterated personal names** that occur in different Chinese texts are referring to the same person. This is an important scenario as, for instance, transliteration of a European family name to Chinese written language might involve fuzziness, mapping different European names to the same Chinese transliteration or vice versa. Addressing this issue

[16]Leidner et al. (ibid.) didn't carry out formal evaluation; they only discussed some example cases, illustrating application of their heuristics on two documents of the news domain.

[17]**Swiss-Prot** is a manually curated biological database of protein sequences. It is now maintained by the international UniProt consortium. (See http://www.ebi.ac.uk/uniprot/)

[18]The **Enron email dataset** contains about 500,000 emails of ca. 150 users. It was collected during the investigation of the Federal Energy Regulatory Commission on the Enron case. (See http://www.cs.cmu.edu/~enron/)

is important for various application types, e.g. cross-document summarization. Wang et al. devise a clustering algorithm for cross-document transliterated personal name coreference resolution based on the vector space model, referring to external biographical resources as the base for grounding. This gives evidence that anaphora processing technology might as well play an important role in multilingual application cases.

Summarization of Consumer Test Reports **Stede et al.** [36] describe an application of intra-document coreference resolution as part of a hybrid statistical/linguistic system SUMMaR that accomplishes multi-document **summarization of consumer test reports.**[19] Contribution of anaphora processing is restricted to the intra-document level, employing object coreference resolution and third-person pronominal anaphora resolution, which is accomplished by applying the robust rule-based off-the-shelf system ROSANA (Stuckardt [37]). In this application scenario, anaphora processing is employed to **enabling coherence** of summaries: based on the identification of the object coreference chains of the whole document, it is checked whether, in the subsequence of sentences selected for the summary, a pronoun would lose its antecedent and would thus not be intelligible to the reader; if so, then this pronoun will be substituted by an informative antecedent as identified through pronominal anaphora resolution. While this is a fairly obvious way of employing anaphora processing to enhancing a chiefly statistical approach to text summarization, it illustrates an important point: in particular application scenarios, it might be relevant to give precision priority over recall. As there is some degree of freedom which sentences to select for the summary, only those sentences containing pronouns should be chosen for which the anaphora processing component signals high confidence regarding the correct understandability of the pronoun and, as far as applicable, the correctness of the substituted informative antecedent. This boils down to a respective criterion to be taken into account in the requirements analysis and technology selection phase of the procedure model described below.

Further Work **Hong and Park** [17] describe an application of anaphora processing in the narration/story domain. They consider a **text animation** scenario, employing anaphor resolution for keeping track with the overall behavior of characters, dealing not only with object, but as well with event/action anaphora.

Kuo and Chen [23] consider an application case in the news domain related to text summarization: coreference resolution is employed for **event clustering on streaming news**, aiming at grouping documents by events automatically. This is a cross-document scenario, which involves intra-document coreference resolution followed by cross-document event clustering that refers to features derived by object anaphora processing. By resorting to manually annotated rather than automatically determined coreference chains, the application case is studied at the conceptual level.

[19] Among the microdomains considered are hotel test reports and film reviews.

Popescu-Belis and Lalanne [30] work on a multimodal application case in which transcripts of **spoken-language press review meeting dialogues** (held in French) are to be referentially interpreted. In particular, this amounts to resolving references to commonly discussed document structure entries such as headlines, subheadings, and paragraphs. According to Popescu-Belis and Lalanne, the set of referents is known a priori in this scenario, which could thus be understood as a task of reference resolution (or, to be precise: entity grounding) over a restricted domain.[20] Envisaged particular application scenarios are meeting transcript retrieval and review, e.g., to support users who have missed a meeting.

3 The Procedure Model

Looking at the above survey of cases, recommendations for the systematic design and development of anaphora processing technology to be employed in an application scenario can be distilled. The following itemization is to be considered as a checklist that aids the NLP engineer in taking into account all relevant issues in an appropriate order; examples, which are taken from the above-discussed cases, are included wherever appropriate (written in italicized letters). The length of the checklist underlines the inherent complexity of the development of anaphora processing applications.

1. **Identify application domain and microdomain.**
2. **Identify generic application type(s).**
   It has to be taken into account that there are scenarios in which anaphora processing serves multiple purposes, e.g., intra-document information extraction combined with subsequent cross-document summarization.
3. **Identify the key requirements of anaphora processing:**
   If there are multiple generic application types, the following questions need to be answered separately for each type.

   a. What are the target entities of the generic application type?
      In the case of protein-interaction IE, relational entities corresponding to protein interactions; in the case of attorney / judge / expert witness IE in the legal domain, object entities corresponding to people working in this area.
   b. What are the target entities of anaphora processing?
      E.g., proteins; people working in the legal domain.
   c. How do mentions of the anaphor resolution target entities look like?
      E.g., proper nouns, pronouns, and definite NP.
   d. Contextual conditions: what are the structural and semantic properties of the context in which these mentions typically occur?

[20] It might be objected that the transcribed press review dialogues will typically center around document *content* as well.

In the protein interaction case, mentions of proteins participating in biological interaction relations, which are expressed by a respective verb or deverbative.

e. Taking into account the contextual conditions, which are the distributional and microdistributional characteristics of the mentions (in particular, the anaphoric ones)?
   In the protein interaction case, 95 % of the relevant protein mentions are accomplished through the third-person non-possessive pronoun it.
f. Are these distributional characteristics typical or atypical for the considered text corpora?[21]
   In biomedical research articles, bioentity mentions are mostly accomplished through names and definite NP (including cases of sortal and associative anaphora), while pronouns are atypically prevailing if only considering descriptions of protein interactions.
g. Are there requirements of cross-document coreference resolution?
   Biomedical information extraction typically involves implicit cross-document coreference resolution, as it includes the task of identifying syntactic variants of bioentity spellings, which might vary from corpus to corpus.
h. Are there requirements of entity grounding (typically as a means to accomplish cross-document coreference resolution)?
   In the above-described BioAR application scenario, cross-document protein name resolution is to be accomplished through relating protein mentions with respective entries of the proteome database Swiss-Prot.
i. Are there requirements of biasing particular stages of anaphora processing towards high precision?
   As discussed for the consumer test report summarization case, it can be relevant to bias pronoun resolution towards high precision (at the expense of recall), which might be accomplished by referring to decision confidence feedback.

4. **Identify the resources required:**

   a. **Mention extraction:** identify

      - which base technology is required;
      - whether, in the considered particular scenario, this is a straightforward task, enabling employment of an off-the-shelf solution;
        else,
      - whether there are domain characteristics to be exploited, and
      - whether there are suitable reusable domain- or scenario-specific tools, extraction pattern libraries, dictionaries, etc.

[21]This might help to decide whether components of previous work in the same application domain can be reused in the considered particular application scenario.

In the protein interaction case, this led to reusing available technology for biodomain-specific PoS-tagging and named entity recognition, as required for recognizing the domain-specific syntax of gene mentions.

b. **Anaphor resolution proper[22]—reusing existing resources:** check whether (parts of) the job be accomplished

- with a generic off-the-shelf solution;
- with resources custom-made for the domain and/or scenario (possibly from an own predecessor project), exploiting their structural and semantic characteristics;
- with domain-independent resources custom-made for applications of the same generic type?

For resolving pronouns, if domain-independent linguistic knowledge is considered sufficient (as in the protein interaction case), GuiTAR or MARS might be reasonable candidates.

c. **Anaphor resolution proper—devising a custom-made approach:** as far as there are no reusable resources,

- identify the sources of evidence to be referred to for resolving the relevant types of anaphoric expressions—this might involve a sneak preview of the available domain resources as to be discussed in the next step;
  In the gene database curation case, associative anaphor resolution was identified to require part-whole *evidence, which led to employing Sequence Ontology.*
- decide which corpus- and/or rule-based approach(es) to employ—this decision requires in-depth understanding of the anaphors to be dealt with and the contextual conditions, as gathered in the above requirements analysis phase.
  Again, in the gene database curation scenario, the availability of rich domain resources led to chiefly applying semi-supervised and rule-based techniques.

d. **Domain resources**—identifying ontologies, domain-annotated corpora,[23] world models for entity grounding, and other knowledge sources:

- ontologies;
  E.g., Sequence Ontology, UMLS Metathesaurus.
- corpora annotated with domain-specific information;
  E.g., the GENIA corpus, which is annotated according to the GENIA Ontology.
- databases for entity grounding;

[22]This is to be understood to cover antecedent determination only, as the mention extraction step is considered separately above.

[23]Not to be confounded with referentially annotated corpora as employed for evaluation (see below).

E.g., Swiss-Prot, Westlaw Legal Directory, geographical databases.

- other resources:
  E.g., professional license information, expert taxonomy (as employed in the above-described legal domain application).

Check whether the required resources are readily available; in case additional (possibly laborious) manual domain knowledge engineering proves necessary, then proceed analogously to referential annotation below (deciding which annotation tool(s)/guidelines/annotators to employ).[24]

e. **Evaluation criteria**—decide which of the following type(s) of evaluation to employ:

- intrinsic evaluation of the anaphora processing technology.
  In the case of coreference resolution, coreference classes can be scored according to the MUC metric or one of its refinements (B-Cubed, CEAF)—see chapters "Evaluation Metrics" and "Evaluation Campaigns" on coreference evaluation metrics and evaluation campaigns.
- extrinsic evaluation at generic application level;
  If anaphora processing is employed to enhance IE recall, its achievements can be evaluated indirectly by measuring the IE (P,R) gain.
- extrinsic evaluation at application scenario level.
  A usability evaluation can be conducted, determining overall performance at the level of the global application scenario; for instance, user performance with vs. without NLP/anaphora processing support can be compared.

If we know the anaphora processing performance to be expected and/or if we employ off-the-shelf technology that doesn't require or permit adaptation, extrinsic evaluation might be sufficient.

f. **Evaluation tools:** depending upon the selected evaluation measures, decide whether software support is required; if so, decide whether to reuse an existing tool or to custom-build one.
As coreference scoring measures such as MUC, B-Cubed, and CEAF are somewhat tricky to compute, it might be an option to reuse the scoring software employed at the SemEval and CoNLL contests—see chapter "Evaluation Campaigns" on evaluation campaigns.

g. **Referentially annotated corpora, annotation tools, and guidelines:**

- check whether they are required for evaluation;
  The answer is "no" in case that we use extrinsic evaluation only.
- check whether they are required for training purposes;
  This will be the case if a corpus-based approach is employed.
- If annotated corpora are required: refer to domain-specific previous work and check whether corpora with the required type of annotation (covering

[24]This might have repercussions for decisions related to the previous step.

mentions and referential relations) can be directly reused or adapted, thus avoiding or reducing own annotation efforts;

- If it turns out that own annotation efforts are necessary:
  - develop an understanding of the size of the corpus to be annotated—partly, this depends upon the particular corpus-based approach employed and upon whether the corpus shall be used for evaluation and/or training purposes;
  - check whether suitable (generic or domain-specific) annotation tools can be reused;
  - check whether suitable annotation guidelines are available;
  - develop an understanding of the annotator competence required, i.e., whether domain expert knowledge is necessary for achieving a sufficient annotation quality;
  - decide about which annotation tool(s)/guidelines/annotators to employ.

  According to the methodological study of Watters et al. [46] in the biomedical domain, laymen knowledge and an annotation tool with a simple user interface suffices in the case of pronouns, while non-pronominal anaphora typically requires domain-specific expert rather than linguistic knowledge and a more sophisticated software support for annotation.

5. **Feasibility assessment:** determine cost, benefit, and risk estimates[25] for all identified anaphora processing implementation options.
6. **Considering further options:** if none of the anaphora processing options considered so far fulfils the budget and/or technical requirements, then reiterate the above steps if there are further options available.
7. **Decision:** if one or several suitable approaches have been identified, decide which particular approach to implement.
8. **Proceed with the usual steps of IT project planning and specification,** duly taking into account the typically vanguard character of applications based on innovative natural language processing technology.[26]

---

[25]**Estimating risks** that are specific to applications of natural language processing technology is an intricate issue that certainly deserves to be investigated in more detail. In the case of anaphora processing applications, particular NLP-related risks are: (1) difficulty to estimate the extraction quality achievable for new types of mentions that are specific to a previously unseen (micro-)domain and/or language; (2) difficulty to estimate the resolution quality achievable for previously unconsidered types of anaphoric relations, particularly such relations that are specific to the (micro-)domain considered and chiefly based on non-linguistic knowledge; (3) difficulty to estimate beforehand whether corpus annotation efforts will remain within bearable limits—relevant factors are: corpus size required (depending upon learning behaviour of corpus-based classifiers), knowledge required for annotation (laymen vs. domain expert), complexity of tools required for annotation (annotation software and guidelines), and, importantly, achievable annotation quality (interannotator agreement). In general, reusing existing resources as far as possible will reduce risks or at least enable a better risk estimation.

[26]Essentially, this amounts to adequately reflecting the estimates of the NLP-related risks; see the above step 5.

The leading four items address the core tasks related to anaphora processing: points 1–3 constitute the application requirements analysis phase as motivated in the initial sections of this chapter, whereas point 4 embodies the resources requirements identification phase. Details on how to appropriately address the specific technical issues mentioned in points 3 and 4 can be found in the respective dedicated chapters in the *Algorithms* and *Resources* parts. In fact, these points and their subitems are representing a synopsis of all key issues related to operational, practical anaphora processing. The reader is supposed to find the relevant technical background information in the above chapters.

4 Conclusion

The procedure model that has been derived above embodies a serious attempt to capture all essentials of anaphora processing application development, as it is based on a quite comprehensive survey of several ten concrete application scenarios in different domains. It is, however, likely that future will bring about further significant technical and methodological advances as well as further innovative application scenarios. Quite probably, this will lead to the creation of additional resources—e.g., off-the-shelf tools covering particular types of non-pronominal anaphora that currently require non-standard treatment; checking for applicability of this new technology has to be accomplished through additional standardized steps to be included in item 4b of the procedure model. The procedure model should thus be understood as an approximation of the state of the art of anaphora processing application development; it should be subject to iterative refinement based on the further evolution of the discipline. As this is a very diverse and complex research field with numerous publications per year, the author is necessarily far from being omniscient. Fellow researchers are thus invited to actively contribute to enhancing the procedure model based on their detailed knowledge of their own work.

In this regard, consistently documenting one's work according to the above outline might greatly contribute to further advancing the art of anaphora processing application development. In fact, the procedure model not only embodies a checklist that guides the development process; interpreted statically, it can be used as a comprehensive template for thoroughly documenting all key aspects of concrete application systems, covering anaphora processing requirements, technical design decisions including employed resources, and evaluation criteria. Combined with evaluation results, this greatly enhances visibility and comparability of contributions and achievements of particular application systems. Most importantly, this establishes a proper base for reusing previous work or for drawing lessons from less successful experiments, which are as well worth to be documented. It would thus be of extraordinary use to the research community if there were a central point of reference (i.e., a web page) at which such standardized documentation could be collected, made available, and discussed.

Basically and essentially, this amounts to entering an enhanced level of standardization beyond mere employment of well-defined evaluation criteria that enable numerical performance comparison. Whereas classical research on the basic anaphora processing algorithms gave rise to defining quantitative evaluation measures and respective standardized result reporting procedures (see, for instance, Byron: [2]), the movement towards concrete application scenarios now calls for appropriate *qualitative* extensions of the employed standardization scheme. This is the rationale behind the proposal that has been put forward in the preceding paragraphs: promoting further advances in the discipline by enabling visibility and, thus, comparability of approaches at a refined granularity as required for adequately capturing the intricacy of concrete application scenarios.

Eventually, this should entail important repercussions at the base technology level. A detailed understanding of the requirements of concrete applications is expected to foster the further refinement of anaphora processing algorithms and resources, as it enables focusing on the key issues. In particular, it might lead to respective refinements of off-the-shelf toolkits: instead of merely offering basic domain-independent component technology,[27] algorithms and resources for particular domains and application requirements might be provided, establishing diversity by employing fine-grained distinctions along the above lines.

As this gives a perspective of how to further tame the apparent eclecticism in present-day work on anaphora processing (as identified in the initial chapter), this closes the circle. The book at hand provides an extensive and hopefully highly useful documentation of recent theoretical and practical research on anaphora processing. Presumably, however, this completes only part of the job: further consolidation of the insights gathered in the last decade seems indispensable. This might be partly accomplished as delineated above, that is, driven by a standardized and centralized documentation of concrete application achievements. Ultimately, theoretically oriented research should gain from this as well, as enhancements in resource availability (e.g., by diversification according to domain and specific scenario) will enable respectively finer-grained studies on important discourse-theoretic concepts such as centering and salience, thus contributing to the overall advancement of the anaphora processing discipline.

References

1. Bin, C., Xiaofeng, Y., Jian, S., Lim, T.C.: Other-anaphora resolution in biomedical texts with automatically mined patterns. In: COLING '08: Proceedings of the 22nd International Conference on Computational Linguistics, pp. 121–128. Association for Computational Linguistics, Morristown (2008)
2. Byron, D.K.: The uncommon denominator: a proposal for consistent reporting of pronoun resolution results. Comput. Linguist. **27**(4), 569–577 (2001)

[27]E.g., an algorithm for third-person pronoun resolution that employs linguistic knowledge only.

3. Castaño, J., Zhang, J., Pustejovsky, J.: Anaphora resolution in biomedical literature. In: Proceedings of the International Symposium on Reference Resolution for NLP, Alicante (2002)
4. Cohen, K., Demner-Fushman, D., Ananiadou, S., ichi Tsujii, J. (eds.): Proceedings of BioNLP 2014. Association for Computational Linguistics, Baltimore (2014). http://www.aclweb.org/anthology/W/W14/W14-34
5. Cooper, J.W., Kershenbaum, A.: Discovery of protein-protein interactions using a combination of linguistic, statistical and graphical information. BMC Bioinform. **6** (2005)
6. Dozier, C., Zielund, T.: Cross-document coreference resolution applications for people in the legal domain. In: Proceedings of the ACL-2004 Workshop on Reference Resolution and Its Applications, pp. 9–16. Association for Computational Linguistics, Barcelona (2004)
7. D'Souza, J., Ng, V.: Anaphora resolution in biomedical literature: a hybrid approach. In: Proceedings of the 3rd ACM Conference on Bioinformatics, Computational Biology and Biomedicine, pp. 113–122. ACM, Orlando (2012)
8. Eilbeck, K., Lewis, S.E., Mungall, C.J., Yandell, M., Stein, L., Durbin, R., Ashburner, M.: The sequence ontology: a tool for the unification of genome annotations. Genome Biol. **6**(5), R44+ (2005). doi:10.1186/gb-2005-6-5-r44. http://dx.doi.org/10.1186/gb-2005-6-5-r44
9. Elsayed, T., Oard, D.W., Namata, G.: Resolving personal names in email using context expansion. In: Proceedings of ACL-08: HLT, pp. 941–949. Association for Computational Linguistics, Columbus (2008). http://www.aclweb.org/anthology/P/P08/P08-1107
10. Gasperin, C.: Semi-supervised anaphora resolution in biomedical texts. In: BioNLP '06: Proceedings of the Workshop on Linking Natural Language Processing and Biology, pp. 96–103. Association for Computational Linguistics, Morristown (2006)
11. Gasperin, C.: Statistical anaphora resolution in biomedical texts. PhD thesis. Tech. Rep. UCAM-CL-TR-764, University of Cambridge, Computer Laboratory (2009). http://www.cl.cam.ac.uk/techreports/UCAM-CL-TR-764.pdf
12. Gasperin, C., Briscoe, T.: Statistical anaphora resolution in biomedical texts. In: COLING '08: Proceedings of the 22nd International Conference on Computational Linguistics, pp. 257–264. Association for Computational Linguistics, Morristown (2008)
13. Gasperin, C., Karamanis, N., Seal, R.: Annotation of anaphoric relations in biomedical full-text articles using a domain-relevant scheme. In: Proceedings of DAARC 2007, pp. 19–24. CLUP – Center for Linguistics of the University of Oporto, Lagos (Algarve) (2007)
14. Hachey, B., Nguyen, H., Nissim, M., Alex, B., Grover, C.: Grounding gene mentions with respect to gene database identifiers. In: BioCreAtIvE Workshop Handouts, Granada (2004)
15. Hahn, U., Cohen, K.B., Garten, Y., Shah, N.H.: Mining the pharmacogenomics literature—a survey of the state of the art. Brief. Bioinform. **13**(4), 460–494 (2012)
16. He, T.Y.: Coreference resolution on entities and events for hospital discharge summaries. Ph.D. thesis, Massachusetts Institute of Technology, Department of Electrical Engineering and Computer Science (2007)
17. Hong, K., Park, J.C.: Anaphora resolution in text animation. In: Proceedings of the IASTED International Conference on Artificial Intelligence and Applications (AIA) (2004)
18. Karamanis, N., Seal, R., Lewin, I., McQuilton, P., Vlachos, A., Gasperin, C., Drysdale, R.A., Briscoe, T.: Natural language processing in aid of flybase curators. BMC Bioinform. **9** (2008)
19. Kennedy, C., Boguraev, B.: Anaphora for everyone: pronominal anaphora resolution without a parser. In: Proceedings of the 16th International Conference on Computational Linguistics (COLING), pp. 113–118 (1996)
20. Kilicoglu, H., Demner-Fushman, D.: Coreference resolution for structured drug product labels. In: Proceedings of BioNLP 2014, pp. 45–53. Association for Computational Linguistics, Baltimore (2014). http://www.aclweb.org/anthology/W/W14/W14-3407
21. Kim, J.J., Park, J.C.: Bioar: anaphora resolution for relating protein names to proteome database entries. In: Proceedings of the ACL-2004 Workshop on Reference Resolution and Its Applications, pp. 79–86. Association for Computational Linguistics, Barcelona (2004)
22. Kim, J.J., Park, J.C.: Bioie: retargetable information extraction and ontological annotation of biological interactions from the literature. J. Bioinform. Comput. Biol. **2**(3), 551–568 (2004)

23. Kuo, J.J., Chen, H.H.: Event clustering on streaming news using co-reference chains and event words. In: Proceedings of the ACL-2004 Workshop on Reference Resolution and Its Applications, pp. 17–23. Association for Computational Linguistics, Barcelona (2004)
24. Lappin, S., Leass, H.J.: An algorithm for pronominal anaphora resolution. Comput. Linguist. **20**(4), 535–561 (1994)
25. Leidner, J.L.: Toponym Resolution in Text. Universal-Publishers (2008). http://dissertation.com/book.php?book=1581123841&method=ISBN
26. Leidner, J.L., Sinclair, G., Webber, B.: Grounding spatial named entities for information extraction and question answering. In: Proceedings of the HLT-NAACL 2003 Workshop on Analysis of Geographic References, pp. 31–38. Association for Computational Linguistics, Morristown (2003). doi:http://dx.doi.org/10.3115/1119394.1119399
27. Nguyen, N.L.T., Kim, J.D.: Exploring domain differences for the design of pronoun resolution systems for biomedical text. In: COLING '08: Proceedings of the 22nd International Conference on Computational Linguistics, pp. 625–632. Association for Computational Linguistics, Morristown (2008)
28. Nguyen, N.L.T., Kim, J.D., Miwa, M., Matsuzaki, T., Tsujii, J.: Improving protein coreference resolution by simple semantic classification. BMC Bioinform. **13**, 304 (2012)
29. Poesio, M., Kabadjov, M.A.: A general-purpose, off-the-shelf anaphora resolution module: Implementation and preliminary evaluation. In: Proceedings of the 4th International Conference on Language Resources and Evaluation (LREC), Lisbon, pp. 663–666 (2004)
30. Popescu-Belis, A., Lalanne, D.: Reference resolution over a restricted domain: references to documents. In: Proceedings of the ACL-2004 Workshop on Reference Resolution and Its Applications, pp. 71–78. Association for Computational Linguistics, Barcelona (2004)
31. Sanchez-Graillet, O., Poesio, M., Kabadjov, M.A., Tesar, R.: What kind of problems do protein interactions raise for anaphora resolution?—a preliminary analysis. In: Proceedings of the Second International Symposium on Semantic Mining in Biomedicine, Jena, pp. 109–112 (2006)
32. Savova, G., Chapman, W., Zheng, J., Crowley, R.: Anaphoric relations in the clinical narrative: corpus creation. J. Am. Med. Inform. Assoc. **18**(4), 459–465 (2011)
33. Segura-Bedmar, I., Crespo, M., de Pablo-Sanchez, C., Martinez, P.: Resolving anaphoras for the extraction of drug-drug interactions in pharmacological documents. BMC Bioinform. **11**(Suppl 2), S1 (2010)
34. Settles, B.: Biomedical named entity recognition using conditional random fields and rich feature sets. In: Proceedings of the International Joint Workshop on Natural Language Processing in Biomedicine and Its Applications (NLPBA), pp. 104–107. Association for Computational Linguistics, Stroudsburg (2004)
35. Son, R., Taira, R., Kangarloo, H.: Inter-document coreference resolution of abnorman findings in radiology documents. In: Proceedings of the 11th World Congress on Medical Informatics (MEDINFO). IOS Press, Amsterdam (2004)
36. Stede, M., Bieler, H., Dipper, S., Suriyawongkul, A.: Summar: combining linguistics and statistics for text summarization. In: Proceeding of the 2006 conference on ECAI 2006, pp. 827–828. IOS Press, Amsterdam (2006)
37. Stuckardt, R.: Design and enhanced evaluation of a robust anaphor resolution algorithm. Comput. Linguist. **27**(4), 479–506 (2001)
38. Su, J., Yang, X., Hong, H., Tateisi, Y., Tsujii, J.: Coreference resolution in biomedical texts: a machine learning approach. In: Proceedings of the Dagstuhl Seminar on Ontologies and Text Mining for Life Sciences, Dagstuhl (2008)
39. Taira, R.K., Soderland, S.G., Jakobovits, R.M.: Automatic structuring of radiology free-text reports. Radiographics **21**(1), 237–245 (2001). http://www.biomedsearch.com/nih/Automatic-structuring-radiology-free-text/11158658.html

40. Tsuruoka, Y., Tateishi, Y., Kim, J.D., Ohta, T., McNaught, J., Ananiadou, S., ichi Tsujii, J.: Developing a robust part-of-speech tagger for biomedical text. In: Advances in Informatics, Proceedings of the 10th Panhellenic Conference on Informatics, PCI 2005, Volos, 11–13 Nov 2005. Lecture Notes in Computer Science, vol. 3746, pp. 382–392. Springer, Berlin/New York (2005)
41. Vilain, M., Burger, J., Aberdeen, J., Connolly, D., Hirschman, L.: A model-theoretic coreference scoring scheme. In: Proceedings of the 6th Message Understanding Conference (MUC-6), pp. 45–52. Morgan Kaufmann, San Francisco (1996). doi:http://dx.doi.org/10.3115/1072399.1072405
42. Vlachos, A., Gasperin, C.: Bootstrapping and evaluating named entity recognition in the biomedical domain. In: BioNLP '06: Proceedings of the Workshop on Linking Natural Language Processing and Biology, pp. 138–145. Association for Computational Linguistics, Morristown (2006)
43. Vlachos, A., Gasperin, C., Lewin, I., Briscoe, T.: Bootstrapping the recognition and anaphoric linking of named entities in drosophila articles. In: Proceedings of the Pacific Symposium on Biocomputing, Hawaii, pp. 100–111 (2006)
44. Wang, H.: Cross-document transliterated personal name coreference resolution. In: Lecture Notes in Computer Science 3614: Fuzzy Systems and Knowledge Discovery, Proceedings of the Second International Conference, FSKD 2005, Changsha, 27–29 Aug 2005, Part II, pp. 11–20 (2005)
45. Wang, Y., Melton, G.B., Pakhomov, S.: It's about "this" and "that": a description of anaphoric expressions in clinical text. In: Proceedings of the American Medical Informatics Association Annual Symposium (AMIA 2011), Washington, DC, pp. 1471–1480 (2011)
46. Watters, S., McInnes, B., McKoskey, D., Miller, T., Boley, D., Gini, M., Schuler, W., Polukeyeva, A., Gundel, J., Savova, S.P.G.: Using volunteers to annotate biomedical corpora for anaphora resolution. In: Proceedings of 2005 AAAI Spring Symposium on Knowledge Collection from Volunteer Contributors (KCVC05), Stanford (2005)
47. Wellner, B., Castaño, J., Pustejovsky, J.: Adaptive string similarity metrics for biomedical reference resolution. In: ISMB '05: Proceedings of the ACL-ISMB Workshop on Linking Biological Literature, Ontologies and Databases, pp. 9–16. Association for Computational Linguistics, Morristown (2005)
48. Zheng, J., Chapman, W.W., Crowley, R.S., Savova, G.K.: Coreference resolution: a review of general methodologies and applications in the clinical domain. J. Biomed. Inform. **44**(6), 1113–1122 (2011). http://www.sciencedirect.com/science/article/pii/S153204641100133X

Part V
Outlook

Challenges and Directions of Further Research

Massimo Poesio, Roland Stuckardt, and Yannick Versley

Abstract In this final chapter, the prospects of the research field of anaphora processing shall be briefly discussed, identifying promising directions of further research, new application scenarios, and interdisciplinary cooperation. In order to obtain the broadest-possible view of the discipline's future, an inspiring survey with respective pertinent questions has been conducted among all contributors to this book in order to poll their individual opinions. This chapter thus gathers contributions by multiple authors, which will be summarized and evaluated.

Keywords Challenges and directions survey • Challenges in coreference resolution • Coreference resolution

1 Anaphora Resolution in the Twenty-First Century

Looking back at the individual book chapters, it seems safe to conclude that the research field of anaphora and coreference resolution has reached a state of maturity. Empirical, corpus-based, and machine learning approaches are understood to play a key role, and the paramount importance of shared resources (such as annotated corpora, evaluation infrastructure, and software components for diverse preprocessing tasks) is widely acknowledged. The research presented in this book illustrates that there is now a shift of attention towards particular problems that have been neglected in earlier work on anaphora resolution, which dealt with much more fundamental issues of robust natural language processing, e.g. how to work on the fragmentary output of a robust parser, etc.

M. Poesio (✉)
School of Computer Science and Electronic Engineering, University of Essex, Colchester, UK
e-mail: poesio@essex.ac.uk

R. Stuckardt
IT-Beratung, Sprachtechnologie, Medienanalyse, D-60433 Frankfurt am Main, Germany
e-mail: roland@stuckardt.de

Y. Versley
ICL Universität Heidelberg, Heidelberg, Germany
e-mail: versley@cl.uni-heidelberg.de

M. Poesio et al. (eds.), *Anaphora Resolution*, Theory and Applications of Natural Language Processing, DOI 10.1007/978-3-662-47909-4_17

For instance, it is now widely recognized that the task of mention extraction constitutes a non-trivial problem, and that it thus makes a huge difference whether we evaluate an anaphora resolution system on gold mentions or require the system to provide its own—that is: less than perfect—mention extraction subcomponent. In a similar vein, it is commonly understood that we have to properly reflect the transitivity property of the coreference relation, and that it thus makes a difference whether we accomplish reference processing according to the mention pair or the entity mention model. While some of these issues (such as the transitivity problem) have already been recognized more than a decade ago, it seems to have taken until recently for them to eventually reach the full awareness of the research community.

Hence, in dealing with these specific issues, some recent research on anaphora processing carries a quite technical flavor. Annotation schemes are getting more and more elaborated, and there is now a plethora of different evaluation measures and task definitions, distinguishing among many different ways to formally define the reference processing task. Some quite advanced and specialized work on algorithms now focuses on particular subproblems, thus explicitly addressing rather technical issues that have been largely neglected, or merely mentioned *en passant*, in classical research.

In accordance with the general trend in computational linguistics, anaphora processing has thus become a decent discipline of natural language *engineering*, acknowledging the full technical complexity of the task rather than approaching the problem at a merely conceptual level, devising pseudo-formal notations with virtually no practical value from a software engineering and application perspective. This shift of attention is definitely commendable. If, however, one looks at the discipline from the side of the phenomenon (i.e. language, discourse structure, and—ultimately—*content*), we might arrive at the somewhat sobering intermediate conclusion that, after more than four decades of research, we are yet far away from the ambitious discourse processing proposals propagated by the classical theoretical work. That is, instead of investigating the celestial realms of rhetorical and thematic structure, we're yet occupied with rather mundane issues such as advanced string matching heuristics for common and proper nouns, or appropriate lexical resources for elementary strategies, e.g. number-gender matching etc.

If we further take into account that it is yet quite hard to beat the long-known baseline algorithms for pronoun or entity coreference resolution, we might reach the conclusion that we should become more ambitious again in order to eventually enhance the performance level of our systems. That is, after more than one decade of detail-oriented engineering work on certainly highly relevant basic problems, we should possibly shift our attention towards the higher levels of discourse processing—*nota bene*, while definitely retaining our engineering approach to anaphora processing.

In the introductory chapter, it has been suggested to refer to the current anaphora processing research period by the name *post-modern phase*; moreover, it has been argued in favor of an ensuing second phase of *consolidation*. The appraisal of recent research as conducted in this book is aimed as a fertilizer. This book, however, would not be complete without a brief discussion of the prospects of the discipline, identifying promising directions of further research, new application scenarios, and interdisciplinary cooperation. A particularly appropriate way to obtain the broadest-possible view of our discipline's future should be to consult leading researchers about their individual informed opinion. We have thus devised a survey with respective pertinent questions and circulated it among all contributors to this book in order to poll their opinions.

As we think that the survey might be of general inspiring value for systematically thinking about the prospects of anaphora processing research, we are including it verbatim below. In the ensuing section, we will then summarize and discuss the answers received.

2 Survey

Suppose you have just been awarded the Grand Research Prize of the Republic of San Serriffe, which gives you Euro 10.000.000 over the next ten years for research and development to further the state of the art of anaphora and coreference resolution. You are in charge of devising a strategy for investing the money in the most promising and effective way. That is, you have to decide where to set the focal points of research, and which measures to support in order to foster the wider cooperation of the research community.

Below is a list of possible research issues to be considered. However, feel free to express your ideas and visions on any anaphora-resolution-related issue that you think should/will be key during the next decade:

1. Guideline question that might help identifying particular focal points of research: what are the most persistent theoretical and practical problems (solvable or not) that anaphora and coreference resolution would have to overcome to get closer to human-like performance?
2. What is your opinion about where to focus regarding the further development of the research community's shared resources? Headwords:
    - annotated corpora
    - evaluation criteria
    - evaluation contests (covering additional anaphora types etc.)
    - preprocessing technology
    - semantic/encyclopedic knowledge sources
    - off-the-shelf systems
    - other ...
3. Where do you think should subsequent work on algorithms center on?
    a. corpus-based methods:
        - general strategy (mention-pair, entity-mention, etc.)
        - which particular ML and statistical methods to be further explored

- further requirements on resources (types of annotations, corpus size, etc.)

b. rule-based components (possibly for particular subtasks)
c. algorithms for particular/related subtasks:

- resolution of non-standard types of anaphora (beyond object anaphora etc.)
- mention extraction and classification
- knowledge acquisition

4. Which role do you think that subsequent theoretical research on local coherence, focus, discourse structure, etc. will play for further advances in the area of robust/operational/fully-implemented anaphora resolution systems?
5. How should theoretical and practical, application-oriented research be intertwined in order to further enhance cross-fertilization?
6. Any further generic and particular application scenarios of anaphora and coreference resolution that you think will become important during the next couple of years? Think about possible new, groundbreaking practical applications (social network analysis, semantic enterprise and web search, etc.) as well as about more research-oriented applications (discourse structure analysis, content comparison, etc.). Which related further demands on resources could be identified?
7. Put even more generally/open-ended: where and how do you think that cooperation between anaphora and coreference resolution, and neighboring fields such as (formal/cognitive/psycho)-linguistics, information extraction, psychology etc., should be encouraged more strongly?
8. Which particular measures would you suggest to be taken in order to further enhance the collaboration of the international research community and thus fostering the advances in the research field?
9. Wildcard query: any other thoughts, ideas, visions etc. you'd like to express about our research field's further development?

3 Answers Received

The answers have been slightly edited in order to resolve any dangling references to those parts of the survey questions that are not repeated below; the replies are ordered alphabetically according to surname.

1. What are the most persistent theoretical and practical problems(solvable or not) that anaphora and coreference resolution would have to overcome to get closer to human-like performance?

Massimo Poesio: I share Marta Recasens' sense in her comments that we have reached a plateau in anaphora resolution both from an engineering perspective and from a theoretical understanding perspective, and that moving on from this plateau will require a better understanding of the phenomenon both in linguistic terms and in terms of what applications actually need. Basically, we know how to handle the simplest cases of anaphoric reference/coreference, and anything beyond that is a challenge.

From a theoretical perspective, the key point to me seems that the availability of larger corpora is revealing a number of aspects of anaphoric interpretation for which we don't really have good theories. To make just two examples from those discussed in chapter "Detecting Non-reference and Non-anaphoricity" I would mention (i) the question of which nominal expressions are genuinely referential (there are a number of cases like nominal modifiers or expletives whose referential status is really unclear) and (ii) what is the interpretation of references to abstract objects. And large datasets like OntoNotes and especially the Phrase Detectives corpus (which also contains longer texts) are revealing a number of cases where we simply don't know what the interpretation of an "anaphoric" expression should be, or indeed whether that expression counts as anaphoric.

By the way: what is human performance on this task is also a difficult question—humans don't agree that much on the interpretation of expressions in the Phrase Detectives corpus!

Sameer Pradhan: Getting a better handle on identifying mentions with disparate heads or what was called "opaque" mentions in a paper last year would certainly help the task of coreference. How we go about getting that information annotated other than annotating hordes more text is not quite clear. It does seem to be the case that annotating full document coreference might lead to diminishing returns on annotator time as many of the cases are simpler to annotate and don't add much information for the learning algorithm.

Kepa Rodriguez: In my opinion (lexical mostly) semantic problems are yet far from being solved: problem of modification, lexical relationships like synonymy or hypo-/hyperonymy, contribution (or not) of meronymy, etc.

Roland Stuckardt: Dealing with referential relations beyond basic coreference is definitely among the most important issues. Not only do we require the appropriate semantic and encyclopedic resources; in particular, we are facing fundamental problems how to formally define the anaphora processing task to be solved: can we render this definition sufficiently exact in order to achieve high enough inter-annotator agreement of the annotated corpora employed for scoring? The more elaborated the considered referential relations are, the less clear it becomes what "*human-like performance*" really amounts to. Eventually—since the reference processing task to be accomplished is too "vague" and thus not amenable to a sufficiently exact definition—, we might come to the conclusion that it is difficult to evaluate such systems in isolation, so that we have to move one level upwards and to evaluate their contribution chiefly extrinsically at application level.

Yannick Versley: The most persistent problems you need to solve to get current state-of-the-art results in a particular language seem to be: (i) good-quality preprocessing, including both reliable parsing/morph/lemmatization and a way of identifying mentions that is appropriate for the targeted annotation scheme—while this is a solved problem for English, fully automated preprocessing of text can be a vexing problem in other languages. (ii) named entity recognition and linking or classification—this is crucial in resolving "the X" anaphora, where X is a common class of NEs, (iii) good alias features and (iv) knowledge for pronoun resolution. Many of these need lexical knowledge, which means that you could not easily scale from English-plus-DARPA-languages to, say, a hundred languages.

A particularly puzzling theoretical problem is the relation between coreference and information structure. There are already some resources for this (including the German DIRNDL corpus of Baumann and Riester, 2013, and the Prague Dependency Treebank), but both information structure itself and anaphoric or bridging relations beyond coreference are very hard to model.

2. What is your opinion about where to focus regarding the further development of the research community's shared resources?

Massimo Poesio: It seems to me that for the near future we will have our hands full exploiting the resources that have recently become available, both in terms of corpora (e.g. OntoNotes and ARRAU give a much more realistic picture of the anaphoric phenomenon than previous corpora, and we don't know how to handle a lot of that) and in terms of lexical and encyclopedic knowledge (e.g. developing the first large-scale models of the role of inference in anaphora resolution).

In the longer term, I think we need to work in two distinct directions. In order to improve our handling of the "basic" anaphoric phenomena, particularly in languages like Italian and Japanese, where a lot of anaphoric phenomena involve unrealized elements of argument structure, or even morphological structure, such as clitics, we need to develop more resources in which the annotation of anaphora is closely linked to morphological structure, argument structure and nominal structure, as done, e.g., in the Prague Dependency Treebank.

At the other extreme, we need to find ways to free our annotation from too close a link to text in order to annotate aspects of anaphora like plural anaphora or abstract anaphora where the antecedent is not directly expressed by text.

Sameer Pradhan: Probably the semantic/encyclopedic knowledge sources would have the most impact. How to go about creating them without turning into Cyc is an open question.

Kepa Rodriguez: I think that semantic and encyclopedic knowledge sources are especially important regarding to coreference resolution, for instance if a system has to be able to distinguish chains of mentions referring to two different entities (mostly named entities or domain entities in the use cases that I know better) represented by the same string. Moreover, off-the-shelf systemsshould be in the focus of development as well.

Roland Stuckardt: As I have said above, the more elaborate the anaphora processing task becomes, the more likely it seems that we require respective application-oriented evaluation campaigns. This might amount to considering enhanced scenarios well beyond classical information extraction over internet pages, e-mails, transcribed telephone conversations, etc., where reference processing evaluation is then conducted indirectly at application level.

In this regard, another thought comes into my mind. Current evaluation campaigns constitute a dust-dry matter, involving sophisticated annotation schemes, fine-grained annotation instructions, and quite technical accompanying distinctions (whether to evaluate on gold or system mentions, etc.) so that it proves more and more difficult to keep being in the know and to understand what has been accomplished by the participating systems. Couldn't we do better and devise an evaluation mode that provides a more sensual experience? My ideal conception would be an evaluation scenario that involves two or more systems at once that compete against each other, where the probability to prevail chiefly depends upon the system's referential processing capabilities.

For instance, such a competition could take place in an enhanced "blocks world" or computer game environment, where reference processing is employed for successfully accomplishing a task-oriented dialogue in order to achieve some particular goal against an adversary system in the considered miniworld. These competitions could be broadcast via the internet, which should amount to lots of fun and further motivation to improve one's system. E.g., in the computer chess world, live-broadcast system tournaments have long proven to generate a strong momentum that decisively fosters the further advancement of the discipline.

Yannick Versley: Looking at English, we see that the OntoNotes corpus and the CoNLL-2011/2012 shared task have done much to rekindle interest in coreference resolution among practitioners, and that both the amount of data available and the richness and consistency play a role. We also see that, in the CoNLL-2012 shared task as well as in the SemEval-2010 shared task—covering languages as diverse as German, Spanish, Italian, Arabic, and Chinese, besides English, yet leaving out, e.g. Slavic languages—the incompatibility of semantic and encyclopedic knowledge sources across languages was a large hindrance to their adoption. In the meantime, we find resources that provide semantic and encyclopedic knowledge in a uniform way across languages, such as UBY, DBPedia Spotlight, or even try to bridge across languages, such as Babelfy.

In the area of preprocessing, I find it exciting that projects such as the Google Universal Treebank [2] or HamleDT [5] would make it very easy to use preprocessing components with a single representation across many languages, which might one day enable the portability of coreference systems across languages.

3. Where do you think should subsequent work on algorithms center on?

Massimo Poesio: As I said in answer to point 2, I think for the near future our work on algorithms should concentrate on developing models that do a better job at capturing the richer notion of anaphora encoded in the latest corpora, as well as using lexical and encyclopedic knowledge better.

As far as the first range of problems, the most obvious need is for better mention detection, especially for languages where zero anaphora is prevalent.

In order to use lexical and encyclopedic resources better, moving on from simple look-up, I think we will need to develop large-scale models of the use of inference. The work on Markov Logic Networks is promising but so far it has only been small-scale due to the limitations of the current MLN engines.

Sameer Pradhan: The latent tree model seems very promising. Annotating non-standard type such as bridging might be useful for tasks as annotating more of other cases probably would only add marginally to the technology.

Kepa Rodriguez: Knowledge acquisition seems very important.

Roland Stuckardt: Of course, developing algorithms for dealing with bridging references. Moreover, we should focus parts of our attention on the relationship between discourse parsing/discourse structure and anaphora processing: could we devise an algorithm to (robustly) construct a hierarchical discurse structure that contributes to referential processing? In this regard: what are the interdependencies between discourse parsing and anaphora resolution? How should the underlying discourse model be defined? Could we approach this in a fairly generic way or would we be better off employing an application-specific approach?

Yannick Versley: There are currently two strands of coreference resolution that seem very promising to me: one is the Stanford Sieve approach, which Chen and Ng (2012) showed can be extended with a simple set of parameters for tuning; such an approach does not need much data, but needs rules to be written that model each phenomenon; the other would be most typical for systems such as the one of Fernandez et al. (2012) or for HOTCoref (Björkelund et al.), where machine learning is used to cluster entities in a bottom-up fashion, with techniques that are also used in other structured learning tasks for complex inference problems.

4. Which role do you think that subsequent theoretical research on local coherence, focus, discourse structure, etc. will play for further advances in the area of robust/operational/fully-implemented anaphora resolution systems?

Massimo Poesio: Like Yannick, I think the disconnect between, on one hand, the very solid linguistic and psychological evidence about the importance of salience in anaphoric interpretation and, on the other hand, the very limited success achieved when trying to incorporate such information in anaphora resolution systems is one of the most surprising aspects of modern work on anaphora resolution. I expect those findings will become more important when we expand the range of anaphoric phenomena our systems handle to types of anaphoric expressions in which salience plays a key role, such as zero anaphora and bridging.

Yannick Versley: The interaction of discourse structure, focus (and/or information structure), and referential structure has been the subject of much inspired and inspiring theoretical research, ranging from Grosz and Sidner's (1986) model of focus and discourse segments to Lascarides and Asher's [1] views on bridging or Cristea's Veins theory. Unfortunately, discourse structure and information structure have revealed themselves to be hairy and difficult notions when applied to complex real-world texts. Theoretical research on deceptive discourses (where the common ground is not necessarily common and plausibility may or may not be your ally) or on the patterning of reference structure in texts of various authors and genres may give us a peek of a deeper understanding that, so far, has always been around the next corner.

5. How should theoretical and practical, application-oriented research be intertwined in order to further enhance cross-fertilization?

Massimo Poesio: It seems to me that we have just witnessed an excellent example of what for me is the best way for theoretical research to affect application-oriented work. The creation of anaphorically annotated corpora such as AnCora, ARRAU, OntoNotes, Tüba D/Z that are less application-oriented than previous resources such as MUC or ACE has naturally led to a great deal of interest in phenomena such as event anaphora that were not previously considered.

Kepa Rodriguez: I think cooperative work between different research communities offers excellent perspectives for that. I think areas related to information and documentation sciences (archives, libraries, and digital document repositories), projects in social sciences, network analysis, digital humanities, etc. are places in which useful cross-fertilization could happen.

Roland Stuckardt: I think that we should reconsider the classical theoretical work on discourse and pursue further research on the *empirical* groundings of its central concepts; shared resources such as annotated corpora will prove useful in this regard. This should enable us to eventually devise an empirically founded algorithmic discourse model suitable to be employed in the context of robust, operational anaphora processing.

Yannick Versley: My intuition on this is that the linguistic/theoretical side and the application-oriented/engineering side generally need to work hand in hand, but that they need to do so with an interface between the disciplines that allows both to evolve independently from each other. As an example, the most effective coreference systems in the time of the MUC evaluations were based on foundations such as FASTUS or GATE that allow to state rules in a declarative fashion; modern feature-based systems, including BART or HOTCoref combine the treatment of linguistic data structures with a mechanism that allows to combine feature functions with machine learning. Approaches for feature learning, which are already very dominant in image processing and have been successful as a means to improve some areas of natural language processing, may shift the boundary between the language dependent learning and inference and the more specific part of linguistic description and theory further.

6. Any further generic and particular application scenarios of anaphora and coreference resolution that you think will become important during the next couple of years?

Massimo Poesio: I am glad to see that we are finally moving away from the obsessive focus on news. New annotated corpora in information extraction domains (e.g. biomedical), new dialogue corpora, new fiction corpora are now available, and I think they will all become important domains. Like a couple of other respondents, I also think social media data will become important, and we have been involved in the creation of datasets of this type.

Sameer Pradhan: I am currently working on improving clinical informatics and there is rich information available in a patient's clinical notes. It appears though that in order to get to a point where one can provide useful input to physicians, it would be important to tackle the problem of cross document event coreference. There is a much vaguer distinction between entities and events in the medical notes and so what I am talking about is essentially cross-document entity/event coreference. I believe this is a much harder problem than in the case of general or the newswire domain and would be very useful. This also requires the fading of distinctions between bridging and other possible variations but it is not clear what level of distinction would be best suitable for this purpose.

Kepa Rodriguez: I think the areas of social network analysis, semantic enterprise and web search as well as discourse structure analysis and content comparison are good candidates indeed. If the scope of the research is to resolve coreference connecting mentions with entities of the real world (or controlled vocabularies, ontologies, etc.) another issue to think about is the use for linked data and semantic web. In the same context, integration of partially structured and indexed data for which we don't have the possibility of a complete manual resolution of mappings will be relevant.

Roland Stuckardt: Automatic content extraction from social networks as well as cross-document coreference resolution (including real world entity grounding) over the internet will certainly be among the most important application fields. But I hope that there will be as well other innovative application scenarios and respective technological advances that neither play directly into the hands of, nor are funded by, NSA, GCHQ, DoD & Co.[1]—for instance, in the areas of enhanced information retrieval and extraction for the humanities, the life sciences, etc.

Yannick Versley: One area where coreference will in all likelihood become more important are applications including a generation component, such as summarization (see chapter "Coreference Applications to Summarization") and machine translation (see Hardtmeier et al.'s work on pronoun translation). Where it was previously sufficient to leave things as they are (summarization) or to trust a model with no discourse information (MT), ongoing progress in the other parts of the

[1]The Science Applications International Corporation (SAIC), which once played a leading role in the MUC evaluation campaigns and the DARPA-TIPSTER program, is now involved in the development of the (in-)famous spy software XKeyscore.

models will make it more and more appealing to attack problems in handling referential expressions.

7. How do you think that cooperation between anaphora and coreference resolution, and neighboring fields such as (formal/cognitive/psycho)-linguistics, information extraction, psychology etc., should be encouraged more strongly?

Massimo Poesio: As I already wrote in answer to point 5, I am in complete agreement with Yannick here—the best way to achieve cooperation with linguistics and information extraction is via resource creation. The interaction with psychology is more complex since developing more cognitively plausible models is a different undertaking than developing better performing systems, but again the creation of more "natural" datasets e.g. of spontaneous interaction might help.

Kepa Rodriguez: I see a high potential in information retrieval if anaphora resolution is linked to the use of semantic resources that help to find anaphoric relationships between mentions of the same entity realized by different NP strings (of course, not pronouns, that is not the issue). That would help to improve document indexing and retrieval some for cases of "synonymy" that aren't covered by the control vocabularies used to index the data.

Yannick Versley: To put out an uncomfortable truth here, I believe that encoding linguistic facts in corpora will result in a better basis for working anaphora and coreference resolution than any given set of linguistic or psycholinguistic assumptions about single phenomena, because coreference systems either profit from concepts that linguists would find very boring (name matching), or from subregularities that linguists find very unsatisfactory. Then again, corpus annotation—our favorite, or only way of encoding linguistic facts, can profit enormously from careful linguistic analysis (see Versley, [6] or Recasens, Hovy, and Martí, [4]).

8. Which particular measures would you suggest to be taken in order to further enhance the collaboration of the international research community?

Massimo Poesio: I am glad Sameer enjoyed RAIS, which I co-organized with Arndt Riester. I also found it extremely stimulating and hope more such events will take place—e.g., I hope that DAARC will continue, since I have always found it a great mix.

Sameer Pradhan: I think the RAIS[2] workshop was very helpful for me to get the connection between anaphora and information structure. If we can find funding for meeting such as these, it would be very useful and encourage collaboration that would otherwise not be possible.

Yannick Versley: If we look at languages other than English, we find a lot of phenomena such as clitics, the absence of definite articles, or zero pronouns, that are

[2]RAIS = (**R**ethinking (the Annotation of) **A**naphora and **I**nformation **S**tructure)

"normal" in these languages but conspicuously absent from models that are created based on English. To get a full account of these phenomena, we would have to treat them not as "niche" phenomena, but as first-class citizens, which could be helped by having compatible datasets in an even more diverse set of languages than SemEval-2010 or CoNLL-2012.

Not referring directly to particular questions of this survey, several researchers expressed some additional thoughts which seem to fit best into the wildcard query bucket. Moreover, Marta Recasens submitted a comprehensive general answer, which will as well be displayed below.

9. Any other thoughts, ideas, visions etc. you'd like to express about our research field's further development?

Massimo Poesio: Overall, it seems to me, also from the answers to the survey, that a split is beginning to emerge between two lines of research on anaphora resolution:

- Natural language engineering: work most concerned with improving the performance of anaphoric resolvers. For instance, work on improving mention detection is mostly engineering work. I see the Stanford Sieve work as going in this direction, as well as Björkelund's work. I have as well the impression that this is Yannick Versley's main interest.
- Using empirical evidence to improve our understanding of anaphora: there is no question in my mind that computational modelling is throwing up a lot of challenges to traditional linguistic theories of anaphora. This is my main concern, although I see myself as being interested in engineering as well, and I would guess Marta's as well.

I don't see this as a negative development, on the contrary! Also, I think that many people, like me, are active in both types of research. But I think it's important to keep this in mind as we analyze the results of the survey. Also it is important to make sure that cross-fertilization continues.

Marta Recasens: I think that research on coreference resolution has stagnated. It is very hard to beat the baseline these days, state-of-the-art coreference outputs are far from perfect, and conferences receive less and less submissions on coreference. What's the problem? The community has managed to do our best with the "cheapest" and simplest features (e.g., string match, gender agreement), plus a few more sophisticated semantic features, and this is enough to cover about 60 % of the coreference relations that occur in a document like a news article, but successfully resolving the relations that are left requires a rich discourse model that is workable so that inferences at different levels can be carried out. This is a problem hindering research not only on coreference resolution but many other NLP tasks. Therefore, I'd spend the Grand Research Prize on developing a computationally tractable discourse model.

Two types of common challenging coreference relations that state-of-the-art systems struggle with are: (1) competing antecedents, e.g., when a pronoun has two potential antecedents (agreeing in number, gender, not violating binding constraints, etc.) and only semantics/discourse information has the clue of which antecedent is the correct one; and (2) coreference relations involving proper and common nouns, such as *Woody Allen* and *the 79-year old* or *college students* and *the new entrepreneurs*, which require both world knowledge and discourse understanding (of the local context) to be resolved.

Another issue at a more theoretical level is the treatment of coreference relations as discrete. As a discourse evolves, coreference intertwines with other anaphoric relations in complicated ways, and it is not even possible sometimes for a human to decide whether two mentions corefer or not. This becomes a problem for computational systems, especially at evaluation time, when every single pair of mentions is considered as either coreferent or not. It would be interesting to investigate if a more flexible formulation of the problem would capture the linguistic phenomenon in a richer way so that it can be evaluated in a fairer way and more precise algorithms can be developed.

Similarly to the discreteness problem, multiple other simplifications have been made to reduce the complexity of the phenomenon, but this has also introduced inaccuracies that often mislead the algorithms and trained systems. For example, the case of split antecedents and discourse deixis. Even if some corpora annotate these phenomena, they are ignored in practice, and the corresponding coreferent mentions are thus treated as singletons. Improving the way we handle these is initially expensive but I believe it will pay off in the long run.

Yannick Versley: I think that the split between natural language engineering and improving our understanding of anaphora was there all along—maybe since the empirical turn of the 1990s. Probably because empirical evaluation forces you to look at details and minor points that don't necessarily add up to a good story about language understanding. E.g., while Soon et al.'s seminal publication (2001) or Ng's reranking paper [3] focus on engineering issues, Vieira and Poesio's work furthers our understanding of anaphora and thus is interesting both for insights into what aspects of anaphora we're currently modeling and as a recipe on how to get a particular subproblem resolved.

And I think that work in the second category always needs work in the first, and vice versa, all while having clearly separate goals. Point to be made, both Marta Recasens and myself have published work in either area (e.g. on near-identity questions in the annotation, or see Marta's work with the singleton classifier).

Of course we also have work such as Finley and Joachims, or Culotta et al., which is interested mostly in developing inference techniques rather than producing real-world coreference resolution or learning about anaphora. And even that work, if we consider the transition over to ranking and ILP resolvers to the beam search models that are at the core of Durrett and Klein's or Björkelund et al.'s systems, has its influence on the first two lines of work: it both eases the construction of sensible systems and makes it easier to get interpretable results than mention-pair models with pairwise classification.

Reference

1. Asher, N., Lascarides, A.: Bridging. J. Semant. **15**(1), 83–113 (1998)
2. McDonald, R., Nivre, J., Quirmbach-Brundage, Y., Goldberg, Y., Das, D., Ganchev, K., Hall, K., Petrov, S., Zhang, H., Täckström, O., Bedini, C., Bertomeu Castelló, N., Lee, J.: Universal dependency annotation for multilingual parsing. In: Proceedings of the 51st Annual Meeting of the Association for Computational Linguistics, Sofia, vol. 2, pp. 92–97 (2013)
3. Ng, V.: Learning noun phrase anaphoricity to improve conference resolution: issues in representation and optimization. In: Proceedings of the 42nd Meeting of the Association for Computational Linguistics (ACL'04), Barcelona, pp. 151–158 (2004)
4. Recasens, M., Hovy, E., Martí, M.A.: Identity, non-identity, and near-identity: addressing the complexity of coreference. Lingua **121**(6), 1138–1152 (2011)
5. Rosa, R., Mašek, J., Mareček, D., Popel, M., Zeman, D., Žabokrtský, Z.: HamleDT 2.0: Thirty Dependency Treebanks Stanfordized (LREC), Reykjavik (2014)
6. Versley, Y.: Vagueness and referential ambiguity in a large-scale annotated corpus. Res. Lang. Comput. 6(3), 333–353 (2008)

Index

M. Poesio et al. (eds.), *Anaphora Resolution*, Theory and Applications of Natural Language Processing, DOI 10.1007/978-3-662-47909-4